ASTER FAMILY FLOWER

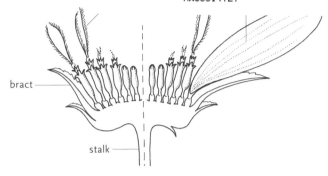

bract

stalk

INFLORESCENCES

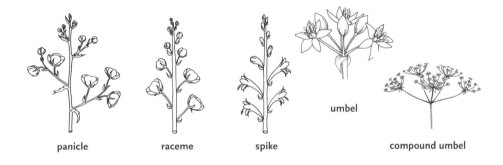

panicle   raceme   spike   umbel   compound umbel

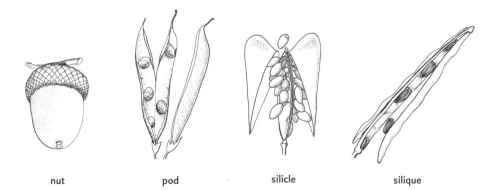

nut   pod   silicle   silique

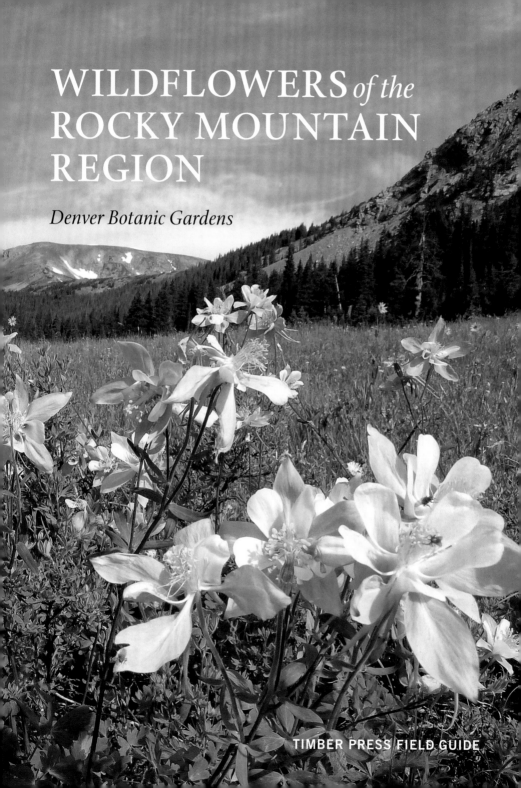

WILDFLOWERS *of the* ROCKY MOUNTAIN REGION

Denver Botanic Gardens

TIMBER PRESS FIELD GUIDE

This book is dedicated to Loraine Yeatts and
Janet Wingate for their decades of contributions to botany in the
Rocky Mountain region and service to Denver Botanic Gardens.

Published in 2018 by Timber Press, Inc.

Endpapers by Alan Bryan
Regional map by David Deis
Frontispiece: Wildflower vista, Southern Rockies
Title page: *Aquilegia coerulea* (Colorado blue columbine),
Herman Gulch, Colorado
Photo credits appear on page 470.

Timber Press
The Haseltine Building
133 S.W. Second Avenue, Suite 450
Portland, Oregon 97204-3527
timberpress.com

Printed in China
Cover and text design by Susan Applegate

Library of Congress Cataloging-in-Publication Data

Names: Denver Botanic Gardens.
Title: Wildflowers of the Rocky Mountain region / Denver Botanic Gardens.
Description: Portland, Oregon: Timber Press, 2018. | Series: Timber Press field guide | Includes
    bibliographical references and index. | Identifiers: LCCN 2018011959 (print) | LCCN 2018015768
    (ebook) | ISBN 9781604698695 () | ISBN 9781604696448 (pbk., flexible plastic/vinyl cover)
Subjects: LCSH: Wild flowers—Rocky Mountains—Identification.
Classification: LCC QK139 (ebook) | LCC QK139 .A53 2018 (print) | DDC 582.130978—dc23
LC record available at https://lccn.loc.gov/2018011959

CONTENTS

FOREWORD

The *Encyclopedia Britannica* lists the Rocky Mountains as number one of the seven great mountain ranges on Earth, followed by the Alps, Atlas Mountains, Himalayas, Andes, Ethiopian Highlands, and Australia's Great Dividing Range. Made up of more than 100 separate mountain ranges spreading from Alberta and British Columbia in the north to New Mexico in the south, the Rocky Mountains are a massive cordillera inspiring everyone from mountain climbers, hikers, skiers, and explorers to songwriters like John Denver. In the contiguous United States, Colorado has the highest number

(53) of fourteeners (mountain peaks with an elevation of at least 14,000 feet); climbing them all is a popular activity by peak baggers. In addition, the multitude of wildflowers that bloom throughout the season attracts many visitors; a favorite annual event is the Wildflower Festival at Crested Butte in Colorado.

With so many wildflower books on the market, why another one? Almost all the wildflower books currently available are specific to a particular region and mostly separate the Canadian and the U.S. Rockies. This book covers the entire Rocky Mountain

Independence Pass, Colorado

range from Canada, south to New Mexico, separated into three main regions: the Northern Rockies, the Middle Rockies, and the Southern Rockies. Within these regions are numerous habitats harboring a diversity of plants. This Timber Press publication was conceived to satisfy the need for a handy guide with photos that will make the plants easy to identify in the field and maps showing the locations where one could encounter them.

This book is a work of passion developed over a period of three years by and supported by years of experience from numerous plant and horticulture experts at Denver Botanic Gardens. Countless hours were spent poring over plant lists and finally narrowing the list down to 1,200 plants that a hiker or visitor in the Rocky Mountains is likely to encounter. Then came the photographs. Many of the authors took special trips to various sites to capture plants in their peak blooming stage. Then came the writing of plant descriptions and sorting thousands of photos, followed by incorporating the maps. I hope you will find this book useful in helping you identify plants on a hike in the magnificent Rocky Mountains and expand your knowledge about the wildflowers and the various habitats they grow in. I also hope you will enjoy the book as much as we have enjoyed putting it together.

—Sarada Krishnan, Ph.D.

Director of Horticulture and Center for Global Initiatives

Denver Botanic Gardens

Kootenay Rockies, British Columbia

Arizona–New Mexico Plateau

ACKNOWLEDGMENTS

Wildflowers of the Rocky Mountain Region owes its success to the support, time, expertise, and patience of many people.

A special thank-you is due to Savannah Putnam, who started as an intern to provide additional help with the book but quickly turned into a true project manager; Savannah managed all aspects of the project including keeping ten people on track with photographing, chasing down photos, researching, and writing. She was truly a force of nature, managing the project with a level of grace and competence that few could muster.

Thank you also to our families and friends for being supportive of our extra work in the field photographing plants, long days in the office, evenings of researching and writing, and for listening to our many updates on the current status of the book.

Thank you to the editors and staff at Timber Press, who helped us with every step and allowed us more time to create a more comprehensive field guide.

We would like to thank those who have come before us in writing floras and field guides of this vast and floristically diverse region. Their important contributions were foundational for this project. Much work remains to sort out some taxonomic ambiguities, and the region continues to surprise with new records and species.

Thank you to the National Science Foundation for supporting the digitization of data, creation of websites, and funding of scientific research of plants all over the globe.

A multitude of individuals generously shared their photos, and without them this book would not have been possible. Thank you Adam Burch, Al Schneider, Alan Schroder, Amy Taylor, Ann DeBolt, Barry Breckling, Ben Legler, Bryan Hobby, Christopher Christie, Curtis Björk, Emily Kachergis, Ernie Marx, Frank Morrey, Gary A. Monroe, Gary Waggoner, Gerald and Buff Corsi, Ginny Maffitt, Janét Bare, Jay Lunn, Jean Pawek, Jeff Thompson, Jim Pisarowicz, Jo Panosky, Johan Nilsson, Karen Vail, Keir Morse, Linda Vaxvick, Loraine Yeatts, Lori Skulski, Mary Winter, Max Licher, Mike Ireland, Mikel R. Stevens, Neide Bollinger, Pam Eveleigh, Phyllis Weyand, RT Hawke, Sharon Chester, Suzanne Putnam, Todd Boland, Tom Zeiner, and William Adams.

In addition to contributing photos, the following individuals and organizations provided advice and information for which we are eternally grateful: Curtis Björk, Phyllis Gustafson (*Wildflowers of the Pacific Northwest*), Pam Eveleigh (Primula World), Loraine Yeatts, Janet Wingate (Denver Botanic Gardens' Kathryn Kalmbach Herbarium), Bonnie Heidel (University of Wyoming), Al Schneider (swcoloradowildflowers.com), Ernie Marx (*Eastern Colorado Wildflowers*), Scott Smith, Karen Vail (Yampatika, Steamboat Springs, CO), John T. Kartesz (Biota of North America Program), Ann DeBolt, Roger Rosentreter, Jennifer Ackerfield (Colorado State University Herbarium and *Flora of Colorado*), University of Wyoming's Rocky Mountain Herbarium, and the University of Colorado Museum Herbarium.

We would like to thank Julie Casault, Kevin Williams, Bryan Fischer, Gary Waggoner, Janét Bare, Pat Roth, Lisa Negri, and Ali Zvada Schade, who put in countless hours making the individual distribution maps for each species. We would also like to thank Ann Frazier, Bryan Fischer, and many other members of our own DBG staff for providing additional support in this project.

Lastly we would like to thank the native plant societies in the region for their devotion to conservation of the region's native plants, and for connecting people to the flora of this region.

INTRODUCTION

The Rocky Mountains have been famous as magnets for winter sports for decades, but the appeal of the Rockies has grown exponentially in the summer months as well, as residents of the burgeoning Front Range flee the summer heat by driving to the heights on weekends. Tourists in droves from across North America and the world pay homage to the numerous national parks that stud the region. The incomparable displays of wildflowers that bloom reliably throughout the growing season are a large part of the draw. Crested Butte has celebrated a Wildflower Festival for decades, but truth be told, the Mardi Gras of flowers in the Rockies is never-ending, beginning in late winter and extending to the last days of fall.

Thirty years ago, Denver Botanic Gardens published *Rocky Mountain Alpines*, a coffee-table tome with authors from around the world celebrating the unique flora of this region. Since then, the native plant collections at the Gardens have expanded enormously. They have become a focal point of interest for keen gardeners who visit. This book is a testament to the Gardens' commitment to our native flora.

Throughout the growing season, the Rocky Mountain region boasts colorful displays at different elevations, and first-time visitors are justified in being somewhat confused and overwhelmed by the flora they encounter. The first flowers begin to appear in March most years (a few harbingers even before that at the lowest elevations and in special microclimates): regional flower buffs are always seeking the first pasqueflowers, springbeauties, or Townsend daisies on the fringes of the Great Plains. It's not till May most years that the lower foothills and plains explode with color, and June is when the higher mountains begin their floral pageant. July and August are the months for glorious bloom across the higher mountains. Although autumn arrives mid-August at the heights, the color only deepens as foliage on Ross' avens (*Geum rossii*) turns bright scarlet, the asters and gentians blaze with bright blue color, and a hundred yellow composites burgeon everywhere, making this book all the more important to have along to help sort them out!

Elevation, rainfall, and aspect have an extraordinary impact on the character and nature of floral displays in the Rockies—perhaps more than almost any other part of our country. You can drive countless miles at lower elevations through dry sagebrush or prairie where there may be nothing in bloom to speak of, but if you rise a few hundred feet in elevation, the meadows suddenly fill with flowers. Aspect (the orientation toward the sun) is magnified in dry, continental climates. One quickly notices that north slopes are more heavily wooded—the place to seek out orchids and ferns. Lower-elevation flora invariably climbs higher on south-facing slopes—where cacti and yucca can be found thousands of feet higher in elevation than one would expect. In spring or later during wet years, the lowland vegetation can rival the alpine heights in floral display. Timing is key to understanding and appreciating the richness of this flora. Mid-June to mid-August virtually guarantee visitors wonderful flower displays at higher elevations—the Fourth of July weekend is often the peak at the heights. But during drought cycles, the season shifts earlier, and during cold, snowy winters, the flower displays can be postponed almost a month at higher elevations.

It is not uncommon to return to the very same spot on the very same date a few years later and not find a single wildflower that once occurred by the thousands or millions blooming there. The season can be so delayed the plants may simply not have emerged yet. Or they may be past. Or some, like monument plant (*Frasera speciosa*), may bloom prolifically one year, and then for several years not a single stalk may rise in a colony. This phenomenon is common in mountains everywhere but seems to be more pronounced in the Rockies.

The Rocky Mountains can be said to have a predictably good flower display every year, but locals come to realize that certain years are spectacular. Especially when snow and rains are heavy in spring and early summer, you can expect the flowers to increase in quantity and size enormously. These "miracle years"—particularly at lower elevations—are worth a special trip, as few places on earth can offer the diversity of flower color and type you can find in sagebrush country in a wet spring! It is astonishing so many drivers whiz by on interstates in years like that, oblivious to the Persian carpet of phlox, buckwheat, paintbrush, milkvetch, penstemon, and daisy in every bright hue imaginable, blooming prolifically among the sagebrush like a painting come to life.

The species makeup can vary enormously from one valley to the next: the public lands of the Rockies are North America's wildflower treasure chests, and this book can be the key to unlock them!

Climate

It would be hard to exaggerate the climatic extremes of the Rocky Mountain region. You can be roasting on the plains around Denver, but drive 40 miles to Mt. Goliath and freeze in a snowy blizzard. Temperatures vary dramatically through the seasons, and even within a single day. This book focuses mostly on plants found at higher elevations (above 5,000 feet); but the flora of the "lowlands"—the Great Plains grassland steppe in the east and the intermountain sagebrush steppe on the western slope of the Rockies—often occurs well up into the hills, especially in the warm microclimates of southern exposures. The complex mosaic of vegetation is a reflection of the variability inherent in steppe climates: here the sun shines throughout much of the year, but the extreme heat of summer months and the extreme cold of the winters is often interrupted by contrary weather fronts. Short-sleeve weather and sunny days can occur throughout the winter months, and likewise snow squalls have occurred even on the plains in late spring and as early as Labor Day weekend.

For wildflower lovers, this climate provides endless opportunities for finding flowers. If you have missed the first pasqueflowers on the plains in March, you can find them a month later in the foothills, or two months later in the subalpine zone. I have found pasqueflowers blooming well into July above treeline in Colorado and Wyoming.

Climate Change

Climate change is present throughout the Rockies, with several noticeable effects. Wildflowers are blooming earlier than they once did, as confirmed by regional phenology studies. Snowpacks are melting earlier, creating lower river flows in mid to late summer. Earlier melting snowpack also means many high-elevation flowers are blooming earlier, potentially leaving them out of sync with many of their pollinators.

Mountain pine beetle outbreaks are increasingly common. A large outbreak in northern Colorado and southern Wyoming recently killed millions of trees and saw the beetle moving into high-elevation timberline areas where they had previously not been a large issue. Similar effects are being seen in the Middle and Northern Rockies, with outbreaks in whitebark pines at high elevations. Other insects have had large outbreaks as well, perhaps due to the longer and warmer growing season.

Wildfires, an important part of the cycle of regeneration in many Rocky Mountain plant communities, are more intense and at times more frequent than in the past. Some of this is due to poor land management and the spread of invasive species. In many cases climate change is exacerbating the effects. For much of the late 19th and until the late 20th century, forest fires were suppressed, allowing forests to become much thicker, accumulating more fuel than previously recorded. When these forests burn, they burn with much more intensity than in the past. Earlier seasonal warming also means that fuels dry out faster and more thoroughly. Fires can burn so intensely that even fire-adapted species such as ponderosa pines do not regenerate as they once did. The spread of cheatgrass, a Eurasian introduction, is causing sagebrush steppe to burn at such a frequent rate that natives are bring displaced by cheatgrass in a vicious cycle; what's more, the amazing plasticity of cheatgrass allows it to spread higher and higher as it adapts to cooler climates.

While plants exhibit great adaptability, many live in vulnerable habitats. For those that survive only at an isolated seep, or depend on a single obligate pollinator, or those that live only in the high tundra, there are few choices and nowhere to go. It is our great opportunity to learn all we can about them and to strive to ensure their continued existence.

Mountain pine beetle damage

The dramatic nature of this climate can present some real challenges to visitors from lower elevations and cloudier regions. The harsh light at all elevations here in the summer months will challenge photographic skills: visitors are often surprised by how bleached a picture can look when taken by digital cameras or even smartphones. You learn to seek out cloudy weather or shade (or otherwise compensate for the light intensity) to obtain true colors.

Weather and Wildlife: Danger for Hikers!

Weather can pose great dangers to tourists and even locals who don't think they need hats or sunscreen: the intensity of summer sun at any elevation (but especially the alpine) cannot be overstated. Sunstroke and sunburn are an omnipresent danger: you can never bring along quite enough water for extended hikes at any elevation! A severe sunburn not only adds pain to a visit but can increase the risk of melanoma.

Severe weather presents a more immediate danger: many forget that mountains create their own weather. Snowfall in June, July, or August—sometimes accumulating to many inches—is not unheard of from montane to alpine elevations. Night temperatures regularly plunge to or below freezing at the heights during the summer months. Sudden torrential rain or hail can lead to hypothermia and worse. The most common mistake visitors make is to forget to bring warm clothing and rain gear on long alpine hikes. A sunny morning lulls one into complacency—you leave the poncho behind. A few hours into your hike you notice that clouds are building, and before you know it rain is pelting down. The downpour can turn into a deluge with

Mountains create their own weather

Pronghorn antelope on the plains

no protection above treeline, and of course, trees are potential lightning rods lower down. Colorado ranks third among the states for lightning-caused death: several are struck by lightning every year.

You will discover quickly that local flower lovers seek the heights as early as possible in the day, and few seasoned flower lovers will be found in exposed areas when the daily thunderstorms arise. It's a good idea to stock a backpack with extra water, food, warm clothes, matches, and ponchos—inexpensive plastic ponchos are available in sporting goods stores everywhere in this area—and they can truly be lifesavers.

It is easy to get lost, especially if you bushwhack or wander off trails. The solution? Stick to trails unless you are a seasoned hiker with the proper geolocation equipment and local experience. People are reported lost in the Rockies every year, often leading to expensive and unnecessary retrieval efforts. Some are never found.

Wildlife presents the other peril throughout the region: curious tourists are gored by bison in Yellowstone National Park every year, and bison herds are now found in ranches and reserves throughout the Rockies—often where visitors can drive near to them. Don't risk a close encounter! Grizzly bears are found in parts of the Middle and Northern Rockies: important precautions include making noise while hiking, carrying bear spray, and using bear canisters or hanging food from trees. Check in with local authorities before you venture long distances in grizzly country. Erwin Evert, one of the leading field botanists of

Watch your backpacks!

keeping your eyes on paths and watching where you place your hands when climbing is only logical. Obviously, seek immediate medical assistance should you be bitten by a venomous snake.

Few other wildlife present this sort of peril: unfortunately, ignorant visitors often feed rodents and birds, which can lead to encounters that ultimately harm the animals more often than the visitor: black bears that lose fear of humans and persistently visit towns are often eventually "eliminated." We do not advise taking selfies alongside the charismatic and often deceptively docile mountain goats that you may encounter on some high-altitude drives.

Botanical History

The interaction of native peoples and wildflowers throughout the Rockies is a story that has yet to be fully researched and told. There is no doubt that the native peoples utilized plants for food, medicine, fiber, and construction of dwellings. Much pre-Columbian lore is still being gathered, and much can be deduced through anthropological study. Most may have been lost forever. Many plants utilized by first peoples, such as *Ligusticum porteri* (osha), have become important (and efficacious) contemporary herbal remedies sold around the world.

Lewis and Clark transected the Rockies en route to the Pacific Ocean in 1805 and re-crossed them on their return in 1806: their journals are filled with references to plants of all kinds—both to their ornamental character and usefulness as food. Of the 174 species of plants brought back from the expedition, most were new to science and described from their collections. The

the Middle Rockies, was killed by a grizzly bear in 2010 while hiking near Yellowstone. Black bears may be smaller than grizzlies, but they have been known to raid camps and have led to loss of life. Mountain lions are rarely seen, even by seasoned hikers— but they see you! And moose are as potentially lethal as bison and should be given an equally wide berth.

Few visitors are bitten by rattlesnakes, although several species are not uncommon in and around the Rockies. They are increasingly rare as you rise above the Great Plains or intermountain sagebrush country and essentially absent in subalpine and alpine areas. There are Coloradoans who've hiked the hills their entire lives and never seen a rattlesnake. Most strikes occur when you step on or next to a snake—so

Zebulon Pike expedition (1806–07) produced no new plant discoveries. The next major expedition (and the first to really explore the Southern Rockies scientifically) was the Stephen Long expedition of 1818–20. Edwin James was the officer accompanying this trip in charge of geological and botanical discoveries; he ultimately wrote the two-volume account of the expedition that famously characterized the Great Plains as the "Great American Desert." James was responsible for the scientific description of the Colorado blue columbine (*Aquilegia coerulea*), which he observed and collected between Denver and Colorado Springs. He is commemorated in the genus *Jamesia* and in a number of species epithets, including *Telesonix jamesii*, the spectacular endemic saxifrage best known from Pikes Peak.

John C. Fremont conducted four hectic, exploratory expeditions that crisscrossed the Rockies repeatedly in the 1840s, resulting in a number of new plant findings as well as a great deal of data on the intermountain region. But it wasn't until the 1850s, when a series of five well-funded expeditions seeking to find the best transcontinental route for a railroad were staged, that the scientific floodgates burst with new species in eastern publications.

Four of the five Pacific Railroad Surveys crossed or concentrated on the Rockies, and their leaders and officers, including Joseph Whipple Congdon, John Williams Gunnison, Edward Griffin Beckwith, and Isaac Stevens, are commemorated in many scientific names. The accounts of these expeditions were published and widely disseminated from 1855 to 1860, expanding the awareness and knowledge of the region's flora enormously. Further expeditions by

George Montague Wheeler, Ferdinand Hayden, Clarence King, and John Wesley Powell over the next few decades were accompanied by the researches of many independent and private botanists who were attracted to this region for its novelty—and profit: herbarium specimens sold to European herbaria fetched a price that funded many an itinerant botanist. Many of America's greatest 19th-century botanists began their careers in this region.

Edward Greene and Marcus Jones started as Protestant ministers, the former an Anglican, the latter a Presbyterian, in Greeley and Denver, respectively. Both explored throughout the West over the next half century, publishing competing botanical journals and authoring thousands of taxa. Alice Eastwood was born in Canada but grew up in Denver, where she finished high school and became a teacher at East High School; she published *Popular Flora of Denver* in 1893—the first local flora of the Rocky Mountain region.

In the first half of the 20th century, more and more scientific research was undertaken by systematic botanists researching specific genera for monographs, such as James Reveal on *Eriogonum*. Intensive exploration of certain areas has been undertaken by many botanists, such as E. H. Moss and John G. Packer (Alberta), Robert Dorn and Ron Hartman (Wyoming, Montana), Peter Lesica and Klaus Lackschewitz (Montana), Ray Davis (Idaho), Stanley Welsh and Arthur Holmgren (Utah), and William Weber, Jennifer Ackerfield, and Barney Lipscomb (Colorado). Noel and Patricia Holmgren have combed the entire intermountain region, and the staff and students of the Rocky Mountain Herbarium in Laramie, Wyoming, have ventured far across the Rockies. Most of the aformentioned have produced exhaustive floras of their respective regions.

Scientific exploration has continued unabated, and new taxa are still being found in the region although the rate has dropped to a half dozen or more a year. Many of these are spectacular, and some occur near centers of population—the flora in its entirety may not be fully known for decades! The Rockies consist of dozens of mountain ranges spanning 1000 miles: botanists and keen field workers are often guilty of visiting the same fruitful places, leaving vast areas untouched. Much more is surely still to be found, and keen wildflower enthusiasts like yourself are often the ones who find new things first!

Plant Distribution in the Rockies

Striking patterns of plant distribution become apparent to observant visitors. A large percentage of high-elevation wildflowers are found throughout the northern hemisphere: moss campion (*Silene acaulis*) and mountain-avens (*Dryas octopetala*) are not only common throughout the higher mountains of the West but across much of Canada, Alaska, Siberia—all the way to the Alps and northern Europe. These are often referred to as having circumboreal distribution. Many of the commonest, most conspicuous genera in this region, including *Aquilegia*, *Gentiana*, *Geranium*, and *Primula*, are circumboreal in their distributions. Our local species in these genera may be distinct but closely related to similar species in Eurasia. While many circumboreal plants are widespread and common, some are quite local and rare, such as the yellow lady's slipper (*Cypripedium parviflorum*).

Another suite of natives occurs throughout mountains from Alaska to New Mexico: elephant's head (*Pedicularis groenlandica*), brook saxifrage (*Micranthes odontoloma*), spiny phlox (*Phlox hoodii*), and many more could all be characterized as Cordilleran species, referring to the Rocky Mountain cordillera, or range. This group seems to be especially prevalent at subalpine and montane elevations.

A particularly distinctive group of plants, including those of the genus *Yucca*, have their centers of distribution far to the south; these are often referred to as Madrean in their distribution, from the Sierra Madre of Mexico. Many of the largest genera in this volume, with the most species and greatest variety, have their centers of distribution in the American Southwest and northern Mexico: *Castilleja*, *Eriogonum*, *Penstemon*, and *Phlox* are major garden genera around the world—and the American Southwest is their greatest concentration of speciation. These and many more are conspicuous and richly diversified throughout the Rocky Mountains region.

For the plant enthusiast, however, the plants that possess a special cachet are those that grow only in this area (termed endemics by biologists). These are sometimes rare and difficult to find. Three miniature, high-mountain columbines serve as examples of native endemics. Jones' columbine (*Aquilegia jonesii*) is the commonest of these, found sporadically over a wide swath of the Middle and Northern Rockies. The Rocky Mountain blue columbine (*A. saximontana*) is largely confined to near treeline in the Colorado Front Range: few visitors are lucky to find this. And the Laramie columbine (*A. laramiensis*) is entirely confined to its namesake mountain range—very few of its stations are near roads, and I doubt more than a few people will see this blooming in any given year. *Telesonix jamesii*, the purple mountain saxifrage of Pikes Peak and the Tarryall mountains, and *T. heucheriformis*, its more modest cousin in the Middle Rockies, are not only endemic species, but the genus is confined to the area covered by this book. Most of these endemic taxa are relatively uncommon in nature and should be cherished. We can only hope that attempts will be made to ensure their future. There are dozens—nay hundreds—of these special plants. Seek them out. Fortunately, unlike birds, wildflowers will quietly stay put, just waiting for you to visit!

The Regions

Many of the plants in this book are found commonly from Alberta to the heights of the Sangre de Cristo in New Mexico; these generalists, which tend to be found in montane levels upward, are marked in the text as RM (Rocky Mountains). A large percentage of the meadow flora of the Rockies, such as the common blue lupines, *Lupinus argenteus* and *L. sericeus*, is common throughout. Most of the montane and subalpine shrubs and trees are widely distributed across the Rockies, especially ponderosa and lodgepole pine, aspen, and the omnipresent Engelmann spruce and subalpine fir below treeline. Twinflower (*Linnaea borealis*) and twinberry honeysuckle (*Lonicera involucrata*) are two members of the Caprifoliaceae that are common in subalpine woodlands throughout the Rockies.

An especially distinct assortment of woodland flowers are found in shady woodlands at high elevations throughout: the popular fairy slipper (*Calypso bulbosa*) and a few less showy orchids can be quite common in the right spot in early summer. Later in the summer, a suite of pipsissewa (*Chimaphila umbellata*), single delight (*Moneses uniflora*), bunchberry dogwood (*Cornus canadensis*), and many bilberries (*Vaccinium* spp.) are found again and again under the highest forest canopy. The very same species of woodlanders are dominant in much of the Hudsonian zone in Canada—and these have been called the "Canadian Carpet." Many are found across the Bering Strait across the taiga of Eurasia as well!

The Northern Rockies

The Northern Rockies (NR) encompasses all of southern Canada treated in this book, primarily the mountains in Alberta and easternmost British Columbia, as well as the mountains along the Canadian border in Montana and Idaho. This was the most severely glaciated portion of the Rocky Mountains, and the only place covered by this book where glaciers are still prominent. The largest of these, the Columbia Icefields, covers 125 square miles partly contained by Banff and Jasper national parks, straddling the Continental Divide in both British Columbia and Alberta. This is the last remnant of the continental glaciation in our area that covered much of Canada during the Pleistocene era.

As a consequence of that glaciation, many of the plants of the Canadian Rocky Mountains have fewer endemic taxa than might be found farther south. There were areas in this region, however, that must have escaped glaciation at higher elevations. The locoweeds *Oxytropis podocarpa* and *O. splendens* and several milkvetches (*Astragalus* spp.) in particular have a fascinating range on scattered high peaks from

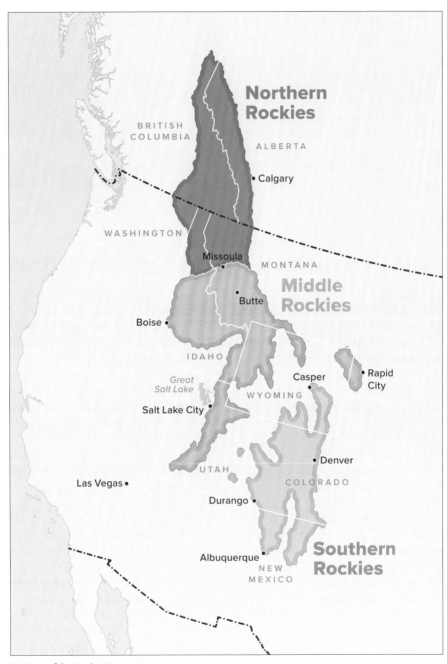

Regions of the Rocky Mountains

The Northern Rockies

Alaska to Colorado—growing profusely on a few high places and absent for hundreds of miles in between. *Eriogonum androsaceum* is a beautiful endemic taxon entirely restricted to the Northern Rockies.

The alpine heath community, including two species of both *Cassiope* and *Phyllodoce* as well as the more widespread *Kalmia microphylla*, is much more prevalent in the Northern Rockies than in the ranges to the south. Many arctic species, such as *Chamerion latifolium* and *Dryas drummondii*, form vast colonies here.

Although not nearly as high in elevation as the Southern Rockies, the glacier-clad Northern Rockies actually feel much higher—and the scenic views and vistas are as spectacular as the Alps or even the Himalayas. As a consequence, tourism in the summer months is monumental in Canada's provincial parks, although the size and scope of the region is such that there are many areas where visitors are few. The subalpine larch (*Larix lyallii*) is a special endemic tree of the Northern Rockies (with one disjunction in Washington state): this deciduous conifer is found only at the highest elevations below treeline, sometimes forming specimens that rival the five-needle pines of the Southern and Middle Rockies in their gnarly, bonsai-like form.

The floristics in the Northern Rockies of Montana and Idaho become increasingly complex. Many plants that are most commonly found in the maritime forests along the Pacific coast are found in northern Idaho and Montana as well: swordfern (*Polystichum munitum*), western redcedar

Canadian Rockies

The Middle Rockies

(*Thuja plicata*), western larch (*Larix occidentalis*), mountain hemlock (*Tsuga mertensiana*), and even Pacific dogwood (*Cornus nuttallii*), and many shrubs and herbaceous plants (e.g., *Lilium columbianum*, *Clintonia uniflora*) more commonly found in the Cascades make their only Rocky Mountain appearance in the Idaho panhandle and neighboring northwestern Montana. An unsuspecting botanist transported magically here might well think they're in the Olympic peninsula or Alaskan panhandle rather than far inland in the Rockies! This area also harbors many unusual and local endemics, including darkwoods violet (*Viola orbiculata*).

The most popular destinations for wildflower lovers in the Northern Rockies are the numerous national parks in Canada and Glacier National Park in the United States.

The Middle Rockies

Unlike the Northern and Southern Rockies, which consist of more cohesive and unified mountain ranges that are physically connected, the Middle Rockies (MR) are more of an archipelago of ranges situated in a sea of sagebrush, stretching from the Bitterroot range south to the Uinta and Wasatch ranges. There is much commonality of trees and shrubs at higher elevations, but the many mountain ranges that make up the Middle Rockies possess many spectacular species that are missing farther south and a much higher percentage of endemic plants than the Northern Rockies.

Rocky Mountain dwarf primrose (*Androsace montana*) and Howard's forget-me-not (*Eritrichium howardii*), two of the most beautiful and distinctive native wildflowers, are remarkably abundant in the Middle Rockies, from the sagebrush and grasslands of the Great Plains of Montana and northern Wyoming to the summits of alpine peaks.

Yellowstone National Park is the centerpiece of the Middle Rockies. Best known for the fantastic geothermal and geologic features, tourists flock here to see the abundant wildlife. There are not many plants restricted to this park, but many fine displays of wildflowers justify the visit for plant lovers as well; unfortunately, peak wildflower season in the park coincides with the maximum traffic jams of Winnebagos and Airstreams. Savvy visitors know it is best to rise early and beat the behemoths of the highway if you need to slip through the park quickly.

Two popular destinations to see wildflower fields at their best are the Bighorn Mountains of Wyoming and Beartooth Pass between Cody, Wyoming, and Red Lodge, Montana. A full day at least is required to even taste these two spectacular ranges—so nearby to one another and yet so utterly different. The Bighorns are an enormous uplift, with Dolomitic limestone around the edges and a granitic heart. Much of the range consists of rolling plateaus that display unparalleled fields of wildflowers from mid-June to late August: acres of lupines, penstemons, shootingstars, milkvetches, and more composites than you can imagine make for very slow driving if you're with wildflower lovers. The occasional sighting of moose or elk enhances a typical drive here.

In the Bighorn Mountains, the cliffs along Shell and Tensleep Canyons, the Medicine Wheel National Historic Landmark, and Hunt Mountain are the most accessible locations to find some of the special endemics of the region: the rock-hard Kelsey moss (*Kelseya uniflora*) is known

Medicine Wheel, Wyoming

from only a very few ranges in Montana, Idaho, and north-central Wyoming—but it can be abundant here in the Bighorns. It is undoubtedly the most congested member of the rose family, forming moss-like masses on sheer cliffs. Few people find this in full bloom since it is very early, flowering in late May or early June, before the masses arrive. Soon thereafter, Jones' columbine (*Aquilegia jonesii*) can be found in a few of these same spots; it is also found on scattered mountain ranges to the north and west, forming dense mounds with dozens of deep blue flowers on scree and crevices of limestone. Last summer we met a ranch couple on Hunt Mountain who drove 200 miles every June just to come find and admire this columbine. It extends sparingly to the Northern Rockies in Glacier National Park

and southernmost Alberta, but the Middle Rockies are the stronghold of this diminutive and lovely Rocky Mountain endemic.

The Beartooth Highway—approached either from Mammoth in Yellowstone or from Cody, Wyoming, is certainly one of the most scenic drives in the United States. Towering mountains in several ranges make for dizzying and constantly changing views the whole way. Many miles of the highway extend above treeline—and every imaginable habitat from meadow, bog, lakeside, cliff, scree, and tundra are found here in abundance. Alpines typical of the Southern Rockies, like old man of the mountain (*Hymenoxys grandiflora*), are found here, as well as alpines more common farther north, like pink mountain heath (*Phyllodoce empetriformis*) and purple mountain saxifrage

(*Saxifraga oppositifolia*). Pacific hulsea (*Hulsea algida*), which is common in the Sierra and Cascade alpine, has its southeasternmost stations here.

The mountain and alpine flora is so charismatic that many miss the greatest diversity the region has to offer: the sagebrush and grassland around the many islands of mountains here have even greater numbers of wildflowers than the peaks above them. Only two or three species of *Penstemon* are found above treeline in the Middle Rockies, but dozens are found among the sagebrush. The same is true for the giant genera of *Eriogonum*, *Erigeron*, and *Phlox*. You can find cushion phlox (*P. pulvinata*) above treeline, but drop to the sagebrush and longleaf phlox (*P. longifolia*), Kelsey's phlox (*P. kelseyi*), whitemargin phlox (*P. albomarginata*), and a half-dozen more might be encountered.

The sagebrush sea of the intermountain west, and the Middle Rockies in particular, has become the focus of energy development: the vast surface mines are now outnumbered by oil and natural gas installations, but energy and mineral exploitation, severe overgrazing in some areas, and off-road vehicle use have severely impacted some of America's richest biodiversity and will only continue to do so. Wildflower appreciation should be factored into the "Multiple Uses" and abuses of BLM and other public lands management agencies.

The Southern Rockies

One of the axioms of biogeography is that the closer you approach the equator, the greater the biodiversity. Naturally, one would suppose that being farther south, the Southern Rockies (SR) would have the greatest number of species of the region, and this is very likely the case. I remember once commenting to Peter Goldblatt—the leading authority on southern Africa flora—that it seemed to me South Africa was the richest temperate region in terms of species per acre I'd encountered. He responded huffily, "Mexico is much richer"—with approximately 40,000 species of plants, most of them endemic. The Madrean flora that characterizes much of Mexico can be said to find its northern terminus in the Southern Rockies. Typical wildflowers that characterize the Chihuahuan desert and steppe in Mexico, such as tree cholla (*Cylindropuntia imbricata*), make their last stand in the Southern Rockies.

The mountains themselves encompass all the mountains of Colorado, and the nearby ranges in neighboring states: the Sierra Madre, Medicine Bow, and Laramie ranges of Wyoming, the Abajo and La Sal mountains of Utah, and the northernmost mountains of New Mexico—especially the Sangre de Cristo. A great many classic alpines of the Southern Rockies are found on practically all these above treeline and nowhere else, including alpine kittentails (*Besseya alpina*), featherleaf fleabane (*Erigeron pinnatisectus*), Brandegee's Jacob's-ladder (*Polemonium brandegeei*), alpine primrose (*Primula angustifolia*), and the list goes on!

A special feature of these mountains are "parklands"—enormous, flat prairie-like expanses that occur in Colorado especially at 9,000 feet: these include Estes and Taylor Park, and the larger North, Middle, and South Park in the very heart of the Southern Rockies. The largest of all is the San Luis Valley: these represent the terminal moraines of various glaciations, which ended at much higher elevations than

The Southern Rockies

glaciers farther north. At one time, many of these parks had enormous lakes and wetlands, many of which have been drained to "enhance" ranching. These parks often boast rare and sometimes endemic taxa, such as Osterhout's milkvetch (*Astragalus osterhoutii*), Penland's penstemon (*Penstemon penlandii*), and North Park phacelia (*Phacelia formosula*). The famous alkaline fens of South Park possess rare disjuncts from the Arctic, like white willow (*Salix candida*) and Greenland primrose (*Primula egaliksensis*). Since the alluvia in the parklands contains concentrations of gold, the parklands have also attracted gold mining from the very beginning of statehood, and huge placer mines are still active. Where not disturbed by vacation homes or other touristic development, the mountain parks

are still among the most scenic and floriferous spots in the Southern Rockies—and the least protected parts of our mountain ecosystems. The great bulk of forest land, however, lies within national forests.

More than a thousand peaks rise above treeline in the Southern Rockies, and the mountain towns have transformed from sleepy mining hamlets with a gas station or one or two shops into small cities brimming with condominiums and mega-mansion second homes. There are dozens of ski areas that used to slumber through the summer—but almost all now have music festivals and a bustling summer season where people from all over come to cool off!

Since so much of the land is public, and so many roads and passes crisscross the region, this area has become a major destination for flower-seeking tourists. This book therefore contains a major focus on plants of the Southern Rockies.

Leave No Trace

Every year seems to see an increase in visitation to the Rockies. Human impact is evident in more and more backcountry locales, and heavily trafficked areas can be devastated by vehicles and foot traffic. Wildflower lovers are apt to be the most responsible of visitors, but it never hurts to remind ourselves that we can help effect a new ethic of environmental responsibility. I remember the time when picnickers would toss apple cores and cherry pits into the bushes around the campground, when picking wildflowers was a charming pastime. Multiply these by the millions of visitors in this area, and you can begin to see that the time has come to tread ever more lightly when we visit.

The Rockies are blessed with vast stretches of public lands—many free for hiking. Access fees are assessed on many areas that are heavily trafficked or vulnerable—ignoring these can lead to fines and tickets. You would probably object to strangers wandering at will in your private garden—so respect the privacy of the large private holdings: obtain permission to visit these and don't trespass. There really is no need to dig, pluck, or remove wildflowers, no matter how abundant they may appear: remember the passenger pigeon and bison were once countless in their numbers. Researchers and others with special projects can obtain permits from the Forest Service or Bureau of Land Management to harvest specimens. Picking or otherwise impacting the plants found in national or provincial parks is strictly illegal. There has been a long tradition of wildcrafting (harvesting

Shrine Ridge, Colorado

herbs, wild greens, mushrooms, and other forest products) on other public lands. Knowledgeable wildcrafters know to gather only a tiny fraction of a population, and to exercise great caution in eating either herbs or mushrooms. Beginners should consider taking classes or joining along in club forays with knowledgeable guides before sampling herbs.

Parking your car, pitching your tent, building a fire ring—all can leave marks on a landscape years after you passed through. Remember not to bring unwanted seed or contaminants to the mountains as well. Make sure your boots and pant cuffs and pockets haven't accumulated weed seed from your last foray. Pests can hitchhike on lumber or firewood and contaminate new areas. Check yourself as carefully before you head to the hills as you do when you come back, looking for ticks and other hitchhikers of the hills.

The Rockies are crisscrossed with innumerable trails, livestock paths, game trails, and passes. As foot traffic on these increases, they often become braided—especially where they are partly flooded by late winter snowmelt. Avoid further widening these paths if possible and try particularly *never* to take shortcuts on switchbacks, as tempting as it is to cut corners. Our collective feet can erode whole mountains. The most vulnerable terrain tends to be desert pavement and boggy areas—where a footprint can last decades. Take lots of pictures and try *not* to leave even a footprint!

—Panayoti Kelaidis

HOW TO USE THIS BOOK

In the pages that follow, you can expect to find most of the conspicuous and commoner wildflowers of the Rockies, approximately 1,200 in total, representing perhaps a third of the species that might be encountered in the area covered. So what's missing? Woody plants are mostly excluded, as are ferns, grasses, sedges, and rushes. Some of the showiest or otherwise significant rare plants are here, but many inconspicuous, obscure, or questionable species have been left out. Even so, many of the giant genera that are heavily concentrated in the Rockies (*Erigeron, Eriogonum, Penstemon*) are well represented but not complete. There are just too many of these—they almost demand to have their own special guides!

Descriptions

We begin our descriptions with basic information—the plant's scientific name and family, any useful synonyms, common name(s), range (Southern, Middle, or Northern Rockies), general habitats, abundance, bloom season, growth cycle, and height. Next, we describe the overall habit of the plant, followed by stem, leaf, flower, fruit, and detailed habitat descriptions. Often, we provide an interesting tidbit about the plant. We also include if a plant is native or introduced.

Plant Names

Each plant is identified by its scientific name (genus and species) and family; some species are further split into subspecies (ssp.) and varieties (var.), if variations are distinctive. But plant nomenclature is a constantly changing and evolving science, especially given the recent advancement of genetic analysis and online data sharing. Scientific names that were once accepted are changed, lumped, split, created, and deconstructed, which causes confusion for plant identification. In our book we have decided to largely follow the accepted names found on The Plant List (theplantlist.org), which is an effort put forth by a multitude of botanic gardens, societies, and universities around the world to universalize the accepted scientific names of plants. Most synonyms found in this book are past accepted names.

We have included at least one common name for each species. Common names can and do vary extremely over different state and country lines and should be used more for amusement than reliable identification purposes. As William A. Weber once wrote, "[Common names are] an insult to intelligence and a crime against good taste." He argued that we are dumbing down society by assuming children and non-botanists cannot memorize and pronounce scientific names.

Abundance

Botanists use the term "population" to describe a grouping of individual plants in close proximity to each other. The density of these individuals determines the abundance of the population. Common, uncommon, rare, endemic, locally abundant, infrequent—all are terms used to describe abundance.

Common plants are prolific and found in a wide range of locations, habitats, and elevation. Locally abundant plants are more selective in their abundance; some plants may be plentiful at higher elevations but absent at lower. Uncommon plants are plentiful in only a few geographical locations. Infrequent plants have only a few individuals in a wider range of locations. Rare plants are the most elusive, with only a small number of individuals in very few places.

Endemic plants are species that are found only in specific places in the Rocky Mountains. For example, the beautiful Rocky Mountain blue columbine (*Aquilegia saximontana*) is a small, uncommon flower found only in the central Rockies of Colorado.

Abundance is a useful but hard-to-define idea. The Rocky Mountains cover such a large distance that many plants will fall under multiple definitions. The level of occurrence of each plant helps determine the likelihood that the plant is correctly identified. In general, the more rare the plant, the less certain you can be of your identification. Use the range maps provided next to each plant to see if your identification makes sense.

Bloom Season

This is one of the most subjective areas of our descriptions, as each species can bloom at different times of the year based on snow melt, precipitation, elevation, location, and other (often shifting) environmental factors. Spring can begin as soon as early March, summer in the middle of June; and fall begins to be felt in the middle of August. Generally, each species has a range of time (e.g., Spring–Fall) when it is most likely to be blooming.

Growth Cycle

Most plants fall under one of three categories—annual, perennial, and biennial. Annuals bloom, produce seeds, and die within one year. Perennials live for many years; generally they bloom and produce seeds every year, but they can also become dormant for years at a time and flower only randomly, sometimes opting for vegetative reproduction over seed production in harsh alpine environments. Biennials take two years to bloom: the first year, the seed germinates and produces roots and leaves; the second year, the plant blooms and produces seeds. Rarely, species can exhibit multiple growth cycles.

Height

Height too can be extremely variable in high-elevation plants due to extreme growing conditions. At lower elevations with less wind, snowpack, and other environmental stresses, plants can look very different in size, which is why many of the species in this book have such wide height ranges. When not otherwise noted, measurements in the body of the entry refer to height or length.

Life Zones

A plant's habitat is one of its most defining features. Some species will be found only in grasslands, others only in the highest alpine tundra. We use the following general habitats in the upper part of the descriptions: alpine, subalpine, montane, foothills, pinyon-juniper, sagebrush steppe, intermountain parks, grasslands, and wetlands. The term "throughout" is used when a plant occurs in all (or most of) these life zones.

Alpine. From above treeline to over 14,000 feet, this is the highest life zone

Alpine

in the Rockies. In the vast, diverse Rocky Mountain region, treeline varies depending on latitude, topography, and distance from the ocean (the more continental the climate, the higher the treeline). For example, in northern New Mexico and southern Colorado timberline begins around 12,000 feet; in northern Wyoming and southern Montana it begins between 9,500 and 10,000 feet; in northern Idaho and northwest Montana, 6,500–7,000 feet; and in Jasper, Alberta, treeline starts around 7,000 feet.

Despite generally low temperatures, windy conditions, and a short growing season—all physical characteristics in common with true Arctic tundra found much farther north—the alpine tundra in the Rockies differs in several ways. First, while frost and snow can occur any day of the year

in the Rockies, there are few areas of true permafrost (frozen ground). Furthermore, although a long snowy season can stretch from September through early June, the Rockies are not high enough to have a nival zone where permanent snow and ice keep plants from growing. There are, however, glaciers and snowfields, and these become progressively larger and more common as one travels farther north. Finally, the Rockies boasts higher average wind speeds, shorter daylight hours, greater precipitation, and much higher solar radiation due to both the elevation and latitude.

In spite of the harsh conditions and short growing season of the alpine life zone, it is rich in plant life. Approximately 400 species of vascular plants (mostly herbaceous plants and low shrubs) are found in the alpine tundra of Colorado. This zone is well known for its brief but often spectacular flowering of dwarf plants with large, brightly colored flowers. Alpine plants are highly adapted to their harsh environment and tolerate conditions that would kill most other plants. However, despite their adaptations, these plants are extremely delicate and can be damaged or killed when stepped on. Trail widening and side trails are one of the greatest threats to these flowers, along with human-caused climate change. Some common wildflowers encountered throughout this habitat include *Silene acaulis*, *Geum rossii*, and various species of *Potentilla*, *Saxifraga*, *Senecio*, and *Gentiana*. Each of the three regions of the Rockies also has its own special alpine species, some of which are endemic.

Subalpine. The subalpine life zone begins around 10,000 feet in the Southern Rockies and ends at treeline. Like all life zones, the subalpine becomes progressively lower as one goes farther north: in southwestern and south-central Montana it is between 6,500 and 9,500 feet; in northern Idaho and in northwestern Montana, from 5,500 to 7,000 feet. A zone of both dense well-developed forests and large open meadows, the subalpine offers a wide variety of habitats for many types of wildflowers. At its highest limits this zone is defined by krummholz, the dwarf wind-scoured trees found at treeline. Dominant tree species include Engelmann spruce and subalpine fir, which occur throughout the Rockies. Other species of pines are intermixed: bristlecone pine is found in the Southern

Subalpine

Rockies, while limber pine occurs throughout. Whitebark pine is an important component of the Middle and Northern Rockies, and alpine larch is an unusual addition to the Northern Rockies. This zone is similar in temperature and appearance to the boreal or Hudsonian zone, which stretches around the high latitudes of the globe just south of the Arctic tundra. Some of the most spectacular displays of wildflowers occur from summer to early autumn. Many circumboreal species, such as *Chamerion angustifolium* and *Potentilla fruticosa*, are present in this life zone.

Montane. Starting around 8,000 feet or higher in the Southern Rockies, this is a zone of well-developed forests, meadows, and many intermountain parks (intermountain parks are absent in the Northern

Rockies). In northwestern Montana, montane is found from 2,500 to 5,500 feet; in the more continental climate east of the divide in Montana, it is found from 4,500 to 7,000 feet. The montane can have deep, winter-long snow cover, though on the east side of the mountains the snowpack is usually less and can be periodic through the winter. Forests of ponderosa, lodgepole pine, Douglas-fir, and aspen predominate. Aspen are particularly common in the Southern Rockies in the montane to lower subalpine; watered by the summer monsoons, they are especially lush in New Mexico, Colorado, and Utah. Aspen do not dominate the life zone again until the Northern Rockies of Montana and Alberta, where they form large stands. From the Middle section of Colorado and Utah northward,

Montane

Foothills

Pinyon-juniper

lodgepole pine are very common and form dense forests reaching to the lower subalpine. These dense forests are often dark and species-poor. However, several species of orchids, pinesap, wintergreen and other ericaceous plants call this life zone their home. Habitats within the montane that have spectacular displays of wildflowers include aspen forests and meadows.

Foothills. The foothills zone is one of transition. In the Southern Rockies, it is a defined life zone, beginning where the plains meet the mountains, generally 4,000–6,000 feet, depending on latitude. In Colorado, it is generally defined as 6,000–8,000 feet. Snow can come and go throughout the winter, and here the summer monsoon is an important source of moisture during the growing season. This zone is often heavily affected by chinooks, warm down-sloping winds that occur from fall to spring. The dominant vegetation includes ponderosa pine, Rocky Mountain juniper, assorted shrubs, mountain mahogany, Gambel oak, and wavyleaf oak (as far north as Denver).

As one moves north, the term "foothills" refers less to the life zone and instead becomes a geologic descriptor of the smaller mountains at the base of the Rockies. Here, the montane zone may abut either aspen parkland or prairie without the "foothills" transition. The vegetation is a mix of the montane and the drier life zones below. In the Middle and Northern Rockies, this can either be shrubs, ponderosa pine, Douglas-fir, or aspen. In the Bighorn Mountains of northern Wyoming and into central Montana, the dominant tree is often ponderosa pine; from Yellowstone and points north and west, it is often Douglas-fir.

Pinyon-juniper. In the Southern Rockies below the ponderosa pine/montane forest belt is the pinyon-juniper zone. This zone typically ranges in elevation from 4,000 to 7,000 feet depending on the latitude; however, in rain shadows, this zone can reach heights of over 9,000 feet. The climate is semi-arid with sporadic precipitation throughout the year and long hot and dry periods. The range of many of its species is determined by the limits of the summer monsoon. Winter snowpack is generally light and often only on north-facing slopes. This life zone is found on the eastern slope of the mountains as far north as Colorado Springs, and on the western slope as far north as southern Idaho and far southwestern Wyoming. This vegetation zone represents the northernmost extension of the Madrean flora. Depending on location and latitude, one to several dwarf oaks (*Quercus gambelii, Q. ×pauciloba, Q. grisea, Q. turbinella*) often accompany the pines and junipers.

Sagebrush steppe. Found throughout the Rockies as far north as central British Columbia, this life zone can vary greatly in elevation. In Colorado, it is found between 5,000 and 10,000 feet, mainly west of the Continental Divide. In Utah, it is found throughout the state, and in Wyoming it spills over the Continental Divide and can be found integrating with the shortgrass prairie of the Great Plains grassland around Casper and Douglas. In Montana, the sagebrush steppe is found throughout the state, however, in Alberta, it is found only in the vicinity of Waterton National Park, making it a very rare biome there. It is always found in rain shadows on fine soils that rarely experience fires. The climate is arid to semi-arid with more precipitation falling in the winter months and little to none in the summer. Winter precipitation percolating deeply into the soil is one of the factors determining if an area is sagebrush steppe or grasslands. Like all life zones it deserves protection, yet it is one of the least protected biomes in the western United States.

Intermountain parks. These large open valleys found in the Southern and Middle Rockies tend to be dominated by grasses or sagebrush steppe. Trees are only along rivers or on favorable topography.

High plains. This zone stretches east of the Rockies from Alberta and Saskatchewan, south to New Mexico. It can be found between 4,000 and 6,000 feet in the south and as low as 3,000 feet or below in the north. Dominated by grasses more than shrubs, it tends to exist in areas that have more precipitation in summer than in winter, and also in areas with higher fire frequencies. Grasses are well adapted to absorbing quick heavy downpours and are unbothered by frequent fires, since their growth structures are below ground. As one moves north, warm-season grasses are increasingly replaced by species of *Festuca*, *Poa*, and other cool-season grasses. Starting in northern Montana and continuing into Alberta is an ever-widening band of aspen mixed with prairie grasses; this aspen parkland fills in as the transition zone between plains and mountains in the Northern Rockies.

Wetlands. These aquatic zones vary from streams and ponds to lakes, rivers, marshes, and manmade ditches. They tend to be fed by surface-water flow and some underground flow.

Sagebrush steppe

Intermountain parks

High plains

Wetlands

Detailed Habitat Descriptions

Plant entries often include references to preferred exposure; in general, woodland plants favor shade, either moist or dry, but most wildflowers prefer open, full-sun locations that rarely have tree or shrub cover. The following are some other, frequently encountered habitat terms, each illustrated.

Riparian. Found along watercourses and bodies of water.

Pine parklands. Open forests often dominated by ponderosa pines. These stretch from south of the region covered by this book into British Columbia. Ponderosa pine habitat stops near Great Falls, Montana, on the east side of the Rockies; the species is not native to Alberta. In places west of the divide this could constitute open Douglas-fir forest as well.

Coniferous/aspen/mixed. Forests of pine, fir, and spruce or aspen. The type of tree cover, along with the wildflowers found within these forests, depends upon elevation, soil, and microclimate.

Meadows/sage meadows. Found at most elevations except alpine, these are open areas within forested areas. They often have a rich display of wildflowers depending on the season and precipitation.

Moist meadows/fens/bogs. All three habitats are defined by water. Moist meadows and fens are typically fed by some source of ground water percolating through the soil; both can be alkaline or acidic, depending on the surrounding rock types and ground water. Bogs are specialized habitats fed by precipitation, not ground water; they tend to be acidic in nature and become increasingly common as one goes farther north in the Rockies. Both fens and bogs can accumulate deep deposits of poorly decomposed organic matter known as peat.

Barrens. Often found in the intermountain parks and the areas west of the Continental Divide in Colorado, Utah, and Wyoming. These areas are often bare of dense vegetation due to the soil content, which can either have various toxic substances in it, or have a texture that precludes the establishment of widespread seedlings.

Rock scree. Moving fragments of rock on a steep slope are often found in the subalpine and alpine life zones. This habitat can be found anywhere there are crumbling cliffs and steep slopes. These areas often have specialized plants that are adapted to constantly shifting material.

Tundra. Existing above the treeline throughout the Rockies, tundra is dominated by small, mainly herbaceous plants and small dwarfed woody plants. A wide variety of microclimates can be found here, and they greatly influence what species of plants are present.

Seeps. Found at all elevations throughout the region. These springs usually emerge between layers of rock strata, creating small pockets of moist soil nearby and sustaining a flora that is drastically different from surrounding areas. Seeps can run seasonally or all year. The hanging gardens found on the Colorado Plateau are a specialized type of seep.

Rock ledges. Found in all life zones, these are specialized habitats where smaller plants can find a foothold. The species composition changes with the type of rock. Limestone and other calcareous rocks often have their own associated floras. Some plants are found only on granitic rocks.

Disturbed. These human-disturbed habitats are extremely widespread. They include roadsides, abandoned lots in urban areas, mine tailings and agricultural fields. Many of the plants found in these sites are exotics that coevolved with the land use techniques that Europeans brought with them to the Americas. A few North American native plants evolved to grow in areas disturbed by bison or other large animals.

Woodlands. These vary in species composition with elevation, latitude, precipitation, and soil.

Dry slopes. These tend to be dry open slopes devoid of heavy vegetation. They often offer habitat to species that are poor competitors.

Dunes/sandhills. Found throughout the region, both of these habitats range in size from a few acres to thousands of acres. Sandhills are stabilized by vegetation, while sand dunes are not. In Colorado, some of the most notable are the dunes in North Park and in the Great Sand Dunes National Park. Large and highly dispersed dunes can be found in central Wyoming; smaller sets of dunes and sandhills occur into Alberta.

Photos

Many species naturally exhibit a lot of variation in size, color, and growth patterns—but especially so when they hail from such a wide range of both longitude and elevation. In choosing the photos for this book, we have attempted to show the most true-to-form example of each species, including the most common flower color. Occasionally, we use insets of distinctive fruit to round out the wildflower portrait.

Maps

We have included range maps for each species, showing where in the Rocky Mountain region it has been found. The data were collected by various herbaria, botanic gardens, institutions, conservancies, universities, and government agencies over many years and compiled by the Biota of North America Program (BONAP). Canadian data and the few maps that were not found on BONAP were made from information supplied by the University of British Columbia Herbarium, Beaty Biodiversity Museum, SEINet, Consortium of Pacific Northwest Herbaria, Canadensys, University of Alberta Vascular Plant Herbarium, *Flora of Alberta* by E. H. Moss, and a few additional scientific papers. The maps are to be used as a guide, not as the final word. Much research and fieldwork remains to be conducted before we can consider the species of the Rocky Mountains mapped to perfection.

PLANT FAMILIES

Botanists classify plants in increasing levels of detail starting with two broad classes: angiosperms (flowering plants) and gymnosperms (nonflowering plants). The angiosperms are divided into two subclasses, monocots (having one seed leaf) and dicots (having two seed leaves). The next levels, superorders and orders, are not often used and are followed by plant families.

The family is the highest botanical classification level in common usage. Plants in the same family share many characteristics that are usually easily distinguished by the layperson. For instance, it is easy to recognize a member of the iris family, Iridaceae, by the flower parts coming in threes and by the flat stems and leaves. Some families are further divided into subfamilies, tribes, and subtribes, but these divisions are usually of interest only to serious botanists.

Learning about plant families and their major characteristics is one tool you can use to help you understand the relationships among the various plants you find. Some families are large, with many genera and species, while others have only a few members. Each family treated in this field guide is described here.

Adoxaceae—moschatel or elderberry family. Herbs, shrubs, or small trees. Leaves opposite, simple or pinnately compound and with entire or serrated margins. Inflorescence a terminal spike- or panicle-like cluster of perfect and radial flowers. Fruit a fleshy drupe.

Alismataceae—water-plantain family. Freshwater plants floating or growing on mud.

Leaves palmately veined, submersed, generally linear to oval, blades above water linear to arrow-shaped. Flowers 3 green sepals and 3 large white or pink petals, many stamens.

Amaranthaceae—pigweed family. Annual, monoecious or dioecious herbs. Leaves opposite or alternate and simple. Inconspicuous flowers, sometimes enclosed by 3 green bracts, in dense clusters; 4 or 5 sepals, petals lacking; imperfect or perfect and usually actinomorphic. Fruit a capsule or sometimes a utricle.

Amaryllidaceae—amaryllis family. Perennial herbs with leafless scapes that emerge each year from underground bulbs. Leaves basal, somewhat succulent. Inflorescence often an umbel subtended by bracts. Actinomorphic flowers with 6 tepals. Fruit a capsule. A prevalent genus of this family in the Rocky Mountain region, *Allium*, has a distinct onion smell. Some authors place *Allium in Alliaceae.*

Anacardiaceae—sumac family. Shrubs or trees. Leaves simple, compound, deciduous or evergreen. Flowers with 5 sepals fused at base, 5 petals free. Fruit with a single seed. Plants in our region toxic, may produce contact dermatitis.

Apiaceae—parsley family. Hollow stems with ribs, arising from ground. Leaves basal and on stem, usually compound. Small flowers in umbels, 5 petals.

Apocynaceae—dogbane family. Milky sap. Erect. Leaves not compound, entire. Flower clusters of 1 to many, axillary or terminal blossoms. Sepals fused at base, petals fused in bell shape.

Araceae—arum family. Many small flowers crowded on a spadix and partially surrounded by a spathe, as in yellow skunk cabbage, the only member of this family in our area.

Araliaceae—ginseng family. Shrubs or woody vines. Stems branched. Leaves simple or compound, alternate. Tiny flowers in umbels. Flowers with 5 petals alternating with 5 stamens. Fruit is a berry.

Aristolochiaceae—pipevine family. Leaves heart-shaped. Flowers solitary, 3 sepals partly fused into bowl shape with 3 long thin "tails" and 12 stamens, no petals. Seed with fleshy appendage. Ovary inferior or partly inferior.

Asparagaceae—asparagus family. Perennial herbs or subshrubs. Deciduous except in *Yucca*. Leaves alternate, basal or along stem, parallel-veined, and entire. Small, radial, greenish yellow flowers with 6 tepals are solitary or paired along stem forming a raceme or umbel. Fruit a green, red, or black berry or capsule. Some authors place portions of this family in Ruscaceae.

Asteraceae—aster family. Largest family on earth. Mostly herbs. Leaves various. What appears to be a single flower is a tightly crowded compound head of numerous small flowers of 2 types: ray flowers, with a ligule, often on outer edge of head; and disc flowers, with complete tubes and no ligule. All combinations of ray and disc flowers occur.

Balsaminaceae—touch-me-not family. Annuals with juicy sap. Leaves simple, alternate. Flowers showy, of irregular shape. Sepals 3: 2 small, green; 1 large, colored, forming a spur. Petals 5, fused into unequal lobes. Pods explode when ripe.

Berberidaceae—barberry family. Spreading to erect shrubs or herbs from rhizomes. Leaves are simple or pinnately compound. Sepals and petals 6 or 9, in whorls of 3. Berry usually purple-black.

Boraginaceae—borage family. Prostrate to erect. Leaves usually simple, entire. Flowers in clusters or 1-sided coil, uncoiling in

seed; each flower a 5-lobed tube usually with 5 appendages at top, alternating with 5 stamens and sometimes arching over tube.

Brassicaceae—mustard family. Leaves alternate. Flowers with 4 sepals shorter than the 4 petals, held in a double cross shape. Seedpods unique, with outer covering over a single row of seeds on each side of a papery division.

Cactaceae—cactus family. Thick, fleshy, round to flat structures with spines. Flowers solitary, with many petals.

Campanulaceae—bellflower family. Leaves on stems, simple. Flowers in clusters, spikes, or solitary. Flowers either bell-shaped or 2-lipped, petals fused at base or almost entirely. Stamens 5, free or fused.

Cannabaceae—hemp family. Annual or perennial, taprooted or rhizomatous herbs that are erect or climbing; foliage hairy-glandular and sometimes aromatic. Leaves simple, palmately lobed or compound with serrate or entire margins. Flowers unisexual: staminate flowers 5-merous and greenish white; pistillate flowers often surrounded by bracts.

Caprifoliaceae—honeysuckle family. Herbaceous perennials, shrubs, or vines. Leaves simple or compound, opposite. Narrow tubular flowers with 5 lobes held in pairs. Some authors place *Valeriana* in Valerianaceae.

Caryophyllaceae—pink family. Leaves usually opposite, not divided. Flowers few to many in open cluster or solitary in leaf axil. Sepals 4 or 5, free or fused, tube with lobes. Petals 4 or 5, very small or larger than sepals, usually notched or divided. Stamens 10 or fewer.

Celastraceae—staff-tree family. Herbs, shrubs (ours), vines, or trees. Leaves simple, evergreen (ours), or deciduous. Flowers in clusters at leaf axils, cup-like with 4 or 5 sepals and 4 or 5 tiny petals. Fruit a capsule.

Cleomaceae—cleome family. Unpleasant-smelling annual and perennial herbs or shrubs. Leaves alternate and usually palmately compound with 3–5 leaflets and entire margins. Flowers solitary, in a raceme, or a flat-topped cluster; radial or slightly bilateral and 4-merous. Stamens often conspicuously protruding. Fruit a linear capsule resembling a mustard pod, but without the central partition.

Commelinaceae—spiderwort family. Annual or perennial herbs with fleshy roots. Basal or alternate stem leaves often succulent and with parallel venation and entire margins; bases sheathing. Radial or bilateral flowers have 3 sepals and 3 petals: 2 petals often larger and showier than 3rd. Fruit a capsule.

Convolvulaceae—morning-glory family. Twining or trailing. Flowers single or in cluster, with 5 free sepals overlapping; petals fused, bell-shaped, pleated, twisted in bud.

Cornaceae—dogwood family. Leaves with parallel veins, opposite or whorled, deciduous. Tiny flowers white, green, or pale yellow, surrounded by large white petal-like bracts. Ovary inferior. Fruit red, white, or blue, soft on outside, 1 or 2 hard stones inside.

Crassulaceae—stonecrop family. Fleshy. Leaves basal and on stem, not compound. Flowers in clusters, usually with bracts. Flower sepals 3–5, free; petals 3–5, free or fused. Stamens same number as sepals. Seedpods with 3–5 chambers, many seeds.

Droseraceae—sundew family. Bog dwellers. Carnivorous. Leaves in flattened rosette with insect-catching hairs on upper surface. Flowers in parts of 5, single to few on long leafless stem.

Ericaceae—heath family. Bark peeling. Leaves simple, evergreen or deciduous. Flowers in cluster or solitary, usually with bracts. Petals 4 or 5, usually free or fused. Stamens 8–10. Fruit is a capsule or berry.

Euphorbiaceae—spurge family. Milky sap. Petals absent. Petal-like bracts often brightly colored; stamens and glands in a central cluster or a 3-lobed ovary hanging to one side of the stamens.

Fabaceae—pea family. Shrubs, herbs, or trees. Leaves compound. Flower shape unique to this family, with 5 petals, 1 large at top, 2 lower joined to form crescent-shaped keel. Ovary superior. Fruit is a pod, often inflated, with 1 or 2 rows of seeds attached along one edge.

Gentianaceae—gentian family. Flowers large, with 4 or 5 petals fused, forming flattened to narrow bell shape with spreading lobes. Stamens 4 or 5, fused to wall, alternate with lobes. Sinuses between lobes often with various uniquely shaped appendages. Ovary superior on stalk.

Geraniaceae—geranium family. Leaves palmately lobed or divided. Flowers in loose clusters in parts of 5, with 10 stamens. Mature seed clings to elongated style, and coils, driving seed into soil.

Grossulariaceae—gooseberry family. Shrubs with erect stems, with or without many spines. Simple, deciduous leaves clustered on tips of twigs, palmately 3- to 5-lobed. Flowers usually in hanging clusters. Sepals usually 5 and spreading, 5 petals fused at base, alternating with 5 stamens. Berries of many colors.

Hydrangeaceae—hydrangea family. Trees, shrubs, or vines. Leaves opposite, simple, entire, lobed or toothed, deciduous or evergreen. Flowers in clusters or solitary at tip or on upper stem. Sepals and petals 4–7, free. Stamens at least twice the number of petals. Seeds many, small.

Hypericaceae—St. John's wort family. Annual or perennial herbs, subshrubs, or shrubs, usually with angular stems. Leaves simple, usually opposite, sessile or nearly so, and with entire margins; blades often with translucent glandular dots. Bisexual flowers solitary or in a cymose raceme. Stamens in cluster of 5. Fruit a capsule. Some authors place portions of this family in Clusiaceae.

Iridaceae—iris family. Leaves usually strap-like, with parallel veins, arranged in fans. Flower parts, in 3s, are the same on each side. Ovary inferior.

Lamiaceae—mint family. Stems erect, 4-sided. Leaves entire to deeply lobed, opposite. Flowers usually clustered around stem or at top, subtended by leaves or bracts. Flowers 1- or 2-lipped; upper lip entire or lobed, flat to hood-shaped but occasionally none; lower lip 3-lobed. Fruit is a nutlet. Plants often have a mint smell.

Lentibulariaceae—bladderwort family. Carnivorous. Growing in wet places or in water. Leaves none or in basal rosette, entire. Flowers in cluster or single, on long leafless stem. Sepals united, flower united, 2 lips, upper lip with 2 lobes, lower lip with 3 lobes and spur at base. Small seed in capsule.

Liliaceae—lily family. Leaves with parallel veins. Flowers with 3 petals and sepals, and 3 or 6 stamens. Ovary superior.

Linaceae—flax family. Long thin stems. Leaves on stem, usually linear. Flower cluster open to dense, nodding in bud, petals short-lived. Stamens 4 or 5, alternate, with 4 or 5 petals.

Loasaceae—blazing-star family. Rough or stinging hairs. Leaves alternate, pinnately lobed. Flowers with 5 sepals persistent in seed; 5 free petals. Many stamens with thread-like filaments. Many seeds in capsules.

Lythraceae—loosestrife family. Stems sometimes 4-angled. Leaves entire. Flowers radially symmetrical, sepals and petals 4–6 alternating. Ovary superior but inside fused sepals.

Malvaceae—mallow family. Leaves lobed, somewhat maple-like. Juice sticky. Flower sepals form 5-lobed calyx; petals 5, free, wide. Stamens fused at base, forming column around long pistil with style tips extending above.

Melanthiaceae—false-hellebore family. Perennial herbs that are rhizomatous or from bulbs. Leaves basal or alternate along stem have parallel venation and entire margins. Inflorescence a raceme or panicle (or flowers solitary) of radial, perfect flowers with 6 tepals (or 3 petals and 3 sepals) and 6 stamens. Fruit a capsule. Some authors place this family in Liliaceae. *Xerophyllum is sometimes placed in Xerophyllaceae.*

Menyanthaceae—buckbean family. Aquatic. Leaves simple or 3 sessile leaflets. Flowers with 5-lobed calyx; corolla 5-lobed, flat to funnel-shaped; stamens 5; pistil 1. Ovary superior or partially inferior. Few to many seeds in capsule.

Montiaceae—miner's lettuce family. Annual, biennial, or perennial, succulent herbs typically with opposite leaves. Flowers radial, bisexual, usually with 2 sepals and 5 petals; however, in the case of *Lewisia* there can be up to 18 petals. Fruit a capsule.

Nyctaginaceae—four-o'clock family. Leaves opposite, entire, not usually same size. Bracts free or fused into calyx-like unit with solitary flower or cluster of flowers. Petal-like sepals fused into trumpet shape with 4 or 5 lobes and the tube constricted at base. No true petals. Ovary superior.

Nymphaeaceae—water lily family. Aquatic. Floating or submersed leaves arising from roots on long petioles. Flowers solitary, large, showy.

Onagraceae—evening primrose family. Flowers in spikes, clusters, or solitary, often open at dusk or dawn, darkening in color with age. Flowers in parts of 4, free. Pollen on interconnected threads. Ovary inferior.

Orchidaceae—orchid family. Leaves with parallel veins. Flowers irregularly shaped, ovary inferior. Sepals 3 petal-like, petals 3, lowest usually different, often enlarged. Stamen 1 fused with stigma.

Orobanchaceae—broomrape family. Erect, fleshy, nongreen parasites. No leaves. Flowers in spike, cluster, or solitary. Calyx tubular or cup-shaped, lobes 0–5. Corolla

2-lipped, 5-lobed, with 4 stamens. Capsules with many small seeds.

Paeoniaceae—peony family. Perennials. Stems several, clustered. Leaves large, deeply dissected or compound. Flowers solitary or few in cluster. Sepals 5, persistent after flowering. Petals 5–10. Pistils 2–5, large, coarse. Seeds large, black.

Papaveraceae—poppy family. Annuals to trees. Yellowish sap. Leaves basal and on stem, toothed or dissected. Flowers radially symmetrical. Ovary superior. Sepals 2 or 3, fall as flower bud opens. Petals 4–6, free, many stamens.

Phrymaceae—lopseed family. Annual or perennial herbs with simple, basal or opposite stem leaves with toothed or entire margins. Inflorescence pairs of perfect, 5-merous, bilateral, and bilabiate tubular-campanulate flowers in upper leaf axils. Fruit an ellipsoidal capsule.

Plantaginaceae—plantain family. Leaves in basal rosette. Flowers in dense spike at top of long leafless stem. A single bract is just under each tiny flower, 4 sepals form calyx holding bell-shaped tube with 4 spreading to erect colorless lobes. Dries brown and papery. Ovary superior.

Polemoniaceae—phlox family. Simple or compound leaves on stem or in basal rosette. Flowers in clusters, heads, or solitary. Flowers bell-shaped or a short tube with flattened lobes and open throat.

Polygalaceae—milkwort family. Leaves simple, pinnately veined, entire. Flowers in cluster are pea-like; sepals and petals free or fused together.

Polygonaceae—buckwheat family. Leaves alternate, with a paper sheath around the node where the petiole attaches, each a different shape. Flowers small with colored sepals and no true petals. Stamens 2–9, often in whorls.

Primulaceae—primrose family. Annuals or perennials, hairless or with glands. Leaves simple. Flowers sometimes on long leafless stems. Flower parts 4 or 5. Calyx deeply lobed; petals spreading to reflexed; ovary usually superior. Seed a capsule with few to many small seeds.

Ranunculaceae—buttercup family. Leaves basal and alternate on stem; petioles usually flat at base. Flowers radially symmetrical or irregular with spurs, as in *Delphinium*. Sepals and petals usually 5 to many; sepals green, withering early or petal-like when no petals are present. Stamens 10 to many. Fruit is a cluster of many hard seeds, a berry, or many seeds in a dry pod.

Rhamnaceae—buckthorn family. Shrubs, vines, or trees. Plants sometimes thorny. Simple leaves with petioles, clustered on short shoots. Flowers in small to large clusters atop stems or solitary in axils. Sepals 4 or 5; petals none or 4 or 5, often narrowing toward the base. Seed in stone in 2–5 fused fleshy cells.

Rosaceae—rose family. Leaves usually pinnately or palmately compound, alternate with stipules. Flowers in groups or solitary. Sepals 5, often alternate with bractlets; petals 5, free; stamens 5 to many; pistils 1 to many. Fruit can vary in form: pome (apple), raspberry-like, achene, or follicle.

Rubiaceae—madder family. Stems rough, with 4 sides. Leaves in pairs or whorls. Flowers in clusters or solitary. Calyx 4-lobed or missing. Flower petals small, with 4 lobes fused at base forming cross. Ovary inferior, forming 2 rounded seeds.

Santalaceae—sandalwood family. Herbs, shrubs, or trees. Parasites on roots of other plants. Leaves stemless, entire. Flowers small clusters in axils on upper plant. Calyx tubular to bell-shaped, with 4 or 5 lobes. No petals. Ovary inferior or superior. Single-seeded fruit in persistent calyx.

Sarcobataceae—greasewood family. Deciduous, monoecious, much-branched, spiny shrubs. Leaves fleshy to succulent and green. Inflorescences spikes with either male or female flowers. The lone genus has only 2 species, both of which are halophytic.

Saxifragaceae—saxifrage family. Plant hairy, usually glandular. Leaves oblong to round, entire to maple-like. Flowers 1 to many. Petals sometimes spotted, 10 stamens, filaments generally flat.

Scrophulariaceae—figwort family. Generally glandular. Leaves alternate. Flowers in spike or cluster with bracts, or in axils. Petals 4 or 5, united, 2-lipped. Stamens usually 4 in 2 pairs, sometimes sterile staminode. Flower shapes include wide tube with 2 flaring lips; narrow tube with upper lip arching to pointed spout; radially symmetrical.

Smilacaceae—greenbrier family. Perennial, rhizomatous, dioecious shrubs, herbs, or lianas that are often prickly and bearing tendrils. Leaves opposite or alternate, simple and with 3 prominent veins and reticulation between veins. Inflorescence often a spike-like cluster with imperfect, radial, 3-merous, small and yellowish green flowers. Fruit a berry.

Solanaceae—nightshade family. Simple leaves with petiole, entire or deeply lobed. Flower calyx with 5 lobes. Petals 5, fused, trumpet-shaped or flattened. Fruit is a tomato-like berry or capsule.

Tofieldiaceae—tofieldia family. Perennial, sometimes rhizomatous, deciduous herbs with erect aerial stems. Leaves mostly basal, grass-like and with smooth surfaces and parallel venation; when present, stem leaves alternate. Inflorescence globose, or nearly so, and with 4–15 small flowers. Fruit a capsule.

Typhaceae—cattail family. Wetland plants. Stems round, stiff. Leaves flat, stiff, with parallel veins. Flowers in thick cylindrical spike, male flowers separate above female flowers.

Urticaceae—nettle family. The lone plant in our region, stinging nettle, is covered with stinging hairs. Flowers tiny, green, without petals, in small clusters of hanging stems. Leaves opposite.

Verbenaceae—vervain family. Leaves opposite, toothed. Flowers in spike or head, slightly 2-lipped. Ovary not lobed, later separating as 4 nutlets. Without mint-like odor.

Violaceae—violet family. Leaves basal or on stem, sometimes both. Flowers usually solitary in parts of 5. Irregular shape. Larger petal at bottom, with spur or pouch at base; pair of side petals and another pair of petals at top. Lower 2 stamens with nectaries project into spur. Pistil with unique peak; ovary superior.

Zygophyllaceae—caltrop family. The single species in our region forms large mats with pinnately divided leaves. Flowers single in axils. Seed nutlet with stout spines.

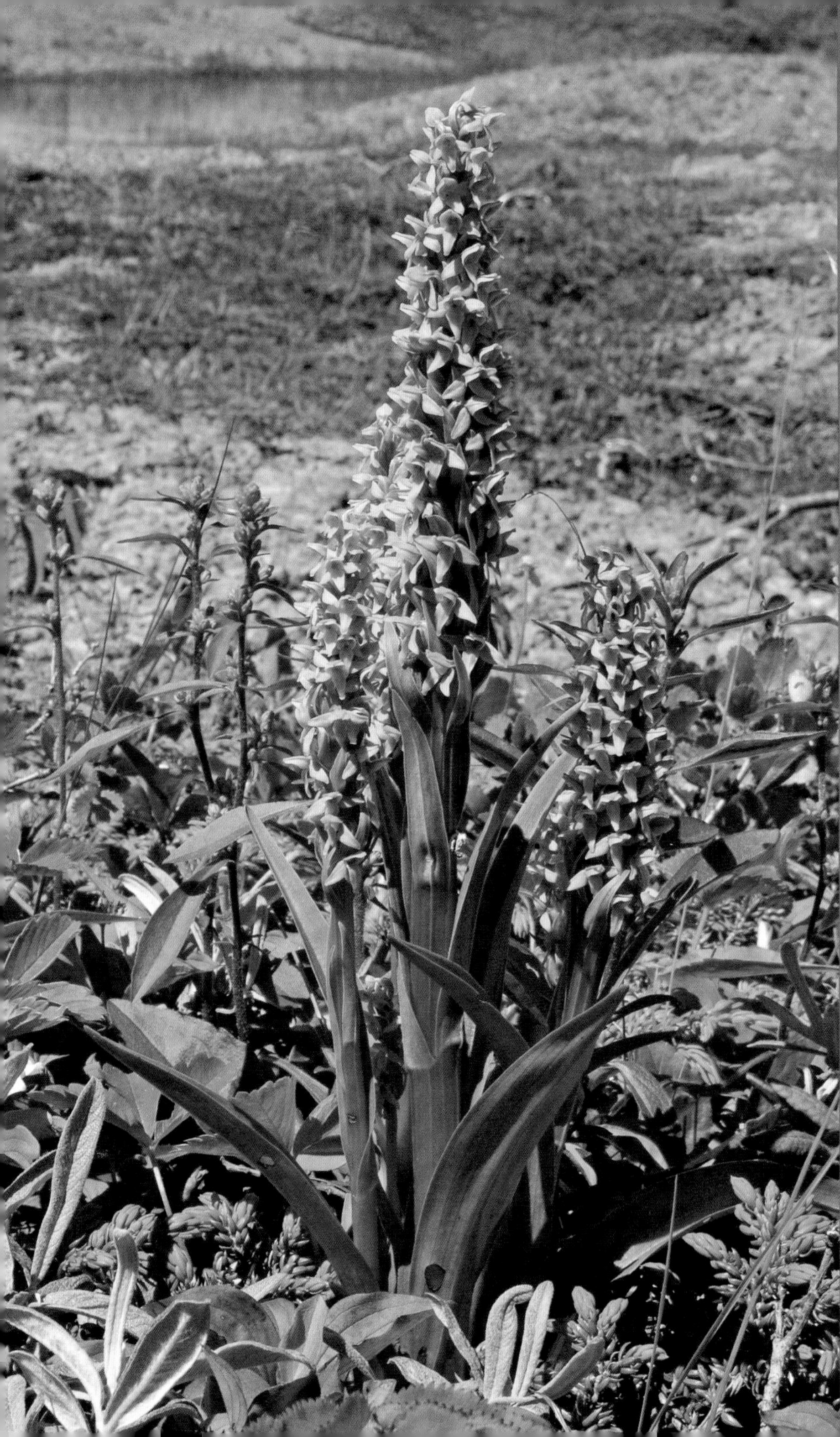

Plantago major PLANTAGINACEAE
common plantain
RM, subalpine, montane, sagebrush steppe, grasslands, common, Spring–Summer, perennial, 2–16 in.
Herbaceous perennial with basal rosette. Flowering stems erect, several, unbranched. Leaves broad, oval to egg-shaped, entire to somewhat toothed, with 3 to several distinct parallel veins. Inflorescence a dense, narrow, 2- to 7-in.-long spike of tiny green flowers, topping a leafless stem. Fruit a capsule. Disturbed areas including lawns, gardens, roadsides, and urban areas. Introduced.

Humulus lupulus var. *neomexicanus*
(*H. neomexicanus*) CANNABACEAE
New Mexican hop
RM, montane, foothills, common, L Spring–Summer, perennial, 7–30 ft.
Herbaceous (woody at base), rhizomatous, twining vine; climbs shrubs, trees, and boulders. Leaves opposite, 4 in. or longer; 5 palmate lobes, serrated margins; surfaces rough-hairy. Dioecious, male/female flowers on separate plants: female inflorescence a cylindric spike with pairs of apetalous flowers under greenish yellow bracts; male inflorescence a panicle of yellowish or whitish green apetalous flowers. Fruit an achene in pendulous papery cone-like arrangement. Grows in moist, shady canyons, alluvial forests, and on riverbanks. Native.

Thalictrum fendleri
RANUNCULACEAE
Fendler's meadow-rue
RM, subalpine, montane, foothills, common, Spring–Fall, perennial, 1–2 ft.
Herbaceous, rhizomatous. Stems erect to spreading. Leaves basal and alternate on stems; short-stalked, green, 3 or 4 times ternately compound; leaflets round in outline, 3-lobed, margins crenate. Inflorescence branched panicles, open, many-flowered. Flowers with no obvious petals, dioecious (male/female flowers on separate plants). Sepals green to white, filaments greenish yellow to purple, and stigma purple. Fruit achenes. Occurs in ponderosa forests. Common in MR and SR, uncommon in NR. Native.

Sarcobatus vermiculatus

SARCOBATACEAE
greasewood
RM, pinyon-juniper, sagebrush steppe,
intermountain parks, common,
L Spring–Summer, perennial, 3–8 ft.

Shrubby asymmetrical mounds of spiny evergreen growth. Spiny stems light when young,
aging dark. Leaves linear, succulent, mostly
glabrous, 0.75–1.5 in. long. Female and male
flowers are formed in separate cone-like cat-
kins on the same plant. Seedpods resemble flat, flaky flowers. A dominant plant covering acres of alkaline flats in
the intermountain region, and dry and dense soils. Toxic
to grazers in large quantities. Can resemble *Atriplex canescens*, with which it often grows. Native.

Urtica dioica URTICACEAE

stinging nettle
RM, montane, foothills, wetlands,
common, Spring, perennial, 4–6 ft.

Rhizomatous plant can form large colonies.
Stems are 4-sided and hairy. Leaves are narrow, lanceolate, and often toothed, 1.5–6 in.
long, the surface covered in hairs with glands.
Flowers tiny, often green or whitish, in small
clusters at leaf axils. Found in the montane
zones in wet areas and often at the base of rocky or talus
slopes. Mature plants cause stinging, itching, and burning
when in contact with bare skin; very young plants can be
eaten raw or boiled in soups. Native.

Aralia racemosa ARALIACEAE

American spikenard
SR, montane, foothills, rare,
Summer, perennial, 2–7 ft.

Herbaceous, shrub-like. Stems stout, maroon, branched, glabrous or finely hairy. Basal
leaves to 2 ft. around, alternate, pinnate, twice
compound, with dentate margins; leaflets on
small stalks to 5.5 in. long, oval, sharply tapering to a point. Flowers in long, irregular
branched panicle; larger clusters made up of
smaller stalked umbels; pale green, less than 0.2 in. wide
with 5 long white stamens, petals reflexed; stems densely
hairy. Found in shade, moist ravines, and woodlands. Conspicuous spikes of reddish purple berries in fall. Native.

Smilax lasioneura
(*S. herbacea* ssp. *lasioneura*)
SMILACACEAE
Blue Ridge carrionflower
MR, SR, foothills, infrequent, L Spring–
Summer, perennial, 10–15 ft.

Small liana with herbaceous stems twining
upward over adjacent vegetation. Branched
stems annual, erect to ascending. Glabrous,
cordate, entire, alternate leaves; veins raised
on reverse; green tendrils. Round clusters
of many malodorous flowers from leaf axils,
peduncle to over 5 in.; become black fleshy fruit; unisexual in separate clusters. Found at east edge of our range,
disjuncts from a primarily Midwestern population. Open
woodlands along foothills. Native.

Euphorbia esula EUPHORBIACEAE
leafy spurge
RM, foothills, pinyon-juniper, sagebrush
steppe, grasslands, common, Spring–
Summer, perennial, 12–32 in.

Stems upright, multiple, glabrous to hairy,
with a milky latex if broken. Leaves alternate, linear to lanceolate, entire, to 2.5 in.
long, hairless. Flower stems with multiple
flowers in umbels. Individual flowers small,
with broadly heart-shaped yellowish green
bracts being the showiest part of the flower. Found in
fields, moist areas, roadsides and other disturbed habitats.
Native to Eurasia and classified as a noxious weed throughout the Rockies. Introduced and invasive.

Coeloglossum viride
(*Habenaria viridis*) ORCHIDACEAE
longbract frog orchid
RM, subalpine, montane, foothills,
grasslands, wetlands, infrequent, L
Spring–Summer, perennial, 12–28 in.

Stout single stem from several basal leaves.
Oblanceolate leaves below, reducing above,
alternate, clasping, transform into ascending bracts among flowers. Flowers green to
light green, often with tinges of brown or
pink. The spurs located behind the hood are swollen to
form a bladder. The lower lip is elongated to sometimes
twice the length of the hood. One of the more common orchids to encounter in mixed coniferous forests, found on
grassy slopes, in clearings. Native.

Corallorhiza trifida
(*C. corallorhiza*) ORCHIDACEAE
early coralroot, yellow coralroot
RM, montane, foothills, infrequent,
Spring–Summer, perennial, 3–14 in.

Similar to *C. maculata* but smaller in all its
parts, and stems always green to yellow, solitary or in dense groups. Leaves reduced to a
few alternate sheaths on lower stem. Flowers
share stem color on 3 sepals and 2 upper petals; labellum white, not spotted. Shaded coniferous woodlands, mixed forests, in undisturbed duff soils.
Partial nutrition obtained from other plants, mostly trees,
through a mycorrhizal relationship. Circumboreal. Native.

Epipactis helleborine
(*E. latifolia*) ORCHIDACEAE
broadleaf helleborine
RM, montane, foothills, infrequent, locally
abundant, Summer, perennial, 1.5–3 ft.

Tall stems, most leafy toward the middle.
Leaves lanceolate, 2–4 in. long, alternate,
clasping stem, horizontal and curved downward, parallel venation. Flowers with leafy
bracts; less than 1 in. across in terminal spike,
not at each leaf axil as *E. gigantea*; variable
shades of pinkish green. 3 sepals, 2 similar
petals, labellum flared with 2 lobes at lip. Found in moist
to dry woodlands, roadsides, in partial shade. Sparse in the
NR. This European orchid can become weedy. Introduced.

Listera cordata
(*Neottia cordata*) ORCHIDACEAE
heartleaf twayblade
RM, subalpine, montane, foothills, locally
abundant, Summer, perennial, 2–12 in.

Small herb from slender rhizomes and fibrous roots; stems glabrous to glandular
above the leaves. Leaves 2, opposite, broadly
ovate-cordate, tipped with a sharp point. Few
to several yellowish green flowers in a terminal raceme; lip deeply cleft into 2 lobes with 2
teeth at the base. Fruit an egg-shaped capsule.
Our native orchids live in sensitive habitats and should
never be disturbed. Grows in shade, moist forests, bogs,
thickets, and mossy areas along streams. Native.

3 or 6 petals, elongated clusters, bilateral

Piperia unalascensis
(*Habenaria unalascensis*) ORCHIDACEAE
slender-spire orchid, Alaska rein orchid
RM, montane, foothills, uncommon,
Spring, perennial, 12–26 in.

Herbaceous, scapose, from tuberous roots.
Leaves 1, basal, 1.5–6 in. long, 0.3–2 in.
wide, smooth, oblanceolate, prominent midvein, blunt tip. Inflorescence a sparse terminal spike. Flowers pale to whitish green,
0.1–0.25 in., resupinate. Upper sepal roundish, erect to arching over column; 2 adjacent
petals curve upward, creating a hood; lower
2 sepals bend backward; lower lip greenish
white, terminates in a tapered curved spur. Fruit a capsule.
Shady moist forests, riparian areas. Native.

Platanthera aquilonis (*Habenaria*
hyperborea) ORCHIDACEAE
northern green orchid
RM, throughout, common, L
Spring–Fall, perennial, 2–24 in.
Herbaceous with erect stems. Leaves ascending to erect, oblong to lance-shaped,
smooth, 1.5–10 in. long, 2 in. wide. Inflorescence a terminal spike, sparse to dense.
Flowers green to greenish yellow, resupinate. Upper sepal and 2 petals together
form a hood; 2 sepals extend horizontally
from center in opposite directions; lower lip projecting to
descending. Spur is cylindrical, rounded, slightly curved
forward. Fruit a capsule. Moist meadows, fens, tundra,
streambanks, ditches, seeps, open forest. Native.

Platanthera huronensis
(*Habenaria huronensis*)
ORCHIDACEAE
Huron green orchid
RM, alpine, subalpine, montane,
wetlands, locally abundant, L
Spring–Fall, perennial, 6–36 in.
Herbaceous with spindle-shaped stems
from fibrous roots. Leaves 3 or more, ascending to arching, 4–12 in., distally reduced to bracts, broadly linear with rounded
tip. Inflorescence a terminal spike. Flowers whitish green,
petals often whiter than sepals. Upper sepal and upper
2 petals form a hood. 2 lateral sepals extend horizontally
to downward, may be reflexed. Lower lip terminates in a
cylindrical, rounded, curved spur. Fruit a capsule. Wet
meadows, tundra, riparian areas, fens, seeps, ditches.
Shade to sun. Native.

Platanthera obtusata
(*Habenaria obtusata*) ORCHIDACEAE
bluntleaved orchid
RM, montane, wetlands, common,
Summer, perennial, 2–14 in.

Herbaceous, scapose, from tuberous roots.
Leaves 1 (rarely 2), basal, 1.5–6 in. long by 0.3–
2 in. wide, smooth, oblanceolate, prominent
midvein, blunt tip. Inflorescence a terminal
spike, sparsely flowered. Flowers pale green to
whitish green, 0.1–0.25 in., resupinate. Upper
sepal nearly round, erect to arching over column; 2 adjacent petals curve upward, creating
a hood; lower 2 sepals bent backward; lower lip
greenish white, descending, terminates in spur. Spur slender, tapering, somewhat curving. Fruit a capsule. Shady
moist forests and riparian areas. Native.

Platanthera stricta
(*Habenaria saccata*) ORCHIDACEAE
slender bog orchid
NR, MR, subalpine, montane,
foothills, wetlands, common,
Summer–Fall, perennial, 8–32 in.

Herbaceous from tuberous roots with erect
narrow stems. Leaves alternate, 1–6 in. long,
oblong to lanceolate; lower leaves bluntly
tipped, upper leaves pointed, eventually reduced to bracts. Inflorescence a terminal
spike of numerous green, bilateral flowers;
2 lateral sepals, 1 upper sepal slightly hooded at tip;
2 upper petals flank hood, lower lip points down; spur
equal to or shorter than lip. Fruit a capsule. Found in
moist meadows, thickets, forest openings,
often in non-calcareous soils. Native.

Veratrum viride
(*V. eschscholtzianum*) MELANTHIACEAE
green false hellebore, green corn lily
NR, MR, subalpine, montane, locally
abundant, Summer, perennial, 2–6 ft.

Robust stems in clusters or large colonies,
from short rhizomes. Leaves alternate, elliptical, 4–12 in. long by 3–6 in. wide; upright,
clasping stem, heavily pleated; smooth above,
hairy below, reduced to smaller bracts among flowers.
Flowering stem upright, 1–3 ft. tall above leaves; woolly,
with drooping branches in loose panicles; flowers 0.75 in.
across, 6 tepals light to deep green; seed capsule glabrous,
0.5–0.75 in. long. Sunny areas of wet meadows, subalpine
slopes, forest openings. Native.

Rumex salicifolius POLYGONACEAE
willow dock
RM, subalpine, montane, common, L
Spring–E Summer, perennial, 8–32 in.
Upright herb with stems branching from
base into multiple side branches. Leaves
mostly on stems, alternate, linear and
willow-like to 6 in. long. Inflorescence
a panicle 4–8 in. long with dense, spiky
branches. Flowers in whorls of 7–20, with 6
tepals, greenish; 3 inner tepals mature into
rounded fruit, a brown achene. Found in moist meadows and riparian areas. Approximately 17 *Rumex* spp. are
native or introduced to the Rockies; mature fruit is often
needed for positive identification. Native.

Frasera speciosa
(*Swertia radiata*) GENTIANACEAE
monument plant
RM, subalpine, montane, sagebrush steppe,
common, Summer, perennial, 1–7 ft.
Thick stems from basal rosette; leaves
whorled and smaller up the stem. Leaves
3–10 in., lanceolate, glabrous, lighter central vein. Flower racemes at all but lowest
whorls; 4 long sepals, 4 petals opening wide,
speckled purple; hairy central gland split
lengthwise. Grows in sunny areas, moist meadows, forest
edges and openings, and steppe. Monocarpic; plants may
live 20–60 years before flowering and dying; colonies often
bloom en masse. Native.

Galium coloradoense
(*G. multiflorum* var. *coloradoense*)
RUBIACEAE
Colorado bedstraw
SR, montane, foothills, pinyon-juniper,
sagebrush steppe, uncommon, L
Spring–Summer, perennial, 6–16 in.
Dioecious herb with numerous erect, glabrous, square stems from creeping rhizomes; woody at base. Leaves along stem in
whorls of 4, linear to lanceolate, with smooth
surfaces and a prominent midrib. Flowers campanulate,
yellowish green, white, or cream, and in groups of few on
branchlets along stem. Fruit covered in white or yellowish brown bristles. Grows on sandstone ledges, cliffs, and
other dry, rocky habitats of the Colorado Plateau. Discovered in southwestern CO by Alice Eastwood. Native.

Frasera albomarginata (*Swertia albomarginata*) GENTIANACEAE

desert frasera

SR, pinyon-juniper, sagebrush steppe, common, Spring–Summer, perennial, 8–16 in.

Single stem from basal rosette, openly branched in flower. Leaves 3–5 in. long, linear, concave, often very wavy, with clear white edge; whorled or opposite along stem, branched from axils. Flowers green-white in open, paniculate cyme; 4 petals spotted blue-purple with fringed green horizontal gland. A Four Corners species, reaching the pinyon and sage habitats and open ponderosa forests in southwestern CO, southern UT. Native.

Heuchera richardsonii

SAXIFRAGACEAE

Richardson's alumroot

RM, montane, foothills, grasslands, rare, locally abundant, Spring–Summer, perennial, 8–37 in.

Herb with erect stems covered in stalked glands. Leaves basal, with 5–7 deep lobes, toothed margins, and smooth surfaces (sometimes with stalked glands). Inflorescence a dense to spreading cluster of greenish white (rarely pink) campanulate flowers with bilateral hypanthia. Sepals erect with green tips. Styles protruding and stamens sometimes protruding. Grows in pine forests, meadows, on gravelly lakeshores, and in open woodlands. Disjunct populations in CO, where it is rare. Native.

Oplopanax horridus (*Echinopanax horridus*) ARALIACEAE

devilsclub

NR, montane, foothills, wetlands, locally abundant, L Spring–E Summer, perennial, 3–10 ft.

Thicket-forming shrub with spiny stems. Alternate maple-like leaves enormous at 4–10 in. across, palmate with toothed and serrated lobes, spiny petioles and veins. Green flowers in a 4- to 10-in.-long terminal panicle; flowers around 0.2 in. wide, exserted stamens; mature into scarlet berries. Forms thickets along streams, marshes, wet woods at middle and lower elevations, disjunct from its primary coastal habitats. Native.

Orthilia secunda
(*Pyrola secunda*) ERICACEAE
sidebells, one-sided wintergreen
RM, alpine, subalpine, montane,
foothills, common, L Spring–Summer,
perennial, 2–10 in.

Rhizomatous, evergreen, herbaceous subshrub with green to reddish stems from
basal cluster of leaves. Leaves oval, to 2 in.
long, shiny and darker on top, light green
below. Margins entire or finely toothed. Inflorescence a terminal raceme with 4–20
greenish white urn-shaped flowers hanging
from one side of arching stem. Light-green
styles protrude from flowers and curve downward. Fruit a
rounded, flattened capsule that persists through the winter.
Moist, coniferous forests, often in small colonies. Native.

Pyrola chlorantha
(*P. virens*) ERICACEAE
green-flowered wintergreen
RM, subalpine, montane,
foothills, common, L Spring–
Summer, perennial, 4–10 in.

Rhizomatous evergreen herb to subshrub
with erect reddish stems from basal cluster
of leaves (sometimes absent). Leaves leathery, round or ovate, to 2 in., shiny and dark
green on top, pale green below. Veins light
but not conspicuously white like *P. picta*. Inflorescence an elongated terminal raceme of 2–8 greenish
to yellowish, weakly bilateral, nodding white flowers with
projecting, down-curved styles and a cluster of included
yellow stamens. Shady coniferous forests,
often where moist. Native.

Heuchera bracteata
SAXIFRAGACEAE
Rocky Mountain alumroot
SR, alpine, subalpine, montane,
foothills, common, L Spring–
Summer, perennial, 3–15 in.

Herb with erect stems from dense cluster of basal leaves. Stem leaves alternate,
to 1.5 in. across with 5–7 shallow, rounded
lobes and sharply toothed margins. Leaf surfaces covered in long stalked glands. Inflorescence a dense, 1-sided
spike of small yellowish green to greenish white, narrowly
bell-shaped flowers. Styles and stamens protrude past corolla. Shady rocky ledges, cracks in cliffsides. Native.

Mitella pentandra
(Pectiantia pentandra) SAXIFRAGACEAE
five-stamened mitrewort
RM, alpine, subalpine, montane, common,
Spring–Summer, perennial, 3–16 in.

Rhizomatous (can be stoloniferous) herb;
slender, erect leafless stems from basal cluster of leaves; forms dense colonies. Leaves to
3 in. wide, 5–9 lobes, sharp-toothed margins;
lobes and teeth with pointed tips. Raceme of
6–25 pinwheel-like flowers remote from each
other. Erect, triangularly lobed sepals alternate with yellowish green pinnatifid petals and surround a disc-shaped,
gland-lined hypanthium. Seeds reddish brown. Grows in
moist shady woods, streambanks, wet meadows, fens, and
on talus slopes. Native.

Adoxa moschatellina ADOXACEAE
muskroot, moschatel
RM, alpine, subalpine, montane,
foothills, uncommon, L Spring–
E Summer, perennial, 2–8 in.

Delicate, herbaceous plant from rhizome.
Stems erect. Basal leaves long-stalked, ternately divided 2 or 3 times, with smooth
surfaces; stem leaves, 1 pair above middle of
flowering stem, opposite and reduced. Inflorescence a cluster of 5 terminal flowers with 4 yellowish
green petals; lateral flowers with 5 petals. Stamens equal
to number of petals, but filaments so deeply divided they
appear twice as numerous. Fruit a dry green drupe. Flowers produce a musky scent. Grows in moist
shady forests and alpine rockslides. Native.

Asclepias asperula APOCYNACEAE
spider milkweed, antelope horns
MR, SR, foothills, pinyon-juniper, sagebrush
steppe, grasslands, locally abundant,
Spring–Summer, perennial, 1–2 ft.

Ascending stems with milky sap. Leaves opposite to irregularly whorled with short petioles; lanceolate to nearly linear, pointed, 4–8
in. long. Flowers bowl-shaped, in terminal
clusters more than 3 in. wide; yellowish green corolla and
reddish violet hood; corolla lobes not reflexed; follicle 2–4
in. long. Found in sandy or gravelly soil in dry plains and
slopes, pinyon-juniper communities, openings in ponderosa pine forests of the plains, and foothills. Maturing seedpods curve, resembling antelope horns. Native.

Asclepias cryptoceras

APOCYNACEAE

pallid milkweed, cow cabbage
MR, SR, pinyon-juniper, sagebrush steppe,
locally abundant, L Spring–
E Summer, perennial, to 1.5 ft.

Stems spreading or reclining, from a central crown. Leaves opposite, ovate to nearly round, thick, veined, 0.75–3 in. long. Flowers in large terminal umbel, sometimes with smaller lateral ones. Pale yellowish green corolla 0.3–0.6 in. long with lobes often strongly reflexed; 5 reddish purple hoods are crown-like, attached to the central column. Follicle 2–2.75 in. long. Sandy, clay, and serpentine soils in sagebrush, pinyon-juniper, and aspen communities; scattered in the high deserts, sometimes occupying dry openings in oak and aspen habitats. Native.

Asclepias viridiflora

(*Acerates lanceolata*) APOCYNACEAE

green comet milkweed
RM, foothills, grasslands, common,
Summer, perennial, 4–24 in.

Slender stems from thickened rhizomatous roots. Leaves opposite, commonly lanceolate, can be more ovate, 1.2–5.5 in. long. Flowers in 1- to 1.5-in. umbels from upper leaf axils, 1 per leaf pair. Corolla green, hoods greenish yellow; sharply reflexed corolla lobes make flowers resemble a streaking comet, hence the common name. Silky-haired seeds in 1 or 2 follicles per node. A prairie species, entering our region along the eastern edge in sunny dry grasslands and foothills, in sandy, rocky, or calcareous soils. Native.

Geocaulon lividum

(*Comandra lividum*) SANTALACEAE

false toadflax, northern comandra
NR, MR, subalpine, montane,
wetlands, common, L Spring–
Summer, perennial, 4–8 in.

Clumps of 1 to several, erect, herbaceous stems from rhizomes. Leaves alternate, entire, short-petiolate, narrowly ovate to oblanceolate, thin. Clusters of 3 yellowish green flowers from axils of middle to upper leaves; no petals, 5 sepals. Fruit an orange to red fleshy drupe, with remnants of sepals on top. Hemiparasitic in association with spruce, pine, birch, and others. Coniferous and deciduous forests, bogs. Native.

Lithospermum ruderale
(*L. pilosum*) BORAGINACEAE
western stoneseed, western gromwell
RM, montane, foothills, pinyon-juniper,
sagebrush steppe, intermountain
parks, grasslands, common, Spring–
Summer, perennial, 10–20 in.

Husky taprooted herb. Often quite multistemmed and robust, with stems spreading
in all directions. Corollas greater than tube
length. Leaves linear, broader at base, 1.2–3.1
in. long. Flowers funnel-shaped, small, yellowish green, 0.4 in. wide; the strange chartreuse flowers should distinguish it from all other gromwells. Fruit
4 white to brown nutlets, conspicuous late in the season.
Found in dry sunny or partly shaded slopes, disturbed
sites, and sage meadows. Native.

Paronychia depressa
(*P. depressa* var. *diffusa*)
CARYOPHYLLACEAE
spreading nailwort
MR, SR, montane, foothills, pinyon-
juniper, sagebrush steppe, intermountain
parks, grasslands, locally abundant,
Spring–E Summer, perennial, 1–2 in.

Prickly, woody, mat-forming herb. Stems
branched, sprawling 3–6 in., and mostly
puberulent. Leaves fleshy, entire, leathery, puberulent,
and linear. Flowers a muted chartreuse, tiny and distinct, to 0.14 in. with a star-like appearance; sepals green
to purple-brown. Generally occurs in sparse grasslands,
rocky ridges, hillsides, with other miniature
species, like creeping alpine phloxes. Native.

Paronychia pulvinata
CARYOPHYLLACEAE
Rocky Mountain nailwort
SR, alpine, subalpine, common,
Summer, perennial, 0.5–1 in.

Cushion-forming woody perennial. Stems
prostrate to 2–4 in. wide, puberulent,
branched. Leaves fleshy, vary from elliptic
oblong to elliptic-oblanceolate, and glabrous.
Flowers tiny, yellow-green, star-like, to 0.1 in.; sepals whitish to green. Widespread and common tundra cushion
plant, found on rocky slopes and scree. Makes hard cushions on fellfields with almost inconspicuous chartreuse
bloom at height of summer color; easily picked out by this
habit in summer. Native.

Paronychia sessiliflora

CARYOPHYLLACEAE

creeping nailwort
RM, foothills, pinyon-juniper, sagebrush steppe, intermountain parks, grasslands, locally abundant, Spring–E Summer, perennial, 2–10 in.

Loose mats of prickly foliage form tufted cushions. Stems erect to ascending, branched, and 2–10 in. tall. Leaves tiny, fleshy, linear-subulate, leathery, glabrous to finely puberulent. Flowers tiny, star-like, a muted chartreuse, to 0.2 in.; sepals green to red-brown. Widespread in dry, stony areas and barren habitats on east and west slope of the Rockies. Native.

Matricaria discoidea
(*M. matricarioides*) ASTERACEAE

disc mayweed, pineapple weed
RM, montane, foothills, common, Spring–Fall, annual, 2–16 in.

Herbaceous upright stems with finely pinnate alternate leaves to 3 in. long. Flowerheads usually solitary, rounded, lacking ray flowers, with multiple green-yellow disc flowers topping a ring of cup-like green bracts. Found along roadsides and in disturbed sites. This plant is native to portions of North America but is often reported as being introduced, as it is weedy in places. Lewis and Clark collected it in ID in 1806. Native.

Echinocereus viridiflorus

CACTACEAE

nylon hedgehog cactus
MR, SR, foothills, pinyon-juniper, sagebrush steppe, grasslands, common, L Spring–Summer, perennial, 3–12 in.

Succulent stems erect, cylindrical; often solitary but may be branched; may form small clumps up to 12 stems. Spines are stiff, straight or slightly curved, and may be red and white or yellow, often with dark tips. Typically 0–17 central spines, and 12–38 radial spines per areole. Flowers are usually shiny yellowish green, 0.5–1.5 in., inner petals often shades of yellow or brown. Fruits green, may be tinged reddish, typically 0.5 in. across. Found in open woodlands, in dry, gravelly soils, from plains to foothills. Native.

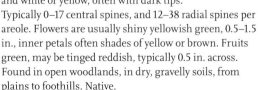

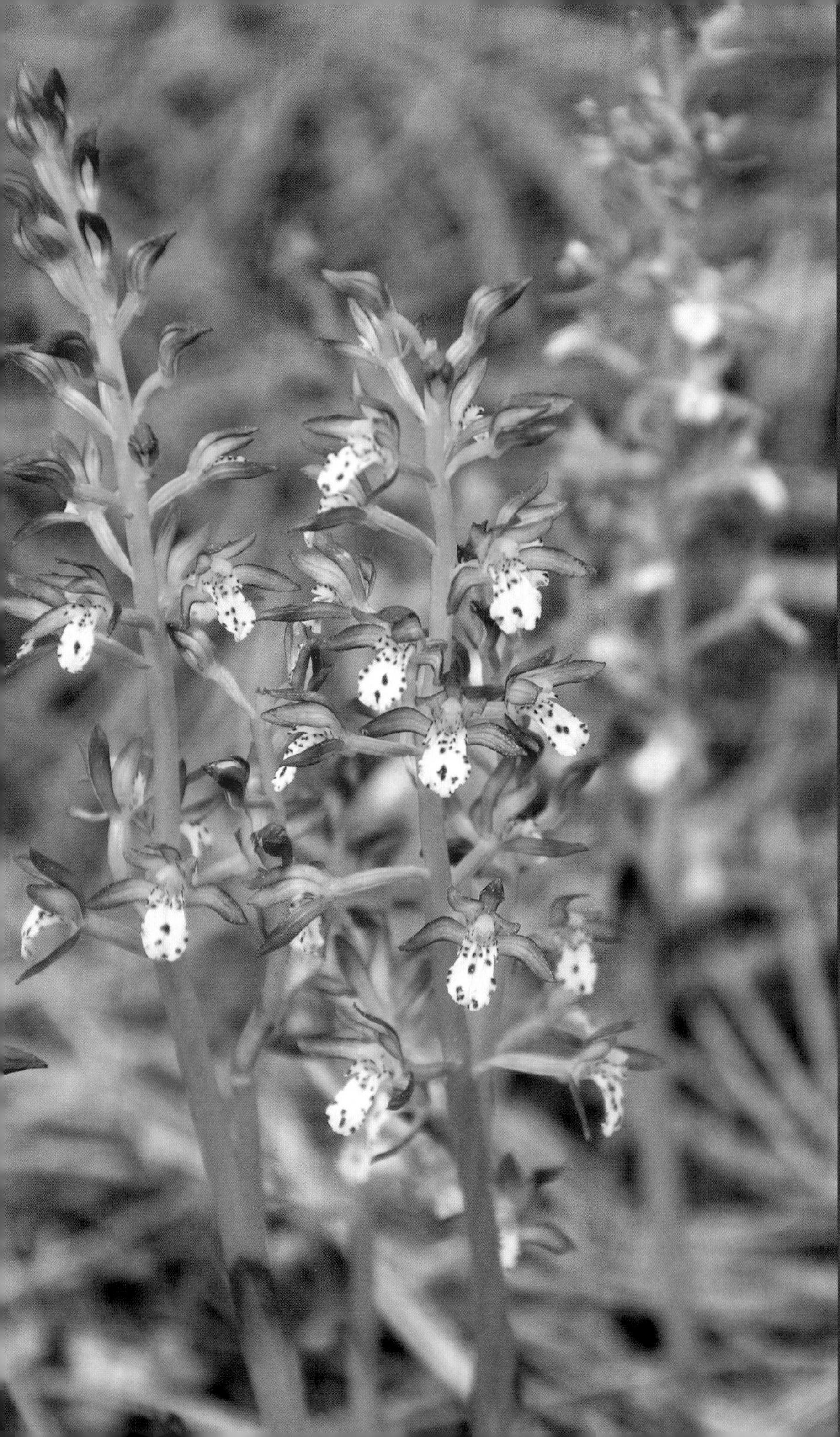

Maroon and Brown Flowers

Plantago tweedyi
(*P. eriopoda* var. *tweedyi*)

PLANTAGINACEAE
Tweedy's plantain
MR, SR, subalpine, montane, common,
Summer–Fall, perennial, 5–10 in.

Herb with smooth basal leaves on stalks.
Leaves are lance-shaped, 1–4 in. long, margins with few shallow teeth, 5 prominent parallel veins on underside. Inflorescence a dense spike 0.8–4 in. long. Flowers are tiny and brown. Fruit a capsule. Grows in moist meadows, forests, and riparian areas. Native.

Thalictrum alpinum RANUNCULACEAE
alpine meadow-rue
MR, SR, alpine, subalpine, montane,
wetlands, infrequent, L Spring–
Fall, perennial, 2–10 in.

Rhizomatous herb. Stem erect, leafless or nearly so, bluish gray, smooth. Leaf 2 times pinnately compound, basal, bluish gray, smooth, 0.8–4 in., sometimes 1 stem leaf near base. Leaflet rounded in outline, 3- to 5-lobed, smooth, rolled margins. Sparse raceme erect to ascending; flowers on slender stalks, sepals brownish maroon, early deciduous. Stamens 8–15; anthers yellow, 0.1 in. long, longer than the purple filaments; stigma purple. Fruits 2–6 spreading achenes on down-curved stalks. Moist areas, tundra. Native.

Typha latifolia TYPHACEAE
broadleaf cattail
RM, montane, foothills, grasslands,
wetlands, common, locally abundant,
Summer, perennial, 3–10 ft.

Unbranched, cylindrical, hard, pithy stems from extensive aquatic rhizomes. Leaves long and narrow, linear, alternate, sheathing, broad, light green. Numerous flowers in a densely crowded terminal cylindrical spike 6–12 in. long; female flowers lower, brown; male flowers above but contiguous, sloughing away to leave dry terminal stem behind. Fruit a small achene with abundant fluff, carried far and wide on the wind. Found in sunny areas, small ponds, streams, lakeshores, marshes, and wet ditches. Native.

Corallorhiza maculata

ORCHIDACEAE

spotted coralroot

RM, montane, foothills, infrequent,
Spring–Summer, perennial, 8–20 in.

Stems smooth, waxy, reddish brown to orange
or yellow, solitary or in dense groups. Leaves
similar to stem color (not green), and are reduced to a few alternate sheaths on lower
stem. Flowers also share stem color on the 3
sepals and 2 upper petals, hood-like; labellum
white with purple or burgundy spots, many
flowers in a slender spire. Roots reddish; *Corallorhiza* spp.
lack chlorophyll and form complex parasitic relationships
with nearby plants. Dust-like seed in pendent pods. Found
in shaded woodlands, mixed forests, in undisturbed duff
soils. Native.

Corallorhiza striata ORCHIDACEAE

striped coralroot

RM, montane, foothills, grasslands,
infrequent, Spring–Summer,
perennial, 5–18 in.

Stems smooth, waxy, light reddish purple to
yellow, solitary or in dense groups. Leaves
lighter than stem color (not green), and are reduced to a few alternate sheaths, close or overlapping on lower stem. Flowers in a slender
spire; sepals and petals share stem color, but striped, not
spotted; labellum often a darker color, also striped. Similar
to *C. maculata*, but plant is generally smaller and flowers
larger, to 1.5 in. across. Mixed woodlands, grassy meadows,
part shade, in undisturbed duff soils. Native.

Corallorhiza wisteriana

ORCHIDACEAE

Wister's coralroot, spring coralroot

MR, SR, montane, foothills, common,
Spring–Summer, perennial, 2–21 in.

Stems smooth, waxy, reddish purple to yellow, solitary or in dense groups. Leaves smilar
to stem color, and reduced to a few alternate
sheaths on lower stem. Flowers also share
stem color on the 3 sepals and 2 upper petals,
hood-like; labellum white and often spotted with purple,
2–25 flowers in a slender spire. Roots reddish. Found in
shaded, moist woodlands, mixed forests, in richer soils
than other coralroots. Rarely takes other color forms of
green, light yellow, pink, and red. Native.

Stenanthium occidentale
(Stenanthella occidentalis)
MELANTHIACEAE
western featherbells, bronze bells
NR, MR, alpine, subalpine,
montane, uncommon, L Spring–
Summer, perennial, 6–20 in.

Herbaceous plant from an oval onion-like
bulb 0.5–1.5 in. long. Stems ascending to
erect. Basal leaves 2 or 3, grass-like, 4–8 in.
long, smooth, sheathed, entire. Stem leaves 2
or 3, reduced to bracts. Inflorescence a loosely
flowered terminal raceme with 3–20 nodding, narrowly
bell-shaped flowers on 0.5- to 1-in.-long stems. Flowers purplish maroon to yellowish green, narrow tepals fused at
base; gradually tapering tips reflexed. Occurs on wet cliffs,
moist meadows, and scree. Sun. Native.

Rumex densiflorus POLYGONACEAE
dense-flowered dock
SR, alpine, subalpine, montane,
wetlands, common, locally abundant,
L Spring–Summer, perennial, 1–3 ft.
Upright herb with stout, erect stems that
branch in the inflorescence. Young basal
leaves start out only 2 in. long after snowmelt, and grow into tough 13-in.-long, narrow leaves; alternate, entire, lanceolate, and
weakly cordate. Inflorescence is an upright, dense cluster
of tiny yellow, red, and green flowers. Within a few weeks,
flowers become showy, dense clusters of pink, red, and
brown seeds. Grows in large colonies, sunny areas and
moist meadows. Native.

Cypripedium fasciculatum
ORCHIDACEAE
clustered lady's slipper
RM, subalpine, montane, rare,
Spring–Summer, perennial, 2–8 in.
Stems hairy, solitary or in small groups. Single sheath clasps the stem base; leaves 2, opposite, broadly elliptic, 1–3 in. long, near top
of stem. Flowers 1–9, clustered on bent stem
above leaves; 3 sepals, upper sepal centered
above pouch, lower 2 fused below pouch; 2 similar petals,
3rd petal is pouch-shaped; all striped or blushed reddish
brown on greenish background. Grows in shade and coniferous forests in undisturbed duff soils. Rare, with complex
soil fungi associations. Native.

Cypripedium montanum

ORCHIDACEAE

mountain lady's slipper
NR, MR, subalpine, montane,
uncommon, locally abundant, Spring–
Summer, perennial, 8–24 in.

Stems hairy, sturdy, upright; lowest 1 or 2
leaves sheath-like at the stem base. 4–6 leaves,
alternate, 2–7 in. long, elliptical, hairy below,
glabrous above, along entire stem. Flowers
fragrant; color variable; tannish leafy bract
and wavy sepal above; 2 linear twisting petals to each side;
2 fused sepals below; the large white pouch often with purplish veins; central parts yellow. Dust-like seeds in brown
upright pods. Found in shady, undisturbed duff soils in
open mixed or coniferous forests. Grows only
with complex soil fungi associations. Native.

Epipactis gigantea ORCHIDACEAE
stream orchid
RM, wetlands, rare, Spring–Summer,
perennial, 1–3 ft.

Tall stems from short rhizomes, may be rough
or glabrous. Alternate leaves clasping stem,
oval to lanceolate, 2–8 in. long, smaller on
upper stem, curled upward, parallel venation.
Variable flowers to 1.25 in. across in leaf axils;
3 spreading sepals yellowish or reddish green with darker
netting; 2 upper petals orange to pinkish green, striped.
Labellum pouch striped within, narrow toward tip. Limited to precise conditions near springs, cliff seeps, fens;
rare in this region. Native.

Asarum caudatum

ARISTOLOCHIACEAE

wild ginger
NR, montane, foothills, common,
L Spring–Summer, perennial, to 1 ft.

Herbaceous groundcover from shallow rhizomes. Leaves heart-shaped, hairy surface
and petioles. Flowers distinctive, 1–2 in. long,
hairy exterior, 3 long-tipped burgundy petals, creamy heart, near ground level. Grows
in shady to partially shady areas; extensive groundcover
in evergreen forests, with ferns, other woodland species. Crushed or bruised leaves give off a spicy citrus
lemon-ginger smell. Roots are edible and have been used
as a substitute for ginger. Native.

Fritillaria affinis LILIACEAE
checker lily, chocolate lily
NR, montane, foothills, grasslands,
common, locally abundant, Spring–
Summer, perennial, 8–36 in.

Smooth stems from a scaly bulb. Leaves 2–6
in. long, lanceolate, glabrous, in 1 or more
whorls of 3–5 on lower stem; leaves alternate
and single above. Flowers 1–7, nodding from
upper leaf axils; tepals 6, ovate to lanceolate in open bells, to 1.25 in. long; mottled
maroon-brown and yellowish green, variable. Seed capsules mature upright. Several similar species. This west
coast species is also found in ID and BC. Seasonally damp
meadows, cool slopes, grasslands, and woodland openings. Native.

Fritillaria atropurpurea LILIACEAE
spotted fritillary
RM, montane, foothills, sagebrush
steppe, grasslands, infrequent,
Spring–Summer, perennial, 5–20 in.

Smooth slender stem from a scaly bulb.
Leaves 2–5 in. long, linear to lanceolate, alternate or in 1 or 2 loose whorls of 2–4 below
the flowers, and 1–3 at upper nodes. Flowers
1–4, pendent or outfacing; 6 lanceolate tepals mottled maroon-brown and yellow, variable. Several
species are similar. Widespread but seldom abundant;
among shrubs, in dryish forest openings, sage meadows,
or grasslands. Native.

Paxistima myrsinites
CELASTRACEAE
Oregon boxwood, mountain lover
RM, subalpine, montane, foothills,
sagebrush steppe, common,
locally abundant, L Spring–
E Summer, perennial, 0.5–3 ft.

Low, dense, evergreen shrub with green
to reddish brown 4-angled stems. Leaves
glossy, leathery, opposite, to 1 in.; lanceolate
to elliptic, with crenate to serrate margins.
Inflorescence an axillary cyme with 1 to many tiny, fragrant, reddish maroon flowers. 4 sepals, 4 maroon petals,
and 4 stamens surround broad disc. Fruit an ovoid capsule that splits upon drying and persists through winter.
Found in shady forests. Floral scent is said to resemble
myrrh, hence the specific epithet. Native.

Scrophularia lanceolata

SCROPHULARIACEAE

lanceleaf figwort

RM, montane, foothills, pinyon-juniper, intermountain parks, grasslands, wetlands, locally abundant, L Spring–Summer, perennial, 24–50 in.

Herbaceous with tall, erect, clustered, 4-sided sticky stems from a main crown. Lanceolate leaves are opposite, clasping, coarsely dentate. The zygomorphic flowers are 1 in. or less; 5 petals fused; 2 hood-like and pointing forward; one on each side, the lower folded back; resulting in a small, brownish green somewhat fish-shaped corolla. Grows in moist meadows, woodlands, and riparian openings. Attracts hummingbirds. Native.

Angelica grayi APIACEAE

Gray's angelica

SR, alpine, subalpine, montane, common, Summer, perennial, 6–24 in.

Herbaceous stems very stout but hollow; single, occasionally multiple. Leaves deciduous, pinnate, bipinnate, or ternate pinnate, often with a noticeable sheath around the stem. Leaflets 0.4–2 in. long, lanceolate to ovate with serrated margins. Inflorescence a flat-topped, compound umbel, with distinctive ball-like clusters, turning from a tannish green to a yellow-maroon in the fall. Flowers purplish brown. Grows in moist meadows, tundra, and scree. Monocarpic. Native.

Geum rivale ROSACEAE

purple avens, water avens

RM, montane, wetlands, common, L Spring–Summer, perennial, 10–28 in.

Upright herb with hairy stems and leaves. Basal leaves pinnately compound to 8 in. long with 2–6 larger egg-shaped, toothed leaflets and several minute ones; the terminal leaflet to 4 in. long, triangular and lobed. Inflorescence an upright cyme with bracts, leaves, and 3–7 flowers. Flowerheads often nodding, with conspicuous hairy purplish maroon sepals; petals less visible and shorter, pink to yellowish, with purple veins. Fruit an achene with long, stiff, S-shaped hairs. Found in moist meadows and fens, marshes, riparian and open forests. Native.

Rudbeckia montana
(*R. occidentalis* var. *montana*)
ASTERACEAE
montane coneflower
SR, montane, foothills, locally abundant,
Summer, perennial, 1.5–6 ft.
Herbaceous stems from stout rhizomes, not
colony-forming but can be abundant. Leaves
alternate, greenish blue, glabrous, elliptic to
ovate, pinnatifid to pinnately lobed. Flowers in tall cone-shaped terminal heads, disc
flowers maroon below, greenish above; ray flowers absent,
pappus a short crown. Found only in CO and UT. Grows
in sunny areas, moist hillsides and meadows, streamsides,
seeps, and aspen forests. Native.

Rudbeckia occidentalis
ASTERACEAE
western coneflower
RM, montane, foothills, common,
Summer–Fall, perennial, 20–79 in.
Herbaceous stems from rhizomes, nearly
glabrous. Leaves alternate, broadly ovate to
lanceolate, entire or toothed, basal leaves
petiolate, stem leaves usually sessile. Flowers in dark conical heads to 1 in. tall; ray
flowers absent, disc flowers black, involucre bracts reflexed, pappus a short crown. Grows in sunny
areas in moist, open forests, meadows, streamsides, and
seeps. Native.

Paeonia brownii PAEONIACEAE
Brown's peony
MR, foothills, sagebrush steppe,
intermountain parks, infrequent,
Spring–E Summer, perennial, 12–14 in.
Showy mounds of glaucous, divided foliage. Leaves 5–8 per shoot, primary divisions
1.2–2.4 in. long by 0.8–1.6 in. wide, ultimate
divisions elliptic to obovate. Nodding, waxy
mahogany flowers, with yellowish or greenish margins, often shorter than the inner sepals. Filaments many, yellow, and 0.8–1.6 in.
This cousin of the spectacular Eurasian peonies is widespread in the West, especially the Pacific coast, but extends
into some select habitats in the intermountain region.
A treat to find. Native.

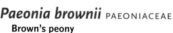

Orange Flowers

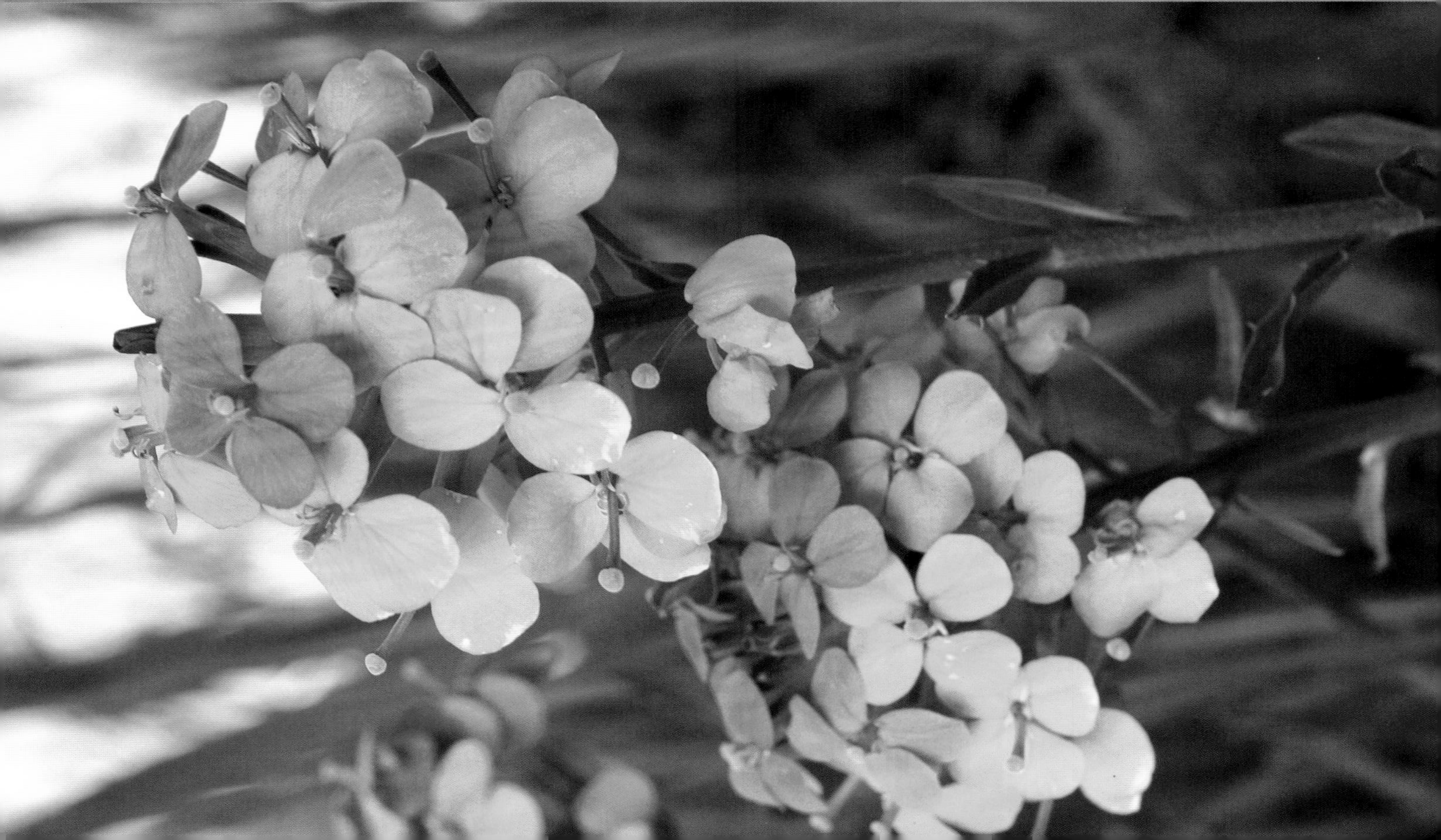

Lilium columbianum
(*L. canadense* var. *parviflorum*)

LILIACEAE

Columbia lily, tiger lily
NR, subalpine, montane, foothills, common, L Spring–Summer, perennial, 15–36 in.

Sturdy stems from a scaly whitish underground bulb. Leaves glabrous, shiny, 2–4 in. long, in widely spaced whorls of 6–9; fewer scattered, alternate on upper stem. Flowers showy, nodding, in open terminal raceme of 2–12 or more; each 1–2.5 in. across, 6 golden to deep orange tepals, recurved, inner surface speckled reddish brown toward base; long protruding pistil; 6 green stamens with orangish brown anthers. Full or part sun, moist meadows, open woodlands; higher elevations inland. Native.

Lilium philadelphicum LILIACEAE
wood lily
RM, montane, foothills, sagebrush steppe, rare, Summer, perennial, 1–2 ft.

Sturdy, smooth, single stem from a small scaly whitish bulb. Leaves glabrous, lanceolate, 2–4 in. long, alternate on lower stem, whorled at top. Showy terminal flower 3–4 in. across, usually single, upfacing; 6 spoon-shaped tepals are recurved, blushed yellow near base with red-brown spots; erect pistil and stamens match flower color. Found in sunny areas, moist meadows, and forest edges or openings. Spectacular but fragile; should always be left undisturbed. Native.

Penstemon rostriflorus

PLANTAGINACEAE

bridge penstemon
SR, montane, foothills, pinyon-juniper, sagebrush steppe, uncommon, Summer–Fall, perennial, 12–40 in.

Subshrub with scraggly stems from a woody base. Leaves green, opposite, 0.8–2.8 in. long, linear to lanceolate or oblanceolate. Basal rosette absent. Inflorescence a sparse elongated cluster of scarlet or orange-red flowers. Grows in sunny and shady locations on rock ledges, pine parklands, dry slopes, and sage meadows. Can be found at high elevations in central UT. Native.

Sphaeralcea coccinea MALVACEAE
scarlet globemallow
RM, montane, foothills, pinyon-juniper,
sagebrush steppe, intermountain
parks, grasslands, common, Spring–
Summer, perennial, 4–12 in.

Decumbent herb from spreading rhizomes.
Stems ascending, branching, covered with
silver hairs. Leaves alternate, deeply 3- to
5-lobed, hairy, margins entire. Simple flowers in racemes, few to many, salmon to
red-orange, 0.8 in. across, stamens united into column.
The unusual color stands out in sunny prairies, dry slopes
and meadows, and shrublands. Historically used by Native
Americans for medicinal and nutritional purposes. Native.

Sphaeralcea fendleri MALVACEAE
Fendler's globemallow
SR, montane, foothills, pinyon-juniper,
sagebrush steppe, grasslands, common,
Spring–Summer, perennial, 3–4 ft.

Upright subshrub with many branches and
hairy stems, almost woody. Stems gray to
gray-green, sometimes dark purple. Leaves
green above, hairy-gray to gray-green below;
1.2–2.8 in. long, alternate; deep-veined,
ovate-oblong, 3-lobed with terminal lobe lon-
ger. Inflorescence an elongated cluster, with simple orange
to pinkish purple flowers, with all 5 petals held nearly flat.
Found in sunny areas of coniferous forests, sage meadows,
and dry riverbanks. Native.

Sphaeralcea grossulariifolia
MALVACEAE
gooseberryleaf globemallow
MR, SR, foothills, pinyon-juniper,
sagebrush steppe, grasslands, common,
Spring–Summer, perennial, 2–3 ft.

Herbaceous, erect stems, green tinged with
purple, arising from woody base; hairy,
appearing gray. Leaves alternate, simple,
palmately 3-lobed with dentate to crenate margins. Inflorescence paniculate, with simple
orange-red flowers arranged into crowded elongated clusters, rarely solitary. Grows in sunny and disturbed areas
and dry rocky or sandy soils. Native.

Sphaeralcea munroana
(*Malva munroana*) MALVACEAE
Munro's globemallow
RM, foothills, sagebrush steppe, grasslands, common, Spring– Summer, perennial, 8–31 in.

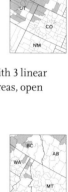

Herbaceous, branched stems, ascending to erect, gray-hairy to greenish, from thick roots. Stem leaves alternate, kidney-shaped, shallowly 3- to 5-lobed, no basal leaves. Simple flowers pink to orange-red, color is variable; in compound raceme, 5 petals, calyx with 3 linear bracteoles. Grows in sunny and disturbed areas, open forests, and sage meadows. Native.

Impatiens capensis
(*I. biflora*) BALSAMINACEAE
jewelweed, spotted jewelweed
NR, SR, foothills, wetlands, locally abundant, Summer, annual, 20–40 in.

Upright herb; stems succulent, variably branched, hairless, and larger at axils. Leaves to 4 in., oval, toothed, alternate. Flowers from upper axils on thin stalks; yellow tubular flower with a curled spur and 4 orangish yellow speckled petals. Grows in riparian areas, ditches. Commonest along streams along the Front Range Piedmont, where you can find both yellow and orange variants. Introduced.

Asclepias tuberosa ssp. *interior*
APOCYNACEAE
butterfly milkweed
SR, pinyon-juniper, intermountain parks, grasslands, common, Summer, perennial, 8–19 in.

Stems with short stiff hairs; upright to vase-shaped, from a tuberous root; stems of this species lack milky sap. Leaves lanceolate, 1.5–3.5 in. long. Corolla lobes red-orange to yellow, 0.2–0.3 in. long; hoods with horns. Follicles upright 2.75–4.75 in. long. Found in sandy, gravelly, or calcareous soils in the plains, open woodlands, and pinyon-juniper communities. Nectar attracts butterflies, hummingbirds, bees, and other insects. Serves as larval food for Monarch butterflies. The type is widespread in eastern U.S.; ours is scattered in the Wasatch range and Four Corners states. Native.

Hypericum anagalloides
HYPERICACEAE
tinker's penny
NR, MR, subalpine, montane,
wetlands, common, L Spring–
Summer, perennial, 1–5 in.

Low spreading stems form loose mats, rooting at nodes; upright portions have terminal flowers. Leaves opposite, oval to round, to 0.5 in. wide, clasping stem. Flowers, orange to salmon-yellow, solitary or in small cymes, to 0.75 in. across; 5 oval petals and erect stamens. Found in sunny wet meadows, fens, streambanks, and lake margins. Native.

Agoseris aurantiaca ASTERACEAE
orange agoseris
RM, alpine, subalpine, montane,
intermountain parks, common,
Summer, perennial, 4–24 in.

Herbaceous, with solitary, leafless stems. Leaves all basal to 15 in. long, lanceolate or oblanceolate, entire to lacy-pinnate with purplish petioles. Torn leaves excrete a milky sap. Flower stems leafless, heads solitary. Involucre bracts narrow, pointed, in 2 or 3 series. Ray flowers numerous, usually orange (sometimes yellow, pink, red, purple, or white). Seeds wind-distributed. Forest openings, meadows, shrublands, near streams. Our region has 2 varieties, differentiated by the shape of the phyllaries. Native.

Tephroseris lindstroemii
(*Senecio lindstroemii*) ASTERACEAE
orange arctic-groundsel
MR, alpine, locally abundant,
Summer, perennial, 3–10 in.

Herbaceous plant from creeping or sub-erect rhizomes. Single and multistemmed leaves silvery and woolly. Flowers orange or orange-yellow, with 13–21 ray florets and 50–80 or more disc florets. Very showy and distinctive. Grows in meadows and open tundra. *Tephroseris* is largely Eurasian and consists of 50 species; this species is amphiberingian (found on both sides of the Bering Strait), then disjunct to the Beartooth Plateau of MT/WY. Native.

numerous petals, simple-shaped, radial

Cylindropuntia ×*anasaziensis*
CACTACEAE
Anasazi cholla

SR, foothills, pinyon-juniper, endemic,
rare, Summer, perennial, 3–4 ft.

Upright, shrubby cactus with
much-branched cane-like stems, usually
only 3 ft. tall or little more. Flowers variable,
pinkish to yellowish, with distinct orange
shading. Possibly originated as a complex
hybrid with *C. whipplei*, and is somewhat
intermediate in character. While you may encounter this
plant in scattered locations in southwestern CO, the name
is not yet recognized, and exact lineage remains the sub-
ject of speculation. Found on sunny slopes, in woodland
clearings, within sagebrush, ponderosa pines, and
Gambel oaks. Native.

Chenopodium capitatum
(*Blitum capitatum*) AMARANTHACEAE
blite goosefoot, strawberry goosefoot
RM, subalpine, montane, foothills,
intermountain parks, wetlands, common,
L Spring–Summer, annual, 12–36 in.
Stems erect to ascending or sprawling,
branched from base. Red fruit much showier than small green flowers. Leaves alternate, smooth, fleshy, lanceolate or
arrow-shaped, margins sharply toothed or
entire, tip sharply to slightly pointed. Inflorescence green,
becoming small but conspicuous fleshy red-pink fruit clusters, sessile in upper leaf axils forming terminal spikes 2–8
in. long. Occurs in woodland openings or edges, disturbed
soils. Fruit is tasteless. Native.

Oxyria digyna
(*Rumex digyna*) POLYGONACEAE
alpine mountain-sorrel
RM, alpine, subalpine, montane, common,
Summer–Fall, perennial, 2–14 in.
Hairless herb with reddish, clustered stems
from thick root crowns. Basal leaves 0.4–1.6
in. long, entire, and cordate to reniform.
Inflorescence with many groups of tiny
greenish red flowers densely clustered along
slender stalks above leaves. Seeds are reddish and broadly
winged. Grows in sunny and shady areas, tundra, rock
scree, and rock ledges. Leaves are a sharp, vinegary addition to salads; Native Americans included them in drinks
and soups and used them as a thickening
agent in cakes. Native.

Grayia spinosa
(*Atriplex grayi*) AMARANTHACEAE
spiny hopsage
RM, foothills, pinyon-juniper,
sagebrush steppe, common, Spring–
Summer, perennial, 1.5–4.5 ft.
Dense rounded shrub with spine-tipped
branches. Leaves to 1 in., narrowly ovate,
fleshy, alternate. Flowers greenish, dioecious, male/female on separate plants; not showy—males
in tight clusters, females in short spikes at leaf axils. The
clustered fruits are more noteworthy: papery, to 0.7 in.
across, maturing pale to vivid pink. Floodplains, alkali
flats, sage meadows, pinyon-juniper openings. Native.

Sanguisorba minor
(*Poterium sanguisorba*) ROSACEAE
small burnet, salad burnet
RM, montane, foothills, pinyon-
juniper, grasslands, common, Spring–
Summer, perennial, 6–25 in.

Herbaceous evergreen with ascending stems
from a taproot; sometimes weakly rhizomatous. Leaves are oval to oblong, 4 in. long,
coarsely serrate; oval leaflets 9–17 with serrated edges. Pink flowers, imperfect, densely
packed in a 3- to 8-in. elongated round spike; petals absent,
with 12 filiform stamens; lower flowers staminate, upper
flowers pistillate or perfect. Found in sunny and moist
places. Introduced for erosion control, but slow growth
kept it from becoming noxious. Leaves are
edible and often used in salads. Introduced.

Eriogonum racemosum

POLYGONACEAE
redroot buckwheat
SR, throughout, common, Summer–
Fall, perennial, 1–3 ft.

Stems are erect to slightly spreading,
and loose to dense. Leaves basal, gray,
linear-oblanceolate, 0.6–2.4 in., densely covered with white hairs. 6-petaled flowers white,
aging pink. Grows in sunny areas, rock ledges, scree, barrens, dry slopes, and sage meadows; all life zones except
alpine and wetlands. Distinctive flower spires; few species,
except *E. niveum*, resemble it. The Navajo (or Diné) people
use the roots as a medicine in the treatment
of poisoning and diarrhea and as an analgesic
and orthopedic aid. Native.

Rumex paucifolius
(*Acetosella paucifolia*) POLYGONACEAE
alpine sheep sorrel
RM, alpine, subalpine, montane, common,
L Spring–Summer, perennial, 4–20 in.

Herb. Stems solitary or few from base; plant
not hairy. Leaves basal and alternate, lanceolate, 1–3.25 in. long by 0.4–1.25 in. wide. Inflorescence terminal, in panicles with narrow spike-like
branches on upper third of stems; 6 tepals reddish in color;
3 inner tepals enlarging at maturity into rounded papery
winged fruit with heart-shaped base; seed a brown achene.
Found in moist meadows and along streams. Native.

Rumex venosus POLYGONACEAE
veiny dock, wild begonia
RM, sagebrush steppe, grasslands,
common, locally abundant, L Spring–
Summer, perennial, 6–18 in.

Upright herb with stout, reddish, leafy
stems, producing basal auxiliary shoots.
Leaves 1.5–4.5 in. long, alternate, leathery, entire, and lanceolate. Inflorescence
an upright, thick cluster of large red to
pink, slightly translucent flowers. Foli-
age and flowers appear early, then dry and vanish during
summer heat. Grows in sunny disturbed areas, spreading densely on sandhills and roadsides; the vast network
of shoestring-like roots helps stabilize sand dunes. Early
Spanish settlers used tannin extracted from
its roots for tanning hides. Native.

Calypso bulbosa ORCHIDACEAE
fairy slipper
RM, subalpine, montane, infrequent,
Spring–Summer, perennial, 2–6 in.
Herb. Stout stem with a single flower; several bracts sheathing the stem. Corm-like
root. Leaves basal, single, elliptic-cordate,
1–3 in., smooth, appearing in autumn,
withering in summer. Flower sepals and
petals 6: 5 pink, erect, linear to oblong, may be twisted;
1 pouch-like labellum below, pink-white, dark interior
stripes; central column hood-like over pouch; entry yellow
with bristles. Var. *americana* has a yellow lip apron; var. *occidentalis*, a white lip apron. Grows in deep
old soils of evergreen woods—do not disturb
the site. Circumboreal. Native.

Polygala subspinosa
POLYGALACEAE
spiny milkwort
SR, pinyon-juniper, sagebrush steppe,
intermountain parks, infrequent,
Spring–E Summer, perennial, 3–14 in.
Compact, spiny shrub of the Colorado Plateau and Great Basin. Leaves ovate, alternate,
to 1 in. long. Forms tiny, blue-gray mounds of foliage with
vivid magenta papillionaceous flowers in spring, more
than 1 in. across with contrasting yellow keels. Very distinctive and beautiful. Found on sunny dry slopes, sage
meadows, and exposed barrens. Rare in western CO and
northern NM, more common in UT. Native.

Allium acuminatum

AMARYLLIDACEAE
tapertip onion
RM, montane, foothills, sagebrush steppe, common, Spring, perennial, 4–14 in.

Herb. Bulb with 2–4 basal leaves shorter than the flower stalk; leaves withered by flowering time. Flowering stem with 2 papery bracts directly beneath rounded flower umbel; 10–40 individual flowers pink to purple or white with 6 petals; outer 3 petal tips strongly flared backward. Grows in dry, open spaces including hills and plains. Both the specific epithet and common name reference the long, tapering petal tips. Native.

Allium brevistylum AMARYLLIDACEAE

shortstyle onion
MR, SR, montane, foothills, common, L Spring–Summer, perennial, 8–24 in.

Herb. Bulb with 2–5 basal leaves, flattened and still green at flowering time. Flowering stems with 2 bracts directly beneath rounded flower umbel. 7–20 individual flowers are typically rosy pink with 6 narrowly pointed petals, narrowing near the top before flaring slightly. Grows in riparian areas and in moist, swampy meadows, sometimes in wooded areas. Found only in the Rocky Mountains. Native.

Allium cernuum AMARYLLIDACEAE

nodding onion
RM, throughout, common, L Spring–Fall, perennial, 4–20 in.

Evergreen herb from bulb, with 2 or more thick, erect, leafless stems. 3–7 flattened to channeled, sheathing basal leaves almost as tall as the flowering stem; pungent when bruised. Inflorescence a loose, nodding umbel of pink, rose-purple, or whitish bell-shaped flowers with 6 distinct tepals and protruding stamens. Fruit a capsule. The most widespread *Allium* sp. in North America. Found in sunny locations in all life zones except alpine and wetlands. Occurrence decreases with increasing precipitation and latitude. Native.

Allium geyeri AMARYLLIDACEAE

Geyer's onion
RM, alpine, subalpine, montane,
foothills, grasslands, common,
Spring–Summer, perennial, 4–20 in.
Herb. Bulb with 2 or 3 basal leaves, flat-tened and still green at flowering time. A pa-pery sheath up to one-quarter of leaf height often present. Flowering stems have 2 or 3 bracts beneath the rounded flower umbel. 10–25 individual flowers per umbel are pink (sometimes white) with 6 petal-like tepals. Grows in riparian areas, moist slopes and meadows. Native.

Allium geyeri var. tenerum
(*A. rubrum*) AMARYLLIDACEAE

bulbil onion
RM, alpine, subalpine, montane,
sagebrush steppe, common, Spring–
Summer, perennial, 4–20 in.
Bulbs, often in clusters, with 2 or 3 leaves each. Leaves linear, flat and persisting at flowering time, up to a foot long with pa-pery sheath up to one-quarter of leaf length. Flowering stems usually taller than leaves with 0–5 pink flowers on short stalks and bulbils sessile on the rounded umbel. The bulbils are red and rounded. Found in meadows and along streams, in woodlands and thickets. Flowers are mostly sterile, and the plant reproduces through the bulbils instead of seeds. Native.

Allium macropetalum

AMARYLLIDACEAE
largeflower onion
SR, foothills, sagebrush steppe, grasslands,
locally abundant, Spring, perennial, 2–8 in.
Herb. Bulb with 2 basal leaves still green at flowering time. Upright flowering stems with 2 or 3 bracts beneath the rounded flower umbel; flowers with 6 tepals. 10–20 individual flowers per umbel, pink to rarely white with a dark pink center line. Grows on dry hills and desert areas. This short-statured species occurs in the southern part of the region and extends into Mexico. Native.

Eriogonum bicolor
(*E. microthecum* ssp. *bicolor*)

POLYGONACEAE
pretty buckwheat
SR, pinyon-juniper, endemic, rare,
Spring–E Summer, perennial, 0.75–3 in.

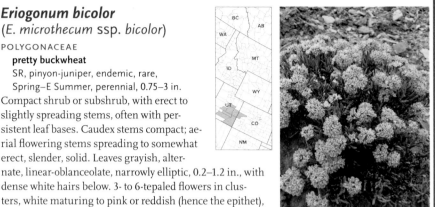

Compact shrub or subshrub, with erect to slightly spreading stems, often with persistent leaf bases. Caudex stems compact; aerial flowering stems spreading to somewhat erect, slender, solid. Leaves grayish, alternate, linear-oblanceolate, narrowly elliptic, 0.2–1.2 in., with dense white hairs below. 3- to 6-tepaled flowers in clusters, white maturing to pink or reddish (hence the epithet), rounded, and unbranched. Grows in sunny areas, barrens, rock ledges, dry slopes, and meadows. A beautiful distinctive little buckwheat. Native.

Eriogonum lonchophyllum

POLYGONACEAE
spearleaf buckwheat
SR, montane, foothills, pinyon-juniper, sagebrush steppe, intermountain parks, grasslands, locally abundant, L Spring–Fall, perennial, 3–31 in.

Stems are in a shrub or subshrub form, spreading to erect. Leaves are green to grayish, linear-oblanceolate, 0.6–2 in., and densely hairy on both surfaces. Inflorescence a cyme, dense to more commonly open. Flowers 6-tepaled, to 0.15 in., white aging to pink. Grows in sunny areas, rock ledges, barrens, dry slopes, sage meadows, roadsides. Incredibly variable throughout its range. Native.

Eriogonum ovalifolium

POLYGONACEAE
cushion buckwheat
RM, throughout, common, L Spring–Summer, perennial, 1–20 in.

Slender, leafless stems form a cushion. Leaves grayish, rounded-oblanceolate, 0.1–2.4 in., densely hairy on both surfaces. 6-tepaled flowers form dense, pompom-like clusters; pink to rose or cream to yellow. Grows in sunny areas, rock ledges, scree, barrens, dry slopes, and sage meadows. Highly variable, with many named varieties occurring in all life zones but wetlands. In general, if it has rounded leaves *and* tight pompoms, it is simply *E. ovalifolium*. Native.

Olsynium douglasii var. inflatum
(*Sisyrinchium douglasii* var. *inflatum*) IRIDACEAE

inflated grasswidow
NR, MR, montane, foothills, pinyon-juniper, sagebrush steppe, grasslands, locally abundant, Spring–Summer, perennial, 1–16 in.

Erect herb with round flowering stems. Leaves basal, grass-like, parallel-veined. Flowers few per stem; pink to purple (occasionally white), saucer-shaped, 6-petaled, and with 3 yellow stamens shorter than style. Filament cluster is distinctly flared at base, petals are pointed at the apex. Found in open, vernally moist areas. Native.

Calochortus flexuosus LILIACEAE

winding mariposa lily
SR, pinyon-juniper, sagebrush steppe, common, locally abundant, Spring–E Summer, perennial, to 8 in.

Herbaceous from deep bulb. Wiry flower stem to 8 in., often bent or twisted lower under weight of flowers. 1 or 2 narrow basal leaves and small leaves along stem. Flowers 1–5; 3 petals deep pink to nearly white, smooth, with yellow bases and orange nectaries with small hairs; 3 greenish pink sepals about half the length of petals. Anthers often pink. Slender 3-chambered seed capsule. High desert plant of Four Corners region, near the southern Wasatch. Native.

Calochortus macrocarpus

LILIACEAE
sagebrush mariposa lily
NR, MR, sagebrush steppe, grasslands, common, Spring–Summer, perennial, 8–20 in.

Herbaceous from deep bulb. Stout stem, grass-like leaves and smaller alternate leaves up the stem. 1–3 flowers, lavender-pink or white, to 4 in. across. Colorful narrow sepals longer than petals with green reverse; petals with narrow green stripe on reverse; creamy center sometimes ringed in wine-red; hairy below the ring; dark nectaries; lavender stain at the base. Grassy foothills, sagebrush meadows of NR. Native.

Chamerion angustifolium
(Epilobium angustifolium)
ONAGRACEAE
fireweed
RM, alpine, subalpine, montane, common,
Summer–Fall, perennial, 2–6 ft.

Herbaceous stems, often reddish, unbranched
or sparsely so, from rhizomatous roots. Leaves
alternate, 2–8 in. long, willow-like; distinct
white midrib, leaf veins uniquely rounded,
do not end at leaf edge. Terminal racemes of
pink and purple flowers; 4 pink petals, paddle-shaped, alternating with 4 purple, slender sepals; 8 white stamens,
purple-brown anthers; style white, curled tip. Fruit a slender pod, fluffy seeds. Open or disturbed areas, mixed
forests, recent burns or clearcuts, along roadsides, often in conspicuous colonies. Native.

Corydalis caseana PAPAVERACEAE
Sierra fumewort
RM, subalpine, montane, infrequent,
locally abundant, L Spring–
Summer, perennial, 3–6 ft.

Robust hollow stems, often in colonies;
smooth, waxy powder on all parts. Leaves
alternate; pinnately compound; lobed, oval
leaflets. Flowers 0.5–0.75 in. long, in dense
terminal spikes; 2 outer petals spreading at tip, one with
elongated spur behind, often pointing upward; 2 inner
petals smaller, fused, purple tip. Striking when blooming
en masse; pink forms especially showy. Several subspecies
identified; ssp. *brandegeei* found only in the
SR. Grows in sun, part shade, moist meadows, ravines, open woodlands. Native.

Oenothera curtiflora
(Gaura mollis) ONAGRACEAE
velvetweed
MR, SR, foothills, pinyon-juniper,
sagebrush steppe, grasslands, common,
L Spring–Summer, annual, 2–5 ft.

Fast-growing annual, lower half unbranched,
upper portion with gangly branching. Leaves
4 in., alternate, lanceolate, velvety, smaller on upper
branches. Flowers, in terminal elongating spikes, 0.4 in.
across, 4 wilty pink petals open in evening in ascending
sequence. Found in meadows, ditches, roadsides, and
disturbed sites at lower elevations. Native.

Dicentra uniflora PAPAVERACEAE
longhorn steer's head
RM, subalpine, montane, foothills, rare,
Spring–Summer, perennial, 2–4 in.

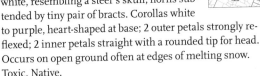

A tiny plant, leaves and flower stalks emerge
from deep tuberous roots. Leaves glaucous,
1 to several on long petioles, each 3 times
compound. Flowers solitary on leafless
stalks just above the leaves. Flowers pink or
white, resembling a steer's skull, horns subtended by tiny pair of bracts. Corollas white
to purple, heart-shaped at base; 2 outer petals strongly reflexed; 2 inner petals straight with a rounded tip for head.
Occurs on open ground often at edges of melting snow.
Toxic. Native.

Vaccinium oxycoccos ERICACEAE
small cranberry
NR, alpine, subalpine, montane,
wetlands, locally abundant,
Summer, perennial, 1–5 in.

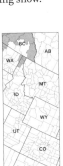

Evergreen subshrub, stems mostly prostrate, becoming erect when in fruit. Leaves
0.2–0.6 in., alternate, glabrous, oval to
lance-shaped; glossy dark green above,
gray-green below; leathery, edges rolled
under. Flowers 1 to few, nodding on short
smooth stalks with 2 small down-curved bractlets. Petals
reflexed, similar to *Dodecatheon* spp.; flowers begin dark
pink, lighten as petals curve backward; 8 dark stamens
hang down. Berries pale pink to deep red. Grows in wet
sphagnum moss in bogs in the boreal forest.
Native.

Clarkia pulchella ONAGRACEAE
pinkfairies
NR, MR, montane, foothills, pinyon-juniper,
sagebrush steppe, intermountain
parks, grasslands, uncommon,
L Spring–Summer, annual, 4–20 in.

Stems simple to freely branched; short
taproot. Leaves alternate, linear to
spoon-shaped, 1–3 in. long, entire or slightly
toothed. Few-flowered short raceme; petals rose-pink
to lavender, veins lighter, 0.5–1 in. long, deeply 3-lobed,
middle lobe widest; narrow at base, small tooth on either
side; pistil resembles small white multi-petaled flower; 4
purple-pink stamens fertile; 4 shorter, cream, infertile.
Rocky, sandy soils in pine woodlands and valleys. Native.

9

Cleome serrulata
(*Peritoma serrulata*) CLEOMACEAE
Rocky Mountain beeplant, spider-flower
RM, montane, foothills, sagebrush
steppe, grasslands, common, Spring–
Summer, annual, 0.5–5 ft.

Herb with erect, freely branched, smooth to
soft-hairy stems. Stem leaves alternate, to 2.75
in., trifoliate, with linear to lanceolate leaflets; margins entire. Inflorescence a terminal
bracted raceme elongating in fruiting. Calyx
lobes purple to green. Pale pink to reddish purple (rarely
white) petals narrowly ovate, their bases tapering to a claw.
6 stamens twice as long as petals. Fruit a pendent capsule
to 4 in. Grows on sandy slopes, disturbed sites, and pastures. Attracts bees, butterflies, wasps, and
hummingbirds. Native.

Menziesia ferruginea
(*M. glabella*) ERICACEAE
rusty menziesia, fool's huckleberry
NR, MR, subalpine, montane, foothills,
common, Spring–Summer, perennial, 2–9 ft.
Erect to spreading, sparingly branched, deciduous shrub; emits a musky odor when bruised.
Twigs with rusty-colored hairs, becoming
smooth or shredding. Bluish green leaves
clustered at stem tips; alternate, oval to elliptic with finely
toothed margins and soft, glandular hairs. Inflorescence
a hanging cluster of 1–10 salmon-pink to greenish orange
urn-shaped flowers, on terminal shoots. Fruit a brown,
ovoid capsule. Forests, moist shady woods, on
streambanks, and north-facing slopes. Native.

Chamerion latifolium
(*Epilobium latifolium*) ONAGRACEAE
dwarf fireweed, river beauty willowherb
RM, alpine, subalpine, montane, uncommon,
Summer–Fall, perennial, 4–20 in.
Herbaceous stems simple to freely branched,
erect to ascending, clustered from woody caudex; colony-forming. Leaves alternate, nearly
unstalked, glaucous; 1–2.5 in. long, longer
above, broadly lanceolate, entire to finely toothed. Short
terminal raceme, 3–12 flowers, pink-rose-purple (rarely
white); petals oval, 0.6–1 in. long, upper wider. Sepals linear, purplish, between petals. Style shorter than stamens.
Fruit a capsule. Streambanks and drier subalpine to alpine
talus slopes. Native.

Epilobium anagallidifolium

ONAGRACEAE

pimpernel willowherb, alpine willowherb
RM, alpine, wetlands, common,
L Spring–Summer, perennial, 4–8 in.

Stems arising from rhizomes. Leaves narrowly lanceolate, opposite, entire or with a few teeth to 1.25 in. long. Flowers to 0.5 in. wide, usually nodding on long, slender pedicels that elongate to 2.25 in. in fruit. Petals pink and notched, sepals often red and erect. Found in moist meadows and riparian zones, along streams and lakes. Hybridization is common in *Epilobium*; seeds are needed for confident species identification. Native.

Epilobium brachycarpum
(*E. paniculatum*) ONAGRACEAE

tall annual willowherb, panicled willowherb
RM, montane, grasslands, common,
L Spring–Summer, annual, 8–40 in.

Upright stems with mostly alternate, linear leaves to 2.75 in. long; leaves may be entire or toothed. Flowering stems branching with small flowers on stalks less than 1 in. long. The 4 purplish pink to white petals are deeply cut on the tips and to 0.3 in. long. Fruit a narrow capsule to 1.2 in. long, held upright on stems, opening longitudinally to reveal tufted silky hairs attached to the seeds. Found in moist meadows, forests, and riparian areas. Native.

Epilobium ciliatum ONAGRACEAE
fringed willowherb
RM, montane, wetlands, common,
Spring, perennial, 12–40 in.

Upright herb with stems branching, and minutely hairy. Leaves opposite, ovate to elliptical, 1–4.75 in. long and slightly toothed. Var. *ciliatum* flowers in upright racemes with several pink or white flowers with notches at the end of the petals; var. *glandulosum*'s flowers (pictured) are simple. Both have slender pedicels to 0.8 in. long in fruit. The capsules are to 4 in. long. Found in riparian areas, seeps, and moist meadows. Native.

Epilobium obcordatum

ONAGRACEAE
rockfringe, rockfringe willowherb
MR, alpine, subalpine, locally abundant,
Summer, perennial, 3–8 in.

Striking, mounding, mat-forming herb.
Stems numerous, clustered. Leaves alternate, egg-shaped, to 0.75 in. long, often looking frosted with a bluish tint. Flowers a very
showy bright magenta, to 0.8 in., each petal
heart-shaped, with a large notch at tip. Fruit a
capsule. Usually found at high elevations, often on rocky
sites, cliffs, scree slopes, and dry meadows, from the Sierra
Nevada to the MR. Native.

Epilobium saximontanum

ONAGRACEAE
Rocky Mountain willowherb
RM, subalpine, montane, wetlands, common,
L Spring–Summer, perennial, 2–22 in.

Slightly hairy upright herbaceous stems.
Leaves opposite, usually clasping the stem;
lanceolate to elliptic to 2.4 in. long by 1 in.
wide; entire or slightly toothed; stiff hairs
along edges. Inflorescence sometimes nodding in bud; flowers pink to purple (sometimes white), with notches at top of petal.
Found in riparian sites, moist meadows, and bogs. Several
similar species are native to the Rockies, most occurring
in moist environments. Native.

Houstonia rubra

(*Hedyotis rubra*) RUBIACEAE
red bluet
SR, montane, foothills, pinyon-juniper,
sagebrush steppe, grasslands, common,
Spring–Fall, perennial, to 2 in.

Densely tufted herbaceous perennial with
woody taproot. Leaves linear, opposite, erect to
ascending; fleshy, margins sometimes rolled
under; lower leaves oblanceolate. Flowers tubular, pink, red, white, or lavender; yellow
at center. Corolla 0.3–1.5 in. long, abruptly
spreads wide into 4 distinct petals. Style length varies
within the species. Found in the Rockies of NM in washes
and with pinyon-juniper. Native.

Astragalus thompsoniae
(*A. mollissimus* var. *thompsoniae*)
FABACEAE
Thompson's milkvetch
SR, pinyon-juniper, common, Spring–
E Summer, perennial, 4–12 in.

Very hairy clump-forming herb with numerous stems. Leaves pinnately compound; leaflets small, gray, very soft to the touch from the hairs; keeled, in tidy up-pointing rows on arched rachis. Flowers pink-purple in short upright clusters held above the leaves; each flower is narrow with a distinctive flare upward at the tip. Pods silvery pink and very hairy. Grows on dry slopes, woodlands, shrublands, and sunny forest openings. Native.

Astragalus tridactylicus
(*Orophaca tridactylica*) FABACEAE
foothill milkvetch
SR, foothills, sagebrush steppe, grasslands, common, locally abundant, Spring–Summer, perennial, 1–4 in.

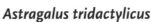

Stems cushion- and mat-forming, and tend to retain dead leaves and stems. Leaves silvery, compound with 3 leaflets, and very hairy. Flowers among the first of spring's legumes; pea-shaped, and pink-purple. Pods are pea-like. Grows in sun on barrens, dry slopes, rock ledges, pine parklands, and sage meadows. Sometimes confused or grouped with *A. sericoleucus*, which has slightly smaller flowers and tends to form mats with less dead material. Native.

Hedysarum boreale FABACEAE
Utah sweetvetch, northern chainpod
RM, montane, foothills, sagebrush steppe, common, Spring–Summer, perennial, 6–24 in.

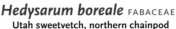

Stems erect or leaning on adjacent supports, from a central crown. Leaves green, elliptic to oblong, pinnate; 7–15 leaflets are 0.4–1.4 in. long and exhibit venation. Pea-shaped flowers, bright red-purple, pink, or white, surround the stem in tall terminal clusters. Calyces 0.8–1.4 in. long with linear lobes. Thin, flat, pea-like pods have 2–7 segments. Grows in barrens, dry slopes, sage meadows, and meadows. Found at lower elevations than other hedysarums. Large keel and unusual, segmented fruit differentiate this species. Native.

Hedysarum occidentale FABACEAE
western sweetvetch
RM, alpine, subalpine, montane,
foothills, common, Spring–
Summer, perennial, 12–32 in.

Several to many stems originate from base.
Leaves green, pinnate; 11–17 leaflets, ovate
to elliptic-lanceolate, 0.2–0.6 in. long, with
secondary venation present. Pea-shaped
5-petaled flowers, red-purple to pink
(rarely white), upper keel reflexed upward;
upright-leaning spikes, flowers often hang to one side.
Thin, flat, pea-like pods have 2–5 segments with netted venation. Grows on rock scree, dry slopes, and in mixed forests, usually at higher elevations than *H. boreale*. Native.

Oxytropis besseyi FABACEAE
Bessey's locoweed
RM, subalpine, montane, foothills,
sagebrush steppe, grasslands, common,
Spring–Summer, perennial, 1–10 in.

Herb with erect, leafless stems. Basal leaves
deciduous, pinnately compound; 5–23 leaflets
depending on the variety, with hairy, silvery
surfaces. Inflorescence a short upright to globose spike of pea-shaped flowers, magenta
fading to blue. Pods ascending and covered
with long, spreading white hairs that do not hide the surface. Grows in barrens, pine parklands, dry slopes, and
meadows. Blooms several weeks later than *O. lagopus*. Extremely variable, with at least 3 subspecies: ssp. *obnapi-
formis* has 17–23 leaflets, ssp. *besseyi* 9–21, and
ssp. *argophylla* 5–9. Native.

Robinia neomexicana FABACEAE
New Mexico locust
SR, montane, foothills, sagebrush
steppe, common, L Spring–
Summer, perennial, 6–25 ft.

Shrub to small tree with suckering
habit, forms dense thickets; stems with 2
down-turned thorns at the alternate leaf
nodes. Leaves pinnate; 15–21 oval leaflets to
1.5 in. long, with fine hairs. Showy flowers 0.75 in. across,
fragrant, pea-like; in dense, often pendulous racemes with
hairy calyces. Fruit a hanging 3-in. pod, bristly or smooth,
with hard bean-like seeds, toxic. Sun or part shade; ravines, riparian areas, disturbed sites, rocky slopes. Native.

Agastache pallidiflora LAMIACEAE
**Bill Williams Mountain giant hyssop,
New Mexico giant hyssop**
SR, montane, intermountain parks,
common, Summer, perennial, 1–3.5 ft.

Multiple square-shaped stems upright with woody base. Leaves opposite, triangular to ovate, to 2.75 in. long and half as wide, with obtuse, truncate or heart-shaped base; margins serrate-crenate; dull green. Flowers on upright spike of up to 15 whorls; calyx green, pink or rosy-purple and showy even after flower fades; corolla tube bilabiate, pink, white, or blue-lavender; filaments and style usually protrude from flower. Rocky outcroppings, meadows, aspen forests and streams. Native.

Agastache urticifolia LAMIACEAE
nettleleaf giant hyssop
RM, montane, intermountain parks, common, L Spring–Summer, perennial, 2–6 ft.

Multiple upright square stems with strong minty odor. Leaves opposite, broadly triangular with rounded to heart-shaped base, sharply toothed margins, 1–3 in. long, lighter green on underside. Flowers on dense, upright spike to 6 in. long with leaf-like bract at base. Calyx green to pink and more showy than true flower; corolla tubular to 0.6 in. long with upper 2 lobes shorter than lower 3 lobes; rose, violet, or white. Found on rocky outcroppings, in meadows and forest openings. Occurs throughout western North America, mostly west of the Continental Divide. Native.

Castilleja chromosa
(*C. angustifolia* var. *dubia*)
OROBANCHACEAE
northwestern Indian paintbrush
MR, SR, pinyon-juniper, sagebrush steppe, common, Spring–E Summer, perennial, 6–16 in.

Erect stems stiff and often branched. Lower leaves alternate, linear or sometimes lobed, to 2.75 in. long; upper leaves alternate with 3–5 narrow lobes. Bracts 3-parted, bright red, orange, or yellow. Calyx to 1 in. long and notched. Tubular green to yellow flowers to 1.25 in. long with the hood-like galea about half the length of corolla. Grows on dry hillsides and in sagebrush meadows. Native.

Castilleja haydenii OROBANCHACEAE
Hayden's Indian paintbrush
SR, alpine, locally abundant,
Summer, perennial, 4–6 in.

Short hairy stems in small clusters. Leaves
alternate, linear to narrow-lanceolate to 3 in.
long; lower leaves entire and upper leaves
with 1 or 2 pairs of lateral lobes. Flowering
stem and bracts finely hairy; bracts notched
and pink, red, or purple. Corolla tube to 1 in.
long, hood-like galea to 0.3 in. long, lower lip
less than half galea length. Found on tundra. Similar to
C. rhexifolia, but distinguishable by its smaller size and
higher tundra habitat. Native.

Castilleja integra OROBANCHACEAE
wholeleaf Indian paintbrush
SR, montane, foothills, pinyon-juniper,
intermountain parks, grasslands, common,
Spring–Summer, perennial, 4–12 in.

Herbaceous, 1 to several erect stems, short
whitish tomentose hairs. Leaves alternate,
hairless on top and hairy below; linear to
narrowly lanceolate, entire, sometimes involute; not divided into lobes or forks like
others in genus. Inflorescence a short, broad
crimson-orange spike; rounded, entire or
shallowly cleft bracts subtend minute, slightly protruding
green flowers. Grows in sunny forest openings, dry foothills, and into the plains in rocky, gravelly soil. Hemiparasitic. A host plant for Fulvia Checkerspot butterfly. Native.

Castilleja linariifolia
(C. linearis) OROBANCHACEAE
Wyoming Indian paintbrush
MR, SR, montane, foothills, pinyon-juniper,
sagebrush steppe, grasslands, common,
L Spring–Summer, perennial, 12–32 in.

Erect stems, sometimes branching above
base. Leaves less than 2.5 in. long, alternate,
linear-lanceolate, entire or with a pair of linear lobes. Flowering stems and bracts quite
hairy; bracts red to red-orange, with a pair of
lateral lobes. Calyx to 1.2 in. long, red to orange-red with
back lobes less notched than those in the front. Corolla
tube visibly extends beyond the calyx, to 1.75 in. long, the
hood-like galea to 1 in. long. Widespread in dry habitats;
long-flowering, often showy into fall. State flower of WY.
Native.

Castilleja miniata

OROBANCHACEAE

giant red Indian paintbrush
RM, alpine, subalpine, montane,
foothills, grasslands, common,
L Spring–Summer, perennial, 10–32 in.

Stems erect, base somewhat woody. Leaves alternate, linear-lanceolate to 3.2 in. long, flat, entire (upper are rarely cleft), tips pointed. Flowering stem and bracts hairy; bracts red to red-orange, rarely yellow or white (western MT); calyx to 1.2 in., with lobes more deeply cut in front than in back, with segments to 0.3 in. long; corolla greenish to 1.75 in. long, the hood-like galea to 0.75 in. long. Grows in many different habitats, including forests, riparian areas, and moist meadows. Native.

Castilleja pulchella

OROBANCHACEAE

beautiful Indian paintbrush, showy Indian paintbrush
MR, alpine, subalpine, endemic,
L Spring–Summer, perennial, 1.5–6 in.

Stems erect. Leaves alternate, linear, entire or with a pair of lateral lobes on upper leaves with middle lobe rounded. Flowering stems hairy; bracts reddish-purplish with 1 or 2 lobes, shorter than the flowers; calyx to 1 in. long; corolla longer than calyx with hood-like galea less than a third of the length of flower tube, and longer than lower lip. Limited to tundra and high rocky meadows. Native.

Castilleja rhexifolia

OROBANCHACEAE

rosy paintbrush, alpine paintbrush
RM, alpine, subalpine, montane,
foothills, common, L Spring–
Summer, perennial, 4–24 in.

Stems erect or curving upward in showy groups. Leaves alternate, linear to lanceolate, entire, 1.2–2.7 in. long. Flowering stems and bracts hairy or rarely smooth. Bracts reddish purple to rich pink, occasionally red; ovate, entire or with a pair of small lateral lobes near the tip. Calyx to 1 in. long, nearly equally notched both above and below; corolla 0.75–1.4 in. long, with hood-like galea to 0.5 in. long and tube to 1 in. long. Grows in riparian areas, moist meadows, and forests. Native.

Castilleja sessiliflora

OROBANCHACEAE

downy paintedcup, downy Indian paintbrush
RM, foothills, grasslands, common,
Spring–Summer, perennial, 4–12 in.

Herbaceous compact mounds of multiple
hairy, short stems. Leaves 1–3 in. long, narrow, lobed into 3 sections or rounded, pubescent, and entire. Inflorescence a dense, leafy
spike with 1-in.-long lobed, pale yellow-green
flowers. Unusually for *Castilleja*, clearly evident true greenish flowers extend 1 in. or more beyond
the salmon to pinkish green bracts. Almost always grows
among blue grama or buffalograss in the shortgrass
prairie or nearby hills. Native.

Orthocarpus tenuifolius

OROBANCHACEAE

thinleaved owl's-clover
NR, MR, montane, foothills, sagebrush
steppe, grasslands, uncommon, locally
abundant, L Spring–Summer, annual, 4–12 in.

Slender herb with erect, usually simple,
short-hairy stems. Leaves cauline, alternate,
sessile, to 2 in. long, short-hairy, entire; lower
leaves linear, upper with 1 or 2 pairs of slender lobes. Bracts purplish pink, broader and
blunter-tipped than leaves. Inflorescence a dense spike
of 2-lipped, tubular flowers: upper lip hooded, lower lip
shorter, inflated, minutely 3-toothed. Purplish-tipped and
yellow flowers nearly hidden by the showy bracts. Grows
in meadows, valleys, and open woods. Native.

Pedicularis crenulata

(*P. albomarginata*) OROBANCHACEAE

meadow lousewort
MR, SR, subalpine, montane,
foothills, locally abundant, L Spring–
Summer, perennial, 6–20 in.

Soft-haired, herbaceous perennial with clusters of erect stems. Basal and alternate stem
leaves to 4 in., linear to lanceolate (not pinnatifid), with serrate to crenate, cartilaginous
margins. Inflorescence a dense, spike-like raceme of pink,
red, or purple flowers with soft, shaggy-haired calyces;
subtended by leaf-like bracts. Corolla 2-lipped: upper lip
with inconspicuous beak. Grows in riparian meadows and
marshes. Native.

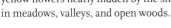

Pedicularis groenlandica OROBANCHACEAE
elephant's head

RM, alpine, subalpine, montane, common,
L Spring–Summer, perennial, 4–28 in.

Glabrous herb with erect, unbranched,
stems. Fern-like leaves basal and alternate
along stem, 2–10 in. long (reducing upward),
pinnatifid with toothed, sometimes cartilaginous margins. Inflorescence a dense spike
of pink to purple (rarely white) flowers subtended by shorter, pinnately divided bracts.
Calyx with conspicuous veins. Corolla
2-lipped: lower lobes spreading to resemble
elephant ears and upper lip strongly hooded
with a long, slender, upcurved beak. Grows in wet mountain meadows, seeps, and along streams. Native.

Pedicularis sudetica ssp. *scopulorum*

OROBANCHACEAE
sudetic lousewort

SR, alpine, subalpine, uncommon,
locally abundant, L Spring–
Summer, perennial, 1–3 ft.

Rhizomatous, smooth to hairy herb with
erect, unbranched, purplish stems. Basal
leaves 1–3 in. long, pinnately lobed or deeply
cleft with toothed margins; 2 or 3 alternate
stem leaves reduced or absent. A short terminal spike of pink to purple flowers subtended by leaf-like bracts. Corolla 2-lipped:
upper lip hood-like, arched, beakless; lower lip shorter,
spotted. Calyx smooth to white-woolly. Found in open forests, moist meadows, along streams, and on the tundra.
Native.

Digitalis purpurea

PLANTAGINACEAE
purple foxglove

RM, montane, foothills, infrequent,
L Spring–Summer, biennial, 3–6 ft.

Usually biennial herb. Year 1: lush lanceolate basal leaves 5–15 in. long, coarse teeth,
hairy. Year 2: robust upright stems to 6 ft.
with terminal flower spike. Leaves alternate, decreasing in size up stem. Flowers
opening from base upward along one side of
stem; petals fused into pendent, lobed tubular corolla 1–3
in. long, shades of pink-purple to white; lower lobe heavily
speckled with dark spots. Fruit a 4-valved capsule with fine
seeds. Naturalized garden escapee, sunny meadows, roadsides, woodland edges, disturbed sites. Introduced.

Penstemon barbatus

PLANTAGINACEAE

beardlip penstemon

SR, subalpine, montane, foothills, pinyon-juniper, grasslands, locally abundant, Spring–Summer, perennial, 12–14 in.

Several stems form a slender upright clump. Rosette leaves are linear to lanceolate with entire margins; stem leaves are opposite, linear and smooth, with no hairs; basal leaves evergreen. Inflorescence an elongated cluster of tubular red to orange-red flowers, openly spaced, on thin stems. Grows on rock ledges, dry slopes, in pine parklands, and meadows. One of the few true red species in the SR. Pollinated by hummingbirds. Native.

Penstemon cyathophorus

PLANTAGINACEAE

sagebrush penstemon

SR, montane, foothills, sagebrush steppe, intermountain parks, grasslands, endemic, locally abundant, Summer, perennial, 6–24 in.

Several erect stems from a semi-woody base. Basal leaves spatula-shaped to rounded, entire, evergreen; stem leaves clasp the stem; all leaves waxy and blue-green. Inflorescence a sparse elongated cluster of pinkish to violet-blue tubular flowers. All 4 anthers exserted from the throat. Found on rock ledges, dry slopes, and in sage meadows in CO's North and Middle Parks, and southern WY. Native.

Penstemon eatonii PLANTAGINACEAE

firecracker penstemon

MR, SR, montane, foothills, pinyon-juniper, sagebrush steppe, common, Spring–Summer, perennial, 6–40 in.

Herb with several stems arising from basal rosette of evergreen leaves. Basal and alternate stem leaves bright green to gray-green; linear to lanceolate with glossy, smooth to minutely hairy surfaces. Inflorescence a spike of red to orange-red tubular flowers. Grows in sunny and shady locations on rock scree, rock ledges, pine parklands, dry slopes, sage meadows, and disturbed habitats. A most eye-catching penstemon and among the earliest red wildflowers to bloom; often planted along highways and found outside its native range. Native.

Penstemon palmeri

PLANTAGINACEAE

Palmer's penstemon

RM, montane, pinyon-juniper, sagebrush steppe, grasslands, uncommon, L Spring–Summer, perennial, 20–55 in.

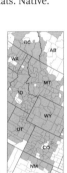

Several tall, erect stems from a semi-woody base. Basal leaves evergreen, ovate, with conspicuously large-toothed margins; upper opposite. Inflorescence a tall spire of pale pink or lavender (rarely white) fragrant tubular flowers hanging from one side of the stem. Prominent red lines inside of tube and densely yellow-haired staminode. Grows in sunny locations, rock ledges, dry slopes, meadows, disturbed habitats. Native.

Cynoglossum officinale

BORAGINACEAE

gypsyflower, houndstongue

RM, subalpine, montane, sagebrush steppe, grasslands, common, Spring–Summer, biennial, 1–4.5 ft.

Bristly-haired herb. Rosette in first year, tall flowering bolt in second year. Leaves to 1 ft. with distinct veins, smooth margins, and pointed tips. Basal and rosette leaves broader and stemmed; stem leaves alternate, clasping, lance-shaped and smaller. Inflorescence small clusters of panicles that originate in the leaf axils; 5-petaled flowers purplish red. Fruit a 4-barbed nutlet about 0.25 in. long. Coniferous forests, riparian areas, dry meadows, disturbed sites. Seeds distributed by clinging to animal fur or clothing. Introduced and invasive.

Silene drummondii

CARYOPHYLLACEAE

Drummond's campion

RM, throughout, common, L Spring–Summer, perennial, 8–24 in.

Herb with stout upright stems. Basal leaves on long petioles; stem leaves in 2–5 opposite pairs, linear to lanceolate, to 3.5 in., hairy. Cymes with up to 20 glandular or hairy flowers. Calyx with 10 veins, not inflated, to 0.7 in. Petals purplish pink to off-white. Found in meadows and forests. The type occurs at lower elevations; narrowed base of petal does not exceed calyx's length. Ssp. *striata* has pink to purple flowers and narrowed base of petal is longer than calyx; occurs from foothills to alpine. Native.

Pterospora andromedea ERICACEAE
pinedrops
RM, montane, foothills, common,
Summer, perennial, 1–3 ft.
Erect herb with reddish pink or brownish,
fleshy and glandular-hairy stems. Leaves
alternate; inconspicuous scale-like bracts
found mostly on lower portion of stem. Inflorescence an elongated terminal raceme of
nodding, urn-shaped flowers, pink, creamy
white, or yellow. Fruit a round, flattened capsule, which persists on rust-colored stems through winter. Grows in coniferous forests in pine needle duff. This
achlorophyllous plant is mycotrophic. Native.

Pyrola asarifolia ERICACEAE
pink wintergreen
RM, subalpine, montane, foothills, common,
L Spring–Summer, perennial, 4–18 in.
Rhizomatous, herbaceous, evergreen subshrub with erect stems. Basal cluster of
round, egg- or heart-shaped leaves; leathery,
shiny and dark green on top and often purplish on underside; margins entire to toothed.
Inflorescence an elongated terminal raceme
with 5–25 nodding, light pink to purplish red
flowers; waxy, weakly bilaterally symmetric,
with protruding light green, down-curved styles; included
cluster of stamens with dark pink tips. Grows in shady
coniferous forests, along streambanks, and in wet meadows. Native.

Dalea purpurea FABACEAE
purple prairie clover
RM, foothills, grasslands, common,
L Spring–Summer, perennial, 8–20 in.
Many tough slender stems, upright, spreading in a vase-shaped cluster; sometimes
branched. Leaves alternate, fine, pinnately
compound, 3–7 leaflets linear to 0.75 in.
with fine hairs. Flowers in compact terminal
spikes 1–2.5 in. long; florets dense, tiny, with 5
petals, protruding orange stamens; maturing
into small 1-seeded pods in dense spike. Found on sunny
slopes and roadsides at lower elevations. Native.

Ribes laxiflorum
(*R. coloradense*) GROSSULARIACEAE
trailing black currant
NR, SR, subalpine, montane, common,
Spring–Summer, perennial, 1–3 ft.
Deciduous shrub, spineless, loosely
branched, decumbent to spreading. Stems
reddish brown with fine hairs, sparse
glands. Leaves alternate, to 4 in. across;
maple-shaped, typically 5-lobed; crenate
margins. Upper surface smooth and hairy,
glandular below. Erect to ascending racemes
with 6–18 shallowly bowl-shaped flowers; calyces reddish purple to greenish white, pubescent; petals reddish
purple; stamens with reddish filaments. Berries ovoid,
waxy-coated, with bristly glands. Grows in moist woods,
along streams, on rocky slopes, and in open
sunny locations. Native.

Sidalcea oregana MALVACEAE
Oregon checkerbloom
NR, MR, montane, sagebrush
steppe, grasslands, infrequent,
L Spring–Fall, perennial, 8–60 in.
Stems slender, erect, hairier below,
smoother above; several from a branched
taprooted crown. Leaves highly variable.
Lower leaves long-stalked and shallowly
lobed. Higher leaves smaller, shorter-stalked and more
deeply lobed. Inflorescence a terminal raceme of many
small pink flowers; 10–20 or more, densely to loosely
arranged. Fruit a capsule. Found in sage meadows at mid
elevations. Native.

Ipomopsis aggregata
(*Gilia aggregata*) POLEMONIACEAE
scarlet gilia, skyrocket
RM, subalpine, montane, foothills,
sagebrush steppe, grasslands, common,
Spring–Summer, biennial, 7–40 in.
Hairy, glandular stems, 1 to several, originate from a taprooted base. Year 1: finely
dissected pinnate leaves form an evergreen
basal rosette up to 4 in. across. Year 2: flowering stems grow quickly, often branching, with alternate
leaves. Tubular red (pink, white) flowers 0.6–1 in. long nod
from branch tips throughout. Grows in disturbed areas,
barrens, rock scree, ledges, dry slopes, and sage meadows. Variation has led to many different described names.
Long-flowering, attracts hummingbirds. Native.

Ipomopsis tenuituba
(Gilia tenuituba) POLEMONIACEAE
slendertube skyrocket
MR, SR, subalpine, montane, foothills,
sagebrush steppe, grasslands, common,
Summer, biennial, 8–40 in.
Single stem (rarely more) with woolly hairs
from basal rosette. Leaves pinnatifid to sub-
pinnatifid. Tubular flowers, 5-petaled, soft
pink or lavender to white. Sunny, disturbed
areas, rock slopes, sage meadows. Fragrant in
the evening, pollinated by moths. Native.

Persicaria amphibia
(Polygonum amphibium) POLYGONACEAE
water smartweed, longroot smartweed
RM, subalpine, montane, foothills,
sagebrush steppe, wetlands, common,
Summer–Fall, perennial, 1–3 ft.
Rhizomatous or stoloniferous herb; stems
ranging from prostrate to erect, branched,
variably hairy, and ribbed. Leaves light to
dark green, alternate, to 8 in. long by 3 in.
wide, entire; variably tipped, textured, and
stalked. Inflorescence a terminal raceme
2–4 in. long; bright pink flowers (mostly
bisexual) with 5 tepals and long stamens;
barrel- to thimble-shaped depending on species location.
Leaf stalk has variably hairy sheath at base, often brown
and thin, sometimes green and flared. Found in shallows
of ponds, lakes, streams, and occasionally creeps into wetlands. Native.

Spiraea douglasii ROSACEAE
rose spirea, hardhack spirea
RM, subalpine, montane, locally abundant,
Spring–Summer, perennial, 3–8 in.
Upright branching shrub spreading by
suckers in dense thickets. Stems slender,
erect to ascending. Leaves oblanceolate, 1–4
in., serrated toward the tip. Inflorescence a
branched, cone-shaped, fuzzy spike of tiny
bright pink-purple flowers. Found in damp
meadows, bogs, and streamsides; primarily distributed
in Pacific NW, extending to the humid woodlands of ID
and WA, with a disjunct population in northwestern CO.
Native.

Telesonix heucheriformis
(*Boykinia heucheriformis*)
SAXIFRAGACEAE
alumroot brookfoam
NR, MR, alpine, subalpine, montane, locally abundant, Summer, perennial, 2–8 in.
Rhizomatous herb with erect to ascending, glandular-hairy stems from basal rosette; forms dense colonies. Leaves succulent, to 2.75 in. wide, reniform to round, with shallowly lobed or doubly crenate margins. Stem leaves reduced. Inflorescence a paniculate cyme (flowers sometimes solitary) subtended by leafy bracts. Sepals erect. Pale pink to violet-purple (white) petals, ovate to spatulate, taper to a claw. Fruit an ovoid, 2-beaked capsule. Moist rock crevices, on cliffs and talus slopes; frequently on calcareous substrates. Native.

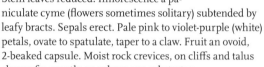

Telesonix jamesii
(*Boykinia jamesii*) SAXIFRAGACEAE
James' telesonix
SR, alpine, subalpine, montane, endemic, infrequent, locally abundant, Summer, perennial, 4–10 in.
Rhizomatous, mat-forming herb with erect to ascending, glandular-hairy stems from basal cluster of leaves. Leaves to 1.5 in. wide, with rounded lobes and crenate margins. Stem leaves reduced and alternate. Inflorescence a paniculate cyme or solitary flower. Sepals erect. Reddish pink, spatulate petals taper to claw. Grows on talus slopes, cliffs, cool crevices, and ledges. Found on Pikes Peak granite in the Platte River drainage and on Precambrian schist and gneiss in Rocky Mountain NP. Endemic to CO. Native.

Astragalus purshii FABACEAE
woollypod milkvetch, Pursh's milkvetch
RM, montane, foothills, pinyon-juniper, sagebrush steppe, intermountain parks, grasslands, locally abundant, Spring, perennial, 0.5–8 in.
Clump-forming, stemless or with short stems. Leaves silvery to gray-green, pinnately compound, 5–19 leaflets, densely hairy. Flowers 5-petaled, pea-shaped, bright pink, red, and purple to whitish pale yellow. Pods, pea-like, densely hairy. Sunny areas, barrens, rock scree, dry slopes, sage meadows. The very woolly pods that tend to ring the plant and woolly leaves are distinctive. Native.

Lathyrus pauciflorus FABACEAE
fewflower pea
RM, montane, foothills, sagebrush
steppe, common, Spring–E Summer,
perennial, 8–24 in.

Trailing to erect herbaceous stems, not
winged, from taproot and short rhizomes.
Leaves alternate, pinnate with 8–10 leaflets,
linear to ovate, thick; stipules half the size of
leaflets. Pinkish to violet pea-shaped flowers
in racemes of 4–7 flowers; banner purplish
on back, wings lighter than banner and shorter. Smooth
pods are 1–2 in. long. Grows in sun to part shade in open
forests. Native.

Onobrychis viciifolia
(*Hedysarum onobrychis*) FABACEAE
sainfoin
RM, foothills, intermountain parks,
grasslands, infrequent, L Spring–
E Summer, perennial, 12–28 in.

Herbaceous stems spreading, upright, and
robust. Leaves odd-pinnate with 15–21 oblong
leaflets, 0.5–1 in. long. Flowers pea-like in
terminal spikes; salmon-pink, dark stripes,
around 0.5 in.; blunt keel longer than wings.
Grows along sunny roadsides and in other
disturbed sites. Can resemble its native relatives, but this
is Eurasian, frequently escaping cultivation where grown
as fodder in colorful fields. Introduced.

Erythranthe lewisii
(*Mimulus lewisii*) PHRYMACEAE
purple monkeyflower, Lewis' monkeyflower
RM, alpine, subalpine, montane,
uncommon, Summer, perennial, 12–40 in.

Herbaceous, rhizomatous, with stems clustered; often found in large, showy groups.
Leaves opposite, sessile, ovate, pointed, 1.2–
2.8 in. long and prominently veined; margins
entire to toothed. Flowers on upper stems,
solitary in the leaf axils; pink to rose, 1 in.
long, yellow markings and reddish speckles
in throat. Moist habitats at mid to high elevations; disjunct
population found in northwestern CO and southern WY.
Named for Meriwether Lewis. Recent genetic work re-
vealed that *Mimulus* is an Australian genus, and *Erythran-
the* is the North American genus. Native.

Erythranthe nana
(*Mimulus nanus*) PHRYMACEAE
dwarf purple monkeyflower
NR, MR, subalpine, montane, foothills,
sagebrush steppe, uncommon,
L Spring–Summer, annual, 0.5–4 in.

A tiny plant covered with glandular hairs.
Stems with 1 to many branches. Flowers
bright rose, bilaterally symmetrical, on
short stalks in upper leaf axils. Flowers tubular and 5-lobed; upper 2 lobes larger than
lower 3; 2 yellow stripes run parallel on the tube's bottom
in stark contrast to the magenta flowers; reddish markings
also decorate the throat. A desert annual that will spread
and bloom profusely with good rainfall. Grows in dry and
sunny open areas. Native.

Astragalus amphioxys var.
vespertinus FABACEAE
crescent milkvetch
SR, montane, foothills, pinyon-juniper,
sagebrush steppe, common, Spring–
E Summer, perennial, 0.5–6 in.

Clump-forming herb with sprawling leaves
and stems. Leaves pinnate, gray-green
with 5–21 leaflets. Flowers pea-shaped,
pink-purple, in loose small clusters that
often lay on the ground. Fruit a pod, sparsely hairy and
sometimes mottled, tapering sharply at both ends. Grows
on dry slopes, rock ledges, and meadows. Native.

Astragalus chamaeleuce
FABACEAE
cicada milkvetch
MR, SR, pinyon-juniper, sagebrush
steppe, locally abundant, L Spring–
E Summer, perennial, 1–3 in.

Nearly stemless. Leaves pinnately compound, silvery gray-green, covered in dense
hairs, usually with 5–15 leaflets. Flowers
are creamy rose-pink to magenta with a
purple-tipped keel. Without fruit, it is easily
confused with *A. amphioxys*, which typically
has 11–21 leaflets. Grows in meadows, barrens, and
woodlands. Native.

Astragalus detritalis FABACEAE
debris milkvetch
MR, SR, montane, foothills, sagebrush
steppe, endemic, rare, Spring–
E Summer, perennial, 2–8 in.

Dense clump of basal leaves, stemless until
flowering. Leaves green, pinnately compound with 3–7 leaflets, deciduous. Flowers
pea-shaped, 5-petaled, brightly pink-purple,
with 2–8 flowers in each cluster. Pods point
up, are pea-like, not swollen, and are often
mottled and hairy. Found in sunny open barrens, rocky
ledges, dry hills, especially on shale slopes. In harsh
environments, bright pink flowers stand out beautifully.
Endemic to the Green and Yampa River Valleys of UT
and CO. Native.

Astragalus missouriensis FABACEAE
Missouri milkvetch
RM, foothills, pinyon-juniper,
sagebrush steppe, common, Spring–
Summer, perennial, 0.5–8 in.

Short clump-forming stems from taproots;
can grow in small ground-covering colonies.
Leaves silvery to gray-green, uniform and tidy,
with 7–19 oval leaflets. Flowers pea-shaped,
5-petaled, pink-purple; in small but showy
clusters on short stems. Pea-like pods are less than 1 in.
and can be hairy or smooth. Environmentally adaptable,
growing in sun and shade, barrens, pine parklands, dry
slopes, sage meadows. Variable in Four Corners region,
uniform elsewhere. Native.

Astragalus shortianus FABACEAE
Short's milkvetch
MR, SR, montane, foothills, sagebrush
steppe, intermountain parks, grasslands,
common, Spring–Summer, perennial, 1–6 in.

Clump-forming stems very similar to previous. Leaves deciduous, gray-green, pinnately
compound with 9–17 leaflets, and thinly
hairy on the underside. Flowers pea-shaped,
purple-pink. Pea-like pods are red on top, display a groove along their side, and are green underneath.
Grows in sunny areas, barrens, dry slopes, coniferous and
aspen forests, and sage meadows. Easily confused with *A.
missouriensis*, but the seedpods of *A. shortianus* are 1 in. or
longer and curved. Microscopic differences in leaf hairs.
Native.

Astragalus spatulatus FABACEAE
tufted milkvetch

RM, montane, foothills, sagebrush steppe,
intermountain parks, grasslands, common,
Spring–Summer, perennial, 1–4 in.

Stems mat- or tuft-forming. Leaves silvery,
simple, linear-spatulate, very hairy, with
an occasional compound leaflet. Flowers
pea-shaped and pink-purple. Pods pea-like,
point up, covered in hairs. Grows in sunny
areas, barrens, dry slopes, rock ledges, and
sage meadows. Locally common and distinct throughout the Rockies, its short tufted habit and simple leaves
differentiate it from many species. The leaves are not
spine-tipped like *A. kentrophyta* var. *tegetarius* and are not
found in 3s like *A. aretioides*. Native.

Astragalus utahensis FABACEAE
Utah milkvetch

MR, foothills, sagebrush
steppe, grasslands, common,
Spring, perennial, 1–4 in.

Stems cushion- and mat-forming; can create
carpets of silver and purple. Leaves silvery,
hairy, and pinnately compound with numerous leaflets. Flowers pea-shaped, 5-petaled,
and pink-purple. Pods are pea-like and thick
with dense white coiling hairs covering their surface.
Grows in sunny habitats, barrens, dry slopes, rock ledges,
and sage meadows. Very showy. Native.

Oxytropis lagopus FABACEAE
haresfoot locoweed

RM, alpine, subalpine, montane, foothills,
sagebrush steppe, grasslands, common,
Spring–Summer, perennial, 1–6 in.

Deciduous, cushion-forming, stemless unless flowering. Leaves pinnately compound,
7–15 lanceolate leaflets; silvery-hairy. Inflorescence stems leafless, upright to sprawling; length surpassing the leaves. Flowers
5–10, pea-like, magenta fading purple. Calyx
covered in dense white and shorter black
hairs. Pods spreading, inflated, 0.4–0.8 in. long, covered in
white hairs. Tundra, coniferous or mixed forest, pine parklands, dry slopes, meadows, often on limestone, mostly
east of the divide. At least 3 varieties: var. *conjugans* (endemic, central MT and AB), var. *lagopus*, and var. *atropur-
purea*. Native.

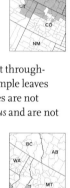

Oxytropis multiceps FABACEAE
Nuttall's oxytrope
MR, SR, subalpine, montane, foothills,
sagebrush steppe, grasslands, locally
abundant, Spring–E Summer,
perennial, 0.5–2 in.

Deciduous, cushion-forming herb. Flower
stems usually same height as foliage.
Leaves basal, pinnately compound with 5–9
elliptic-lanceolate-oblanceolate leaflets; surfaces hairy and silvery. Inflorescence a spike
of 2–4 pea-shaped, pink-purple (rarely white), 0.6- to 1-in.
flowers. Calyx covered in dense white hairs. Pods erect,
0.4–0.8 in. long, with long beak; leathery or woolly. Grows
in barrens, rock ledges, pine parklands, dry slopes, and
meadows. Favors granitic soils. Native.

Oxytropis nana FABACEAE
Wyoming locoweed
MR, SR, subalpine, montane, foothills,
sagebrush steppe, grasslands, locally
abundant, Spring–E Summer,
perennial, 0.5–2 in.

Deciduous, cushion-forming herb. Flower
stems usually same height as foliage.
Leaves pinnately compound with 5–9
elliptic-lanceolate-oblanceolate leaflets; surfaces hairy and silvery. Inflorescence a spike
of 2–4 pea-shaped, pink-purple (rarely white), 0.6- to 1-in.
flowers. Calyx covered in dense white hairs. Pods erect,
0.4–0.8 in. long, with long beak; leathery or woolly. Sunny
barrens, rock ledges, pine parklands, dry
slopes, and meadows. Native.

Oxytropis splendens FABACEAE
showy locoweed
RM, alpine, subalpine, montane, foothills,
common, Spring–Summer, perennial, 4–16 in.
Deciduous, clump-forming herb with several
to many leafless stems. 7–15 whorls of leaves,
each with 3 or 4 elliptic, oblong-lanceolate,
or lanceolate leaflets; surfaces hairy and silvery. Inflorescence an erect spike of 9–35
pea-shaped, magenta, pink, or bright red flowers. Calyx
covered in dense white hairs. Pods erect, sessile, 0.4–0.8
in. long, often with white and black hairs; walls thin.
Grows in tundra, barrens, rock ledges, pine parklands, dry
slopes, and meadows. Found at lower altitudes northward.
Native.

Oxytropis viscida
(*O. borealis* var. *viscida*) FABACEAE
sticky locoweed
RM, alpine, subalpine, montane,
locally abundant, Spring–
Summer, perennial, 3–12 in.

Deciduous, clump-forming herb from a
woody branched caudex. Leaves with 25–39
(rarely 15) ovate or oblong-lanceolate leaflets. Flower stems leafless; 3–20 pea-shaped,
red-purple or purple flowers in a spike;
calyx with light or dark hairs. Pods erect, 0.4–0.6 in. long,
sticky, with white or black hairs. Grows in tundra, barrens,
rock ledges, pine parklands, dry slopes, and meadows. An
eye-catching plant, often more showy than *O. splendens*.
Native.

Trifolium andinum FABACEAE
intermountain clover
MR, SR, montane, pinyon-juniper,
sagebrush steppe, locally abundant,
L Spring–Summer, perennial, to 2 in.
Mat-forming herb from woody base.
Leaves compound with 3 leaflets to 0.6 in.
long, with short-toothed margins near the
acute tip, hairy or not, frequently folded.
Flowerheads pink, sessile, with 5–12
upward-growing flowers, multiple leaf-like bracts below;
calyx with long soft hairs to almost hairless; flowers with a
pink to purple 0.5-in. banner. Fruit an elliptic pod to 0.2 in.
long with sparse hairs. Uncommon in CO. Found in sandy
soil, often with sagebrush, *Pinus edulis*, or
Cercocarpus spp. Native.

Trifolium arvense FABACEAE
rabbitfoot clover
NR, MR, montane, sagebrush steppe,
grasslands, uncommon,
L Spring–Summer, annual, 4–16 in.
Stems softly hairy, erect and branching.
Leaves alternate, palmately compound with
leaflets in 3s, to 1 in. long, entire, stipules
to 0.4 in. long. Flower racemes egg-shaped,
axillary and terminal, with a multitude of tiny light pink
flowers and lacking leaf-like bracts; calyces hairy to feathery and showiest part of flower, longer than the corollas. Fruit a tiny pod with 1 seed. Found in disturbed sites,
sandy soils, dunes, and roadsides. The common name
refers to the appearance of the flowerhead. Introduced.

Trifolium attenuatum
(*T. bracteolatum*) FABACEAE
Rocky Mountain clover
SR, alpine, subalpine, locally abundant,
L Spring–Summer, perennial, 4–8 in.

Stemless herb with compound leaves. Leaflets in 3s, to 2 in. long, linear to egg-shaped
with a pointed tip, entire, hairy, often folded
inward. Flowerheads rounded with 5–20 pink
to purple flowers to 0.7 in. long. Flowers reflexing with age. Fruit a pod to 0.25 in. long,
egg-shaped. Found in dry meadows, tundra, and talus.
Forms large, eye-catching mats, sometimes several feet in
diameter, at high elevations. Native.

Trifolium brandegeei
(*T. kingii* var. *brandegeei*) FABACEAE
Brandegee's clover
SR, alpine, subalpine, locally abundant,
L Spring–Summer, perennial, 2–6 in.

Mat-forming herb with compound leaves.
Leaflets in 3s, to 1.2 in. long, egg-shaped to elliptical, entire to toothed, not hairy. Flowerheads topping leafless stems with 5–15 bright
pink, iridescent, reflexed flowers. Calyx to 0.35
in. long and also bright pink. Fruit a pod to
0.25 in. long, not hairy. Found in moist meadows and forests at high elevations. Named for botanist
Townshend Brandegee, who collected the species in 1874
on the Hayden expedition. Native.

Trifolium dasyphyllum FABACEAE
alpine clover
MR, SR, alpine, subalpine, common,
L Spring–Summer, perennial, to 2 in.

Low-growing, almost stemless herb. Compound leaves with leaflets in 3s, rounded to
lanceolate, up to 1.2 in. long with silvery hairs
on lower surface and sometimes on upper
surface. Flowerheads rounded, up to 1 in.
across, terminal with 5–15 individual bicolored flowers, with pink-red keel and wings
and lavender-white (or yellow) banner. Found

in moist meadows, fens, and fellfields. Most comparable to
T. attenuatum but has a much wider range and bicolored
flowers. Native.

Trifolium gymnocarpon FABACEAE
hollyleaf clover

MR, SR, montane, pinyon-juniper,
sagebrush steppe, common,
Spring, perennial, 1.5–3.5 in.

Low-growing, almost stemless herb, with
flattened long hairs. Leaves palmately compound; leaflets in 3s or 5s, to 0.8 in. long,
often marked with a white chevron; leaflets
elliptic to oblong and often folding inward,
margins sharply toothed; stipules to 0.4 in.
long. Flowerheads sprawling with 4–15 light pink to yellowish white flowers ascending or reflexed, to 0.5 in. long.
Fruit a rounded pod to 0.2 in. Found in dry slopes, sagebrush meadows, woodland openings. Native.

Trifolium nanum FABACEAE
dwarf clover

MR, SR, alpine, common, L Spring–
Summer, perennial, to 3.5 in.

Mat-forming herb with small compound
leaves in 3s; leaflets lance-shaped to 0.5 in.
long with slightly toothed margins. Flowerheads with 1–4 upright, pink to purple flowers; flowers are larger than leaves, up to 0.7
in. long with 4 small bracts united below.
Found in fellfields at high elevations. Individual plants may grow up to a foot in diameter. Native.

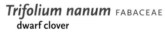

Trifolium pratense FABACEAE
red clover

RM, montane, sagebrush steppe,
grasslands, wetlands, common,
Spring–Fall, perennial, 2–32 in.

Upright short-lived herb. Compound leaves
with leaflets in 3s; leaflets rounded with
white chevron in center, up to 2 in. long,
toothed, hairy. Flower stems with numerous
flowers in terminal rounded cluster up to 1.2
in. wide; a pair of leaves directly below flowerhead; flowers red-purple or white. Found
in disturbed sites, moist meadows, and
along streams. Native to Europe and named
by Linnaeus. Introduced.

Castilleja scabrida OROBANCHACEAE
rough Indian paintbrush
MR, SR, pinyon-juniper, sagebrush steppe,
common, Spring–Fall, perennial, 3–8 in.

Herbaceous stems commonly purple in color
due to a lack of chlorophyll, covered in fine
hairs. Densely downy tufts of linear leaves
often divided into 3 segments along very short
stems, producing compact, bright red-orange
bracted inflorescence in spring and fall. Compact flower clusters usually more rounded
than elongated. This species grows most commonly in
tiny cracks of red sandstone in the Colorado Plateau,
although it can be found on gravelly, open sites as well.
Native.

Cymopterus bulbosus
(*Vesper bulbosus*) APIACEAE
spring biscuitroot, bulbous springparsley
MR, SR, montane, foothills, pinyon-
juniper, sagebrush steppe, common,
Spring–E Summer, perennial, 3–11 in.
Stems from a basal cluster. 2 or 3 basal pinnate leaves; deciduous, hairless, blue-green.
Flowers umbellate, 5-petaled, purplish pink
or white. Fruit 0.2–0.4 in., noticeable 0.1-in.
wings. Grows in sunny habitats, dry slopes,
rocky slopes, sage meadows, and meadows. One of the
first spring wildflowers. Similar to *C. constancei* but prefers lower elevations and clay soil. Bracts on *C. constancei* are narrower and joined for a third of their length; *C.
bulbosus*'s bracts are joined for up to half their
length. Native.

Cymopterus planosus APIACEAE
Rocky Mountain springparsley
SR, montane, foothills, pinyon-juniper,
sagebrush steppe, endemic, common,
Spring–E Summer, perennial, 2–12 in.
Several stems with basal leaves. The flower
stems barely exceed the leaves. Leaves deciduous, hairless, blue- or mint-green, 3 times pinnate on the stem; ultimate segments less than
0.04 in. wide. Flowers red-purple or yellow, 5-petaled; in an
umbel. Grows in sunny areas on dry slopes, aspen and sage
meadows, open meadows. Often found on clay and shale
slopes, this plant can dominate areas in the spring. Later
in the season the hillside appears devoid of life. Native.

Lomatium orientale
(*Cogswellia orientalis*) APIACEAE
salt and pepper biscuitroot
MR, SR, montane, foothills, sagebrush
steppe, grasslands, common,
Spring, perennial, 4–16 in.

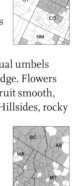

Leaves basal, triply pinnate, softly hairy,
to 3.25 in. long; ultimate leaf segments
crowded, linear to 0.2 in. long. Flower stems
leafless to 8 in. with few-flowered compound umbels, branches to 1.2 in. long and
not equal in length; bractlets under individual umbels
linear to 0.15 in. long with a membranous edge. Flowers
5-petaled, pink to white with red anthers. Fruit smooth,
elliptic to 0.35 in. long with narrow wings. Hillsides, rocky
slopes, sagebrush meadows. Native.

Apocynum androsaemifolium
(*A. pumilum*) APOCYNACEAE
spreading dogbane
RM, montane, foothills, pinyon-juniper,
intermountain parks, grasslands, wetlands,
common, Summer, perennial, to 3 ft.
Herb, often in large colonies, stems only
slightly branching. Leaves are round to
slightly cordate and dark green, opposite or
alternate, usually with edges curled under.
Fragrant flowers in clusters of nodding pink to pink-tinged
white bells, generally striped with a deeper pink. Plants
adapt to a wide range of conditions and soil types; often
but not exclusively found in disturbed sites. Native.

Asclepias hallii APOCYNACEAE
Hall's milkweed
MR, SR, pinyon-juniper, sagebrush steppe,
rare, Summer, perennial, 6–24 in.
Erect herb. Leaves alternate, petiolate, lanceolate to ovate, to 5.5 in. long, uniformly hairy
to glabrate. Umbels slightly hairy; pink,
reddish cream, or purple corolla 0.2–0.3 in.
long; hoods spreading widely with pale rose
to cream or white horns. Follicles 3–4.75 in.
long. Inhabits sandy and gravelly soils along
roadsides and sagebrush, pinyon-juniper, and cottonwood
communities. Rare species with a NatureServe Global
Conservation Status of G3, a ranking reserved for plants
characterized as vulnerable due to limited habitats and
regional threats. Native.

Asclepias incarnata APOCYNACEAE
swamp milkweed
MR, SR, foothills, grasslands, wetlands, common, Summer, perennial, 1.3–5 ft.

Tall, moisture-loving herb, arising from shallow, fibrous root system. Opposite, lanceolate leaves 4–6 in. long. Umbels slightly hairy; corolla 0.1–0.2 in. long, pink (rarely white); hoods white or dark pink on older flowers with white or dark pink horns. Follicles erect on erect pedicels, 2–3.5 in. long. Grows along ditches, swales, streamsides, and other wet areas. Attracts numerous butterflies, especially the Monarch, providing nectar for adults and food for larvae. Native.

Asclepias speciosa
(*A. giffordii*) APOCYNACEAE
showy milkweed
RM, foothills, sagebrush steppe, grasslands, common, Summer, perennial, 1.3–4 ft.

Herb with stems ascending to erect, densely pubescent with whitish, woolly hairs; deep rhizomes. Leaves opposite, mostly ovate, 4–8 in. long and 1.5–4 in. wide. Showy inflorescences are the largest of all *Asclepias* spp. Very pale or deep pink to purple corolla 0.3–0.6 in. long, hoods pinkish to nearly white; horns present. Follicles 2.4–4.7 in. long. Common in sandy, loamy, or gravelly soils in disturbed areas such as roadsides, ditches, and fields, and along streams. Vital larval food for Monarch butterflies. Native.

Symphoricarpos albus
CAPRIFOLIACEAE
common snowberry, white snowberry
RM, montane, foothills, sagebrush steppe, grasslands, common, Spring–Summer, perennial, 2–9 ft.

Deciduous, rhizomatous, erect, much-branched shrub, often forming dense colonies. Stems becoming dark grayish brown and shreddy. Leaves opposite, to 2 in. long, ovate to elliptic; margins entire or with few irregular teeth. Inflorescence a cluster of 2–5 flowers at ends of twigs and in upper leaf axils. Corolla pink to white, campanulate, with 5 shallow to slightly spreading lobes; densely hairy inside. Style and stamens not exserted. Berry-like drupes white, ellipsoid. Grows in forests, meadows, shrublands, and on open hillsides. Native.

Symphoricarpos occidentalis

CAPRIFOLIACEAE

western snowberry, wolfberry
RM, montane, foothills, sagebrush
steppe, grasslands, common,
L Spring–Summer, perennial, 1–9 ft.
Deciduous, rhizomatous, erect shrub.
Twigs reddish brown becoming dark gray
and shreddy. Thick leathery leaves opposite, to 3 in.; ovate to elliptic; margins entire
or with few irregular teeth. Inflorescence a
cluster of flowers at ends of twigs and in upper leaf axils.
Corolla pale pink to white, campanulate, with 5 spreading
lobes, equal to or longer than tube; densely hairy within.
Berry-like drupes white and round. Grows in dense colonies along streams, lakes, forest margins,
and in meadows. Native.

Symphoricarpos rotundifolius

CAPRIFOLIACEAE

mountain snowberry
SR, subalpine, montane, foothills,
sagebrush steppe, grasslands, common,
L Spring–Summer, perennial, 2–9 ft.
Deciduous, much-branched shrub with
erect to spreading, reddish brown and
soft-hairy stems becoming gray and
shreddy. Leaves opposite, to 2 in. long, ovate to round, with
few-toothed or few-lobed margins. Leaf surfaces smooth
to hairy, paler and more conspicuously veined below. 1 or 2
flowers in leaf axils and on terminal racemes. Corolla pink
to white, narrowly bell-shaped, with 5 erect
lobes; hairy at lower part of tube. Berry-like
drupes white and ovoid. Meadows, canyons,
shrublands, open forests. Native.

Saponaria officinalis

CARYOPHYLLACEAE

bouncing bet
RM, montane, foothills, pinyon-juniper,
grasslands, common, L Spring–Summer,
perennial, 1–3 ft.
Glabrous, clump-forming herb with erect
stems that are simple or branched above; from branched
rhizomes. Leaves opposite, elliptic to oblanceolate, entire,
short-petiolate to sessile; lower leaves absent at flowering.
Numerous showy, fragrant, pink to white flowers in terminal or axillary clusters; 5 petals, 5 sepals. Sunny locations,
disturbed habitats. Introduced.

Rhodiola integrifolia
(*Sedum integrifolium*) CRASSULACEAE
king's crown
RM, alpine, subalpine, common, L Spring–
Summer, perennial, 2–20 in.

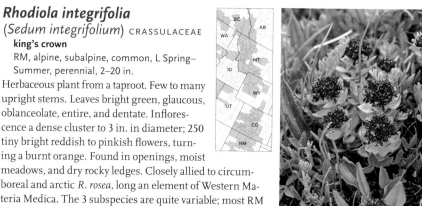

Herbaceous plant from a taproot. Few to many
upright stems. Leaves bright green, glaucous,
oblanceolate, entire, and dentate. Inflorescence a dense cluster to 3 in. in diameter; 250
tiny bright reddish to pinkish flowers, turning a burnt orange. Found in openings, moist
meadows, and dry rocky ledges. Closely allied to circumboreal and arctic *R. rosea,* long an element of Western Ma-
teria Medica. The 3 subspecies are quite variable; most RM
forms are a deep red-maroon to nearly black in color. Native.

Rhodiola rhodantha
(*Clementsia rhodantha*)
CRASSULACEAE
rose crown, queen's crown
MR, SR, alpine, subalpine, common,
L Spring–Summer, perennial, 2–16 in.

Upright stems from a branched woody crown.
Leaves succulent, alternate, but closely set on
all sides of stem; usually entire, flat, lance-
to egg-shaped, 1.2 in. long by 0.25 in. wide.
Flowers in rounded clusters on upper part of
stems; 5 pink sepals shorter than the 5 pink to white petals. Found in moist meadows and along streams at high elevations. Flowers are a clear pink, much lighter than those
of *R. integrifolia.* Native.

Arctostaphylos patula
(*A. pinetorum*) ERICACEAE
greenleaf manzanita
MR, SR, montane, foothills, pinyon-
juniper, sagebrush steppe, common,
Spring–E Summer, perennial, 3–10 ft.

Woody, spreading shrub; older bark smooth,
reddish brown. Leaves evergreen, alternate,
ovate-lanceolate to rotund, with pointed tips
and bright green, glabrous surfaces. Pink
(sometimes white), urn-shaped flowers with
5 petals form panicle. Berries brownish to dull orange.
Common in the Wasatch and Colorado Plateau, less so in
western SR; rare occurrence in western MT is likely *A.
×media.* Grows in open pine forests, sandstone outcrops,
montane chaparral, and other sunny locations. Native.

Arctostaphylos uva-ursi
(*A. adenotricha*) ERICACEAE
kinnikinnick
RM, montane, foothills, pinyon-juniper,
common, Spring–E Summer,
perennial, 4–20 in.

Woody, mat-forming shrub with prostrate
stems and sparsely hairy twigs. Leaves evergreen, alternate, oblanceolate, with entire
margins; light green below, dark green and
shiny above. Pink, urn-shaped flowers hang
in simple or 1-branched racemes. Berries bright red, small.
Grows in acidic, sandy, rocky soils, in sunny or shady locations and open forests, frequently as a monoculture under
lodgepole pines. Native.

Chimaphila umbellata ERICACEAE
pipsissewa, prince's pine
RM, subalpine, montane,
foothills, common, L Spring–
Summer, perennial, 4–14 in.

Rhizomatous, evergreen shrub or subshrub
with upright, branched, stems. Leaves opposite or in whorls on lower half of stem;
lanceolate, shiny, leathery and dark green,
with serrated margins (sharpest near apex).
Inflorescence a nodding cluster of 3–7 pink
to red waxy flowers; spreading petals surround a shiny
green ovary. Fruit a 5-sectioned capsule, drying to dark
brown and persisting through winter. Found in dry, deeply
shaded coniferous forests. Native.

Kalmia microphylla
(*K. occidentalis*) ERICACEAE
alpine laurel, western bog laurel
RM, alpine, subalpine, montane,
wetlands, common, locally abundant,
Spring–Summer, perennial, 2–20 in.

Rhizomatous, evergreen shrub or subshrub with woody, spreading to erect stems.
Branchlets round or slightly 2-angled.
Leathery leaves opposite, lacking petioles, with oblong to lanceolate blades that
are shiny green on top and white below due to fine dense
hairs. Leaf margins entire and curling under. Showy, dark
pinkish purple, parasol-shaped flowers 0.75 in. across may
be solitary or in terminal clusters. Grows on streambanks,
lake margins, in wet meadows and peat bogs. Native.

Phyllodoce empetriformis

ERICACEAE

pink mountain heath, pink mountain heather
NR, MR, alpine, subalpine, montane,
common, locally abundant,
Summer, perennial, 2–16 in.

Erect to spreading, much-branched evergreen
shrub; mat-forming. Twigs glandular-hairy,
becoming smooth. Dark, leathery leaves alternate, linear, crowded. Leaf margins revolute,
lower surface whitish. Rosy pink campanulate
flowers, clustered at stem tips or singly in leaf axils. Corolla with 5 spreading lobes surrounds a protruding style.
Found in meadows, open forests, seeps, heath, and on
moist slopes. Native.

Ribes cereum GROSSULARIACEAE

wax currant, white currant
RM, throughout, common, Spring–
Summer, perennial, 1.5–6 ft.

Deciduous, spineless, loosely branched shrub;
erect to spreading stems, grayish to reddish
brown bark. Leaves alternate, palmately 3- to
5-lobed, dentate margins; surfaces smooth or
with stalked glands. Inflorescence a cluster of
2–8 tubular flowers. Calyces greenish white,
lobes spreading; 5 pink to white petals covered
in glandular hairs. Berries ovoid, translucent, red-orange,
smooth to sparsely glandular. Grows in canyons, gulches,
woodlands, on hillsides in all life zones except wetlands.
Native.

Ribes montigenum

GROSSULARIACEAE

alpine prickly currant
RM, alpine, subalpine, montane,
common, L Spring–Summer,
perennial, 1–5 ft.

Deciduous, freely branched, spiny shrub;
spreading to decumbent pubescent stems,
tan becoming gray. Leaves alternate, to 1 in.
across, deeply 5-cleft with toothed margins;
surfaces hairy-glandular. Inflorescence a
hanging cluster of 3–8 flowers. Reflexed, green to pinkish
sepals; pink, red, or purplish petals surround yellowish
pink disc bearing stalked glands. Yellow stamens equal to
petals. Berries round, bright red, sparsely covered in glandular hairs. Somewhat palatable. Grows on forest floors,
along streams, and on talus slopes. Native.

Ribes viscosissimum

GROSSULARIACEAE

sticky currant

RM, subalpine, montane, foothills, locally abundant, L Spring–Summer, perennial, 1.5–6.5 ft.

Deciduous, spineless, loosely branched shrub with spreading to erect stems becoming reddish brown. Gray-green leaves alternate, to 4 in. across, with 3–5 rounded lobes and toothed margins; surfaces rough with hairs and glands. Inflorescence an erect to drooping raceme of 4–16 tubular-campanulate flowers. Sepals greenish yellow to yellowish white; petals pinkish, cream, or white. Berries ovoid, deep bluish black, and smooth to stalked glandular. Grows in woodlands, forest openings, sagebrush shrublands, and on avalanche tracks. Plant is fragrant. Native.

Collomia linearis POLEMONIACEAE

tiny trumpet

RM, subalpine, montane, foothills, sagebrush steppe, intermountain parks, grasslands, common, Spring–Summer, annual, 2–10 in.

Herb with simple stems. Leaves alternate, linear, hairy, slightly sticky to the touch, with glands that shine in the sun. Flowers simple, 5-petaled, and pink, purple, or white. Grows in sunny, shady, and disturbed habitats, coniferous and aspen or mixed forests, pine parklands, dry slopes, and meadows. This sticky plant often collects dust and debris on its foliage; the tiny flowers bloom for a long season. Very common but often overlooked. Native.

Microsteris gracilis

(*Phlox gracilis*) POLEMONIACEAE

slender phlox

RM, montane, foothills, grasslands, common, Spring, annual, 1–8 in.

Simple to branched, herbaceous, hairy to glandular stems. Leaves alternate above, lower ones opposite; linear to elliptic, entire, glandular to hairy, more so above. Pink to white flowers in pairs or solitary at tips of stems and branches, 5 petals, 1 flower usually stalked, tubes yellowish. Grows in sun; moist to dry meadows, sagebrush slopes, streamsides, forest openings. Native.

Phlox longifolia POLEMONIACEAE
longleaf phlox
RM, montane, foothills, pinyon-juniper,
sagebrush steppe, intermountain
parks, grasslands, common, Spring–
E Summer, perennial, 5–10 in.

Colony-forming herb to subshrub with upright stems; from taproot, which is often
branched. Stems smooth, glandular, or hairy.
Widely spaced leaves opposite, to 3 in., linear
to elliptic, with pointed tips. Inflorescence a
loose cluster of 3–12 pink (rarely white), sweetly scented
flowers. Petals obovate. A common, widespread species
found in sagebrush meadows, dry slopes, prairie edges,
and often along roadsides. Native.

Primula parryi PRIMULACEAE
Parry's primrose
MR, SR, alpine, subalpine, wetlands,
common, Summer–Fall, perennial, 6–20 in.

Herb with a basal rosette, usually clumped.
Leaves leathery and oblong, 3–10 in. long,
margins dentate, winged stalk. Inflorescence
a terminal raceme of 5–25 showy, bright pink
flowers atop a stout, leafless flower stalk.
Flowers yellow in center. Contact with leaves
releases an unpleasant odor. Occurs in subalpine bogs, wet meadows; common at or just above edges of
cold streams. Showiest primrose in North America, most
common species in the West. Native.

Spiraea splendens
(*S. densiflora*) ROSACEAE
rose meadowsweet, subalpine spirea
NR, MR, subalpine, montane,
infrequent, locally abundant,
Summer–Fall, perennial, 20–40 in.

Deciduous shrub with reddish brown bark;
from rhizomes. Leaves alternate, egg-shaped,
entire toward base, serrate toward apex. Inflorescence a rounded cluster up to 2 in. wide of
many small pink flowers. Stamens are many
and project beyond the petals. Fruit a follicle.
Grows in wet subalpine meadows, avalanche chutes, rocky
slopes in sun. Also in the Cascades, Siskiyous, and Sierra
Nevada. Native.

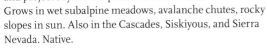

Lithophragma glabrum

(*L. bulbiferum*) SAXIFRAGACEAE

bulbous woodland-star, smooth fringecup
RM, subalpine, montane, foothills,
sagebrush steppe, grasslands, common,
Spring–Summer, perennial, 3–14 in.
Rhizomatous herb; erect, sticky, reddish
purple hairy stems. Basal leaves 3-lobed,
sometimes lobed again. Stem leaves alternate, reduced. Clusters of 1–5 star-like flowers; petals pinkish (or white), spreading,
3- to 5-lobed, so deeply cut they almost appear linear. Flowers often replaced by purple bulblets toward top of stem;
these bulblets fall to the ground, root, and produce geneti-
cally identical plants. Grows in sagebrush, meadows,
coniferous forests. Native.

Lithophragma tenellum

SAXIFRAGACEAE

slender woodland-star, slender fringecup
RM, montane, foothills, sagebrush
steppe, grasslands, common, Spring–
E Summer, perennial, 3–12 in.
Rhizomatous herb with erect, slender,
sticky, hairy stems from basal cluster of
leaves. Leaves often twice 3-lobed with shallow, rounded teeth; surfaces stiff-hairy; 2 or
3 stem leaves alternate, more deeply lobed, and reduced.
Inflorescence a congested raceme of 5–10 star-like flowers
elongating as flowers open. 5 pinkish to white petals each
divided into 5–7 lobes. Found in sagebrush, meadows,
coniferous forests. Native.

Saxifraga nivalis

(*Micranthes nivalis*) SAXIFRAGACEAE

alpine saxifrage, snow saxifrage
NR, alpine, subalpine, infrequent,
L Spring–Summer, perennial, 3–8 in.
Herb with thick, erect, glandular-hairy, leafless stems. Leaves in a basal rosette, 1–3
in. long, leathery, grayish green (often red
beneath), spatulate and with smooth surfaces (sometimes hairy below) and toothed
margins; persistent. Small round to elongated clusters of
reddish pink, greenish yellow, or white flowers with 12
conspicuous yellow to tan stamens. Calyx and ovary often
deep red. Found in crevices and ledges of rocks and cliffs
in shady, often north-facing sites. Native.

Orobanche uniflora
(*Aphyllon uniflorum*) OROBANCHACEAE
oneflowered broomrape
RM, montane, foothills, sagebrush
steppe, infrequent, Spring–
Summer, perennial, 0.5–3 in.

Parasitic plant lacking chlorophyll, from a
fleshy root. Flowers pedicellate, stalks single or clustered, smooth to finely glandular, joined to true stem at or below ground;
true stem leaves small, alternate, lanceolate,
scale-like, smooth. Single flower per leaf-
less stalk, 1 to many stalks per plant; pinkish red (cream),
finely fringed. Fruits angled capsules, net-veined. Parasitic
on sedums, saxifrages, various asters. Found in moist,
open forests, meadows,
riparian areas. Native.

Stephanomeria tenuifolia
(*S. minor*) ASTERACEAE
lesser wirelettuce
RM, foothills, pinyon-juniper, sagebrush
steppe, common, Summer, perennial, 1–2 ft.

Herb with skeletal gray-green stems branching at wide angles, forming a wiry dome.
Brown stems from previous season often
present. Leaves alternate, slender, linear, to 1
in., resembling the stems, but usually withering by flowering. Flowers at stem tips, usually 5 florets
per involucre with pale pink ray petals, toothed at tips;
maturing to achenes with conspicuous tufted feathery
pappus. Grows on dry slopes, canyon sides, washes of
lower elevations or foothills. Native.

Linnaea borealis CAPRIFOLIACEAE
twinflower
RM, alpine, subalpine, montane,
foothills, common, L Spring–Summer,
perennial, 2–6 in.

Evergreen herb or subshrub; forms colonies
that carpet forest floor. Stems slender, erect,
and leafy. Dark green leaves shiny, leathery,
opposite, ovate to round; margins shallowly
toothed toward leaf tip. Inflorescence a nodding pair of pink to white bell-shaped flowers on leafless,
Y-shaped stalks. Corolla with hairy throat and 5 flaring
lobes. Found in moist, shady, coniferous forests and on
alpine slopes. The genus name honors Swedish botanist
Carl Linnaeus (1707–1778), the father of binomial nomenclature. Circumpolar. Native.

Silene acaulis CARYOPHYLLACEAE
moss campion
RM, alpine, locally abundant,
Summer, perennial, 1–2 in.

Deep roots secure this cushion plant. Stems from woody base branch to form mounds 2–20 in. across. Leaves are tiny, linear, pointed, sparsely hairy, basal, and persist for many years. Flowers range in color from bright pink to light purple (rarely white), single, and somewhat toothed on round tip. Found in disturbed areas, on rocky slopes, and tundra. A distinctive tundra plant, and one of the northernmost plants in the world; larger cushions can be over a century old. Native.

Silene uralensis CARYOPHYLLACEAE
apetalous catchfly
RM, alpine, uncommon, Summer,
perennial, to 1 ft.

Low-growing herb from woody base. Leaves mostly basal, narrowly lanceolate to 5 in. long; stem leaves in 1–5 pairs, much reduced. Flowers usually solitary, erect or nodding. Calyx with 10 purple or brown veins, inflated, and to 0.7 in. long. Petals pink, purple, or red, and reflexing just beyond end of calyx, extending shorter than length of calyx; 5 styles shorter than petals. Circumpolar. Native.

Gaultheria humifusa ERICACEAE
alpine spicy-wintergreen
RM, alpine, subalpine, montane,
infrequent, locally abundant, L Spring–
Summer, perennial, 0.5–1 in.

Low, creeping evergreen shrub or subshrub; prostrate to ascending, smooth to finely hairy stems. Leaves alternate, thin, leathery, to 1 in. long, with nearly round blades, conspicuous lateral veins, and entire to toothed, thickened margins; bracts green with reddish margins. Solitary flowers in leaf axils; small, bell-shaped, pinkish to greenish white. Stamens included. Fruit a round, red, edible, berry-like capsule. Grows in cool, moist forests, riparian meadows, and fens. The leaves, reported to taste like wintergreen, can be used to make tea. Native.

Vaccinium cespitosum ERICACEAE
dwarf bilberry, dwarf huckleberry
RM, alpine, subalpine, montane, common,
L Spring–Summer, perennial, 4–20 in.
Rhizomatous, deciduous, often mat-forming
shrub. Woody stems upright, smooth, yellowish green to reddish and finely hairy. Leaves
alternate, to 1 in. long, light green, oval to elliptic, broadest above the middle, often with
rounded teeth on the margins. Pink to whitish urn-shaped nodding flowers, singly in

axils. Berries round, glaucous, usually blue, rarely black.
Grows in moist forests, meadows, bogs, and on rocky
ridges. The sweet and edible berries are sought after by
mammals and birds. Native.

Vaccinium myrtillus ERICACEAE
whortleberry, bilberry
RM, alpine, subalpine, montane,
foothills, common, L Spring–
Summer, perennial, 4–12 in.
Rhizomatous, deciduous, much-branched
shrub, often forming open colonies. Stems
upright, woody, with green to greenish brown,
strongly 3-angled, often puberulent branchlets. Light green leaves alternate, to 1.2 in.,
with elliptic to ovate blades and sharp-toothed

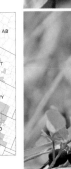

margins. Bell- to urn-shaped pink or cream-colored flowers nod singly in leaf axils. Round berries bluish black,
rarely red, and sweet. Found on coniferous forest floors
and rocky, alpine ridges. Plants produce few flowers and
thus few fruit. Native.

Vaccinium scoparium ERICACEAE
grouse whortleberry, dwarf red whortleberry
RM, alpine, subalpine, montane,
foothills, common, L Spring–
Summer, perennial, 4–12 in.
Rhizomatous, deciduous, colony-forming
shrub with a dense broom-like habit. Upright,
woody stems smooth, greenish or yellowish green, with strongly angled branchlets. Smooth, light green leaves alternate,

less than 0.5 in., are lance-shaped to oval and have finely
toothed margins. Broadly urn-shaped pinkish flowers,
singly in leaf axils. Berries round, red or bluish purple.
Grows on forest floors, talus slopes, in meadows, and near
high-elevation lakes. Soft and tart berries were gathered by
many Native American tribes. Native.

Erodium cicutarium GERANIACEAE
redstem stork's bill
RM, montane, foothills, pinyon-juniper,
sagebrush steppe, grasslands, common,
Spring–Summer, annual/biennial, 1–8 in.
Low herb with basal rosette. Leaves 3–8 in.,
pinnate, lobed, fern-like, hairy; smaller and
alternate on flowering stems. May be purplish red in cool weather. Flowers 3–7 per
umbel, to 0.5 in. across, with 5 oval petals.
Sharp-pointed seeds mature with styles
elongated and joined in an up-pointing "stork's bill."
Mature seeds spring away, the twisting style drilling into
the soil when moisture is present. Plants flower when tiny
in harsh conditions, or become large, lush when favorable.
Abundant weed of roadsides, fields, and disturbed sites. Introduced and invasive.

Geranium caespitosum
(*G. fremontii*) GERANIACEAE
pineywoods geranium
MR, SR, montane, foothills, pinyon-
juniper, sagebrush steppe,
intermountain parks, common,
L Spring–Summer, perennial, 6–18 in.
Low-growing, sprawling herb with branching, often red stems. Leaves mostly basal;
reduced opposite leaves present on flowering stems.
Leaves often deeply cut with 3–5 palmate lobes and
equally-toothed margins; surfaces hairy. Flowers magenta
to lilac (rarely white). Plants grow at middle elevations in
coniferous forests and adjacent meadows in
sun to part shade. Native.

Geranium carolinianum
GERANIACEAE
Carolina geranium
RM, montane, foothills, grasslands,
common, Summer–Fall, annual, 8–12 in.
Herb with ascending to erect, branched
stems. Leaves most often opposite (occasionally alternate), to 3 in. wide, heart-shaped,
hairy; cut palmately, usually into 5 sections
with smaller lobes. Inflorescence several to many light
pink to white flowers, with each petal slightly notched.
Fruit a compact cluster of capsules with short beaks; when
mature, the capsule splits into sections, flinging seeds
far and wide. Grows in sandy and rocky soil in sunny disturbed sites and clearings. Native.

Geranium viscosissimum

GERANIACEAE
sticky purple geranium
RM, subalpine, montane, foothills,
grasslands, common, L Spring–
Summer, perennial, 1–2 ft.

Herb with ascending to erect, branched
stems covered with sticky glands (glands
yellow-tipped, at least above). Basal leaves on
long stalks and stem leaves opposite and reduced; both usually palmately 5- to 7-parted
and toothed, with stiff-hairy surfaces. Inflorescence of several to many pink or purple (rarely white) flowers with reddish purple veins and soft-hairy bases. Fruit a carpel with
stalked glands. Grows in aspen forests, meadows, and on
dry slopes. Intensely aromatic when crushed.
Native.

Malva neglecta MALVACEAE

common mallow
RM, montane, foothills, sagebrush
steppe, grasslands, common, Spring–
Fall, perennial/annual, 6–18 in.

Short-lived herb. Stems spreading or upright
at ends, from taprooted crown. Leaves alternate, rounded, wavy, lobed, with palmate
venation, on 1- to 3-in. petioles. Several pale
pink or nearly white flowers at leaf axils. Petals 5, to 0.5 in.
across with dark pink stripes. Seeds in flat wheel-shaped
arrangement to 0.4 in. across. Grows in sunny disturbed
sites below subalpine zone. Introduced.

Mirabilis linearis

(*Oxybaphus linearis*) NYCTAGINACEAE
narrowleaf four o'clock
RM, montane, foothills, grasslands,
common, Summer, perennial, 8–60 in.

Herb or subshrub with ascending or trailing,
smooth stems from taproot. Smooth, waxy
leaves simple, opposite, nearly sessile, narrowly linear to lanceolate, with entire margins. Inflorescence paniculate, branched,
sparsely hairy. Flowers lacking petals; united
involucre bracts pale green and hairy; calyx bell-shaped,
white to pink, with 5 fused lobes. Flowers open in afternoon and close in morning. Fruit egg-shaped, hairy,
brownish, 5-ribbed. Grows in dry sandy or rocky soils,
plains, open places in mountain valleys in the sun. Native.

Mirabilis multiflora
(*Oxybaphus multiflorus*)
NYCTAGINACEAE
Colorado four o'clock
SR, foothills, pinyon-juniper, sagebrush steppe, grasslands, common, Summer, perennial, 1–2 ft.

Herbaceous with decumbent, hairy or smooth, repeatedly forked stems; forms mounds to 4 ft. wide from fleshy thick taproot. Leaves glabrous, simple, opposite, triangular-cordate; margins entire. Tubular flowers, 3–6 in leaf axils, subtended by large bracts. Flaring calyx petal-like, pink-magenta; true petals absent. Flowers open late afternoon, close next morning. Fruit brownish, ovoid-globose, 0.5 in., hairy or smooth. Grows in dry, open ground, roadsides, and shale outcrops in the sun. Native.

Phlox austromontana
POLEMONIACEAE
mountain phlox, desert phlox
RM, foothills, pinyon-juniper, sagebrush steppe, intermountain parks, grasslands, common, Spring, perennial, 2–4 in.

Spreading plants forming low, dense mats. Leaves linear, opposite, sharply acute, 0.3–0.8 in. long, sparse covering of white hairs mostly on upper surfaces. Inflorescence solitary with primarily pink or pink-tinged white flowers; corolla tubes 0.3–0.6 in. long, corolla lobes rounded at tips; calyx sparsely villous with keeled intercostal membranes. Found in dry ridgetops, shale slopes, and sandy soils in semi-desert foothills, canyons, and shrublands. Native.

Phlox diffusa POLEMONIACEAE
spreading phlox
NR, MR, alpine, subalpine, common, locally abundant, L Spring–E Summer, perennial, 1–4 in.

Tufted, mat-forming herb to subshrub with prostrate to ascending stems from taproot; hairless to white-hairy, but not glandular. Leaves opposite, linear, soft, with smooth green surfaces. Flowers at branch tips, solitary, unstalked; palest pink or white to lavender-blue. Overlapping petals narrow or round. Calyx with loose, soft hairs. Found in open, rocky areas on slopes and in forests. Native.

Phlox hoodii POLEMONIACEAE
spiny phlox, carpet phlox
RM, montane, foothills, pinyon-juniper,
sagebrush steppe, intermountain
parks, grasslands, common, Spring–
E Summer, perennial, 0.5–1 in.

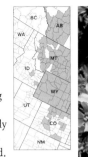

Mat- or cushion-forming, small, low-growing
plant producing multiple branches, typically
hairy. Leaves linear, opposite, woolly or loosely
pubescent, with sharp needle-like points. Inflorescence solitary and sessile; petals 5-lobed,
commonly white or pink to pale blue or purple; petal lobes
0.15–0.3 in. long. Found on bluffs, ridgetops, or dry slopes
in meadows, prairie, and open dry forests. Several subspecies have been recognized. Native.

Phlox speciosa POLEMONIACEAE
showy phlox
NR, MR, foothills, pinyon-juniper, sagebrush
steppe, intermountain parks, grasslands,
infrequent, Spring, perennial, 3–8 in.

Herb to subshrub from woody taproot, often
growing in mounds or mat-forming; stems
erect and branched, smooth below and
soft-hairy above. Leaves opposite, to 2.75 in.,
linear to lanceolate, with pointed tips. Inflorescence a loose cluster of several bright pink,
white, or purple flowers with white throats; petals usually
notched at tips; subtended by leafy bracts. Scattered in our
region; widespread in the NR, Columbia Basin, northern
CA; var. *woodhousei* at mid-high elevations in northern
AZ. Grows in sagebrush, meadows, and open
pine forests. Native.

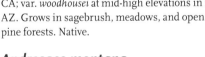

Androsace montana
(Douglasia montana) PRIMULACEAE
Rocky Mountain dwarf primrose
NR, MR, alpine, subalpine, montane,
foothills, sagebrush steppe, grasslands,
uncommon, Summer, perennial, 1–2 in.

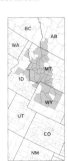

Herb forming small cushions; stems prostrate to ascending. Foliage nearly brown for
much of the growing season. Diminutive and
almost succulent leaves arranged in rosettes. Flowers are
5-petaled and an intense carmine to magenta. At the center of flowers is a yellow ring that turns pink once flower
is pollinated. Grows in rocky soil on exposed slopes, fellfields, and ridges in sunny locations. Native.

Primula angustifolia PRIMULACEAE
alpine primrose

SR, alpine, subalpine, common, locally abundant, Summer, perennial, 1–4 in. Herbaceous perennial, leaves in basal rosettes, simple, linear to oblong, sometimes spoon-shaped, 0.5 in. long, fleshy, mostly entire, smooth. Flowers solitary, sometimes paired; calyx green, cylindric; corolla bright rose-pink (sometimes white), tubular, 5-lobed; stamens 5. Occurs in rocky alpine tundra, subalpine meadows. Native.

Primula conjugens
(*Dodecatheon conjugens*) PRIMULACEAE
Bonneville shootingstar

NR, MR, montane, foothills, sagebrush steppe, uncommon, locally abundant, Spring–E Summer, perennial, 3–10 in. Herb. Flowering stems in spring are slightly pubescent and leafless, above a basal rosette. Leaves 1–6 in. long, spoon- or egg-shaped, pubescent above and below with small marginal hairs, which distinguish this species. Flowers 1–7 in nodding umbel; petals 5, reflexed upward, pink-purple to magenta (rarely white); yellow and white at base, pointed center structures dark maroon. Grows in sun or part shade, in vernally moist open woodlands, meadows, or slopes. Native.

Primula jeffreyi
(*Dodecatheon jeffreyi*) PRIMULACEAE
tall mountain shootingstar

NR, MR, montane, uncommon, L Spring–Summer, perennial, 5–20 in. Herb. Leafless stem to 20 in. above basal leaf rosette, smooth or with some glandular hairs. Leaves 3–18 in. long, lanceolate to oval, upright, usually glabrous and without teeth. Flowers 3–20 in loose umbels; 4 or 5 petals reflexed, white at base with reddish ring just inside floral tube, central structures dark. Grows in sun or part shade in moist meadows, stream or lake margins, bogs, and open coniferous woodlands. Widespread in the Pacific NW, reaching ID, MT. Rare specimens may be white or yellow. Native.

Primula pauciflora
(*Dodecatheon pulchellum*)

PRIMULACEAE

darkthroat shootingstar
RM, throughout, common, locally abundant,
Spring–Summer, perennial, 4–20 in.
Herb. Leafless stem above basal leaf rosette,
glabrous. Ovate leaves to 6 in. long, glabrous,
may have small teeth; spreading to upright.
Flowers 1–10 in terminal umbel, each 0.75 in.
long; petals reflexed, magenta-pink (rarely
white), with white to yellow base and fine red
ring; central structures dark. Variable throughout its huge
range with several subspecies. Found in wet meadows,
slopes, streamsides, open woodlands, grasslands. Native.

Aquilegia elegantula

RANUNCULACEAE

western red columbine
SR, subalpine, montane, pinyon-juniper,
sagebrush steppe, locally abundant,
L Spring–Summer, perennial, 12–18 in.
Herb. Basal leaves biternately compound and
shorter than flowering stems; surfaces glabrous. Flowers pendulous, mostly red with
yellow at tips; more cylindrical than *A. deserto-
rum* or *A. formosa*, whose ranges overlap to the
south and west, respectively. Spurs straight and to 0.5 in.
long, parallel to flower axis and tapering to a slightly bulbous end. Stamens to 0.75 in. Sepals mostly yellow to green
and parallel with spurs and blades. Grows in moist coniferous forests and along shady streams. Native.

Aquilegia formosa
(*A. fosteri*) RANUNCULACEAE

western columbine
RM, throughout, uncommon,
Spring–Fall, perennial, 12–40 in.
Herb with erect stems, spreading branches.
Leaves mostly basal, blue-green, biternate,
smooth to soft-hairy. Stem leaves alternate,
reduced, and shorter-stalked. Flowers red
with yellow, nodding; stout spurs abruptly
narrowed near middle, with rounded tips. Numerous protruding stamens. Fruit 5-chambered follicle. Occurs in all
zones except alpine and wetlands, in mesic to moist meadows, rocky slopes, thickets, clearings, and open forests in
sun or part shade. Visited by hummingbirds and butterflies. Native.

Geum triflorum
(*Erythrocoma triflora*) ROSACEAE
old man's whiskers, prairie smoke
RM, alpine, subalpine, montane,
foothills, sagebrush steppe, common,
Spring–Summer, perennial, 4–20 in.

Herb. Basal leaves spreading, pinnately
compound, to 7.5 in. long, and hairy; flower
stems with pair of reduced opposite leaves
below the cyme. Flowers usually 3 per cyme,
nodding; sepals cup-shaped, conspicuous,
dark pink, hairy, with 5 pointed radiating
bracts. Petals cream-colored, same length as sepals; they
remain tightly enclosed in sepals. Fruit eye-catching with
hairy, purplish, feathery tails, up to 2 in. long, radiating
from the now-open sepals. Found in meadows/sage meadows, woodlands, forest openings, and riparian areas. Native.

Kelseya uniflora
(*Eriogynia uniflora*) ROSACEAE
Kelsey moss, rock spirea
MR, alpine, subalpine, montane,
infrequent, Spring, perennial, 0.5–3 in.
Dense, cushion- or mat-like shrub. Pale
to grayish green leaves becoming brownish; crowded and overlapping along stem.
Tiny flowers can cover the cushion in May
or early June, but bloom is usually finished by summer tourist season. Almost always grows in crevices of
north-facing, vertical cliffs of dolomitic limestone at or just
below treeline in sunny locations. Known only from a few
restricted ranges in 3 states. Native.

Rosa acicularis
(*R. sayi*) ROSACEAE
prickly rose, wild rose
RM, subalpine, montane, foothills,
sagebrush steppe, grasslands, common,
L Spring–E Summer, perennial, to 5 ft.
Rhizomatous shrub. Stems open, spreading; covered in thin, straight prickles, except smooth flower stalks. Leaves alternate,
to 2 in., pinnate, with 5–7 narrow oval leaflets; margins with glands and sawtoothed. Surfaces dark
green, hairless above, paler and glandular-hairy below.
Narrow, lance-shaped sepals and leaf stipules glandular.
Solitary flowers pink to rose, to 2 in. Fruit a hip, round to
pear-shaped, red-purple. Forests, meadows, riparian areas,
usually where moist. Native.

Rosa nutkana ROSACEAE
Nootka rose
RM, montane, common, Spring–
Summer, perennial, to 5 ft.

Shrub. Stems with dark, reddish brown bark, erect to open-spreading, singular or rhizoma-tous, thicket-forming. Stems not very prickly; pairs of large curved prickles at nodes. Stem leaves alternate, pinnate, with 5–7 oval saw-tooth leaflets 0.75–2 in., green and glan-dular. Sepals flattened at tip, with stalked glands, persist after flowering. Solitary flowers pale pink to deep rose, petals 0.75–1.5 in.; followed by a large round red-purple hip to 0.75 in. Found in forest openings and ri-parian areas. Important plant of traditional medicine, and for animal forage. Native.

Rosa woodsii
(*R. blanda*) ROSACEAE
Woods' rose
RM, throughout, common,
Summer, perennial, to 6.5 ft.

Rhizomatous shrub. Stems with dark red to gray bark; open-spreading or thicket-forming. Stems with fine, straight round prickles, nodes with straight or slightly curved pairs. Leaves alternate, pinnate, with 5–9 oval leaf-lets toothed at tip; glands absent. 2 or more pink to deep rose, fragrant flowers in corymbs or panicles. Hips to 0.5 in., red, sometimes orangish or purplish, ovoid to round. Found on dry, rocky slopes, streambanks, and open forests in all zones but alpine and wetlands. Morphol-ogy highly variable. Most common wild rose in the Rockies. Native.

Rubus acaulis
(*R. arcticus* ssp. *acaulis*) ROSACEAE
dwarf raspberry
RM, subalpine, montane, uncommon,
Spring, perennial, 1–6 in.

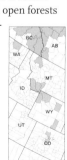

Short-growing rhizomatous herb without prickles. Leaves alternate, compound in 3s with leaflets rounded to ovate and less than 2 in. long; edges toothed. Flowers usually solitary, pink. Petals 5 or 6, to 0.75 in. long. Fruit a reddish, rounded raspberry to 0.4 in. Found in moist riparian areas, along creeks, bogs, hummocks in sphagnum fens, moist mead-ows. The fruit is edible. Native.

Antennaria rosea ASTERACEAE
rosy pussytoes
RM, throughout, common, Spring–
Summer, perennial, 1.5–16 in.

Low-growing herb, spreading by short
stolons. Basal leaves mostly in a rosette,
spoon-shaped, gray, hairy on upper sides,
with a bluntly pointed tip. Inflorescence has
only female flowers, with 3–20 clustered
in elliptical heads. Involucre bracts may
be gray, green, red, yellow, or white but are
frequently pink. Found in open meadows, rocky slopes,
wooded forests, sage meadows, outcrops, and fellfields.
The specific epithet refers to the pink-colored bracts. This
is the most widespread *Antennaria* sp. in North America.
Native.

Arctium minus
(*Lappa minor*) ASTERACEAE
lesser burdock
RM, montane, foothills, sagebrush
steppe, intermountain parks, grasslands,
common, Summer–Fall, biennial, 2–10 ft.
Erect, thick, branching stems. Basal rosette
of thick cobwebby-hairy leaves establishes
in first year; leaves heart-shaped, alternate,
coarsely toothed to nearly entire with hollow
petioles. Numerous heads in raceme or panicle-like clusters; disc flowers pink or purple (rarely white), surrounded
by hooked spiny bracts but lacking ray flowers. Bracts
dry into bur around seed. Found in disturbed sites, often
moist soils, roadsides, fields, streambanks.
A noxious weed. Introduced and invasive.

Centaurea nigra ASTERACEAE
black knapweed
NR, montane, foothills, grasslands, locally
abundant, Summer, perennial, 1–3 ft.
Robust plant with pubescent herbage and
branched stems. Lower leaves with irregular
lobes, decreasing up the stem and becoming
oblong or lanceolate. Disc flowers pinkish
purple, like small thistles; base covered by
dark bracts and bristly, comb-like teeth. Ray petals lacking, but corollas of outer florets sometimes elongated, like
fringed petals, especially in hybrids with *C. jacea*. Both
species aggressive weeds in the northeastern U.S. and Pacific NW, especially in agricultural lands, roadsides, forming inpenetrable monocultures. Introduced and invasive.

Centaurea stoebe ASTERACEAE
spotted knapweed
RM, foothills, pinyon-juniper,
sagebrush steppe, intermountain parks,
grasslands, common, locally abundant,
Summer–Fall, perennial, 1–4 ft.

Flowering stems shrub-like, blue-green with
ridges, cobwebby, from vigorous rosettes to 14
in. across. Leaves pinnately lobed, alternate,
lower broader than upper, which become linear and unlobed. Flowers like small pink thistles, outer florets providing a longer fringe.
Phyllaries green or brown overlapping scales "spotted" by
dark, fringed tips. Disturbed areas, roadsides, farm fields.
Difficult to eradicate. Introduced and invasive.

Cirsium arvense
(*Carduus arvensis*) ASTERACEAE
Canada thistle
RM, subalpine, montane, foothills,
sagebrush steppe, grasslands, common,
L Spring–Summer, perennial, 1–6 ft.

Rhizomatous, colony-forming herb; erect,
smooth to gray-woolly stems; branched above.
Basal (soon deciduous) and alternate stem
leaves sessile, 2–8 in., reducing upward, lanceolate, shallow to deep pinnate lobes (or unlobed), with spiny-toothed margins; surfaces
smooth, green above, white-woolly below. Inflorescence a
corymb of small, unisexual discoid heads with pink-purple
(rarely white) flowers. Phyllaries smooth to cobwebby, imbricate and appressed, with weak spines. Fields, meadows,
along roadsides, disturbed sites.
Introduced and invasive.

Cirsium clavatum var. *osterhoutii*
(*C. osterhoutii*) ASTERACEAE
Osterhout's thistle
SR, alpine, subalpine, montane,
endemic, locally abundant, Summer,
biennial/perennial, 0.5–6 ft.

Herb with erect, purplish, hairy stems; from
taproot. Basal and alternate stem leaves to 14
in., decurrent, pinnatifid, with spiny-toothed
margins. Surfaces smooth to sparsely hairy above and
white-woolly below. Few to many discoid heads with pinkish to white flowers atop a soft-hairy involucre. Phyllaries
with narrow glutinous ridges and purple centers. Grows
on rocky slopes, mountain meadows, coniferous forests,
and along streams. Native.

Cirsium drummondii
(*C. coccinatum*) ASTERACEAE
Drummond's thistle, dwarf thistle
NR, MR, montane, sagebrush steppe,
grasslands, rare, locally abundant,
L Spring–Summer, biennial, 0.2–4 ft.

Stout, fleshy, woolly-hairy, erect, unbranched stems (sometimes without stem);
from taproot. Basal and alternate stem leaves
6–12 in., sessile, oblanceolate to lanceolate,
pinnatifid, segments oblong-triangular with
spiny-toothed margins. Surfaces smooth
to soft-hairy. 1–9 large discoid heads with
purplish red to pink (rarely white) flowers. Phyllaries have
smooth dorsal ridge, spines erect to ascending. Grows
in prairies, meadows, open forests, and along roadsides.
Native.

Cirsium ochrocentrum
ASTERACEAE
yellowspine thistle
MR, SR, montane, foothills, pinyon-juniper,
intermountain parks, grasslands, common,
L Spring–Summer, biennial, 0.5–3 ft.
Clumps of erect to ascending, simple to
branched, grayish to white-woolly, leafy
stems; may be perennial. Basal and alternate stem leaves 3–9 in., decurrent, elliptic
to oblanceolate, deeply pinnatifid or coarsely
toothed with yellow spines. Surfaces green and cobwebby
above; white-woolly below. Discoid flowers, 1 to few, with
pink, purple, reddish purple (rarely white) petals. Involucres smooth; phyllaries with a glutinous dorsal ridge
and reflexed outer spines. Grows in dry soil along roads
and on open slopes, prairies. Native.

Echinacea angustifolia
ASTERACEAE
blacksamson echinacea
RM, foothills, grasslands, uncommon,
locally abundant, L Spring–Summer,
perennial, 15–30 in.
Herb with 1 or more stiff upright stems,
sometimes branched, coarsely hairy. Leaves
2–12 in. long, alternate, lanceolate, rough,
hairy, 3 prominent veins; lower leaves with petiole; upper
sessile, smaller. Flowers 1.5–3 in. across, with narrow overlapping bracts below in 3 or 4 rows. Rounded central cone
of stiffly pointed red/orange disc flowers; narrow ray petals
0.75–1.75 in. long, horizontal to drooping. Found in sunny
grasslands, open pine woodlands, and rocky meadows.
Native.

Erigeron acris ASTERACEAE
bitter fleabane, blue fleabane
RM, subalpine, montane, common,
Spring–Summer, biennial, 4–30 in.
Tall branched stems with many half-open
pink to purple (occasionally white) daisies
with large, dark involucres. Widespread, but
not terribly showy, and often overlooked.
Leaves are oblanceolate, entire and smooth.
Basal foliage is often dried at flowering time.
Fleabanes are often very similar in appear-
ance, separated into species based on geographical distributions. With its height and small flowers, this species is
more distinctive. Sun. Native.

Erigeron pumilus ASTERACEAE
shaggy fleabane
RM, foothills, pinyon-juniper, sagebrush
steppe, intermountain parks,
grasslands, common, Spring–E Summer,
perennial, 3–8 in.
Herb with cluster of erect, stiff-hairy and
slightly sticky stems. Basal leaves oblanceolate
to narrowly spatulate and very hairy; sometimes soon deciduous. Stem leaves similar
and reducing upward or sometimes absent.
Flowers 1 to many, with ray and disc flowers:
ray flowers pale pink or blue, often white. Phyllaries green
with an orange to yellow midrib and densely glandular.
Abundant on sunny, exposed sites in grasslands
and shrublands throughout the Rockies. Native.

Lygodesmia grandiflora
(*Erythremia grandiflora*) ASTERACEAE
largeflower skeletonplant, showy rushpink
MR, SR, montane, foothills, pinyon-juniper,
sagebrush steppe, intermountain
parks, grasslands, locally abundant,
L Spring–Summer, perennial, 3–18 in.
Lactiferous, twiggy herb with solitary, erect,
simple to sparingly branched stems. Basal
and alternate stem leaves linear, reducing upward to scales; margins entire. Inflorescence
of 1–5 flowers. Ray flowers 5–10, pink or lavender-blue
(sometimes white) and disc flowers absent. A showy, distinctive plant of sunny habitats including sparse grassland, barrens, roadsides and other disturbed habitats;
often grows in sand and shale. Native.

Xanthisma coloradoense
(*Machaeranthera coloradoensis*)
ASTERACEAE

Colorado tansyaster
SR, alpine, subalpine, montane, sagebrush steppe, intermountain parks, uncommon, Summer, perennial, 2–5 in.
Low, mat-forming herb from taproot. Stems with soft gray to white hairs. Leaves oblanceolate to spatulate, with densely hairy surfaces, margins toothed and teeth bristle-tipped. Large, solitary flowers with disc and ray flowers: ray flowers pink, rosy, or purple. Rare on tundra, but locally abundant in sunny sites such as barrens, rocky outcrops, and mountain parks. A sensitive species that occurs in the western counties of CO and the south-central counties of WY. Described in 1874 from the San Juan Mountains. Native.

Lythrum salicaria LYTHRACEAE
purple loosestrife
RM, wetlands, common, locally abundant, Summer, perennial, 2–6 ft.
Vigorous rhizomatous herb. Stems upright with fine hairs, 4-angled, simple or branched near top. Leaves lanceolate, sessile, opposite or in whorls of 3. Flowers to 0.75 in. across, terminal spikes to 20 in. long; 5–7 narrowly oval petals. Hairy cylindrical calyx aging brown, with 2-celled capsule of tiny seeds. Very showy but extremely invasive via seeds and roots: this plant is now banned from cultivation in most regions as it replaces rich wetland habitats with unproductive monocultures. Introduced and invasive.

Cylindropuntia imbricata
(*Opuntia imbricata*) CACTACEAE
tree cholla
SR, pinyon-juniper, grasslands, common, Summer, perennial, 4–6 ft.
Large, much-branched shrub with upright, succulent, cylindric to clavate, widely branching stems; stem segments gray-green, often whorled. 5–30 red, tan, or brown barbed spines per areole; rarely spineless. Pale yellow glochids in dense tufts. Flowers dark pink to magenta, more than 3 in. across. Filaments green becoming magenta or pink upward; anthers yellow. Fleshy obovoid fruit, yellow in late summer, persists till next spring. Grows in sunny, open, dry habitats in sandy to gravelly soil. Native.

Echinocereus triglochidiatus

CACTACEAE
claret cup cactus
SR, montane, foothills, pinyon-juniper,
sagebrush steppe, common, locally
abundant, L Spring–E Summer,
perennial, 2–24 in.

Succulent stems green, erect and cylindric,
branched or unbranched. Plants may form
large mounds up to 300 stems. Central spine
solitary or lacking, and 1–10 radial spines per
areole. Spines straight to slightly curved, project outward; white to yellow, gray, or black. Flowers 2–4 in.
and red-orange to dark red. Fruits green to yellow-green
or occasionally pink. Grows on dry, rocky sites, cliffs, rock
ledges, in coniferous forests and pinyon-juniper woodlands. State cactus of CO. Native.

Escobaria vivipara
(*Coryphantha vivipara*) CACTACEAE
spinystar, pincushion cactus
RM, foothills, pinyon-juniper, sagebrush
steppe, grasslands, common, Spring–
Summer, perennial, to 4 in.

Plants with erect, unbranched, succulent
stems. More than half of stem above ground,
but during drought, stems shrink below soil
surface, leaving only top visible. Solitary or
in small clumps with age. Many short spines per areole,
white to reddish brown or multicolored, protruding from
conspicuous tubercles. Simple flowers with many pink,
pointed petals. Juicy green fruits slowly turn a dull brownish red; ovoid with a persistent floral remnant.
Found in sun, diverse substrates, and dry
grassy areas. Native.

Pediocactus simpsonii CACTACEAE
mountain ball cactus
MR, SR, montane, foothills, pinyon-juniper,
sagebrush steppe, grasslands, common,
Spring–E Summer, perennial, 1–7 in.

Succulent, globose to depressed-ovoid stems
solitary, occasionally branched. Spines
smooth, 15–35 radial spines, 4–11 central
spines per areole; reddish brown at tip and cream to yellow at base. Flowers 0.5–1.5 in., typically pink although
white, magenta, or yellow flowers occur. Fruits green,
tinged with red, drying to reddish brown. Grows in sunny
locations in dry open ground, on slopes, forest openings.
Highly variable. Native.

Lewisia pygmaea
(*Oreobroma pygmaeum*)
MONTIACEAE

alpine lewisia, pygmy bitterroot
RM, alpine, subalpine, montane,
common, locally abundant, Spring–
Summer, perennial, 0.5–3 in.

Succulent herb with prostrate to ascending
scapes. Basal rosette of leaves, with linear to
lanceolate blades and entire margins; soon
deciduous; 1 pair of bracts mid-length of
stem. 1 or 2 pink or white flowers; petals 5–10 prominently
veined, often glandular-hairy, and with sharply pointed
tips. A hand lens reveals 2 sepals with jagged teeth (or entire) and glands at tips (or non-glandular); *L. nevadensis*
lacks glands. Grows in gravelly areas and on
tundra. Native.

Lewisia rediviva MONTIACEAE
bitterroot
RM, montane, foothills, pinyon-
juniper, sagebrush steppe,
grasslands, locally abundant, Spring–
Summer, perennial, 1–3 in.

Succulent herb with spreading to erect
stems from basal rosette. Leaves to 3 in.,
linear to club-shaped with entire margins;
wither after flowering. A solitary pink, white, or lavender flower on short stalk, subtended by a whorl of 4–7
floral bracts. Flowers with 10–19 petals to 2 in. across;
6–9 unequal, ovate sepals; numerous stamens. Grows in
well-drained gravelly soils in shrublands,
pinyon-juniper woodlands, and open forests. State flower of MT. Native.

Anemone multifida
RANUNCULACEAE
Pacific anemone, cutleaf anemone
RM, alpine, subalpine, montane,
foothills, common, Spring–E Summer,
perennial, 4–20 in.

Herb with hairy stems from woody base.
Basal leaves on long petioles, 1–4 in. wide,
palmate and deeply dissected, long-hairy on lower surface; stem leaves similar. Flowers with 5–9 petal-like sepals; pink or cream to yellow, tinged with purple or blue;
hairy on outside, smooth on inside. Grows in mixed forests, meadows, riparian areas, avalanche chutes, disturbed
sites. Native.

Amorpha canescens
(A. brachycarpa) FABACEAE
leadplant
MR, SR, foothills, grasslands, common,
Summer, perennial, to 3.5 ft.
Semi-woody clustered stems from a woody
crown. Odd-pinnately compound leaves
1.6–4 in. long with 15–47 leaflets. Stems and
bottoms of leaves densely woolly. Purple
flowers in terminal spike-like racemes; 200–
300 flowers per raceme; single-petaled, with
only banner present. Fruit a densely woolly, curved, indehiscent legume, about 0.2 in. long. Found in open prairies,
hillsides, roadsides, open woodlands, and wet to mesic
sites. The common name is a reference to the plant's silvery gray-hairy foliage and stems. Native.

Orthocarpus purpureoalbus
OROBANCHACEAE
purple-white owl's-clover
SR, montane, foothills, pinyon-juniper,
sagebrush steppe, locally abundant,
L Spring–Summer, annual, 4–16 in.
Slender herb with erect, greenish purple,
glandular-hairy stem branched above the
middle. Green to purplish leaves alternate,
sessile, to 2 in. long, and linear; margins entire or 3-cleft and resembling shorter, 3-lobed floral bracts.
Inflorescence an elongated spike of bicolored pinkish lavender and white 2-lipped tubular flowers: upper lip darker
purple, narrow, straight, and tapering to small spike; lower
lip wider and whitish. Grows in sagebrush
meadows, moist fields and open coniferous
forests. Native.

Aconitum columbianum
RANUNCULACEAE
Columbian monkshood
RM, alpine, subalpine, montane,
foothills, sagebrush steppe, common,
Summer–Fall, perennial, 18–60 in.
Herb with erect, flowering stems emerging
directly from tuberous roots. Leaves alter-
nate along stem. Leaf blades deeply divided into 5–7 lobes
and cleft and toothed. Flowers are commonly blue but can
be white. Sepals form a hood over the 2 true petals. Grows
in mixed forests, sage meadows, and moist meadows.
Native.

Aconitum delphiniifolium
RANUNCULACEAE
larkspurleaf monkshood
NR, alpine, subalpine, montane, uncommon,
Summer–Fall, perennial, 4–48 in.

Herb with slender stems, erect, unbranched;
alternate, mostly cauline leaves. Leaves
stalked, 1–6 in. wide, palmately divided
into 5 segments, margins cleft. Inflorescence a terminal open raceme of few to many
purple-blue, hooded flowers. Flowers bilateral, 1–1.5 in.; hood arches from back to front hiding 2
true petals underneath. Flower rises from linear, sometimes palmately divided bract. Occurs in sunny areas
on meadows, thickets, streambanks, and tundra. Leaves
often more deeply divided and hood more
crescent-shaped than *A. columbianum*.
Highly toxic. Native.

Camassia cusickii ASPARAGACEAE
Cusick's camas
NR, montane, endemic, uncommon,
Spring, perennial, to 3 ft.

Erect stems arise from clusters of bulbs. Usually more than 10 linear leaves from base,
about 1–2 in. wide. 6 pale blue tepals up to 1
in., wither separately on each of the heavily
clustered flower stalks. Endemic to Hells Canyon in OR
and ID; found on rocky, open steep-sloping seeps in thin
clay soils. Native.

Camassia quamash ASPARAGACEAE
small camas, common camas
NR, MR, montane, grasslands,
common, locally abundant, Spring–
Summer, perennial, 8–28 in.

Showy, narrow raceme above fewer than 10
basal, linear, grass-like leaves from a single bulb. Flowers star-shaped, 6 tepals vary
in color from clear to dark blue and violet to
occasionally white, on pedicels that curve
inward; lowest tepal curving outward is a distinguishing feature of this species. Found in
mountain grasslands and moist meadows that dry out in
summer. Historically an important food source and trade
commodity for Native Americans; considered an example
of early "gardening" for food, as large stands were managed meticulously. Native.

Allium schoenoprasum

AMARYLLIDACEAE

wild chives
RM, montane, common,
Summer, perennial, 8–24 in.

Hollow, cylindrical flowering stem, with 1 or 2 sheathed leaves shorter than the inflorescence, growing from a bulb. Stem and leaves persistent. Inflorescence is an erect, compact, congested umbel of 15–50 campanulate flowers, pale purple to deep lilac with a dark midrib, drying to pink. Flowers composed of 6 distinct tepals, lance-shaped with pointed tips becoming papery in fruit and enclosing the capsule. Occurs in sunny wet meadows, rocky/gravelly streambanks, and lakeshores. Commonly cultivated and widely escaped outside its original circumboreal range. Native.

Triteleia grandiflora

ASPARAGACEAE

largeflower triteleia, wild hyacinth
RM, montane, foothills, pinyon-juniper,
sagebrush steppe, grasslands, uncommon,
Spring–Summer, perennial, 8–24 in.

Herbaceous perennial from deep-seated corm. Basal leaves slender, 1–3, smooth, entire, keeled, sheathing at base, as tall as flowers. Scape smooth; inflorescence open, 5- to 20-flowered, terminal umbel. Flowers narrowly bell-shaped, deep to light blue with darker midveins, base rounded; 6 fused lobes, outer 3 egg- to lance-shaped, inner 3 wider and ruffled; stamens 6. Occurs in sagebrush desert, pine forests. Rare in WY; a disjunct population in southwestern CO. Native.

Tradescantia occidentalis

COMMELINACEAE

western spiderwort
MR, SR, montane, foothills, sagebrush
steppe, intermountain parks,
grasslands, common, Spring–
Summer, perennial, 8–24 in.

Stems succulent; several from perennial crown. Leaves alternate, linear, 3–15 in. long, folded V-shaped lengthwise, often bent downward near stem, clasping stem at base; broken leaf reveals fibers and slimy sap. Flowers open in morning, fade by afternoon; to 1 in. across, 3 petals, in terminal clusters; stamens with feathery hairs, anthers yellow. Sunny slopes, woodland openings, rocky meadows. Native.

Iris missouriensis
(*I. longipetala*) IRIDACEAE
Rocky Mountain iris, western blue flag
RM, subalpine, montane, foothills,
sagebrush steppe, intermountain parks,
grasslands, wetlands, common, L Spring–
E Summer, perennial, 10–40 in.
Herb with simple, erect stems from stout rhizome. Leaves bluish green, mostly basal, to 16
in., linear to lanceolate; margins entire. 1 or 2
flowers pale blue or blue-purple (rarely white),
lined with purple; 3 lower petals with yellow-orange bases.
Grows in aspen forests, moist meadows, along streams
and lake margins. Native.

Sisyrinchium idahoense IRIDACEAE
Idaho blue-eyed grass
RM, montane, intermountain
parks, common, L Spring–
Summer, perennial, 10–14 in.
Clumping herb with several erect, simple,
unbranched stems that are flat and winged.
Leaves grass-like, mostly basal, narrowly linear, sheathing, with entire to finely toothed
margins and smooth surfaces. Inflorescence
of 2–5 flowers, blue-violet tepals with darker
streaks and yellow centers. Tepals rounded to
blunt with bristle tips. Anthers yellow. Outer spathe bract
on flower stem less than twice as long as the inner. Grows
in moist meadows, along streams, and in vernally wet
areas that tend to be alkaline or saline. Native.

Sisyrinchium montanum
IRIDACEAE
**strict blue-eyed grass, mountain
blue-eyed grass**
RM, montane, foothills, sagebrush steppe,
intermountain parks, grasslands, common,
L Spring–Summer, perennial, 6–15 in.
Compact herb with several erect, simple, and
unbranched, flat and winged stems. Leaves
grass-like, mostly basal, sheathing, and with
entire to finely toothed margins. Inflorescence
of 1–6 showy flowers with bright blue-violet tepals, yellow
bases, and clearly mucronate tips. Anthers yellow. Outer
bract on flower stem at least twice as long as inner. Found
in marshes, meadows, along streams and other seasonally
wet areas throughout the Rockies. Native.

Anemone patens
(*Pulsatilla patens*) RANUNCULACEAE
cutleaf anemone, eastern pasqueflower
RM, alpine, subalpine, montane,
foothills, common, Spring–
E Summer, perennial, 2–20 in.
Stems, leaves, and sepals all densely hairy.
Basal leaves ternately compound, with leaflets further dividing and thinly dissected;
stem leaves clasp the stem, also thinly dissected. Flowers solitary, 5–8 petal-like se-
pals (typically 6), lightest lavender or blue, 0.75–1.5 in.
long. Fruit an unwinged achene. Dry meadows, forest
openings, plains, hillsides. Among the first wildflowers to
bloom in spring, this species (one set of stem leaves) could
be confused with *Clematis hirsutissima*
(several stem leaves). Native.

Besseya alpina
(*Synthyris alpina*) PLANTAGINACEAE
alpine kittentails
SR, alpine, subalpine, locally abundant,
Summer, perennial, to 6 in.
Herb with densely hairy flowering stalks.
Leaves thick, 2–3 in. long, in coarse rosettes;
egg-shaped, partially folded, and with saw-
toothed margins. Bluish purple flowers in
dense woolly spikes; petals protrude from conspicuous
calyces, and stamens protrude beyond the petals. Found
among alpine vegetation, in rock crevices and meadows in
sunny locations above 10,000 ft. Native.

Besseya wyomingensis
(*Synthyris wyomingensis*)
PLANTAGINACEAE
Wyoming kittentails
RM, alpine, subalpine, montane,
foothills, sagebrush steppe,
uncommon, locally abundant, Spring–
Summer, perennial, 4–10 in.
Herb. Erect, flowering stems hairy with a
few leaves becoming larger upward. Basal
rosettes of hairy, oblong leaves 1–2.5 in.
with toothed edges. Inflorescence a dense terminal spike
of furry calyces; flowers lack petals; stamens conspicuous, colorful, purple to blue, protruding beyond the calyx.
Found in high meadows, sunny openings in pine parklands, sage meadows. Native.

Veronica americana

PLANTAGINACEAE
American speedwell, American brooklime
RM, throughout, common, L Spring–
Summer, perennial, 2–24 in.
Long-stemmed, rhizomatous herbs; stems
often reddish. Leaves on short petioles, opposite, lanceolate to egg-shaped, to 2.5 in. long,
with toothed edges. Flower racemes emerging from leaf axils with 10–25 flowers per
inflorescence. Flowers blue, less than 0.4 in.
wide, with leaf-like bracts surrounding each flower; 4 petals, with upper one the largest; sometimes with white eye.
Found in all but the alpine zone, in moist meadows and
riparian areas, where it may grow submerged in shallow
water. May grow in colonies by rhizomes in
wet areas. Native.

Veronica anagallis-aquatica

PLANTAGINACEAE
water speedwell
RM, subalpine, montane, foothills,
grasslands, wetlands, common,
Spring–Summer, perennial, 4–40 in.
Long-stemmed, rhizomatous herb; stems
sometimes glandular-hairy. Leaves sessile, opposite, elliptic to oval, 0.75–3 in. long by 0.2–
1.5 in. wide, toothed. Flower racemes emerging from leaf
axils with up to 60 flowers per inflorescence. Flowers blue
and white, less than 0.4 in. wide, with leaf-like bracts on inflorescence; 4 petals, with upper one the largest. Found in
riparian areas, including streams and ditches.
Often grows submerged in shallow water.
Introduced.

Veronica cusickii PLANTAGINACEAE
Cusick's speedwell
NR, MR, alpine, subalpine, uncommon,
Summer, perennial, 2–10 in.
Herb with upright stems, sparsely hairy to
glandular. Leaves opposite, sessile, held upright along stem, to 1 in. long, elliptic to
egg-shaped. Flowers occur in terminal ra-
cemes; flowers deep blue-violet, up to 0.5 in. wide, with
leaf-like bracts on inflorescence; 4 petals, with the upper
one the largest; style and stamens long and noticeable.
Fruit a flattened, heart-shaped capsule with a notch at the
top, hairy. Found in moist meadows, forest openings, and
on rocky slopes. Native.

Veronica scutellata

PLANTAGINACEAE
skullcap speedwell
RM, wetlands, uncommon, L Spring–
Summer, perennial, 4–16 in.
Upright, rhizomatous herb. Leaves opposite, sessile, 0.75–3.5 in. long, narrow, linear to lanceolate, sometimes hairy. Flower
racemes emerging from leaf axils; flowers
blue, purple, or pink (rarely white), to 0.2 in.
wide; 4 petals, with the upper one the largest; 2 white stamens and 1 style projecting from center.
Fruit a smooth, kidney-shaped capsule. Found in riparian
areas, including the margins of lakes or ponds. Native.

Veronica serpyllifolia
(Veronicastrum serpyllifolium)

PLANTAGINACEAE
thymeleaf speedwell
RM, subalpine, montane, foothills,
wetlands, common, L Spring–
Summer, perennial, 2–12 in.
Low-growing, rhizomatous herb with hairy
stems. Leaves opposite, on short petioles
below and sessile above, rounded, 0.2–0.6 in.
long. Flowers occur on terminal racemes;
blue to white, to 0.25 in. wide. Fruit a pubescent, kidney-shaped capsule. The type has light blue to
white flowers, non-glandular pedicels, occurs in disturbed
sites, and is introduced; ssp. *humifusa* has blue flowers on
pedicels with glandular hairs, grows in moist and riparian
areas, and is native.

Veronica wormskjoldii

(*V. nutans*) PLANTAGINACEAE
American alpine speedwell
RM, alpine, subalpine, wetlands,
common, Summer, perennial, 4–16 in.
Upright, rhizomatous herb with hairy
stems. Leaves opposite, almost sessile, lanceolate to rounded, with slight toothing;
0.4–1.2 in. long, hairy. Inconspicuous flowers occur in terminal racemes; flowers blue
(rarely white) to 0.4 in. wide with leaf-like bracts on inflorescence; calyx hairy, dark blue. Fruit a long-rounded,
hairy, notched capsule. Found in riparian areas along
streams, moist meadows, and tundra. Native.

Chorispora tenella BRASSICACEAE
crossflower, blue mustard
RM, foothills, sagebrush steppe, grasslands, common, Spring–Summer, perennial, 4–14 in.
Glandular stems branch out and up from base. Basal leaves lance-shaped to oblong, 1–2 in., wavy-toothed, with petioles; stem leaves similar but smaller, sessile, and less toothed to entire. Purplish sepals partly fused into tube around 4 clawed pinkish purple petals that are sometimes twisted. Fruit an ascending silique, often curving upward. All plant parts noticeably glandular, sometimes hairy, emitting a musky scent. Common weed of dry roadsides, disturbed areas, gardens; can cover large areas with color in early spring. Introduced.

Frasera albicaulis
(*Swertia albicaulis*) GENTIANACEAE
whitestem frasera
NR, MR, montane, foothills, sagebrush steppe, locally abundant, L Spring–Summer, perennial, 12–30 in.
Herb with light green flowering stems from a branched caudex. Leaves in a basal rosette, 2–6 in. long, linear with fine white edges; few pairs of opposite leaves on lower half of stem. Before flowering, basal rosettes may resemble those of some penstemons. Flowers to 1 in. across, densely whorled in spike on upper stem; 4 pointed petals with hairy central gland; pale blue (rarely deep blue) to white, and usually with dark flecks. Seeds in dry capsules. Grows in sunny meadows, rocky slopes, and forest openings. Native.

Frasera fastigiata
(*Swertia fastigiata*) GENTIANACEAE
clustered green gentian
NR, montane, common, locally abundant, L Spring–Summer, perennial, 1.5–5 ft.
Herb. Broad-leaved rosette produces solitary robust stem when flowering. Basal leaves ovate, 8–14 in. long, glabrous, smaller and whorled up the stem. Terminal flowers in a dense paniculate cyme, with a few possible at the whorled leaf axils just below main inflorescence. Petals 4, lightly striped with greenish basal nectary gland, fringed at base. Grows in sun or part shade, moist meadows or mixed forest openings. Native.

Mentha arvensis
(*M. canadensis*) LAMIACEAE
wild mint
RM, montane, foothills, wetlands, common, Summer, perennial, 4–20 in.
Ascending to erect, square, softly hairy herbaceous stems, often single, from lengthy rhizomes. Leaves simple, 0.75–2.75 in. long, opposite, egg-shaped with toothed margins and short petioles; highly aromatic. Flowers lavender to pinkish, or buds lavender-tipped opening to white; funnel-shaped with 4 lobes, arranged in whorls around leaf axils from middle stem up. Found in moist places, wetland edges, riparian areas at low elevations. Used medicinally, for teas, and for fragrance. Circumboreal. Native.

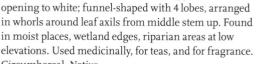

Collinsia parviflora
PLANTAGINACEAE
maiden blue-eyed Mary
RM, subalpine, montane, foothills, common, Spring–Summer, annual, 8–12 in.
Herb from taproot. Stem upright to sprawling, minutely hairy. Leaves 0.5–1.5 in., opposite, entire or nearly so. Leaves rounded proximally, linear distally. Inflorescence cyme-like. Small flowers in upper leaf axils, tubular; 2 white upper lobes; 3 blue lower lobes, the center one keel-like and hidden below the outer 2. Corolla 0.2–0.3 in., abruptly slanting at calyx in downward angle, strongly pouched at bend. Occurs in vernally moist, shady places, often vanishing with summer drought. The less common *C. grandiflora* has longer corolla and smaller pouch at bend. Native.

Boechera lemmonii
(*Arabis lemmonii*) BRASSICACEAE
Lemmon's rockcress
RM, alpine, subalpine, common, Summer, perennial, 2–10 in.
Mat-forming herb from basal rosette. Single stem from each branch of woody caudex. Stem leaves few and egg-shaped; basal leaves spoon-shaped and gray-felted. Lavender flowers surrounded by purplish sepals; never white. Fruits attached to one side of stem, which is a distinguishing attribute. Found in gravelly soils in alpine meadows, talus slopes, fellfields, and cliffs. Begins growing in very early spring. Native.

Boechera lyallii
(*Arabis lyallii*) BRASSICACEAE
Lyall's rockcress
NR, MR, alpine, subalpine, common,
Summer, perennial, 4–10 in.

Glabrous herb with several erect stems arising
from woody caudex. Leaves fleshy, entire,
linear to lanceolate in basal rosette; surfaces covered in trichomes but usually hairless. Stem leaves alternate and oblong to
egg-shaped. Flowers arranged in racemes of
3–15, with 4 hairless purplish sepals surrounding 4 purple
petals. Found primarily on dry talus slopes, gravelly ridges
and cliffs. Native.

Hesperis matronalis BRASSICACEAE
dame's rocket
RM, montane, foothills, common,
locally abundant, L Spring–
Summer, perennial, 1–3 ft.

Upright hairy stems, upper portion branched,
from basal rosette that withers by flowering
time. Hairy, toothed leaves to 6 in., alternate,
lanceolate, reduced up stem, sessile. Flowers
to 1 in. across, fragrant, in rounded raceme;
egg-shaped petals in shades from purple to
white. Fruit a slender silique 3–5 in. long;
seeds brown. Widely naturalized, usually near human
habitation, disturbed sites, roadsides, open woodlands.
Attractive but spreads aggressively by seed, displacing natives and becoming dominant. Introduced and invasive.

Thelypodiopsis elegans
(*Sisymbrium elegans*) BRASSICACEAE
westwater tumblemustard
SR, pinyon-juniper, sagebrush
steppe, common, locally abundant,
Spring–Summer, annual, 6–24 in.

Herb. Stems branched basally and above,
may be pilose throughout. Basal leaves wither
early; cauline leaves to 2 in. long, decreasing
upward; sessile, ovate or obovate, lobes at base
surrounding stem; rarely with dentate mar-
gins. Terminal flower clusters with purplish buds open in
shades of purple to white, each flower more than 0.75 in.
across; gold anthers in center. Grows in sunny, open barrens, clay slopes, shale flats, and hillsides at lower elevations. Native.

Dipsacus fullonum
(*D. sylvestris*) CAPRIFOLIACEAE
fuller's teasel, common teasel
RM, grasslands, wetlands, common,
L Spring–Summer, biennial, 2–6 ft.

Tall, stout herb with erect, few-branched, prickly stems. Stem leaves opposite, sessile, lanceolate to oblanceolate, with entire to toothed margins; underside of midribs prickly. Basal leaves to 1 ft., drying second season. Inflorescence on long prickly leafless stalk, cone-shaped flowerheads persist through winter. Involucre bracts linear, upcurved, prickly, and at least equal to length of head. Flowers open in rings from bottom up. Small corollas purple to white. Fruit a 4-angled, hairy achene. Moist, disturbed sites. Introduced and invasive.

Gentiana prostrata
(*Chondrophylla prostrata*)
GENTIANACEAE
pygmy gentian, moss gentian
RM, alpine, subalpine, locally abundant, Summer, annual/biennial, 0.75–6 in.
Hairless herb with several prostrate to ascending stems. Spatulate basal leaves overlap to form rosette. 3–8 pairs of stem leaves opposite, sheathing and also overlapping. Surfaces light green, waxy, margins whitish. Inflorescence a solitary blue, rarely whitish, flower. Corolla funnel-shaped, with 4 or 5 lobes and broadly triangular plaits between lobes. Calyx green or bluish, with 4 or 5 lobes. Flower twists closed when clouds cover sun. Moist meadows and seeps, tundra. Native.

Gentianella tenella
(*Comastoma tenellum*)
GENTIANACEAE
Dane's gentian, Lapland gentian, slender gentian
RM, alpine, subalpine, montane, rare, locally abundant, Summer, annual, 1.5–7 in.
Small hairless herb with several ascending to erect stems. Basal leaves obovate to elliptic, in a pair or rosette. Stem leaves few or absent, opposite, and lanceolate. Blue, purple, or white flowers solitary, terminal and on long stalks. Tubular corolla 4- or 5-lobed with a pair of fringed scales at base of each lobe. Calyx green, 4- or 5-lobed, swollen at base. Along streams, in moist meadows, boulder fields, tundra. Rare in BC. Native.

Gentianopsis barbellata
(*Gentiana barbellata*) GENTIANACEAE
perennial fringed gentian
MR, SR, alpine, subalpine, montane,
uncommon, Summer, perennial, 2–6 in.

Rhizomatous herb with glabrous, erect
stems. Basal leaves to 3 in., oblanceolate,
long-petioled. 1 or 2 pairs of stem leaves opposite, reduced, linear to oblanceolate and
sessile. 1–3 terminal flowers sessile or on
short stalks, subtended by 2 leaf-like bracts.
Calyx lobes lack purplish midveins. Blue to purplish corolla lobes twist and overlap; fringed margins taper at apex
(whereas the lobes of *G. thermalis* are widest at apices).
Grows on moist slopes, in wet rocky areas, meadows, and
aspen forests. Native.

Gentianopsis thermalis
(*Gentiana elegans*) GENTIANACEAE
Rocky Mountain fringed gentian
MR, SR, alpine, subalpine, montane,
common, locally abundant, Summer,
annual/biennial, 2–20 in.

Hairless herb with several erect stems. Basal
leaves tufted. 2–4 pairs of stem leaves opposite, to 2.75 in., with oblanceolate to elliptic
blades becoming linear above. Solitary flowers
held terminally on long peduncles. Calyx tube with
purplish midvein. Corolla lobes deep blue to purplish
(occasionally white or pink), widest at apices, fringed along
margins, and twisting. Grows in wet meadows, bogs,
snowmelt basins, and along streams. Floral
emblem of Yellowstone. Native.

Clematis columbiana
(*Atragene columbiana*)
RANUNCULACEAE
rock clematis
RM, montane, foothills, common,
L Spring–Summer, perennial, 1–6 ft.

Deciduous vines scrambling over adjacent
plants, or as groundcover; rhizomatous. Leaves
opposite, oval to lanceolate, ternate, with irregular teeth or deep notches. Flowers to 1.5 in. long, solitary,
nodding, with 4 sepals, not fused, and openly bell-shaped;
light purple, blue, often closer to white in NM populations.
Fruit an achene with feathered plumes. Found on moist
slopes, bright open woodlands or ravines. Native.

Clematis hirsutissima
(Coriflora hirsutissima)
RANUNCULACEAE
hairy clematis
RM, montane, foothills, pinyon-
juniper, sagebrush steppe,
intermountain parks, common,
L Spring–Summer, perennial, 6–18 in.
Stems not vining, upright, sturdy, all
parts hirsute. Leaves opposite, lowest ones
smaller, often entire; upper ones pinnately
compound, leaflets linear or lobed, fine textured, very
hairy, with silvery sheen. Terminal flowers leathery, nodding downward, 1–1.75 in. long, exterior very hirsute, 4
sepals fused halfway, bell-shaped, ends spreading or reflexed, often twisted. Seeds in dense heads;
achenes with feathery plumes, showy.
Sunny sites, meadows, woodland openings,
roadsides, sage meadows. Native.

Clematis occidentalis
(C. grosseserrata) RANUNCULACEAE
western blue virgin's bower
RM, montane, foothills, common,
Spring–Summer, perennial, 1–6 ft.
Lax deciduous vine. Leaves opposite, ternate, glabrous to few hairs, petioles winding around adjacent stems for support. Flowers solitary
at stem nodes; pale blue, purple, or white, sepals to 1.5 in.
long, not fused, nodding in open bell shape. Seedheads
clustered achenes with feathery tails. Open woodlands,
shady slopes and ravines, streamsides.
Native.

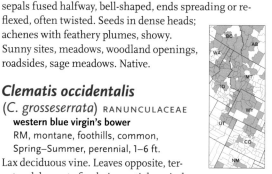

Clematis scottii
(C. hirsutissima var. scottii)
RANUNCULACEAE
Scott's clematis
MR, SR, montane, foothills, intermountain
parks, grasslands, locally abundant,
L Spring–Summer, perennial, 12–18 in.
Stems not vining, upright, some leaning
outward from a robust crown. All parts hirsute or nearly
glabrous. Leaves opposite, pinnate, gray-green; leaflets
ovate to lanceolate, often pointing upward. Sepals fused
and constricted, urn-shaped, down-facing with only the
tips reflexed. Showy feathered seedheads. Grows in grassy
pine parklands, open meadows, and sunny slopes. Native.

Clematis tenuiloba
(*C. columbiana* var. *tenuiloba*)
RANUNCULACEAE
rock clematis
MR, SR, alpine, subalpine, montane,
locally abundant, L Spring–E Summer,
perennial, 3–5 in.

Deciduous stems tufted or short rather than
viny, as compared to the type; rhizomatous.
Leaves opposite, ternate or lobed, and leaflets oval to lanceolate. Violet-blue flowers,
0.6–2 in. long, solitary, nodding, with 4 sepals, not fused,
and openly bell-shaped. Fruit an achene with feathered
plumes. Grows at edges and openings of pine woodlands
or on exposed, alpine slopes and summits; often in calcareous soil. Native.

Lobelia siphilitica CAMPANULACEAE
great blue lobelia
MR, SR, foothills, grasslands, wetlands,
uncommon, Summer–Fall, perennial, 2–5 ft.
Erect herbaceous stems, usually unbranched,
mostly hairless. Leaves alternate, sessile,
toothed, 3–5 in. long, narrowly oval, with
pointed tips and hairy upper surfaces. Inflorescence a single, many-flowered, terminal spike-like raceme 4–12 in. long. Flowers
bright blue, sometimes white. Flowers bilaterally symmetrical: upper lip 2-lobed, lower lip 3-lobed; lobes sharply
pointed, white stripes in throat. Sepals 5, hairy, with
ear-like appendages between lobe bases. Fruit a capsule.
Grows in damp to wet ground often in partial
shade and disturbed riparian habitats. Somewhat toxic. Native.

Astragalus bisulcatus FABACEAE
two-grooved milkvetch
RM, alpine, subalpine, montane, foothills,
common, Spring–Summer, perennial, 1–10 in.
Stem branching from often red-tinged base,
arching out. Leaves green, pinnately compound with 13–15 leaflets, can have hairs on
both sides, deciduous. Upright spike of showy
purple (occasionally white or cream) flowers. The calyx
has black hairs pressed to the surface. Hairy pea-like pods
point down. Common on sunny, dry slopes and meadows.
Very common in favorable sites, especially those with high
selenium. Var. *haydenius* has slightly smaller flowers and
thrives west of the Continental Divide in the SR. Native.

Astragalus flexuosus FABACEAE
flexile milkvetch
RM, throughout, common, L Spring–
Summer, perennial, 4–24 in.
Stems clump-forming. Leaves green, hairless to hairy above and densely hairy below,
pinnately compound with 9–25 leaflets, deciduous. Flowers purplish to whitish, nodding slightly in a raceme of 20–50 flowers.
Calyx hairs white to black. Non-swollen,
hairless pea-like pods point down and
straight out, sometimes mottled with red. Dry slopes,
meadows, sage meadows. One of the most common species on the grasslands at the eastern base of the Rockies
and into the intermountain parks from NM to Canada,
all habitats except wetlands. Native.

Astragalus wingatanus FABACEAE
Fort Wingate milkvetch
SR, pinyon-juniper, sagebrush
steppe, common, Spring–E Summer,
perennial, 6–26 in.
Clump-forming stems spreading outward
from central root. Pinnately compound
leaves, leaflets 3–17; green, not silvery. Purple flowers with white wing tips held in
spikes above the leaves; may be bicolored,
white with purple banner and keel tip. Pods with or without a short stem, hang down, can be mottled. Found in
woodland openings and on dry slopes, among sagebrush.
Native.

Lupinus argenteus FABACEAE
silvery lupine
RM, montane, foothills, sagebrush
steppe, grasslands, common, L Spring–
E Summer, perennial, 1–3 ft.
Herbaceous, branching from caudex. Stems
erect, clustered, covered with silky, silver
hairs. Basal leaves wither by flowering; stem
leaves alternate, palmately compound, 6–9
elliptic folded leaflets hairy below and glabrous above. Spire of pea-shaped flowers,
blue to whitish with glabrous wings; banner without hairy
spot on back; keel fringed along upper edges, slanting forward. Silky calyx with 2 lips, upper 2-toothed. Pods to 1 in.,
densely hairy, 4–6 seeds. Sunny locations, open forests,
sage meadows, roadsides. Native.

Lupinus aridus FABACEAE

desert lupine
NR, MR, subalpine, montane,
foothills, grasslands, common,
Summer, perennial, 1–3 ft.

Herbaceous with several slender, decumbent
to erect, silky-haired stems from a caudex.
Leaves mostly basal, few alternate along stem,
palmately compound; 6–10 oblanceolate,
folded leaflets with silky surfaces. Numerous blue to white pea-shaped flowers whorled
on a terminal raceme; banner smooth and circular; wings
smooth, narrow; keel fringed along upper edges; calyx
with 2 lips cleft for half their length. Pods 0.4–1.2 in.;
2–4 seeds. Grows on dry, open ground and gravelly soils.
Native.

Lupinus bakeri FABACEAE

Baker's lupine
SR, montane, foothills, pinyon-juniper,
grasslands, endemic, locally abundant,
Spring–Summer, perennial, 1–3 ft.

Herbaceous with several erect, hairy stems
arising from a caudex. Leaves alternate, palmately compound; 6–9 oblanceolate leaflets silky-hairy above and below. Numerous
pea-shaped flowers well spaced along terminal raceme; purple to violet with white spot on banner
that darkens with age; banner hairy on back. Pods hairy,
0.8–1.2 in. Sometimes lumped with *L. sericeus*. Grows in
sunny, dry, open areas, meadows, openings in aspen and
oak woodlands and hillsides. Native.

Lupinus caudatus FABACEAE

tailcup lupine
RM, montane, foothills, sagebrush
steppe, common, L Spring–
Summer, perennial, 1–3 ft.

Herbaceous hairy stems, simple or shortly
branched, from woody caudex. Leaves alternate, palmately compound; 5–9 leaflets, flat or
folded, and elliptic; surfaces with silky, silvery
hairs. Purple to light blue pea-shaped flowers
in terminal racemes; banner hairy, light blue with white
in middle; wings smooth, bases hairy; keel with hairy
margin. Spurred calyx. Pods 0.8–1.2 in. Grows on sunny
dry hillsides, roadsides. More frequent in SR. Native.

Lupinus lepidus var. *utahensis*

FABACEAE

Utah lupine
MR, SR, montane, foothills, pinyon-
juniper, sagebrush steppe, intermountain
parks, grasslands, common, Spring–
Summer, perennial, 2–6 in.
Low-growing, from simple or branched caudex, lacking upright stems. Leaves mostly
basal on long, hairy, mostly horizontal petioles; palmately compound with 5–9 oblanceolate leaflets, smooth to silky above, hairy
below. Numerous pea-shaped flowers in dense, sessile racemes among the leafy crown; blue to violet; not spurred;
banner with large white spot, smooth, reflexed. Pods to 0.5
in., hairy, oblong. Sunny meadows. Native.

Lupinus leucophyllus FABACEAE

velvet lupine
NR, MR, montane, foothills, sagebrush
steppe, grasslands, locally abundant,
Summer, perennial, 1–3 ft.
Several simple or branched herbaceous
stems, densely hairy, from a caudex. Leaves
alternate, palmately compound with 7–11
oblanceolate leaflets; densely velvety-silver
on both sides. Numerous pea-shaped,
densely whorled flowers form a slender,
tapering, terminal raceme; lavender to light blue, pale
pink, or white to tan; banner densely hairy on back, wings
glabrous, keel fringed on upper edge, calyx not spurred,
shaggy with lower lip entire. Pods 0.5–1 in., reddish hairs,
4–6 seeds. Sunny, dry hillsides, dry mead-
ows, and open forest. Native.

Lupinus prunophilus

FABACEAE

chokecherry-loving lupine
RM, montane, foothills, sagebrush
steppe, grasslands, common, Spring–
Summer, perennial, 8–40 in.
Erect, simple, smooth herbaceous stems
from a caudex. Basal and alternate stem
leaves palmately compound with 8–12 leaf-
lets; hairy below, smooth above, typically flat, oblanceolate.
Numerous pea-shaped flowers in terminal raceme; bluish
to violet; banner nearly circular, with white spot, shorter
than wings; calyx entire or lightly toothed. Pods curved,
1.2–2 in., densely hairy, 6–10 seeds. Grows in sunny locations, open forests, meadows, roadsides. Native.

Lupinus sericeus FABACEAE
silky lupine
RM, montane, foothills, sagebrush
steppe, intermountain parks, grasslands,
common, locally abundant, L Spring–
Summer, perennial, 1–3 ft.

Erect, hairy herbaceous stems, 1 to several,
from caudex. Leaves basal and alternate along
stems, palmately compound with 6–9 oblanceolate leaflets with pointed tips; surfaces
silky. Numerous, well-spaced pea-shaped
flowers in terminal raceme; variable, flowers not always in precise whorls; purple-violet with white spot on
silky-backed banner that darkens with age; smooth wings;
fringed keel along upper edges; calyx 2-lipped, lower lip
slightly longer. Hairy pods to 1.2 in. with 4–6
seeds. Grows in dry, open, sunny spaces,
meadows, and hillsides. Native.

Lupinus wyethii
FABACEAE
Wyeth's lupine
RM, subalpine, montane, foothills,
pinyon-juniper, common, L Spring–
Summer, perennial, 15–20 in.

Erect, simple, hairy herbaceous stems arising from a caudex. Basal leaves with long petioles; palmately compound with 9–11 narrow, oblanceolate,
often folded leaflets; stem leaves alternate with shorter petioles. Many pea-shaped flowers in terminal racemes above
foliage; violet-purple, banner has white center, smooth
and reflexed; hairy calyx; smooth wings; hairy
keel. Pods hairy, 1–1.6 in. Grows in sunny locations, open ground, and dry slopes. Native.

Oxytropis deflexa FABACEAE
nodding locoweed
RM, alpine, subalpine, montane, foothills,
sagebrush steppe, grasslands, common,
Spring–Summer, perennial, 3–16 in.

Deciduous herb with sprawling to erect, leafless stems. Basal leaves pinnately compound
with 11–30 ovate to lanceolate leaflets; surfaces hairy and silvery. Flowers pea-shaped, purple to pale
bluish, lavender, or whitish, and 0.25–0.5 in. long. Pods
drooping, 0.4–0.8 in. long with a short stem, and covered
in black and white hairs. Grows in tundra, coniferous forests, mixed forests, pine parklands, dry slopes, meadows,
and riparian habitats. Native.

Oxytropis lambertii FABACEAE
purple locoweed
MR, SR, subalpine, montane, foothills,
sagebrush steppe, grasslands, common,
Spring–Summer, perennial, 2–8 in.
Deciduous herb with erect, leafless stems.
Leaves pinnately compound, 5–19 elliptic to
linear-lanceolate leaflets; surfaces hairy, silvery. Inflorescence with 5–20 pea-shaped,
magenta, pink-purple, or violet (rarely white)
flowers. Calyx covered in dense white hairs.
Pods erect, 0.4–0.8 in. long with long beak; leathery or
woolly. Grows in tundra, coniferous forests, mixed forest,
pine parklands, dry slopes, meadows, and riparian habitats. The most common magenta locoweed in the SR, it's
found on the plains farther north. Native.

Oxytropis sericea ×*lambertii*
FABACEAE
locoweed
MR, SR, throughout, common, Spring–
Summer, perennial, 2.75–8 in.
Deciduous, clump-forming with several to
many leafless stems. Leaves pinnately compound; 9–23 leaflets, 0.2–1.25 in. long, ovate
to oblong-lanceolate; surfaces hairy and silvery. Inflorescence an erect spike of 5–20
pea-shaped flowers, lavender or white. Calyx covered in
light to dark hairs. Pods erect, sessile, 0.6–1 in. long, often
with white and black hairs; walls thick and rigid. Tundra,
barrens, rock ledges, pine parklands, dry slopes, meadows,
moist meadows, riparian ecosystems. Intermediate hybrid; map shows where *O. sericea*
and *O. lambertii* overlap on their respective
BONAP maps. Native.

Psoralidium tenuiflorum
(*Psoralea tenuiflora*) FABACEAE
slimflower scurfpea
MR, SR, foothills, grasslands, common,
L Spring–Summer, perennial, 1–4 ft.
Bushy herbs with sprawling to erect stems;
not armed. Leaves alternate, palmately compound with 3 rounded to elliptic leaflets to 1.5 in. long,
dotted with translucent glands. Flowers in a raceme up
to 2.5 in. long; individual flowers lavender to violet, aging
to cream or tan. Fruit an elliptic to egg-shaped, flattened
brown pod to 0.35 in. long. Grows in sandy soils in woodlands, fields, and roadsides. Native.

Vicia americana FABACEAE

American vetch
RM, montane, foothills, pinyon-juniper,
sagebrush steppe, grasslands, common,
Spring–Summer, perennial, 6–20 in.
Herbaceous vine with usually single, trailing
or climbing stems from a rhizome, lightly to
densely hairy. Leaves alternate, pinnately compound; 8–16 leaflets, elliptic to linear, smooth
to hairy, thin to leathery; tendrils simple to
branched. 3–9 pea-shaped, tubular flowers up
to 1 in. long form a loose raceme; blue-purple to reddish
purple (occasionally white). Pods to 1 in., smooth to hairy;
8–14 seeds. Grows in dry soils, aspen forests, meadows,
and streamsides. Native.

Vicia cracca FABACEAE

bird vetch
NR, MR, montane, foothills,
sagebrush steppe, common, Spring–
Summer, perennial, 1–3 ft.
Herbaceous vine with climbing to trailing
stems, finely hairy to smooth, grooved. Leaves
alternate, pinnately compound; 12–18 linear
leaflets with entire margins; branched tendrils at end of each leaf. Axillary, secund raceme with 20–70 densely packed violet-purple
pea-shaped, tubular flowers; calyx half the length of corolla. Pods smooth with 4–8 seeds. Grows in sun to part
shade in disturbed areas, roadsides, and open forests.
Introduced.

Vicia villosa FABACEAE

hairy vetch
RM, foothills, sagebrush steppe, grasslands,
common, Spring–Summer, annual, 1–3 ft.
Herbaceous vine with sprawling or climbing
stems, conspicuously hairy. Leaves alternate,
pinnately compound with 14–18 lanceolate
to linear-oblong entire leaflets to 1.2 in. long;
branched tendrils at terminus of each leaf.
Pea-shaped, tubular flowers form densely
packed axillary raceme; violet or bicolored;
10–40 per raceme. Seedpods usually smooth to about
1 in. long. Grows in sun in cultivated fields, roadsides,
disturbed areas, and meadows. Introduced.

Dracocephalum parviflorum
(*Moldavica parviflora*) LAMIACEAE
American dragonhead

RM, subalpine, montane, foothills,
pinyon-juniper, common, L Spring–
Summer, annual, 8–32 in.
Taprooted annual, biennial, or monocarpic perennial. Stems erect, square, solitary
or branched from base. Leaves opposite,
stalked, lance-shaped to elliptic, 1–3 in. long,
coarsely toothed with spines at tips and minute short hairs. Inflorescence a dense cluster or whorl,
flowers on short stalks, blue to purple, tubular, lower lip
3-lobed, not showy. Bracts leaf-like, unstalked or nearly so,
toothed with spines at tips. Fruit a nutlet. Grows in moist
to dry disturbed soils, rocky slopes, and riparian sites. Native.

Poliomintha incana LAMIACEAE
frosted mint

SR, pinyon-juniper, sagebrush
steppe, locally abundant, Spring–
Summer, perennial, 1–3 ft.
Upright to spreading, tangled shrub; all
parts with soft hairs and a minty or lavender
scent. Leaves linear or narrowly oval to 1 in.,
opposite. Flowers in dense whorls at upper
leaf nodes (resembling true lavender); purple calyx very
hairy; flowers 0.4 in. long, tubular. Petals fused: upper lip
2-lobed; lower 3-lobed with dark purple lines or dots, its
center lobe notched. Grows in sunny sites at low elevations
in sand. Native.

Prunella vulgaris LAMIACEAE
common selfheal, heal-all

RM, subalpine, montane, foothills,
wetlands, common, L Spring–
Summer, perennial, 4–20 in.
Herb with 4-sided stems, upright to prostrate, hairy. Leaves opposite, entire or
slightly toothed, lanceolate, 0.75–3.5 in.
long, hairy. Inflorescence in a bracted spike
0.75–2 in. long; flowers lavender, pink, or
white with upper lip hood-like and lower lip 3-lobed with
central lobe fringed. The type is found in disturbed sites
and is introduced from Eurasia; var. *lanceolata*, with leaves
at least twice as long as wide, is found in moist meadows
and riparian areas and is native.

Stachys palustris var. *pilosa*
(*S. pilosa*) LAMIACEAE
marsh hedgenettle, woundwort, marsh betony
RM, montane, foothills, wetlands, common,
L Spring–Summer, perennial, 6–40 in.

Upright herbs with square stems, somewhat hairy. Leaves opposite, lanceolate to egg-shaped, to 4 in. long, toothed and hairy. Inflorescence in a bracted spike; flowers whorled around the stem in groups of 6, light purple; hood-like upper lobe is shorter than lower lobes; lower lobes with white markings. Calyx sharply pointed, hairy. Found in riparian areas and moist meadows. The leaves are unpleasantly aromatic when bruised. Native.

Chionophila tweedyi
(*Penstemon tweedyi*) PLANTAGINACEAE
Tweedy's snowlover
MR, alpine, subalpine, endemic,
rare, Summer, perennial, 1–12 in.

Herbaceous stems, 1 to few, erect. Basal leaves stalked, oblong to lance-shaped, 0.5–1.5 in. long. Stem leaves opposite, 1 or 2 pairs, lance-shaped, unstalked, smaller. Inflorescence a few-flowered terminal raceme of solitary flowers, 1-sided, held nearly perpendicular to stem. Flowers tubular, 5-lobed, 2-lipped, lavender and white, approximately 0.5 in. long; lips turn up. Stamens 4. Occurs in open forest, meadows, and rock outcrops, often near recent snowmelt. Native.

Penstemon absarokensis
PLANTAGINACEAE
Absaroka Range beardtongue
MR, subalpine, montane, endemic, rare,
Spring–E Summer, perennial, 2.75–7 in.

Several stems from somewhat woody base. Leaves entire to 3.5 in. long by 1 in. wide, somewhat fleshy with waxy coating. Inflorescence an elongated cluster of tubular, bicolored purplish blue, bright blue-mouthed flowers. Grows in sun in barrens, rock scree, rock ledges, dry slopes, and sage meadows. Found in remote parts of Absaroka Range. *P. glaber*, *P. subglaber*, and *P. cyaneus* are similar. Prefers to grow with little competing vegetation. Native.

Penstemon albertinus

(*P. caelestinus*) PLANTAGINACEAE

Alberta beardtongue
NR, MR, subalpine, montane, foothills, grasslands, common, L Spring–E Summer, perennial, 4–16 in.
Stems numerous from woody base. Evergreen leaves entire, occasionally toothed, lanceolate to 1.75 in. long, smooth, hairless. Inflorescence an elongated cluster of bright blue, tubular flowers. Grows in sunny barrens, rock scree, rock ledges, dry slopes, and sage meadows. Compare to *P. virens* and *P. humilis* found farther south. Native.

Penstemon angustifolius

PLANTAGINACEAE

narrowleaf beardtongue
MR, SR, foothills, sagebrush steppe, grasslands, common, Spring–Summer, perennial, 4–24 in.
Several stems form an upright clump. Evergreen leaves linear, smooth with no hairs, blue-green, waxy, slightly fleshy, with entire margins. Inflorescence a dense pointed cluster of large, bright robin's egg–blue tubular flowers. Grows in sun on dry slopes, sage meadows, and sandy areas. One of many sky-blue penstemons found in the Rockies. Related to *P. nitidus*, which has more rounded flower clusters. Native.

Penstemon arenicola

PLANTAGINACEAE

sand penstemon, sand beardtongue
MR, SR, foothills, sagebrush steppe, grasslands, uncommon, Spring–Summer, perennial, 3–12 in.
Several stems form an upright clump. Evergreen leaves linear, smooth, blue-green, waxy, slightly fleshy, lacking hairs and entire. Inflorescence with bright blue and red-violet tubular flowers. Grows in sun on dry slopes, sage meadows, and sandy areas. Another of the many sky-blue penstemons found in the region. Common in WY, especially in the steppe along I-80. It tends to be shorter and have slightly smaller flowers than *P. angustifolius*. Native.

Penstemon aridus PLANTAGINACEAE
stiffleaf penstemon

MR, foothills, sagebrush steppe, grasslands, endemic, Spring–Summer, perennial, 2–10 in. Several-stemmed herb forms upright clump. Rosette leaves linear, margins entire; stem leaves linear, smooth, lacking hairs; evergreen. Inflorescence a sparse, elongated cluster of bright blue, tubular flowers. Grows in sun on rock ledges, in pine parklands, dry slopes, sage meadows, and sandy meadows. Endemic to southwestern MT, adjacent ID, and WY. Easily seen in the Bighorns. Native.

Penstemon attenuatus PLANTAGINACEAE
sulphur penstemon

NR, MR, subalpine, montane, foothills, sagebrush steppe, grasslands, endemic, Spring–Summer, perennial, 2–10 in. Several-stemmed herb forms an upright clump. Rosette leaves linear, margins entire; stem leaves linear and smooth, lacking hairs; evergreen. Inflorescence an elongated cluster of bright blue (occasionally yellow, pink, or white) tubular flowers. Lower lip and 5th stamen often hairy. Grows in sun on rock ledges, in pine parklands, dry slopes, sage meadows, and sandy areas. May have originated as a hybrid between the similar *P. albertinus* and another species. Native.

Penstemon auriberbis PLANTAGINACEAE
Colorado penstemon

SR, subalpine, montane, foothills, sagebrush steppe, grasslands, endemic, Spring–Summer, perennial, 4–14 in. Several stems form an upright clump. Rosette leaves linear with entire margins; stem leaves linear, finely hairy; evergreen. Leaves in whorls of 3 distinguish this species. Inflorescence an elongated cluster of tubular, lavender flowers; bright orange, hairy 5th stamen extending out of flower tube. Grows in sun on rock ledges, in pine parklands, dry slopes, sage meadows, and sandy areas. Native.

Penstemon brandegeei

PLANTAGINACEAE

Brandegee's penstemon

SR, montane, foothills, grasslands, locally abundant, Summer, perennial, 4–32 in. Several stems form upright clump. Basal rosette leaves evergreen, smooth or hairy, lanceolate, margins entire; stem leaves linear to lanceolate, smooth or hairy. Inflorescence an elongated cluster of strikingly large (to 1.6 in. long) bluish purple or deep blue (occasionally pink) tubular flowers. Grows in sun on rock ledges, in pine parklands, dry slopes, and meadows. Native.

Penstemon caespitosus

PLANTAGINACEAE

mat penstemon

MR, SR, montane, foothills, sagebrush steppe, intermountain parks, common, Spring–Summer, perennial, 0.75–4 in. Creeping and mat-forming with many stems, some rooting along their length. Leaves small, linear, rounded, or spatula-shaped, hairy, evergreen. Inflorescence an elongated cluster of bicolored tubular flowers: outside blue to lavender, interior white with red lines. Grows in sun on rock ledges, in rock scree, dry slopes, and sage meadows. Native.

Penstemon comarrhenus PLANTAGINACEAE

dusty penstemon

MR, SR, montane, foothills, pinyon-juniper, sagebrush steppe, grasslands, common, Summer, perennial, 1–4 ft. Herb with several erect stems. Basal leaves rounded to linear, to 4.5 in. long, entire, and evergreen. Inflorescence an elongated cluster of bicolored tubular flowers; exterior pale blue to lavender, rounded throat pinkish white with red-violet lines. Grows on rock ledges, in rock scree, dry slopes, sage meadows, and occasionally moist meadows. Distinctive, with large flowers on tall stems with very few leaves. Native.

Penstemon compactus

PLANTAGINACEAE
Cache penstemon
MR, montane, foothills, pinyon-juniper,
sagebrush steppe, grasslands, endemic,
uncommon, Summer, perennial, 4–8 in.

Several erect stems. Leaves green, opposite, entire, 0.75–4.5 in. long, oblanceolate to lanceolate. Inflorescence a showy, short spike of sky-blue to blue-violet tubular flowers, rather tight, generally on one side of the stem; flowers 0.7–0.9 in. long. Grows on limestone, in rock scree, rock ledges, dry slopes, sage meadows, and occasionally moist meadows. Common name refers to Cache County, UT, where it grows. Native.

Penstemon crandallii

PLANTAGINACEAE
Crandall's penstemon
SR, montane, foothills, sagebrush
steppe, intermountain parks, grasslands,
common, Summer, perennial, 3–7 in.

Mat-forming subshrub with many stems, some rooting along their length. Leaves narrowly egg-shaped to 1.4 in. long, entire, evergreen, and with minute hairs. Inflorescence a dense elongated cluster of light to dark blue tubular flowers covered with glandular hairs; golden yellow 5th stamen. Grows on dry slopes, rock ledges, in coniferous and mixed forests, pine parklands, and meadows. Native.

Penstemon cyananthus

PLANTAGINACEAE
Wasatch penstemon
MR, montane, foothills, sagebrush steppe,
intermountain parks, grasslands, endemic,
common, Summer, perennial, 8–24 in.

Several erect stems. Basal leaves lanceolate to rounded, entire, and evergreen; stem leaves lance-shaped, clasping the stem. Inflorescence a dense elongated cluster of blue to blue-violet tubular flowers. Grows on rock ledges, dry slopes, in coniferous and mixed forests, pine parklands, meadows, and occasionally moist meadows. Endemic to southern ID, southwestern MT, and northwestern WY. Found in the steppe around Jackson, WY. Native.

Penstemon cyaneus

PLANTAGINACEAE
blue penstemon
MR, montane, foothills, sagebrush
steppe, intermountain parks, grasslands,
common, Summer, perennial, 8–24 in.
Evergreen, woody-based subshrub with
erect stems. Basal leaves lance-shaped, up to
6 in. long by 1 in. wide, entire, lacking hairs,
glaucous. Stem leaves smaller, clasping the
stems. Upright inflorescence with vivid blue
flowers to 1.5 in. long. Grows in sagebrush meadows and
dry slopes. Flowers unique in that they typically exhibit
twisted S-shaped anthers. Native.

Penstemon dolius PLANTAGINACEAE

Jones' penstemon
MR, foothills, pinyon-juniper, sagebrush
steppe, endemic, uncommon, L Spring–
Summer, perennial, 1–5 in.
Herb with 1 to several stems from basal rosette. Leaves narrowly oblanceolate to spatulate and densely covered in very fine gray
hairs. Inflorescence an elongated cluster of
tubular blue-violet flowers. Grows in sunny
locations, often in alkaline soils, rock scree,
rock ledges, dry slopes, sage meadows, pine
parklands, and disturbed habitats. A beautiful species
whose deep purple flowers stand out in the harsh environments it favors. Native.

Penstemon fremontii

PLANTAGINACEAE
Fremont's penstemon
MR, SR, montane, foothills, pinyon-juniper,
sagebrush steppe, grasslands, common,
Spring–Summer, perennial, 4–16 in.
Herb with several densely gray-haired
stems arising from basal rosette. Leaves
gray-green, with toothed to minute-haired
margins; upper stem leaves smaller than
basal leaves. Inflorescence an elongated
cluster of large dark blue to blue-purple tubular flowers. Grows in sunny sites, on rock scree, rock
ledges, pine parklands, dry sandy and shale slopes, sage
meadows, and disturbed sites. A strikingly distinctive
species. Native.

Penstemon fruticosus

PLANTAGINACEAE

bush penstemon, shrubby penstemon
NR, MR, alpine, subalpine, montane,
sagebrush steppe, intermountain
parks, grasslands, locally abundant,
Summer–Fall, perennial, 6–12 in.

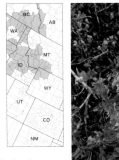

Mat-forming, multistemmed woody subshrub
with both flowering and nonflowering stems.
Leaves evergreen, only along stems, with
noticeably toothed margins and glabrous to
hairy surfaces. Inflorescence a dense cluster of a few lavender to purplish, tubular flowers. Grows on rock scree, rock
ledges, often on granite. Probably the most commonly
encountered shrubby penstemon in the NR and MR. Interestingly, absent in northwestern MT and
Glacier NP but present in Banff. Native.

Penstemon glaber PLANTAGINACEAE

**sawsepal penstemon, western smooth
penstemon**
MR, SR, montane, foothills, grasslands,
locally abundant, Summer, perennial, 4–20 in.

Herb with several upright, stout stems.
Basal leaves evergreen, lanceolate, smooth or
hairy, margins entire; stem leaves lanceolate,
smooth, glossy, and clasping. Inflorescence
a dense elongated cluster of many large blue to lavender
tubular flowers. Grows in sunny locations on rock ledges,
pine parklands, dry slopes, and meadows. *P. brandegeei*
and *P. alpinus* are often considered to be varieties of *P. glaber*. Native.

Penstemon gracilis PLANTAGINACEAE

lilac penstemon
RM, montane, foothills, pinyon-
juniper, grasslands, uncommon,
Spring–Summer, perennial, 5–20 in.

Herb with a clump of several upright, thin
stems from basal rosette. Basal leaves evergreen, lanceolate, oblanceolate, or round, with
toothed margins and smooth surfaces. Stem
leaves opposite, linear to lanceolate and clasping. Inflorescence a dense to sparse elongated cluster of
many pale lavender to mauve tubular flowers. Grows in
sunny and shady locations in pine parklands and meadows. Largely observed on the plains but can be found up to
9,000 ft. in CO. Native.

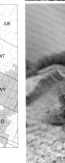

Penstemon griffinii

PLANTAGINACEAE

Griffin's beardtongue

SR, subalpine, montane, foothills, grasslands, endemic, locally abundant, Summer, perennial, 8–12 in.

Herb with clump of several upright, stout stems from basal rosette. Basal leaves evergreen, lanceolate to oblanceolate to 2.4 in. long, with entire margins and smooth surfaces; stem leaves linear. Inflorescence a dense, short, rounded cluster with many bluish to blue-purple tubular flowers. Flower opening and staminode with dense, long golden hairs. Grows on rock ledges, pine parklands, and dry slopes. Endemic to southern CO, northern NM. Native.

Penstemon hallii PLANTAGINACEAE

Hall's penstemon

SR, alpine, subalpine, endemic, locally abundant, Summer, perennial, 4–8 in.

Clump-forming herb with several upright, stout stems from basal rosette. Basal leaves evergreen, lanceolate to oblanceolate with entire or rolled-up margins; surfaces smooth. Stem leaves lanceolate, the upper clasping the stem. Inflorescence a short, dense spike with many bluish to bluish purple tubular flowers. Grows in sunny habitats, rock scree, tundra, on rock ledges, dry slopes and disturbed sites. Endemic to CO's alpine and subalpine meadows and, at these high elevations, not easily confused with other penstemons. Native.

Penstemon humilis

PLANTAGINACEAE

low penstemon

RM, montane, foothills, pinyon-juniper, sagebrush steppe, common, L Spring– Summer, perennial, 2–14 in.

Herbaceous, with several erect stems. Basal leaves 0.6–4.75 in. long by 0.2–1.25 in. wide, oblanceolate or ovate with entire margins, persistent. Stem leaves lanceolate to ovate, smaller. Inflorescence a dense, elongated cluster of blue to purple, glandular-hairy, tubular flowers (to 0.7 in.). Grows on rocky ledges, dry slopes, and in sage meadows. Similar to *P. virens*, *P. aridus*, and *P. albertinus*. Native.

Penstemon lemhiensis

PLANTAGINACEAE

Lemhi penstemon

MR, montane, foothills, sagebrush steppe, grasslands, endemic, uncommon, L Spring–Summer, perennial, 8–28 in.

Herb with several erect stems from basal rosette. Basal leaves persistent, 1–4.75 in. long. Stem leaves opposite, clasping, linear, lanceolate or narrowly ovate with entire margins. Inflorescence an elongated cluster of blue tubular flowers. Grows on rock ledges, in pine parklands, dry slopes, and sage meadows. A sensitive taxon with small populations that are threatened by invasive species and decreased fire regimes. Native.

Penstemon leonardii

PLANTAGINACEAE

Leonard's penstemon

MR, subalpine, montane, foothills, endemic, uncommon, L Spring–Summer, perennial, 10–12 in.

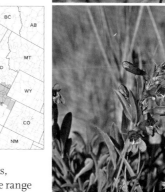

Dwarf subshrub with a woody base. Leaves opposite, narrowly oblanceolate, 0.6–2.5 in. long with entire margins. Inflorescence an elongated cluster of deep blue tubular flowers; flowers up to 0.9 in. long. Grows on rock ledges, dry slopes, sage meadows, and in coniferous, aspen, and mixed forests. Found throughout a wide range of elevations, north on the Wasatch Front and into ID. Native.

Penstemon linarioides ssp. coloradoensis PLANTAGINACEAE

toadflax penstemon

SR, montane, foothills, pinyon-juniper, common, L Spring–Summer, perennial, 4–14 in.

Dwarf subshrub. Leaves opposite, linear, 0.3–1.4 in. long by 0.1 in. wide with gray-green, short-hairy or hairless surfaces. Inflorescence an elongated cluster of lavender to purple (rarely white) tubular flowers covered with shiny glandular hairs; interior white-throated with darker lines. Grows on rock ledges, pine parklands, dry slopes, and sage meadows. Can be mistaken for *P. caespitosus*, but *P. linarioides* tends to be more upright with narrower leaves. The common and scientific names relate to its toadflax-like leaves. Native.

Penstemon luculentus

PLANTAGINACEAE

bright penstemon, brilliant penstemon
SR, montane, foothills, pinyon-
juniper, sagebrush steppe, endemic,
locally abundant, L Spring–
Summer, perennial, 4–14 in.

Herb with erect stems from basal rosette.
Basal leaves linear to lanceolate, often absent
by flowering; stem leaves opposite, linear,
and gray-green (less gray than *P. fremontii*)
with hairs on margins. Inflorescence an elongated cluster of bright blue tubular flowers. Grows in sunny sites in
rocks and on steep, dry shale slopes in the Piceance Creek
drainage and Roan Creek drainage. Described in 2016,
this is a species of concern due to oil and gas
exploration in its habitat. Native.

Penstemon lyallii PLANTAGINACEAE

Lyall's penstemon
NR, subalpine, montane,
foothills, common, L Spring–
Summer, perennial, 4–24 in.

Herb or subshrub with erect stems and
a woody base. Basal rosette absent. Stem
leaves opposite, reducing downward, narrowly lanceolate, with some small teeth,
0.8–4.75 in. long, mostly sessile. Inflorescence a short
cluster of pale lavender tubular flowers. Grows in sunny
locations, rock scree, rock ledges, dry open slopes, roadsides and other disturbed sites. One of the NR's woody
penstemons but with longer, narrower
leaves than *P. fruticosus* or *P. ellipticus*.
Native.

Penstemon mensarum

PLANTAGINACEAE

Grand Mesa penstemon
SR, subalpine, montane, foothills,
endemic, locally abundant, L Spring–
Summer, perennial, 16–40 in.

Herb with erect stems from basal rosette of
elliptic, entire, evergreen leaves. Stem leaves
opposite, oblong or lance-elliptic, and entire. Inflorescence
whorled clusters of dark blue to purple tubular flowers.
Grows in open coniferous forests, oak woodlands, and
meadows. The common name tells where this species is
frequently found. Native.

Penstemon nitidus PLANTAGINACEAE
waxleaf penstemon
NR, MR, subalpine, montane, foothills,
sagebrush steppe, intermountain
parks, grasslands, common, L Spring–
Summer, perennial, 4–14 in.

Herb with multiple erect stems from basal
rosette. Leaves opposite, evergreen, thick,
oblanceolate to oblong, with entire margins
and waxy, gray-green surfaces. Inflorescence
an elongated cluster of deep blue tubular flow-
ers, 0.5–0.75 in. long, shorter than *P. payettensis*. Grows in
sunny locations, rock scree, rock ledges, pine parklands,
dry slopes, and disturbed sites. Often among the first penstemons to bloom, its striking sky-blue flowers contrast
sharply with the sparse hillsides that are its
preferred habitat. Native.

Penstemon ophianthus

PLANTAGINACEAE
coiled anther penstemon
MR, SR, montane, foothills, pinyon-juniper,
sagebrush steppe, common, L Spring–
Summer, perennial, 5–11 in.

Herb with multiple erect stems from basal
rosette. Leaves 1–3 in. long, linear to lanceolate with entire, wavy or toothed margins.
Inflorescence an elongated cluster of pale lavender, violet,
or blue-violet tubular flowers. Grows in sunny locations,
rocky scree, rock ledges, pine parklands, dry slopes, and
disturbed habitats. A plant of the Colorado Plateau. Native.

Penstemon pachyphyllus

PLANTAGINACEAE
thickleaf penstemon
MR, SR, montane, foothills, pinyon-
juniper, sagebrush steppe, grasslands,
common, Summer, perennial, 4–24 in.

Herb with several erect stems. Leaves thick
and waxy with entire margins: basal leaves
evergreen and spatulate to lanceolate, stem
leaves rounded to lanceolate and clasping the
stem. Inflorescence a dense elongated clus-
ter of blue to purplish or pinkish tubular flowers. Grows
on rock ledges, dry slopes, coniferous/mixed forests, pine
parkland, and meadows. Var. *mucronatus* (pictured) is
more lavender-blue to bright blue. The similar *P. confusus*
tends to be more pink. Native.

Penstemon parvus

PLANTAGINACEAE

Aquarius Plateau penstemon
MR, subalpine, montane, sagebrush
steppe, grasslands, endemic, rare,
Summer, perennial, 3–8 in.
Herb with several erect stems. Stem leaves
mostly linear with entire margins; basal
leaves wider and evergreen; 0.25–2.4 in.
long and up to 0.25 in. wide. Inflorescence
a dense, elongated cluster of blue to dark
blue tubular flowers to 0.8 in. long on one side of the stem.
Grows in sun on rock ledges, dry slopes, meadows, sagebrush shrublands, often on volcanic substrate. A distinctive species found only in central UT on the Aquarius and
Fishlake Plateaus. Native.

Penstemon payettensis

PLANTAGINACEAE

Payette penstemon
NR, MR, montane, foothills, sagebrush
steppe, grasslands, uncommon, L Spring–
Summer, perennial, 8–28 in.
Glabrous herb with several tall erect stems.
Leaves thick and firm, the basal leaves ovate
to oblanceolate. Bright blue flowers, 0.7–
1.1 in. long, surround the stem. Grows in
sunny, sandy and gravelly locations on rock ledges,
dry slopes, meadows, and disturbed sites. Native.

Penstemon penlandii

PLANTAGINACEAE

Penland's penstemon
SR, sagebrush steppe, intermountain
parks, endemic, locally abundant,
L Spring–Summer, perennial, 3–10 in.
Herb with several to many erect, short
stems from woody base. Leaves opposite,
green, linear with entire, folded margins.
Inflorescence secund with bright blue to
blue-violet flowers to 0.6 in. long. Grows in
sunny locations, barrens, dry slopes, and
sage meadows. Endemic to selenium-rich,
shale soils of Middle Park in Grand County, CO. An endangered species, protected by law. Though it has one
of the smallest ranges of any penstemon, it is incredibly
abundant in its habitat. Native.

Penstemon perpulcher

PLANTAGINACEAE
Minidoka penstemon
MR, sagebrush steppe, locally abundant,
L Spring–Summer, perennial, to 2 ft.

Herb with erect stems. Basal leaves narrowly oblanceolate and opposite stem leaves becoming linear; surface glabrous. Bright blue flowers with violet tubes, 0.75–1 in. long, partially surrounding the stem. Grows in sunny locations such as sage meadows. Found largely in the Snake River Plain of ID. Superficially similar to *P. payettensis*, but with smaller flowers. Native.

Penstemon platyphyllus

PLANTAGINACEAE
broadleaf penstemon
MR, sagebrush steppe, endemic,
locally abundant, L Spring–
Summer, perennial, 1–2 ft.

Herb with erect stems, somewhat woody base. Basal leaves narrowly oblanceolate; opposite stem leaves more linear, 0.75–2.4 in. long, 0.1–0.6 in. wide; surfaces glabrous. Large purple flowers 0.75–1.2 in. long with violet tube and broad fronts, partially surrounding the stem. Grows in sunny sage meadows. Its leaves are wider than many penstemons, as noted by both its common and scientific names. Native.

Penstemon ramaleyi
(*P. crandallii* ssp. *glabrescens*)

PLANTAGINACEAE
Ramaley's penstemon
SR, montane, sagebrush steppe,
intermountain parks, endemic, uncommon,
L Spring–Summer, perennial, 4–16 in.

Subshrub; stems rise from knobby, woody bases. Basal rosette absent. Leaves green, opposite, 0.6–1.2 in. long, linear. Inflorescence whorled clusters of blue flowers, 0.3–0.6 in. long. Grows on rock ledges, dry slopes, in pine parklands and sage meadows. A distinct taxon endemic to the Cochetopa Hills. Two factors distinguish it from related species: it is winter deciduous and blooms heavily at least twice each growing season. Native.

Penstemon saxosorum

PLANTAGINACEAE

upland penstemon

MR, SR, montane, foothills, sagebrush steppe, common, L Spring–Summer, perennial, 4–24 in.

Herb with few to many erect, stout stems. Basal and opposite stem leaves green, 1–5.5 in. long, linear-oblanceolate to oblanceolate with entire margins. Inflorescence a congested and elongated cluster of deep blue to purplish blue flowers, 0.7–1 in. long. Grows on rock ledges, dry slopes, in pine parklands, and sage meadows. Common in CO in Steamboat Springs and north of the Flattops into southern WY. Native.

Penstemon scariosus

PLANTAGINACEAE

White River beardtongue

MR, SR, montane, foothills, sagebrush steppe, common, L Spring–Summer, perennial, 5–25 in.

Herb with few to many stout stems. Leaves basal and opposite along stem, green, 1.5–7 in. long, linear to narrowly oblanceolate. Inflorescence an elongated cluster of lavender to deep blue flowers, 0.7–1 in. long, on one side of the stem. Grows on rock ledges, dry slopes, in pine parklands and sage meadows. One of the most variable penstemons, with at least 2 varieties (var. *cyanomontanus* is pictured). If you see a lavender-blue, secund-flowered penstemon in UT, it is likely this. Native.

Penstemon secundiflorus

PLANTAGINACEAE

sidebells penstemon

SR, montane, foothills, sagebrush steppe, grasslands, common, L Spring–Summer, perennial, 4–16 in.

Glabrous, often glaucous herb with few to several stout, erect stems. Basal and opposite stem leaves gray-green, entire, fleshy, firm, 0.75–2.75 in. long, and oblanceolate to lanceolate. Inflorescence a conspicuously 1-sided elongated cluster of pinkish purple, lavender-violet, or darker purple flowers, 0.6–1 in. long. Grows on rock ledges, dry gravelly slopes, in pine parklands, grassy meadows, and sage meadows. Dwarf forms occur in South Park, CO. Native.

Penstemon sepalulus

PLANTAGINACEAE
little cup penstemon
MR, montane, foothills, sagebrush
steppe, endemic, rare, L Spring–
Summer, perennial, 17–35 in.

Semi-shrubby with many stout stems. Basal
and opposite stem leaves green, 0.1–0.4 in.
wide, and narrowly elliptic. Inflorescence
an elongated cluster of lavender-violet flowers, 0.7–1.15 in. long, that surround the stem;
red-violet lines in the throat of the lower lip. Grows on rock
ledges, dry slopes, and in pine parklands with sagebrush,
oak, chokecherry, aspen, and Douglas-fir at 5,000–8,200
ft. Native.

Penstemon speciosus

PLANTAGINACEAE
royal penstemon, showy penstemon
NR, MR, subalpine, montane, foothills,
pinyon-juniper, sagebrush steppe,
grasslands, common, L Spring–E Summer,
perennial, 2–36 in.

Herb with few to many erect stems. Leaves
green, opposite, thick, firm, and narrowly elliptic. Basal leaves similar, but evergreen and
often folded lengthwise. Inflorescence an
elongated cluster of 0.4- to 1.5-in.-long, bright blue flowers. Grows on rock ledges, dry slopes, and pine parklands.
Another widespread blue penstemon with significant variation in height and habitat. Its large blue flowers help to
differentiate it from other species. Native.

Penstemon strictus

PLANTAGINACEAE
Rocky Mountain penstemon
MR, SR, subalpine, montane, foothills,
pinyon-juniper, sagebrush steppe,
grasslands, common, L Spring–
Summer, perennial, 1–3 ft.

Evergreen herb with few to many erect, stout
stems from a mat of basal leaves to 6 in. long.
Stem leaves green, opposite, thick, firm,
and narrowly elliptic; leaves often folded lengthwise. Inflorescence an elongated cluster of deep purple to pale
lavender-purple flowers, mostly on one side of the stalk.
Grows on rocky ledges, dry slopes, disturbed habitats, and
pine parklands. Often used in revegetation mixes, can be
found beyond its range. Native.

Penstemon subglaber

PLANTAGINACEAE
smooth penstemon
MR, subalpine, montane, foothills,
sagebrush steppe, endemic, common,
L Spring–Summer, perennial, 1–3 ft.
Herb with few to many erect, stout stems
from a mat of basal leaves. Stem leaves 2–4
in., opposite, entire, elliptic to lanceolate;
0.6–6 in. long by 0.1–1.4 in. wide. Inflorescence an elongated cluster of deep blue flow-
ers that are 0.75–1.25 in. long. Grows on rocky ledges, dry
slopes, pine parklands, and disturbed habitats. Another
widespread blue penstemon that is similar to *P. glaber*,
P. cyananthus, and *P. cyaneus*. Native.

Penstemon uintahensis

PLANTAGINACEAE
Uinta penstemon
MR, alpine, subalpine, endemic, locally
abundant, Summer, perennial, 2–8 in.
Herb with few to many erect, stout stems
from a mat of basal leaves. Basal and opposite stem leaves green, 0.6–2.5 in., narrowly oblanceolate to entire, with entire and
folded margins. Inflorescence an elongated
cluster of sky-blue flowers, 0.7–1 in. long,
on one side of the stem. Grows on tundra, rock ledges, dry
slopes, and in coniferous forests. A small alpine blue penstemon resembling *P. hallii*, although they are never found
together. Endemic to UT's Uinta Mountains. Native.

Penstemon venustus

PLANTAGINACEAE
beautiful penstemon, elegant penstemon
NR, MR, subalpine, montane, locally
abundant, Summer, perennial, 16–36 in.
Shrubby plant with few to many erect stems.
Stem leaves green, opposite, attached directly to stem and with serrated (rarely entire) margins, 1–4 in. long. Basal leaves
absent. Inflorescence an elongated cluster of
blue, dark blue, or violet flowers, 0.9–1.5 in.
long, on one side of the stem. Grows on rock ledges, dry
slopes, disturbed habitats, and in coniferous forests. A very
showy penstemon, often included in seed mixes and therefore found on roadsides outside its range. Native.

Penstemon virens PLANTAGINACEAE
Front Range beardtongue
SR, subalpine, montane, foothills, sagebrush steppe, grasslands, locally abundant, Spring–Summer, perennial, 4–16 in.

Herb with slender stems. Leaves oblanceolate to elliptic with entire or denticulate margins; surfaces smooth, shiny, and bright green; basal to 4 in. long, stem to 2 in. long. Inflorescence an elongated cluster of large blue or blue-violet flowers, to 0.6 in. long, on one side of stem. Grows on rock ledges, dry slopes, disturbed habitats, and in coniferous forests. Similar to *P. humilis* and *P. albertinus*, but their ranges do not overlap. Native.

Penstemon wardii PLANTAGINACEAE
Ward's penstemon
MR, pinyon-juniper, endemic, rare, Summer, perennial, 6–12 in.

Herb with erect stems from evergreen basal leaves. Leaves opposite along stem, 1–2.25 in. long, lanceolate to linear-lanceolate, and covered in felty hair. Inflorescence an elongated cluster of blue, 0.9- to 1.25-in.-long flowers on one side of stem. Found on sunny, dry slopes with clay or loamy soils. Very similar to *P. tidestromii*, which occurs in central UT, but differs in having a smooth staminode and anthers. Endemic to UT. Native.

Penstemon watsonii
PLANTAGINACEAE
Watson's penstemon
MR, SR, subalpine, montane, foothills, pinyon-juniper, sagebrush steppe, common, Summer, perennial, 10–24 in.

Herb with erect stems. Leaves mostly on stem, opposite, 1–2.75 in. long, oblanceolate to lanceolate with entire margins and hairless or sparsely hairy surfaces. Inflorescence an elongated cluster of 0.5- to 0.6-in.-long, blue to violet flowers in loose tiers. Similar to *P. procerus* and *P. rydbergii* but grows in drier areas, lacks basal leaves, and has looser and longer flower clusters. Grows in sunny sites in pine parklands and on dry slopes. Native.

Penstemon whippleanus

PLANTAGINACEAE
Whipple's penstemon
MR, SR, subalpine, montane, foothills,
pinyon-juniper, grasslands, common,
Summer, perennial, 8–24 in.
Erect stems. Basal and opposite stem
leaves 1.5–4 in. long, oblanceolate with entire to dentate margins. Inflorescence an
elongated cluster; flowers drooping, in
whorled clusters; black-purple, violet, blue
to creamy white; 0.75–1.1 in. long, lower lip with long
hairs. Grows in tundra, rock scree, rock ledges, dry slopes,
coniferous-aspen forests, and meadows. Distinctive, with
few morphologically similar species, its typical color, large
flowers, and preference for high elevations
set it apart. Native.

Penstemon yampaensis

PLANTAGINACEAE
Yampa penstemon
SR, montane, foothills, pinyon-juniper,
sagebrush steppe, grasslands, endemic,
uncommon, L Spring–E Summer,
perennial, less than 1 in.
Mat- to cushion-forming herb. Leaves
gray-green, opposite, 0.6–1.2 in. long by 0.07–
0.2 in. wide, oblanceolate and covered in short gray hairs.
Inflorescence with lavender-blue to pale blue tubular flowers, 0.6–0.7 in. long, with golden-haired staminode. Grows
in barrens, sage meadows, on dry slopes and rock ledges.
Native.

Delphinium barbeyi

(*D. exaltatum*) RANUNCULACEAE
subalpine larkspur
MR, SR, alpine, subalpine, locally abundant,
Summer–Fall, perennial, 20–60 in.
Herbaceous perennial from woody rootstock. Stems erect. Leaves alternate, stalked,
deeply dissected and serrate. Inflorescence
a terminal raceme of many dark blue to purple, scented flowers. Showy flaring sepals
5, dark blue. Upper sepal's ascending spur down-curved
at tip. True petals hairy, at center of bloom, 2 upper petals
white and 2 lower purple; petals mostly obscure stamens.
Occurs in moist meadows, streambanks, and moist alpine
tundra. White-flowering and bicolored (white-blue) varieties rare. Highly toxic. Native.

Delphinium bicolor RANUNCULACEAE
little larkspur, low larkspur
RM, subalpine, montane, foothills,
pinyon-juniper, sagebrush steppe,
grasslands, uncommon, Spring–
Summer, perennial, 5–16 in.

Herb with erect stems, many branched,
smooth to slightly hairy, reddish near base.
Leaves rounded, dissected into thin linear
segments, entire, mostly basal. Inflorescence
3- to 12-flowered terminal raceme; sepals 5,
0.6–0.8 in., dark blue to purple, softly hairy;
upper sepal spur ascending, 0.5–0.9 in. long,
down-curved. In center, upper 2 petals fused,
white or pale blue, purple-lined; lower 2 petals dark blue,
sparse white hairs. Sunny areas, open forests, rocky slopes.
Highly toxic. Native.

Delphinium geyeri RANUNCULACEAE
Geyer's larkspur
MR, SR, montane, foothills, pinyon-juniper,
sagebrush steppe, intermountain parks,
grasslands, common, L Spring–Summer,
perennial, 1–2 ft.

Clumping herb with erect, hairy stems often
reddish at base. Leaves mostly basal, light
green, to 2.5 in., hairy, deeply dissected; stem
leaves distinctly smaller. Inflorescence a raceme of 6–30 flowers. Sepals 5, bright blue, to
0.7 in. long, slightly hairy. Upper sepal with
straight to down-curved ascending spur. Upper 2 petals
whitish, blue tips. Lower 2 petals elevated, exposing stamens. Sunny, open slopes and thickets at lower elevations.
Highly toxic. Native.

Delphinium glaucum
(*D. brownii*) RANUNCULACEAE
Sierra larkspur
NR, subalpine, montane, common,
Summer–Fall, perennial, 3–7.5 ft.

Herbaceous, erect stems, few basal leaves, numerous stem leaves. Rounded leaves deeply
divided 5–7 times, in turn divided 2 or 3 more
times, reduced up stem. Inflorescence dense
with 40–90 blue-purple to lavender flowers.
Sepals 5, slightly hairy; lateral sepals pointing forward to spreading; lower sepals downward. Upper
sepal with straight spur, ascending. Central petals small,
obscuring stamens; upper 2 united, bluish white; lower 2
pale to dark blue with white hairs. Open evergreen woods,
wet meadows and thickets, often near streams. Highly
toxic. Native.

Delphinium nuttallianum
(*D. nelsonii*) RANUNCULACEAE
Nuttall's larkspur, twolobe larkspur
RM, subalpine, montane, foothills,
pinyon-juniper, sagebrush steppe,
grasslands, common, Spring–
Summer, perennial, 4–15 in.
Single-stemmed herb, usually unbranched.
Leaves few, on long petiole, on lower stem,
2–4 times divided into linear segments, entire. Few upper leaves smaller with fewer
segments. Inflorescence a raceme of 3–15 bluish purple
flowers (rarely white to pink). Sepals 5, reflexed; top sepal
spurred, straight, ascending; upper 2 united, whitish,
blue-veined, spurred; lower 2 deep purplish blue, white
hairs, elevated, exposing stamens. Sunny,
vernally moist meadows and open forest.
Highly toxic. Native.

Delphinium occidentale
(*D. cucullatum*) RANUNCULACEAE
duncecap larkspur
RM, subalpine, montane, sagebrush steppe,
uncommon, Summer, perennial, 2–4 ft.
Herbaceous stems erect, simple, smooth,
hollow, somewhat bluish and waxy. Leaves
deeply divided into 3 segments, side seg-
ments divided again, but less deeply, irregularly toothed.
Inflorescence a terminal raceme of 25 or more flowers.
Sepals 5, purple to white, slightly hairy, pointing forward.
Lateral sepals 0.35–0.6 in., rounded to pointed. Spur 0.4–
0.6 in. long. Meadows, moist grasslands.
Highly toxic. Native.

Delphinium ramosum
RANUNCULACEAE
mountain larkspur
SR, subalpine, montane, common,
Summer–Fall, perennial, 20–80 in.
Herb. Stems erect, slightly hairy, sometimes reddish at base, 8–24 leaves. Leaves
rounded and deeply lobed into 5 main segments, these further dissected into smaller
toothed segments. Inflorescence a terminal raceme of
few to many flowers. Sepals 5, dark blue, slightly hairy,
forward-pointing to spreading. Top sepal spur straight,
0.35–0.6 in., ascending. Meadows, aspen forests, streambanks. Highly toxic. Native.

Echium vulgare BORAGINACEAE
common viper's bugloss
RM, throughout, common, L Spring–
Summer, biennial, 12–30 in.

Biennial or annual herb. Grows as annual if spring germination; later germinating seeds grow a basal rosette, bloom the next spring. Stems spiny. Leaves lanceolate to 8 in. long, quite hairy. Flowers blue, bell-shaped with red stamens; spirally coiled cymes on an elongated raceme, flowering first at base. An escaped ornamental, aggressive in disturbed areas as well as steppe. Classified as a noxious weed in much of region. Hairs an irritant to those who are sensitive to borages. Introduced and invasive.

Hackelia floribunda BORAGINACEAE
manyflower stickseed
RM, montane, sagebrush steppe, grasslands, wetlands, common, Summer, biennial, to 4 ft.

Few, upright stems from woody base. Leaves oblanceolate to elliptic, entire; basal leaves smaller than stem leaves, wither when flowering. Leafy bracts at base of narrow, elongated cluster of flowers; 5 blue petals fuse into 5-lobed tube, up to 0.5 in. across. Up to 4 nutlets with fused marginal prickles but none on face. Found in wet habitats, from meadows to slopes to riverbanks, also in disturbed areas. Native.

Hackelia micrantha
(*H. jessicae*) BORAGINACEAE
Jessica sticktight
RM, subalpine, montane, sagebrush steppe, grasslands, wetlands, locally abundant, Summer, perennial, to 2.5 ft.

Several stems from a branched, woody base arising from taproot. Leaves oblanceolate to elliptic, petiolate, upper leaves sessile, entire, with short flat or stiff hairs. Basal leaves persistent. Fused flowers with white or yellow eye, up to 0.33 in. across. Flower clusters less dense than *H. floribunda*. Distinguishing feature: nutlets with marginal prickles (as well as several on face). Found in moist meadows, forest openings, riparian areas up to subalpine. Native.

Lappula occidentalis
(L. redowskii var. occidentalis)
BORAGINACEAE
flatspine stickseed
RM, montane, foothills, pinyon-juniper,
sagebrush steppe, intermountain
parks, grasslands, common,
Spring, perennial, 2–16 in.

Herbaceous stems single, often branching above middle, covered in spreading hairs. Leaves softly hairy, basal often deciduous, linear to lance-shaped; linear stem leaves becoming smaller bracts above. Numerous inconspicuous blue to white flowers on raceme; funnel-form to tubular with 5 lobes at top. Small round fruits divided into 4 nutlets with single marginal row of prickles. Circumpolar, native to western U.S. but introduced east. Found in disturbed sites. Native.

Phacelia crenulata BORAGINACEAE
cleftleaf wild heliotrope, notched-leaved phacelia
MR, SR, foothills, uncommon, Spring–
E Summer, annual, 6–24 in.

Herb from a taproot. Leaves narrow, shallowly crenate, rounded lobes; rough or glandular hairs; abruptly reduced distally. Inflorescence a densely flowered, 1-sided spirally coiled cyme. Flowers bell-shaped, lavender to deep purple (rarely white), often with a white throat, on short pedicel. Stamens 5. Stamens and style protrude from corolla. Fruit a capsule. Occurs in desert, rocky areas, clay soil, at low elevations. May cause a rash if handled. Native.

Phacelia gina-glenneae
BORAGINACEAE
Gina's phacelia
SR, foothills, endemic, rare,
Summer–Fall, annual, 2–5 in.

Taprooted herb with stems mostly solitary, sometimes few to several branches from base. Basal leaves lobed to pinnate, glandular hairs present. Stem leaves similar, alternate. Inflorescence 2 or 3 coiling cymes per branch; flower bell-shaped, 0.2 in. long, purple. Seeds reddish brown, hollowed out on both sides of ventral ridge. Discovered by USFWS botanist Gina Glenne in 2009 in Grand County, CO. Found on shale or clay slopes. Native.

Phacelia linearis BORAGINACEAE
threadleaf phacelia
RM, foothills, grasslands, locally abundant,
Spring–Summer, annual, 4–24 in.

Herb with stiff glandular hairs, strong odor.
Stems slender, usually branched, erect, hairy.
Leaves alternate, short-stalked, linear to
lance-shaped, to 2 in. long, entire; some leaves
with a pair of lobes below the middle. Inflorescence few-flowered terminal and axillary
cymes. Flowers light purple, bowl-shaped, 5
petals, white to pale blue center, 0.33 in. across. Stamens
and style protrude. Distinguished from other species by its
large flower and narrow leaves. Occurs in dry, open areas.
Native.

Phacelia sericea BORAGINACEAE
silky phacelia
RM, alpine, subalpine, montane, common,
L Spring–Fall, perennial, 4–24 in.

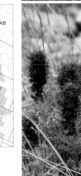

Herb with a taproot and branched caudex.
Stems several, ascending to erect. Herbage
silky-hairy. Leaves oblong to oval in outline,
deeply pinnately lobed; stem leaves alternate, reduced up stem. Inflorescence a dense
terminal panicle of many coiled, dense,
1-sided clusters. Flowers purple, bell-shaped,
5-petaled, to 0.3 in. long. Stamens and style protrude 2–3
times beyond length of corolla. Calyx stiffly hairy. Yellow anthers. Distinguished by inflorescence's cylindrical
shape. Long-lived, occurring in open, often rocky areas at
mid to high elevations. Native.

Campanula rapunculoides
CAMPANULACEAE
creeping bellflower
RM, montane, foothills, pinyon-
juniper, locally abundant, Summer–
Fall, perennial, 2–3 ft.

Herb. Central stems coarse, rough hairs;
sometimes branched. Leaves coarsely toothed,
lower leaves cordate, petiolate; upper more
lanceolate, sessile. Flowers pendent, in spike,
along one side on upper half of stem; 5 petals fused halfway or more into bell shape. Spreads by rhizomes and
seed; attractive but pernicious weed indicative of human
disturbance, in farm country, woodland edges, roadsides,
rural communities, escaping into natural habitats. Introduced and invasive.

Gentiana affinis

GENTIANACEAE

Rocky Mountain gentian, prairie gentian, pleated gentian

RM, subalpine, montane, intermountain parks, common, locally abundant, Summer, perennial, 4–20 in.

Herb with 1 to several decumbent to erect stems. Basal leaves absent. 6–12 pairs of stem leaves opposite, to 1.5 in. long, reduced toward base, and lance-ovate. Flowers 1 to many, blue-purple, sometimes mottled with green, in upper nodes of stem. Corolla cylindric to funnel-shaped, 5-lobed and toothed pleats between lobes. Calyx with unequal flaring lobes subtended by leaf-like bracts. Grows in dense clusters in dry or moist meadows, fens, and open woodlands. Rare in BC. Native.

Gentianella amarella ssp. acuta

(*G. acuta*) GENTIANACEAE

autumn dwarf gentian, northern gentian

RM, alpine, subalpine, montane, foothills, sagebrush steppe, common, Summer, annual, 2–20 in.

Hairless annual to biennial herb with ascending to erect stems. Basal leaves few and soon deciduous. Stem leaves opposite, oblanceolate to elliptic, clasping, often purplish-tinted. Inflorescence an axillary or terminal, loose to dense cluster of violet-blue (occasionally pink or white) flowers. Calyx 4- or 5-lobed, subtended by bractlets. Corolla tubular with 4 or 5 lobes, fringed on the base of the inside. Moist meadows, open forests, along streams and roads. Native.

Swertia perennis GENTIANACEAE

felwort, star gentian

RM, alpine, subalpine, montane, common, Summer–Fall, perennial, 5–24 in.

Herbaceous, rhizomatous. Stem is sturdy, simple, solitary, smooth. Basal leaves 2–4 in., oblanceolate, smooth, entire, stalked. Stem leaves opposite, progressively reduced, short stalked or unstalked. Inflorescence few-flowered cymes from leaf axils. Calyx 5-lobed, lobes lance-shaped, spreading. Corolla blue to violet with prominent veins, 5 narrowly long lobes. Pedicels 0.4–2 in. long. Fruit a capsule. Wet meadows, fens, streambanks, pond edges, open forests. Native.

Polemonium occidentale

POLEMONIACEAE

western polemonium, western Jacob's-ladder
RM, subalpine, montane, foothills,
grasslands, uncommon, Summer,
perennial, 18–36 in.
Rhizomatous herb. Stems solitary, erect,
unbranched. Basal leaves dark green, pinnately compound. Basal and lower leaves
2–8 in. long, on long stalks. Leaflets many,
lance-shaped, entire, 0.4–2 in. long. Upper
leaves reduced. Inflorescence a terminal elongated panicle. Flowers blue, bell-shaped, to 0.6 in. long, on openly
branched stalks. Throat creamy white with dark lines.
Style protrudes. Fruit a capsule. Occurs in wet, open conifer forests and meadows. Native.

Polemonium pulcherrimum

POLEMONIACEAE

Jacob's-ladder
RM, alpine, subalpine, montane, uncommon,
L Spring–Fall, perennial, 2–12 in.
Herb with several stems upright to ascending. Leaves mostly basal, 1–4 per stem, 0.2–1.3
in. long, pinnately divided with 11–23 leaflets.
Leaflets 0.1–0.6 in. long, oval to lance-shaped.
Inflorescence an open to congested terminal
raceme. Flowers stalked, corollas blue-violet with yellow
or white throat, bell-shaped. Anthers and style included
to slightly protruding. Pungent, skunky odor. Fruit a capsule. Occurs in open areas above timberline and moist or
shaded forest areas. Native.

Verbena hastata VERBENACEAE

swamp verbena, blue vervain
RM, grasslands, wetlands, common,
Summer, perennial, 2–5 ft.
Stems rough, upright, square, from perennial
crown. Leaves 2–7 in. long, lanceolate, opposite, with irregular teeth, rough and lightly
hairy. Flowers in branched terminal spikes
3–6 in. long; 5 corolla lobes 0.25 in. across,
reproductive parts within the tubular base;
opening in showy whorls from base of spike upward;
calyx matures with 4 small nutlets. Grows in sunny
damp meadows, swales, ditches, pond margins, and
riparian areas at lower elevations. Native.

Hedeoma drummondii

LAMIACEAE
Drummond's false pennyroyal
MR, SR, pinyon-juniper, sagebrush
steppe, grasslands, common, L Spring–
Summer, perennial, 4–15 in.
Numerous stems, square and covered in
fine recurved hairs, branching from woody
base. Leaves opposite, entire, linear to narrowly oval, glandular and finely hairy, 0.2–
0.8 in. long. Flowers 1–6 per leaf axil on
single stalks, rosy to lavender, tubular with lowest 2 fused
petals longest; 2 stamens; calyx tube hairy, swollen at base,
curved inward, closing after flowering. Found in rocky
soils. Has strong minty scent; used medicinally and for
flavoring. Native.

Scutellaria brittonii LAMIACEAE
Britton's skullcap
SR, montane, foothills, grasslands,
common, Summer, perennial, 4–8 in.
Rhizomatous herb with upright stems, scattered or in small groups. Leaves opposite,
lanceolate and entire with a distinctive con-
vex midvein. Flower petals fused, bilabiate,
rich purple with white or gray striping on
the lower labellum; in pairs at the nodes. A
dried casing that surrounds the seed resembles a type of
medieval helmet (hence skullcap). Found in open pine forest, mainly in foothills and adjacent plains along the Front
Range. Prefers sun, sandy soils. Native.

Pinguicula vulgaris

LENTIBULARIACEAE
common butterwort
NR, throughout, locally abundant,
Spring–Fall, perennial, 2–6 in.
Carnivorous perennial from fibrous roots.
Stem erect, solitary to few, unbranched. 5–7
basal leaves, simple, entire, lance-shaped
to elliptic, 0.5–2 in. long, margins rolled
in; upper surface covered in sticky hairs,
trapping and digesting insects. Flowers solitary. Calyx 5-lobed. Corollas funnel-like, purple, sometimes nearly white, 0.6–1 in. long including spur, flaring
at throat, broadly rounded lobes; upper lip 2-lobed, lower
lip 3-lobed. Stamens 2. Fruit a capsule. Occurs in all zones
but alpine, in swamps, fens, bogs, and seeps. *P. villosa* has
only 1 or 2 basal leaves. Native.

Viola adunca
(V. bellidifolia) VIOLACEAE
hooked-spur violet, western blue violet
RM, alpine, subalpine, montane, foothills,
sagebrush steppe, grasslands, common,
Spring–Summer, perennial, 1–4 in.

Stemless or short-stemmed herb with
blue-green, cordate to ovate leaves, often truncate at base; margins scalloped. Solitary blue
to deep violet flowers, 1 per stem, but often
in masses. Lowest petal with long, slender,
sometimes hooked spur; 3 lowest petals whitish with purple markings; the 2 side petals white-bearded. The most
common blue violet in meadows, open slopes, and open
forests at middle and higher elevations; the much-reduced
var. *bellidifolia* also occurs at all elevations.
Native.

Viola beckwithii VIOLACEAE
Beckwith's violet
MR, foothills, sagebrush steppe,
infrequent, Spring, perennial, 2–8 in.
Herb with cluster of erect stems. Basal and
stem leaves in a dense tuft, succulent, glaucous, and palmately divided into many leaflets. Flowers pansy-like and bicolored: colors
variable, but typically 2 dark purple petals
above and 3 pale lavender petals below; center yellow and
white with dark striations. This unique and unmistakable
violet occurs sparingly in dry rocky sites and in sagebrush
or under pines. Native.

Viola nephrophylla
(V. sororia ssp. affinis) VIOLACEAE
northern bog violet
RM, montane, foothills, wetlands, locally
abundant, Spring–Summer, perennial, 3–7 in.
Stemless herb. Basal leaves rounded to
kidney-shaped with crenate to coarsely
toothed margins, often purplish beneath. Inflorescence above leaves; solitary flowers with
bluish violet petals: the central lower petal
with purple veins and a short bearded spur
and the lower 3 with white, long-hairy bases. The most
common stemless blue violet in the Rockies, this plant
grows along streams, in moist swales and meadows, and
on slopes of shady forests at moderate to low elevations.
Native.

Viola sororia
(*V. papilionacea*) VIOLACEAE
common blue violet, downy blue violet
MR, montane, foothills, wetlands, locally
abundant, Spring–Fall, perennial, 6–9 in.
Stemless herb, often forms colonies. Basal
leaves rounded to kidney-shaped and often
covered with down; crenate to coarsely
toothed margins, cordate base. Inflorescence of solitary flowers with bluish violet,
wine, white, or bicolored petals with contrasting basal stripes: the lateral 2 petals white-bearded,
the spurred petal beardless. Found in woodlands, forests,
and thickets, more frequently in the eastern U.S., where
it is widespread. Native.

Astragalus agrestis FABACEAE
purple milkvetch
RM, montane, foothills, pinyon-juniper,
sagebrush steppe, intermountain
parks, grasslands, wetlands, common,
Spring–Summer, perennial, 2–12 in.
Stem branching, decumbent, from a stout
subterranean crown. Leaves green, pinnately compound with 9–19 leaflets. Flowers
point up and are pea-shaped, purple-pink,
blue-lavender, or bicolored, in clusters of
5–15. Pea-like pods covered with dense, white hairs that
turn black upon ripening. Common in dry and moist
meadows, along streams, and in pine parklands. One of
the most common astragalus from the lowlands up to
the montane zone. Native.

Astragalus bodinii
(*A. yukonis*) FABACEAE
Bodin's milkvetch
MR, SR, montane, foothills, intermountain
parks, grasslands, common, L Spring–
Summer, perennial, 4–16 in.
Herb with very slender and sprawling
stems. Leaves pinnately compound; 11–17
leaflets oblanceolate to rounded and up to
0.6 in. long. Flowers pea-shaped in loose
small clusters of up to 15 flowers, pale purple. This plant
has a wide and disconnected range and never seems
abundant where it is found. Grows in riparian areas, moist
meadows, and aspen forests. Native.

Astragalus ceramicus FABACEAE
painted milkvetch
MR, SR, montane, foothills, pinyon-
juniper, grasslands, uncommon, L Spring–
Summer, perennial, 4–16 in.

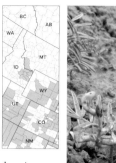

Herb with sprawling, very slender stems;
densely covered in stiff, appressed hairs.
Leaves pinnate with up to 11 linear leaflets; surfaces with silvery hairs. Inflorescence a small, loose cluster of pale purple,
pea-shaped flowers; rounded but lengthen-
ing as it matures. Pods are swollen, pendent, and noticeably maroon-mottled. Found in dunes, sandhills, rock
ledges, and woodlands. The specific epithet refers to the
pottery-like appearance of the seeds. Native.

Astragalus laxmannii ssp. *robustior*
(A. adsurgens var. *robustior)*
FABACEAE
prairie milkvetch
RM, montane, foothills, sagebrush
steppe, intermountain parks, common,
Spring–Summer, perennial, 4–12 in.

Multistemmed clump-forming herb. Leaves
green, pinnately compound, 9–25 leaflets,
deciduous. Flowers in erect rounded cluster,
pea-shaped and up-pointing, 5-petaled, blue-lavender to
purplish, white, or pale yellow. Pods pea-like and small.
Found in mixed forests, pine parklands, dry slopes, moist
and dry meadows. A commonly encountered astragalus in
the West, found over a wide range of habitats
from the plains up to montane. Native.

Astragalus molybdenus FABACEAE
Leadville milkvetch, molybdenum milkvetch
NR, SR, alpine, endemic, locally abundant,
L Spring–Summer, perennial, 1–4 in.

Herb with stems loosely clump-forming.
Leaves gray-green, pinnately compound with
9–25 leaflets, hairy on both surfaces, deciduous. Flowers pea-shaped, pointing upward;
5-petaled, pink-purple, dull lilac, or whitish with purple. Pods are pea-like, small, hairy, hanging
down, and sometimes purple-dotted or -tinged. Found in
sunny areas on tundra, rock scree, rock ledges, and meadows. Often grows on Leadville Limestone and other calcareous rocks. Native.

Astragalus vexilliflexus FABACEAE
bentflower milkvetch
NR, MR, alpine, subalpine, montane, sagebrush steppe, grasslands, common, Spring, perennial, 1–4 in. Stems and structure vary depending on habitat; can be low and cushion-forming, upright and clump-forming, or scraggly. Leaves silvery or green, sparse to dense hairs, pinnately compound with 7–11 leaflets. Flowers pea-shaped, 5-petaled, purple to white. Pods pea-like, flattened, and down-facing. Grows in sunny habitats, barrens, dry slopes, on rock ledges, and sage meadows. Native.

Medicago sativa FABACEAE
alfalfa
RM, montane, foothills, grasslands, common, L Spring–Fall, perennial, 7–40 in. Slender, glabrous to finely hairy, erect to decumbent stems from a taproot. Leaves alternate, pinnately compound with 3 obovate or narrowly lanceolate leaflets to 1 in. long, toothed near tip, sparsely to densely hairy, bluish green. Numerous purple, pea-shaped flowers in a compact raceme; 5 petals, banner longer than wings and keel. Fruit a pod coiled in 2 or 3 spirals, glabrous to hairy. Grows in sunny, disturbed sites, roadsides, and fields. Introduced.

Oxytropis parryi FABACEAE
Parry's locoweed
MR, SR, alpine, subalpine, montane, uncommon, Summer, perennial, 1–4 in. Deciduous, cushion-forming herb. Flower stems usually same height as foliage. Leaves pinnately compound with 7–19 ovate to oblong leaflets; surfaces hairy and silvery. Inflorescence a spike of 1–3 pea-shaped, purple to blue-purple, 0.25- to 0.4-in.-long flowers. Calyx covered in dense white hairs. Pods ascending, 0.6–0.8 in. long, and densely covered in long white and short black hairs. Grows in sunny sites, tundra, coniferous forests, rock ledges, and meadows. An inconspicuous species with possibly cleistogamous flowers that do not seem to open fully. Native.

Oxytropis podocarpa FABACEAE
stalkpod locoweed
RM, alpine, subalpine, locally abundant,
Summer, perennial, 1–4 in.

Deciduous, cushion-forming herb. Leaves
pinnately compound with 9–15 elliptic to
oblong leaflets that are usually folded and
recurved; surfaces hairy and silvery. Inflorescence a spike of 1–3 erect pea-shaped purple
flowers 0.25–0.4 in. long. Calyx covered in
light to dark hairs. Pods stalked, reddish, noticeably inflated, 0.75–1.2 in. long including the beak, and
covered in white or black hairs. Grows in sunny meadows,
rock ledges, and tundra. Scattered throughout the Rockies, prefers calcium-rich soil. Native.

Trifolium parryi FABACEAE
Parry's clover
MR, SR, alpine, subalpine, common,
L Spring–Summer, perennial, 2–8 in.

Upright stems from a woody base. Leaves palmately compound with leaflets in 3s, oval to
1.2 in. long with slight toothing. Flowerheads
to 1.4 in. across with 15–20 individual flowers,
upright on terminal stems; reddish lavender
or purple, up to 0.7 in. long. Found in tundra,
meadows, and coniferous forests at high elevations. Named for 19th-century explorer and naturalist
Charles Parry. Native.

Monarda fistulosa LAMIACEAE
wild bergamot, bee balm
RM, montane, foothills, sagebrush
steppe, grasslands, common,
Summer, perennial, 1–2.5 ft.

Herb with erect square stems from rhizomatous roots; all parts finely hairy, mint-like, aromatic. Leaves lanceolate with teeth, opposite,
1–3 in. long. Flowers purple to pink (rarely
white), in dense terminal whorled cluster
above leafy bracts; fused, tubular, to 1.25 in.
long; narrow upper lip arching with stamens
and pistil; wider 3-lobed lower lip. Found in
sunny meadows, forest openings, streamsides, and damp
hillsides. Showy, attracts hummingbirds and other pollinators. Native.

Pedicularis centranthera

OROBANCHACEAE

dwarf lousewort

MR, SR, foothills, pinyon-juniper,
sagebrush steppe, locally abundant,
Spring, perennial, 1–4 in.

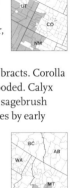

Herb with short to almost no stems. Basal
leaves 1–6 in., wavy, purple-tinged, and pinnately cleft or lobed; margins cartilaginous,
crenate or toothed. Lower leaves often linear,
entire. Inflorescence a raceme of white to
pale yellow flowers with violet to pink tips;
flowers subtended by shorter reddish green bracts. Corolla
2-lipped: upper lip longer than lower and hooded. Calyx
hairy. Grows on dry slopes, gravelly flats, in sagebrush
shrublands and woodlands. Entire plant dries by early
summer. Native.

Pedicularis cystopteridifolia

(*P. elata*) OROBANCHACEAE

fern-leaved lousewort

MR, alpine, subalpine, montane, sagebrush
steppe, endemic, locally abundant,
L Spring–Summer, perennial, 4–16 in.

Herb with erect, solitary unbranched stems.
Basal and stem leaves fern-like, deeply pinnatifid, the segments lobed and dentate.
Stem leaves alternate, reducing upward. Inflorescence a dense terminal spike with soft shaggy hairs
and purple flowers subtended by bracts. Corolla 2-lipped:
upper lip hooded, arched and with an inconspicuous beak.
Grows in open meadows, sagebrush, and on grassy slopes.
Endemic to southwestern MT, northern
and northwestern WY. Native.

Penstemon ellipticus

PLANTAGINACEAE

rocky ledge penstemon

NR, MR, alpine, subalpine, montane,
sagebrush steppe, intermountain
parks, grasslands, locally abundant,
Summer–Fall, perennial, 2–6 in.

Mat-forming multistemmed woody subshrub with both flowering and nonflow-
ering stems. Leaves evergreen, elliptical, to 0.75 in. long,
only along stems and with noticeably toothed margins.
Inflorescence a dense cluster of lavender, tubular 1-in.
flowers. Grows in rock scree and rock ledges near or above
timberline. Can be seen in Glacier and the Canadian
national parks. Native.

Penstemon eriantherus

PLANTAGINACEAE

fuzzytongue penstemon

RM, montane, sagebrush steppe, grasslands, common, Spring–Summer, perennial, 2–12 in.

Herb with several stems arising from basal rosette of evergreen leaves. Leaves gray-green, with toothed to minute-haired margins, to 4 in. long, oblanceolate; upper stem leaves smaller than basal leaves. Inflorescence a rounded cluster of 0.6- to 1.4-in.-long tubular, lavender to pinkish flowers with conspicuous purple lines. The 5th stamen fuzzy, which is diagnostic. Grows in rock scree, rock ledges, pine parklands, dry slopes, sage meadows, and disturbed sites. Native.

Penstemon globosus

PLANTAGINACEAE

globe penstemon

NR, MR, subalpine, endemic, locally abundant, L Spring– Summer, perennial, 4–16 in.

Herb with several upright stout stems in a clump from basal rosette. Basal leaves evergreen, lanceolate to 6 in. long, smooth or hairy, margins entire; stem leaves lanceolate, smooth, the upper leaves clasping the stem. Inflorescence with 1–3 dense, short, rounded clusters of many blue, tubular 0.8-in.-long flowers spaced along stem. Part of a complex of small blue-flowered penstemons found in moist meadows; can be confused with *P. rydbergii.* Native.

Penstemon harbourii

PLANTAGINACEAE

Harbour's penstemon

SR, alpine, subalpine, endemic, locally abundant, Summer, perennial, 2–6 in.

Creeping evergreen herb with weakly erect stems. Leaves opposite; lower spatulate to oblanceolate; upper ovate to lance-ovate, 0.4– 0.8 in. long; surfaces smooth. Inflorescence a short, dense rounded cluster with few to many bluish to bluish purple tubular flowers, 0.6–0.8 in. long, on one side of the stem. Grows in sunny locations on the alpine tundra and in rock scree. Can be confused with *P. crandallii* ssp. *procumbens,* which is found at lower elevations and whose flowers are more mixed into the foliage. Native.

Penstemon montanus

PLANTAGINACEAE
cordroot penstemon
NR, MR, subalpine, common, L Spring–
Summer, perennial, 2–12 in.

Herb or subshrub with many stems (both flowering and nonflowering) from woody base. Basal rosette absent. Leaves green, opposite, narrowly lanceolate, 0.4–1.2 in. long, with teeth, and glandular-hairy surfaces; lower leaves short-stemmed and upper leaves clasping. Inflorescence a rounded cluster of pale lavender, tubular flowers. Grows in sunny locations on rock scree, rock ledges, dry slopes, and disturbed habitats. Native.

Penstemon procerus

PLANTAGINACEAE
littleflower penstemon, pincushion penstemon
RM, throughout, common, L Spring–
Summer, perennial, 6–18 in.

Herb with numerous, erect stems from a mat of basal leaves. Basal leaves oblanceolate, obovate, or lanceolate; stem leaves opposite, more linear; surfaces green and hairless to minutely hairy. Inflorescence with rounded cluster(s) of blue-purple or blue (rarely white or pinkish) flowers, 0.25–0.45 in. long. Grows in tundra, coniferous forests, meadows, riparian habitats, and on rock ledges. A widespread and tremendously varied species, with at least 6 varieties; it is present in every state and province covered in this book. Native.

Penstemon radicosus

PLANTAGINACEAE
matroot penstemon
RM, montane, sagebrush steppe,
uncommon, L Spring–Summer,
perennial, 4–16 in.

Herb with erect stems. Leaves opposite, green, 0.75–2.5 in. long, lanceolate to lance-linear with entire margins. Basal leaves absent. Inflorescence whorled clusters of blue-purple or blue (rarely white or pinkish) flowers, 0.65–0.9 in. long. Grows on rocky ledges, dry slopes, in pine parklands and sage meadows. More of a MR plant, only brushing the SR and present in one county in northern ID. Native.

Penstemon rydbergii

PLANTAGINACEAE
Rydberg's penstemon
RM, alpine, subalpine, montane,
foothills, sagebrush steppe, wetlands,
uncommon, Summer, perennial, 8–20 in.

Herb with many stems arising from a spreading rhizome. Leaves green, oblanceolate to narrowly elliptic, margins entire; basal leaves to 6 in. long; stem leaves opposite to 4 in. long. Inflorescence a dense, rounded cluster of blue-purple flowers, 0.4–0.6 in. Grows in mixed forests, dry slopes, sage meadows, moist meadows, riparian habitats. One of the few penstemons that grows in wet areas, even in temporarily standing water, it can fill entire seasonally moist meadows with color. Native.

Delphinium alpestre
(*D. ramosum* var. *alpestre*)

RANUNCULACEAE
alpine larkspur
SR, alpine, subalpine, uncommon,
Summer, perennial, 2–16 in.

Multistemmed herb. Leaves palmate and divided to 1.2 in. wide. Flowers few per stem, dark blue on the front and blue on the back, spur to 0.35 in. long; 5-petaled; in rounded clusters unlike most delphiniums. Grows in sunny places on tundra, rock scree, and in meadows. Found primarily east of the Continental Divide reaching as far north as Hoosier Pass, where it is never common but can be locally abundant. Some consider this a high-elevation form of *D. ramosum*. Native.

Cymopterus montanus
(*Phellopterus montanus*) APIACEAE

mountain springparsley
MR, SR, subalpine, montane, foothills,
locally abundant, Spring, perennial, 2–13 in.

Multistemmed herb arising from a woody crown. Basal leaves 2 or 3 times pinnate. Inflorescence a pseudoscape, topped with a compact umbel of many small purple to white flowers. Bracts have a prominent green vein. Grows in plains and woodlands; largely a Great Plains species. Prefers sandy areas. Differs from *C. acaulis* in having shinier leaves and green bracts. *Lomatium orientale* has red anthers. Native.

Amsonia jonesii APOCYNACEAE
Jones' bluestar
MR, SR, pinyon-juniper, sagebrush steppe, grasslands, rare, Spring–E Summer, perennial, to 18 in.

Herb with many branched stems that arise from the base. Leaves typically soft green and smooth, linear to lanceolate. Flowers are a terminal compound cyme. Tubular flowers to 0.8 in. long are blue with darker blue sepals behind. One of several species in the genus that grows in dry rocky environs. Foliage turns a bright golden yellow in fall. Sun. Native.

Eritrichium aretioides
(*E. nanum*) BORAGINACEAE
alpine forget-me-not
MR, SR, alpine, subalpine, common, Summer, perennial, 1–4 in.

Stems form a dense cushion, with only the flowering stems present. Leaves rounded and densely hairy, packed into tight rosettes. Flowers 5-petaled, simple, bright blue (occasionally white). Grows in sunny areas, tundra, rock scree, and meadows. Found in the Yukon, but interestingly skips most of the NR and reappears south of Glacier NP. It is very common in the SR. One of the emblematic alpine flowers. Native.

Eritrichium howardii BORAGINACEAE
Howard's forget-me-not
NR, MR, alpine, subalpine, montane, foothills, grasslands, endemic, infrequent, locally abundant, Spring–Summer, perennial, 1–4 in.

Stems form cushions and mats. Leaves linear, densely hairy, and not packed into tight rosettes. Flowers 5-petaled, simple, blue or white. Grows in sunny areas, barrens, rock ledges, dry slopes, and sage meadows. Tends to be found on limestone east of the Continental Divide, its bright flowers easily spotted from a passing vehicle. Very similar to *E. aretioides*. Native.

Hydrophyllum capitatum

BORAGINACEAE
ballhead waterleaf, wool breeches
RM, subalpine, montane, foothills,
sagebrush steppe, common, Spring–
Summer, perennial, 4–18 in.
Fibrous-rooted herb. Stems ascending to
erect. Leaves 2–5 in. long, pinnately divided
into 5–7 simple or lobed leaflets on somewhat
hairy long petioles. Inflorescence a dense,
ball-like cluster of many bell-shaped lavender
to white 5-petaled flowers, often obscured by the leaves.
Stamens and style protrude beyond corolla. Found in
shade, moist to mesic open forests, meadows, and slopes.
Fuzzy in bud, hence "wool breeches." Seeds may be
distributed by ants. Native.

Mertensia alpina BORAGINACEAE

alpine bluebells
MR, SR, alpine, locally abundant,
L Spring–Summer, perennial, 1–12 in.
Herb with upright stems. Leaves alternate,
lance-shaped to rounded, up to 2.75 in. long by
1.2 in. wide, hairy above and lacking obvious
lateral veins, margins entire. Flowers face up
(the only species with this character), bright
blue. Fragrant. The glaucous mound, almost a
rosette, of prostrate leaves can be practically obscured
with showy flowers; a striking plant in the areas where it
occurs. Found in sunny, moist meadows and tundra at
high elevations. Native.

Mertensia bakeri BORAGINACEAE

oblongleaf bluebells
RM, alpine, subalpine, montane,
locally abundant, Spring–Summer,
perennial, 5–10 in.
Upright herb. Ephemeral of middle elevations with linear to oval leaves up to 4.3 in.
long with hairs on both surfaces; hairs more
flattened on top surface. Calyx usually hairy
on back and margins. Flowers in a loose panicle; tube usually longer than the petal's lobes.
Found in moist meadows, moraines, rocky areas, tundra.
Sometimes lumped with *M. viridis*: both are extremely
variable in their size, leaf shape, and flowers. Native.

Mertensia brevistyla
(M. alpina var. brevistyla)
BORAGINACEAE
shortstyle bluebells
MR, SR, montane, foothills, pinyon-
juniper, sagebrush steppe, intermountain
parks, grasslands, locally abundant,
Spring–Summer, perennial, 5–15 in.
Upright ephemeral herb, usually with 2 or
more stout, hairy stems from a fusiform
root. Basal leaves broadly lanceolate to ob-
long, to 5 in. long by 1.6 in. wide with longer petioles, lacking obvious lateral veins; stem leaves smaller, rounded to
elliptic; upper surfaces stiffly hairy, glabrous below. Inflorescence with many blue flowers, bell-shaped; calyx lobes
hairy. Found in aspen woods, meadows,
and dry slopes. Often found with *Phlox multiflora* ssp. *depressa*. Native.

Mertensia ciliata BORAGINACEAE
tall fringed bluebells, mountain bluebells
RM, subalpine, montane,
wetlands, common, L Spring–
Summer, perennial, 15–50 in.
Upright multistemmed herb. Basal leaves
to 6 in. long, up to 4 in. wide, shape variable;
stem leaves lance-shaped to rounded, lower
leaves on short petioles and upper leaves sessile; hairy
edges, upper surfaces papillate. Pendulous clusters of blue
and pink flowers arise from the leaf axils. Widespread
along streams and creeks. The specific epithet refers to the
minutely hairy leaf margins. Native.

Mertensia fusiformis
BORAGINACEAE
spindle-rooted bluebells
RM, montane, foothills, pinyon-juniper,
sagebrush steppe, intermountain parks,
grasslands, endemic, locally abundant,
Spring–E Summer, perennial, 5–12 in.
Erect herb from stout fusiform root. Stems
smooth or slightly hairy. Basal leaves
densely hairy above with hairs pointed to
edges, elliptic to 4.75 in. long by 1.25 in. wide, on a long
petiole; stem leaves linear to rounded and slightly smaller
with rounded tip. Inflorescence densely crowded, nodding;
flowers blue; calyx with ciliate hairs. Found on slopes,
aspen groves, and open woodlands. Difficult to separate
from *M. lanceolata* in CO. Native.

Mertensia lanceolata

(*M. linearis*) BORAGINACEAE
prairie bluebells, languid ladies
RM, throughout, common, Spring–
Summer, perennial, 4–18 in.

Upright herb lacking a fusiform root. Basal leaves ovate-lanceolate to 5.5 in. long, with 1–7 parallel veins; stem leaves lance-shaped to oblong, to 4 in. long; leaves either hairy or glabrous. Inflorescence a coiled cyme; flowers bell-shaped, blue, 5 petals, with a dense ring of hairs near the inner base and anthers projecting beyond the throat. Found in sunny, open meadows and mountain slopes, all habitats except wetlands. Several varieties occur in the region. Native.

Mertensia longiflora BORAGINACEAE

long-flower bluebells, small bluebells
NR, MR, montane, pinyon-juniper,
sagebrush steppe, intermountain
parks, grasslands, locally abundant,
Spring–E Summer, perennial, 2–10 in.

Tuberous rooted herb with solitary stems curving upward or erect. Basal leaves rare; stem leaves sessile, to 2.5 in. long, broadly elliptic with the lower leaf or leaves reduced; lateral veins not apparent. Inflorescence with multiple narrowly bell-shaped, pendulous flowers to 1 in. long, with the tube 2–3 times longer than the not-much-expanded petal lobes. Found in sun or part shade in woodlands, spring wet/summer dry sagebrush meadows, rocky hillsides. Native.

Mertensia oblongifolia

BORAGINACEAE
oblongleaf bluebells, sagebrush bluebells
RM, montane, foothills, pinyon-juniper,
sagebrush steppe, intermountain
parks, grasslands, locally abundant,
Spring–E Summer, perennial, 4–16 in.

Herb from a branching caudex. Leaves narrow to broad elliptic, hairy above, glabrous below; basal leaves 0.75–6 in. long by 0.25–2.4 in. wide; stem leaves sessile or short-petioled, to 3.2 in. long by 0.6 in. wide. Flowers blue and hanging in bell-shaped clusters, the tube narrow, to 0.8 in. long and up to twice as long as the expanded petal lobes. Found in woodlands, sagebrush meadows, dry slopes, open forest, and rocky areas. Native.

Mertensia paniculata

BORAGINACEAE
tall bluebells, tall lungwort
NR, alpine, subalpine, montane,
wetlands, common, L Spring–
Summer, perennial, 2–5 ft.
Hirsute stems from a woody caudex. Basal
leaves to 8 in. long, on a long petiole; stem
leaves to 7 in. long, on a short petiole or sessile; elliptic to egg-shaped. Leaves pubescent
on both surfaces. Inflorescence starts out
congested and matures to paniculate. Flowers blue, to 0.6
in. long, with tube shorter than the expanded petal lobes.
Found along streams in sun to part shade. Native.

Mertensia viridis
(*M. lanceolata* var. *nivalis*)

BORAGINACEAE
snowy bluebells, mountain bluebells
RM, alpine, subalpine, common,
L Spring–Summer, perennial, 2–14 in.
Few- or many-stemmed herb. Petiolate basal
leaves, lance-shaped to rounded, to 4 in.
long, short stiff hairs on top, smooth below,
sometimes with obvious lateral veins. Stem
leaves similar except sessile, to 2.75 in. long.
Inflorescence a crowded cyme. Calyx divided
to the base. Flowers fragrant, blue, tube to 0.35 in. long,
ring of hairs in interior; expanded portion of petals to 0.35
in. long. The silver var. *cana* is found in north-central CO
and Bald Mountain, UT. Found in sun, on
rocky cliffs and crevices, slopes and meadows. Sometimes lumped with *M. oblongifo-
lia*. Native.

Myosotis asiatica
(*M. alpestris*) BORAGINACEAE

Asian forget-me-not
RM, alpine, subalpine, locally abundant,
L Spring–E Summer, perennial, 3–10 in.
Low spreading stems, short rhizomes. Basal
leaves are oblanceolate, stem leaves are half
the length of basal. Flowers in clusters on
leafless stems, mostly 5-petaled, blue (occasionally pink or
white). Found on exposed alpine and subalpine slopes, in
rocky ground or tundra. Fragrant flowers. Sun. Native.

Myosotis scorpioides
(*M. palustris*) BORAGINACEAE
true forget-me-not
RM, foothills, grasslands, wetlands,
infrequent, Spring–E Summer,
perennial, 8–12 in.

Loosely branched flowering stems; may creep
and root along ground. The blossoms appear
on fiddleneck-type stem, clear blue with a
yellow eye. Found along streams and marshy
areas. Sun to part shade. An occasional es-
capee, likely from gardens, not often persisting or encountered in remote areas. This is often put into wildflower
seed mixes and is one of the most recognizable blue flowers of early spring. Introduced.

Phacelia bakeri BORAGINACEAE
Baker's phacelia
SR, alpine, subalpine, montane, infrequent,
Summer–Fall, annual, 1–5 in.

Herb from a taproot. Stems erect, somewhat
branched. Leaves basal and alternate, 0.5–4 in.
long, deeply pinnately divided. Inflorescence
terminal and axillary cymes. Flowers purple,
bell-shaped, to 0.3 in. long; stamens and style
protrude; lower third of style hairy; anthers
greenish. Herbage is sticky, strongly scented
from glandular hairs. Seeds on one side of ventral ridge.
Occurs in open rocky areas and on eroding slopes. Found
at higher elevations than *P. glandulosa*. Native.

Phacelia formosula BORAGINACEAE
North Park phacelia
SR, montane, intermountain
parks, endemic, locally abundant,
Summer–Fall, biennial, 6–9 in.

Herb from a taproot. Stems stout, erect to
spreading, branched, grayish, hairy. Leaves
pinnately dissected. Inflorescence a spirally
coiled cyme. Flowers purple, bell-shaped,
5-lobed, to 0.25 in. long. Seeds dark brown.
Found on shale slopes and sandstone in the
Coalmont Formation, a coal-bearing substrate. An endangered species whose primary threats are
motorized recreation, livestock trampling/grazing, energy
and residential development, and loss of native pollinators
and their habitat. Native.

Phacelia glandulosa

BORAGINACEAE

glandular phacelia, glandular scorpionweed
MR, SR, montane, foothills, sagebrush
steppe, uncommon, L Spring–
Summer, annual/biennial, 4–15 in.
Herb from a taproot. Stems erect,
few-branched. Leaves basal and alternate,
0.5–4 in. long, deeply pinnately divided. Inflorescence in terminal and axillary cymes.
Flowers purple, bell-shaped to 0.27 in. long,
stamens and style protrude, anthers yellow or greenish.
Style pubescent on lower fourth. Herbage is sticky and
strongly scented. Seeds on both sides of ventral ridge.
Open rocky areas and on eroding slopes. Native.

Gentiana parryi
(*Pneumonanthe parryi*)

GENTIANACEAE

Parry's gentian
MR, SR, alpine, subalpine, montane,
common, Summer, perennial, 3–16 in.
Herb with decumbent to erect stems. Stem
leaves opposite, to 1.5 in. long, lance-ovate,
fine-haired margins. Inflorescence a dense
apical cluster (sometimes a single terminal flower) of blue (occasionally white) flowers, with greenish streaks and speckles. Flower bell- to
funnel-shaped to 2 in. long, with 5 rounded to pointed
lobes and 2-cleft pleats between lobes. Calyx with 5 variable lobes. Flowers subtended by leaf-like bracts. Streams,
moist meadows, forest openings. Native.

Monardella odoratissima
(*M. glauca*) LAMIACEAE

coyote mint
RM, montane, foothills, common,
Summer, perennial, 8–20 in.
Upright to spreading 4-angled stems from a
woody taprooted crown; all parts aromatic.
Leaves lanceolate to 1.5 in., opposite, can be
hairy. Terminal flower clusters 1.5 in. across,
with leafy bracts below; tubular flowers project from hairy calyces, appearing to have 5 spreading petals, actually a 2-lobed upper lip, 3-lobed lower lip, with fine
hairs, 4 projecting stamens. Sunny woodland openings,
rocky dry meadows, sage meadows, slopes. Native.

Aliciella pinnatifida
(*Gilia pinnatifida*) POLEMONIACEAE
sticky gilia

MR, SR, pinyon-juniper, sagebrush steppe,
locally abundant, Summer, annual, 8–12 in.

Herb with erect stems. Leaves 1–3 in., conspicuously pinnatifid, and gray-green due to
the glandular hairs. Inflorescence panicu-
lately cymose. Individual flowers are purple,
and the tepals surrounding the floral tube
are very glandular. Long filaments support
blue anthers well beyond the floral tube. Found in gravelly
and disturbed soils where there is little competition for re-
sources. Prefers sun. The genus name honors CO and CA
botanist Alice Eastwood. Native.

Collomia debilis POLEMONIACEAE
alpine collomia, alpine mountain trumpet

NR, MR, alpine, subalpine, montane, locally
abundant, Summer, perennial, 4–12 in.

Stems creeping, often hidden. Leaves alternate, hairy, and slightly sticky to the touch,
crowded toward the tip. Flowers 5-petaled,
blue to rose-pink or white. Grows in sunny
habitats, rock screes and rock slides, from a
deep taproot and is often largely concealed in
the scree. Its low compact habit helps protect
it from cold mountain winds. Native.

Polemonium confertum
(*P. grayanum*) POLEMONIACEAE
Rocky Mountain Jacob's-ladder,
Rocky Mountain sky pilot

SR, alpine, endemic, uncommon,
Summer, perennial, 4–12 in.

Herb. Leaves alternate, pinnatifid to pinnately
compound, succulent-like, upright to ascending. Inflorescence a rounded cluster about
the size of a tennis ball. Flowers light blue
to light purple, widely open to 0.6 in., corolla
twice the length of calyx. Anthers orange.
Sweet-smelling; pollinated by ants. Occurs
above 11,000 ft. on tundra, talus, and rock
scree. Similar to *P. viscosum* but lighter in flower color.
Native.

Polemonium foliosissimum

POLEMONIACEAE

towering Jacob's-ladder

MR, SR, alpine, subalpine, montane, common, Summer, perennial, 2–3 ft.

Herb with open airy habit. Stems 1 to several, branched or unbranched, smooth and hairless to softly hairy. Pinnately compound foliage; leaves 1.2–4 in. long; leaflets oval to lance-shaped, 15–27, 0.2–1 in. long with soft short hairs. Inflorescence a flat-topped cyme, loose or compact. Corolla lavender to white or yellow, funnel-shaped flowers. Stamens and style protrude. Fruit a capsule. Grows in colonies. More common in the SR. Native.

Polemonium viscosum

POLEMONIACEAE

sticky polemonium, sky pilot

RM, subalpine, montane, common, Spring–Summer, perennial, 4–8 in.

Herb from branching caudex. Stems in clumps. Leaves and stems covered in sticky glandular hairs. Leaves succulent- and fern-like, bright green, in tufts. Leaves divided into thick segments with whorls of small leaflets. Inflorescence loose terminal head-like cluster. Flowers funnel-shaped, deep purple to blue-violet, 0.6–1.2 in. long. Stamens with golden yellow anthers protruding from the throat. Fruit a capsule. Sunny subalpine meadows, open woods near timberline, south-facing scree slopes. Pollinated by flies. Native.

Primula incana

(*P. americana*) PRIMULACEAE

silvery primrose, mealy primrose

MR, SR, subalpine, montane, intermountain parks, wetlands, uncommon, Spring–E Summer, perennial, 1–18 in.

Herbage powdery-covered throughout, especially when young. Leaves a basal rosette. Leaves spoon-shaped, 0.5–2.5 in. long, leaf stalk winged, margins irregularly toothed toward apex, often rolled under. Inflorescence a rounded umbel with 4–19 flowers on a leafless scape. Flowers pale lilac, yellow center, 0.4 in. wide, slight fragrance. Petals cleft. Moist meadows, streambanks, ledges, disturbed areas in part shade. Native.

Solanum dulcamara SOLANACEAE
climbing nightshade
RM, montane, foothills, grasslands,
common, Spring–Summer, perennial, 3–10 ft.

Climbing or scrambling herbaceous vines
from rhizomes. Leaves alternate, petiolate,
often with 2 small lobes near the base, smooth
to hairy, 2.75–4.75 in. long by 1.5–3.5 in. wide;
no tendrils and unarmed. Violet flowers in
clusters from leaf axils or stem tips; 5 petals,
strongly reflexed; conspicuous yellow sta-
mens surround a single style. Berries bright red, globose
to ovoid, to 0.5 in. Grows in open woods, thickets, moist
soils, streamsides, and disturbed areas. Poisonous to humans. Introduced.

Glandularia bipinnatifida
(*Verbena bipinnatifida*) VERBENACEAE
prairie verbena
MR, SR, grasslands, common, Spring–
Summer, perennial, 6–18 in.

Herb with prostrate to ascending stems; heavily branched from base, hairy to densely hairy.
Leaves simple, petiolate, opposite, pinnate to
tripinnate, hairy, margins curve downward,
to 2.4 in. long. Lavender-violet to pink clusters
of flowers in a rounded terminal cluster that
elongates as oldest flowers fade; 5 notched petals fused at
base. Fruit a 4-pitted nutlet. Grows in dry prairies,
pastures, disturbed areas, rocky slopes, and roadsides.
Present in Black Hills. Native.

Astragalus kentrophyta var. *tegetarius* FABACEAE
spiny milkvetch
RM, montane, foothills, sagebrush
steppe, intermountain parks,
common, locally abundant, Spring–
Summer, perennial, 1–12 in.

Plants mat- and cushion-forming with deciduous, silvery-hairy leaves with 3–7 leaflets,
each spine-tipped. Flowers covering the plant,
pea-shaped, 5-petaled, purplish to white, with
the keel often purple. Pods pea-like, small, may be mottled. Grows in sun, tundra, barrens, rock scree, pine parklands, dry slopes, meadows, sage meadows. Dense, small
mats in montane and intermountain parks, larger cushions on western CO and UT steppe. Leaf tip spines and
matting habit distinctive. Native.

Campanula lasiocarpa
(*C. latisepala*) CAMPANULACEAE
Alaska harebell
NR, alpine, subalpine, infrequent, locally
abundant, Summer, perennial, 1–6 in.
Stemless until flowering. Basal leaves oblong, to 2.5 in., coarsely toothed, in small
rosettes from slender underground rhizomes; smaller, alternate on stems.
Flowers bell-shaped to 1.25 in., solitary,
lavender-blue, 5 petals, bases fused, up- or
outfacing on lax stems. Found in meadows, rocky/grav-
elly ground, stream edges. Rare in the Cascades of WA
(Snohomish and King counties); locally abundant from BC
north and west through AK, to Kamchatka,
northern Japan. Native.

Campanula parryi
CAMPANULACEAE
Parry's bellflower
RM, subalpine, montane, uncommon,
Summer, perennial, 2–12 in.
Wiry stems, basal rosette; all leaves narrow,
linear (unlike rounded basal leaves of *C. ro-
tundifolia*). Flowers solitary, terminal, generally upfacing; 5 petals fused half the length
into a bell-shaped corolla. Widespread but
seldom abundant. Sunny streambanks, open meadows,
pine parklands where moisture is adequate. A showy
species. Native.

Campanula rotundifolia
CAMPANULACEAE
bluebell
RM, throughout, common, L Spring–Fall,
perennial, 6–12 in.
Slender stems, top-branching, multiple
flowers. Basal rosette leaves rounded, often
withered by flowering time; not rhizomatous. Stem leaves small, linear, alternate.
Blue (sometimes white) corolla bell-shaped,
nodding, 5 petals, lower two-thirds fused.
Widespread at all elevations, growing in
well-drained slopes, crevices, meadows. Circumboreal,
variable, and especially adaptable. Native.

Campanula uniflora

CAMPANULACEAE
arctic bellflower
RM, alpine, uncommon,
Summer, perennial, 1–5 in.

Deep taproot, woody caudex, short slender branched stems. Deciduous leaves linear, glabrous, sparsely toothed, 0.5–1.5 in. long in small rosettes; small and alternate on stems. Blue flowers solitary, 5 petals fused halfway, forming a narrowly bell-shaped corolla just 0.5 in. long; upper stem dark with hairy linear sepals. Alpine to arctic species, circumpolar, extends its range down the spine of the Rockies into CO. Moist meadows, cool open slopes above treeline. Native.

Gentiana calycosa
(*Pneumonanthe calycosa*)

GENTIANACEAE
mountain bog gentian, explorer's gentian
NR, MR, alpine, subalpine, montane, rare,
locally abundant, Summer, perennial, 2–14 in.

Herbaceous, glabrous plant with 1 to several erect to decumbent stems. Stem leaves opposite, in 7–9 pairs, to 1 in., sessile, elliptic to ovate, reduced and sheathing toward base. Inflorescence 1–3 deep blue terminal flowers with greenish streaks and mottling. Corolla funnel-shaped, with 5 pointed lobes and fringed pleats between lobes. 5 purplish to greenish calyx lobes highly variable (sometimes absent). Flower subtended by bracteoles. Grows in moist meadows and along streams. Especially rare in southeastern BC. Native.

Lomatogonium rotatum
(*Pleurogyne rotata*) GENTIANACEAE
marsh felwort
RM, alpine, subalpine, montane, rare,
Summer, annual/biennial, 2–20 in.

Hairless herb with slender, erect, unbranched stems. Pairs of opposite leaves, to 1 in. long, lanceolate and entire. Inflorescence a terminal or axillary cluster of 1–3 flowers of palest blue or bluish white petals with grayish blue stripes. Corolla 4- or 5-lobed with fringed scales at bases of lobes. Conspicuous linear, green, leaf-like sepals alternate with petals. Grows in moist, alkaline meadows, fens, and near lakes and streams. Circumpolar and circumboreal. Native.

Linum lewisii LINACEAE
prairie flax, blue flax
RM, throughout, common, L Spring–
Summer, perennial, 8–28 in.

Glabrous, somewhat glaucous herb with simple, ascending to spreading, wiry stems; from woody base and taproot. Leaves alternate, linear, margins entire. Inflorescence a loose terminal cluster of blue to whitish blue (rarely white), saucer-shaped flowers with yellow centers; petals drop by early afternoon when conditions are hot and sunny. Grows in open forests, mesic to dry meadows, and along roads, in all life zones except wetlands. Species is abundant throughout its range. Native.

Linum perenne LINACEAE
blue flax
SR, intermountain parks,
grasslands, infrequent, L Spring–
Summer, perennial, 10–30 in.

Glabrous, tufted herb with simple, erect stems from woody base and taproot. Leaves alternate, linear and with entire margins. Inflorescence a loose terminal cluster of deep blue flowers that open for only a day. Naturalized along roadsides that have been revegetated by highway departments. So similar to our native *L. lewisii* that it has been lumped by many botanists. This European cousin is found in ruderal habitats, and its much darker blue flowers are heterostylic. *L. lewisii* is homostylic. Introduced.

Phlox kelseyi POLEMONIACEAE
Kelsey's phlox, marsh phlox
NR, MR, montane, foothills, pinyon-
juniper, sagebrush steppe, intermountain
parks, grasslands, locally abundant,
Spring–E Summer, perennial, 1–1.5 in.

Low-growing plant forming loose to dense mats. Stems prostrate to ascending, 1–5 in. long, glabrous or sparsely hirsute and glandular. Leaves lance-linear, succulent, to 1 in. long, ciliate toward the base. Inflorescence solitary, calyx glabrous to villous with flat intercostal membrane; corolla typically white to lavender-purple, lobes 0.2–0.35 in. long. Grows in alkaline meadows and seasonally (summer) dry fens. Native.

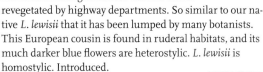

Phlox pulvinata
(*P. caespitosa* ssp. *platyphylla*)

POLEMONIACEAE

cushion phlox

RM, alpine, common, Summer,
perennial, 1–2 in.

Very dense mat- to mound-forming plant.
Leaves linear to 0.6 in. long. Flowers solitary,
expressing enormous variability in color,
blue to white. The most common phlox above
treeline, capable of forming vast colonies at
the highest elevations, even in exposed tundra. Always
intensely and sweetly fragrant. Native.

Primula cusickiana PRIMULACEAE

Cusick's primrose

MR, subalpine, montane, foothills, rare,
Spring–Summer, perennial, 2–4 in.

Herbaceous perennial, leaves lance- to
spoon-shaped, 1–3 in. long, stalk winged,
margins mostly entire. Inflorescence 2- to
8-flowered. Flowers deep purple to pink,
yellow-eyed, 5 slightly cleft lobes. Fruit a capsule. Plants leggier at lower elevations, more
compact higher. Blooms at edges of recent
snowmelt and in cool, moist microclimates. It
is found in the Wallowa Mountains of northeastern OR and in central and west-central ID, where it
blooms from foothills to subalpine slopes immediately
after snowmelt, on rough, unpromising ground. Native.

Aquilegia brevistyla

RANUNCULACEAE

smallflower columbine

NR, MR, alpine, subalpine, montane,
foothills, locally abundant,
Summer, perennial, to 2 ft.

Slender, sparingly branched, perennial,
lightly pubescent below and glandular above.
Leaves are biternately compound and glabrous
on top and bottom, occasionally pilose. Blue
flowers point downward and have hooked
spurs. Nodding flowers are small, 0.5–1 in.
long, atop tall graceful stems. Blades of the sepals are
white to cream and about twice as long as the spurs. Seed
capsules 5-lobed, pubescent. Found in open woods, meadows, shores, and rock outcrops, growing in shade or sun.
Native.

Aquilegia coerulea
(*A. caerulea*) RANUNCULACEAE
Colorado blue columbine
RM, alpine, subalpine, montane,
foothills, common, locally abundant,
Spring–Summer, perennial, 1–2 ft.
Branched stems from perennial crown;
leaves rounded, blue-green, biternately compound; smaller, alternate on stems. Flowers
showy, 1.5–3 in. across, color variable: deep
blue-purple, cream, white. Typically white
central petals end in long bluish spurs containing nectar.
Sepals blue, star-like, spreading perpendicular to floral
axis. Anthers yellow. 4 varieties identified. Found in sun,
light shade; meadows, mixed forests to alpine slopes.
State flower of CO. This and all columbines
hybridize freely. Native.

Aquilegia jonesii RANUNCULACEAE
Jones' columbine
NR, MR, alpine, subalpine, montane,
endemic, rare, Summer, perennial, 2–3 in.
Basal leaves ternate, occasionally biternately
compound, most often sessile, very glaucous. Foliage densely clustered, forming
small cushions with ruffled appearance.
Single flowers are held just above the foli-
age. Sepals are perpendicular to the floral axis and are blue
to dark purple. Blades are almost twice as long as the short
spurs and are consistently blue to purple. Stamens are
shorter than the blades and often lack staminodes. Plants
are restricted to sunny rocky limestone soils
at high elevations, rarely down to the montane zone, and occur only in central WY and
northward. Native.

Aquilegia saximontana
RANUNCULACEAE
**Rocky Mountain blue columbine, Rocky
Mountain columbine**
SR, alpine, subalpine, endemic,
uncommon, Summer, perennial, 4–6 in.
Herb with basal leaves biternately com-
pound and usually clustered but not as tightly as *A. jonesii*.
Leaves are green above and glabrous beneath. Flowers are
quite small to only 0.5 in. across and not very floriferous.
Blades white to soft yellow with blue spurs. One of 3 spe-
cies with hooked spurs. Confined to the central part of CO
in the SR, in shade and sun. Native.

Aquilegia scopulorum

RANUNCULACEAE
Utah columbine
MR, alpine, subalpine, endemic,
uncommon, Summer, perennial, 3–5 in.

Basal leaves are biternately compound and
glaucous on both sides. Leaflets densely clustered. Flowers erect, on stems slightly above
the clustered foliage. Flowers up to 2 in.
across, up- or outfacing. Sepals, from light
sky-blue to almost purple, are not quite fully
perpendicular to the flower axis. Petals slightly cleft, commonly white but can shade into blue; spurs are straight
and most commonly blue. Stamens rarely project past the
petals. Plants most abundant in the Wasatch of UT, with a
few outliers in CO and NV. Sun. Native.

Saxifraga oppositifolia

SAXIFRAGACEAE
purple mountain saxifrage
NR, MR, alpine, subalpine, locally abundant,
L Spring–Summer, perennial, 0.75–3 in.

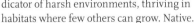

Rhizomatous herb with erect flowering stems
and numerous trailing sterile stems; forms
mats to 8 in. across. Stem leaves opposite,
crowded, purplish-tinged, leathery, sessile,
spatulate to ovate, with entire to coarse-haired
margins. Inflorescence a solitary flower with a cup-shaped
calyx and purple to pink (rarely white) erect to spreading
fleshy petals. Found on slopes, rocky outcroppings, fellfields, and in moist to mesic meadows. Plant often an in-
dicator of harsh environments, thriving in
habitats where few others can grow. Native.

Carduus nutans

(*C. macrocephalus*) ASTERACEAE
nodding plumeless thistle, musk thistle
RM, montane, foothills, grasslands,
common, L Spring–Fall, biennial, 1–6 ft.

Upright stems with spiny wings; leaves basal
and alternate to 8 in., reduced upward; pinnate, lobed and spiny on edges. Flowerheads
solitary, sometimes nodding, to 1.6 in. Flower
stalks to 1 ft. long. Phyllaries lance-shaped, outer reflexed,
inner unarmed; disc flowers to 1 in. long, purple. Ray flowers absent. Found in disturbed areas, meadows, roadsides,
and open fields. May hybridize with *C. acanthoides*, which
is less widespread and differentiated by having multiple
flowerheads per stem. Introduced and invasive.

Cichorium intybus ASTERACEAE
chicory
RM, montane, foothills, sagebrush
steppe, grasslands, locally abundant,
Summer–Fall, perennial, 1–4 ft.
Upright stems, coarsely branched. Basal
leaves to 8 in. long, lanceolate with deep
toothed lobes, smaller and less lobed up the
stems; all parts with milky sap. Distinctive
clear blue flowers have no central disc; all
florets have 0.5- to 1-in. ray petals, their tips
cut with 4 or 5 small notches. Escaped cultivation to become a common roadside weed. Introduced.

Cirsium barnebyi ASTERACEAE
Barneby's thistle
MR, SR, pinyon-juniper, sagebrush
steppe, endemic, locally abundant, L
Spring–Summer, perennial, 0.5–2 ft.
Smooth to gray-woolly erect stems, branched
above middle; from taproot. Basal and alternate stem leaves decurrent, 4–12 in., reducing
upward, oblong-elliptic, undulate to deeply
pinnatifid; lobed, spiny-toothed margins; surfaces white-woolly. Flowers in a corymb of
1–20 small discoid heads clustered at branch
tips; palest lavender-purple. Phyllaries imbricate, smooth to cobwebby, with or without glutinous dorsal
ridge; spines spreading to ascending. Shale slopes, in limestone and sandstone. Endemic mainly in Garfield and Rio
Blanco counties in CO. Of conservation concern. Native.

Cirsium undulatum
(*Carduus undulatus*) ASTERACEAE
wavyleaf thistle
RM, montane, foothills, sagebrush
steppe, grasslands, common, L Spring–
Summer, biennial, 1–5 ft.
Slender, erect, white-hairy stems from taproot; may be short-lived perennial. Basal
and alternate stem leaves 4–17 in., reducing upward, sessile to decurrent, lanceolate
and coarsely toothed, undulate, or pinnatifid
with yellow-spiny margins. Surfaces smooth to sparse cobwebby above, white-woolly below. Discoid flowers solitary
and terminal or on branch ends. Petals pink-purple. Involucres round to bell-shaped; phyllaries with dorsal ridge,
spines reflexed. Grows in sandy or gravelly soil in meadows, open forests, and on dry hillsides. Native.

Cirsium vulgare ASTERACEAE
bull thistle
RM, montane, foothills, sagebrush
steppe, grasslands, common,
Summer, biennial, 2–6 ft.

Erect, branched, hairy, spiny-winged stems;
from taproot. Basal and alternate stem leaves
5–12 in. long, reducing upward; strongly
decurrent, lanceolate, pinnatifid, with
spiny-toothed margins; surfaces rough,
stiff-haired and sharp-spiny above and white-
woolly to stiff-haired below. Inflorescence several to many
discoid heads on branches; flowers purple (rarely white).
Phyllaries cobwebby and without glutinous dorsal ridge;
spines yellow and spreading. A noxious weed that grows
in disturbed habitats, roadsides, pastures, and
moist meadows. Introduced and invasive.

Cyanus segetum
(*Centaurea cyanus*) ASTERACEAE
garden cornflower, bachelor's button
RM, montane, foothills, grasslands,
infrequent, locally abundant, L Spring–
Summer, annual, 8–40 in.

Erect stem, usually 1, branching toward top,
covered in soft hairs. Basal leaves linear to
lance-shaped, 1–4 in., entire or with lin-
ear lobes, stem leaves similar but always entire. Florets
composed of discs, with outer enlarged, funnel-shaped,
reminiscent of rays. Found in disturbed areas, roadsides.
Originally called cornflower for its abundance in agricultural fields and now also found in seed mixes.
Introduced.

Dieteria bigelovii
(*Machaeranthera bigelovii*)
ASTERACEAE
Bigelow's tansyaster
MR, SR, throughout, common,
Summer–Fall, biennial, 1–4 ft.

Herb with erect, branching stems, sometimes
covered in short, soft, white-gray hairs; from
taproot. Forms mounds by fall. Leaves alter-
nate, typically lanceolate, irregularly serrate or toothed,
and smooth or soft-hairy. Ray flowers blue to purple. Involucre bracts in 5–10 series and spreading to reflexed. Plant
variable in size and habit. Very widespread along sunny
roadsides at many elevations, contributing to late summer
color. Usually monocarpic. Native.

Erigeron eximius
(*E. superbus*) ASTERACEAE
sprucefir fleabane
MR, SR, alpine, subalpine,
montane, foothills, common,
Summer, perennial, 8–20 in.

Stems upright in colonies from spreading
rhizomes and surface stolons. Basal leaves
normally have obvious elongated petioles,
while stem leaves are clasping and reducing
in size as they progress upward. Daisy-like,
40–80 narrow rays, from soft shades of blue or pink to
white. Showy and common component of summer meadows throughout its range. Plants often grow in shaded
woodland or meadow edges, with stems leaning toward
the nearest open sky. Native.

Erigeron formosissimus
(*E. glabellus* var. *viscidus*)
ASTERACEAE
beautiful fleabane
MR, SR, alpine, subalpine,
montane, foothills, common,
Summer, perennial, 8–20 in.

Herbaceous; flowering stems curve upward
from base, from vigorous rhizomes that
form expansive colonies. Leaves are lanceo-
late and often undulate, may be glabrous to slightly hairy,
stem leaves often cupped inward. Daisy-like and similar
to *E. eximius*, but with more ray florets (70–150). Phyllaries
are reflexed, hairy and purple at the tips. Widespread and
variable fleabane, providing summer color at
higher elevations. Sun or part shade. Native.

Erigeron glacialis
(*E. peregrinus*) ASTERACEAE
subalpine fleabane
RM, alpine, subalpine, montane, common,
L Spring–Summer, perennial, 4–20 in.

Perennial herb. Flowering stems from
thickened caudices, spreading by rhizomes.
Leaves variable, linear to lanceolate to spatulate; glabrous to hirsute; 1–6 in. long and
reduced upward. Showy daisies in soft shades of blue/pur-
ple; distinctive ray flowers are up to 0.3 in. wide—much
wider than most other species. Phyllaries are moderately
hairy and have red tips. Common high-altitude meadow
fleabane, forming mats of colorful bloom. Native.

Erigeron grandiflorus
(*E. simplex*) ASTERACEAE
onestem fleabane, largeflower fleabane
RM, alpine, subalpine, common,
L Spring–Summer, perennial, 2–8 in.

Diminutive plant with solitary flowers on
short stems. Dense tufts of shiny green
leaves are lanceolate to spatulate, 1–5 in. long,
hairy, reduced upward. Showy flowers 1.25
in. across, usually blue-purple to pink (rarely
white). Phyllaries are covered with abundant
purple hairs. Commonest blue-purple entire-leaved aster
above treeline in its range. Grows only in sunny meadows.
Native.

Erigeron leiomerus ASTERACEAE
rockslide fleabane
MR, SR, alpine, subalpine,
montane, common, L Spring–
Summer, perennial, 2–4 in.

Densely matted, caespitose herb. Blue-green
foliage is commonly folded inward, leaves
1–2 in. long, linear. Ray flowers usually
lavender-blue (rarely white). Purple phyllaries
are glabrous to slightly glandular. Involucre
composed of few, broad, dark bracts. Commonest mat-forming blue-flowered fleabane
on sunny RM tundra, especially screes. Native.

Erigeron pinnatisectus
(*E. compositus* var. *pinnatisectus*) ASTERACEAE
featherleaf fleabane
SR, alpine, subalpine, montane, common,
L Spring–Summer, perennial, 2–7 in.

Clump-forming, perennial herb. Common
on tundra. The only fleabane with fern-like
pinnatifid leaves; the other cutleaf daisies
are trifid. Basal foliage is dark blue-green,
mainly glabrous on the upper and sometimes
sparsely hirsute underneath. Ray flowers are
usually a rich blue-purple. Phyllaries are minutely glandular. Sun. Native.

numerous petals, composite, radial

Erigeron rydbergii ASTERACEAE
Rydberg's fleabane
MR, alpine, subalpine, locally abundant,
Spring–E Summer, perennial, 3–7 in.
Compact, tufted clump-former, with hairy
oblanceolate, persistent foliage and sparse
linear stem leaves. Vivid purple ray flowers.
Plants grow in sunny, open subalpine and
alpine slopes, occasionally at lower altitudes
in forest openings; usually in stony ground
and non-calcareous soils. Named for Per
Axel Rydberg (1860–1931), Swedish-born botanist who
authored several pioneer floras of this region. Native.

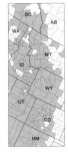

Erigeron speciosus ASTERACEAE
Aspen fleabane, showy fleabane
RM, alpine, subalpine, montane,
grasslands, common, L Spring–Summer,
perennial, 8–18 in.
Herb. Stems clustered. Leaves basal and
cauline, oblong to spoon-shaped, openly
spaced along the stem, stalks smooth. Stem
leaves sessile. Inflorescence a corymb of
1–13 colorful daisy-like flowers: blue, lavender (rarely white) rays in multiple planes.
Fruit an achene. Widespread, showy "Aspen
daisy" of high-elevation meadows and open
forest. Native.

Erigeron subtrinervis ASTERACEAE
threenerve fleabane, hairy showy daisy
RM, alpine, subalpine, montane,
foothills, common, L Spring–Summer,
perennial, 8–28 in.
Rhizomatous mats with leafy stems. Basal
foliage is oblanceolate and usually senesces
at flowering. Ray flowers are numerous,
nearly filiform, lavender-pink (rarely white),
with yellow disc. Inflorescence a corymbiform array of up to 9 flowerheads. Common
along sunny roadsides and disturbed areas,
often in drier habitats than the similar *E.
speciosus*. Native.

Erigeron tweedyi ASTERACEAE
Tweedy's fleabane
MR, alpine, subalpine, montane, foothills,
sagebrush steppe, common,
L Spring–Summer, perennial, 4–12 in.

Herb with erect to ascending stems; from
taproot. Stems with dense, stiff, appressed
hairs. Leaves basal and along stem, spatulate
to elliptic, margins entire and surfaces with
gray-white hairs. Stem leaves reduce upward.
Ray flowers 20–50, 0.2–0.4 in. long, blue or
purple (sometimes white). Phyllaries are in 3 or 4 series,
hairy and sparsely glandular. Grows on sunny dry slopes,
rock outcrops, screes, open meadows, in a wide variety of
soil types. Native.

Erigeron ursinus ASTERACEAE
Bear River fleabane
MR, SR, alpine, subalpine,
montane, common, L Spring–
Summer, perennial, 3–8 in.

Shiny, rhizomatous mats with dark green
leaves and lavender daisies in summer. This
will form large, very loose colonies. Phyllaries are in 4 rows, often purple with distinctly
reflexed tips. Named for the Bear River canyon in the Uinta mountains, where it was first
discovered on a high ridge. Common on high scree slopes,
also in high meadows, forest openings in sun to part
shade. Native.

Erigeron vetensis ASTERACEAE
early bluetop fleabane
SR, foothills, sagebrush steppe,
intermountain parks, grasslands, common,
Spring–Summer, perennial, 3–10 in.

Small loose cushions from a branched caudex that often retains some dead leaves. Basal
leaves linear and cupping inward, persistent
through flowering; stem leaves are linear and
smaller. Flowerheads are singular on smooth
or slightly hirsute stems. Phyllaries have a
green to white midrib. Found on sunny, rocky
slopes from the lower foothills to sparse intermountain
meadows, and common on the steppe. Native.

numerous petals, composite, radial

Herrickia glauca
(Eurybia glauca) ASTERACEAE
gray aster
MR, SR, alpine, subalpine, montane, foothills, common, L Summer–Fall, perennial, 8–27 in.

Herbaceous plant from rhizomes. Stems glabrous and occasionally branched. Leaves alternate, finely serrated, lanceolate to oblong, up to 4.5 in. long and gray-blue-green in color. Flowers have 10–15 lavender ray florets, center of 12–32 yellow (to red and purple) disc florets; each plant can produce over 100 flowers, in a loose corymbiform array. Phyllaries in rows of 4 or 5 and overlap close to the flower; inner are pointed, outer are rounded; maroon-edged. Found on rocky and sandy soils, slopes, woodland edges, and openings. Native.

Lactuca tatarica
(Mulgedium oblongifolium)
ASTERACEAE
blue lettuce
RM, montane, foothills, sagebrush steppe, intermountain parks, grasslands, common, Summer–Fall, perennial/biennial, 10–40 in.

Stems erect, branched especially near upper inflorescence; often reddish green with milky sap. Leaves alternate, thin, smooth, with shallow and irregular pointed lobes. The striking blue flowers have ray flowers only, no disc; in open panicles of up to 20 blooms. Sunny meadows, roadsides, disturbed sites; can make mats of glaucous foliage in damp swales. Native.

Machaeranthera canescens
(Dieteria canescens) ASTERACEAE
hoary tansyaster
RM, montane, foothills, pinyon-juniper, sagebrush steppe, intermountain parks, grasslands, common, L Summer–Fall, biennial, 1–3 ft.

Biennial or annual herb rising from a taproot. Stem leaves and branches are canescent. Often forms prickly, symmetrical mounds of lavender flowers in fall at lower elevations. Flowerheads, with around 20 ray flowers, are lavender-blue (occasionally white). Involucre bracts are distinctly spine-tipped. Extremely common, especially in sunny grasslands or disturbed habitats. Native.

Machaeranthera pattersonii

(*Aster pattersonii*) ASTERACEAE

Patterson's tansyaster

SR, alpine, subalpine, uncommon,
Summer, perennial, 3–12 in.

Perennial herb, forming compact mounds
of lax rosettes with deeply lobed green leaves
2–4 in. long. Flowers are large, 3 in. across,
and nearly stemless. Very local, showy miniature of a few high peaks in the Colorado
Front Range. This has been confused, and
even lumped, with the much larger *Dieteria
bigelovii*, which is often branched and is usually monocarpic. Long-lived. Sun. Native.

Machaeranthera tanacetifolia

(*Aster tanacetifolius*) ASTERACEAE

tansyleaf tansyaster, Tahoka daisy

RM, sagebrush steppe, grasslands,
common, Summer–Fall, annual, 1–3 ft.

Very dissected fern-like gray-green foliage
and many branched stems with single flowers at the apex, forming twiggy mounds of
bright blooms in wet years. Purple flowers
with a yellow center. Plants are common along
sunny roadsides and in disturbed sites. One
of the few showy annuals on the Great Plains.
Native.

Onoropordum acanthium ASTERACEAE

Scotch cottonthistle

RM, throughout, common,
Summer, biennial, to 10 ft.

Erect branching stems from taproot, covered
in flat, soft hairs and spiny wings. Leaves
woolly, gray-green, toothed to pinnately lobed,
with spines on edges; basal usually gone by
flowering; stem leaves alternate, elliptic, and

smaller toward top, up to 2 ft. Flowers usually
1–3, with many purple discs but lacking rays,
spherical to 2 in., surrounded by spiny bracts.
Found in disturbed areas up to 10,000 ft. This
Eurasian species is widespread in all but the
alpine zone and can form impenetrable clusters. Introduced and invasive.

Saussurea nuda ASTERACEAE
nutty saw-wort
NR, alpine, rare, Summer, perennial, 2–7 in.
Compact herb from woody stem base;
stems erect, hairy. Leaves in a rosette-like
arrangement; stem leaves alternate, bright
blue-green, elliptic to ovate with almost entire, wavy or toothed margins, and almost
prickly; becoming unstalked upward. Flowerheads showy, in clusters of 3–20 or more,
each with numerous pale purple ray flowers.
Grows in scree, talus, and dry meadows at high elevations.
Species is restricted northward in our region. Native.

Saussurea weberi ASTERACEAE
Weber's saw-wort
MR, SR, alpine, endemic, infrequent,
Summer, perennial, 2–8 in.
Herb. Leaves alternate, elliptic to ovate, to
3 in.; stalked below and unstalked above.
Heads in clusters of 1–15, with purple disc
flowers; ray flowers absent. Purplish involucre covered in long white hairs. Grows in
gravelly soil and scree slopes and substrate
derived from Manitou Dolomite and Leadville Limestone; in meadows of the Mos-
quito and Collegiate ranges of CO; a few
disjunct populations northward. Closely related *S. nuda*
has foliage less gray, flowers brighter purple. The genus is
primarily distributed in the Himalaya. Native.

Symphyotrichum ascendens
(*Aster ascendens*) ASTERACEAE
western aster
RM, throughout, common, Summer–
Fall, perennial, 18–26 in.
Short-lived herb, often occurs in large
patches. Green leaves alternate, variable in
length with appressed hairs, clasping stem
with winged sheath; lower leaves often senesce at flowering. Flowers many; phyllaries are alternately stacked like roof tiles with
a distinctive pointed tip and white margins,
lowest row distinctly rounded and not pointed. Flowers
purple to pink and sometimes white. Sunny sage meadows, forest openings, disturbed sites, grasslands where
moisture is adequate; all life zones except alpine and
wetlands. Native.

Symphyotrichum foliaceum
(*Aster foliaceus*) ASTERACEAE
alpine leafybract aster
RM, throughout, locally abundant,
Summer, perennial, to 1 ft.

Stems often hairy and dark reddish to
brown. Leaves are often glabrous, sometimes
sparsely hairy; individual leaves are almost
spoon-shaped and very narrow at the attachment to the stem. Flowers vary—blue, lavender, pink, or white. The broad almost leaf-like
phyllaries are the distinguishing characteristic. Found in
woodland openings, riparian areas, and moist meadows
in sun or light shade. Native.

Symphyotrichum laeve
(*Aster laevis*) ASTERACEAE
smooth blue aster
RM, throughout, common, Summer–
Fall, perennial, 8–20 in.

Herb with upright stems that are branched
above. Leaves to 6 in. long, oblong to lanceolate, entire to slightly serrate and glabrous. Inflorescence a multi-flowered, round
to flat-topped panicle. Ray flowers 15–30
and blue to purple. Phyllaries in 4–6 series,
diamond-shaped and distinctly dark green at
ends. Plants have a wide distribution throughout North
America and are found in a range of elevations in sunny
meadows, forest openings, and near streams. Native.

Symphyotrichum spathulatum
(*Aster spathulatus*) ASTERACEAE
western mountain aster
RM, subalpine, montane, intermountain
parks, grasslands, common,
Summer–Fall, perennial, 6–30 in.

Herb with ascending to erect stems that are
branched above; rhizomatous. Leaves to 6 in.,
linear to elliptic and sparsely pubescent to glabrous. Basal leaves soon deciduous. Phyllaries
variable but typically long; green at rounded
tips and white in middle and toward base.
Flowers few per stem in open inflorescence. 15–50 palest
lavender (apparently white in very bright light) to purple or
blue ray flowers surround yellow disc flowers. Plants variable throughout range; hybridization occurs. Sunny areas,
mesic to moist meadows, open forests. Native.

Townsendia montana
(*T. alpigena*) ASTERACEAE
Wyoming Townsend daisy

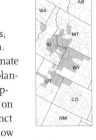

NR, MR, alpine, subalpine, grasslands, infrequent, Summer, perennial, 1–2 in. Herb with erect stems. Basal and alternate stem leaves dark green, spatulate to oblanceolate, and covered with short, stiff, appressed hairs or smooth. Flowerheads on stalks or sessile; ray flowers are a distinct dark violet and surround orangish yellow disc flowers. Involucre bracts oblanceolate with obtuse to acute tips. Grows in meadows, sagebrush, dry forests, and woodlands, often on calcareous substrates. Native.

Townsendia parryi ASTERACEAE
Parry's Townsend daisy

NR, MR, alpine, subalpine, montane, foothills, uncommon, L Spring–Summer, perennial, 1–2 in. Herb with 1 to several reclining to erect stems. Basal and alternate leaves spatulate, tufted, reducing upward, persistent; surfaces smooth or with short, stiff, appressed hairs; first-year rosette has fine hairs. Flowerheads comparatively enormous, with purplish to blue (rarely white or pink) ray flowers. Involucre bracts lanceolate, lightly hairy, and with fringed margins. Grows on dry rocky or grassy slopes and meadows at high elevations. A very showy and common plant in its range. Monocarpic. Native.

Townsendia rothrockii
ASTERACEAE
Rothrock's Townsend daisy

SR, alpine, subalpine, montane, intermountain parks, endemic, rare, Summer, perennial, 1–2 in. Herb with erect stems from blue-green rosettes. Basal and alternate stem leaves spatulate, fleshy; surfaces smooth or lightly covered in short, stiff, appressed hairs. Flowerheads sessile or on short stalks; ray flowers pale lavender (never white). Involucre bracts often reddish purple and anthocyanic, ovate to obovate, with obtuse to acute tips. Grows in dry, open places, rocky soil, especially in alpine fellfields. Found near alpine snowfields in central CO and on rocky subalpine ledges in western CO. Native.

Liatris punctata ASTERACEAE
dotted blazingstar, dotted gayfeather

RM, foothills, sagebrush steppe, grasslands, common, Summer–Fall, perennial, 8–20 in. Herb. Stems upright, in clusters from vertical tuberous root. Leaves densely clothing stem on all sides, alternate, linear, edges with hairs; 2–6 in. long, shorter on upper stem. Flowers in a fluffy spike; 4–6 disc flowers emerging from a cylindrical involucre of pointed phyllaries (no ray florets). Corollas with 5 recurved lobes, to 0.4 in. across. Fruit a fluffy achene, dispersing seeds slowly over winter. Grows on sunny hillsides, meadows, and forest openings. Attractive to a range of pollinators. Native.

numerous petals, elongated clusters, radial

230

0 petals, elongated clusters, bilateral

0 petals, elongated clusters, radial

Plantago patagonica
PLANTAGINACEAE
woolly plantain
RM, foothills, intermountain parks,
grasslands, common, Spring–
Summer, annual, 2–12 in.
Herbaceous annual from a taproot. Herbage
white-woolly. Stems erect, several, simple.
Leaves 0.1–5 in. long, oblanceolate to linear,
in often upright basal rosette. Inflorescence
topped with dense, woolly flower spike,
0.6–4 in. long; flowers white, bracts firm and linear. Calyx
and corolla 4-lobed. Stamens 4. Fruit a capsule. Occurs in
dry openings, canyons at lower elevations. Can become
weedy in certain areas. Native.

Thalictrum dasycarpum
(*T. hypoglaucum*) RANUNCULACEAE
purple meadow-rue
RM, montane, foothills, grasslands,
uncommon, L Spring–Fall, perennial, 2–5 ft.
Herbaceous stems erect, stout. Leaves basal
and alternate; basal and lower stem leaves
stalked. Upper stem leaves sessile or nearly
so. All leaves 3–5 times ternately compound.
Leaflets dark to bright green or brownish,
leathery, rounded, 2- or 3-lobed, prominent
veins underneath; margins entire, often rolled under.
Many-flowered panicles, no obvious petals, dioecious,
male/female flowers on separate plants. Sepals whitish.
Filaments white to purplish. Fruit numerous achenes.
Found in wet meadows, thickets, ditches,
disturbed areas, and streambanks. Native.

Petrophytum caespitosum
ROSACEAE
mat rockspirea
MR, SR, alpine, subalpine, montane,
sagebrush steppe, common,
Summer, perennial, 3–8 in.
Extremely compact, mound-forming shrub
restricted largely to vertical limestone cliffs.
The blue-green rosettes, always an inch or
more across, distinguish this from the tiny, blue-green of
its cousin, *Kelseya uniflora*, with which it is often found.
The flowers occur in late summer, with showy, exserted
stamens. Native.

Sanguisorba canadensis
(*S. sitchensis*) ROSACEAE
Canadian burnet
NR, montane, foothills, locally
abundant, L Spring–E Summer,
annual/perennial, 10–40 in.
Herbaceous plant with ascending stems;
short-lived, or several seasons. Leaves are
oblong-ovate to lance-oblong, 1–5 in. long, divided pinnately; leaflets 9–17, sessile, toothed
and oval. Inflorescence a long round spike
of 250–500 or more greenish white flowers, lacking petals. Found in bogs, streamsides, seeps, and wet meadows.
Similar to *S. annua*, which has lobed leaflets. Native.

Trautvetteria caroliniensis
RANUNCULACEAE
Carolina bugbane
RM, subalpine, montane, infrequent,
Summer, perennial, 15–40 in.
Few tall stems from spreading rhizomes.
Leaves basal, 5–7 palmate lobes, coarsely
toothed; few alternate on stems. Flower clus-
ters flat-topped with small hooked hairs; con-
spicuous cluster of showy white stamens.
Shaded forests. Odd distribution: Appala-
chian mountains; widely scattered in MR and
SR; abundant in NR and Pacific NW; also in Japan. Native.

Amerorchis rotundifolia
(*Galearis rotundifolia*) ORCHIDACEAE
roundleaf orchid
NR, MR, montane, wetlands, uncommon,
Summer, perennial, 12–16 in.
Plants produce only 1 leaf per flowering stem.
Leaves are oblong blades to 5 in. long. Plants
produce leaves every year but not flowers.
Inflorescence can have up to 15 flowers per
stem. Flowers are showy but quite small; all
face the same direction on raceme. A pair of
sepals form a hood over the functional flower
parts; the lower labellum is lobed, often spotted pink to magenta. Uncommon in the MR,
becoming more common to the north; the majority of the
plant's distribution is in Canada. Grows in light shade in
damp woodlands, bogs, and fens. Native.

Goodyera oblongifolia
(*G. decipiens*) ORCHIDACEAE
western rattlesnake plantain
RM, subalpine, montane, foothills,
common, locally abundant,
Summer–Fall, perennial, 6–16 in.

Herb with dark green basal leaves, 1–4 in.
long, narrowly elliptic to oval, tip pointed,
margins entire, usually with white midrib
and sometimes white variegation. Inflorescence a terminal spike, 2–5.5 in. long,
spiraled or 1-sided. Flowers white to greenish, sessile,
tubular-shaped, resupinate. Upper petals and sepals form
a hood over lower. Fruit a capsule. Moist or dry coniferous
or mixed woods. Confined to higher elevations in the SR,
in spruce-fir forests. Native.

Platanthera dilatata
(*Habenaria dilatata*) ORCHIDACEAE
scentbottle
RM, throughout, common, Summer–
Fall, perennial, 6–36 in.

Herbaceous from few fibrous roots. Stem
erect, spindle-shaped. Leaves few to several,
ascending to arching, alternate, broadly linear, rounded tip, 4–12 in., distally reduced to
bracts. Inflorescence a terminal spike, 5–30
white flowers, 0.5 in., unstalked, fragrant. Upper sepal and
upper 2 petals form a hood. 2 lateral sepals extend horizontally, reflexed or not. Lip terminates in a spur. Fruit a
capsule. Moist meadows and open, riparian areas, in all
life zones except alpine and wetlands. Part
shade to sun. Native.

Spiranthes romanzoffiana
ORCHIDACEAE
hooded lady's tresses
RM, subalpine, montane, foothills, locally
abundant, Summer–Fall, perennial, 3–22 in.

Herbaceous perennial from long, fleshy, tuberous roots. Basal leaves linear to oblanceolate, 2–8 in. long, less than 0.5 in. wide.
Stem leaves few, alternate, quickly reduced
to short, sheathing bracts above. Inflorescence a dense cylindrical spike. Flowers white to cream, usually in 3 spiraling vertical rows. Upper sepal and petals form a hood over
the protruding lip. Fruit a capsule. Wet meadows, fens.
Infrequent in the NR above 55 degrees north and frequent
below. Native.

Polygala alba POLYGALACEAE
white milkwort
RM, grasslands, locally abundant,
L Spring–Summer, perennial, 7–16 in.

Upright herb. Leaves linear above and narrowly oblanceolate below, 1.5 in., alternate along stem, glabrous. Inflorescence a slender spike of 0.3-in. zygomorphic flowers with characteristic fringed beard of genus. Flowers white with green centers, 5 sepals, 2 lateral sepals larger and petal-like, 3 rounded petals united into a tube that is split on back and fused with 8 stamens. Widespread on the Great Plains, and rare westward in rocky grassland at lower elevations. Dry slopes, rocky outcrops and ledges. Native.

Sagittaria cuneata
(*S. arifolia*) ALISMATACEAE
arumleaf arrowhead
RM, subalpine, montane, foothills, sagebrush steppe, grasslands, wetlands, common,
L Spring–Summer, perennial, 6–20 in.

Aquatic or semi-aquatic, rhizomatous, scapose herb. Leaves basal, 3–18 in.; emersed are sagittate with entire margins; floating or submerged, linear; all with smooth surfaces. Inflorescence a bracteate raceme of 2–10 white, 3-merous flowers in whorls of 3. Male flowers with bright yellow stamens; female flowers with green, globose clusters of pistils. Grows on shorelines and along slow-moving streams. Native.

Maianthemum racemosum
ssp. *amplexicaule*
(*Smilacina racemosa*) ASPARAGACEAE
feathery false lily-of-the-valley, false Solomon's seal
RM, subalpine, montane, foothills, common, locally abundant, Spring–Fall, perennial, 12–40 in.

Rhizomatous herb with upright to arching stems. 5–12 glossy alternate stem leaves, elliptic to egg-shaped, short-stalked or unstalked, frequently clasping, 2–8 in. long, hairy below, margins entire, parallel venation. Inflorescence a terminal branched panicle 2–4.5 in. long of numerous white flowers; 6 similar but distinct tepals; stamens 6. Berries mottled green and red when immature, red when mature. Moist to mesic forests, streambanks, meadows, clearings, avalanche slopes. Native.

Maianthemum stellatum
(*Smilacina stellata*) ASPARAGACEAE
starry false lily-of-the-valley
RM, subalpine, montane, foothills, grasslands, common, locally abundant, Spring, perennial, 8–24 in.

Rhizomatous herb with stems erect to arching, straight to zigzag. Leaves 5–11, narrowly oval, pointed, flat to folded, 2–6 in. long, sessile or clasping, margins entire, prominent parallel venation. Inflorescence a sparsely flowered terminal raceme, 0.8–2.8 in. long, rachis zigzag or straight. Flowers creamy white, star-shaped, 6 similar but distinct tepals, 6 stamens. Berries yellow-green with purple longitudinal stripes, maturing dark blue to reddish black. Moist to mesic, sometimes dry, forests, streambanks, meadows, clearings. Native.

Yucca baccata
(*Y. vespertina*) ASPARAGACEAE
banana yucca
SR, foothills, pinyon-juniper, grasslands, common, locally abundant, Spring–Summer, perennial, 4–6 ft.

Large rosette-forming plants are typically stemless and evergreen. Thick, rigid 1- to 2-ft. leaves are bluish green with brown margins, sharp, pointed tips. Edges of leaves are fibrous and up-curled. Cream-colored 6-petaled flowers are nodding, up to 4 in. long, in panicles on a woody stalk that rarely extends past the leaf tips. Fruit is green, indehiscent, and very fleshy. Sun; coniferous forests, dry ridges and slopes, canyon rims. Native.

Yucca glauca
(*Y. angustifolia*) ASPARAGACEAE
soapweed yucca
RM, montane, foothills, grasslands, common, locally abundant, Spring–Summer, perennial, 16–24 in.

Typically stemless rosette-forming semi-woody shrub, slowly expanding by rhizomes. Leaves glabrous, evergreen, stiff, sharp-tipped; narrowly linear, 0.25–0.5 in. wide by up to 18 in. long; margins with white, curly spreading fibers. 15–50 bell-shaped greenish white to cream flowers, some blushed burgundy, nodding from a raceme. Fruit a non-constricted capsule, 6 sides, numerous flat, dark seeds. Dry slopes, sandy substrates, disturbed areas. Native.

Yucca harrimaniae ASPARAGACEAE
dollhouse yucca
MR, SR, foothills, pinyon-juniper,
sagebrush steppe, grasslands, common,
Spring–Summer, perennial, 6–24 in.
Small rosette-forming plants, stemless and
evergreen, may form dense or open colonies.
Linear leaves are rigid and thin but flexible, green with entire margins and white to
brown, curly filaments. Pendent, bell-shaped
flowers, with 3 purple-tinged cream petals
and 3 white or green sepals, arise on a woody stalk. De-
hiscent fruit is dry and deeply constricted toward the center. Sun; plateaus, dry rocky slopes, sandy flats, canyon
shelves. Native.

Veratrum californicum
(V. tenuipetalum) MELANTHIACEAE
California false hellebore, corn lily
RM, subalpine, montane, intermountain
parks, common, locally abundant,
Summer, perennial, 3–6 ft.
Robust stems from spreading black rhizomes.
Leaves 8–15 in. long, oval, heavily pleated; base
clasping stem and holding leaf upward. Flowers in 1.5- to 2.5-ft.-tall branched panicles above
leaves; 1-in. starry blooms have 6 creamy to
greenish petals, green at base; maturing as brown capsules
to 1.25 in. long; flat winged seeds. Sunny damp meadows,
streamsides, forest openings; often in impressive colonies;
flowering only with plentiful moisture. Native.

Xerophyllum tenax MELANTHIACEAE
common beargrass, squaw grass
NR, MR, subalpine, montane, common,
Spring–E Summer, perennial, 40–70 in.
Herbaceous perennial from a stout, somewhat
woody rhizome. Stems erect. Basal leaves numerous, in clumps, 8–26 in. long by 0.07–0.15
in. wide, rigid, wiry, grass-like. Stem leaves
alternate, otherwise similar. Leaf margins
rough and harsh, reduced upward becoming
bract-like. Inflorescence a terminal raceme
up to 16 in. long, taller than leaves, linear-oblong, emerging bulbous and nippled, then elongates. Flowers many,
stalked, white to cream, saucer-shaped, fragrant. Tepals 6,
similar but distinct. Fruit is a capsule. Open woods, rocky
slopes, clearings. Native.

Zigadenus elegans
(*Anticlea elegans*) MELANTHIACEAE
mountain death camas
RM, alpine, subalpine, montane,
grasslands, common, locally abundant,
Summer, perennial, 8–30 in.
Flowering stems from non-clumping bulbs.
Leaves 2–10 in. long, grass-like, keeled, light
waxy coating; smaller, alternate along stem.
Flower pedicels 0.5–1 in. long; 1-in. creamy
flowers foul-smelling, in upright or nodding
spikes to 6 in. long with short lower branches possible; 6
star-like tepals, green nectaries at base; 3-chambered seed
capsule egg-shaped with pointed tips on spreading pedicels. Sun; high damp meadows, lakeshores, rocky slopes,
forest openings. All parts extremely toxic!
Native.

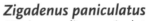

Zigadenus paniculatus
(*Toxicoscordion paniculatum*)
MELANTHIACEAE
foothill death camas
RM, foothills, sagebrush steppe,
grasslands, uncommon, Spring–
E Summer, perennial, 1–2 ft.
Flowering stems from non-clumping bulbs.
Leaves 6–14 in. long, grass-like, keeled; a
few smaller, alternate along stem. Flowers 0.5 in. wide
in panicles on a narrow terminal raceme; those on side
branches often staminate only; 6 star-like tepals, creamy,
with yellow-green nectary at base of each; mature capsule
3-chambered, upright in narrow spike. Sun;
meadows, rocky slopes, forest openings. All
parts extremely toxic! Native.

Allium brandegeei
(*A. tribracteatum* var. *diehlii*)
AMARYLLIDACEAE
Brandegee's onion
MR, SR, montane, sagebrush
steppe, grasslands, common,
Spring, perennial, to 4 in.
Bulb with 2 linear, grooved basal leaves
persisting through flowering. Flowering stem is half the
height of leaves and topped with a rounded umbel of up to
25 flowers. Flowers bell-shaped, white to light pink with
green or purplish midveins; petal-like tepals up to 0.3 in.
long and stamens not protruding beyond tepals. Cliffs and
outcrops, dry, sandy soil. Native.

Allium fibrillum AMARYLLIDACEAE
Cuddy Mountain onion, Blue Mountain onion, fringed onion
NR, MR, alpine, subalpine, montane, locally abundant, L Spring–E Summer, perennial, 2–8 in.

Bulb with 2 flat or channeled linear leaves to 6 in. long, tip withering by flowering; basal sheaths not extending much beyond soil surface. Flowering stem solitary, upright, round or slightly flattened with rounded to half-spherical umbel of 10–20 flowers; each bell-shaped, white with green midveins; petal-like tepals to 0.4 in. long; stamens not protruding beyond tepals. Rocky soils, meadows, forests, moist grasslands. Flower scape height approximates the leaf height of the similar *A. brandegeei.*

Allium textile AMARYLLIDACEAE
wild onion
RM, subalpine, montane, pinyon-juniper, sagebrush steppe, common, Spring–Summer, perennial, 4–16 in.

Bulbs in clusters of 1–3. Leaves linear, flat, and persisting at flowering time, 4–16 in. long, and sheathed. Flowering stem solitary and upright with 15–30 flowers in a round cluster, white (rarely pink), with a purplish midrib running down the middle of every tepal. Bracts 3, each with a single vein. Found in sunny and sandy areas along roadsides, in prairies, pinyon-juniper communities, and deserts. Specific epithet is a reference to the mesh of fibrous tissue around the bulb. Native.

Eriogonum annuum POLYGONACEAE
annual wild buckwheat
MR, SR, foothills, sagebrush steppe, grasslands, common, Spring–Fall, annual, 4–40 in.

Stems 1 to several, sometimes branching. Leaves grayish, alternate, oblanceolate-oblong, 0.75–2 in., densely hairy. Basal leaves wither before flowering. 6-tepaled flowers in clusters, white to cream and sometimes pink-tinged; upper flowering branchlets elegantly arched and spreading upward. Grows in sunny areas, barrens, dry slopes, meadows, sand dunes, and roadsides. One of the only large annual eriogonums in the region. Prefers sandy soils. Native.

Eriogonum cernuum

POLYGONACEAE

nodding buckwheat

RM, montane, foothills, pinyon-juniper, sagebrush steppe, grasslands, common, Summer–Fall, annual, 2–24 in.

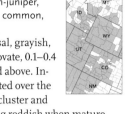

Stems branching. Leaves all basal, grayish, alternate, orbiculate to broadly ovate, 0.1–0.4 in., dense white hairs below and above. Inflorescences are evenly distributed over the plant. 6-petaled flowers form a cluster and are white to pink-tinged, turning reddish when mature. Grows in sunny areas, barrens, rock ledges, dry slopes, meadows, and sandy areas. One of the 2 most commonly encountered small eriogonums. Native.

Eriogonum coloradense

POLYGONACEAE

Colorado buckwheat

SR, alpine, subalpine, montane, sagebrush steppe, grasslands, endemic, uncommon, Summer–Fall, perennial, 1.2–2.4 in.

Densely matted perennial with numerous underground caudices. Leaves all basal, grayish, alternate, lanceolate to orbiculate, 0.4–2 in., dense white hairs above and below. Flowering stems are glabrous, scapose, bearing 3 or 4 involucres per head. 6-tepaled flowers in clusters, pink-tinged white. Grows in sunny areas, tundra, rock screes, rock ledges, barrens, dry slopes, and meadows. Has been documented on every type of soil texture, slope, and aspect. Native.

Eriogonum corymbosum

POLYGONACEAE

crispleaf buckwheat

MR, SR, montane, foothills, pinyon-juniper, sagebrush steppe, grasslands, common, Summer–Fall, perennial, 7–60 in.

Shrubby stems are woody and persistent, with intricately branched dome-like habit. Leaves are all on stems, not basal; grayish, alternate, lanceolate to orbiculate and spoon-shaped, 0.2–1.8 in., dense white hairs below and above. 6-tepaled flowers in clusters; white, cream, pink, or yellow. Grows in sunny areas, barrens, canyon rims and ledges, dry slopes, roadsides. Native.

Eriogonum exilifolium

POLYGONACEAE

dropleaf buckwheat

SR, montane, foothills, sagebrush steppe,
intermountain parks, grasslands, endemic,
uncommon, Summer, perennial, 1.2–4 in.

Stems mat-forming and spreading. Leaves
all basal, green to grayish, alternate, linear to linear-oblanceolate, 0.8–2.4 in., dense
white hairs below, not as hairy above. White
6-tepaled flowers in clusters. Grows in sunny
areas, rock ledges, barrens, dry slopes, and sage meadows.
Although an insignificant plant, blending into its native
habitat, it illustrates the remarkable diversity of the buckwheats in the varied environments of the West. Native.

Eriogonum heracleoides

POLYGONACEAE

parsnipflower buckwheat

RM, montane, foothills, sagebrush steppe,
intermountain parks, grasslands, common,
Summer–Fall, perennial, 3–24 in.

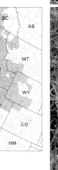

Stems mat-forming, upright, with bracts
midway. Leaves all basal, green to grayish,
linear-oblanceolate, 0.6–2 in., with dense
white hairs below. Umbels of 6-tepaled flowers in clusters, creamy white to pale yellow.
Grows in sunny areas, rock ledges, barrens, dry slopes,
and sage meadows. Sometimes possesses bract whorls
mid stem; these are diagnostic. Can resemble *E. umbellatum* var. *majus* but has longer, more linear basal leaves.
Largely found west of the Continental Divide
except in WY and MT. Native.

Eriogonum jamesii POLYGONACEAE

James' buckwheat

SR, montane, foothills, pinyon-juniper,
sagebrush steppe, intermountain
parks, grasslands, common,
Summer–Fall, perennial, 2–10 in.

Stems are mat-forming. Aerial flowering
stems erect, slender, arising directly from a
taproot. Leaves are all basal, green to grayish,
linear-oblanceolate, 0.6–2 in., and densely hairy on both
surfaces. 6-tepaled flowers in clusters, in a white, cream,
or pale pink umbel. Grows in sunny areas, rock ledges,
barrens, dry slopes, and sage meadows. Considered "life
medicines" by Native Americans and used ceremonially.
Native.

Eriogonum panguicense
(*E. pauciflorum* var. *panguicense*)
POLYGONACEAE
cushion buckwheat
SR, throughout, endemic, locally abundant,
L Spring–Summer, perennial, 1–8 in.
Slender, leafless red flowering stems
from a leafy cushion. Leaves are greenish,
linear-oblanceolate, 0.2–1.5 in., hairless
or hairy above, densely white-hairy below.
6-tepaled white flowers with conspicuously
purplish red anthers form dense pompom clusters. Grows
in sunny areas, rock ledges, scree, barrens, dry slopes, and
sage meadows, all life zones except wetlands. Endemic to
the high country of UT. Native.

Eriogonum pauciflorum
(*E. depauperatum*) POLYGONACEAE
fewflower buckwheat
NR, MR, sagebrush steppe,
grasslands, common, L Spring–
Summer, perennial, 8–12 in.
Loose mat-forming plant. Persistent, spreading stems have leafy bases. Foliage is mostly
basal and densely tomentose and silver,
oblanceolate to elliptic, 0.5–1.5 in. long.
Flowers are on a capitate head and can range
from white to rose-pink, tepals to 0.1 in. long, hairy (rarely
glabrous). Found on clay to gravelly flats, washes, and
slopes in grassland and sagebrush communities, juniper
woodlands. Native.

Eriogonum soliceps POLYGONACEAE
Railroad Canyon wild buckwheat
MR, montane, sagebrush steppe, endemic,
rare, Summer, perennial, 0.5–2.5 in.
Mat-forming herb. Leaves all basal, oblanceolate, covered in hairs. Flowers in dense
cluster, white with greenish midribs that
mature to pinkish red. Most closely related
to *E. mancum*, from which it differs in having only 1 involucre per stem. Only a few
populations of this species exist. Found on
both calcareous and non-calcareous soils in 4 counties in
southwestern MT and adjacent ID. First described in 2004.
Native.

Eriogonum tumulosum

POLYGONACEAE
woodside buckwheat
SR, foothills, pinyon-juniper, sagebrush
steppe, intermountain parks, grasslands,
endemic, locally abundant, L Spring–
Summer, perennial, 1–2 in.
Stems form a dense, tight cushion. Leaves
green, oblanceolate to elliptic, 0.1–0.3 in.,
woolly, with thickened margins. 6-tepaled
flowers form dense pompoms that are white
to rose in color, fading to dark brown. Grows in sunny
areas, rock ledges, scree, barrens, dry slopes, and sage
meadows. Rare and distinctive, with its very tight green
cushions. It is larger than *E. acaule* and has more linear
and green leaves than *E. shockleyi*. Native.

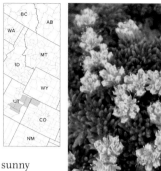

Galium trifidum

(*G. brandegeei*) RUBIACEAE
threepetal bedstraw, small bedstraw
RM, subalpine, montane, foothills, common,
Spring–Summer, perennial, 3–24 in.
Herbaceous, rhizomatous plant with many
weak, branching stems that sprawl or scram-
ble on other plants. Leaves in whorls of 4
(rarely 5 or 6) along stem, each leaflet to 0.75
in. long, blades linear-oblanceolate to narrowly
elliptic, tips rounded, surfaces covered in sandpaper-like
hairs. Many axillary or terminal clusters of 1–3 minute
white flowers, each with 3 petals. Fruit a pair of smooth,
round nutlets somewhat larger than flowers. Grows in
moist forests, along shady streams and lakes,
and in wet meadows. Circumboreal. Native.

Triantha glutinosa

(*Tofieldia glutinosa*) TOFIELDIACEAE
sticky false asphodel
NR, alpine, subalpine, montane, common,
L Spring–Summer, perennial, 2–18 in.
Herbaceous stems upright, unbranched,
and densely glandular at the top. Most of the
leaves are basal, thin, 2–7 in. long, erect, and
smooth; occasional stem leaves are alternate
up the stem and smaller. Flowers buds are tinged pink,
becoming white when blooming; 1–3 flowers at each node
of the spike-like raceme, with 3–30 flowers in each cluster.
Found in sunny and wet areas, fens, seeps, and meadows.
Native.

Trillium ovatum MELANTHIACEAE
Pacific trillium, western wakerobin
RM, subalpine, montane, foothills,
common, locally abundant, Spring–
Summer, perennial, 4–12 in.

Stems erect, unbranched, round, smooth,
from somewhat rhizomatous bulbs. 3
whorled leaves 2–6 in., sessile to stalked,
veined, egg-shaped, pointed tip. Inflorescence solitary terminal flower, 3 spreading to recurved petals, on upright-nodding
stalk. Green sepals. Petals white, margins flat to wavy, fading to pink, purple/red with age. Stamens 6, shorter than
petals. Fruit a green to yellowish red berry-like capsule.
Occurs in open to dense moist forests, often vernally moist
to boggy. Several disjunct populations in
WY, CO. Native.

Asparagus officinalis
ASPARAGACEAE
   garden asparagus
   RM, montane, foothills, pinyon-
   juniper, sagebrush steppe, grasslands,
   common, Summer, perennial, to 6 ft.
Herbaceous plant with finely dissected
branches. Stems green and photosynthetic.
Form familiar new shoots in spring, become
feathery alternately branched plumes with tiny leaves. Inflorescence is an axillary raceme, 1- to 3-flowered. Many
tiny cream flowers nod singly on upper stems. Seldom
in wild habitats; common in farm country along ditches,
rural roadsides, old homesites. Dioecious,
females produce small red berries in late
summer. Introduced.

Leucocrinum montanum
ASPARAGACEAE
   common starlily
   RM, foothills, pinyon-juniper, sagebrush
   steppe, intermountain parks, grasslands,
   common, Spring, perennial, 2–6 in.
Striking monocot with intensely fragrant,
waxy flowers framed by glaucous, narrow
strap–shaped, channeled leaves. Leaves go dormant by
early summer. Surprisingly common in varying habitats
from the Great Plains to sunny canyons in the foothills
and locally across the intermountain region. A favorite
early spring wildflower wherever it grows. Native.

Sisyrinchium septentrionale

IRIDACEAE

northern blue-eyed grass

NR, montane, sagebrush steppe,
intermountain parks, grasslands, infrequent,
L Spring–Summer, perennial, 7–12 in.

Tufted, slender, and glabrous herb with several simple, flat, 2-winged stems. Leaves mostly basal, narrowly linear, sheathing and with entire margins. Inflorescence of 1–5 flowers with white, pale blue, or light bluish violet tepals with yellow bases, rounded tips, and short bristles. Anthers yellow. Flowers subtended by bracts, the outer longer than the inner. Grows in dry to mesic meadows and along streams. Red-listed in BC and rare in MT. Native.

Calochortus apiculatus LILIACEAE

pointedtip mariposa lily

NR, montane, foothills, intermountain
parks, common, L Spring–
Summer, perennial, 4–16 in.

Stems usually not branching, straight, scape-like, stout. Flower stems wiry. Single linear leaf, basal, usually shorter than stem, parallel venation, resembling a small tulip leaf, from deeply buried bulb. Inflorescence consists of 1 to several cream/white blooms. 3 large petals, short hairs from mid-petal inward, brushed golden, a single dark spot (nectary) a short distance from the base; otherwise not ornately patterned as some species; 3 smaller pointed sepals. Found on dry, rocky slopes in coniferous/mixed woodlands, pine parklands, meadows. Native.

Calochortus eurycarpus LILIACEAE

white mariposa lily

NR, MR, montane, foothills, common,
L Spring–Summer, perennial, to 18 in.

Bulb-forming perennial with straight stems. Flower stems wiry. Single linear leaf, parallel venation, resembling a small tulip leaf, from deeply buried bulb. Blooms 1 to several, cream/white (sometimes pink). 3 large petals with rounded to crescent-shaped magenta-wine blotch; golden crescent nectary with long filaments near base; reverse has green central blotch. 3 narrow pointed greenish white sepals. Large 3-chambered seed capsule conspicuous late in season. Open coniferous forests among grasses. Native.

Calochortus gunnisonii LILIACEAE

Gunnison's mariposa lily
MR, SR, montane, foothills,
grasslands, common, L Spring–
Summer, perennial, to 14 in.
Sturdy slender stem has 1 or 2 slender leaves;
narrow linear basal leaves wither early. 1–3
flowers white (sometimes pink). Petals ornately marked, burgundy ring where golden
green hairs begin; crescent-shaped nectaries
below, burgundy blotches near base. Vari-
able. Sepals narrow, shorter than petals, greenish exterior.
Anthers pink or lavender. Found in undisturbed areas,
pine parklands, montane meadows. Native.

Calochortus nuttallii LILIACEAE

Sego lily
MR, SR, foothills, sagebrush steppe,
intermountain parks, grasslands, common,
Spring–Summer, perennial, to 24 in.
Stems mostly leafless. Narrow grass-like
basal leaves. 1–3 flowers white or pink. Sepals shorter than petals; both may have
rust/wine crescents or spots, golden center,
fringed nectaries. Intricate patterns vary:
highly ornamented specimens are reminiscent of gazing through a kaleidoscope.
Found in open grassland, forest openings, dry slopes.
Small edible bulbs helped avert starvation in desperate
times. Native.

Clintonia uniflora
(*Smilacina borealis* var. *uniflora*)
LILIACEAE

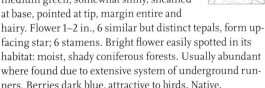

bride's bonnet
NR, MR, subalpine, montane, common,
L Spring–Fall, perennial, 6–10 in.
Rhizomatous, groundcover-like. Flower
stem erect, unbranched, hairy; 1 small bract
and 1 (rarely 2) blooms. Rosette of 2 or 3
leaves, oblong, 3–8 in. long by 1–2 in. wide,
medium green, somewhat shiny, sheathed
at base, pointed at tip, margin entire and
hairy. Flower 1–2 in., 6 similar but distinct tepals, form upfacing star; 6 stamens. Bright flower easily spotted in its
habitat: moist, shady coniferous forests. Usually abundant
where found due to extensive system of underground runners. Berries dark blue, attractive to birds. Native.

Lloydia serotina
(*Gagea serotina*) LILIACEAE
common alplily
RM, alpine, subalpine, common,
L Spring–Summer, perennial, 3–7 in.
Delicate herb with erect flowering stems,
from thick rhizome attached to a bulb.
Grass-like, fleshy leaves basal or alternate
along stem. Inflorescence usually a solitary,
nodding flower (rarely 2). Tepals white to
yellowish: green or purple lines on inside,
purplish-tinged on outside, usually with a small, nectariferous groove near base adaxially. Grows in gravelly meadows, scree, or rock crevices. Foliage resembles the tiny
sedges with which it grows. A famous link to the circumboreal flora. Native.

Prosartes trachycarpa
(*Disporum trachycarpum*) LILIACEAE
roughfruit fairybells, roughfruited mandarin
RM, subalpine, montane, foothills,
grasslands, common, L Spring–
Summer, perennial, 12–32 in.
Herbaceous perennial from a rhizome. Stem
arched, sparsely branched. Leaves oval, 1–4 in.
long, smooth above, somewhat hairy below,
pointed at tip. Leaves are unstalked, somewhat clasping, margins entire or somewhat hairy, distinct
parallel veins. Flowers 1–4, on stout, hairy pedicels. Flowers pendent, 0.5 in., narrowly bell-shaped, creamy white.
Tepals 6; stamens 6; ovary superior. Berries green, becoming red to orange. Occurs in coniferous forests, aspen groves, along streambanks. Native.

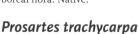

Streptopus amplexifolius LILIACEAE
claspleaf twistedstalk, white mandarin
RM, subalpine, montane, foothills,
wetlands, uncommon, L Spring–
Summer, perennial, 12–48 in.
Herbaceous perennial from rhizomes. Stem
zigzags. Leaves alternate, elliptic to ovate,
pointed at tip, 2–6 in. long by 1–2 in. wide, sessile, mostly clasping. Flowers small, solitary
in leaf axils, radially symmetrical. Tepals 6, white to green;
stamens 6; ovary superior. Flower stalks twist at an angle,
so flower hangs down like a bell. Berries fleshy, white to
green when immature, red to orange with age. Occurs in
moist shady mountain forests and streambanks. Native.

3 or 6 petals, simple-shaped, radial

Argemone hispida PAPAVERACEAE
rough pricklypoppy
SR, foothills, pinyon-juniper, sagebrush
steppe, grasslands, common,
Spring–Summer, perennial, 1–2 ft.
Large, showy, white flowers atop an unbranched, gray-silver, densely prickly stem.
Leaves alternate, toothed margins, deeply
lobed, sparsely to densely covered with bristles between veins. Leaf underside most
prickly on main veins/midribs, upper sur-
face less so. Leaves stalked near bottom of stem, clasping
upward. Flower buds oblong, prickly. Flowers 2.7–4 in.,
stamens numerous, filaments pale yellow. Fruit a prickly
egg-shaped capsule. Occurs at lower elevations in sunny
prairies, slopes, eastern foothills, and disturbed areas. Native.

Argemone munita PAPAVERACEAE
flatbud pricklypoppy
MR, foothills, pinyon-juniper, sagebrush
steppe, common, L Spring–Summer,
annual/perennial, 2–3 ft.
Stems stout and upright, branched, densely
to sparingly prickly. Leaves sessile, covered
with spines on both sides; oblong, 2–6 in.
long; distinctly rounded, marginal teeth.
Flowers at stem tips, above bracts covered with upright
spines; 6 silky white petals, 1–2 in. long. Seedpod cylindrical, densely spiny. Closely resembles *A. polyanthemos* of
the Great Plains but occurs farther west, from Baja to the
Wasatch, southern ID, southwestern OR.
Native.

Argemone polyanthemos
(A. intermedia) PAPAVERACEAE
crested pricklypoppy
MR, SR, foothills, pinyon-juniper, sagebrush
steppe, grasslands, common, Spring–
Summer, biennial/perennial, to 2.5 ft.
Upright stems branching, blue-gray; alternate leaves ruffled, coarse, pinnately lobed,
blue-green with lighter venation; sharp
prickles on leaves and stems. Stems herbaceous, smaller
basal leaves may be evergreen. Large white flowers, dense
gold stamens. Fruit a prickly bur, black seeds. Milky
sap bright yellow. Conspicuous among drying summer
grasses, in plains, open meadows, dry slopes, pine parklands. Native.

4 petals, elongated clusters, bilateral

Polanisia dodecandra CLEOMACEAE
redwhisker clammyweed
MR, SR, pinyon-juniper, sagebrush steppe, grasslands, common, Summer, annual, 1–2 ft.
All parts hairy, sticky, with skunky odor. Stems branched upward. Leaves alternate; on lower parts, 3 palmately set oval leaflets 1.5 in. long on equal petiole. Upper flowering parts: small single leaves close to stem. Flowers in elongating cluster; 4 upright petals, spatulate and notched to 0.5 in.; long reddish pink stamens below petals lend bristly appearance. Mature seedpods to 1.5 in. long on ascending pedicel, small seeds snail-shaped. Sand, gravel washes, roadsides, slopes, disturbed sites at lower elevations. Native.

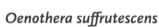

Oenothera suffrutescens
(*Gaura coccinea*) ONAGRACEAE
scarlet beeblossom, scarlet gaura
RM, montane, foothills, sagebrush steppe, grasslands, common, Spring–Summer, perennial, 8–24 in.
Herb with smooth to hairy, ascending to erect, simple to branched stems. Leaves alternate, sessile, to 1.6 in., reducing upward; lanceolate to oblong, entire or with few shallow teeth. Inflorescence a many-flowered terminal spike, sometimes nodding at tip. Slender calyx tube with 4 reflexed lobes. Clawed and spatulate petals white, maturing pink to red, surround 8 conspicuous stamens and a 4-lobed style. Fruit a nut-like capsule. Grows on dry slopes, in sandy soil. Native.

Dicentra cucullaria
(*Bicuculla cucullaria*) PAPAVERACEAE
Dutchman's breeches
NR, foothills, uncommon, locally abundant, Spring–E Summer, perennial, 8–14 in.
Scapose and glaucous herb from rice-like underground bulblets. Leaves emerge from ground on red, tan, or brown petioles. Blades ternately divided 3 or 4 times, fern-like. Inflorescence a raceme of 3–8 pendent flowers on one side of arching stem. Flowers 0.75 in. long, distinctly resemble a pair of breeches hanging upside down. Petals 4, pinkish white. Inner 2 petals tipped orange-yellow, flare outward revealing stamens. Outer 2 petals each form a spur, tips divergent. Occurs in moist woods and on gravelly banks. Spring ephemeral. Toxic. Native.

Besseya plantaginea
(*Synthyris plantaginea*)
PLANTAGINACEAE
White River kittentails
SR, subalpine, montane, foothills,
common, locally abundant, L Spring–
Summer, perennial, to 14 in.

Flowering spikes to 1 ft. above herbaceous
basal rosettes. Elongated 2- to 5-in. hairy
basal leaves; stem clothed with smaller
leaves below the inflorescence. Flowers
barely emerge from the hairy 4- or 5-lobed calyces with
only the upper corolla visible, white or soft pink; the projecting pistil and stamens give a bristly appearance. Found
in fens and other moist areas, mixed forests, moist meadows. Native.

Maianthemum canadense
ASPARAGACEAE
Canada mayflower, wild lily-of-the-valley
NR, MR, montane, locally abundant,
L Spring–Fall, perennial, 2–20 in.

Rhizomatous herb creates carpet-like colonies; stem often zigzags. Leaves 2 or 3,
stalked to unstalked, smooth above, hairy
below, glossy; margins entire and hairy; base
heart-shaped; parallel venation. Leaves often
in 2 rows along stem. Inflorescence bottlebrush-like; 12–25
flowers cream to white, star-shaped, 0.4 in. wide. Stamens
4. Berries round, red, mottled when immature. Occurs in
moist to mesic deciduous forests and clearings. Native.

Capsella bursa-pastoris
BRASSICACEAE
shepherd's purse
RM, montane, foothills, grasslands,
common, Spring–E Summer,
annual, 4–20 in.

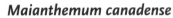

Herb with pinnately lobed basal leaves up to
4 in. long; stem leaves egg-shaped to linear
and up to 2.25 in. long, alternate and clasping the stem. Flowers with 4 petals, white,
arranged in a spiraling raceme. Lower flow-
ers bloom first, changing to flattened heart-shaped silicles
before the upper flowers finish blooming. Found in disturbed sites, meadows, roadsides, and gardens throughout
North America. The common name refers to the shape of
the fruit. Introduced.

Lepidium alyssoides
(L. montanum ssp. *alyssoides)*
BRASSICACEAE

mesa pepperwort
SR, montane, foothills, pinyon-juniper,
sagebrush steppe, common, L Spring–
E Summer, perennial, 7–22 in.

Several smooth, ascending, branched stems
from a woody base. Leaves smooth, linear,
alternate on stems. Many clusters of simple bright white flowers with 4 round petals;
oval thickened seedpods. Common in sunny areas on dry
washes, slopes, roadsides. The genus holds many similar
crucifers from Central Asia, underscoring the close floris-
tic ties of these regions: the emphatic white petals are
universal. Native.

Noccaea fendleri
(Thlaspi montanum) BRASSICACEAE
**Fendler's pennycress, alpine pennycress,
Idaho pennycress**
RM, throughout, common,
Spring, perennial, 2–7 in.

Single or lightly branched stems arising from
small leafy rosettes. Basal foliage is ovate to
oblong, gray-green, with toothed margins.
Clustered terminal flowerheads 1.25 in. in diameter; usually solitary, can be branching. Small flowers
with 4 petals on stem that elongates as they mature into
thin siliques. Can form large colonies in sunny, disturbed
sites where there is little to no competition. Often hosts a
rust that turns leaves yellow. Among the first
flowers to bloom in its many habitats. Native.

Stanleya albescens BRASSICACEAE
white prince's plume
SR, foothills, pinyon-juniper, sagebrush
steppe, uncommon, Spring–
E Summer, biennial, 6–24 in.

Herbaceous, waxy, glabrous stems; unbranched or occasionally branched. Basal
leaves broadly lanceolate; margins pinnatifid or lyrate. Stem leaves petiolate, similar
to basal leaves; margins entire or lyrate-pinnatifid. Simple flowers in tall dense racemes; pale cream to white; 4
oblong-linear sepals; 4 orbicular to obovate petals. Fruit
a silique; suberect to ascending, curved inward, 1–2.5 in.
Grows on sunny dry slopes, Mancos shale, or clay barrens,
often in soils with abundant selenium. Native.

Thlaspi arvense BRASSICACEAE
field pennycress
RM, montane, foothills, sagebrush
steppe, grasslands, common,
Spring–Summer, annual, 4–24 in.
Upright branching stems. Basal leaves
spoon-shaped, either entire or with toothed
edges, 0.75–2.4 in. long, withering early;
stem leaves similar but reduced, often with
ear-like lobes near base, alternate. Flowers
in racemes with individual flower stalks to
0.5 in. long. 4 white rounded petals in cross to H shape
atop pointed green sepals. Fruit is a silicle with flattened
edges and heart-shaped upper edge. Found in meadows,
disturbed soils, roadsides, and fields. Widespread across
North America, currently being investigated
as a potential biofuel crop. Introduced.

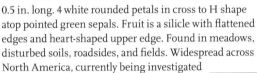

Galium boreale
(G. septentrionale) RUBIACEAE
northern bedstraw
RM, subalpine, montane, foothills,
sagebrush steppe, common, L Spring–
Summer, perennial, 8–30 in.
Rhizomatous, sticky herb with numerous
erect to ascending, simple to much-branched
stems; short beards below nodes, other-
wise smooth to slightly rough. Basal leaves ephemeral and
stem leaves in whorls of 4. Leaves linear to lanceolate, with
rounded tips, and smooth to stiff-haired surfaces. Inflorescence a pyramid-like cluster of minute white or cream
flowers, each with 4 petals. Nutlets covered
in curved hairs or smooth. Grows in forests, woodlands, meadows, shrublands, and
along streams. Circumboreal. Native.

Braya glabella BRASSICACEAE
smooth northern-rockcress
RM, alpine, uncommon,
Summer, perennial, 2–8 in.
Stems leafless, bearing flowers only. Basal
leaves are linear to spoon-shaped, generally fleshy, and occasionally toothed. Flow-
ers are simple, 4-petaled, and white to purplish in color.
Pods are thick, elongated, and often hairy. Grows in sunny
and disturbed habitats, tundra, rock scree, and on rock
ledges. Prefers rocky, alpine soils and abandoned mine
sites. Highly variable. *B. humilis* differs in having at least 2
leaves on the stems. Native.

Cardamine cordifolia BRASSICACEAE
heartleaf bittercress
RM, subalpine, montane, foothills,
locally abundant, L Spring–
Summer, perennial, 8–24 in.

Many vigorous erect stems, unbranched or branched distally, from extensive system of underground runners. Leaves mostly cauline, alternate, simple, broadly rounded; toothed or strongly wavy margins. Inflorescence a terminal raceme without bracts, flower stalks spreading to erect. Flowers 0.6 in. across, 4 white petals, 0.25–0.5 in. long, egg-shaped narrowing at base. Species easily distinguished from others whose flowers are tinted pink or are quite small. Leaves of most other species often deeply divided with heart-shaped bases. Occurs in wet soils near ponds and streams, moist meadows, and forests. Native.

Draba hitchcockii BRASSICACEAE
Lost River draba, Hitchcock's draba
MR, alpine, subalpine, endemic, rare,
L Spring–E Summer, perennial, 0.4–5 in.

Multiple unbranched stems arise from rosettes. Basal leaves with 2- to 4-rayed hairs form a dense gray-green cushion; oblanceolate to oblong-linear, entire, and often pubescent. 4–15 white flowers 0.25–0.5 in. wide, in an upright cluster that lengthens as seedpods develop. Grows on gravelly soil, rock ledges, and on limestone. Endemic to just a few ranges in ID, where it is of conservation concern. A fairly distinctive species with comparatively large white flowers for the genus. Native.

Draba lonchocarpa BRASSICACEAE
lancepod draba
RM, alpine, rare, Summer, perennial, 0.4–4 in.

Short stems are hairless, or have hairs with 8–12 rays; leaves may or may not be present. Leaves are gray-green, oblanceolate, and have star-shaped hairs with 8–12 rays. White, 4-petaled flowers form a 0.25-in.-wide cluster. Grows on rock ledges. Found on limestone, rare in CO. One of several smaller white-flowered drabas not arising from a cushion. Native.

Nasturtium officinale
(*Rorippa nasturtium-aquaticum*)

BRASSICACEAE

watercress

MR, wetlands, common, locally abundant,
Spring–Summer, perennial, 3–12 in.

Succulent stems creeping or floating, to
30 in. long, rooting at nodes. Leaves 1.5–4
in. long, smooth, alternate; pinnate, 3–7
egg-shaped leaflets, terminal one largest; edible with crisp, peppery flavor. Flowers each
0.25 in. across, 4 petals; in rounded cluster to 1.5 in. across,
elongating as they mature. Seeds in curved siliques to 0.7
in. long. Found in sunny wet areas: streamsides, pond
margins, springs, ditches. Introduced.

Smelowskia americana
(*S. calycina* var. *americana*)

BRASSICACEAE

alpine smelowskia, western smelowskia

RM, alpine, subalpine, locally abundant,
Summer, perennial, 2–8 in.

Mat-forming herb from much-branched
crown; flowering stems few and erect.
Leaves 0.4–4 in. long, pinnately divided,
grayish, with thin petioles equal to length
of leaf blade. Stem leaves similar, alternate,
several, reduced. Inflorescence a flat-topped terminal raceme. Sepals 4, white to purple-tinged, early deciduous.
Petals 4, spoon-shaped, white to purplish-tinged. Stamens
6. Fruit a silique. Found in rocky areas,
tundra, and fellfields. Native.

Cornus sericea
(*C. stolonifera*) CORNACEAE

redosier dogwood

RM, subalpine, montane, foothills,
wetlands, common, Spring–
Summer, perennial, 2–8 ft.

Deciduous shrub. Stems smooth, maroon
to bright red in winter, more greenish in
summer. Leaves ovate, pointed tip, opposite,
clear lateral veins; to 4 in. long, 2 in. wide;
wine-red in fall. Flowers 0.25 in. across, 4 petals, in terminal flat or mounded clusters to 3 in. across. Berries white,
0.25 in. Abundant along streams, sunny moist meadows;
stems colorful en masse with native willows in winter.
Variable; many stem-color forms, including yellow. Native.

Clematis ligusticifolia

RANUNCULACEAE
western virgin's bower
RM, montane, foothills, pinyon-juniper,
sagebrush steppe, common,
L Spring–Summer, perennial, 1–20 ft.

Vigorous vine, rhizomatous, deciduous; can reach 20 ft. or more. Leaves glabrous, ternate or pinnate; leaflets lanceolate to oval, variable with irregular teeth and notches; petioles winding around nearby stems to assist climbing. Flowers 0.75 in. across, in clusters up to 20; 4 or 5 white sepals and many white stamens. Fluffy seedheads of many plumed achenes. Scrambles high into riparian trees, along riverbanks, open slopes, fencelines. Native.

Cornus canadensis
(*Chamaepericlymenum canadense*)

CORNACEAE
bunchberry dogwood
RM, subalpine, montane, locally abundant,
L Spring–Summer, perennial, 1–6 in.

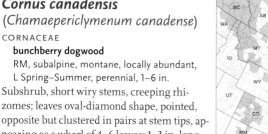

Subshrub, short wiry stems, creeping rhizomes; leaves oval-diamond shape, pointed, opposite but clustered in pairs at stem tips, appearing as a whorl of 4–6 leaves; 1–3 in. long, heavily veined; small pair of bract-like leaves less than 0.5 in. along stem. True flowers tiny in terminal central cluster, creamy, dark style in center; 4 surrounding white bracts, showy, to 2 in. across. Berries red. Abundant in NR, infrequent in CO, NM. Cool, moist evergreen or mixed woodlands in shade. Native.

Cornus unalaschkensis
(*Chamaepericlymenum unalaschkense*) CORNACEAE

Alaskan bunchberry
NR, montane, common, Spring–
Summer, perennial, 2–8 in.

Wiry subshrub similar in most respects to *C. canadensis*, but stems often have a pair of small leaves midway. Leaves 4–6, ovate, pointed tip, to 3 in. long, paired but appearing as terminal whorl. True flowers tiny, clustered, 4 showy bracts. Red fruits to 0.5 in. follow. Cool moist evergreen or mixed forests in duff soils, shade. Most common farther west; its range overlaps with *C. canadensis* in ID, BC. Native.

Fendlera rupicola HYDRANGEACEAE
cliff fendlerbush
SR, foothills, pinyon-juniper,
sagebrush steppe, common, Spring–
Summer, perennial, 4–6 ft.

Upright to arching shrub, gray stems,
woody base; often vase-shaped with age;
deciduous; semi-evergreen in far southern
range. Leaves opposite, clustered at twig
ends, to 1.5 in., oval to lanceolate, edges
curled under, fuzzy below. Showy flowers
to 1.75 in. across; 4 white spoon-shaped petals, buds and
petals may be blushed pink; often fragrant. Brown oblong
seeds in 4-chambered egg-shaped pod to 0.6 in. long.
Canyons, rocky slopes, forest openings. Native.

Philadelphus lewisii
HYDRANGEACEAE
Lewis' mock orange
NR, MR, montane, foothills, sagebrush
steppe, grasslands, common,
L Spring–Summer, perennial, 3–9 ft.
Upright to arching shrub; stems red/brown,
aging to gray, flaking layers. Glabrous leaves
elliptical, 1–3 in. long, usually smooth, entire, but may have few teeth; conspicuously
veined. Flowers 1 in. across in terminal racemes of 3–6 on lateral branches; 4 oval petals, stamens
white, anthers yellow; fragrant. Open woodlands, ravines,
moist slopes, grasslands and steppe. More northern distribution than the next. Native.

Philadelphus microphyllus
(*P. occidentalis*) HYDRANGEACEAE
littleleaf mock orange
MR, SR, montane, foothills,
pinyon-juniper, sagebrush steppe,
common, locally abundant, Spring–
Summer, perennial, 2–6 ft.
Shrub with heavily branched upright to
arching stems, newer ones striped rusty
brown, aging gray. Leaves opposite, ovate,
with 3 parallel veins, pubescent below, to
1.5 in. long on short petioles. Flowers 1 in. across, lightly
fragrant, 1–3 at tips of stems; 4 oval petals, yellow anthers;
matures to woody 4-chambered capsule. Similar to *Fend-
lera* spp., but petals not spatulate and leaves wider. Found
in woodland openings, shrub meadows, cliffs or slopes in
riparian zones, sun or part shade. Native.

Epilobium clavatum
(*E. alpinum* var. *clavatum*)
ONAGRACEAE
talus willowherb, clavatefruit willowherb
RM, alpine, subalpine, locally abundant,
Summer, perennial, 2–8 in.
Upright, spreading herb with multiple
stems; finely hairy. Leaves opposite, elliptic
to egg-shaped to 1.2 in. long, entire or slightly
toothed with pointed or blunt tips. Small flowers on slender pedicels to 0.7 in. long; white or
pink petals less than 0.3 in. long with slight notch at end
of each petal. Fruit capsules to 1.6 in. long, narrow. Found
in moist meadows, scree and talus, occasionally along
streams. Native.

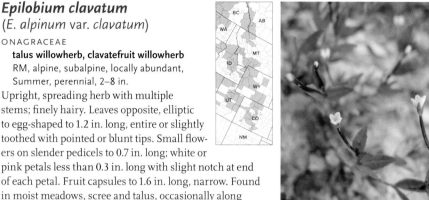

Oenothera albicaulis ONAGRACEAE
white-stem evening primrose
RM, montane, pinyon-juniper,
sagebrush steppe, grasslands, common,
Spring–Summer, annual, 2–6 in.
Basal rosette from taproot. Leaves pubescent, ovate to lanceolate, 1–5 in. long; may be
entire, partially lobed, or pinnate, even on
one plant; procumbent stems have smaller
leaves. Flower buds nodding, opening white;
4 heart-shaped petals opening in evening and
lasting several days, fading pink. Fruit a cylindric ribbed
capsule 1–1.5 in. long. Sandy prairies, washes, sunny roadsides, often in great masses under favorable conditions.
Native.

Oenothera caespitosa ONAGRACEAE
tufted evening primrose
RM, montane, foothills, pinyon-juniper,
sagebrush steppe, grasslands, common,
Spring–Summer, perennial, 2–5 in.
Basal rosettes, rhizomatous, forming small
colonies. Leaves pubescent, lanceolate, entire
or irregularly toothed, 2–7 in. long. Flowers to
4.5 in. across; 4 white petals opening in evening, shifting to soft or deep pink as they fade
the next morning. Sunny dry slopes, rocky
meadows, clay slopes or flats, roadsides, openings in lower
forests, high desert. Native.

Oenothera coronopifolia
ONAGRACEAE
crownleaf evening primrose
MR, SR, montane, foothills, sagebrush
steppe, grasslands, common,
Summer, perennial, 6–14 in.

Slender stems from rhizomatous roots.
Leaves alternate, 1 in. long, pinnately lobed.
Generally pubescent, flower buds and
fruit capsules may have longer white hairs.
Flowers terminal and in leaf axils; 1–1.3 in.
across, 4 white petals opening in evening, fading to pink
the next day. Fruit capsules cylindrical, 0.75 in. long. Common in sunny prairies, may be found in forest openings,
dry meadows, slopes. Native.

Oenothera nuttallii ONAGRACEAE
Nuttall's evening primrose
RM, montane, foothills, sagebrush
steppe, grasslands, common,
L Spring–Summer, perennial, 1–2.5 ft.

Loosely branched stems from slender rhizomes; smooth, papery, peeling whitish surface. Leaves 1–2.25 in. long, linear, alternate,
entire or with few tiny teeth. Buds nodding;
flowers glandular, 1.75 in. across; 4 rounded
or heart-shaped petals with shallow notch
at tip, opening in evening, fading to pink by the next afternoon. Common prairie species; sun, sandy soils in sage
meadows, lower forests, roadsides. Native.

Oenothera pallida ONAGRACEAE
pale evening primrose
RM, foothills, pinyon-juniper,
sagebrush steppe, grasslands,
common, locally abundant, Spring–
Summer, perennial, 12–18 in.

Rhizomatous; may grow as a subshrub;
stems fleshy, reddish, aging white and
peeling. Basal rosettes early, withering
as stems grow; 1- to 2-in. leaves alternate,
lanceolate, margins entire or with small
teeth. Buds red/pink, nodding; 4 rounded
or heart-shaped white petals, gold-green at base, opening
each evening, fading to pink next day; sepals joined and
reflexed to one side when open. Seed capsules 0.75–1.25 in.
long, curved or twisted. Grows in sun, sandy soil in steppe,
washes, roadsides or disturbed sites. Native.

Astragalus australis
(*A. aboriginorum*) FABACEAE
Indian milkvetch
RM, alpine, subalpine, montane,
foothills, uncommon, Spring–
Summer, perennial, 1–10 in.

Stem branching from the base, arching out.
Leaves gray-green, pinnately compound with
7–15 leaflets, deciduous. Foliage can have
hairs on both sides. Flowers white or cream
with a purple keel. Pods are pea-like and point
down, ranging from green to reddish with spots. Uncommon throughout its range, in tundra, rocky slopes, pine
parklands. Native.

Astragalus canadensis FABACEAE
Canadian milkvetch
RM, montane, foothills, grasslands,
uncommon, Spring–Summer,
perennial, 6–48 in.

Stem branching from base, arching out.
Leaves green, pinnately compound with 7–35
leaflets, can have hairs on both sides, deciduous. Flowers white or cream, an upright spike
of many flowers. Pods are pea-like, green,
point out, and are generally smooth; cylindrical, not at all compressed. Ranges from CA
to the Midwest, moist meadows, sun/shade. One of our
larger milkvetches, it is often found leaning on surrounding vegetation. Native.

Astragalus cicer FABACEAE
chickpea milkvetch
RM, alpine, subalpine, montane,
foothills, grasslands, common, Spring–
Summer, perennial, 12–32 in.

Stem branching from base, arching out.
Leaves green, pinnately compound with 17
leaflets, can have hairs on both sides, deciduous. Flowers cream, pale yellow, or
pink-purple; up to 60 flowers per spike. The
calyx has black hairs pressed to the surface.
Pods pea-like and point out, swollen; green
turning to black with short white hairs; cylindrical, not at
all compressed; persist. Common in disturbed areas, used
for revegetation along roads, trailheads, and campgrounds.
It can cover large areas. Pods more notable than flowers.
One of the few non-native *Astragalus* spp. Introduced.

Astragalus convallarius FABACEAE
lesser rushy milkvetch
RM, montane, foothills, pinyon-juniper, sagebrush steppe, intermountain parks, common, locally abundant, Spring–Summer, perennial, 8–28 in.

Stem branching from base, arching out, rhizomatous. Leaves green, simple to pinnately compound with up to 13 leaflets, deciduous. Foliage very thin, resembling stems. Flowers white, cream, pale yellow, or purplish. Pea-like pods hang down; reddish or green, short hairs. Frequent on dry slopes, barrens, and meadows; occasional in aspen, more common in pinyon-juniper, shrub oak, or sagebrush. Becomes less frequent north of WY; can be common in western CO and UT. Occasional leafless rachises give it a broom- or grass-like appearance when out of bloom or seed. Native.

Astragalus drummondii FABACEAE
Drummond's milkvetch
RM, montane, foothills, sagebrush steppe, intermountain parks, grasslands, common, L Spring–Summer, perennial, 12–28 in.
Clumping with deciduous, pinnately compound, gray-green leaves with 17 or more leaflets. Covered in dense hairs. Flowers white and nodding slightly; in a raceme of 20–50 flowers. Calyx has white to black hairs. Pea-like pods point down, not swollen, often mottled and hairless. Barrens, rocky ledges, dry slopes, meadows, sage meadows. One of the most common species throughout the region, from grasslands of the eastern Rockies through mountain parks; more limited but locally abundant west of the divide. Native.

Astragalus miser FABACEAE
timber milkvetch
RM, throughout, common, Spring–Summer, perennial, 2–6 in.

Stem clump-forming. Leaves green, pinnately compound with 9–21 leaflets, hairless above, deciduous. Flowers whitish, occasionally with purple veins, and pointing up. Pods are small, hairy, sometimes purple-dotted or tinged, hanging down. Mixed forest, pine parklands, dry slopes, moist and dry meadows. One of the most commonly encountered *Astragalus* spp. in the West, found over a wide range of habitats from the plains up to the alpine. Native.

Astragalus osterhoutii FABACEAE
Osterhout's milkvetch
SR, sagebrush steppe, intermountain
parks, endemic, uncommon,
Summer, perennial, 12–20 in.

Roots can be rhizomatous, stems forming upright clumps. Hairy, deciduous, bright green,
pinnately compound leaves display 7–15 leaflets, and elevated margins. Bright white flowers point down. Pods are reddish, and hang

down. Grows in sunny areas, barrens, dry
slopes, and sage meadows. Endemic to Grand County, CO,
where it is a listed endangered species protected by law.
Found on selenium-rich clay and shale slopes. Large, clean
white flowers and specialized habitat distinguish it from
other species. Native.

Astragalus pattersonii FABACEAE
Patterson's milkvetch
SR, montane, foothills, pinyon-juniper,
sagebrush steppe, intermountain
parks, grasslands, locally abundant,
Spring–Summer, perennial, 8–28 in.

Stems clump-forming, red, and upright.
Leaves deciduous, gray-green, pinnately com-
pound with 13 leaflets, and smooth on top.
Flowers white, aging to yellow. Calyx has

black hairs and is distinctively fringed. Pods hang down,
almost hairless. Grows in sunny areas, barrens, rock scree,
dry slopes, and sage meadows. Often found on shale or clay
slopes. Has a strong selenium odor. Native.

Astragalus praelongus FABACEAE
stinking milkvetch
MR, SR, foothills, pinyon-juniper,
sagebrush steppe, intermountain
parks, grasslands, locally abundant,
Spring–Summer, perennial, 15–36 in.

Stems clump-forming and upright. Leaves
deciduous, green, pinnately compound
with 13 leaflets, and smooth on top. Flowers
yellow-white to pale yellow. Pods almost hairless, and point in all directions. Often found

on shale or clay slopes. Has a strong selenium
odor. The stems and pods of previous year often persist.
Native.

Astragalus scopulorum FABACEAE
Rocky Mountain milkvetch
MR, SR, subalpine, montane, foothills,
pinyon-juniper, sagebrush steppe,
intermountain parks, common,
Spring–Summer, perennial, 6–18 in.
Stems clump-forming, light red, often lean
and then turn up at the ends. Leaves deciduous, green, pinnately compound with 7–35
leaflets, hairy on the underside. Flowers
creamy white and pale yellow. Pods reddish
on top and green underneath with a groove on the side.
Grows in sunny areas, barrens, dry slopes, coniferous and
aspen forests, and sage meadows. Native.

Astragalus tenellus
(*A. multiflorus*) FABACEAE
looseflower milkvetch
RM, subalpine, montane, foothills,
sagebrush steppe, intermountain
parks, grasslands, common, Spring–
Summer, perennial, 8–16 in.
Clump-forming stems with very hairy,
green, compound leaves with 13 leaflets.
Flowers small and compressed, pointing
down. Grows in sunny areas, barrens, dry
slopes, rock ledges, mixed forests, pine
parklands, and sage meadows. Sometimes confused with
A. miser, *A. tenellus* differs in several ways: reddish lower
stem, wider inward-folding leaflets, longer flower spikes,
and larger flowers. Native.

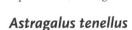

Glycyrrhiza lepidota FABACEAE
American licorice
RM, pinyon-juniper, sagebrush
steppe, intermountain parks,
grasslands, wetlands, common,
Spring–Summer, perennial, to 4 ft.
Erect glandular stems from long rhizomes and deep fleshy aromatic roots.
Leaves alternate and odd-pinnate, with 7–19
lance-shaped leaflets up to 1.5 in. that come
to a sharp point. Spike of clustered creamy
white pea-shaped flowers; seedpods oval, bur-like up to
1 in., spread by animals. Found in disturbed sites, from
grasslands to forest, especially in riparian zones. Historically an important source of food and medicine for Native
Americans; contains the compound used in licorice candy.
Native.

Hedysarum sulphurescens

FABACEAE

yellow sweetvetch, white sweetvetch
NR, MR, alpine, subalpine, montane,
grasslands, locally abundant, Spring–
Summer, perennial, 6–20 in.

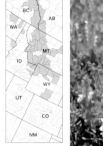

Several to many stems originate from a
base. Leaves are green, pinnate, with 9–17
ovate to lanceolate leaflets 0.06–0.25 in. long.
5-petaled flowers in a dull white to light yellow white elongated cluster, the only *Hedysarum* sp. so colored. Calyx is 0.6–0.8 in. long. Pods have
netted venation and are thin, flat, and pea-like, with 1–4
segments. Grows in sunny areas, rock scree, dry slopes,
mixed forests, riparian. Often found on calcareous soil.
Native.

Melilotus albus FABACEAE

white sweetclover
RM, montane, foothills, pinyon-juniper,
sagebrush steppe, intermountain
parks, grasslands, common,
L Spring–Summer, annual, 2–5 ft.

Stems usually glabrous, loosely branched
throughout. Leaves alternate, pinnate with
3 oblong leaflets up to 1.5 in. long, finely
toothed, with stipules at stem. Flowers small,
pea-like, in axillary racemes of 20–50, sweetly fragrant.
Generally similar to *M. officinalis*, but usually smaller and
with white flowers. A common global weed, has been cultivated as a crop and for beekeeping, but now found in
disturbed sites, roadsides, fields everywhere.
Introduced and invasive.

Oxytropis sericea FABACEAE

white locoweed, silky locoweed
RM, throughout, common, Spring–
Summer, perennial, 2.75–8 in.

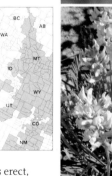

Deciduous, clump-forming herb with several
to many leafless stems. Leaves pinnately compound with 9–23 ovate to oblong-lanceolate
leaflets; surfaces hairy and silvery. Infferes-
cence a spike of 5–20 white to pale yellow
flowers. Calyx covered in light to dark hairs. Pods erect,
sessile, 0.6–1 in. long and often covered in white and black
hairs; walls thick and rigid. Grows in tundra, barrens, rock
ledges, pine parklands, dry slopes, meadows. The largest
and showiest of the white locoweeds, it is the only common
species that tends to be a clear white. Native.

Sophora nuttalliana
(*Vexibia nuttalliana*) FABACEAE
silky sophora
MR, SR, foothills, pinyon-juniper,
sagebrush steppe, intermountain
parks, grasslands, common, L Spring–
Summer, perennial, 6–20 in.

Lax to upright stems from rhizomatous network of roots. Gray-green pinnate leaves are
silky, alternate, with graceful spikes of white
pea-like flowers, often with lavender-gray
calyx. Can be mistaken for a large, stemmed oxytropis,
but seedpods are distinctly constricted between each seed.
Herb of sandy prairie and sparse grassland. Native.

Marrubium vulgare LAMIACEAE
horehound
RM, montane, foothills, pinyon-juniper,
sagebrush steppe, grasslands, common,
Spring–Summer, perennial, 6–36 in.
Upright or decumbent 4-angled stems,
woolly white hairs, from taprooted crown.
Leaves opposite, 1–2 in. across, rounded;
wavy edges are round-notched; textured
velvety surface; horizontal or down-curved
on short petioles. White to pink flowers
in dense whorls at leaf axils, tubular from

fringed hairy calyces; upper lip 2-lobed, pointed; lower lip
wider, 3-lobed. Sun, anywhere below subalpine: disturbed
sites, roadsides, trails, human habitation. Introduced.

Nepeta cataria LAMIACEAE
catnip
RM, foothills, sagebrush steppe,
common, locally abundant,
Summer–Fall, perennial, 1–3 ft.
Erect square stems, grooved, lightly pubescent, from perennial crown. Triangular
leaves opposite, to 4 in. long, toothed edges,
surface raised between veins; all parts with
catnip fragrance. Flowers in dense whorls;
fuzzy 2-lipped calyx; petals fused, tubular,
upper lip 2-lobed, lower lip 3-lobed with serrated edge; white with small purple or pink dots. Grows
in disturbed sites, habitations, streamsides, open woods,
rocky moist or dry slopes. Can be aggressively weedy in
some habitats. Introduced.

Pedicularis contorta

OROBANCHACEAE

coiled lousewort
NR, MR, alpine, subalpine,
montane, common, L Spring–
Summer, perennial, 6–24 in.

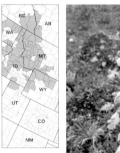

Hairless herb with cluster of erect, unbranched stems. Basal leaves pinnate, to 7 in.,
the segments serrated. Stem leaves few, alternate, reduced upward. Inflorescence an elongated terminal spike of white to pale yellow
flowers, often with pink or purplish markings. Flowers
subtended by shorter narrow and divided bracts. Corolla
2-lipped: lower lip with 3 lobes; upper lip hooded, strongly
arched, tapering to a down-curved beak. Dry slopes, in
open forests and meadows. Native.

Pedicularis racemosa

OROBANCHACEAE

sickletop lousewort
RM, alpine, subalpine, montane,
foothills, common, L Spring–
Summer, perennial, 6–20 in.

Glabrous herb with clusters of erect stems.
Leaves alternate, to 4 in., narrowly lanceolate (not pinnatifid), with toothed margins.
Basal leaves reduced or absent. Inflores-
cence a loose, elongated raceme of white, cream, pinkish,
or purplish flowers subtended by leaf-like bracts. Lower
flowers sometimes in leaf axils. Corolla 2-lipped: lower lip
3-lobed and spreading; upper lip arched, hooded, and tapering to down-curved beak. Moist meadows,
spruce-fir forests, and rocky slopes. Native.

Chionophila jamesii

PLANTAGINACEAE

Rocky Mountain snowlover
SR, alpine, endemic, rare,
Summer, perennial, 2–12 in.

Flowering stems 1 to several above basal
rosette. Basal leaves lance-shaped, thick,
margins entire. Stem leaves few, smaller, opposite, clasping. Inflorescence 1-sided, densely
clustered. Flowers greenish white to cream with areas of
contrasting purple shading; 2-lipped, somewhat flattened;
upper lip erect with small indentations along the edge;
lower lip bearded; edges browning. Occurs where snow has
recently melted, often in groups of a dozen or more. Native.

Penstemon albidus

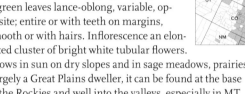

PLANTAGINACEAE
white penstemon
RM, foothills, sagebrush steppe,
grasslands, common, Spring–
Summer, perennial, 4–22 in.
Several stems form an upright clump. Evergreen leaves lance-oblong, variable, opposite; entire or with teeth on margins,
smooth or with hairs. Inflorescence an elongated cluster of bright white tubular flowers.
Grows in sun on dry slopes and in sage meadows, prairies.
Largely a Great Plains dweller, it can be found at the base
of the Rockies and well into the valleys, especially in MT.
Native.

Penstemon deustus

PLANTAGINACEAE
hotrock penstemon
NR, MR, montane, foothills,
sagebrush steppe, intermountain
parks, grasslands, locally abundant,
Summer, perennial, 4–12 in.
Multistemmed subshrub. All leaves evergreen, opposite, noticeably toothed, and
present on the stems. Inflorescence an elongated cluster of white tubular flowers, often
with red veins in the throat. Grows on rock ledges, dry
slopes, in rock scree, pine parklands, sage meadows, and
disturbed areas. Loves rocky roadsides. Native.

Penstemon laricifolius

PLANTAGINACEAE
larchleaf penstemon
MR, SR, montane, foothills, sagebrush
steppe, grasslands, common,
L Spring–Summer, perennial, 4–8 in.
Cushion-forming herb with several stems.
Leaves narrow, larch-like, 0.4–1.6 in.; stem
leaves opposite, basal leaves persistent. Inflorescence an elongated cluster of white
or pink (occasionally burgundy) tubular
flowers. Grows in sun and shade on rocky
ledges, dry slopes, sage meadows, often on calcareous
rocks. Unique for its grassy tufts and narrow, bright green
leaves. Var. *exilifolius* (pictured) tends to be white and is
found in the southern part of the range; the type is more
pink and is found farther north. Varieties overlap extensively in WY. Native.

Sambucus racemosa ADOXACEAE
red elderberry, black elderberry
RM, subalpine, montane, foothills,
sagebrush steppe, common, Spring–
Summer, perennial, 6–18 ft.

Deciduous, erect shrub to small tree with soft,
pithy, waxy stems and reddish brown bark.
Leaves opposite, to 6 in.; pinnately compound
with 5–7 lanceolate leaflets; margins serrated.
Lower surface hairy, upper surface glabrous
and dark green. Inflorescence a pyramidal
cluster of creamy white flowers. Fruit a round berry-like
drupe; not glaucous. Var. *melanocarpa* has purplish black
berries; var. *microbotrys* has red or yellowish berries.
Grows along streams, on moist slopes, avalanche tracks,
and in aspen forests. Native.

Orogenia linearifolia APIACEAE
Great Basin Indian potato
RM, montane, foothills, common,
Spring, perennial, to 4 in.

Herb. Single, leafless, hairless stem from a
spherical to spindle-like root, 0.75–2.75 in.
below the soil. Up to 3 basal leaves divided ternately, into long, thin, entire leaflets to 1.75 in.
Inflorescence a tight cluster of white flowers
with dark purple anthers. Found, if you are
lucky, on open slopes in valleys and meadows, as it flowers
early and all but disappears after blooming. Root is edible,
reminiscent of a potato. Native.

Oreocarya celosioides
(*Cryptantha celosioides*)
BORAGINACEAE
butte candle
RM, montane, sagebrush steppe,
grasslands, common, Spring–
E Summer, perennial/biennial, 3–20 in.

Short-lived herb with multiple stems, one
usually taller than the others. Spoon-shaped
basal and alternate stem leaves, 0.75–3.25 in.
long by 0.2–0.6 in. wide, with long white hairs;
raised blisters at the bases of the hairs. Flowers, 0.25–0.5 in. across, in slightly separated clusters along
stem. Petals 5, white, fused in short tube with raised yellow appendages ringing the center. Fruit, an egg-shaped
nutlet, is needed for identification. Found from the desert
to the mountains in stony, sandy soils. Native.

Oreocarya spiculifera
(*Cryptantha spiculifera*)

BORAGINACEAE

Snake River cryptantha
NR, MR, pinyon-juniper, sagebrush
steppe, locally abundant, Spring–
E Summer, perennial, 6–16 in.

Branching from woody base, stems erect.
Basal leaves linear to oblanceolate to 2.5 in.
long, hairy. Flowering stems with leaves alternate and reduced, flowers clustered along
stems and arising from leaf axils; 5 white petals fused in a
short tube with raised yellow appendages ringing the center, the flattened part of the petal extending up to 0.3 in.
Fruit similar to *O. humilis*, plant similar to *O. celosioides*.
Sandy or stony soil, open slopes, sagebrush
or juniper communities. Native.

Oreocarya thyrsiflora
(*Cryptantha thyrsiflora*)

BORAGINACEAE

calcareous cryptantha
MR, SR, sagebrush steppe,
grasslands, common, Spring–
Summer, perennial, 8–16 in.

White-hairy upright herb with multiple
stems. Rounded-lanceolate basal leaves to 4
in. long. Stem leaves alternate and slightly reduced. White
flowers in clusters at ends of stems create a tiered appearance. Flower shape otherwise similar to *O. spiculifera*.
Fruit, with 2–4 small, ovate, wrinkled nutlets, is required
for identification. Found in rocky soils, outcroppings, and dry pastures. Native.

Oreocarya virgata
(*Cryptantha virgata*) BORAGINACEAE

miner's candle
SR, montane, foothills, common,
L Spring–Summer, biennial, 12–40 in.

Tall, prickly unbranched stem from previous year's rosette. Leaves alternate, linear,
with sharp hairs, reduced above. This is a
strict biennial: rosette of hairy, linear foliage first year; spectacular spike of white flowers the next.
Largely restricted to slopes of the Front Range of CO. The
common name is well established, and the plant is distinctive and unmistakable. Native.

Phacelia heterophylla

BORAGINACEAE

varileaf phacelia
RM, montane, foothills, sagebrush
steppe, grasslands, uncommon,
L Spring–Summer, biennial, 8–32 in.

Herbaceous biennial or short-lived monocarpic perennial from a taproot. Stems erect,
often solitary, usually simple. Leaves basal
and alternate, broadly lance-shaped, entire,
prominently veined, 0.8–4 in. long, with 1 or
2 leaflets at the base. Inflorescence terminal and axillary
cymes, helicoid. Flowers dull white to blue; bell-shaped,
5-lobed, stamens and style protrude. Calyx hairy, glandular. Fruit a capsule. Occurs in dry open areas. Native.

Valeriana dioica CAPRIFOLIACEAE

marsh valerian, wood valerian
NR, MR, subalpine, montane, common,
Spring–Summer, perennial, 4–16 in.

Herbaceous, rhizomatous plant with smooth,
slender, erect stems. Basal leaves well developed on long petioles; to 3 in. long and 1 in.
wide, ovate to spatulate, and mostly unlobed.
Stem leaves opposite, in 2–4 pairs, reduced,
nearly sessile, and pinnately cleft. Inflorescence a compact cluster (elongating in fruit) of

white flowers, 3 stamens conspicuously protruding. Some
plants with imperfect flowers. Fruit a lanceolate, glabrous
achene with radial feather-like plumes. Moist meadows
and along streams. Native.

Valeriana edulis CAPRIFOLIACEAE

tobacco root, hairy valerian
RM, alpine, subalpine, montane, foothills,
sagebrush steppe, common,
L Spring–Summer, perennial, 0.3–4 ft.

Herbaceous, with sturdy, upright, glabrous,
solitary stems. Basal leaves numerous, thick,
linear to ovate, blade tapering to petiole, with
nearly parallel venation; margins entire to
few-lobed. 2–6 pairs of stem leaves, opposite, reduced and pinnatifid. Inflorescence

a panicle of white to cream flowers, compact becoming
spreading. Stamens slightly protruding. Some plants with
perfect flowers, others with imperfect flowers. Fruit an
ovate achene with radial feather-like plumes. Grows in
sunny meadows, forest openings, and on gravelly hillsides.
Native.

Silene scouleri CARYOPHYLLACEAE
simple campion
RM, alpine, subalpine, montane,
infrequent, Summer, perennial, 4–32 in.
Stems erect from a woody base. Basal leaves
oblanceolate, 2–10 in. long, hairy; stem
leaves lanceolate to linear, up to 12 pairs.
Flowers in cymes with up to 20 flowers in
pairs or many-flowered whorls. Calyx prominently 10-veined, tubular to 0.8 in. long.
Petals 5, white to pink, expanding flatly
outward, longer than calyx, deeply 2- to 4-lobed. Found in
meadows and forests. Ssp. *hallii* (pictured) is found in CO
and north; ssp. *pringlei* in northern NM. Native.

Silene vulgaris
(S. cucubalus) CARYOPHYLLACEAE
maidenstears
MR, montane, foothills, grasslands,
uncommon, Summer–Fall,
perennial, 8–32 in.
Stems erect, branching from woody base.
Leaves mostly along stems, lanceolate,
paired, almost clasping, reduced upward,
to 3.1 in. long. Flowers in cymes with long
secondary axis and 5–40 flowers; flowers
sometimes unisexual (female only). Calyx
pale green, sometimes purplish, veins obscure, inflated to
0.5 in. long in flower, increasing in fruit, papery. Petals 5,
white, broad, twice the length of calyx. Grows in disturbed
areas, roadsides, and streambanks. Introduced.

Drosera anglica
(D. longifolia) DROSERACEAE
English sundew
RM, montane, foothills, wetlands,
rare, locally abundant, Summer,
perennial, 2–18 in.
Insectivorous, herbaceous plant with erect
flowering stems. Leaves basal, erect, oblong
to spoon-shaped, 1–2 in.; showy red hairs
on upper surface gland-tipped with sticky,
insect-trapping fluid. 1–7 perfect inconspicuous white flowers in a terminal cyme; open in full sun
on one side of stem. Fruits black, egg-shaped capsules.
Found in swamps, bogs, fens, wet areas in steppe, moist
meadows. A small, disjunct population is in southern CO.
Should never be collected. Native.

Drosera rotundifolia DROSERACEAE
roundleaf sundew
NR, SR, montane, foothills, sagebrush
steppe, wetlands, rare, locally abundant,
Summer, perennial, 2–10 in.

Insectivorous, herbaceous plant with erect
flowering stems. Leaves basal, erect, orbicular, 0.7–3.5 in.; showy red hairs on upper surface gland-tipped with sticky, insect-trapping
fluid. 1–8 perfect inconspicuous flowers
with white to pink petals in a terminal cyme;
open in full sun on one side of stem. Fruits light brown,
spindle-shaped capsules. Found in swamps, bogs, fens,
moist meadows, lakeshores. Very rare in CO. Should never
be collected. Native.

Monotropa hypopitys
(*Hypopitys monotropa*) ERICACEAE
pinesap
RM, montane, foothills, uncommon,
Summer, perennial, 5–12 in.

Glabrous herb with bent to erect, simple,
fleshy stems. Plant creamy white to pinkish
red, drying to black. Thick, scale-like, reduced
leaves alternate, lanceolate, with entire to
coarse-haired margins. Inflorescence a terminal raceme with nodding vase-like flowers,
creamy white (sometimes orange or red), often hanging
from one side. Fruit a capsule. Grows in the shade of pine
and spruce forests. This pale plant lacks chlorophyll and is
mycotrophic, obtaining nutrients by parasitizing mycorrhizal fungi associated with conifers: a great
ice-breaking tidbit for parties! Circumboreal.
Native.

Pyrola minor ERICACEAE
lesser wintergreen
RM, subalpine, montane, common,
L Spring–Summer, perennial, 3–10 in.

Rhizomatous, evergreen herbaceous subshrub with erect, solitary stems. Leaves basal,
leathery, to 1 in., ovate to round with crenate
margins, darker green above and paler below.
Inflorescence a crowded terminal raceme with 3–11 nodding white or pale pink flowers. Unlike many other pyro-
las, which have long, curved styles, *P. minor* has a short,
straight, included style. Grows in moist, coniferous forests
and on shaded streambanks. Occasionally hybridizes with
P. asarifolia where their ranges overlap. Native.

Pyrola picta ERICACEAE
whiteveined wintergreen
RM, subalpine, montane,
foothills, uncommon, L Spring–
Fall, perennial, 6–18 in.
Rhizomatous, evergreen herbaceous subshrub with 1 to several erect, reddish brown
flowering stems. Leaves basal, leathery, to
2.75 in., ovate to elliptic-round with entire
to serrulate margins, darker green and conspicuously white-veined above, purplish
(sometimes when young) below. Inflorescence an elongated raceme of 10–25 yellowish to greenish white flowers.
Calyces purplish. Style exserted and curved downward.
Dry to mesic forests, especially ponderosa pine forests.
Native.

Ribes americanum
GROSSULARIACEAE
American black currant
MR, SR, foothills, grasslands, uncommon,
locally abundant, Spring–
E Summer, perennial, 3–5 ft.
Deciduous, spineless shrub with erect to
spreading, gray to black stems. Leaves alternate, to 3 in. across, palmately 3- to 5-lobed,
with toothed margins. Lower surface pubescent and with golden glands. Inflorescence with 5–15
tubular-campanulate flowers. Sepals green to white, typically reflexed, and covered with fine hairs. Petals white and
erect. Berries smooth, round, black; unpalatable unless
cooked. Streambanks, in forests, wet meadows, moist ravines. Native.

Ribes hudsonianum
GROSSULARIACEAE
northern black currant
NR, MR, subalpine, montane, common,
Spring–Summer, perennial, 1.5–6.5 ft.
Deciduous, spineless, loosely branched
shrub, erect to spreading tan to gray stems
dotted with yellow glands and bristly hairs.
Leaves alternate, palmately 3-lobed, with
double-toothed margins; lower surfaces often with yellow
glands. Inflorescence an elongated cluster of 6–15 flowers.
Calyces spreading and white. White petals widely separated. Berries round, often waxy-coated; bitter. Grows on
streambanks, in moist woods, shady rock outcrops, coniferous forests. Plant has sweet but unpleasant odor. Native.

Ribes inerme GROSSULARIACEAE
whitestem gooseberry
RM, subalpine, montane, foothills,
wetlands, common, locally abundant,
Spring–E Summer, perennial, 3–7 ft.

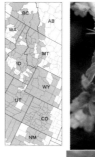

Loosely branched, deciduous, spiny (0–3
at nodes) shrub, erect to spreading grayish stems. Leaves alternate, to 3 in. across,
shallowly palmately 3- to 5-lobed, coarsely
toothed to crenate margins; surfaces smooth
to densely hairy. Inflorescence a drooping raceme of 1–4 white to pink tubular-campanulate flowers.
Sepals greenish white, often reddish at base. Stamens protruding. Berries smooth, round, reddish purple or black;
edible. Found on streambanks, woodlands, forests, meadows, and dry slopes. Although the specific
epithet means "unarmed," this plant typically
has spines. Native.

Iliamna rivularis MALVACEAE
streambank wild hollyhock
MR, SR, montane, foothills, wetlands,
common, Summer, perennial, 3–6.5 ft.
Herb. Erect stems, often branched, from
a woody base. Leaves to 6 in., broadly
heart-shaped with 3–7 triangular lobes,
coarsely rounded teeth, long petioles and covered in fine star-shaped hairs. Flowers 1 to several per leaf
axil, with 5 white to rose-pink petals to 1 in. surrounded by
a hairy, 5-pointed lobed calyx. Found in moist, disturbed
areas, commonly in riparian areas, and distinctive from all
else. Forage for elk and deer. Seeds have been
found still viable after 100 years. Native.

Sidalcea candida MALVACEAE
white checkerbloom
MR, SR, subalpine, montane,
foothills, wetlands, common,
L Spring–Summer, perennial, 1–3 ft.
Herbaceous plant that spreads easily by rhizomes. Stems erect, single, nearly glabrous,
and clustered in older plants. Leaves basal and
mostly cauline; ovate, deeply palmately divided, nearly glabrous, and very distinctive. Flowers grow
in clusters at the top of the stem, are white with a hint of
pink or yellow, often look crowded, and have characteristic
purplish blue anthers. Often found in dense clumps car-
peting the ground in wet areas by streamsides. Native.

Menyanthes trifoliata

MENYANTHACEAE

buckbean, bogbean
RM, subalpine, montane, foothills,
sagebrush steppe, wetlands, common,
L Spring–Summer, perennial, 6–16 in.
Semi-aquatic, rhizomatous, glabrous herb
with fleshy, prostrate or ascending stems.
Basal leaves alternate, trifoliate, each leaflet
elliptic with coarsely wavy margins. Stem
leaves absent. Inflorescence a terminal cluster of white, purplish-tinged flowers. Corollas with reflexed lobes, covered in white scaly long hairs on inside.
Fruit a shiny, oval, brownish yellow, buoyant capsule.
Grows in shallow water of ponds and lakes,
slow-moving streams, marshes. Native.

Ipomopsis aggregata ssp. *candida*

(*Gilia candida*) POLEMONIACEAE

scarlet gilia (white form), white skyrocket
SR, subalpine, montane, foothills,
sagebrush steppe, grasslands, common,
Spring–Summer, biennial/perennial, 7–40 in.
Leaves form an evergreen basal rosette. In
second year, 1 stem (rarely several) originates
from the base. Tubular 5-petaled flowers, 0.8
to 1.6 in. long, form a white or pink (rarely red) elongated
cluster. Grows in sunny and disturbed areas, barrens, rock
scree, rock ledges, dry slopes, and sage meadows. Largely
found on the Front Range of CO. Native.

Ipomopsis aggregata ssp. *weberi*

(*I. aggregata* var. *attenuata*)

POLEMONIACEAE

rabbit ears gilia
MR, SR, subalpine, montane, sagebrush
steppe, grasslands, common, Spring–
Summer, perennial, 7–40 in.
Single stem (rarely several) originates
from an evergreen basal rosette. Tubular 5-petaled flowers form a bright white
to creamy yellow, pink, or red elongated cluster. Sunny
and disturbed areas, barrens, rock scree, rock ledges, dry
slopes, and sage meadows. Found in northern CO around
Rabbit Ears Pass, southcentral WY, and ID. Native.

Polemonium brandegeei

POLEMONIACEAE

Brandegee's Jacob's-ladder

MR, SR, alpine, subalpine, montane,
uncommon, locally abundant,
Summer, perennial, 6–24 in.

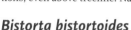

Herbaceous. Leaves are both basal and alternate, narrow, grayish, pinnately divided, somewhat fern-like and delicate-looking. Inflorescence a loose, terminal cyme. Flowers white to yellow often with a reddish blush; long, tubular, often somewhat nodding. Profuse bloomer found on cliffs and in crevices at middle to higher elevations, even above treeline. Native.

Bistorta bistortoides
(Polygonum bistortoides)

POLYGONACEAE

American bistort

RM, alpine, subalpine, montane,
common, locally abundant, L Spring–
Summer, perennial, to 20 in.

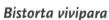

Stems 12–20 in. Linear basal leaves 4–7 in., conspicuous lighter central vein; 3 or 4 leaves in decreasing size on the flowering stems, a papery sheath at each node. Flowers small, 5-lobed, white or blushed pink, in compact 1- to 2-in. terminal spikes, unpleasant scent. Sunny damp meadows, fens at high elevations, tundra. Native.

Bistorta vivipara
(Polygonum viviparum)

POLYGONACEAE

alpine bistort

RM, alpine, subalpine, common,
Summer, perennial, 3–12 in.

Flowering stems from basal rosette; few short leaves along stem with clasping papery sheath. Basal leaves petiolate, smooth, lanceolate to 3 in., edges rolled. Flowers creamy white or tinged pink, 5 petals, mostly sterile, 0.25 in., many in a terminal spike; small bulblets in same arrangement just below flowers are main method of reproduction. Sun; tundra, wet meadows, fens. Circumboreal. Native.

Ceanothus fendleri
(*C. subsericeus*) RHAMNACEAE
Fendler's ceanothus, buckbrush
MR, SR, montane, foothills,
common, locally abundant, L Spring–
Summer, perennial, to 2 ft.

Wide-spreading shrub with thorn-tipped
branches and a shallow root system.
New growth grayish green and hairy.
Lanceolate-elliptic to oblong-ovate leaves,
semi-evergreen, 1 in. long, untoothed,
densely gray-tomentose below and green above. Inflorescence an elongated panicle of corymbs with small white
flowers in clusters. Incurved sepals, tiny spatulate petals,
about 0.1 in. long. Fruit a black capsule, 0.15–0.2 in. long.
Important browse species for deer. Native.

Ceanothus velutinus RHAMNACEAE
snowbrush ceanothus, varnish-leaf
RM, montane, foothills, common, locally
abundant, Summer, perennial, 2–9 ft.

Sprawling, spicy-scented shrub, forming thickets. Olive-green twigs. Leaves
evergreen, alternate, toothed, glandular
and glossy above; elliptic to ovate-elliptic.
Tiny, white, star-shaped flowers have 5
cupped petals, about 0.1 in. long, in dense,
pyramid-shaped clusters. Fruit capsules deeply 3-lobed
and glandular sticky, 0.15–0.2 in. long, ejecting 3 shiny
seeds when mature. When very abundant, plants are a
potential fire hazard due to the presence of volatile oils in
their foliage; favorite deer browse. Native.

Chamaebatiaria millefolium
ROSACEAE
fern bush
MR, montane, foothills, pinyon-
juniper, sagebrush steppe, common,
Spring–Fall, perennial, 3–6 ft.

Coarsely branched shrub, branches reddish
brown to gray, brittle, smooth. Leaves to 3
in., finely fern-like, resinous, fragrant, alternate, closely tufted at branch tips. Flowers
in 4- to 5-in. terminal panicles, each 0.5 in. across with 5
rounded petals and gold central anthers, like tiny roses.
Found on sunny dry slopes, canyons, sage meadows, forest
openings. Loved by bees. Native.

Chamaerhodos erecta ROSACEAE
little ground rose
RM, montane, foothills, sagebrush steppe,
intermountain parks, grasslands, locally
abundant, Summer–Fall, biennial, 4–12 in.

Stems single, branching above. Basal and
stem leaves are deeply divided into many
segments with long hairs. Flowers simple,
5-petaled, white. Grows in sunny and disturbed habitats, barrens, dry slopes, on rock
ledges, sage meadows, and riparian areas. It
can spread in gravelly areas of the intermountain valleys,
plains, and gravel bars of streambeds. Also found in Eurasia. This small plant's flowers resemble miniature wild
roses. Native.

Holodiscus discolor
(Spiraea discolor) ROSACEAE
oceanspray, cream bush
NR, MR, subalpine, montane, pinyon-
juniper, wetlands, common, Spring–
Summer, perennial, 3–10 ft.

Numerous spreading, erect stems; brown
to red bark turning gray and peeling with
age, arching when in flower. Leaves 1–2 in.
long, alternate, egg-shaped or oblong, deeply
toothed or lobed, green above and white
below, with soft hairs more prevalent on underside. Dense,
multibranched inflorescence a nodding pyramid-shaped
panicle, with many fragrant, creamy white flowers that
fade to rust and persist. Along steep riverbanks, open forest, rocky dry to moist areas. Attracts benefi-
cial insects; many traditional uses. Native.

Holodiscus dumosus
(H. discolor var. dumosus) ROSACEAE
rockspirea, glandular oceanspray
MR, SR, montane, foothills, pinyon-juniper,
common, Summer, perennial, to 5 ft.

Numerous spreading, densely branched, erect
stems, dominated by short shoots. Leaves narrower length to width, egg-shaped, with indis-
tinct petioles. Inflorescence loose, irregular
branching panicle of creamy white flowers, smaller than
H. discolor. Found primarily in dry, rocky sites, on cliffs
and in canyons, distinctly different from the wetter habitats of H. discolor. Native.

Prunus americana ROSACEAE
wild plum, American plum
RM, montane, foothills, grasslands,
common, Spring, perennial, 10–25 ft.

Erect shrub to small tree; older bark
thick, gray; twigs reddish to gray; thorns
present. Leaves alternate; obovate to
lanceolate-obovate, doubly serrate margins;
glabrous above, hairy below; deciduous.
Flowers in clusters of 2–5; to 1 in. across; 5
white petals; 5 reddish to greenish reflexed
sepals. Fruit a reddish purple or yellowish drupe about
1 in. in diameter; 1 seed; edible, sweet and juicy. Rocky
slopes, roadsides, riparian areas. Native.

Prunus virginiana var. *melanocarpa*
(Padus virginiana ssp. *melanocarpa)* ROSACEAE
western chokecherry, black chokecherry
RM, subalpine, montane, foothills,
grasslands, common, locally abundant,
Spring, perennial, 10–25 ft.

Shrub to small tree; smooth, brownish to
gray bark; no thorns. Stoloniferous growth
habit can lead to dense thickets. Leaves
2–5 in., simple, alternate, ovate to elliptic,
serrate, glabrous, deciduous. Flowers white, fragrant, in
racemes. Fruits red to dark purple or black; sepals disappear as fruit develops and matures. Important for wildlife.
Found in sun and shade on rocky slopes,
along streams, in open forest. Native.

Purshia stansburiana
(Cowania stansburiana) ROSACEAE
Stansbury cliffrose
MR, SR, pinyon-juniper, sagebrush
steppe, grasslands, common, Spring–
Summer, perennial, 2–12 ft.

Irregular upright stems with close inter-
nodes, young stems reddish gray, aging to
dark papery shredding bark. Leaves to 0.75
in., alternate, densely clustered at nodes; 6–9
pinnate lobes; leathery, edges curled under, evergreen; distinguished by white resin dots and quinine odor. Flowers 1
in. across; 5 creamy white petals and gold central stamens;
sweet fragrance. Sunny dry hills, canyons, high desert tran-
sitional zones of the Wasatch and Colorado Plateau. Native.

Heuchera cylindrica SAXIFRAGACEAE
roundleaf alumroot, poker alumroot
NR, MR, alpine, subalpine, montane,
foothills, common, Spring–Summer,
perennial, 0.5–3 ft.

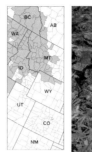

Rhizomatous herb with erect, smooth to
glandular-hairy stems from cluster of basal
leaves. Leaves with 5–7 deeply palmate lobes,
toothed margins, smooth to glandular leaf
surfaces. Inflorescence a dense to open spike
of cream or yellow, weakly bilateral, narrowly
campanulate flowers. Sepals erect, sometimes reddish.
Petals often absent. Styles and stamens not protruding.
Grows on cliffsides and talus slopes. Displays great variation in vegetative and floral morphology. Native.

Heuchera hallii SAXIFRAGACEAE
Front Range alumroot
SR, alpine, subalpine, montane,
foothills, endemic, infrequent,
L Spring–Summer, perennial, 4–12 in.

Herb with erect stems from basal cluster of
leaves. Leaves with 5–7 deep lobes, toothed
margins, smooth to glandular surfaces; purple below. Inflorescence a dense, sometimes
1-sided spike of whitish, greenish, or pinkish
yellow broadly bell-shaped flowers. Sepals
erect. The shape and size of flowers and inflorescence resemble *H. bracteata*, but *H. hallii* has included styles and
stamens. Grows in rocky crevices and on cliffsides. Endemic to central CO. Native.

Leptarrhena pyrolifolia
(*Saxifraga pyrolifolia*) SAXIFRAGACEAE
fireleaf leptarrhena, leatherleaf saxifrage
NR, alpine, subalpine, montane, common,
L Spring–Summer, perennial, 4–16 in.

Rhizomatous herb with erect, reddish stems
from cluster of shiny, leathery, dark green
basal leaves. Leaves to 4 in., obovate to elliptic,
with serrated to crenate margins. 1–3 small,
alternate stem leaves sessile and clasping. Inflorescence a terminal, congested cluster of
white or pinkish saucer-shaped flowers with red calyces
that mature to red seedheads. Stamens exserted. Grows
in wet meadows, fens, along streams, wet cliffs, and talus
slopes. The Aleuts made infusions of the leaves as an
influenza remedy. Native.

Micranthes ferruginea
(Saxifraga ferruginea)
SAXIFRAGACEAE

rusty-hair saxifrage, Alaska saxifrage
NR, MR, alpine, subalpine, montane,
foothills, common, L Spring–
Summer, perennial, 6–16 in.
Rhizomatous herb with erect branching red
stems from basal rosette. Leaves to 3 in.,
fleshy, hairy, oblanceolate to wedge-shaped,
with irregularly toothed margins. A panicle
of 20–30 flowers extends nearly to base of stem. Reddish
purple sepals reflexed. Petals claw-shaped and white: 3
broader with 2 yellow spots near bases and 2 smaller without spots. 10 filaments with pinkish anthers. Wet ledges,
seepage sites, gravelly slopes, sunny streambanks. Native.

Micranthes lyallii
(Saxifraga lyallii) SAXIFRAGACEAE
red-stemmed saxifrage
NR, alpine, subalpine, montane,
common, Summer, perennial, 4–16 in.
Rhizomatous herb; slender, erect, reddish
stems, solitary or mat-forming. Basal rosette,
leaves spatulate-ovate; toothed margins,
glossy or covered in soft, brown hairs. Stem
leaves small, bract-like or absent. Inflorescence a cyme, up
to 15 flowers. Sepals reddish, reflexed; clawed petals also
reflexed, white aging pink, each with 2 basal yellowish
green spots. 10 stamens, white filaments. Wet rocky meadows, wet ledges, streambanks. Native.

Micranthes occidentalis
(Saxifraga occidentalis)
SAXIFRAGACEAE

Alberta saxifrage, western saxifrage
NR, MR, alpine, subalpine, montane,
common, locally abundant, Spring–
Summer, perennial, 4–12 in.
Rhizomatous herb with 1–3 erect,
soft-hairy, leafless stems from basal cluster;
colony-forming. Leaves fleshy, leathery, egg-
to diamond-shaped with coarse, rounded teeth; glabrous
above, reddish brown hairs below. Inflorescence an open
to compact, pyramidal cluster of 10–30 white to pink flowers. Petals unspotted, nearly round, tapering to a claw;
10 stamens, club-shaped filaments. Rocky crevices, meadows, gravelly slopes, streambanks. Native.

Micranthes odontoloma
(Saxifraga odontoloma)
SAXIFRAGACEAE
brook saxifrage
RM, alpine, subalpine, montane, foothills,
common, Summer, perennial, 5–24 in.

Rhizomatous herb with erect, slender stems
from basal cluster of leaves; forming colonies. Leaves 1–3 in., slightly fleshy, round or
reniform with gland-tipped triangular teeth.
Inflorescence an open panicle of 10–30 flowers. Sepals purplish, bent downward. Petals whitish,
nearly round, narrowing to claw with 2 yellow spots. 10
club-shaped stamens with white filaments and purplish
anthers. Wet meadows, streambanks, fens. Native.

Micranthes oregana
(Saxifraga oregana) SAXIFRAGACEAE
Oregon saxifrage
RM, alpine, subalpine, montane, common,
Spring–Summer, perennial, 0.5–3 ft.

Rhizomatous herb with erect, leafless stem
from basal rosette; solitary to colony-forming.
Fleshy, flat leaves linear to ovate; margins entire to toothed; slightly hairy to smooth. Inflorescence an open to congested cluster of
30–50 flowers. Sepals bent backward. Petals
whitish, oval, unequal in size. Wet meadows, fens, and
streambanks. Important early source of nectar for native
pollinators. Native.

Mitella stauropetala
SAXIFRAGACEAE
**side-flowered mitrewort, smallflower
mitrewort**
RM, alpine, subalpine, montane, foothills,
common, Spring–Summer, perennial, 4–20 in.

Rhizomatous herb with slender, erect, leafless
flowering stems from basal cluster of leaves.
Leaves slightly hairy, reniform to cordate with
5–7 lobes, margins round-toothed. Inflorescence a 1-sided simple raceme of 10–45 small,
delicate-looking white flowers distant from
each other. Erect, greenish white, rounded sepals alternate
with narrowly forked petals and surround a saucer-shaped
hypanthium. When petals and sepals fall away, cups of
black seeds remain on the stalk. Open to dense forests,
moist meadows, streambanks. Native.

Mitella trifida SAXIFRAGACEAE
threeparted mitrewort
NR, MR, montane, infrequent,
L Spring–Summer, perennial, 5–18 in.

Rhizomatous perennial. Stems often clustered, hairy. Basal leaves almost round with a heart-shaped base on a long stalk, shallowly lobed. Cauline leaves absent. Inflorescence a spike of white flowers; 3-lobed petals sometimes tinged with purple; calyces bell-shaped. Calyx lobes 5. Stamens 5. Fruit a capsule. Native.

Saxifraga caespitosa SAXIFRAGACEAE
tufted alpine saxifrage
NR, alpine, subalpine, common,
Summer–Fall, perennial, 4–6 in.

Rhizomatous, mat-forming subshrub. Leaves marcescent; basal leaves twice ternately dissected, bright green in basal tufts. Cauline leaves alternate, reduced in size. Inflorescence a dense terminal spike-like raceme, erect to ascending. Flowers 5-petaled, small, whitish to creamy, sometimes yellow-tinged, up to 20 stamens per flower. Fruit a follicle. Grows in moist or shady mountain areas where snow persists. Superficially resembles *Luetkea pectinata* (partridgefoot); indeed, the divided leaves are shaped like birds' feet. Native.

Sullivantia hapemanii SAXIFRAGACEAE
Hapeman's coolwort
MR, SR, subalpine, montane,
foothills, endemic, uncommon,
Summer, perennial, 9–16 in.

Herb with erect, wiry, glandular-hairy, alternately branched stems. Basal leaves with long petioles, orbicular, 1–4 in. across, with 5–13 palmate lobes and toothed to nearly crenulate margins. Stem leaves alternate, reduced, and with shorter petioles. Inflorescence an open panicle of small white flowers. Calyx green, campanulate and 5-lobed. Grows on limestone or calcareous rock faces in hanging gardens and in seepage areas of cliffs in the shade. A regional endemic found in ID, MT, CO, and WY, sensitive to hydrological disruption. Native.

Tiarella trifoliata SAXIFRAGACEAE

threeleaf foamflower, lace foamflower

NR, subalpine, montane, common, locally abundant, L Spring–Summer, perennial, 8–20 in.

Rhizomatous herb with erect, glandular-pubescent stems. Basal leaves to 3.75 in. across, cordate but variable; 3–5 palmate lobes or trifoliate, hairy; margins toothed. Stem leaves absent or few and reduced. Inflorescence an elongated panicle of white flowers. Calyx campanulate with 5 lobes, top lobe largest. Petals white, linear, similar to filaments. 10 stamens, those alternate with petals longer and those opposite shorter. Grows in moist woods, meadows, and streambanks. Native.

Verbascum blattaria

SCROPHULARIACEAE

moth mullein

RM, foothills, grasslands, common, L Spring–Summer, biennial, 2–5 ft.

Taprooted herb; basal rosette first year, then upright flowering stem, mainly glabrous. Basal leaves to 10 in. long, ovate to lanceolate, coarsely toothed, not hairy; stem leaves reduced upward, alternate, mainly absent among flowers. Flowering stem solitary or branched just above leaves, with glandular hairs; flowers outfacing in narrow spike; 5 petals, white or yellow, to 1.25 in. across, stamens red/pink, fuzzy; round seed capsule when mature. Grows in sun, roadsides, disturbed sites, farm fields. Introduced and invasive.

Lathyrus lanszwertii var. *leucanthus*

(*L. leucanthus*) FABACEAE

whiteflower pea

SR, montane, foothills, grasslands, common, Spring–Summer, perennial, 8–48 in.

Sprawling to erect herbaceous stems; tendrils reduced to a simple, uncoiled bristle. Leaves alternate, even-pinnately compound, 4–8 leaflets, linear to elliptic. Inflorescence a raceme of 2–10 white pea-shaped flowers; 5 petals; banner occasionally with purple veins. Pods smooth, 0.75–1.5 in. long. Grows in sun to part shade; open, coniferous forests; meadows; slopes. Native.

Lathyrus ochroleucus FABACEAE
cream pea
NR, MR, montane, foothills, common,
Spring–Summer, perennial, 1–3 ft.
Erect to trailing herbaceous stems from a
rhizome; smooth; not winged. Leaves alternate, pinnate with 6–8 leaflets, narrowly
ovate to elliptic; tendrils branching; stipules
to half the length of leaflets. Pea-shaped
flowers 6–14 per raceme, white to pale yellow; wings and keel shorter than banner.
Pods smooth, to 2.5 in., turning brown. Grows in sun to
shade, moist open forests, meadows, rocky slopes. Native.

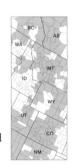

Viola canadensis VIOLACEAE
Canadian white violet
RM, montane, foothills, common,
L Spring–E Summer, perennial, 4–15 in.
Herb with prostrate to erect stems. Basal
and stem leaves soft green, heart-shaped,
with subtle dentation on margins. Petioles
reduced upward. Solitary, white or pale lavender flowers in leaf axils. Petals with yellow bases; the lower petal with a short spur,
the lower 3 with purplish nectar guides, and
the 2 side petals with beards at bases. Widespread and common in woodlands, moist
forests, and on streambanks throughout the
Rockies. Native.

Viola canadensis ssp. *scopulorum*
(*V. scopulorum*) VIOLACEAE
Canadian white violet
SR, montane, foothills, common,
L Spring–Summer, perennial, 4–15 in.
Perennial herb with branching, erect stems.
Basal and stem leaves light green, cordate,
with crenate margins. White or pale pink
flowers in leaf axils. Petals (especially lower
ones) with distinct short dark nectar guides.
Locally common in woodlands, moist for-
ests, and on streambanks throughout the
Rockies, commonest in the montane and
upper foothills. This is the prevailing subspecies in the
SR. Native.

Viola macloskeyi VIOLACEAE
small white violet, smooth white violet
RM, subalpine, montane, infrequent,
L Spring–E Summer, perennial, 2–5 in.

Delicate, stemless herb with orbicular to
heart-shaped leaves that have nearly entire to
crenulate margins. Inflorescence of solitary,
white to pale lavender flowers. Lower petal
with prominent spur, lower 3 heavily striped
with purple guide lines toward the ovary, and
the 2 side petals bearded or not. Upper 2 petals often curving back. Scattered throughout the Rockies
in moist, shady canyons, mossy streamsides, bogs, and
woodlands. Native.

Viola palustris VIOLACEAE
marsh violet
RM, subalpine, montane,
foothills, infrequent, L Spring–
Summer, perennial, 3–7 in.

Smooth, stemless, upright herb. Leaves ovate
to round, heart, or kidney-shaped and with
crenulate margins and smooth surfaces.
Flowers solitary, nearly white to palest lavender with a pouched spur, the lower 3 petals with purplish veins and the 2 side petals
sparsely bearded (beards sometimes absent).
Shade-loving violet found on mossy streambanks, moist
forests, meadows, and fens. Native.

Viola renifolia VIOLACEAE
white violet
RM, subalpine, montane, wetlands, common,
L Spring–E Summer, perennial, to 8 in.

Herb from fleshy rhizome. 2–5 rounded to
kidney-shaped 1.5-in. leaves arise from each
rhizome. Leaf margin entire to finely toothed,
typically villous, sometimes glabrous, unlobed. Flowers are single, on long pedicels,
most often white with purple veins, although
can be pink to lavender. Plants grow in wet
areas along streams and in upland forests and
willow thickets. Shade. Native.

Astragalus alpinus FABACEAE
alpine milkvetch
RM, alpine, subalpine, montane, common,
Spring–Summer, perennial, 2–10 in.
Stems branching, forming colonies from underground rhizomes. Leaves green, pinnately compound with 11–27 leaflets, deciduous. Flowers pea-shaped, 5-petaled, bicolored, with the wings white and the banner and keel tip purple to varying degrees. Pods pea-like, pointing down, covered with hairs. Grows in tundra, aspen or coniferous forests, dry and moist meadows, and along streams. One of the most common milkvetches throughout the West. The leaflets are usually arched, and flower stalk is leafless. Native.

Astragalus crassicarpus FABACEAE
groundplum milkvetch
NR, throughout, common, Spring–Summer, perennial, 4–20 in.
Stems branching from base, arching out, often creeping but sometimes found upright. Leaves green, pinnately compound with 13 leaflets, deciduous. Flowers pea-shaped, 5-petaled, bicolored: white, cream, pink, lavender, or purplish. Most noticeable in fruit: pods are round, swollen, hairless, reddish or greenish "groundplums." Grows on sunny dry slopes, barrens, and meadows. Ranges eastward into the Midwest past the 100th meridian, and farther north is found largely on the plains, not in the mountains. Native.

Astragalus gilviflorus
(*A. triphyllus*) FABACEAE
plains milkvetch
MR, montane, foothills, sagebrush steppe, intermountain parks, grasslands, common, locally abundant, Spring, perennial, 1–5 in.
Stems short, clump- or cushion-forming. Leaves covered in silvery hairs, compound with 3 leaflets, deciduous. Flowers pea-shaped, 5-petaled, white to purplish, with the keel often purple, covering the plant. Pods are pea-like and covered in dense hairs. Grows in sun, barrens, dry slopes, meadows, sage meadows. Found over a wide range but only grows within the MR of WY and southern MT; elsewhere it is a plains-dwelling species. Native.

Astragalus parryi FABACEAE
Parry's milkvetch
SR, montane, foothills, intermountain
parks, grasslands, common,
Summer, perennial, 0.5–8 in.

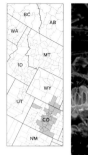

Stems clump-forming. Leaves deciduous,
gray-green, pinnately compound with 4–14
leaflets, hairy on both surfaces. Flowers clean
white and sparse; 4–8 per plant, 5-petaled,
pea-shaped. Pods are pea-like and very hairy.
Grows in sunny areas, pine parklands, dry
slopes, and meadows. Often seen with ponderosa pine.
The leaves display unusually long marginate hairs. Native.

Psoralidium lanceolatum
(*Psoralea lanceolata*) FABACEAE
lemon scurfpea
RM, montane, foothills, grasslands, common,
L Spring–E Summer, perennial, 8–24 in.

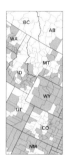

Bushy with erect stems from woody base;
not armed. Leaves alternate, palmately compound with 3 narrowly linear to lanceolate
leaflets to 1.5 in. long, yellow-green and dotted
with translucent glands. Flowers in a raceme
up to 1.5 in. long; individual flowers white to
cream-colored with a purple-tipped keel. Fruit
a rounded and hairy pod to 0.25 in. Found in
sandy sites. The leaves have a lemony aroma and oily feel.
Native.

Trifolium hybridum
(*T. elegans*) FABACEAE
alsike clover
RM, montane, foothills, sagebrush
steppe, grasslands, common,
Spring–Fall, perennial, 4–24 in.

Sprawling to upright, short-lived herb. Compound leaves in 3s, elliptical to 1.2 in. long;
stipules to 0.75 in. long, tapering to sharp
point. Flowerheads rounded with numerous
white to pink or reddish, reflexed 0.6-in.-long
flowers; calyx smooth. Fruit a small pod on a
short stalk with 2–4 seeds. Found in meadows
and disturbed sites, along roadsides, near streams. Similar
to *T. pratense* but lacks white markings on leaves and a pair
of leaves directly below flowerhead. Introduced.

Trifolium longipes FABACEAE
longstalk clover
MR, SR, subalpine, montane,
wetlands, common, L Spring–
Summer, perennial, 2–12 in.
Rhizomatous herb with a woody base.
Stems upright. Compound leaves in 3s; leaflets rounded to linear, to 2 in. long; stipules
green. Flowerheads rounded, with individual flowers upright and spreading; white,
yellowish, purple, or bicolored, to 0.7 in.
long; calyx teeth to 0.25 in. long. Fruit a stalked pod with
1–4 seeds. Found in shady locations in wet meadows, along
streams, and woodlands. Sometimes confused with *T.
pratense* or *T. repens*. Native.

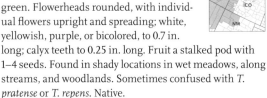

Trifolium repens FABACEAE
white clover
RM, subalpine, montane, foothills,
grasslands, wetlands, common,
Spring–Summer, perennial, 2–24 in.
Stoloniferous herb with long stems. Leaves
alternate, compound with leaflets in 3s; leaflets elliptic to rounded, to 1 in. long, often
with a whitish V-shaped mark. Flowerheads
round to 1.2 in. across, terminal with individual flowers spreading to reflexed; flowers
white, aging to pink, to 0.4 in. long. Found in disturbed
sites, lawns, roadsides, and meadows. Originally imported
as a cover crop and sometimes used in crop rotation.
Introduced.

Sambucus caerulea
(S. nigra ssp. *cerulea)* ADOXACEAE
blue elderberry
RM, montane, foothills, sagebrush
steppe, grasslands, locally abundant,
L Spring–Summer, perennial, 4–20 ft.
Coarse, deciduous, erect shrub to small tree,
usually as wide as tall, with smooth, pithy,
waxy stems and grayish to dark brown bark.
Leaves opposite, pinnately compound with
5–9 lanceolate to elliptic leaflets, each 1–6 in.
long; margins serrated and surfaces smooth. Inflorescence
a flat-topped cluster, to 1 ft. wide, of small, creamy white,
fragrant flowers. Fruit a round, bluish black or purplish
black berry-like drupe covered in a powdery blue bloom.
Found along streams and on moist open slopes. Native.

Viburnum edule
(*V. pauciflorum*) ADOXACEAE
squashberry, highbush cranberry
RM, subalpine, montane, foothills, locally
abundant, Spring–Summer, perennial, 2–9 ft.
Deciduous, rhizomatous shrub with spreading to erect, smooth, reddish gray branches.
Leaves opposite, to 4 in. across, 3-lobed to unlobed, hairy lower surfaces, serrated margins;
often a pair of glandular teeth where blade
meets petiole. Inflorescence a compact cluster of whitish, bell-shaped 0.25-in. flowers with spreading lobes, subtended by a pair of leaves. Fruit a cluster of
orange to red berry-like drupes. Grows along streams,
in moist shady locations, and in spruce-fir forests. Dark
green leaves turn brilliant red in autumn.
Native.

Toxicodendron rydbergii
(*Rhus radicans* var. *rydbergii*)
ANACARDIACEAE
western poison ivy
RM, montane, foothills, uncommon, locally
abundant, Spring–Fall, perennial, 4–20 in.
Rhizomatous, slender shrub. Stems erect
and branched, exude milky sap when broken. Leaves shiny, trifoliate with long stalks.
Leaflets egg-shaped with pointy tips, often folded inward.
Inflorescence an axillary panicle. Flowers 0.25 in. across,
white to cream. Fruit a white berry-like drupe. Contact
with this plant, dead or alive, even from clothing or
animal fur that has contacted it, can cause a
severe dermatitis for some people. Photo inset
is fruiting winter form. Native.

Angelica ampla APIACEAE
giant angelica
SR, montane, foothills, infrequent, locally
abundant, Summer, perennial, 3–7 ft.
Single-stemmed (occasionally multi-) herb
with very stout, hollow stems. Leaves deciduous, ternate and bipinnate. Leaflets 1.2–8 in.
long, ovate, serrate. Inflorescence a rounded
umbel with 30–45 rays. Flowers white. Grows in moist
meadows and along streams. Largest *Angelica* sp. in SR, it
stands out from all others due to its size. Plant has a weak
anise scent. Monocarpic. Native.

Angelica arguta APIACEAE
white angelica
NR, MR, subalpine, montane, common,
Summer, perennial, 2–6 ft.
Herb with single (occasionally multiple),
erect, hollow, and very stout stems. Leaves
deciduous, bipinnate. Leaflets 1.2–4 in. long,
ovate to narrowly elliptic, serrate. Inflorescence a flat umbel, 0.8–1.6 in. across, of
20–60 small white to pinkish flowers, with
uneven rays 0.8–3.1 in. long and petals 0.04–
0.08 in. long. Grows in moist meadows, woodlands, and
along streams. Native.

Angelica pinnata APIACEAE
small-leaf angelica
RM, subalpine, montane, foothills,
grasslands, wetlands, locally abundant,
Summer, perennial, 10–35 in.
Single (occasionally multiple) stout but hollow stems. Leaves deciduous, pinnately
compound or incomplete bipinnate, arising
from base and along stem. Leaflets 1.2–3.5
in. long, lanceolate to ovate, with serrate
margins. Inflorescence a flat-topped, compound umbel consisting of 6–25 flowers.
Rays are uneven and 1.6–2.4 in. long; petals
0.04 in. long. Flowers white or pinkish. Easily found in
riparian areas, aspen, moist meadows, seeps. Native.

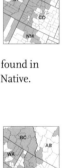

Cicuta douglasii APIACEAE
western water hemlock
NR, MR, montane, intermountain
parks, wetlands, common,
Summer, perennial, 1–4 ft.
Single-stemmed (occasionally multi-) herb
with very stout, hollow stems. Leaves deciduous, leaflets 0.6–2.4 in. long, lanceolate to
ovate, serrate. Inflorescence an umbel with
0.8- to 2-in.-long uneven rays. Flowers white
to pinkish. Grows in riparian areas, moist
meadows, seeps. The roots of *Cicuta* spp.
have a distinctive channeled pattern. One of
the most poisonous plants in North America. Very similar
to *C. maculata*. Native.

Cicuta maculata APIACEAE

spotted water hemlock
RM, montane, foothills, grasslands, wetlands, common, Summer, perennial, 1–4 ft.
Single-stemmed (occasionally multi-) herb with very stout, hollow stems. Leaves deciduous, twice pinnate, leaflets variable, 1.2–4 in. long in CO and 0.8–2.75 in. long in MT, lanceolate, serrate. Inflorescence an umbel with 0.8- to 2-in.-long uneven rays. Flowers white to pinkish. Grows in riparian areas, moist meadows, seeps. The roots of *Cicuta* spp. have a distinctive channeled pattern. Extremely poisonous, found throughout North America. Native.

Conium maculatum APIACEAE

poison hemlock
RM, montane, foothills, grasslands, wetlands, common, L Spring–Summer, biennial, 1.5–10 ft.
Herbaceous stems erect with purple spots or streaks; leaf blades to 1 ft. long, pinnately compound and fern-like, either once or 3 times divided with ultimate segments small. Unpleasant smell if crushed. Small white 5-petaled flowers on a fairly flat compound umbel. Found in wet meadows, riparian areas, disturbed sites, and ditches. All parts of this plant are highly poisonous, and consuming even a small leaf may lead to severe illness. Introduced.

Cymopterus acaulis
(*C. glomeratus*) APIACEAE

plains springparsley
RM, foothills, sagebrush steppe, grasslands, common, Spring, perennial, 1–12 in.
Open flattened rosette of 2 or 3 times pinnate basal leaves. Flowers small, white, in dense rounded umbel; stemless or nearly so. Sun; meadows, barrens, dry slopes. This plant is easily confused with *Lomatium orientale* but has shinier and more narrow leaves. It also tends to be found in sandier soils. Native.

Heracleum maximum
(*H. lanatum*) APIACEAE
common cowparsnip
RM, alpine, subalpine, montane, common,
L Spring–E Summer, perennial, 3–10 ft.
Strong-smelling herbaceous plant from
thick taproot. Stems erect, single, hairy,
branched, hollow. Leaves enormous, from
long stalks with enlarged base; alternate,
palmately lobed, resembling maple leaves.
Inflorescence a round, flat umbel that can
be more than 10 in. across in full bloom, with small white
flowers. Found in wetlands, meadows, and streamsides.
The genus is named for the Greek hero Hercules (Hera-
cles), a nod to the large size of its members. Native.

Ligusticum filicinum APIACEAE
Utah ligusticum, fernleaf licorice-root
RM, subalpine, montane, foothills, locally
abundant, Summer, perennial, 1.5–4 ft.
Many stems; tall, erect, stout, and hollow.
Leaves largely basal, tripinnate, 4.8–11.2 in.,
smallest division linear to deltoid, 0.1–0.7 in.
Flowers white, 5-petaled, in umbels. Fruit
is 0.2–0.3 in. long. Grows in sun and shade,
coniferous and aspen forests, and sage and
moist meadows. Leaves are more dissected
than *L. porteri*. Several similar *Ligusticum* spp. are found
in the NR and MR of ID, MT and UT: *L. canbyi*, *L. grayi*,
and *L. verticillatum*. Native.

Ligusticum porteri APIACEAE
osha, love root, Porter's lovage
MR, SR, alpine, subalpine,
montane, foothills, common,
Summer, perennial, 2–4 ft.
Several to many stems; tall, erect, stout, and
hollow. Leaves fern-like, largely basal, finely
divided in 3s. Flowers white, 5-petaled, in
umbels. Grows in sun and shade, coniferous
and aspen forests, sage and moist meadows,
and riparian areas. Hollow stems and anise
scent differentiate from a bracken fern when
not in bloom. Extremely common in meadows and aspen
groves of CO. Native.

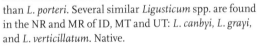

Ligusticum tenuifolium
(*L. filicinum* var. *tenuifolium*)

APIACEAE

slender ligusticum
MR, SR, alpine, subalpine, montane, foothills,
common, Summer, perennial, 4–28 in.

Erect stems, 1 to several. Leaves basal, 1 small
stem leaf; bipinnate, 0.8–5.9 in. long, linear
to deeply lobed. Segments 3 times longer
than wide. Flowers white, 5-petaled, in umbels. Fruit is 0.08–0.2 in. long. Grows in sun
and shade in riparian areas, coniferous and aspen forests,
moist meadows. Fruit size and leaf dissection are defining
characteristics. Smaller and less robust than *L. porteri* and
other ligusticums. Possibly hybridizes with *L. filicinum* in
MT. Native.

Lomatium macrocarpum
(*Peucedanum macrocarpum*)

APIACEAE

bigseed biscuitroot
RM, montane, foothills, pinyon-juniper,
sagebrush steppe, grasslands, locally
abundant, Spring, perennial, 4–12 in.

Unbranched stems and leaves arise from a
compact crown. Leaves pinnately to ternately
dissected, 1.2–2.4 in., with the smallest divisions linear, about 0.1 in. Flowers white, 5-petaled, pinkish in bud, in umbels with fine hairs. Fruit has marginal
wings less than 0.1 in. wide. Grows in sunny areas, barrens, dry slopes, sage meadows, and meadows.
One of the most widespread lomatiums in
the region. Native.

Osmorhiza berteroi
(*O. chilensis*) APIACEAE

sweetcicely
RM, subalpine, montane, foothills,
locally abundant, L Spring–
Summer, perennial, 8–30 in.

Herb from taproot with 1–3 erect branching
stems. Numerous long-stemmed basal and
alternate stem leaves are twice divided into
3 leaflets with lobed to toothed margins and hairy surfaces. Inflorescence a compound umbel of small, white to
greenish white flowers. Fruit a nearly cylindrical, hispid
schizocarp with beak-like tip. Shady woods, open forests,
streambanks. Native.

Osmorhiza depauperata
(*O. obtusa*) APIACEAE
blunt sweetcicely, bluntseed sweetroot
RM, subalpine, montane,
foothills, common, Spring–
Summer, perennial, 4–28 in.

Delicate herb from taproot with 1–3 erect
branching stems. Long-stemmed basal and
alternate stem leaves are twice divided into
3 leaflets with lobed to toothed margins and
hairy surfaces. Inflorescence a compound
umbel of small, white to greenish white (occasionally pink
or purple) flowers. Fruit a club-shaped, hispid schizocarp
without a beak-like tip. Grows in woods, open forests, and
on streambanks. Roots smell like anise. Native.

Oxypolis fendleri APIACEAE
Fendler's cowbane
MR, SR, subalpine, montane, common,
locally abundant, Summer, perennial, 1–3 ft.

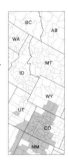

Slender, glabrous, solitary stems from clustered, tuberous roots. Leaves mainly basal,
pinnate, 3–7 in. long, a few smaller along
lower stem; leaflets variable, ovate to lanceolate, 1–2.5 in. long, can have somewhat
rounded teeth. Flowers in small umbels
up to 2 in. across. Grows in shade or partial
sun, wet meadows and especially streamsides. Native.

Perideridia montana
(*P. gairdneri* ssp. *borealis*) APIACEAE
common yampah
RM, alpine, subalpine, montane, foothills,
sagebrush steppe, intermountain
parks, common, locally abundant,
Spring–Summer, perennial, 1–3 ft.

Slender upright caraway-scented stems,
upper part branched, from perennial tuberous roots. Leaves pinnately divided into
pairs of narrow segments 3–12 in. long;
basal leaves withering, cauline leaves alternate, less divided. Flowers in umbels to 3 in.
wide, each section with as many as 40 tiny,
white to pinkish flowers. Subspecies distinguished by venation in the tiny petals. Edible roots were used by Native
Americans. Found in open woodlands, seasonally damp
meadows at all elevations. Native.

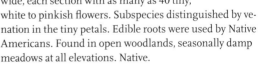

Sanicula marilandica APIACEAE

Maryland sanicle, Maryland black snakeroot
RM, montane, foothills, infrequent,
Spring–E Summer, perennial, 12–30 in.

Upright stem with whorls of leaves at branch
stem axils. Lush green, palmate, basal leaves
are 5- to 7-parted, dentate. Flowers are tiny,
white, sometimes tinged green; 5 sharp linear
petals exceeding the sepals; forming small
round clusters in sparse umbel. Flower with
conspicuous exserted style developing a bristly, green spherical seedpod. Shady woodlands and meadows. Disjunct in the Rockies from eastern U.S. Native.

Sium suave
(*S. cicutifolium*) APIACEAE

hemlock waterparsnip
RM, montane, foothills, grasslands, wetlands,
common, Summer, perennial, 2–4 ft.

Thick, hollow stems with angular ridges,
from fibrous roots. Leaves to 1 ft. long, glabrous, once pinnate, lowest leaves may be
very finely divided, especially if submerged.
Cauline leaves have serrated margins, distinguished from similar species by the fine
veins, which often lead to the tooth tips but
not tooth bases. Flowers in compound umbels
up to 4.5 in. across, with linear bracts below. Once pinnate
leaves distinguish this from the poisonous *Cicuta maculata*, which are twice pinnate. Sunny wetlands, pond and
stream margins, ditches. Native.

Apocynum cannabinum

APOCYNACEAE

Indian hemp, hemp dogbane
RM, subalpine, montane, pinyon-juniper,
sagebrush steppe, intermountain
parks, grasslands, common, Spring–
Summer, perennial, 4–6 ft.

Plants form large colonies. Stems branch
slightly near the top. Leaves yellow-green,
mostly opposite but not always; much more
lanceolate and with a much more visible
venation pattern than those of *A. androsaemifolium*. Flowers, up to 30, in clusters. Flowers are quite small and are
white or often pale green. Grows in shade or sun and
adapted to many soil types. Found in disturbed sites and
roadcuts. Native.

Asclepias pumila APOCYNACEAE
plains milkweed
MR, SR, foothills, grasslands, common,
Summer, perennial, 2–14 ft.

Low herb with 1 to several stems, rhizomatous roots. Leaves linear, irregularly whorled and densely crowded along the stem, up to 2 in. in length, petiole absent. Groups of 4–20 flowers about 0.25 in. long arise from peduncles on the leaf axils. Greenish white corolla, often tinged rose or yellow-green, is 0.1–0.2 in. long. Horns are present on the hood. Fruit, 1.2–3.2 in. long, is held upright. Grows on dry sites in sandy, clay or rocky calcareous soils. Native.

Asclepias subverticillata
(*A. galioides*) APOCYNACEAE
horsetail milkweed, whorled milkweed
MR, SR, montane, foothills, sagebrush steppe, intermountain parks, common, Summer, perennial, 1–2.3 ft.

Erect, spreading herb with multiple branches or unbranched. Leaves linear, 1.5–5 in. long, arranged in a whorl of 3 or 4 leaves, blades narrowly lance-shaped, with short petioles or subsessile. White to cream flowers from lateral and upper leaf axils, corolla 0.1–0.2 in. long; white hoods with horns present. Follicles are 2–3.5 in. long. Common in sandy or rocky soils along ditches and streams and in sagebrush and open ponderosa pine communities. Native.

Hydrophyllum fendleri
BORAGINACEAE
Fendler's waterleaf
RM, subalpine, montane, locally abundant, Spring–Fall, perennial, 8–32 in.

Herbaceous, fibrous-rooted perennial with hairy stems. Leaves 2–12 in. long, mostly basal, spreading, pinnately divided into 7–13 leaflets, simple or toothed with stiff hairs on both sides. Inflorescence many-flowered, loose clusters of bell-shaped white to lavender flowers. Flowers either obscured by foliage or rise just above it. Stamens 5. Stamens and style protrude beyond corolla. Fruit a capsule. Shade. Grows in thickets and moist open places at mid elevations. Common in the SR; infrequent in the MR and NR. Native.

Oreocarya caespitosa
(Cryptantha caespitosa)
BORAGINACEAE
tufted cryptantha
MR, SR, foothills, pinyon-juniper,
sagebrush steppe, intermountain parks,
grasslands, infrequent, locally abundant,
Spring–E Summer, perennial, 1–3 in.
Similar to *O. humilis*, but mat-forming to
mounded. Leaves 0.25–1.25 in., linear,
silky-hairy. Can form almost bowling-ball-
sized mounds in shale barrens. Flowers in small clusters
appearing capitate. Limited distribution on exposed shale
in sagebrush or pinyon-juniper zone. Native.

Oreocarya fulvocanescens
(Cryptantha fulvocanescens)
BORAGINACEAE
tawny cryptantha
SR, pinyon-juniper, sagebrush steppe,
uncommon, Spring, perennial, 3–12 in.
Dense herb, multiple stems from woody base;
basal leaves lance- to spoon-shaped to 2.75 in.
long, uniformly hairy with blisters at bases
mostly on lower surface; stem leaves few, reduced, alternate. Inflorescence covered in
white or yellow hair-like bristles; flowers white
with 5 fused petals, the yellow floral tube visible beyond
calyx, 5 distinctly raised yellow appendages ring the center, the flattened part of the petals extending 0.35 in. Fruit,
a lance-ovate nutlet, is needed for identification.
Sunny, sandy, rocky areas. Native.

Oreocarya humilis
(Cryptantha humilis) BORAGINACEAE
low cryptantha
MR, SR, montane, pinyon-juniper,
sagebrush steppe, locally abundant,
Spring, perennial, to 8 in.
Low, spreading herb with spoon-shaped basal
leaves 0.6–2.4 in. long. Leaves silvery-haired
with blisters at bases of hairs on both surfaces. Flower stems conspicuously hairy.
Flowers cream, similar to *O. fulvocanescens,* except the flattened part of the petals extends up to 0.4 in. Fruit, with 1–4
lance- to round-lance-shaped nutlets, is required for identification. Sandy soil, open places. More common in UT and
NV. Native.

Phacelia hastata BORAGINACEAE
silverleaf phacelia
RM, subalpine, montane, foothills,
sagebrush steppe, common,
L Spring–Fall, perennial, 2–16 in.

Herbaceous plant from a branched caudex. Stems trailing to erect, usually several.
Herbage silvery-hirsute, some thick stiff
hairs, glandless. Leaves basal and alternate,
broadly lance-shaped to oval, 0.8–4 in. long,
usually entire, sometimes with lateral lobes
at base, prominently veined, progressively reduced. Inflorescence a short, compact, coiled, 1-sided cyme. Flowers
white to lavender, bell-shaped, petals fused, 5-lobed, stamens pubescent. Stamens and style protrude.
Occurs in stony, sparsely vegetated soil. Distinguished from close relatives by its prominent leaf veins. Native.

Romanzoffia sitchensis
BORAGINACEAE
Sitka mistmaiden
NR, subalpine, montane, infrequent,
L Spring–E Summer, perennial, 3–8 in.

Delicate herb with slender, weak flowering
stems. Basal leaves palmately notched or
lobed, hairy. Campanulate flowers with yellow centers in lightly branched raceme. Usually found
on cliffs and rock crevices near waterfalls. Disjunct from
Pacific coastal distribution of genus. Native.

Valeriana acutiloba
(*V. capitata* var. *acutiloba*)
CAPRIFOLIACEAE
sharpleaf valerian, Cordilleran valerian
RM, alpine, subalpine, common,
L Spring–Summer, perennial, 4–24 in.

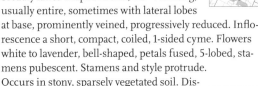

Herbaceous, rhizomatous plant with slender, erect, minutely stiff-hairy stems. Basal
leaves well developed, to 3 in. long, ovate
to spatulate, with entire to coarsely dentate
margins. 1–3 pairs of stem leaves opposite,
reduced and mostly pinnately lobed. Inflorescence a cluster (not elongating much in fruit) with
white to pinkish flowers somewhat hairy on outside. Stamens conspicuously protruding. Fruit a lanceolate achene
with feather-like plume. Grows on moist, rocky slopes, in
conifer forests, moist meadows. Native.

Valeriana occidentalis

CAPRIFOLIACEAE
western valerian
RM, subalpine, montane, foothills, common,
L Spring–Summer, perennial, 1–3 ft.

Herbaceous, rhizomatous plant with erect,
hairless stems. Basal leaves thin, to 4 in. long,
ovate to elliptic, unlobed or with 1 or 2 pairs of
small lateral lobes; margins typically entire.
2–4 pairs of opposite stem leaves, pinnatifid or
undivided. Inflorescence a round-topped cluster of white flowers with conspicuously exserted stamens.
Fruit a lanceolate achene with feather-like plume. Grows
in wet meadows, along streams, and in open forests, thickets, usually where soil is moist. More common
on the western slope. Native.

Valeriana sitchensis CAPRIFOLIACEAE

Sitka valerian
NR, MR, alpine, subalpine,
montane, common, L Spring–
Summer, perennial, 1–4 ft.

Herbaceous, rhizomatous plant with erect,
sturdy stems. Basal leaves few, reduced, or
absent. 2–5 pairs of stem leaves opposite, to
4 in. long, lanceolate to ovate with deep lobes
or coarsely toothed margins, and smooth to

slightly hairy surfaces. Inflorescence a flat, dense cluster of
many flowers with white or pink 5-lobed corollas; stamens
and pistil conspicuously protruding. Cluster spreads when
in fruit, with smooth, ovoid, feathery-plumed achenes.
Grows along streams, in meadows, forests,
and on avalanche tracks. Native.

Eremogone congesta

(*Arenaria congesta*) CARYOPHYLLACEAE
ballhead sandwort
RM, alpine, subalpine, montane,
foothills, common, L Spring–
Summer, perennial, 1–15 in.

Herb from a woody base and thick underground roots. Stems erect to spreading, loosely
matted or tufted. Leaves thin, thread- to
needle-like, 0.5–3 in. long. Cauline leaves similar, opposite,
upper leaves reduced. Inflorescence 1 to several loose to
dense clusters of white flowers. Flowers 5-petaled, 0.5 in.,
on leafless stalk rising above basal leaves. Sepals 5. Fruit a
capsule. Found in woodland openings and tundra. Native.

Eremogone fendleri
(Arenaria fendleri var. *diffusa)*
CARYOPHYLLACEAE
Fendler's sandwort
SR, alpine, subalpine, montane, foothills, pinyon-juniper, sagebrush steppe, common, L Spring–Fall, perennial, 4–15 in. Herb from a woody base. Tight tufts of very narrow, upright basal leaves form mats up to a foot in diameter. Cauline leaves 1–4 in. long, linear, opposite, several pairs. Inflorescence a terminal cyme of white flowers on numerous long stalks. Petals 5, white, oblong to spoon-shaped, 0.2–0.3 in. Sepals 5, green, purple-tinged. Stamens usually 10, pink anthers. Fruit a capsule. Found in sagebrush plains, pine forests. Native.

Eremogone hookeri
(Arenaria hookeri) CARYOPHYLLACEAE
Hooker's sandwort
MR, SR, montane, foothills, sagebrush steppe, grasslands, uncommon, Spring–Summer, perennial, 0.2–6 in. Densely to loosely mat-forming herb; green, somewhat woody base. Basal leaves 0.5–1 in. long, needle-like. Stems unbranched. Cauline leaves in 1–4 pairs, usually larger than basal leaves. Inflorescence many-flowered, congested. Flowers white, 5-petaled, oblong. Fruit a capsule. Occurs at lower elevations, often on open, eroding slopes. Forms dense cushions on dry slopes. Native.

Minuartia nuttallii
(Arenaria nuttallii)
CARYOPHYLLACEAE
Nuttall's sandwort
RM, montane, pinyon-juniper, sagebrush steppe, intermountain parks, grasslands, locally abundant, Spring–E Summer, perennial, 1–4 in. Low, multibranched herb, forming prickly, loose mats, sometimes 16 in. or more across. Leaves narrow, linear, and 0.5–1 in. long. Each leafy stem produces a short, branched inflorescence just above the leaves with 5-petaled, white star-like flowers opening sequentially over several weeks. The common mat sandwort of steppe habitats. Native.

Minuartia rubella
(*Arenaria propinqua*)
CARYOPHYLLACEAE
beautiful sandwort
RM, alpine, locally abundant,
Summer, perennial, 0.5–1 in.

Caespitose herb, forming compact cushions
or small mats 3–6 in. across or more. Slightly
curved, needle-like leaves less than 0.3 in.
long. Petals 0.2 in. long and white. Multiple
flowers in compact cymes on short stems just
above the foliage. Often on moister, shadier substrates
than other alpine sandworts. *Minuartia macrantha* and *M.
stricta* are similar but less common caespitose sandworts
that occur in much the same range. This diminutive
alpine is often overlooked. Native.

Silene douglasii CARYOPHYLLACEAE
Douglas' catchfly
NR, MR, subalpine, montane, sagebrush
steppe, grasslands, common,
L Spring–Summer, perennial, 4–20 in.

Multiple stems, mostly unbranched from
woody base. Basal leaves oblong, pointed;
stem leaves opposite, linear, at nodes on
stems, to 1.5 in. long. Inflorescence with 1–3
flowers per cyme. Calyx green to purple with
10 veins, tubular in flower, inflating as it matures into
fruit. Petals 5, creamy white, 2 shallow lobes at ends; a
2-lobed appendage ringing the center of the flower.
Dry meadows, shrublands, open forests. The similar
S. parryi does not have short, gray-white hairs
on calyx, lacks glands. Native.

Silene latifolia CARYOPHYLLACEAE
bladder campion
RM, montane, foothills, grasslands, common,
L Spring–Summer, annual, 16–40 in.

Stems erect, hairy. Leaves hairy; basal usually
withering by flowering; stem leaves lanceolate
to 4.75 in. long, opposite and reduced upward.
Flower stems with several flowers in cymes.
Flowers unisexual, with plants having either
male or female flowers. Female flowers with 20 veins on
calyx; male with 10 veins. Petals 5, white, twice the length
of calyx. Found throughout much of U.S. and Canada and
sometimes confused with *S. noctiflora*. Introduced.

Silene menziesii CARYOPHYLLACEAE
Menzies' campion
RM, montane, common, L Spring–E Summer, perennial, 2–27 in.
Plants colonizing by underground roots. Stems decumbent to erect. Leaves elliptic-lanceolate, hairy, 2.5 in. long. Flowers in a cyme or solitary. Calyx obscurely 10-veined, hairy and glandular, to 0.3 in. long. Petals white, 5, up to 1.5 times the length of the calyx. Found in forests, moist meadows, and along creeks. Native.

Silene noctiflora
(Melandrium noctiflorum)
CARYOPHYLLACEAE
nightflowering catchfly
RM, montane, foothills, uncommon, L Spring–Summer, annual, 8–32 in.
Stems erect, few branches, hairy. Leaves basal and opposite, lanceolate to elliptic, to 4.5 in. long, densely hairy; reducing upward. Inflorescence a cyme with up to 15 flowers on stalks. Calyx with 10 veins, inflating as it matures into fruit. Petals 5, white or tinged pink, deeply cleft, with a ruffled appendage attached at mouth of the throat. Disturbed sites and along roadsides. *Noctiflora* means "night-blooming": the flowers close in early morning. Introduced.

Silene parryi
(S. macounii) CARYOPHYLLACEAE
Parry's silene
RM, alpine, subalpine, montane, common, L Spring–Summer, perennial, 2–20 in.
Stems glandular and erect from branched, woody base. Leaves mostly basal, lanceolate to linear, to 3.2 in. long; stem leaves in 2–4 pairs, linear-lanceolate; hairy. Flowering stems with 3–7 flowers, stalks usually longer than the purple-striped 10-veined, inflated, glandular calyx. Petals white or purple-tinged, 5, with 4 rounded lobes on each petal. Found on rocky slopes, scree, dry meadows, and open forests. The similar *S. douglasii* has 2-lobed petals. Native.

Arctostaphylos rubra

(*Arctous rubra*) ERICACEAE

red fruit bearberry, alpine bearberry
NR, MR, alpine, subalpine, montane,
common, Spring, perennial, 4–8 in.
Mat-forming, prostrate shrub with peeling
bark. Leaves alternate, simple, oblanceolate to
ovate, deciduous, veiny, turn red in fall, margins lightly toothed. Flowers in few-flowered
terminal racemes; white to yellow-green,
urn-shaped, 5 petals, 5 sepals. Berries bright
red. A disjunct population exists in Shoshone NF in WY.
Grows in sun, peaty soils, open coniferous forests, rocky
tundra, meadows. Circumboreal. Native.

Cassiope mertensiana ERICACEAE

western bell heather, white mountain heather
NR, MR, alpine, subalpine, common, locally
abundant, Summer, perennial, 2–12 in.
Low, mat-forming evergreen shrub or subshrub, ascending stems nearly hidden
by overlapping leaves. Opposite, sessile,
ovate-lanceolate leaves to 0.25 in. form 4 distinct rows. Groove on underside of leaf only
at base. Inflorescence a cluster of nodding,
bell-shaped flowers, red pedicels, near branch
tips. Conspicuous sepals reddish, snow-white
petals fused to a third of their length. Fruit a round capsule. Forests, open rocky areas, meadows, and near late
snowmelt at high elevations. Native.

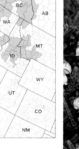

Cassiope tetragona ERICACEAE

**arctic bell heather, four-angled mountain
heather**
NR, alpine, subalpine, locally abundant,
L Spring–Summer, perennial, 2–12 in.
Low, mat-forming evergreen shrub with reclining to erect hairy stems nearly hidden by
overlapping leaves. Opposite, sessile, triangular leaves in 4 distinct rows. Deep groove
on underside of leaf. Inflorescence a cluster
of nodding bell-shaped flowers. Sepals red or
green. White to yellowish petals fused to half
their length. Grows in talus, meadows, and tundra. Inuit
peoples used this plant (which they knew as *itsutit*, "fuel
for fire") for igniting fires to boil water for tea. Native.

Phyllodoce glanduliflora
(P. aleutica ssp. *glanduliflora)*
ERICACEAE
yellow mountain heath
NR, MR, alpine, subalpine, montane,
common, locally abundant,
Summer, perennial, 4–16 in.
Prostrate, ascending or erect,
much-branched, evergreen shrub with hairy
twigs (becoming hairless); forms large mats.
Leaves dark green, alternate, crowded, lin-
ear, with revolute margins. Inflorescence a cluster of yellowish to greenish white urn-shaped nodding flowers, in
clusters at stem tips or singly on hairy green stalks in leaf
axils. Petals fused with 5 small lobes; style included. Fruit
a round 5-segmented capsule. Meadows,
seeps, bogs, heath, and rocky sites in coniferous forests. Native.

Rhododendron albiflorum
(Azaleastrum albiflorum) ERICACEAE
white-flowered rhododendron, white azalea
NR, SR, subalpine, montane, common,
L Spring–Summer, perennial, 2–7 ft.
Rhizomatous deciduous shrub with erect
branched stems; herbage with stiff reddish hairs. Leaves alternate or clustered,
crinkled, deep green, elliptic to oval with entire to serrated margins. Inflorescence a pendulous cluster of white
bowl-shaped flowers, scented of vanilla and jasmine. Fruit
a 5-sectioned capsule, the seed with a
distinct tail. Spruce-fir forests, streambanks, seeps on rock outcrops. Native.

Rhododendron columbianum
(Ledum glandulosum) ERICACEAE
Labrador tea, trapper's tea
NR, MR, subalpine, montane,
locally abundant, Spring–E
Summer, perennial, 15–50 in.
Upright shrub with erect, finely hairy, glandular branched stems. Leaves alternate, evergreen, narrow, with a wrinkled-looking
upper surface and a lighter green, glandular-hairy under
surface; margins usually entire. Inflorescence a terminal
raceme of cream to white flowers with 5 spreading petals
and 8–10 exserted stamens. Fruit a round to egg-shaped
capsule. All parts aromatic when crushed. Found near
streams or moist to wet meadows and forests. Native.

Gentiana algida

(*Gentianodes algida*) GENTIANACEAE
arctic gentian, white gentian
MR, SR, alpine, subalpine, locally
abundant, Summer, perennial, 2–8 in.

Rhizomatous, glabrous herb with 1 to several stems from basal rosette. Leaves to 4 in.,
linear to lanceolate. Stem leaves opposite.
Inflorescence 1–3 tubular to funnel-shaped
terminal flowers. Corolla with 5 short lobes,
whitish or pale yellowish, spotted with purple
or green; pointed. Purple plaits between lobes. Calyx with
5 purplish blotched lobes. Grows along rills, streambanks,
and meadows. Native.

Ribes oxyacanthoides

GROSSULARIACEAE
Canadian gooseberry
RM, grasslands, common, Spring–
Summer, perennial, 1.5–5 ft.

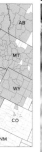

Deciduous spiny shrub; erect to spreading
stems, yellowish becoming gray, covered in
bristly hairs. Leaves alternate, to 1.5 in. across,
round to reniform, with 3–5 (rarely 7) palmate
lobes, coarsely toothed margins. Leaf surfaces
soft-hairy and often glandular below. Inflorescence a raceme with 1–3 drooping, tubular
to bell-shaped flowers. Petals white or pinkish. Calyx with
spreading greenish yellow lobes. Berries round, reddish
or deep bluish purple, palatable. Thickets, woodlands, on
rocky slopes, and along streams. Native.

Ribes wolfii

(*R. mogollonicum*) GROSSULARIACEAE
Wolf's currant
MR, SR, subalpine, montane, foothills, locally
abundant, Spring–Summer, perennial, 3–6 ft.

Deciduous spineless shrub with spreading
to erect tan stems, aging gray, covered with
fine hairs and black glands. Leaves alternate,
mapleleaf-shaped, 3- to 5-lobed, margins
toothed, smooth or glandular-hairy surfaces.
Inflorescence an erect to spreading raceme
of 7–25 flowers, each subtended by yellowish white or reddish bracts. Sepals spreading, greenish or pinkish white;
petals cream, yellowish green, or pinkish, erect, widely
separated, surrounding a cup-shaped hypanthium. Berries black, ovoid, glandular-hairy, and palatable. Grows in
woodlands and along streams. Native.

Jamesia americana
(*Edwinia americana*)
HYDRANGEACEAE

fivepetal cliffbush, waxflower
MR, SR, montane, foothills, pinyon-juniper,
common, Summer, perennial, to 4 ft.

Stems spreading to ascending, forming a rounded to columnar shrub; bark
reddish-orangish brown, weathering to
peeling gray. Leaves opposite, to 1.5 in.,
green, coarsely toothed with recessed veins
above and white-woolly below. Flowers fragrant, white to
pinkish, hairy, in round, dense flat-topped clusters. Seeds
housed in dry capsule; traditionally used as food. Found in
moist, shady, rocky slopes and cliffs. Native.

Claytonia cordifolia
(*C. sibirica* var. *cordifolia*)
MONTIACEAE

heartleaf springbeauty
NR, MR, subalpine, montane,
locally abundant, Spring–
Summer, perennial, 4–12 in.

Herbaceous, rhizomatous, somewhat succulent plant with 1 to several erect stems; often
colony-forming. Basal leaves to 2 in. long,
heart-shaped to triangular, taper to long petioles; reduced stem leaves opposite, in pairs, lanceolate to
ovate, and sessile. Inflorescence an open raceme of 3–10
flowers without bracts; 2 sepals, 5 white petals without
lines, 5 stamens, and 3 linear stigmas.
Grows along streams, ponds, in seepage
sites, meadows, and spruce forests. Native.

Claytonia lanceolata MONTIACEAE
**lanceleaf springbeauty, western
springbeauty**
RM, alpine, subalpine, montane,
foothills, sagebrush steppe, common,
Spring–Summer, perennial, 1–10 in.

Fleshy herb with 1 to several ascending to
erect stems. 1–6 basal leaves, to 6 in., linear to lanceolate, with partially buried,
thread-like stalks; basal leaves may be absent during flowering; 1 pair of clasping stem leaves opposite, reduced. Inflorescence a 1-sided cluster of 3–20 flowers; petals white to
pink (rarely yellow or orange), often with pink lines. Grows
in moist meadows, shrublands, and forests. Native.

Claytonia megarhiza MONTIACEAE
alpine springbeauty
RM, alpine, common, Summer,
perennial, 2–10 in.

Fleshy, glabrous herb with 1 to several ascending to erect stems from thick, very deep taproot. Greenish to reddish leaves in dense basal rosette, to 4 in. long, smooth, oblanceolate to spatulate; 1 pair of stem leaves opposite, reduced, and linear-oblanceolate. Inflorescence a round-topped raceme with 2–9 white to pink flowers subtended by bracts. Found in rocky crevices, gravelly soil, and talus slopes in the alpine, where it thrives. Rare in southeastern BC. Native.

Montia chamissoi
(*Claytonia chamissoi*) MONTIACEAE
water minerslettuce
MR, SR, subalpine, montane, foothills,
common, Spring–Summer, perennial, 2–10 in.

Herbaceous, rhizomatous, stoloniferous, succulent plant with erect, solitary stem. Basal leaves absent or reduced. Stem leaves opposite, in several pairs, to 2 in. long, elliptic or oblanceolate, tapering to petiole. Inflorescence a loose cluster of 3–10 white or pinkish flowers on terminal and axillary racemes. Inflorescence subtended by solitary bract. 2 sepals much shorter than petals. Bulblets often found on freely rooting stolons. Grows in the shade along streams, lakes, and in spruce-fir forests. Native.

Abronia elliptica
(*A. fragrans* var. *elliptica*)
NYCTAGINACEAE
fragrant white sand verbena
MR, SR, pinyon-juniper, sagebrush steppe,
grasslands, common, locally abundant,
L Spring–Summer, perennial, 1–3 in.

Plants are low to the ground; flowering stems may ascend. Oblong leaves are glabrous and appear waxy. Flowers tubular in clusters of 15–25. Floral tubes are greenish cream to pink, flaring into a wavy face of small notched white petals. Flowers very fragrant, especially in evening. Separated from *A. fragrans* based on the morphology of the seed. Grows in sun, especially in sandy soil, dunes. Native.

Abronia fragrans NYCTAGINACEAE
snowball sand verbena
SR, foothills, pinyon-juniper,
grasslands, locally abundant, L
Spring–Summer, perennial, 1–3 ft.

Stems trailing to semierect, slightly
branched, glandular-pubescent, sticky.
Leaves opposite, ovate, lanceolate or triangular, 1–4 in. long by 0.3–2 in. wide; margins
entire to wavy, green to somewhat glaucous,
hairy. Flower cluster a ball with long white
(sometimes reddish or greenish) calyx tubes. Individual flowers to 1 in. long by 0.35 in. wide; noticeable part is
calyx, not petals. Flowers open late afternoon, close next
morning; fragrant. Sandy soils of lower elevations extending onto plains, dunes. Native.

Abronia mellifera NYCTAGINACEAE
white sand verbena
MR, sagebrush steppe, grasslands,
common, locally abundant, L Spring–
Summer, perennial, 1–3 in.

Plants low, spreading. Leaves lanceolate to elliptical, glabrous to quite glandular. Flowers on usually upright stems in
showy clusters of 15–25. Floral tubes can be
white, pink, or greenish. The specific epithet ("bearing honey") alludes to the sweet fragrance and
high nectar content of the white flowers. Grows in sunny
meadows and sage habitats, often in disturbed sandy soils,
dunes. Native.

Tripterocalyx micranthus
(*Abronia micrantha*) NYCTAGINACEAE
smallflower sandverbena
MR, SR, montane, foothills, pinyon-
juniper, sagebrush steppe, intermountain
parks, grasslands, infrequent, L
Spring–Summer, annual, 8–20 in.

Nearly succulent spreading stems. Thick,
orbicular leaves with short stiff glandular
hairs. Round clusters of 10–20 long-tubed,
small flowers with hairy calyces, developing
into comparatively huge, winged seed clusters by midsummer. An infrequent but nonetheless widespread plant of
open sandy areas at lower elevations and a few mountain
parklands. Native.

Ipomopsis congesta
(Gilia congesta) POLEMONIACEAE
ballhead gilia
RM, subalpine, montane, foothills,
pinyon-juniper, sagebrush steppe,
grasslands, common, Spring–
Summer, perennial, 2–20 in.

Single (rarely several) stem originates from
a base. Small thickened linear leaves entire,
pinnatifid, or trifid, forming an evergreen
basal rosette. Inflorescence a dense (hence
the epithet) cluster of tubular 5-petaled flowers. Grows
in sunny and disturbed areas, barrens, rock scree, rock
ledges, pine parklands, dry slopes, and sage meadows. Can
be very abundant in a wide range of habitats. Harsh areas
produce very small plants; lusher conditions
produce large robust plants. Native.

Ipomopsis globularis
(I. spicata ssp. *capitata)*
POLEMONIACEAE
Hoosier Pass ipomopsis
SR, alpine, rare, locally abundant,
Summer, perennial, 2.5–5 in.

Single (rarely several) stem with woolly hairs
originates from base. Leaves linear and entire, rarely pinnatifid, covered in dense woolly
hairs, forming a basal rosette. Tubular 5-petaled white or
cream flowers form a rounded cluster. Grows in sunny and
disturbed areas, tundra, rock scree, and rock ledges. Found
only in central CO, mainly on calcareous rocks. Intensely
fragrant flowers have bluish cast. Native.

Ipomopsis spicata
(Gilia spicata) POLEMONIACEAE
spiked ipomopsis
RM, throughout, common, Spring–
Summer, perennial, 2–16 in.

Single stem (rarely several) with woolly hairs.
Leaves form a linear, entire, rarely pinnatifid, 0.4-in.-long basal rosette. Terminal inflorescence of tubular 5-petaled flowers, white,
cream, pale yellow, or tan. Grows in sun, in all
life zones except wetlands: disturbed areas, tundra, rock
scree, rock ledges, pine parklands, sage meadows, and
meadows. Front Range variant has tan-white flowers; ssp.
orchidacea, with dense, white, ball-like inflorescence, is
found in the alpine of MT, WY, ID. Native.

Linanthus pungens
(*Leptodactylon pungens*)
POLEMONIACEAE

granite prickly phlox, granite gilia
RM, montane, foothills, pinyon-juniper,
sagebrush steppe, intermountain
parks, grasslands, common, L Spring–
Summer, perennial, 6–17 in.

Shrub or subshrub with open, erect
branches forming asymmetrical mounds.
Stems densely covered with narrow,
sharp-pointed leaves. Leaves alternate or subopposite
above, opposite below. Flowers solitary or in clusters at
ends of stems, 5-merous, corolla cream to yellowish, often
tinged with purple below. Fruit a cylindrical capsule with
3 valves, each with 5–10 seeds. Dry hillsides
and meadows, open forests. Aromatic flowers open in the evening. Native.

Eriogonum androsaceum
(*E. flavum* ssp. *androsaceum*)
POLYGONACEAE

rockjasmine buckwheat
MR, NR, alpine, subalpine, endemic,
infrequent, locally abundant,
Summer, perennial, 0.5–2.4 in.

Stems form a dense mat. Leaves are entire,
narrowly oblong and narrowly elliptic, densely hairy
below and sparsely hairy above. 5-petaled flowers form
a cluster, creamy white to pale yellow fading to pink or
orange. Sunny areas, rock scree, rock ledges,
dry slopes, sage meadows, often on
calcium-rich rocks. Native.

Eriogonum umbellatum
var. majus
(*E. heracleoides* var. *subalpinum*)
POLYGONACEAE

subalpine sulphur-flower
RM, throughout, common, Summer–
Fall, perennial, 2–20 in.

Leafless, erect to spreading stems form a
mat or subshrub. Leaves are green to grayish, oblong-ovate
to oblanceolate to elliptic, 0.1–1.6 in., and white below.
Flowers 5-petaled, cream, pale yellow, or pinkish in an
umbel. Sunny areas, rock ledges, scree, barrens, pine parklands, dry slopes, sage meadows, usually found higher
than yellow forms of *E. umbellatum*. Distinct throughout
the Rockies, in all life zones except wetlands. Native.

Androsace chamaejasme

PRIMULACEAE

sweetflower rockjasmine

RM, alpine, subalpine, uncommon, Summer, perennial, 0.5–1 in.

Plants form loose to dense mats of rosettes. Leaves are green and oblong, glabrous to hirsute with simple hairs. Inflorescences are 3- to 6-flowered heads. The pedicels are upright and hairy. Flowers are broadly campanulate and white with yellow at the opening of the corolla tube; this yellow eye fades to pink once the flower is pollinated. Ours are sometimes considered ssp. *carinata* or ssp. *lehmanniana*. Sun. Native.

Androsace septentrionalis

PRIMULACEAE

pygmyflower rockjasmine, northern rockjasmine

RM, throughout, common, Summer– Fall, annual/biennial, to 2 in.

Plants form single rosettes and are usually annual. Leaves are typically glabrescent, occasionally mildly ciliate. Flower scapes can be numerous, with inflorescence having up to 20 flowers. Flowers are narrowly campanulate with prominent ridges. Corolla tube is shorter than, or equal in length to, the calyx. This is the most common of the annual species; it is very difficult to distinguish the others, *A. filiformis* and *A. occidentalis*. Grows in shade and sun, in mostly disturbed areas. Native.

Primula alcalina PRIMULACEAE

bluedome primrose, alkali primrose

MR, alpine, subalpine, wetlands, endemic, rare, L Spring–E Summer, perennial, 6–10 in.

Herbaceous; leaves in a basal rosette, elliptic, 0.4–1.8 in. long, margins wavy or toothed, taper to a short-winged stalk. May be mealy when young, becoming smooth with age. Flowering stem leafless, whitish green with some red. Inflorescence an unbranched terminal umbel of 3–10 flowers. Flowers tubular, white to lavender, lobes deeply cleft. Grows in fens, such as Birch Creek Fen in ID. Endemic, found only in east-central ID and adjacent MT. Native.

Primula egaliksensis
(*P. groenlandica*) PRIMULACEAE
Greenland primrose
RM, alpine, subalpine, montane,
rare, Summer, perennial, 1–5 in.
Herb; leaves basal, margins entire to wavy,
somewhat toothed, elliptic, 1–5 in. long,
smooth. Inflorescence 1–3 flowers. Calyx
green or with purple stripes, cylindric; corolla white or lavender. Fruit a capsule.
Occurs in fens, such as in South Park, a
high-altitude basin in CO, and Swamp Lake in Shoshone
NF in northwestern WY. Native.

Primula latiloba
(*Dodecatheon dentatum*)
PRIMULACEAE
white shootingstar
NR, montane, uncommon, L Spring–
Summer, perennial, 6–12 in.
Leafless flowering stems glabrous, above
basal leaf rosette. Leaves glabrous, oval or
egg-shaped, 2–7 in. long, with petioles; margins slightly to quite toothed. Flowers 1–6 in
terminal umbel, 5 reflexed white petals yellow at base; central parts maroon, or yellow
in some populations. Widely disjunct populations in the Pacific NW, UT (where flowers may be pink),
and AZ/NM. Moist meadows, cliffs, woodland or stream
edges, in sun or shade. Native.

Ranunculus aquatilis
(*Batrachium aquatile*)
RANUNCULACEAE
white water crowfoot
RM, subalpine, montane, foothills,
wetlands, locally abundant, L Spring–
Summer, perennial, 11–28 in.
Aquatic herb with submerged, deeply divided, linear foliage, alternately attached,
to 0.75 in. long and 1 in. wide. Single white
flowers rise above water on short pedicels
arising from a leaf axil, 0.3–0.6 in. across;
5 oval petals with a spot of yellow at the base, many yellow
stamens surrounding a yellow center maturing to green;
5 rounded green sepals much shorter than petals, behind
the flower. Found in ditches, ponds, alder swamps, and on
wet ground. Native.

Amelanchier utahensis
(A. alnifolia ssp. *utahensis)*
ROSACEAE
Utah serviceberry
RM, montane, foothills, pinyon-juniper,
sagebrush steppe, intermountain parks,
locally abundant, Spring, perennial, to 6 ft.
Shrub, smaller than *A. alnifolia* (which see,
page 327). Leaves oval to obovate, usually
evenly toothed on the margins, tomentose on
both sides. Flowers white, petals almost as
wide as they are long. Styles 2 or 3, separated to the base.
Most abundant on the western slope of the MR and SR.
Sun. Native.

Crataegus erythropoda ROSACEAE
cerro hawthorn
SR, montane, foothills, pinyon-
juniper, infrequent, Spring–
Summer, perennial, 4–15 ft.
Shrub to small tree, densely spreading, new
stems smooth, 1-in. thorns. Leaves alternate,
ovate, smooth upper surface shiny, many
small, black-tipped teeth, few larger notches.
Flowers 1 in. across, clustered 5–10; 5 rounded
petals. Fruit elongated, dark purplish red, in
clusters late summer–fall; relished by wildlife.
Sun, part shade; moist ravines, hillsides, along streams.
Native.

Crataegus rivularis
(C. douglasii) ROSACEAE
river hawthorn
MR, SR, montane, foothills, common,
Spring–Summer, perennial, 3–12 ft.
Shrub to small tree, forming thickets;
1-in. thorns, often curved, patchy gray to
rust-colored stems. Leaves glabrous, oval, 1–3
in. long, serrated edges, not notched as some
hawthorns. Flowers 0.75 in. across, 6–12 in
loose corymbs, 5 rounded petals. Fruits 0.5 in.
across, deep red to blackish. Most common in
western CO, the Wasatch, southeastern ID.
Sun, part shade; streambanks, ravines, woodland edges.
Native.

Fragaria virginiana ROSACEAE
wild strawberry
MR, SR, subalpine, montane,
foothills, common, Spring–
Summer, perennial, 1–6 in.
Basal leaf rosette, red runners spread to
increase colony. Leaves blue-green, hairy
below, more glabrous above; not prominently veined as *F. vesca*. Ternate with 3 oval
leaflets, toothed along upper edge, center
tooth shorter than adjacent ones. Flowers
with 5 rounded petals, 0.75–1 in. across, in loose clusters
of 2–12; stem usually shorter than leaves. Fruit a red strawberry, 0.5 in. or more; seeds set into small pits on surface.
Meadows, moist or dryish slopes, woodland openings,
sandy soils. Native.

Physocarpus malvaceus
ROSACEAE
mallow ninebark
RM, montane, foothills, common,
L Spring–Fall, perennial, 1–6 ft.
Deciduous, vase-shaped shrub. Stems
brown to grayish black, bark in layers and
exfoliating, not prickly. Leaves 1.5–3 in.
wide, alternate, simple, palmately lobed,
sparsely hairy and dark green above, paler
and densely hairy below. Inflorescence a densely flowered
corymb. Flowers white, 0.5 in. wide. Petals 5, round. Stamens 20–40; pistils usually 2. Fruit a follicle, begins red,
turns reddish brown. Occurs on dry, rocky
hillsides and in open forest. Native.

Physocarpus monogynus
ROSACEAE
mountain ninebark
MR, SR, subalpine, montane,
foothills, common, L Spring–
Summer, perennial, 1–4 ft.
Deciduous, vase-shaped shrub with arching stems. Bark yellow-orange to red-brown,
exfoliates in long strips, especially on older
stems. Leaves alternate, palmately lobed,
0.8–2.2 in., stipules early deciduous. Inflorescence a
densely flowered cluster, numerous white flowers. Flowers
1.5 in., petals 5, almost round. Fruit a follicle, July to Octo-
ber. Occurs on streambanks, dry slopes, moist mixed conifer forests. Leaves *Ribes*-like, but the peeling bark and fruit
are quite different. Native.

Potentilla arguta
(*Drymocallis arguta*) ROSACEAE
tall cinquefoil
NR, MR, subalpine, montane,
sagebrush steppe, uncommon,
Summer, perennial, 1–3 ft.

Stout, erect stems covered in white hairs;
slightly branched into clusters of creamy
white to light yellow flowers. Leaves mostly
basal, stem leaves alternate, pinnate, 4–10 in.,
with 7–11 egg-shaped leaflets that get smaller
toward stem, coarsely toothed, covered in white sticky
hairs. Petals surrounded by 5 green sepals that are only
slightly smaller. Found in moist meadows, along streambeds, in sage meadows. *Potentilla* ("powerful")
suggests the potent medicinal properties of
the genus. Native.

Prunus emarginata ROSACEAE
bitter cherry
NR, montane, foothills, common,
Spring, perennial, 7–50 ft.

Shrub to small tree; brownish to gray bark
with horizontal lenticels. Leaves alternate, elliptic to oblong, finely serrate, smooth above,
hairy below, deciduous. Flowers in a short,
flat-topped raceme, 3–10 flowers per clus-
ter, white, hairy below. Fruits dark red to black, 1 seed,
very bitter. It is the common cherry of the NR, growing in
sun, shade, moist woodlands, rocky slopes, streambanks.
Native.

Prunus pensylvanica
(*Cerasus pensylvanica*) ROSACEAE
pin cherry
RM, montane, foothills, grasslands,
common, Spring, perennial, 15–35 ft.

Erect shrub to small tree; bark reddish to gray,
peels in horizontal strips; noticeable horizontal lenticels along stems. No thorns. Leaves
glabrous, simple, alternate; lanceolate to elliptic; serrate margins with gland-tipped teeth;
deciduous. White flowers, 3–7 per umbel,
emerge with leaves. Fruit bright red, shiny to 0.25 in. with
a single seed. Grows in sun, shade, along streams, open
forests. Native.

Rubus idaeus ROSACEAE
American red raspberry
RM, subalpine, montane,
foothills, common, L Spring–
Summer, perennial, 8–60 in.
Shrub with slender prickles on stems.
Smaller stems glandular hairy; older stems
with peeling bark. Leaves compound with
3–5 oval to elliptic leaflets up to 4 in. long
and toothed; undersides gray, hairy. Inflorescence with multiple flowers in a raceme.
Flowers white with 5 petals to 0.4 in. long. Fruit is a red
edible raspberry produced on 2-year-old stems. Found in
forests, disturbed sites, riparian areas, and dry slopes. Ssp.
strigosus is native to the Rockies. Circumboreal. Native.

Rubus leucodermis ROSACEAE
white bark raspberry
NR, MR, montane, grasslands, uncommon,
L Spring–Summer, perennial, to 6 ft.
Upright shrub. Arching and curving stems
covered densely with stout, flattened prickles and waxy, whitish coating. Leaves palmately or ternately compound with 3–5
narrowly ovate leaflets to 2.75 in. long;
toothed or lobed; white and hairy on underside. Inflorescence a flat-topped cyme with
up to 12 flowers. Flowers white, 5 oblong petals up to 0.3
in. long; petals shorter than sepals. Fruits red when immature ripening to purple; 0.5 in. across. Open coniferous forests, moist or dry rocky areas and thickets. Used to
make the "blue raspberry" flavor in candy
and syrups. Native.

Rubus parviflorus ROSACEAE
thimbleberry
RM, subalpine, montane,
foothills, common, L Spring–
Summer, perennial, to 5 ft.
Shrub with upright stems without prickles;
older bark shedding. Leaves simple, large
and rounded up to 8 in. long by 10 in. wide
with a heart-shaped base and 5 lobes, toothed
edges. Inflorescence a cyme with up to 15 white flowers.
Petals up to 1 in. long and rounded. Fruits red and rounded
to 0.7 in. and hairy. Found in shady, moist, cool areas including open aspen or coniferous forests, seeps, thickets,
and streambanks. As the common name suggests, the edible raspberry fruit resembles a thimble. Native.

Sorbus scopulina ROSACEAE
Greene's mountain ash
RM, subalpine, montane, locally abundant,
L Spring–E Summer, perennial, 4–15 ft.
Multistemmed shrub to small tree. Glossy,
bright green, pinnate leaves with 9–13 leaflets with dentate margins. Inflorescences of
5-petaled flowers form large showy clusters of
bright orange-red fruit in late summer. Found
on rocky slopes or stream margins at higher
elevations with aspen, conifers. Native.

Spiraea lucida
(*S. betulifolia*) ROSACEAE
white spirea, shiny-leaf spirea
NR, MR, subalpine, montane, foothills, locally
abundant, Spring–Summer, perennial, 1–3 ft.
Shrub with fine, densely branched stems
from vigorous rhizomes. Leaves 1–2.5 in.
long; oval, opposite, clearly toothed toward the
tip. Rounded white flowers with prominent
stamens, in flat-topped racemes. Forms thickets on moist shady slopes and screes. Native.

Comandra umbellata SANTALACEAE
bastard toadflax
RM, throughout, common,
Spring–Summer, perennial, 2–12 in.
Rhizomatous herb with waxy, stout, erect, branched
stems; colony-forming. Stem leaves alternate, thick, fleshy,
pale green, to 2 in., with linear to narrowly ovate blades
and entire margins. Inflorescence a compact,
terminal cluster of star-shaped flowers with
5 (rarely 4) white or whitish green to pinkish
petal-like spreading sepals; 5 stamens opposite sepals. Petals absent. Plant obtains some
nutrition by parasitizing roots of other plants.
Grows in dry, sandy, rocky, often disturbed
habitats in all zones except wetlands and alpine. Native.

Lithophragma parviflorum

SAXIFRAGACEAE

smallflower woodland-star
RM, montane, foothills, sagebrush
steppe, grasslands, uncommon,
Spring, perennial, 4–20 in.

Rhizomatous herb with slender, erect,
green, sticky, hairy stems. Leaves mostly
basal; alternate, reduced stem leaves also
present. Leaves hairy, 3- to 5-lobed, sometimes divided again, and with sharply
toothed margins. 2 or 3 inflorescences per plant with 4–14
white (occasionally pink) star-like flowers. Petals with 3
deep lobes. Occurs in sagebrush shrublands, meadows,
and coniferous forests. Native.

Micranthes rhomboidea
(*Saxifraga rhomboidea*)

SAXIFRAGACEAE

diamondleaf saxifrage, snowball saxifrage
RM, alpine, subalpine, montane, foothills,
sagebrush steppe, grasslands, common,
Spring–Summer, perennial, 4–12 in.

Rhizomatous, solitary to tufted herb with
erect stems from basal rosette; bulbils on
woody base. Leaves fleshy, triangular to
rhombic, smooth above and hairy below;
margins toothed and hairy. Inflorescence a snowball-like
cluster of 10–40 white flowers. Found in seasonally wet
areas, meadows, along alpine ridges, and on sagebrush
slopes. Sometimes mistaken for *Bistorta bistortoides*, but
the latter has some stem leaves whereas *M.
rhomboidea* has only basal leaves. Native.

Micranthes tolmiei
(*Saxifraga tolmiei*) SAXIFRAGACEAE

Tolmie's saxifrage
NR, alpine, subalpine, rare,
Summer, perennial, 1–5 in.

Evergreen mat-forming herb with trailing to
erect flowering stems and numerous leafy,
sterile stems. Leaves fleshy, to 0.75 in., spatulate to oblanceolate, crowded near stem base.
1–3 alternate stem leaves reduced or lacking. Inflorescence
1 terminal flower or a loose cluster of 2–4 flowers. Petals
white or creamy, unspotted, linear to oblanceolate; 10 white,
often petal-like filaments present. Grows in rock crevices,
scree, tundra, meadows, and on streambanks. Native.

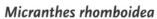

Saxifraga adscendens
(*Muscaria adscendens*)

SAXIFRAGACEAE
wedgeleaf saxifrage, ascending saxifrage
RM, alpine, subalpine, uncommon,
Summer, perennial, 1–4 in.

Evergreen herb with erect, glandular-hairy,
often red-tinged stems from basal cluster of
leaves; plant solitary, tufted. Leaves fleshy,
often reddish purple, sessile, oblanceolate to
obovate, with shallowly lobed or few-toothed
margins. Stem leaves alternate, reduced. Inflorescence
a loose cluster of 6–15 white flowers, not spotted. Sepals
erect, reddish purple, and petals spreading, ovate, tapering
to a claw. 10 stamens. Grows on moist cliffs, scree slopes,
along streams, and in meadows. Native.

Saxifraga rivularis
(*S. debilis*) SAXIFRAGACEAE
weak saxifrage
RM, alpine, subalpine, montane,
common, Summer, perennial, 1–6 in.

Delicate herb with erect stems from basal
cluster of leaves. Leaves slightly fleshy, glabrous, with 3–7 rounded lobes; alternate
along stem. Leaf margins smooth to slightly
glandular-hairy. Inflorescence a cyme, with
2–5 broadly campanulate flowers nodding on weak stems.
Erect sepals and white to pale purple petals. Grows in
dense clusters in moist shady areas, ravines, streamsides,
and under rock ledges in spruce-fir forests. Native.

Saxifraga tricuspidata
(*Leptasea tricuspidata*)

SAXIFRAGACEAE
three-toothed saxifrage
NR, alpine, subalpine, montane,
locally abundant, L Spring–
Summer, perennial, 2–7 in.

Evergreen cushion-forming herb with numerous stems. Basal and alternate stem leaves
are distinctly 3-toothed at tips; in untoothed
variants, margins are glandular-ciliate (in the
similar *S. bronchialis*, margins are smooth or with teeth).
Petals white to yellowish with small yellow to red spots.
Calyx sometimes purplish and sepals erect. Grows in
sandy, gravelly, or rocky soils, dry meadows, forest openings, rock outcroppings, and tundra. Native.

Triantha occidentalis
(*Tofieldia occidentalis*)
TOFIELDIACEAE
western false asphodel
NR, MR, alpine, subalpine, montane,
foothills, grasslands, wetlands,
common, locally abundant,
Summer, perennial, 3–18 in.

Flowering stems from spreading rhizomes
in small colonies. Leaves basal, linear, 2–8
in. long; then upright, alternate, clasping
stem. Flowers white to yellow-green, in short terminal
spikes to 2.5 in. long; 2 or 3 at each node with sticky stalks.
Upright fruit capsules 3-lobed and beaked, red or yellowish. Grows in sunny wet ledges and meadows,
bogs, streambanks. Native.

Euploca convolvulacea
(*Heliotropium convolvulaceum*)
BORAGINACEAE
phlox heliotrope
MR, SR, sagebrush steppe, intermountain
parks, grasslands, locally abundant,
Summer–Fall, annual, 8–17 in.

Herbaceous, with erect branches rising
from a single stout stem. Leaves ovate or lanceolate, silvery blue with adpressed hairs.
Fragrant white salverform flowers (resembling a phlox
or even morning glory) up to 1 in. across, produced on a
fiddleneck-like cyme from June to September, depending
on rains. Found in the intermountain region,
on the Great Plains and Colorado Plateau,
often on steep sandy cuts or dunes. Most
common on sandy soils. Native.

Hesperochiron pumilus
(*H. villosulus*) BORAGINACEAE
dwarf hesperochiron
NR, MR, subalpine, montane, foothills,
grasslands, wetlands, common,
Spring–Summer, perennial, 2–4 in.

Up to 5 low, leafless stalks, spreading to ascending, from basal rosette. Leaves oblanceolate to egg-shaped, 2.75 in. long, hairless except edges.
Single flower from stalk, saucer-shaped with hairless
purple-veined white lobes surrounding a hairy yellowish
tube. Lobes at least twice as long as tube. Found in moist
open areas, meadows, and seeps. Native.

Lonicera utahensis CAPRIFOLIACEAE
Utah honeysuckle
NR, MR, subalpine, montane, foothills,
sagebrush steppe, grasslands, common,
L Spring–Summer, perennial, 2–12 ft.

Erect to spreading deciduous shrub with
smooth twigs. Leaves on short stalks, opposite, to 3 in., elliptic to ovate; smooth on top
surface and smooth to thinly hairy below.
Inflorescence a pair of nodding flowers in
leaf axils. Flowers cream to pale yellow,
funnel-shaped, with 5 unequal corolla lobes and minute
bracts. Berries bright red, round, slightly fused at base.
Grows in meadows, shrublands, and open forests. Not yet
reported in CO, but near the border in UT. Native.

Cerastium arvense ssp. *strictum*
(*C. strictum*) CARYOPHYLLACEAE
prairie mouse-ear
RM, alpine, subalpine, montane,
foothills, grasslands, common,
Spring–Summer, perennial, 2–8 in.

Rhizomatous herb; forms mats or clumps.
Flowering stems reclining to ascending,
green to straw-colored, sometimes purplish.
Stem leaves opposite, with tufts of secondary
leaves in axils of lower leaves. Leaves linear to
lanceolate, surfaces hairless to glandular-soft-hairy, grayish green. Basal leaves absent. Inflorescence a cluster of
3–6 white flowers, each with soft-hairy sepals and 2-cleft
petals twice as long as sepals. 10 stamens. Grows in meadows and openings in forests, never in wet-
lands. Native.

Cerastium beeringianum
CARYOPHYLLACEAE
Bering chickweed
NR, MR, alpine, common,
Summer, perennial, 2–8 in.

Tufted, spreading alpine mat. Flower stems
4 in., sometimes more. Leaves alternate,
gray-green, oblong-lanceolate, largest on the
stems, lightly hirsute, central vein. Flowers
single or in small cymes, delicate white, 5 petals, each cleft
one-third their length; greenish to yellowish center. Grows
in sun, thin alpine soils, talus slopes, meadows. From Siberia through AK to AZ. Native.

Minuartia biflora
(*Arenaria sajanensis*)
CARYOPHYLLACEAE
mountain stitchwort
NR, alpine, subalpine, common,
Summer, perennial, 0.5–1 in.

Prostrate, mat-forming herb, with dense
mounds or mats sometimes more than
a foot across; has a stout woody taproot.
Curved, blunt, linear leaves to 0.5 in. long.
Flowers white, starry—petals at least twice
as long as sepals. Found on sunny areas of moist scree or
open tundra from near treeline to high alpine. A southerly
extension of a primarily arctic-alpine species. Native.

Minuartia obtusiloba
(*Arenaria obtusiloba*)
CARYOPHYLLACEAE
twinflower sandwort, alpine stitchwort
RM, alpine, subalpine, common,
L Spring–Summer, perennial, 0.5–1 in.

Stems densely matted, prostrate, forming glandular cushions often 1 ft. or more
across. Leaves short, needle-thin, linear but
not prickly, less than 0.3 in. long. Stemless
white flowers 0.2–0.4 in. across often cover
the cushion shortly after snowmelt. The
most common alpine sandwort of the Rockies, ubiquitous
on tundra. Native.

Moehringia lateriflora
(*Arenaria lateriflora*)
CARYOPHYLLACEAE
bluntleaf sandwort
RM, montane, foothills, common, locally
abundant, Summer, perennial, 1–8 in.

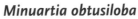

Several ascending to erect, herbaceous,
branched or unbranched, slender stems covered in short hairs from a branched stem
base and thin rhizome. Leaves opposite, elliptic to oblanceolate, rounded to obtuse tips,
hairy around edges with midvein on under-
side, sessile. Terminal and lateral clusters of 5 or 6 white
flowers with 5 (rarely 4) petals and an equal number of
green sepals with white margins. Grows in sun to shade,
forests, streamsides, meadows. Native.

Pseudostellaria jamesiana
(*Stellaria jamesiana*)

CARYOPHYLLACEAE

tuber starwort
RM, montane, foothills, grasslands,
wetlands, common, Spring–
E Summer, perennial, 4–24 in.

Rhizomatous plants with upright stems.
Leaves opposite, linear to lanceolate, 0.75–6
in. long. Inflorescence a cyme. Flowers with
5 lanceolate, glandular sepals; 5 white petals
to 0.4 in. long with deep cleft in center of each; 10 stamens
surrounding the superior ovary. Found in sage meadows
and coniferous/aspen forests. Similar to *Cerastium arvense*
ssp. *strictum* but lacks the tufts of secondary leaves and the
sepals are glandular, not hairy. Native.

Stellaria longipes CARYOPHYLLACEAE
longstalk starwort
RM, alpine, subalpine, montane,
foothills, common, L Spring–
Summer, perennial, 1–12 in.

Rhizomatous herb with several ascending to
erect, slender, 4-angled stems; forms tufts or
mats. Stem leaves opposite, sessile, stiff, linear to lanceolate, glabrous or hairy and often
bluish gray. Basal leaves few and soon deciduous. Inflorescence an open cluster of 1–3 white flowers
on long stalks. 5 petals, each with 2 lobes. Sepals 3-nerved
and slightly shorter than petals. A variable species that
grows in meadows and open forests, on streambanks and
dry rocky slopes. Native.

Parnassia fimbriata CELASTRACEAE
fringed grass-of-Parnassus
RM, alpine, subalpine, montane,
foothills, common, locally abundant,
Summer, perennial, 3–20 in.

Rhizomatous herb with 1 to several erect
stems from clusters of basal leaves. Solitary,
clasping bract mid-length of stem. Leaves cordate to reniform, to 1.5 in. wide, shiny with
conspicuous parallel veins; margins entire.
Inflorescence a solitary white terminal flower. Calyx with
coarse edges at tips. Petals oval, 5- to 7-nerved, lower half
fringed, upper half entire. 5 fertile stamens, alternate petals, and sterile yellowish, thickly scaled stamens opposite
petals. Found on streambanks, in moist meadows, fens,
and seepage sites in forests. Native.

Parnassia kotzebuei CELASTRACEAE

Kotzebue's grass-of-Parnassus
RM, alpine, subalpine, montane,
rare, Summer, perennial, 1–15 in.
Herbaceous plant with 1–3 erect, hairless,
leafless stems from basal cluster of leaves.
Leaves glabrous, to 0.75 in. wide, ovate, tapered at base, with entire margins. Inflorescence a solitary terminal white flower
with 3-veined calyx lobes and 1- to 3-veined
ovate petals; 5 fertile stamens, alternate with
petals; sterile stamens also present, short, narrow scales.
Found in wet meadows, seeps, tundra, on streambanks
and rock ledges. Rare throughout region, except frequent
in northeast BC. Native.

Convolvulus arvensis

CONVOLVULACEAE
field bindweed
RM, throughout, common, Spring–
Fall, perennial, 6–48 in.
Lax, twining stems from aggressive rhizomatous roots. Leaves glabrous, arrow-shaped
to lanceolate, alternate, largest on vigorous
growth. Flowers 1 or more at leaf nodes,
5 white petals fused into typical morning
glory corolla 1–1.5 in. across, sometimes
striped or shaded pale to dark pink. Can be showy—don't
be fooled! Pernicious weed of gardens, roadsides, farmland, disturbed sites; aggressively invading wildlands everywhere it is present. Tolerant of drought, resistant to
most controls. Introduced and invasive.

Moneses uniflora
(*Pyrola uniflora*) ERICACEAE
single delight, wood nymph
RM, subalpine, montane, common,
L Spring–Summer, perennial, 2–4 in.
Herbaceous evergreen with erect stem from
basal rosette. Leaves shiny and green, ovate
to round, with sharp- or round-toothed
margins. Solitary white star-shaped flower
to 0.75 in. across, waxy, fragrant, nodding
down from stem; 10 stout stamens surround large, shiny
green ovary with conspicuous stigma. Grows in moist coniferous forests and along shaded streams, in pine duff,
rotting wood, and near moss. Native.

Geranium richardsonii

GERANIACEAE

Richardson's geranium

RM, subalpine, montane, foothills, common,
L Spring–Summer, perennial, 15–30 in.

Herb with ascending to erect, branched stems
that are often smooth below and glandular above; glands purple-tipped. Basal leaves
on long stalks and stem leaves opposite, unstalked, and reduced; both usually palmately
5- to 7-parted, sometimes divided again and
with sparingly hairy surfaces. Inflorescence with a few
white to light pink flowers with purple veins and soft-hairy
bases. Fruit a carpel with stiff hairs. Grows in woods,
aspen forests, moist meadows, and streams. Native.

Claytonia rubra MONTIACEAE

redstem springbeauty

RM, montane, foothills, sagebrush
steppe, uncommon, locally abundant,
Spring–Summer, annual, 0.3–7 in.

Fleshy annual to biennial herb with several
erect to ascending, red or green stems; from
taproot. Numerous long-petiolate leaves form
flat to somewhat erect basal rosettes. Leaves
with red pigmentation; rhombic, ovate, or
spatulate. Stem leaves also ovate, distinct,
fused to stem on one side, or 1 leaf encircling stem. Inflorescence a cluster of white to pale pink flowers, subtended
by 1 bract. Grows in moist, shady sites including canyons
and ravines, dry woods, and on sand dunes. Native.

Linanthus nuttallii
(*Leptosiphon nuttallii*)

POLEMONIACEAE

Nuttall's linanthus

MR, SR, subalpine, montane, foothills,
common, Summer, perennial, 5–12 in.

Round subshrubby mounds with erect stems,
branching at the base, glabrous to short pubescent. The airy, whorled foliage is distinctive; lobes 4–9, linear to oblong, spinulose,
short pubescent. Inflorescence compact with
2–5 flowers in terminal clusters. Phlox-like flowers have 5
(sometimes 4 or 6) white petals, white lobes, and a yellow
throat and stamens. Part shade to shade. Plants that have
been cut smell like vanilla. Native.

Phlox albomarginata

POLEMONIACEAE

whitemargin phlox

NR, MR, subalpine, montane, foothills, grasslands, locally abundant, L Spring– E Summer, perennial, 0.5–1 in.

Tufted, often cushioned, taprooted perennial with numerous spreading stems, hairy. Leaves opposite, broadly lanceolate, widest in the middle and sharply pointed tip, with a distinctive white margin. Stalkless or short-stalked flowers solitary at ends of stems; about 0.5 in. across; white to pink or purplish corolla has 5 broad, rounded, spreading lobes, often twice as long as the calyx. Fruit a capsule, splitting along 3 lines with few seeds. Makes small mats on gravelly slopes and sparse meadows. *P. alyssifolia* has larger leaves; otherwise similar. Native.

Phlox andicola POLEMONIACEAE

prairie phlox, moss phlox

MR, SR, foothills, grasslands, common, Spring–E Summer, perennial, 1–2 in.

Herbaceous perennial with loosely tufted white stems arising from creeping rhizomes. Leaves opposite, linear, 5–8 pairs with prominent midveins and whitish bases, 0.4–1 in. long with a sharp point, glabrous to sparsely hairy. Flowers white, 1–5 at stem tips; corolla tubular with 5 petals; calyx also tubular with 5 lobes and tangled long hairs. Found in sandy soils and dry sites in sparsely vegetated outcrops, sandhills, and ponderosa pine woodlands. Native.

Phlox caespitosa POLEMONIACEAE

tufted phlox

NR, MR, subalpine, montane, foothills, sagebrush steppe, grasslands, locally abundant, L Spring–E Summer, perennial, 1–2 in.

Mat-forming herb with short, hairy, glandular stems. Stems lined with very narrow, linear, sharp-tipped leaves less than 0.4 in. in length. Inflorescence consists of solitary flower or a cluster of up to 3 flowers at the tip of each stem. Flowers 5-lobed, white, light pink, or lavender, up to 0.4 in. long; calyx thickened with membranes between flat lobes. Intensely fragrant. Found in open, dry pine forests, sometimes in sagebrush. Native.

Phlox condensata
(P. caespitosa ssp. condensata)
POLEMONIACEAE
dwarf phlox, alpine phlox
SR, alpine, subalpine, common,
Summer, perennial, 1–1.5 in.

Plants form cushion-mats, low to the ground
with sparse to dense hairs. Leaves linear to oblong, 0.15–0.35 in. long with a sharply pointed
tip, fleshy. Inflorescence solitary and sessile.
Flowers white to pink, occasionally with a blue
cast to them, 0.25 in., fragrant. Found in gravelly slopes
and rocky tundra. Native.

Phlox multiflora POLEMONIACEAE
flowery phlox, Rocky Mountain phlox
RM, montane, foothills, sagebrush steppe,
intermountain parks,
grasslands, common, Spring–E Summer,
perennial, 0.5–2 in.

Mat-forming herb from taproot with prostrate
to ascending stems. Leaves opposite, linear,
pliable, and surfaces smooth or slightly rough.
Inflorescence of 1–3 white or lavender-pink
flowers at stem tips; stalkless to short-stalked.
Calyx hairless to cobwebby. Corolla with
rounded lobes. Flowers with a strong, almost
tropical scent. Mountain parklands, sagebrush meadows,
open ponderosa pine forests, along streams. Native.

Anemone canadensis
(Anemonidium canadense)
RANUNCULACEAE
Canadian anemone, meadow anemone
RM, montane, foothills, wetlands, common,
Spring–Summer, perennial, 8–32 in.

Stems upright, hairy. Basal leaves
long-petioled to 8.5 in., with 3–5 deep clefts,
segments lobed and margins toothed on distal third to half. Flower stem leaves sessile,
deeply 3-cleft, 1.2–4 in. long. Inflorescence
solitary, rarely a cyme; 5 white petal-like sepals 0.4–0.8 in. long; flower stalk densely
hairy toward tip. Fruit an achene. Moist meadows, damp
thickets, and along streams. Most abundant in the SR
but also found in Black Hills of SD, along rivers and lakeshores east of the Rockies. Native.

Anemone cylindrica
RANUNCULACEAE
candle anemone, thimbleweed
RM, montane, foothills, common,
L Spring–E Summer, perennial, 1–2 ft.
Stems upright, densely hairy. Basal leaves
on petioles 3.5–8.25 in. long, 3- to 7-lobed
and ternate, margins crenate or serrate
and deeply incised on distal half. Whorls of
stem leaves similar to basal leaves halfway
up flowering stems. Inflorescence solitary
or cyme with 2–8 flowers, 5 (rarely 4) white to greenish
petal-like sepals, silky-haired; flower stalk hairy. Heads of
achene cylindrical and thimble-like in appearance. Prairies, dry open woods, pastures, and roadsides. Native.

Aquilegia laramiensis
RANUNCULACEAE
Laramie columbine
SR, montane, endemic, rare,
Summer, perennial, to 8 in.
Plants are biternately compound, occasionally singly ternate. Foliage is loose, not
clustered; leaves green on top and glabrous
beneath. Flowers rise slightly above the foliage, nodding; mostly solitary (rarely 3–5
flowers per stem). Sepals are white to cream,
occasionally green-tipped, and divergent from the floral
axis. Blades are white and spurs are short. Grows only in
the Laramie mountains in south-central WY, on large rock
outcrops in pockets of soil and rock cracks. Sun. Native.

Aquilegia micrantha
RANUNCULACEAE
Mancos columbine
SR, foothills, pinyon-juniper,
endemic, uncommon, Spring–
Summer, perennial, 18–24 in.
Basal leaves are biternate to triternately compound. Leaflets are green to slightly glabrous above, viscid to pubescent beneath,
and not crowded. Flowers erect or pendulous. Sepals are white to pink and perpendicular to petals. Blades are white to yellow and reflex away
from the center. Spurs are long and slender, most often
white to soft pink. A Colorado Plateau endemic, usually
found in seeps or hanging gardens in the canyonlands of
UT and AZ, infrequent in western CO. Native.

Ranunculus andersonii
(*Beckwithia andersonii*)

RANUNCULACEAE

Anderson's buttercup

MR, subalpine, montane, foothills, pinyon-
juniper, sagebrush steppe, locally abundant,
Spring–E Summer, perennial, 3–8 in.
Small herb with erect stems from short caudices. Leaves glaucous, deeply cleft; basal leaf
blades cordate in outline, ternately 1 or 2 times
compound; leaflets 2 or 3 times parted, segments elliptic to linear, margins entire or with occasional
teeth. Flowers with waxy petals about 0.5 in. long that are
white with much pink suffusion. Grows on well-drained
soils in mid-mountain areas from sagebrush desert to juniper and mountain mahogany zone. Native.

Amelanchier alnifolia ROSACEAE
Saskatoon serviceberry

RM, subalpine, montane, foothills, pinyon-
juniper, sagebrush steppe, intermountain
parks, common, Spring, perennial, to 10 ft.
Common across North America in a wide
range of habitats; plants in the Rockies range
from shrubs to small trees. Leaves elliptic
to oval, less toothed on proximal end, more
toothed on distal end; glabrous above, hairy
beneath. Flowers white; petals oblanceolate, 2–3 times as
long as wide. Styles 4, united at base. Fruits purple-black
pomes, in clusters. Dry hillsides in canyons and in association with aspen, pinyon-juniper, or sagebrush.
Sun. Also see *A. utahensis*, page 311. Native.

Fragaria vesca ROSACEAE
woodland strawberry

RM, subalpine, montane, foothills,
intermountain parks, common,
Spring–Summer, perennial, 1–6 in.
Basal leaf rosette; spreading runners root to
become new plants. All parts hairy. Leaves
green, ternate with 3 oval leaflets, deeply
veined, edges toothed, center tooth longer
than the rest; turning red in fall. Flowers to
0.75 in. across, with 5 rounded petals, 3–12 in an open
cluster on stem that may surpass the leaves. Fruit a small
strawberry ripening red, 0.5 in. across, may be larger;
seeds on smooth surface. Open meadows, moist or dryish
slopes, woodland openings, sandy soils. Native.

Rubus deliciosus
(*Oreobatus deliciosus*) ROSACEAE
delicious raspberry, Rocky Mountain raspberry
SR, montane, foothills, common,
Spring–Summer, perennial, to 5 ft.

Medium-sized shrub without prickles. Stems erect to descending with short hairs or glands, lower peeling with age. Leaves to 2 in. long by 2.75 in. wide with 0.5 in. lance-olate stipules; heart-shaped base and 3 or 5 rounded lobes, toothed edges. Flowers solitary, white, 5 petals to 1.2 in. long and rounded. Fruit dryish dark purple raspberry, rounded to 0.4 in. Riparian zones, rocky hillsides and canyons. The similar *R. neomexicanus*, with hairy leaves and red fruit, intersects its southern range. Native.

Saxifraga cernua SAXIFRAGACEAE
nodding saxifrage
RM, alpine, subalpine, common,
Summer, perennial, 2–10 in.

Herb with erect stems; solitary or in small clusters. Basal and reduced stem leaves 3- to 7-lobed, round to reniform, slightly fleshy, glandular-hairy, and often sticky. Basal leaves usually ephemeral. Inflorescence a large terminal white flower, usually upright, above reddish bulblets in the leaf axils. Grows in cool wet areas, on rock faces, talus slopes, and along moist streambanks. Plant reproduces primarily via bulblets, sometimes via rhizomes, rarely via seeds. Circumpolar. Native.

Solanum triflorum SOLANACEAE
cutleaf nightshade
RM, montane, foothills, pinyon-juniper,
sagebrush steppe, grasslands, common,
Summer–Fall, annual, 4–16 in.

Sprawling annual herb, sparsely pubescent with simple hairs; stems sometimes rooting at nodes; prickles absent. Pinnatifid leaves with linear to lanceolate lobes, hairy and often scurfy, 0.75–2 in. long. Inflorescence short, 1–3 flowers; corolla white, lobes to 0.1 in. long. Berries globular, greenish, 0.25–0.5 in. in diameter. Found in disturbed areas along roadsides, fields, and pastures; in prairie dog towns. Native, but with weedy tendencies.

Achillea millefolium
(*A. lanulosa*) ASTERACEAE
common yarrow, western yarrow
RM, throughout, common,
L Spring–Fall, perennial, 3–12 in.

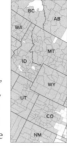

Sturdy upright stems from stoloniferous base,
forming colonies. Leaves lanceolate to oblong,
pinnately divided into fine segments, densely
tomentose to glabrate, aromatic. Flowerheads
flat-topped corymbs; flowers consist of 5 white
ray florets and 10–30 yellowish disc florets.
Fruit a hairless, flattened achene. Grows in very dry to
moist, open sites, mountain meadows, gravelly soil along
roadsides, often in disturbed areas. Used for millennia in
many cultures as a medicine, fumigant, insecticide.
Circumboreal. Native.

Ageratina herbacea
(*Eupatorium herbaceum*) ASTERACEAE
fragrant snakeroot
SR, montane, foothills, pinyon-juniper,
common, Summer–Fall, perennial, 1–3 ft.

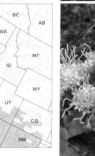

Plants largely herbaceous yet arise from a
woody rhizomal base. Stems upright and
brittle. Opposite leaves triangular, yellow
to green, often covered with gray glandular
hairs. No ray flowers; disc flowers are tubular
and white. Grows in sunny areas on dry slopes, pine parklands, rock ledge, and rock scree. Plants often mistaken for
brickellias yet are quite distinctive with their white flowers
and woody base. Native.

Anaphalis margaritacea
(*A. occidentalis*) ASTERACEAE
western pearly everlasting
RM, throughout, common,
Summer, perennial, 6–24 in.

Stems densely tomentose. Leaves with 3
veins; tomentose on both surfaces; clasping
the stem; leaf edges commonly rolled under.
Flowers in a multi-headed cluster. Numerous
white bracts surround the yellow-tipped disc
flowers; dry phyllaries persistent, ornamental.
Grows in many sunny climates and habitats, not only in
the Rockies but across North America. Can escape cultivation; also native to eastern Asia. Native.

numerous petals, composite, radial

Antennaria alpina ASTERACEAE
alpine pussytoes
NR, MR, alpine, subalpine, infrequent,
Summer, perennial, 1–7 in.

Low-growing, stoloniferous herb. Basal
leaves broadly lanceolate to 1 in. long, hairy
on lower leaf surface; stem leaves linear to
0.75 in. long with papery tips on the upper
ones. Inflorescence a cluster of 2–6 flowerheads. Outer phyllary bracts brown to black
on lower half, upper half greenish black and
pointed; plants mostly just female flowers (male plants uncommon), white. Found in dry to moist tundra, frequently
where snow is slow to melt. Native.

Antennaria anaphaloides
(A. pulcherrima ssp. *anaphaloides)*
ASTERACEAE
pearly pussytoes, handsome pussytoes,
tall pussytoes
RM, throughout, common, L Spring–
Summer, perennial, 6–20 in.
Upright herb without stolons. Narrow el-
liptical basal leaves up to 8 in. long with a
sharp tip, gray hairy on upper leaf surface.
Stem leaves to 3 in. long, usually with pa-
pery tip. Flowers papery, in short-branched
clusters with up to 50 small rounded white or pink flower-
heads; male and female flowers found on separate plants.
Involucre bracts hairy with brown-black spot at the base.
Found in dry meadows and aspen forests. Native.

Antennaria aromatica
ASTERACEAE
scented pussytoes
NR, MR, alpine, subalpine, uncommon,
L Spring–Summer, perennial, 0.75–3 in.
Low-growing herb, spreading by short stolons. Basal leaves oblong with pointed tip
and hairy, sometimes glandular upper surface; citronella-scented. Stem leaves small
and linear, lacking papery tips. Flowerheads
solitary or in white-flowered cluster of 2–5
with male and female flowers found on separate plants. Involucre bracts light to dark brown or olive-green at the tips.
Found in limestone talus and dry habitats. Once thought
to be endemic to southern MT and northwestern WY,
known range now extends as far north as AB. Native.

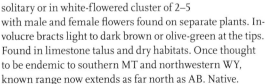

Antennaria dimorpha ASTERACEAE
low pussytoes, cushion pussytoes
RM, foothills, sagebrush steppe, grasslands,
common, Spring, perennial, 0.5–4 in.

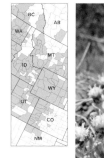

Low-growing herb, not spreading by stolons.
Basal leaves linear or lanceolate to 1.25 in.
long, silvery gray-green and thickly hairy.
Stem leaves linear, without papery tips. Flowerheads solitary, white and large compared to
other pussytoes, with male and female flowers found on separate plants. Involucre bracts
brown on the pointed tips. Found in dry locations with
ponderosa or pinyon pine, sagebrush. Native.

Antennaria lanata ASTERACEAE
woolly pussytoes
NR, MR, alpine, subalpine, common,
L Spring–Summer, perennial, 1–8 in.

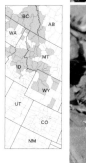

Upright herb, rhizomatous, lacking stolons.
Basal leaves lanceolate, upright to 4 in. long;
densely hairy, silvery green. Stem leaves similar, reduced, more linear up the stem. Inflorescence with 3–10 rounded heads in compact
clusters; dioecious. Involucre bracts on female
plants lance-shaped, dark brown or greenish black below, whitish tips, 0.2–0.3 in. long;
similar but shorter on male plants. Found at
high elevations in moist areas where snow melts late. *A.
racemosa* has similar range, but lives in cool, moist forests;
flowering stems with 3–12 heads in loose panicle up to 20
in. tall. Native.

Antennaria media
(*A. alpina* var. *media*) ASTERACEAE
Rocky Mountain pussytoes
RM, alpine, subalpine, common,
Summer, perennial, 2–6 in.

Low-growing herb. Basal leaves spoon-shaped
to lanceolate, thickly hairy, silvery green, to 1
in. long. Stem leaves similar, becoming linear
and reduced up stem. Flowers white with 3–7
rounded heads per upright flowering stem;
plants with only female flowers (male plants
rare). Involucre bracts lance-shaped with papery part black
to olive-green. Found on rocky slopes, fellfields, moist to
dry meadows. Similar to *A. alpina* but lacking the papery
tips on the stem leaves. Native.

Antennaria microphylla

ASTERACEAE

littleleaf pussytoes
RM, throughout, common, Spring–
Summer, perennial, 3–16 in.

Low-growing herb, spreading by short stolons. Basal leaves spoon-shaped to lanceolate with pointed tip, woolly hairy to 1.25 in.
long; stem leaves linear to lanceolate. Inflorescence white with numerous rounded
to elliptical heads in each compact cluster;
male and female flowers found on separate plants. Involucre bracts brown at the base and white above. Found in
sagebrush meadows, moist meadows, forest openings, and
along streambanks. Could be confused with the closely related *A. rosea*. Native.

Antennaria parvifolia ASTERACEAE

small-leaf pussytoes, Nuttall's pussytoes
RM, subalpine, montane, foothills,
sagebrush steppe, intermountain
parks, common, Spring–
E Summer, perennial, 1–6 in.

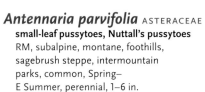

Low-growing mat-forming herb, spreading by stolons. Basal leaves spoon-shaped
to wide lanceolate, to 1.4 in. long with white
hairs; stem leaves linear to lanceolate, unstalked, reduced up stem. Inflorescence white with 3–8
elliptical heads in cluster; male and female flowers on separate plants (male plants uncommon). Involucre bracts
and papery part white to pink, hairy near base. Found in
open meadows, rocky slopes, and open for-
ests. Native.

Antennaria pulcherrima

ASTERACEAE

showy pussytoes
RM, throughout, common, L Spring–
Summer, perennial, 8–26 in.

Upright herb without stolons. Basal leaves
lanceolate to spatula-shaped; to 8 in. long
by 1 in. wide, with pointed tips, long silvery
hairs on upper surfaces; stem leaves linear,
to 5.5 in. long and sometimes with papery tips on upper
leaves. Inflorescence white with 3–30 rounded heads in a
tight cluster; male and female flowers found on separate
plants. Involucre bracts brown or black at tip. Found in
moist meadows, fens, forest openings, willow thickets, and
along streams. Native.

Antennaria umbrinella
(*A. aizoides*) ASTERACEAE
umber pussytoes, brown pussytoes
RM, subalpine, montane, sagebrush
stepp, intermountain parks, common,
Spring–Summer, perennial, 2–8 in.

Low-growing herb, spreading by usually upright, somewhat woody stolons. Basal leaves
narrowly spoon-shaped to triangular, 0.4–0.7
in. long; gray hairy on upper surface and with
a shortly pointed tip; stem leaves linear and
without papery tips. Inflorescence white with 3–8 rounded
heads in a cluster; male and female flowers on separate
plants. Involucre bracts white, yellow, or light brown at tip,
sometimes with some pink streaks. Found in dry sagebrush meadows, rocky slopes, open forests.
Native.

Centaurea diffusa
(*Acosta diffusa*) ASTERACEAE
diffuse knapweed
MR, SR, montane, foothills, pinyon-juniper,
sagebrush steppe, intermountain parks,
common, L Spring–Summer, biennial, 4–20 in.

Year 1: stemless rosette. Year 2: gray-green,
branched shrubby habit, many stems and
flowers. Rosettes to 1 ft., leaves with irregular pinnate lobes; stem leaves small, simple, linear. Disc
flowers like small thistles, white, pink-purple; bracts with
comb-like bristles and longer terminal spine overlap to
cover the involucre. This weedy species hybridizes with
others in the genus. Roadsides and disturbed
sites, aggressive/damaging to rangelands and
sensitive habitats throughout the West. Introduced and invasive.

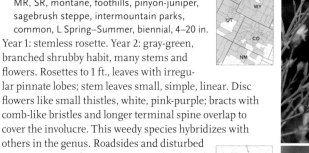

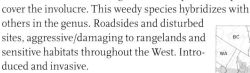

Chaenactis alpina ASTERACEAE
alpine dustymaiden
RM, alpine, subalpine, uncommon,
Summer, perennial, 1–3 in.

Somewhat mat-forming herb from taproot.
Stems erect to spreading. Plants produce only
basal foliage. Foliage is pinnate, fern-like, and
often quite woolly. Scapose flowerheads produce no ray
flowers, are white, cream, or lavender, with style and anthers protruding above the corolla. Fruit 10–20 thin scales.
Grows only in sunny alpine environments on scree or in
crevices. The common name refers to the petticoat-like
froth of the dusty gray-green leaves. Native.

Chaenactis douglasii ASTERACEAE

Douglas' dustymaiden

RM, foothills, pinyon-juniper, sagebrush steppe, intermountain parks, grasslands, common, Spring–Summer, annual, to 1 ft. Short flowering stems from persistent leaf rosettes. Leaves pinnately compound, down-rolled margins give thickened appearance, silvery-hairy, alternate, in basal rosettes and along stems. Flowers in bristly disc of florets with protruding stamen tube and stigma; no ray petals; creamy, some aging pink. Variable, sometimes mat-forming, sometimes with more open growth, in sage meadows and other low-elevation habitats. Native.

Chaetopappa ericoides

(Aster arenosus) ASTERACEAE

rose heath

SR, pinyon-juniper, grasslands, common, Spring–Summer, perennial, to 5 in. Ascending to erect, branching glandular stems from woody base; forms rhizomatous clumps. Basal leaves disappear after flowering; stems with tightly overlapping, alternate, entire, leathery leaves with pronounced midrib. Inflorescence with 12–24 white rays, reflexing midday, tinged pink near the yellow disc flowers. Distinguishing features are unequal phyllaries with white to clear margins; pappi in a series of white barbed bristles. Dry slopes, open areas, forests and meadows. Native.

Cirsium canescens

(C. nebraskense) ASTERACEAE

prairie thistle

MR, SR, montane, foothills, intermountain parks, grasslands, common, L Spring–Summer, biennial, 8–40 in. Biennial or monocarpic perennial with gray-woolly, erect, mostly unbranched stem; from taproot. Alternate stem leaves decurrent, 5–12 in., reducing upward, oblong-elliptic, pinnatifid with spiny-toothed margins; green and cobwebby above, white-woolly below. Several discoid heads at stem tips or in upper leaf axils with creamy white or lavender-tinged flowers. Phyllaries with dark dorsal ridge, spines yellow and reflexed. Dry gravelly soils, roadsides, shortgrass prairie, mountain meadows. Native.

Cirsium eatonii
(*C. tweedyi*) ASTERACEAE
Eaton's thistle
MR, SR, alpine, subalpine, montane, common, locally abundant, Summer, biennial/perennial, 8–40 in.

Stems erect to ascending, often unbranched, smooth to woolly; from taproot. Basal and alternate stem leaves 4–12 in., decurrent, linear-lanceolate, pinnatifid; smooth to sparsely hairy above, white-woolly below; wavy or toothed, spiny margins. Discoid heads, 1 to many, with off-white or lavender-purple flowers. Phyllaries in subequal series, margins with hairs; spines not reflexed. Rocky, open slopes and meadows. Native.

Cirsium foliosum
(*Carduus foliosus*) ASTERACEAE
elk thistle, leafy thistle
MR, alpine, subalpine, montane, grasslands, infrequent, locally abundant, Summer, biennial, 8–40 in.

Biennial or monocarpic perennial with leafy, erect, shaggy to woolly stems; from taproot. Basal and alternate stem leaves 2–10 in., linear-oblanceolate, almost entire, pinnate with spiny-toothed margins; surfaces green and smooth to thinly cobwebby above, gray to white-woolly below. Inflorescence 1–5 discoid heads subtended or hidden by leafy bracts; flowers white to pinkish. Phyllaries imbricate, smooth to sparsely hairy, without glutinous dorsal ridge. Meadows and open forests. Native.

Cirsium hookerianum ASTERACEAE
Hooker's thistle, white thistle
NR, MR, subalpine, montane, sagebrush steppe, intermountain parks, grasslands, infrequent, locally abundant, L Spring– Summer, biennial, 0.5–6.5 ft.

Biennial or short-lived perennial; mostly unbranched, erect, long-hairy stems; from taproot. Basal leaves narrowly oblanceolate, entire or pinnatifid; toothed, weakly spined margins; surfaces light-hairy above, thinly white-woolly below. Stem leaves alternate, decurrent, to 12 in., elliptic-oblong. 1–6 discoid heads in terminal clusters, white to creamy flowers. Phyllaries green or purple, densely cobwebby, slender yellow spine. Meadows, open forests, aspen parklands, roadsides. Native.

numerous petals, composite, radial

Cirsium scariosum
(*C. coloradense*) ASTERACEAE
meadow thistle, elk thistle
RM, alpine, subalpine, montane,
foothills, common, L Spring–
Summer, biennial, 1–40 in.

Biennial or monocarpic perennial with
thick, erect, sparsely hairy stems, or acaulescent (pictured); from taproot. Basal leaves
4–16 in., sessile, oblong, entire or pinnatifid;
marginal yellow spines. Surfaces smooth,
green above; woolly below. Alternate stem leaves overtop
inflorescence. Discoid flowers within basal rosette, at stem
tops or in leaf axils. Petals white, pink, or purplish. Involucres smooth; phyllaries without glutinous dorsal ridge
and spines turned outward. Grows in moist
meadows and open forests, along streams
and roadsides. Native.

Ericameria discoidea ASTERACEAE
whitestem goldenbush
RM, alpine, subalpine, uncommon, locally
abundant, Summer, perennial, 4–15 in.
Low, much-branched shrub; stems white,
tomentose. Alternate leaves oblong, wavy, to
1.25 in. long, midnerve visible; gland-tipped
hairs above and below, and on narrow flower
bracts. Disc flowers only, cream-white to yellow, in small
clusters at branch tips; 10–26 tubular corollas are 0.5 in.
long with protruding stigmas. Sun; rocky slopes, talus.
Native.

Erigeron caespitosus ASTERACEAE
tufted fleabane
RM, montane, foothills, sagebrush
steppe, common, Spring–
E Summer, perennial, 3–7 in.
Mounding caespitose plant from a taproot.
Leaves gray-hairy, narrowly spoon-shaped or
lanceolate, 3-nerved, 1–5 in. long, smaller up
the stems. Mound sometimes hidden with
a dozen or more stems terminating with
pure white or pale pastel daisies. Flowers
have conspicuous boss of yellow disc flowers. Widespread
component of sunny exposed bluffs and open meadows at
lower altitudes. Native.

Erigeron compositus ASTERACEAE
cutleaf daisy, dwarf mountain fleabane
RM, throughout, common, Spring–
Summer, perennial, 2–10 in.

Herb with a stout, branching caudex. Leaves
mostly basal, 0.2–2 in. long, usually ternately
compound and may be divided again, spatulate to obovate-spatulate, and minutely glandular. Flowers with white rays each to 0.5 in.
long. Pink and lavender forms occur at higher
elevations; the rayless var. *discoideus* is found
in some locales. Extremely variable morphologically and in
habitat in its extensive range. Grows in sandy or rocky soil
on slopes, dry meadows, and other open areas. The only
common fleabane with palmate foliage. Native.

Erigeron concinnus
(*E. pumilus* var. *concinnus*)
ASTERACEAE
Navajo fleabane, hairy daisy
RM, pinyon-juniper, sagebrush
steppe, common, Spring–E Summer,
perennial, 3–6 in.

Dense tufts of leaves obscured by flowers
in spring. Leaves to 3 in. long, mostly basal,
oblanceolate, entire, and covered with short,
stiff hairs. Nodding flower buds upturn as
flowers open. Ray flowers white, pink, or deep blue, 0.2–
0.6 in. long. Found in rocky or sandy soil in dry and sunny
habitats, often in pinyon or sagebrush. One of the easier
Erigeron spp. to identify because of the dense hairs covering all parts of the plant. Native.

Erigeron coulteri ASTERACEAE
large mountain fleabane, Coulter's fleabane
RM, subalpine, montane, wetlands, common,
L Spring–Summer, perennial, 8–24 in.

Herb with ascending to erect stems. Forms
loose mats in grass at higher altitudes. Basal
leaves are entire, occasionally slightly toothed.
Leaves on flowering stem are clasping and reduce in length upward. Flowerheads are single, terminal with white ray flowers. Plants
have both light and very dark hairs on the phyllaries.
Grows in high open meadows, along streams, and in open
coniferous forests in sun. Native.

Erigeron divergens ASTERACEAE
spreading fleabane
RM, foothills, intermountain
parks, grasslands, common,
L Spring–Fall, annual, 7–14 in.

Annual, biennial, or short-lived perennial herb. The fine, hairy and branching stem continues to sprout more buds and flowers with recurring rains for much of the summer. Leaves linear to oblanceolate, entire or coarsely toothed and hirsute. Ray flowers white, pink, or blue. Widespread and common on disturbed ground at lower elevations in sunny, dry to mesic meadows, open slopes, and open forest. Also prevalent in the Chihuahuan and Sonoran deserts. Native.

Erigeron eatonii ASTERACEAE
Eaton's fleabane
RM, subalpine, montane, foothills,
pinyon-juniper, sagebrush steppe,
intermountain parks, common,
L Spring–Summer, perennial, 4–18 in.

Tufted herb. Flowering stems seldom erect, usually bending upward. Leaves long, arching downward, crowded at base, narrowly oblanceolate to nearly grass-like, finely stiff-hairy. Flowerheads 0.5–1 in. across, the ray tips pink or purplish in bud, expanding to white (sometimes lavender); usually solitary, occasionally in small clusters. Sunny shrub oak slopes and meadows, open woodlands. Native.

Erigeron elatior ASTERACEAE
tall fleabane
SR, alpine, subalpine, montane, common,
L Spring–Summer, perennial, 8–20 in.
Flowering stems lightly branched near top. All parts hairy. Leaves 1–4 in. long, lanceolate to narrowly oblanceolate, finely stiff-hairy; basal not persistent; cauline slightly smaller, persisting for the season. Flower buds with curled/tangled phyllaries and long dense hairs; emerging rays darker than expanded rays. Flowers 0.5–1 in. across, the rays nearly white to pinkish lavender; solitary or in small clusters. Found in large patches in sunny areas. Native.

Erigeron flagellaris
(*E. nudiflorus*) ASTERACEAE
trailing fleabane
MR, SR, foothills, pinyon-juniper,
grasslands, common, L Spring–
Summer, biennial, 4–14 in.

Herb, biennial or short-lived perennial. Starts
as single rosettes and spreads by leafy runners that root along as the season progresses.
Rampantly spreading pioneer species, usually blooms prolifically; may disappear as
other species of plants encroach. Leaves entire to pinnately
lobed, linear to linear-oblanceolate, hirsute. Ray flowers
white (occasionally pink or blue). Grows in sunny meadows, open forest, and on dry slopes. Native.

Erigeron humilis
(*E. unalaschkensis*) ASTERACEAE
arctic alpine fleabane
RM, alpine, uncommon, L Spring–
Summer, perennial, 3–6 in.

Herb with small single rosettes. Mostly basal
foliage is lanceolate to spatulate and densely
hairy. Stems have few leaves and are covered
in dense purple to black hairs. The white or
blue ray flowers are proportionately much
shorter in length than most fleabanes, usually
0.5 in. long or less. Common in the Arctic region of the
northern hemisphere; the Rockies are an outpost of this
predominantly arctic-alpine species. Sun. Native.

Erigeron lanatus ASTERACEAE
woolly fleabane
RM, alpine, subalpine, rare, L Spring–
Summer, perennial, 2–3 in.

Herb. Stems erect, covered in soft shaggy
hairs. Leaves basal, few on short flower stems,
oblanceolate to narrowly elliptic, margins entire; surfaces with soft straight hairs or woolly.
Ray flowers bright white or sometimes pink,
30–40, spreading nearly as wide as the leaf
rosettes below, 0.3–0.5 in. long. Diminutive,
high-elevation daisy found from CO to AK.
Grows on sunny limestone scree and talus. Native.

Erigeron melanocephalus
(E. uniflorus var. melanocephalus)
ASTERACEAE
blackhead fleabane
SR, alpine, subalpine, common,
L Spring–Summer, perennial, 3–7 in.
Herb. Fibrous-rooted, rhizomatous, with
decumbent caudices. Stems erect, hairs
with black cross walls. Leaves mostly basal,
oblanceolate to spatulate, glabrous or
sparsely hirsute, margins entire. Ray flowers
white to purple, 0.3–0.5 in. long, spreading. Phyllaries are
covered in flattened black hairs, a very distinct identification trait. The most common white alpine fleabane in the
SR, this plant grows in sunny areas on rocky slopes, high
meadows, and subalpine spruce-fir habitats.
Native.

Erigeron nematophyllus
ASTERACEAE
needleleaf fleabane
SR, montane, foothills, sagebrush steppe,
intermountain parks, grasslands, common,
Spring–Summer, perennial, 3–8 in.
Taprooted herb. Stems erect, greenish, hairy
to almost smooth. Leaves mostly basal, linear to linear-oblanceolate; margins entire
and ciliate toward base. Surfaces sparsely hairy to almost
smooth. Ray flowers white to pink, 0.15–0.3 in. long. Phyllaries greenish to purple and slightly hirsute. Grows in
sandy, gravelly, or shale soils, and in rocky meadows or on
ridges and ledges in sunny locations. Native.

Erigeron ochroleucus ASTERACEAE
buff fleabane
RM, alpine, subalpine, montane, foothills,
sagebrush steppe, intermountain
parks, locally abundant, L Spring–
Summer, perennial, 4–15 in.
Plant from thick, woody taproot. Stems usually simple, rarely branched, ascending from
the center of the basal foliage, greenish,
stiff-hairy and sometimes sparsely glandu-
lar. Leaves basal, linear to linear-oblanceolate; margins entire. Flowerheads are solitary. Ray flowers 30–62, 0.3–0.5
in. long, white, pinkish, lavender, or bluish. Grows on
rocky or sandy slopes, talus, meadows, open woodlands,
open forests, often on calcareous soils in sun. Native.

Erigeron philadelphicus

ASTERACEAE

Philadelphia fleabane, fleabane daisy
RM, montane, sagebrush steppe, grasslands,
wetlands, common, locally abundant,
L Spring–Summer, biennial, 10–26 in.

Herb, biennial or sometimes short-lived perennial. Stems erect, greenish, with long,
spreading white hairs, leafy, usually unbranched except toward the inflorescence;
stems rise from a first-year rosette. Leaves
alternate, oblanceolate to obovate, with entire to toothed
margins, surfaces villous to nearly smooth; reduced and
more sparse upward. Flowerheads 0.5–0.75 in. across;
ray flowers 100–300, white to light violet, less commonly
pink, linear and densely distributed. Grows
in sunny meadows, woodland edges, and disturbed sites. Native.

Erigeron vagus ASTERACEAE

rambling fleabane
SR, alpine, infrequent, Summer,
perennial, 2–5 in.

Tiny rosettes from thin stems of a branching
caudex; plant may be only 1–2 in. across, or
forming small mats. Persistent basal leaves
are 3- to 5-lobed with conspicuous long hairs
on all surfaces. Flowerheads are on single stems; ray flowers with pale pink-blue tips before unfurling, opening
white. Phyllaries are in 2 or 3 series and covered in colorless hairs. Always on steep, moving scree slopes above
treeline in sun. Native.

Eucephalus engelmannii
(*Aster elegans* var. *engelmannii*)

ASTERACEAE

Engelmann's aster
RM, subalpine, montane, common,
Summer, perennial, to 4 ft.

Stems ascending to erect, variably hairy and/
or glandular, from a woody base. Leaves up to
4 in., oval to lance-shaped with conspicuous
veins; leaves smaller toward base. Large heads
with 8–13 white to pink rays surrounding yellow discs.
Phyllaries in 4–6 series, pointed, reddish with fringed
margin at tip. Open forests and meadows. Native.

342

Hieracium albiflorum
(*Chlorocrepis albiflora*) ASTERACEAE
white hawkweed
RM, subalpine, montane, foothills,
sagebrush steppe, common,
L Spring–Fall, perennial, 6–15 in.
Herbaceous stems erect, mostly solitary,
somewhat hairy, exude milky sap when broken. Leaves basal, 3–7 in. long, somewhat
hairy and mostly entire. Flowers creamy
white, dandelion-like, several to many in an
open inflorescence. Fruit an achene. Found in coniferous
forests from lower to higher elevations. Native.

Hymenopappus newberryi ASTERACEAE
Newberry's hymenopappus, wild cosmos
SR, subalpine, montane, foothills,
endemic, locally abundant,
Summer, perennial, 8–24 in.
Several to many branching stems originate from base. Finely cut leaves form a
gray-green basal rosette to 5 in. high and
10 in. wide; 1–5 stem leaves. 5-petaled
daisy-shaped flowers form a rounded cluster; ray flowers white, disc flowers are yellow. A showy plant, often found growing on
open grassy slopes in the forests. The finely
cut leaves are similar to those of *H. filifolius*. Occurs
exclusively in a few counties of CO and NM. Native.

Leucanthemum vulgare
(*Chrysanthemum leucanthemum*)
ASTERACEAE
oxeye daisy
RM, montane, foothills, grasslands,
common, Spring–Summer,
perennial, 4–40 in.
Herbaceous stems 1 to many, simple
or branched; basal leaves on petioles,
spoon-shaped to 6 in. long by 1.2 in. wide.
Stem leaves alternate, clasping and usually
lobed or toothed, to 6 in. or more in length
but decreasing on upper stems. Single
daisy-like flower per stem, about 2 in. across, with 15–35
white ray flowers to 1.2 in. long. Central disc flowers yellow. Sunny disturbed sites, roadsides, meadows, seeps,
and clearings. Widespread across North America, initially
grown as an ornamental plant from Eurasia. Introduced
and invasive.

Petasites frigidus var. *sagittatus*
(*P. sagittatus*) ASTERACEAE
arrowleaf sweet coltsfoot
RM, subalpine, montane, wetlands,
infrequent, Spring–E Summer,
perennial, 6–28 in.

Plants arise from rhizomes. Wide mats of
large deltoid to oblong leaves mark the colonies of this imposing marsh plant. Leaves 2–9
in. long, toothed, densely tomentose below.
Heads of off-white flowers emerge shortly
after snow melt. The predominant variety in our region;
plants are found in wet marshes and meadows, in ditches,
and along creeks and streams. Native.

Pseudognaphalium macounii
(*Gnaphalium decurrens*) ASTERACEAE
Macoun's cudweed
RM, montane, foothills, pinyon-juniper,
sagebrush steppe, intermountain
parks, grasslands, common,
Summer, biennial, 14–24 in.

Basal leaves wither as flowering stem develops; stem unbranched below; can be woolly,
branched where flowers appear. Leaves lanceolate, alternate, green above, tomentose below,
2–4 in. long, decreasing up the stem. Flow-
ers in terminal clusters, phyllaries shiny, pointed, white
to cream with soft yellow central disc. Widespread: open
woodlands, disturbed or burned meadows, roadsides.
Native.

Symphyotrichum ericoides
(*Aster ericoides*) ASTERACEAE
white heath aster
RM, foothills, sagebrush steppe, grasslands,
common, L Summer–Fall, perennial, 6–8 in.

Stems hairy, single to multiple from base,
ascending to erect; green initially, turning
brown and woody. Stem hairs appressed or ascending, in contrast to the related *S. falcatum*
(hairs spreading). Leave sessile, linear to lanceolate, withered by flowering time. Phyllar-

ies are numerous and have a distinctive spine at the tips.
Flowers in much-branched panicles; ray flowers white
(very rarely bluish pink). Found in sunny areas on the dry
steppe, disturbed sites, along roadsides. Native.

Symphyotrichum falcatum
(*Aster falcatum*) ASTERACEAE
white prairie aster
RM, montane, foothills, pinyon-juniper,
sagebrush steppe, intermountain parks,
common, Summer–Fall, perennial, 24 in.
Stems ascending to erect, moderately to
densely hairy. Foliage variable in length;
the basal leaves often senesce during flowering. The distinctive characteristic of this
plant is the sickle-shaped phyllaries, which
have a notable spine at the tip. Phyllaries point outward;
they do not clasp the head. Outer tips are green fading to
white at the connection to the plant. Ray flowers 20–35,
white (sometimes blue or pink). Found in sunny areas on
disturbed sites, roadsides, open plains, and
meadows. Native.

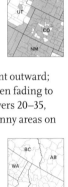

Symphyotrichum porteri
(*Aster porteri*) ASTERACEAE
smooth white aster
SR, montane, foothills, grasslands,
common, locally abundant, Summer–
Fall, perennial, 12–20 in.
Smooth throughout, alternate leaves linear to 3 in. with pointed tip, decreasing in
size up the stems. Flowers are bright and
showy 0.75-in. "daisies" in dense paniculate clusters, white
or less commonly pale pink. Disc florets yellow, aging
maroon-brown. Late summer aster in fields and meadows,
especially along the Front Range of CO, WY,
northern NM. Native.

Townsendia condensata
ASTERACEAE
cushion Townsend daisy
NR, MR, alpine, infrequent,
Summer, perennial, 1–2 in.
Compact, stemless, cushion-forming herb.
Basal and alternate stem leaves spatulate,
covered by long woolly hairs. Flowerheads
more or less sessile; ray flowers are white,
pink, or lavender and surround orangish
yellow disc flowers. Involucre bracts narrowly lanceolate,
with attenuate tips and densely woolly-hairy surfaces. This
high-alpine plant is found in limestone-derived soil, in
scree and talus, and on open, rocky slopes. Monocarpic.
Native.

Townsendia exscapa ASTERACEAE

stemless Townsend daisy
RM, foothills, pinyon-juniper, grasslands,
locally abundant, Spring, perennial, 1–3 in.

Low-growing mounding herb, stemless or
nearly so, often with many clustered rosettes.
Leaves narrowly spatulate to linear, and surfaces with short, stiff, appressed hairs to
nearly smooth. Flowerheads large, showy;
sessile or on short stalks. Ray flowers bright
white or pink. Involucre bracts linear to lanceolate. Grows in dry, sandy or gravelly soils, sagebrush,
open ponderosa pine forests, the Great Plains and nearby
hills. Flowers open in the sun. Native.

Townsendia fendleri ASTERACEAE

Fendler's Townsend daisy
SR, montane, foothills, pinyon-juniper,
uncommon, Summer–Fall, perennial, 4–15 in.
Herb with reclining to erect, much-branched
stems, mounding habit. Basal and alternate
stem leaves oblanceolate to almost linear; surfaces with short, stiff, appressed hairs. Flowerheads smaller and on stalks; ray flowers
white to pinkish. Involucre bracts lanceolate
with acute tips. Grows in dry, open places, on
badland slopes, often with pinyon-juniper,
mountain mahogany, and blue grama. Many flowers in
late summer. Rare in southern CO and in several counties
in NM. Of conservation concern. Native.

Townsendia grandiflora

ASTERACEAE
largeflower Townsend daisy
MR, SR, foothills, intermountain
parks, grasslands, common,
L Spring–Summer, biennial, 7–16 in.
Herb with multiple erect stems (developing the second year) from silvery rosettes
of leaves. Basal and alternate stem leaves
spatulate, oblanceolate, or linear; surfaces
with short, soft to stiff, appressed hairs
(or smooth); not fleshy. Large satiny white
flowerheads on stalks. Involucre bracts lanceolate with
bristly-pointed tips. Grows in open forests, on dry, grassy
slopes, and in gypseous shales. Flowerheads are large,
hence the specific epithet. Native.

numerous petals, composite, radial

numerous petals, composite, radial

Townsendia hookeri ASTERACEAE
Hooker's Townsend daisy
RM, throughout, common, Spring–
E Summer, annual, 1–2 in.
Stemless (or nearly so) herb growing in
huddled rosettes. Leaves linear to narrowly
oblanceolate, and surfaces with short, stiff,
appressed hairs. Flowerheads on short
stalks, with white to pinkish ray flowers. Involucre bracts linear, usually with slender
pointed tips and terminating in a tuft of tangled hairs. This plant is found from the sparse grassland
of the Great Plains to nearly alpine heights, on sunny, dry
slopes and rocky ledges, in all life zones except alpine and
wetlands. Native.

Townsendia incana
(*T. arizonica*) ASTERACEAE
hoary Townsend daisy
MR, SR, pinyon-juniper, sagebrush
steppe, intermountain parks, common,
Spring–Summer, perennial, 1–2 in.
Herb with soft, dense, white-hairy, reclining
to erect stems, forming mats to as much as
10 in. across. Basal and alternate stem leaves
spatulate to oblanceolate; surfaces with
short, stiff, appressed hairs. Flowerheads on
short stalks, and ray flowers bright white to pinkish. Bracts
lance-ovate and acute. Grows in sand or shale soil in dry,
open sites. Widespread in the Colorado Plateau and nearby
pinyon forest. Native.

Townsendia leptotes ASTERACEAE
common Townsend daisy
MR, SR, alpine, subalpine, montane,
intermountain parks, uncommon,
Spring–Summer, perennial, 1–2 in.
Low-growing, stemless (or nearly so) herb
that is similar morphologically to *T. exscapa*. Leaves fleshy, spatulate to linear, and
surfaces nearly smooth to covered with
short, stiff, appressed hairs. Flowerheads
sessile or on short stalks; ray flowers white
(rarely blue). Involucre bracts lanceolate and usually acute.
Grows in dry, open places, rocky ridges, sandy slopes or on
shale, occasionally among rocks on tundra or parkland. A
violet-flowered form occurs in MT. Native.

Tripleurospermum inodorum
(*Chamomilla inodora*) ASTERACEAE
scentless false mayweed, scentless chamomile
RM, subalpine, montane, grasslands, common, L Spring–Fall, annual, 1–2 ft.
Herb, sometimes biennial or perennial. Stems ascending to erect, branching at top, glabrous, with few hairs when young. Leaves 0.75–3 in. long, feathery with thin, branching lobes. Single white flowers are 1–2 in. across with 1–25 ray florets that point downward with age, surrounding a golden dome of disc florets. Found in sunny and disturbed areas, roadsides, dry shorelines, often considered weedy. Pollinated by solitary bees. Introduced and invasive.

Wyethia helianthoides ASTERACEAE
sunflower mule-ears
NR, MR, montane, sagebrush steppe, grasslands, uncommon, locally abundant, Spring–Summer, perennial, 10–24 in.
Flowering stems up to 24 in. from woody base. Leaves basal, elliptical, light green with soft hairs, especially early in the season, hairs becoming more sparse later; 8–12 in. long, margins entire or may have small teeth; smaller and alternate on flowering stem. Solitary terminal flowers 3–4 in. across with 13–21 ray petals; central florets gold, aging brown. Sunny damp meadows, forest openings, sagebrush shrublands. Native.

Xylorhiza glabriuscula
(*Aster glabriuscula*) ASTERACEAE
smooth woodyaster
MR, SR, pinyon-juniper, sagebrush steppe, intermountain parks, locally abundant, L Spring–E Summer, perennial, 7–15 in.
Subshrubby perennial, sessile alternate leaves, oblanceolate, 1–3 in. long, finely hairy with white midrib. White 2-in. daisy flowers with 12–25 ray petals on leafy stems. Grows on sunny slopes or flats, usually on alkaline, selenium-rich clays, with few companions beyond sagebrush, saltbush, and a few grasses. Native.

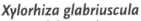

numerous petals, elongated clusters, radial

numerous petals, rounded clusters, radial

numerous petals, simple-shaped, radial

Brickellia grandiflora ASTERACEAE
tasselflower
RM, montane, foothills, pinyon-juniper, sagebrush steppe, grasslands, common, Summer–Fall, perennial, to 3 ft.
Deciduous shrub; heavily toothed alternate triangular leaves, largest and most numerous on lower portions. Inflorescence in branched clusters, pendent rayless flowers to 2 in.; tiny corollas white with bristly protruding cream filaments (tassels). Seeds with bristly white pappus later. Found in coniferous or mixed forests, dry slopes, pine parklands, or riparian areas, sun or shade. Several similar in this genus. Native.

Actaea rubra
(*A. arguta*) RANUNCULACEAE
red baneberry
RM, subalpine, montane, foothills, common, locally abundant, Spring–E Summer, perennial, 1–3 ft.
Large stems have few compound leaves. Leaves ternate and leaflets are toothed. White flowers emerge from leaf axils and ends of stems as fine-textured clusters. The type has bright red berries (pictured); forma *neglecta* has white berries. Berries are very poisonous and should not be eaten. Grows in woodland shade and moist meadow habitats. Native.

Cornus nuttallii CORNACEAE
Pacific dogwood
NR, montane, infrequent, Spring–E Summer, perennial, 10–50 ft.
Small to large tree, horizontal to upright branching, smooth brown bark, in small plates with age. Leaves opposite, ovate, 2–4.5 in. long; red fall color. Rounded flower buds form in fall, open in spring with leaves. Small true flowerheads surrounded by 4–7 showy white bracts 1–4 in. long. Berries red, clustered. A coastal species, with small, disjunct population in ID, struggling with anthracnose. Found along streamsides and valleys in mixed forests. Sun and part shade. Native.

Mentzelia decapetala
(Nuttallia decapetala) LOASACEAE
tenpetal blazingstar
RM, foothills, sagebrush steppe, grasslands, common, Summer, biennial, 1–3 ft.

Erect stems, 1 to several, branched above, whitish bark peeling on lower stem. Leaves alternate, petiolate below, sessile above, lanceolate, pinnatifid; scabrous, attach easily to fabric. Showy, large white flowers to 4 in. across; 10 petals; central boss of yellow stamens shorter than petals, from 1- to few-flowered cyme close to branch tips. Flowers open late afternoon, close next morning. Plants are selenium accumulators. Grows in sun, dry rocky slopes, roadsides, prairies, disturbed sites. Native.

Mentzelia lagarosa
(M. pumila var. lagarosa) LOASACEAE
dwarf mentzelia
MR, SR, foothills, pinyon-juniper, sagebrush steppe, uncommon, L Spring–Summer, biennial, 6–12 in.

Erect, branched, herbaceous, whitish stems from a taproot. Basal leaves lanceolate, petiolate, broadly toothed; stem leaves alternate, sessile, deeply pinnatifid, covered in barbed hairs. Yellowish white to cream, simple star-shaped flowers on stalks of 1–3 flowers, 10 petals. Occasionally perennial. Grows on dry, sandy to rocky slopes and in open woodlands. Native.

Mentzelia nuda
(Nuttallia nuda) LOASACEAE
bractless blazingstar
MR, SR, foothills, sagebrush steppe, grasslands, common, Spring–Summer, perennial, 1–3 ft.

Erect, herbaceous stems, 1 to several, branched, whitish, hairy above. Leaves alternate, petiolate below, sessile above, lanceolate to elliptic, shallowly pinnate, scabrous, easily attaching to fabric. Showy, white to cream flowers, 10 petals, 5 sepals, white stamens almost as long as petals. Flowers open midday, close in evening. Sun; dry slopes at lower elevations, disturbed sites, roadsides, sandy soils, prairies. Native.

350

Lewisia nevadensis
(*L. pygmaea* var. *nevadensis*)
MONTIACEAE

Nevada lewisia

MR, SR, alpine, subalpine, montane, common, locally abundant, Spring–Summer, perennial, 1–4 in.

Succulent herb with 1 to several prostrate to ascending stems; from basal rosette. Leaves linear to oblanceolate with entire margins; wither after flowering; 1 pair of bracts mid-length of stem. Inflorescence 1–3 white (occasionally pink) flowers with 5–10 often glandular-hairy, sharp-tipped petals. With a hand lens, observe 2 sepals with entire or shallow, non-glandular teeth. Grows on wet grassy slopes and moist meadows. Native.

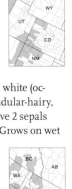

Lewisia triphylla
(*Erocallis triphylla*) MONTIACEAE

threeleaf lewisia

RM, alpine, subalpine, montane, uncommon, locally abundant, Spring–Summer, perennial, 1–4 in.

Succulent herb with 1 to several weak, spreading to erect stems. 1 linear basal leaf, to 2 in., absent by flowering; a semi-whorl of 2–5 stem leaves. Inflorescence a loose, branching cluster of 1–25 white or pinkish flowers sometimes with darker pink venation. 5–9 petals and 2 sepals. Each flower subtended by bracts similar to sepals. Look for this small plant in moist meadows, gravelly slopes, and open forests, often near melting snow. Disjunct populations in the SR. Native.

Trientalis borealis ssp. *latifolia*
PRIMULACEAE

broadleaf starflower, western starflower

NR, montane, foothills, uncommon, Spring–E Summer, perennial, 1–8 in.

Herbaceous, rhizomatous, with upright stems. Leaves simple, in whorls of 5–9 at stem apex; petiolate, lanceolate, 2.5 in. long, widest in the middle, pointed at tip. Petioles 0.5–1.5 in. long, shorter than leaves. Flowers snow-white, aging pink; 1–3 blooms on slender stalks, 0.25–0.5 in. wide, 5–9 petals. Dormant in summer, stem with 1 or 2 capsules remains visible. Occurs in open to dappled shade in moist coniferous forests, boreal forests. Native.

Anemone narcissiflora

RANUNCULACEAE

narcissus anemone

RM, alpine, subalpine, common,
L Spring–Summer, perennial, 2–24 in.

Stems from woody base, often hairy; leaves basal, petiolate, 3–10, ternate with each leaflet deeply divided multiple times. Flowering stem with sessile, ternate leaves at base of cyme; flowers 1–8 in cyme; 5–9 petal-like sepals white or cream to 0.8 in. long; backs of sepals may be blue-tinged. Found in moist meadows, coniferous forests, and rocky slopes. Var. *zephyra* (pictured) is native to CO and WY; var. *monantha* is found in BC. Could be confused with *Trollius albiflorus*. Native.

Anemone occidentalis
(*Pulsatilla occidentalis*)

RANUNCULACEAE

white pasqueflower, western pasqueflower

NR, alpine, subalpine, montane, common,
L Spring–Summer, perennial, 4–24 in.

Erect stems from a woody base, densely hairy. Leaves basal, petiolate, to 8 in.; pinnate with each leaflet finely dissected. Flowers solitary, 1–2 in. wide, 5–7 creamy white petal-like sepals often with blue tinge on underside. Seeds have long silky feather-like tails attached; these create a distinctive mop-like seedhead and assist with wind dispersal. Rocky slopes and moist meadows. Native.

Anemone parviflora

RANUNCULACEAE

smallflower anemone

RM, alpine, subalpine, montane, common,
Spring–Summer, perennial, 2–8 in.

Slender horizontal rhizomes; basal leaves on petioles up to 3.2 in. long and ternately compound with shallowly lobed leaflets, glossy or long-hairy. Flowers solitary, with 4–7 petal-like sepals, white or blue-tinged. Fruit an achene, egg-shaped, not winged and densely hairy, several held in a spherical head. Common in northern regions in moist meadows, seeps, scree, tundra, streambanks, and forest openings; less frequent in alpine regions of SR. Native.

numerous petals, simple-shaped, radial

Caltha leptosepala
RANUNCULACEAE
white marsh marigold
RM, subalpine, montane, wetlands,
common, Spring–Summer, perennial, 10 in.
Herbaceous basal rosettes of leaves emerge
very early, longer than wide, shiny, oblong
with basal lobes where they join the long
petioles. Flowers 1 per stem, many per plant.
6–12 white sepals, yellow stamens, green
pistils. Can be abundant in wet meadows,
streamsides, springs, often appearing as the edges of
snowfields retreat. Native.

Dryas integrifolia ROSACEAE
**entireleaf mountain-avens, white
mountain-avens**
NR, alpine, subalpine, montane, infrequent,
Summer–Fall, perennial, 1–5 in.
Mat-forming shrub with trailing stems
that freely branch and root. Leaves
short-stemmed, oval to lance-shaped, square
to heart-shaped at base, 0.5 in. long, margins
rolled under. Upper leaf surface smooth,
lower covered in white hairs. Scape erect,
leafless and hairy. Flowers solitary, white,
open wide, 8–10 elliptic petals. Calyx somewhat woolly with few dark hairs. Stamens numerous. Fruit
an achene, fluffy with age. Found in dry to moist tundra,
rocky ridges, talus slopes. Native.

Dryas octopetala ssp. hookeriana
(*D. hookeriana*) ROSACEAE
Hooker's mountain-avens
RM, alpine, locally abundant,
Summer, perennial, 1–4 in.
Mat-forming, evergreen subshrub. Branches
prostrate. Leaves alternate, oblong to ellip-
tic, broadest at middle or below; margins
toothed and rolled under; white-hairy below.
Flowers solitary on leafless stalk. Sepals
8–10. Petals 8–10, white to creamy white.
Stamens and pistils numerous. Fruit an achene. Found in
alpine tundra. The flowers are heliotropic. Native.

Atriplex canescens
(*Calligonum canescens*)
AMARANTHACEAE
fourwing saltbush
RM, montane, foothills, pinyon-juniper,
sagebrush steppe, grasslands, common,
Spring–Summer, perennial, 3–6 ft.
Usually dioecious shrub, evergreen; stems
ascending to erect, heavily branched, silvery.
Leaves alternate, sessile, cauline, lanceolate
to oblong, margins entire, silvery-scurfy.
Flowers yellow, inconspicuous, in elongated clusters.
Fruiting bracts very conspicuous, 4-winged with toothed
or entire margins, papery. Very salt tolerant, and dense
deep root system is good for erosion control. Sun; dry,
rocky soils and slopes, canyons, saline areas.
Native.

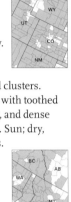

Thalictrum occidentale

RANUNCULACEAE
western meadow-rue
RM, montane, grasslands, common,
Spring–Fall, perennial, 2–5 ft.
Herbaceous perennial with leaves 3–5 times
ternately compound. Leaflets 0.8–1.2 in.,
3-lobed, prominent veins, margins rolled
under, glaucous, somewhat hairy below.
Inflorescence a loose, many-flowered panicle. Flowers
have no obvious petals, unisexual; sepals whitish, anthers
showy, yellow, shorter than filaments. Fruit achenes.
Occurs in wet meadows, thickets, streambanks, and disturbed areas. Common in NR and MR, un-
common in SR. Native.

Lysichiton americanus ARACEAE
yellow skunk cabbage
NR, montane, foothills, wetlands, common,
Spring–E Summer, perennial, 1–3 ft.
Flowers on a thick stem from basal leaf rosette. Bright green leaves emerge with, or
just after, flowers; elliptic to egg-shaped,
1–2 ft. long, with thick petioles; 3–10 leaves
from robust underground rhizomes. Conspicuous large yellow hooded bract opens to reveal a
dense spike 2.5–5 in. long with foul odor. True flowers
tiny, cream-white, maturing into red berries. Part shade,
wet woodlands, bogs, streamsides; more common toward
coast. Native.

Eriogonum alatum
(Pterogonum alatum) POLYGONACEAE
winged buckwheat
MR, SR, montane, foothills, pinyon-
juniper, sagebrush steppe, intermountain
parks, grasslands, common, Spring–
Summer, perennial, 1–8 ft.
Herbaceous, 1 to several stems from an
often-chambered taproot. Leaves in a basal
rosette; oblanceolate, linear-lanceolate, and
densely hairy; few alternate and reduced along
lower stem. Inflorescence a terminal panicle of tiny yellowish to greenish yellow 6-tepaled flowers in small clusters, turning maroon in fruit with winged seeds. Grows
in sunny areas, barrens, rock ledges, pine parklands,
dry slopes, and sage meadows. Monocarpic.
Native.

Cypripedium parviflorum
(C. pubescens) ORCHIDACEAE
yellow lady's slipper
RM, montane, foothills, pinyon-
juniper, sagebrush steppe, rare,
Spring–Summer, perennial, 4–20 in.
Erect herb, leaves 2–6 in., alternate, elliptic, sheathed, parallel veins. Inflorescence 1
or 2 flowers, lower lip inflated, yellow, inner
brown spots. Lateral petals long, often twisted, yellow,
brown marks. Var. *makasin* (NR, MR), sheathing bract
lightly hairy to smooth when young; lip 0.6–1.2 in.; densely
marked sepals and petals; scent intense. Var. *pubescens*
(RM), sheathing bract thickly hairy when
young; lip to 2.2 in., smaller northward; sepals unmarked to spotted, rarely densely;
scent faint. Fens, moist forests, seeps. Native.

Berberis fremontii
(Mahonia fremontii) BERBERIDACEAE
Fremont's mahonia
SR, pinyon-juniper, grasslands, locally
abundant, Spring, perennial, 3–15 ft.
Upright, branching evergreen shrub. Leaves
dark green, pinnately compound with 5–11
strongly lobed or toothed, spine-tipped holly-
like leaflets to about 1 in. long. Bright yellow flowers in short
clusters with 3–6 flowers on racemes up to 2.5 in. long; 6
flat rounded sepals surround the 6 cup-shaped petals. Berries yellow, red, or brown, dry and inflated, less than 0.75 in.
in diameter. Grows on rocky hillsides and slopes. Native.

Berberis repens

(*Mahonia repens*) BERBERIDACEAE
creeping Oregon-grape
RM, montane, foothills, intermountain
parks, common, Spring–
Summer, perennial, 4–12 in.
Woody stems, spreading by rhizomes.
Leaves alternate, pinnate, leaflets ovoid,
coarse sharp-tipped teeth, leathery, evergreen, some red/orange in fall. Flowers to
0.5 in., clustered, 3 outer and 3 inner sepals
surround 6 2-lobed petals, hyacinth-scented; followed by
grape-like cluster of blue berries. Sun, shade; rocky ledges,
hillsides, open pine woodlands. Native.

Eriogonum mancum

(*E. chrysocephalum* ssp. *mancum*)
POLYGONACEAE
imperfect buckwheat
MR, montane, foothills, pinyon-juniper,
sagebrush steppe, intermountain
parks, grasslands, locally abundant,
L Spring–Summer, perennial, 0.5–4 in.
Stems spreading, with persistent leaf bases;
caudex stems matted; aerial flowering stems
scape-like, weakly erect to erect, slender,
solid. Leaves grayish, linear-oblanceolate,
0.2–0.4 in., and densely hairy on both surfaces. 6-tepaled
flowers in dense, pompom-like clusters; bright yellow to
cream, pink to rose. Sunny areas, rock ledges, barrens, dry
slopes, clayey flats and slopes, sage meadows, calcareous
soils at lower elevations. One outlying population in the House Range of UT. Native.

Erythronium grandiflorum

LILIACEAE
yellow avalanche lily, glacier lily
RM, alpine, subalpine, montane,
foothills, locally abundant, Spring–
Summer, perennial, 2–12 in.
Herbaceous perennial from slender bulb.
Leaves basal, 2, fleshy, elliptic, margins
somewhat wavy, about as tall as bloom. Inflorescence 1–5 flowers on leafless flower stalk. Flowers
nodding, lemon to golden yellow; 6 tepals curved strongly
backward revealing large, white stigma and yellow, red,
or white anthers. Fruit a capsule. Abundant in mountain
meadows. Also occurs along streambanks, sagebrush
slopes, and open woods. Native.

Fritillaria pudica LILIACEAE
yellow fritillary
RM, montane, foothills, sagebrush
steppe, grasslands, infrequent, Spring–
Summer, perennial, 6–12 in.

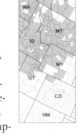

Smooth stem from scaly bulb. Leaves linear,
2–5 in. long, alternate to nearly whorled on
lower stem, occasional on upper stem. Flowers nodding, 1 or 2 on upright stalk; 6 oval tepals to 0.75 in.; yellow, or with few brownish
marks near base, fading orange-red. Seed capsule matures upright. Part shade among shrubs, sage, dry
woodland edges or openings, meadows. Native.

Corydalis aurea
(*C. washingtoniana*) PAPAVERACEAE
golden corydalis
RM, montane, foothills, pinyon-juniper,
sagebrush steppe, grasslands, common,
Spring–Summer, annual, 3–16 in.

Stems clustered, green or reddish, spreading,
smooth. Leaves basal, 3 in. long, alternate,
pinnately compound, lobed, blue-green, often
reaching past the flower racemes. Flowers yellow, to 0.75 in. long, in short terminal spikes;
2 outer petals spreading at tip, one having an
inflated spur behind; 2 inner petals fused.
Fruit a curved capsule, black seeds. *C. micrantha* similar, with taller raceme, smaller flowers. Sun, part shade.
Grows in sandy soil, rocky slopes, disturbed sites, meadows, washes. Native.

Barbarea orthoceras
(*B. americana*) BRASSICACEAE
American yellowrocket
RM, montane, foothills, grasslands,
wetlands, common, Spring–E Summer,
biennial, 8–40 in.

Upright stems with lyrate-pinnatifid basal and
stem leaves. Basal leaves 2.5 in. long on petiole to 2.75 in. long with 1–4 lateral lobe pairs
oblong or ovate. Cauline leaves entire with
terminal lobe 2 in. long by 1.2 in. wide with
conspicuously auriculate base. Flowers spiral up the erect
stems on short pedicels; 4 yellow petals 0.3 in. by 0.1 in.
Fruit a narrow ascending pod 1.75 in. long. Across much
of northern North America, this opportunistic species has
expanded its range widely; in moist areas, roadsides, disturbed sites. Also native to temperate Asia. Native.

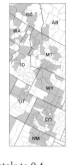

Barbarea vulgaris
(*B. arcuata*) BRASSICACEAE
garden yellowrocket
RM, montane, foothills, grasslands,
wetlands, common, Spring–
E Summer, biennial, 6–40 in.
Upright stems with basal leaves
lyrate-pinnatifid; 1–5 lateral lobe pairs on
leaves to 4 in. long; cauline leaves progressively reduced and usually lobed or toothed
rather than pinnatifid. Flowers spiral up
the erect stems on short pedicels; 4 yellow petals to 0.4
in. long. Fruit 0.6–1.2 in. long and either erect or spreading. Found in disturbed sites, riparian areas, meadows and fields. This species originated in Europe and is
found throughout most of North America.
Introduced.

Descurainia pinnata
(*D. ramosissima*) BRASSICACEAE
western tansymustard
RM, foothills, pinyon-juniper, sagebrush
steppe, grasslands, common,
Spring–Summer, annual, 4–24 in.
Herbaceous, glandular, simple to branched
stems from a taproot. Leaves basal and alternate, lanceolate to oblanceolate, hairy to glabrous, 1 or 2 times pinnate; lower ones petiolate. Bractless
flowers in racemes, 4 petals, pale to bright yellow. Fruits
broad, elliptic siliques. Ours is ssp. *brachycarpa*. Sunny dry
slopes, roadsides, disturbed sites. Native.

Descurainia sophia
(*Sisymbrium sophia*) BRASSICACEAE
herb sophia, flixweed
RM, throughout, common, Spring–
Summer, annual, 6–32 in.
Stems usually solitary, from a taproot, often
in large dense colonies. Leaves gray-green,
pinnate, alternate, very finely dissected.
Small soft yellow flowers in elongating
spikes, quickly maturing into slender upright 1-in. siliques on angled pedicels; each
plant seeding abundantly and becoming very weedy. Extremely widespread and common, especially in arid parts
of the West, but adaptable to all zones except alpine and
wetlands. Sunny disturbed sites, roadsides, gardens.
Introduced.

Rorippa curvisiliqua BRASSICACEAE
curvepod yellowcress
NR, MR, subalpine, montane, wetlands,
common, L Spring–Summer, annual, 1–12 in.
Stems sprawling to ascending with sparse,
backward-curved hairs. Basal leaves wither
early; stem leaves alternate to 2.75 in. long
by 0.75 in. wide, pinnately lobed, with largest lobe at the end. 4 sepals alternate with 4
shorter yellow petals. Fruit a linear silicle to
0.7 in. long and upward-curving, usually hairy
along edges. Found in riparian areas, stream and pond
edges. Native.

Rorippa palustris BRASSICACEAE
bog yellowcress
RM, wetlands, common, L Spring–
Summer, annual, 4–40 in.
Stems erect, usually solitary, often densely
hairy. Basal leaves to 8 in. long by 2 in. wide,
lyrately pinnate; stem leaves similar, clasping
the stems, sometimes with large lobes near
the leaf base, alternate. Flowers in elongated
racemes branching from stem at leaf axils; 4
sepals alternate with 4 spoon-shaped yellow
petals. Fruit is egg-shaped to cylindrical silicle
to 0.6 in. long. Found in moist areas such as
stream and pond edges. Multiple varieties found in our region, each distinguished by hairs on leaf surfaces. Native.

Rorippa sinuata
(*Nasturtium sinuatum*) BRASSICACEAE
spreading yellowcress
RM, montane, foothills, grasslands, wetlands,
common, Spring–E Summer,
annual, 4–18 in.
Stems ascending. Basal and stem leaves 0.75–
2.5 in. long, pinnately lobed on short petioles
with the largest lobe at the end; alternate.
Flowers in elongated racemes; 4 sepals alternate with 4 longer spoon-shaped yellow petals.
Fruit rounded to linear, to 0.6 in. long. Found
in riparian areas, such as streams and pond
edges, from the Mississippi River to CA. Native.

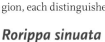

Sisymbrium altissimum
(Norta altissima) BRASSICACEAE
tall tumblemustard
RM, montane, foothills, pinyon-juniper,
sagebrush steppe, grasslands, common,
Spring–Fall, annual, 1.5–5 ft.
Herbaceous erect stems, hairy below, glabrous and branched above. Basal leaves with
pinnatifid margins, broadly lanceolate to
oblanceolate, petiolate; stem leaves alternate,
similar to basal leaves, reduced toward top.
Numerous pale yellow flowers in terminal racemes;
4 sepals, 4 petals longer than sepals. Fruit a spreading,
linear silique. Found in sun in disturbed areas, fields,
and roadsides. Introduced and invasive.

Sisymbrium linifolium
(Schoenocrambe linifolia)
BRASSICACEAE
flaxleaf plainsmustard
RM, montane, foothills, pinyon-juniper,
sagebrush steppe, grasslands, common,
Spring–Summer, perennial, 1–3.5 ft.
Slender, erect stems, 1 to several, simple or
loosely branched, from a rhizome; herbaceous, sparsely hairy or glabrous, glaucous.
Basal leaves entire or pinnatifid; stem leaves
alternate, linear or filiform; entire or rarely dentate; sessile
to short-petiolate; reduced toward top. Flowers yellow, in
a raceme; 4 petals, 4 lanceolate sepals. Fruit a nearly erect
silique. Found on sunny dry slopes, cliffs. Native.

Sisymbrium loeseli BRASSICACEAE
small tumbleweed mustard
RM, montane, foothills, pinyon-juniper,
sagebrush steppe, grasslands, common,
Spring–Summer, annual, 1–5 ft.
Herbaceous, erect, branched stems,
hairy below, glabrous above. Leaves alternate, deltoid-lanceolate to lanceolate,
short-petiolate, pinnatifid, may have toothed
or entire margins. Yellow flowers in racemes; 4 petals, 4 lanceolate sepals. Fruit a
glabrous, linear silique. Found in sunny areas including
roadsides, disturbed or overgrazed areas, streambanks,
and moist to dry fields. Can form large colorful but weedy
displays in damp meadows in late spring. Introduced and
invasive.

Stanleya pinnata BRASSICACEAE
desert prince's plume
RM, montane, foothills, pinyon-juniper,
sagebrush steppe, grasslands, common,
Spring–Summer, perennial, 2–6 ft.

Many herbaceous, mostly erect stems; sometimes branched below, seldom above. Basal
leaves withered at flowering; alternate stem
leaves thick, pale green, entire, waxy, dentate
or pinnately lobed. Simple bright yellow flowers in dense terminal racemes, 2–24 in. long;
4 sepals, 4 petals; long exserted stamens give fluffy appearance. Fruit a silique, linear, 1–3 in. long, spreading or
down-curving. Sun; dry slopes, disturbed, selenium-rich
soils. Dramatic against red canyon walls on the Colorado
Plateau. Native.

Alyssum alyssoides
(*A. calycinum*) BRASSICACEAE
pale madwort
RM, montane, foothills, grasslands,
common, Spring–E Summer, annual, 2–20 in.

Stems single to multiple from base. Stem
leaves subsessile or with short petioles, alternate, 1 in. long by 0.15 in. wide, numerous.
Flowers with persistent sepals, pubescent;
minute petals, 0.15 in. by 0.03 in., pale yellow or white, linear to linear-oblanceolate, petal edge
entire, spiraling around stem on 0.2-in. pedicels. Fruit
stellate-hairy and sepals persistent in fruit, orbicular. Disturbed sites, grassy areas, fields, sagebrush flats, limestone ledges. A handful of other *Alyssum* spp.
are distributed within the region in similar
habitats; all are non-native. Introduced and
invasive.

Draba aurea
(*D. minganensis*) BRASSICACEAE
golden draba
RM, alpine, common, Summer,
perennial, 2–20 in.

One or more hairy stems arise from a rosette
of leaves. Leaves gray-green, basal, and oblanceolate to obovate. Flowers form a spike, are 4-petaled,
yellow, and 0.14–0.2 in. long. Hairs are 3- to 6-rayed. Pods
can be twisted or not. This is one of the most commonly
encountered species. Grows in meadows and forests. It is
more gray-green than *D. spectabilis*. Native.

4 petals, rounded clusters, radial

Draba crassa BRASSICACEAE
thickleaf draba
RM, alpine, subalpine, locally abundant,
Summer, perennial, 2–6 in.
Stems are hairless at the base, becoming
more hairy above. Leaves form a green basal
rosette; oblanceolate, hairless, with entire
ciliate margins. Inflorescence a spike, 0.08–
0.13 in. long. Flowers yellow, 8–25 in a spike.
Petals 4. Common in specific locations in
tundra and scree slopes, often in the shade
of boulders. Few others in the genus have the distinctive,
large, hairless leaves of this species. Native.

Draba crassifolia BRASSICACEAE
snowbed draba
RM, alpine, subalpine, locally abundant,
Summer, annual, 0.4–6 in.
Flowering stems usually hairless, above
small basal rosette. Leaves oblanceolate, 0.2–
1.2 in. long; hairless or with simple 2-rayed
hairs; entire, ciliate margins. Inflorescence
8–25 yellow flowers 0.14–0.25 in. long, with
4 petals; in tiny raceme. Fruit a silique.
Grows in meadows, coniferous forests, and
tundra, especially areas of late snowmelt, in
the shade of boulders and cliffs. Diminutive,
easily overlooked. *D. graminea* is endemic to the San Juan
Mountains, CO, and has larger flowers. Native.

Draba globosa BRASSICACEAE
beavertip draba
MR, SR, alpine, rare, Summer,
perennial, 0.4–2 in.
Cushion-forming with a few leafless flowering stems. Tiny green basal rosettes; leaves
are oblanceolate to linear, hairless, curve
inward, 0.08–0.2 in. long, with ciliate margins. Inflorescence a few-flowered cluster of simple, tiny 4-petaled flowers, yellow
(sometimes creamy white). Grows in moist,
sparsely vegetated soils; rare throughout its
habitat, with widely scattered populations.
Often treated as a variety of *D. densifolia*. Native.

Draba grayana BRASSICACEAE
Gray's draba
SR, alpine, endemic, rare, Summer,
perennial, 0.3–2.4 in.

Short unbranched stems, with simple or 2- to
3-rayed hairs; from a branched caudex. Leaves
0.16–0.8 in. long with simple or 2- to 3-rayed
hairs; in basal rosettes forming a dense green
cushion. Yellow, 4-petaled flowers to 0.3 in.
wide, in short clusters. Grows in tundra and
scree. Endemic almost exclusively to CO,
where it is of conservation concern. Apomictic. Native.

Draba oligosperma BRASSICACEAE
fewseed draba
RM, alpine, subalpine, montane, foothills,
pinyon-juniper, sagebrush steppe,
grasslands, locally abundant, L Spring–
Summer, perennial, 0.4–4 in.

Stems 0.4–1.6 in. long, forming mats. Leaves
gray-green, lower surface having 2- to 5-rayed
hairs; old leaf bases persist. Yellow (rarely
white) flowers up to 0.3 in. across, with 4
petals, in short round clusters above leaves.
Grows in sunny areas, meadows, rock scree,
tundra, rock ledges, and dry slopes. This
plant is incredibly non-diverse throughout its
range. The former *D. juniperina*, now lumped here, is a
lowland version found in WY, CO, and UT. Native.

Draba paysonii BRASSICACEAE
Payson's draba
NR, MR, alpine, subalpine, montane,
locally abundant, L Spring–
Summer, perennial, 0.4–1.5 in.

Leafless flowering stems above small
mat-forming rosettes. Basal leaves are
gray-green, oblanceolate, 0.1–0.3 in. long, entire, with dense, tangled, stalked, branched
hairs and long, simple hairs and cilia. Flowers yellow, 4-petaled, in a cluster. Grows in
sunny and shady areas, meadows, rock scree,
tundra, rock ledges, and dry slopes. Both var.
paysonii and var. *treleasii* are recognized. Tends to be found
on limestone and calcium-rich slopes. *D. novolypicum* is
sometimes lumped here. Native.

Draba streptocarpa BRASSICACEAE
pretty draba, twisted-pod draba
SR, alpine, subalpine, montane,
foothills, locally abundant, L Spring–
Summer, perennial, 0.8–10 in.
Stems 1 to several, with simple and 2-rayed
hairs, rise above a leafy rosette. Basal leaves
are oblanceolate with simple and 2- to
4-rayed hairs. Inflorescence a cluster of yellow, 4-petaled flowers. Grows in sunny and
shady areas, coniferous forests, mixed for-
ests, tundra, rock ledges, and dry slopes. Distinguished by
its characteristic twisted pods. Native.

Erysimum asperum
(*Cheirinia aspera*) BRASSICACEAE
western wallflower
RM, montane, foothills, pinyon-
juniper, common, L Spring–
Summer, biennial, 4–20 in.
Stems 1 to several, often low-branching,
from basal rosette. Lanceolate leaves to 4.5
in. with shallow sparse teeth; alternate up
the stem; gray-green with fine 2-pronged
hairs. Fragrant flowers 0.75 in. across; 4 petals rounded to egg-shaped, in terminal globose racemes that elongate as new flowers
open above and fade below. Variable yellow or orange-red.
Slender seedpods 3–5 in. long, pubescent, perpendicular to stem or curved upward. Sunny roadsides, meadows,
rocky slopes, sandy soils. Native.

Erysimum capitatum
BRASSICACEAE
sanddune wallflower
RM, throughout, common, Spring–
Summer, biennial, 3–24 in.
Upright flowering stems from basal rosette.
Leaves 1–7 in. long, linear, alternate, smaller
up the stem; may be shallowly scalloped
with small teeth; short hairs. Fragrant flowers 0.75 in. across; 4 oval petals; in terminal globose racemes, sometimes branched,
that elongate as upper flowers open. A variable genus
with confused taxonomy: usually yellow but flowers can
be lavender-pink or orange. Slender, smooth seedpods ascending, 4-angled. Sun; sandy soils, open meadows, woodlands, roadsides, tundra. Native.

Erysimum cheiranthoides
(Cheirinia cheiranthoides)
BRASSICACEAE
wormseed wallflower
RM, montane, sagebrush steppe, grasslands,
common, L Spring–Summer, annual, 8–36 in.
Ribbed stems are distinctive. Taprooted
stems, sparsely hairy, sometimes branched.
Withering basal leaves; stem leaves to 4 in.
long, alternate, linear, entire or finely toothed;
fine 3-pronged hairs. Flowers less than 0.33
in. across with 4 narrow rounded petals; in terminal
rounded clusters that elongate as new flowers open above;
slender 1-in. seedpods forming below, spreading or erect.
Sunny fields, roadsides, disturbed sites. Introduced.

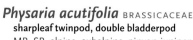

Physaria acutifolia BRASSICACEAE
sharpleaf twinpod, double bladderpod
MR, SR, alpine, subalpine, pinyon-juniper,
sagebrush steppe, intermountain parks,
common, Spring–Summer, perennial, 2–4 in.
Herb forms a basal rosette. Several stems,
prostrate to erect, 2–6 in. long. Basal leaves
ovate to obovate, usually entire; abruptly narrowed to slender, sometimes winged, petiole. Stem leaves spade- or spoon-shaped. All
leaves silvery, covered by tiny star-shaped
hairs. Racemes of yellow flowers, 4 petals. Seedpods inflated, mature from green to purple, in pairs held tightly
to stem. Reseeds well locally. Found in tundra and dry,
gravelly, sandy open areas. Common in Colorado Plateau
screes. Native.

Physaria alpina BRASSICACEAE
Avery Peak twinpod
SR, alpine, subalpine, endemic, locally
abundant, Summer, perennial, 1–3 in.
Herb from taproot, few decumbent stems
from basal rosette. Basal leaves broad, ovate
to obovate, usually entire; abruptly to gradually narrowed to petiole. Stem leaves
spoon-shaped, entire. Tiny star-shaped hairs
cover leaves, creating silvery blue color. Racemes of 3–6 flowers, 4 petals, yellow to egg-yolk orange.
Seedpods not highly inflated, in pairs held tightly to stem.
High-alpine endemic to 4 counties in central CO, usually
found on steep slopes of Leadville Limestone. Native.

Physaria didymocarpa

BRASSICACEAE
common twinpod
NR, MR, subalpine, montane,
foothills, sagebrush steppe,
intermountain parks, grasslands,
common, Spring, perennial, 2–4 in.
Herb from branched caudex forms a basal
rosette. Stems several, decumbent. Basal
leaves obovate, only slightly toothed. Stem
leaves narrowly oblong, usually entire, occasionally toothed. Leaves densely hairy. Dense racemes of
yellow flowers, 4 petals, always showy. Seedpods in pairs
held tightly to stem. Widespread on gravelly slopes. Native.

Physaria floribunda BRASSICACEAE

point-tip twinpod
SR, montane, foothills, sagebrush
steppe, grasslands, locally abundant,
Spring, perennial, 3–4 in.

Several stems, erect to decumbent from
base of leafy rosette. Basal leaves toothed,
broadly oblong, tight, almost overlapping.
Stem leaves entire, spoon-shaped. All leaves
covered in mat of tiny star-shaped hairs, creating a silvery blue color. Loose to congested
showy racemes of yellow flowers, 4 petals.
Rounded inflated seedpods, in pairs, held tightly to stem.
Native.

Physaria ludoviciana
(*Lesquerella ludoviciana*)

BRASSICACEAE
foothill bladderpod, Louisiana bladderpod
MR, SR, montane, foothills, sagebrush
steppe, grasslands, common, Spring–
Summer, perennial, 3–8 in.
Basal rosette with ascending-spreading
stems, 6–10 in. long. Stalkless 1- to 3-in.
basal leaves, narrow-lanceolate to linear, or shallowly dentate. Stem leaves reduced upward, margins rolled inward.
Racemes of yellow flowers, 4 petals. The
silver single-locule elliptical seedpod is smaller than the
twin-podded physarias and not in pairs; held from the
stem on down-curved pedicels. Sandy or gravelly soils.
Native.

Physaria montana
(Lesquerella montana) BRASSICACEAE
mountain bladderpod
MR, SR, montane, foothills, pinyon-juniper,
sagebrush steppe, intermountain parks,
locally abundant, Spring, perennial, 2–4 in.
Small tufted herb with several stems from
base, prostrate to erect. Basal leaves obovate
to elliptic, entire to wavy or shallowly dentate,
covered densely in star-shaped hairs. Stem
leaves linear to obovate, margins entire to
shallowly dentate. Racemes of flowers are dense and compact. Flowers yellow, 4 petals. Unlike other species, commonly found growing on igneous, non-calcareous soils, as well as gravelly soils. Native.

Physaria reediana
(Lesquerella alpina) BRASSICACEAE
alpine bladderpod
MR, SR, subalpine, montane, locally
abundant, Spring, perennial, 2–5 in.
Narrow silver leaves in compact rosette with
upright flowering stems. Stem leaves linear,
margins entire. Dense racemes of flowers.
Flowers yellow, 4 petals. Seedpods oval, not
in pairs, held away from stem. Found in open
areas growing on calcareous soils. More compact than other physarias. Native.

Cleome lutea
(Peritoma lutea) CLEOMACEAE
yellow spiderflower, yellow beeplant
MR, SR, foothills, pinyon-juniper,
sagebrush steppe, common,
Spring–Summer, annual, 1–3 ft.
Smooth to waxy herb with erect, simple to
branched stems. Stem leaves alternate, palmately compound, with 4 or 5 linear to elliptic
2-in. leaflets. Inflorescence a terminal bracteate raceme elongating in fruiting. Calyx lobes
yellowish; egg-shaped petals light yellow. 6
showy yellow stamens protrude well beyond
petals. Fruit a pod-like capsule to 1.6 in. arching downward. Grows in dry, sandy flats, in desert scrub,
and along roads. Important plant for pollinators. Rare in
MT. Native.

Camissonia tanacetifolia
(*Taraxia tanacetifolia*) ONAGRACEAE
tansyleaf evening primrose
NR, MR, sagebrush steppe, intermountain parks, grasslands, common, Spring–Summer, perennial, 1–6 in.
Essentially stemless, or mounding. Basal leaf rosettes 5–15 in. across; leaves with narrow, irregular and deeply pinnate lobes, glabrous or slightly hairy. Flowers bright yellow, short stems, 4 petals, lasting a day, quickly replaced by more in season. Can cover large areas. Found in sunny meadows, roadsides, moist swales, sagebrush meadows into ponderosa forests. Northeastern CA and the Columbia Basin, eastward into southern ID, MT. Native.

Oenothera elata ONAGRACEAE
Hooker's evening primrose
RM, montane, pinyon-juniper, sagebrush steppe, grasslands, common, Summer, biennial, 1.5–3 ft.
Biennial or short-lived perennial; basal rosette first year, then several tall hirsute reddish flowering stems; may be branched. Leaves lanceolate, basal to 6 in. long, reduced and alternate above. Flowers 2–3 in. across, light yellow, fading orange, in leaf axils over long season; 4 heart-shaped petals atop long floral tube. Fruit an upright cylindrical 4-angled pod to 1.5 in. long, at leaf axil. Found on damp slopes or meadows, roadsides, open woodlands in sun, part shade. Native.

Oenothera flava ONAGRACEAE
yellow evening primrose
RM, montane, foothills, pinyon-juniper, grasslands, common, Spring–Summer, perennial, 2–8 in.
Taprooted basal rosette. Lanceolate leaves to 1 ft. long; lower two-thirds dentate or pinnately lobed; leaf tips pointed and mostly entire; glabrous with prominent rib on underside. Flowers lemon-yellow, to 2 in. across, on a long pink floral tube; fragrant, opening quickly in evening and fading to pinkish the next morning. Prefers sunny moist soils, meadows, clay slopes, roadsides, swales, streamsides. Native.

Oenothera howardii
(*Lavauxia howardii*) ONAGRACEAE
Howard's evening primrose
MR, SR, foothills, pinyon-juniper,
sagebrush steppe, grasslands, common,
L Spring–Summer, perennial, 3–6 in.
Basal rosette of upright to spreading lanceolate leaves 2–5 in. long. Margins often wavy,
entire or with shallow irregular lobes; lighter
midrib is pinkish toward base. Flowers 2–3 in.
across, 4 lemon-yellow petals open in evening,
wither to orange the next day. Grows in sunny slopes, canyons, rocky clay soils, shale outcrops. Most common in
UT, AZ, NM; infrequent along Front Range in CO. Native.

Oenothera lavandulifolia
(*Calylophus lavandulifolius*)
ONAGRACEAE
lavenderleaf sundrops
MR, SR, pinyon-juniper, sagebrush steppe,
grasslands, common, locally abundant,
Spring–Summer, perennial, 2–8 in.
Compact mounds of short reddish stems
from a central crown; more open to decumbent with adequate moisture. Green or silvery
leaves closely spaced; alternate, entire, linear,
0.5–2 in. long; margins often inrolled. Flowers day-blooming over a long season. Bud sepals have red/
yellow striped appearance, opening to 2-in. flowers with
crinkled petals and fading to orange. Found in sunny clay
flats or slopes, rocky outcrops, sage meadows,
and shelf rock. Native.

Oenothera villosa ONAGRACEAE
hairy evening primrose
RM, montane, foothills, pinyon-
juniper, sagebrush steppe, grasslands,
common, Summer, biennial, 2–5 ft.
Basal rosette first year, to 10 in. across. Second
year, 1 to several vigorous stems flowering on
upper half; leaves alternate, lanceolate, hairy
and glandular, to 12 in., smaller up the stem.
Buds pinkish, flowers upfacing, 1.5–2 in.
across, loosely spaced; 4 petals opening in evening, fading
in morning. Cylindrical seed capsule ascending, 1–2 in.
long. Found in sunny damp fields, roadsides, habitations,
disturbed sites. Native.

Taraxia subacaulis
(Camissonia subacaulis)
ONAGRACEAE
diffuse-flower evening primrose, northern evening primrose
RM, subalpine, montane, intermountain parks, grasslands, uncommon, Spring–E Summer, perennial, to 2 in.

Low-growing stemless herb. Leaves basal, lanceolate, to 9 in. long, either entire or pinnately lobed. Flowers butter-yellow, 4-petaled, rounded with pointed tips, to 0.6 in. long. Found in moist, high-elevation meadows. This species is most likely to be confused with yellow-flowering oenotheras but, by comparison, has much smaller flowers. Native.

Papaver coloradense
(P. nudicaule ssp. americanum)
PAPAVERACEAE
Rocky Mountain poppy, Uinta poppy
MR, SR, alpine, subalpine, rare, Summer, perennial, 6–18 in.

Plants arise from a branched caudex. Leaves are mostly blue-green, hairy, with deep pinnate lobes. Leaves are all basal but not rosulate, sometimes branched. Flowers are solitary on long pedicels, buds nodding. Flowers range from soft yellow to orange and even white. Fruit a densely hairy capsule. Plants can be quite variable in size. Recent genetic work has brought several species together, distinct from the arctic species. Sun. Native.

Coleogyne ramosissima ROSACEAE
blackbrush
SR, foothills, pinyon-juniper, sagebrush steppe, locally abundant, Spring, perennial, 10–30 in.

Dense gray twigs and dark leaves inspire its common name. Tiny linear 0.5 in. leaves wider toward tip; opposite branching, unusual in rose family. Flowers to 0.6 in., have 4 bright yellow sepals, maturing as 4-chambered pod that splits open when mature. Widespread in canyonlands and lower elevations of the Colorado Plateau and westward. Often a dominant plant over large areas, can be showy in damp spring seasons. Native.

Astragalus flavus FABACEAE
yellow milkvetch
MR, SR, pinyon-juniper, sagebrush
steppe, common, Spring–E Summer,
perennial, 4–10 in.

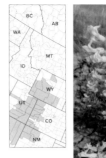

Clump-forming, with flowering stems longer than leaves, radiating in all directions from center. Pinnately compound leaves, 7–17 leaflets, pale blue-green. Flowers pale yellow, pea-shaped, in dense clusters held above foliage. Pods not significantly swollen, point straight out or slightly up. This species can be white in the Four Corners region. Grows in meadows, barrens, dry slopes, and woodlands. Native.

Astragalus pectinatus FABACEAE
narrowleaf milkvetch
RM, montane, foothills, sagebrush
steppe, intermountain parks, common,
Spring–E Summer, perennial, 7–28 in.

Several stems, erect or decumbent. Leaves pinnately compound with 9–17 leaflets. Flowers yellow to white, pea-shaped, in clusters of 10–30. Calyx frequently exhibits black hairs. Pods hang down. Sun; meadows, dry slopes, dunes. Can resemble *A. nelsonianus* but is more yellowish white. Native.

Lupinus arbustus FABACEAE
longspur lupine
NR, MR, montane, foothills, sagebrush steppe,
grasslands, common, locally abundant,
L Spring–Summer, perennial, 7–24 in.

Subshrub with clumped, simple or branched, hairy stems from caudex. Basal and alternate stem leaves palmately compound; 7–11 oblanceolate leaflets, 1–2.5 in., with rounded to sharp-pointed tips, surfaces hairy or glabrous above. Numerous pea-shaped yellow to white flowers, with various tints of pink or purple, in a terminal raceme; banner hairy on center of back, wings smooth, keel with hairs on upper edges; calyx with 2 lips and short spur at base pointing back, lower lip entire. Pods hairy, 3–6 seeds. Grows in sunny sites, open forest, meadows. Native.

Melilotus officinalis
(*M. arvensis*) FABACEAE
yellow sweetclover
RM, throughout, common, L Spring–
Summer, biennial, 2–6 ft.

Coarse erect stems branched throughout.
Leaves alternate, pinnate with 3 oblong leaflets up to 1.5 in. long; finely toothed, with
stipules at stem. Flowers small, pea-like,
in axillary racemes of 20–50, sweetly fragrant. Similar to *M. albus*, but often larger
and with yellow flowers. A common global weed, has been
cultivated as a crop and for beekeeping, but now found in
disturbed sites, roadsides, fields everywhere. Introduced
and invasive.

Oxytropis campestris FABACEAE
field locoweed
RM, alpine, subalpine, montane, foothills,
sagebrush steppe, grasslands, common,
Spring–Summer, perennial, 2–12 in.
Herb with erect, leafless stems. Basal leaves
alternate, pinnately compound with 7–29
lanceolate to ovate leaflets; hairy, silvery
surfaces. Flowers pale yellow to white (occasionally purple). Pods erect, 0.4–0.75 in.
long, with white and black hairs. Grows in
tundra, pine parklands, dry slopes, meadows, and riparian habitats. A variable, circumboreal, common locoweed,
more common in the MR and NR, with at least 3 varieties:
var. *spicata* 17–33 leaflets, var. *cusickii* 7–15 leaflets, and var.
columbiana, which has a white corolla with
purple spots on keel. Native.

Thermopsis divaricarpa FABACEAE
spreadfruit goldenbanner
RM, montane, foothills, pinyon-
juniper, sagebrush steppe,
intermountain parks, common,
Spring–Summer, perennial, 10–20 in.
Herbaceous stems rise early in spring from
vigorous rhizomes that make vast colonies.
Compound leaves, alternate, with 3 leaflets.
Pea-type flowers in open conical racemes. Slightly curved
and spreading seedpods distinguish this, the most common goldenbanner of montane meadows and dry parklands in the SR. All species are similar, and some experts
dispute their differences. Native.

Thermopsis montana
(*T. rhombifolia* var. *montana*)
FABACEAE
mountain goldenbanner, golden pea
RM, subalpine, montane, locally abundant,
Spring–Summer, perennial, 15–36 in.

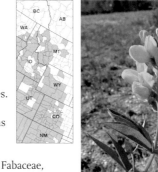

Less rhizomatous than other regional species.
More or less resembles *T. divaricarpa*; generally larger, with straight, upright fruit. Seems
to grow in moister habitats, aspen woods,
bright riparian areas, and lush meadows at
higher elevations. As do many genera in the Fabaceae,
Thermopsis inspires considerable confusion. Native.

Thermopsis rhombifolia
(*T. arenosa*) FABACEAE
prairie thermopsis, prairie goldenbanner
RM, foothills, grasslands, common,
Spring–E Summer, perennial, 8–18 in.

Often shorter than *T. montana*, with shorter,
broader leaves. Typical spreading rhizomes.
Commonest species at lower elevations, grows
in sandy soils, even thriving in the drier habitats of the high desert. This can provide an
early burst of color in otherwise sparsely vegetated areas. Also distinguished by strongly
curved seedpods. Native.

Castilleja cusickii
(*C. lutea*) OROBANCHACEAE
Cusick's Indian paintbrush
NR, MR, subalpine, montane, sagebrush
steppe, intermountain parks, common,
L Spring–E Summer, perennial, 8–24 in.

Erect or ascending stems unbranched. Herbage hairy. Leaves alternate, rounded to 2 in.
long, erect; lower leaves entire, upper leaves
with 1 or 2 pairs of linear lobes. Flower bracts
yellow or yellow-tipped, 1–3 pairs of pointed
lobes. Calyx to 1.1 in. long hides shorter corolla. Petals yellow, hood-like galea, slightly
shorter lower lip, both less than 0.25 in. long.
Found in moist meadows. Similar to *C. flava*
and *C. pallescens*, but both have shorter lower lips. Native.

Castilleja flava OROBANCHACEAE
yellow Indian paintbrush
RM, subalpine, montane, foothills,
sagebrush steppe, grasslands, common,
L Spring–Summer, perennial, 4–20 in.
Erect stems. Leaves alternate, linear to 1.5
in. long, entire or with 1 or 2 pairs of lateral
lobes. Flower bracts yellow to orange, 1 or
2 pairs of lateral lobes; calyx less than 1 in.
long, split to nearly the middle in front, less
so in back, with shorter side segments. Co-
rolla tube greenish yellow, to 1.2 in. long, hood-like galea
less than 0.3 in. long; lower lip half the length of upper.
Grows on dry hillsides and with sagebrush. Native.

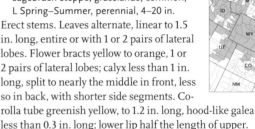

Castilleja occidentalis
OROBANCHACEAE
western Indian paintbrush
NR, SR, alpine, subalpine, common, L
Spring–Summer, perennial, 3–6 in.
Stems erect. Leaves alternate, linear, entire, reduced below; upper leaves may have
2 lateral lobes. Flowering stem and bracts
hairy; bracts yellow, green, occasionally
purple-tipped or reddish; entire or with 2
lateral lobes near tip. Calyx 0.6–0.9 in., lobes
slightly less divided in back, ultimate lobes
to 0.1 in. long. Corolla to 1 in. long; whitish, hood-like galea
to 0.35 in. long. Found in moist meadows, tundra and moraine. Hybridizes with *C. rhexifolia*, creating populations
with white to purple bracts. Native.

Castilleja puberula
OROBANCHACEAE
shortflower Indian paintbrush
MR, SR, alpine, rare, locally abundant,
Summer, perennial, 3–6 in.
Stems erect. Leaves alternate, linear to 1.2
in. long, entire or with a pair of lateral lobes
on upper leaves. Flowering stem and bracts
woolly-hairy; bracts yellow or reddish with 3
lobes. Calyx to 0.6 in. long and notched halfway above and deeper below. Corolla yellow-
ish to 0.8 in. long; the hood-like galea to 0.3 in. long, about
half the length of the corolla tube. Grows in tundra above
treeline. Recent disjunct population found in MT. Native.

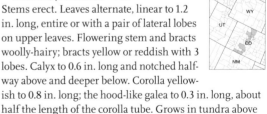

Castilleja sulphurea
(*C. septentrionalis*) OROBANCHACEAE
sulphur Indian paintbrush
RM, subalpine, montane, foothills,
intermountain parks, grasslands, common,
L Spring–Summer, perennial, 6–28 in.
Stems erect or ascending from woody base.
Leaves alternate, lanceolate, entire, 0.7–2.4 in.
long. Flower stems and bracts hairy, glandular; bracts pale yellow with ovate, entire or
shallow lobes near tip. Calyx 0.5–1 in., notches
more prominent in front. Corolla yellow, 0.7–1.2 in.; the
hood-like galea to 0.5 in., corolla tube 0.4–0.8 in. Grows in
meadows, forests, and along streams. Native.

Orthocarpus luteus
OROBANCHACEAE
yellow owl's-clover
RM, montane, foothills, sagebrush
steppe, grasslands, common, L
Spring–Summer, annual, 4–16 in.
Slender herb with erect, usually simple,
glandular-hairy, purplish stems. Numerous
dark green linear leaves alternate, sessile,
to 1.6 in. long, entire; linear leaves become
3-lobed above, resemble broader, more cleft
bracts. Basal leaves absent. Inflorescence a
dense spike, becoming elongate; golden yellow, 2-lipped
tubular flowers: upper lip hooded, beaked and nearly equal
to lower lip, which is minutely 3-toothed. Flowers extend
beyond bracts. Hemiparasitic. Grows in meadows, open
woodlands, disturbed habitats around mines.
Native.

Pedicularis bracteosa
OROBANCHACEAE
bracted lousewort
RM, alpine, subalpine, montane, common,
L Spring–Summer, perennial, 1–3 ft.
Stems unbranched, erect, glabrous below inflorescence. Stem leaves fern-like, alternate,
1–6 in. long, pinnatifid, incised, serrate, reduced upward. Basal leaves often absent.
Inflorescence a dense terminal spike of yellow to cream
flowers (sometimes tinged with red or purple); flowers subtended by hairy, linear bracts. Corolla 2-lipped, with upper
lip hooded, beakless or short-beaked. Found in open forests, thickets, moist meadows, and along streams. Native.

Pedicularis oederi
(*P. versicolor*) OROBANCHACEAE
Oeder's lousewort
MR, alpine, infrequent, Summer,
perennial, 2–10 in.

Herbaceous plant with solitary, erect, un-branched, smooth to hairy stems. Leaves mostly basal, to 4 in., pinnately lobed to cleft, with serrated margins. Stem leaves few, alternate, reduced upward. Inflorescence a compact to elongated terminal spike with yellow flowers, often purple-tipped, subtended by hairy leaf-like bracts. Calyces soft-hairy or long-woolly. Corolla 2-lipped: lower lip 3-lobed; upper lip somewhat arched, hooded, beakless. Grows on rocky slopes, tundra, and in meadows. Members of this genus are hemiparasitic. Native.

Pedicularis parryi OROBANCHACEAE
Parry's lousewort
MR, SR, alpine, subalpine, montane,
common, Summer, perennial, 2–16 in.

Herb with erect, unbranched stems. Leaves fern-like, basal and alternate, 1–6 in. long, deeply pinnatifid with cartilaginous, toothed margins. Inflorescence a dense spike of pale yellow to white flowers subtended by smooth or soft-haired bracts that are pinnately 3- to 7-lobed. Corolla 2-lipped: upper lip a short, straight beak. Grows in meadows and on dry slopes above upper montane. Native.

Pedicularis procera
(*P. grayi*) OROBANCHACEAE
giant lousewort
MR, SR, subalpine, montane,
foothills, common, L Spring–
Summer, perennial, 1–4 ft.

Herbaceous plant with several erect, un-branched stems. Fern-like basal and alternate stem leaves 4–12 in. long, pinnatifid to bipinnatifid, toothed margins. Leaf size reduced upward. Inflorescence a dense terminal spike of pale yellow to cream flowers with reddish to purplish venation. Flowers subtended by linear, hairy bracts. Corolla 2-lipped: lower lip with 3 short lobes; upper lip hooded, beakless or short-beaked. Found in spruce-fir and aspen forests and along streams. Deer and elk browse the flowers. Native.

Linaria dalmatica PLANTAGINACEAE
Dalmatian toadflax
RM, montane, foothills, pinyon-
juniper, sagebrush steppe, grasslands,
common, locally abundant, Spring–
Summer, perennial, 2–4 ft.

Smooth blue-green stems from rhizomatous
crown; upper portion may become heavily
branched through the season. Leaves clasping stem, alternate, closely spaced, pointed,
egg-shaped, waxy blue-green. Flowers 1–2
in. long, snapdragon-like, technically 5 lobes: 3 lower
ones joined as dragon's "mouth," fuzzy and brushed orange at lip, with long spur below; 2 upper are flared above
the "mouth." Fine seeds in brown capsules. Aggressively
spreads in meadows, roadsides, disturbed
sites, and trailsides, disrupting natural habitats. Introduced and invasive.

Linaria vulgaris
(L. linaria) PLANTAGINACEAE
butter and eggs, yellow toadflax
RM, subalpine, montane, foothills,
grasslands, common, locally abundant,
Summer–Fall, perennial, 5–20 in.

Slender smooth stems, may branch near top,
from a network of rhizomes. Leaves alternate,
closely spaced, linear 0.5–3 in., decreasing near top. Flowers in dense terminal spikes 3–6 in. long; 5 petals as previous but smaller, 0.75–1.25 in. including spur. Aggressively
spreads and disrupts natural habitats, forming dense
patches in moist or seasonally dry meadows,
roadsides, farmland. Introduced and invasive.

Ribes aureum GROSSULARIACEAE
golden currant
RM, montane, foothills, sagebrush
steppe, grasslands, common, Spring–
E Summer, perennial, 3–9 ft.

Deciduous, spineless shrub, branches upright,
reddish to grayish. Leaves glossy, alternate, to 2
in. across, palmately 3-lobed; entire to toothed
margins. Inflorescence a raceme of 5–18 tubu-
lar flowers covered in fine hairs. Spreading yellow sepals;
small erect petals maturing to red. Berries round, shiny,
smooth, yellow-red to black. Found along streams, in moist
woods. Flowers with clove scent on warm spring days, at-
tracting the season's earliest hummingbirds. Var. *villosum*
is considered introduced; the type is native.

Heuchera parvifolia
(H. flabellifolia) SAXIFRAGACEAE

littleleaf alumroot, common alumroot
RM, alpine, subalpine, montane, foothills,
pinyon-juniper, sagebrush steppe, common,
Spring–Summer, perennial, 2–28 in.
Herb with slender, erect, short-hairy stems
from basal cluster of leaves. Leaves with 5–7
lobes, toothed margins, and smooth to glandular leaf surfaces. Narrow raceme of yellow
or creamy to green flowers; spike elongates
in fruit. Sepals and petals bend downward, exposing a
yellow-orange saucer-shaped hypanthium. Grows in rock
outcroppings, meadows, open forests, and fellfields. *Parvi-
folia* (Latin, "small leaf") is not to be confused with *parviflora* ("small flower"). Native.

Verbascum thapsus

SCROPHULARIACEAE
common mullein
RM, montane, foothills, pinyon-juniper,
sagebrush steppe, intermountain
parks, grasslands, common, locally
abundant, Summer, biennial, 2–6 ft.
Basal rosette first year; single or sparsely
branched flowering stem in second year. All
parts woolly, gray- or yellowish green. Basal
leaves lanceolate, underside prominently veined, 4–15 in.
long; alternate and reduced upward, absent among flowers. Flowers in compact spike, few open at a time, to 1 in.
across. Found on sunny dry or mesic slopes, roadsides,
disturbed or overgrazed sites of middle and
lower elevations. Introduced and invasive.

Erythranthe guttata
(Mimulus guttatus) PHRYMACEAE

seep monkeyflower, yellow monkeyflower
RM, subalpine, montane, foothills,
common, Spring–Fall, annual, 3–36 in.
Extremely variable, from small and sprawling to large and bushy. Perennial in warmer
zones, annual where colder. Leaves light
green, broadly rounded, margins toothed.
Flowers bright yellow, stalked, in upper leaf axils, red spots
on lower lip. Occurs in wet areas at mid elevations. Uncommon in the SR. Distinguished from other species by
the longer upper tooth on the calyx. Native.

Erythranthe moschata
(*Mimulus moschatus*) PHRYMACEAE
muskflower
RM, subalpine, montane, foothills, common,
L Spring–Summer, perennial, 2–28 in.

Ascending to sprawling stems. Herbage sticky-hairy (occasionally hairless), often slimy, sometimes strongly smells of musk. Leaves opposite, toothed, stalkless or short-stalked, 0.5–3 in. long, oval to elliptic. Leaves prominently veined. Flowers solitary in leaf axils on long stalks, 5-lobed, corolla 0.75–1.25 in. long, deep grooves in the narrow tube floor, red dots or lines in throat. Occurs in moist, shaded mountainous areas. All our erythranthes were separated from *Mimulus*, which is now considered a largely Australian genus. Native.

Erythranthe primuloides
(*Mimulus primuloides*) PHRYMACEAE
primrose monkeyflower
RM, subalpine, montane, foothills,
rare, Summer, perennial, 2–4 in.

Small, rhizomatous, densely mat-forming. Leaves opposite, oblanceolate, crowded, surface lightly hairy to nearly cobwebby. Flowers solitary, 0.25 in., yellow, 5-lobed, on leafless stalks. Corolla less noticeably bilabiate than many species; all lobes relatively deeply notched, flaring; 3 lobes of lower lip usually with maroon dots. Stamens 4. Occurs in moist mountain meadows, along streambanks. Native.

Erythranthe suksdorfii
(*Mimulus suksdorfii*) PHRYMACEAE
Suksdorf's monkeyflower, miniature monkeyflower
RM, subalpine, montane, foothills, pinyon-juniper, sagebrush steppe, uncommon,
L Spring–Summer, annual, 1–4 in.

Small, low-growing herb. Leaves opposite, linear to narrowly oblong, mostly sessile, entire. Herbage with fine glandular hairs. Vegetative parts, including calyx, often red-purple tinted. Flowers solitary, 0.1 in., stalked, in leaf axils. Corolla yellow, faintly spotted, 5-lobed. Lobes notched. Stamens 4. Occurs in open, moist to dry areas in low to mid elevations, occasionally higher. Native.

Erythranthe tilingii
(Mimulus tilingii) PHRYMACEAE
Tiling's monkeyflower, subalpine monkeyflower
RM, alpine, subalpine, montane, foothills, wetlands, common, Summer–Fall, perennial, 2–8 in.
Mat-forming herb. Leaves ovate, opposite, slightly toothed, less than 1 in. long. Flowers larger than expected on such a small plant, bright yellow, 1 in., solitary in leaf axils, lifted above the foliage. On the lower lip are 2 furry humps and reddish spots or markings. Occurs in wet meadows, wet rocky slopes, seeps, mossy streamsides, forming colorful tidy carpets of color. Native.

Viola biflora VIOLACEAE
arctic yellow violet
SR, alpine, subalpine, montane, rare, L
Spring–Summer, perennial, 3–7 in.
Herb with ascending to erect stems that are often 2-leaved. 2–4 basal leaves are heart- to kidney-shaped with scalloped margins; top surface hairy and hairy along veins. Stem leaves similar but with shorter stalks. Flowers solitary, axillary, yellow; lower petal spurred and lower 3 (sometimes all 5) petals with brownish purple striations. Rare herb of cool canyons, moist rock outcrops, shady alpine cliffs, and moist meadows. Also found throughout Eurasia. Native.

Viola glabella VIOLACEAE
pioneer violet
NR, MR, montane, foothills, locally abundant, Spring–Summer, perennial, 3–10 in.
Finely hairy herb with ascending to erect stems. Basal leaves heart- to kidney-shaped, tips pointed, often deeply veined and finely scalloped along the edges. Stem leaves similar, but with shorter stalks. Flowers solitary, deep yellow; lower petal with a short spur, the lower 3 with purplish nectar guides, and the 2 side petals bearded at bases. Woodland violet of the Pacific Coast, extending inland to the humid forests of ID and MT. Also found along streambanks. Native.

Viola nuttallii VIOLACEAE

Nuttall's violet, yellow prairie violet
RM, throughout, common, Spring–
E Summer, perennial, 2–6 in.

Herb with short or no stems. Leaves lanceolate, margins entire to irregularly toothed. Flowers solitary, bright yellow; lower petal with a short spur, lower 3 with brownish purple guide lines, 2 side petals lightly bearded. Early blooming and wide-ranging violet found from plains to above treeline, in all life zones except wetlands. Grows on dry slopes and meadows. Prefers sun, unlike other yellow violets in its range. By far the most common yellow violet in the region. Native.

Viola orbiculata

(*V. sempervirens*) VIOLACEAE
darkwoods violet
NR, MR, subalpine, montane,
locally abundant, Spring–E Summer,
perennial, 3–6 in.

Herb with erect stems. Leaves roundish to nearly heart-shaped, toothed; sometimes evergreen. Flowers lemon-yellow to gold on reddish stalks; lower petal with short, sack-shaped spur, 3 lower petals with maroon stripes, 2 side petals yellow-bearded at base. Violet of the Pacific NW extending to humid, old-growth forests of ID and MT. Grows in open woods, meadows, and forests. Allied to the redwood violet of CA, which is stoloniferous with hairs in corolla. Native.

Viola praemorsa VIOLACEAE

canary violet, yellow montane violet
RM, montane, foothills, common,
Spring–Summer, perennial, 3–6 in.

Several hairy flowering stems from rhizome. Leaves basal, thick, hairy, narrowly oval to egg-shaped, 2–4 in. long, stalk equal or longer. Flower stalks shorter than leaves. Petals 5, yellow, upper 2 with brown underside, lower 3 with brownish lines on front, lateral 2 bearded. Fruit a hairy capsule. Grows in meadows and open forests. Native.

Viola purpurea
(V. utahensis) VIOLACEAE
goosefoot violet
RM, montane, foothills, sagebrush
steppe, locally abundant, Spring–E
Summer, perennial, 2–5 in.

Small, puberulent herb with short erect
stems or no stems. Basal leaves dark green,
thick and fleshy, deeply veined, ovate to
deltoid, with entire to coarsely few-toothed
margins; purplish along the veins and un-
dersurface purple-stained (hence the epithet). Stem leaves
similar, but reduced. Flowers yellow, the central lower
petal with maroon stripes and a very short spur and the 2
side petals with beards. Grows on gravelly slopes among
junipers or sagebrush. Native.

Viola sheltonii
(V. biternata) VIOLACEAE
Shelton's violet
SR, montane, foothills, pinyon-juniper,
infrequent, Spring, perennial, 3–7 in.
Smooth, short to nearly stemless herb; scattered to mat-forming. Leaves glaucous, ternately cleft into 3 lobes and divided into
linear leaflets; lower surfaces purplish.
Flowers yellow, the lower 3 petals with ma-
roon markings, the 2 side petals sparsely bearded, and the
2 top petals with brownish backs. Grows along streams,
in aspen forests, pinyon-juniper or oak woodlands. This is
the only cutleaf yellow violet of the Rockies. It is also found
widely on the Pacific Coast. Native.

Viola vallicola
(V. nuttallii ssp. vallicola) VIOLACEAE
sagebrush violet, yellow violet
RM, subalpine, montane, sagebrush
steppe, locally abundant, L Spring–E
Summer, perennial, 6–12 in.
Plants are often small, and leaves can be
quite variable in the amount of hairs; the
distinguishing factor is that some of or all
the leaves have a truncated base. Plants are
often found at higher elevations than V. nuttallii, which
occurs in lower-elevation steppes mostly on the eastern
slope. Flowers are always yellow. Grows in sunny dry open
areas among sagebrush and in pine forests. Native.

Lonicera dioica
(*L. glaucescens*) CAPRIFOLIACEAE
limber honeysuckle
NR, MR, montane, foothills, common,
Spring–E Summer, perennial, 5–15 ft.

Deciduous semi-erect shrub or liana with
smooth, greenish or purplish twigs becoming grayish brown and shreddy. Leaves very
short-stalked, opposite, to 3 in. long, ovate,
with entire margins; upper 1 or 2 leaf pairs
fused. Inflorescence a cluster of yellow, red,
or maroon stalkless flowers. Corolla sometimes hairy, tubular to funnel-shaped, with 2 lips: upper lip with 4 lobes.
Stamens and style protruding. Berries red, round to oval,
in terminal clusters. Grows in forests and on moist to dry,
rocky slopes. Flowers attract hummingbirds.
Native.

Medicago lupulina FABACEAE
black medick
RM, montane, foothills, sagebrush
steppe, grasslands, common,
Spring–Fall, annual, 3–32 in.

Prostrate or ascending stems, heavily
branched at the base, from a central taproot; glabrous to finely hairy. Leaves alternate, pinnately compound with 3 leaflets,
rhombic-obovate or oblanceolate, sparsely to densely
hairy, margins toothed in upper half. Numerous yellow, pea-shaped flowers form a compact raceme, 5 petals.
Fruits in clusters of kidney-shaped pods, becoming black
at maturity. Grows in sunny disturbed areas,
roadsides, gardens, trailsides, forest openings,
and fields. Introduced and invasive.

Trifolium aureum
(*T. agrarium*) FABACEAE
golden clover, yellow clover
NR, montane, sagebrush steppe, common,
L Spring–Summer, annual, 6–20 in.

Branching, upright, and hairy-stemmed herb.
Leaf petioles with stipules to 0.5 in. long.
Leaflets in 3s to 0.75 in. long, terminal leaflet
unstalked. Flowerheads egg-shaped with up to 100 small
yellow flowers, aging to brown. *T. campestre* and *T. dubium*
also have yellow flowers. All 3 species found along roadsides and in fields. Introduced.

Aletes acaulis APIACEAE
stemless Indian parsley
SR, pinyon-juniper, sagebrush steppe,
locally abundant, Spring–E Summer,
perennial, 3–10 in.
Forms lax mounds of basal, pinnate, shiny
leaves from a rhizome. Foliage is sweetly
aromatic, herbaceous or semi-evergreen.
Flower stems many, unbranched, taller
than foliage. Inflorescence a terminal
compound umbel. Flowers yellow, many.
Found at a range of elevations, always in full sun on
rocky or very sandy soils, often in rock cracks. The type is
white-flowered; all other subspecies are yellow. Native.

Aletes humilis APIACEAE
Colorado aletes
SR, foothills, endemic, rare,
Spring, perennial, 2–4 in.
Mat-forming, can spread up to a foot, from
a taproot. Dense mounds of herbaceous
foliage. Leaves 1 or 2 times pinnately compound, leathery, basal, often obscuring the
flowers. Inflorescence a compound umbel
of many small yellow flowers. Fruits in
summer. Sun to part shade. Grows in rocky
outcrops, in rock cracks, in thin soils of dis-
integrated Silver Plume granite on north-facing slopes.
Endemic to 3 counties in CO, WY. Denver Botanic
Gardens maintains the seed bank for the species. Native.

Bupleurum americanum
APIACEAE
American thorowax
RM, throughout, common, locally
abundant, Summer, perennial, 3–18 in.
Woody caudex, branched stems. Leaves narrow, linear, glaucous, to 5 in., pale parallel
veins, deciduous. Flowers in umbels; yellow,
may be burgundy; each umbel and umbellet
has leafy bracts below. Tiny flowers have 5
incurved petals, a 2-chambered disc, maturing to a dry fruit with raised ribs. Found on
dry slopes, meadows, rocky ledges, and sunny openings
in woodlands. Rare occurrences in southwestern CO and
central NM as well. Most common at alpine elevations.
Native.

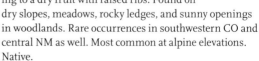

Cymopterus alpinus
(*Oreoxis alpina*) APIACEAE
alpine springparsley
SR, alpine, subalpine, montane,
common, Summer, perennial, 1–5 in.
Tiny plants can be just 2 in. across; deciduous
leaves basal, mostly bipinnate. Tiny flowers
yellow or white, 5-petaled, in an umbel; bractlets under the flower come to a single point.
Grows in sunny habitats, tundra, and meadows. Ranges farther north and west than the
very similar *C. bakeri*, whose bractlets differ in being cut
several times at their tips. Native.

Cymopterus bakeri
(*Oreoxis bakeri*) APIACEAE
Baker's alpine parsley
SR, alpine, locally abundant,
Summer, perennial, 1–2 in.
Tiny rosettes of basal leaves, bipinnate, minutely hairy. Flowers yellow; bractlets under
the flowers are cut several times at their tips.
Grows in the sun in tundra. Easily confused
with *C. alpinus*, this species is found only in
western UT, southern CO, and northern NM,
where both species grow together. Both are
very similar morphologically, but *C. alpinus*
ranges farther north and west, and its bractlets come to a
single point. Native.

Cymopterus hendersonii
(*Pteryxia hendersonii*) APIACEAE
Henderson's springparsley
MR, alpine, subalpine, endemic, locally
abundant, Summer, perennial, 1–3 in.
Mat-forming herb with old leaf petioles persisting. Leaves all basal, linear-lanceolate,
and bipinnate. Flowers yellow. Grows in rock
scree, tundra, on rock ledges and dry slopes.
Endemic to southwestern MT and adjacent
ID. This species has been lumped with *C. longilobus* but differs in being shorter than 3 in.,
having scabrous fruits and more compact um-
bels, and lacking long involucre bracts. Furthermore, it is
found only at high elevations, whereas *C. longilobus* occurs
at both low and high elevations. Native.

Cymopterus humilis
(*Oreoxis humilis*) APIACEAE
Pikes Peak alpineparsley
SR, alpine, endemic, rare,
Summer, perennial, 0.75–4 in.
Compact herb whose stems are
clump-forming. Basal leaves hairless and
deciduous. Flowering stem leafless. Flow-
ers 5-petaled, clustered in a yellow umbel.
Bractlets of involucre are linear, green, and
entire. Grows in sunny habitats, tundra, and
rocky outcrops. Endemic restricted to Pikes Peak in CO.
Native.

Cymopterus lemmonii
(*Pseudocymopterus montanus*)
APIACEAE
alpine false springparsley
SR, alpine, subalpine, montane,
foothills, common, L Spring–
Summer, perennial, 8–20 in.
Several flowering stems rise from basal
leaves. Leaves pinnate or bipinnate with linear leaflets, with 1 or 2 on the stem; deciduous. 5-petaled yellow flowers in an umbel;
some populations red, especially noted in
parts of NM. Grows in sunny and shady hab-
itats, tundra, rocky outcrops, coniferous and aspen forests,
sage meadows, and meadows. Very common and variable;
leaves vary in width, plants vary in height, but a yellow
parsley in middle elevations is most likely this. Native.

Cymopterus longilobus APIACEAE
mountain springparsley
MR, SR, alpine, subalpine,
montane, foothills, pinyon-juniper,
sagebrush steppe, common, Spring–
Summer, perennial, 3–16 in.
Mat-forming herb with old lead petioles persisting. Leaves all basal, bipinnate, the ultimate division linear. Flowers in umbels;
yellow with longer bracts, 0.2–0.4 in. long.
Confused with *C. hendersonii*, this species is
more wide ranging and found from low to high elevations
in the SR. In MT and where it overlaps with *C. hendersonii*,
it tends to be found only at high elevations. See *C. hendersonii* for differences. Native.

Cymopterus longipes APIACEAE
longstalk springparsley
MR, SR, foothills, pinyon-juniper,
sagebrush steppe, common, Spring,
perennial, 2–12 in.

Herb with several stems rising from a taproot,
rarely grows to 20 in. tall. Leaves are basal, 1–3
times pinnately divided, with leaflet sections
distinctively overlapping. Inflorescence is an
umbel of 5-petaled yellow (rarely reddish)
flowers. Grows in sun or shade on dry slopes,
sage meadows, and meadows. Native.

Cymopterus nivalis
(*Aletes nivalis*) APIACEAE
snowline springparsley
NR, MR, alpine, subalpine, montane,
sagebrush steppe, locally abundant,
Spring, perennial, 2–13 in.

Multistemmed herb; red-tinged stems arising from a woody crown with persistent leaf
bases. Basal leaves rough to the touch, can
have a bluish green color; lance-oblong, almost bipinnate to tripinnate, having 4–8 main
pairs of leaves 0.8–4 in. long. Inflorescence a
compact umbel of many small yellow to white
flowers with purple anthers. Grows on gravelly soil on rocky slopes. Native.

Cymopterus purpureus
(*Aulospermum purpureum*) APIACEAE
widewing springparsley
MR, SR, foothills, sagebrush steppe,
locally abundant, Spring–E Summer,
perennial, 2–10 in.

Multistemmed herbaceous plant arising from
a woody crown. Lacks pseudoscape. Flower
and leaf stems often tinged red to purple.
Leaves glabrous, blue-green, 1–3 times pinnate, leaflets egg-shaped to broadly oblong.
Flowers umbellate, start greenish yellow, peak
at yellow, often drying to reddish purple. Locally abundant in sage meadows, woodlands,
and on dry slopes. Native.

388

Cymopterus terebinthinus
(*Pteryxia terebinthina*) APIACEAE
aromatic springparsley
RM, montane, foothills, sagebrush
steppe, grasslands, locally abundant,
Spring–E Summer, perennial, 5–16 in.

Multistemmed herb arising from a woody
crown. Leaves 2–4 times pinnate and widely
spaced and narrow on the main stem. Yellow, 5-petaled flowers borne in umbels.
The plant has a more open appearance than
other cymopterus. The roots and foliage are strongly aromatic (hence the epithet), anise-like. Grows in rocky terrain. Female anise swallowtail butterflies (*Papilio zelicaon*)
lay their eggs on this plant. Native.

Lomatium concinnum APIACEAE
**adobe desert-parsley, Colorado
desert-parsley**
SR, sagebrush steppe, endemic, locally
abundant, Spring, perennial, 4–10 in.
All leaves basal, low-growing, smooth, doubly pinnate with ultimate leaflets narrowly
elliptical or linear-lanceolate and less than
0.5 in. long. Stout flower stems with compound umbel, the branches of the umbel
being all equal or nearly so in length, up to
4 in.; bractlets under the individual umbels to 0.6 in. long.
Flowers yellow, 5 petals. Fruit twice as long as wide with
wings. Found on rocky hills in Mancos Formation soils.
Endemic to CO. Native.

Lomatium cous
(*L. circumdatum*) APIACEAE
cous biscuitroot
NR, MR, alpine, subalpine, montane,
foothills, sagebrush steppe,
grasslands, common, Spring–
Summer, perennial, to 14 in.

Stems often leafless. Leaves basal, mostly
bipinnate, and deciduous after flowering.
Flowers yellow (rarely purple), 5-petaled, in
an umbel with round-tipped bracts. Fruit
rough with marginal wings. Grows in sunny areas, tundra, rocky outcrops, sage meadows, and meadows, as far
north as Canada's Cypress Hills. Prefers shallow, stony
soils. Smells like celery when crushed. The similar *L. attenuatum* has linear-lanceolate involucre bracts and is endemic to southwestern MT and northwestern WY. Native.

Lomatium dissectum APIACEAE
fernleaf biscuitroot
RM, subalpine, montane, foothills,
common, Spring, perennial, 1–5 ft.
Stout, hollow stems, 1 to several, with 1 or 2
leaves. Leaves largely basal, mostly bipinnate,
and deciduous after flowering. 5-petaled flowers yellow (rarely purple), in an umbel. Fruit
has marginal wings. Found from Canada's
Cypress Hills southward, growing in sunny
areas, pine parklands, dry slopes, sage meadows, and meadows. The largest lomatium in the region.
Native.

Lomatium grayi APIACEAE
Gray's biscuitroot
RM, montane, pinyon-juniper, sagebrush
steppe, common, Spring, perennial, 3–16 in.
Several to many stems. Leaves largely basal,
ternate-pinnately dissected, 3–8 in., with the
very fine ultimate division giving it a very
ferny appearance. 5-petaled yellow flowers, fading to whitish, in an umbel. Fruit
has marginal wings. Grows in sunny areas,
pine parklands, dry slopes, sage meadows,
and meadows. An important nursery plant
for sage grouse, providing forage for chicks.
Native.

Lomatium nuttallii
(*Aletes nuttallii*) APIACEAE
Nuttall's biscuitroot
MR, SR, sagebrush steppe, grasslands,
uncommon, Spring, perennial, 6–16 in.
Several to many hollow stems. Leaves 1 or 2
times pinnate or ternate-pinnately dissected,
with smallest divisions linear. Inflorescence
an umbel. Fruit has marginal wings. Grows
in sunny areas, barrens, pine parklands, dry
slopes, sage meadows, and meadows. Most
common in WY, often found on shale or chalk
bluffs. Native.

Musineon divaricatum APIACEAE

leafy wild parsley
RM, foothills, sagebrush steppe,
grasslands, common, Spring–
E Summer, perennial, to 6 in.

Stems 1 to several, but can appear stemless.
Leaves largely basal, 1–3 times pinnately divided, with the smallest divisions oblong or
ovate, 0.1–0.6 in. long. 5-petaled yellow flowers in an umbel. Fruit is 0.08–0.2 in. long.
Grows in sunny areas, rocky outcrops, sage
meadows, and meadows. Has broader, less dissected leaves
than *M. tenuifolium* and is much more common. Native.

Musineon tenuifolium
(*Aletes tenuifolius*) APIACEAE

slender wild parsley
MR, SR, foothills, sagebrush steppe,
grasslands, uncommon, locally abundant,
L Spring–E Summer, perennial, to 6 in.
Stems 1 to several. Leaves largely basal, 1–3
times pinnately divided, smallest divisions
linear, 0.1–1.2 in. long. 5-petaled yellow flowers in an umbel. Fruit is 0.08–0.2 in. long.
Grows in sunny areas, rocky outcrops, sage
meadows, and meadows. A plant of lower
elevations, easily found in sandstone drainages along the trail to Pawnee Buttes in northeastern CO.
Much less common than *M. divaricatum* with narrower
leaves. Native.

Osmorhiza occidentalis
(*Glycosma occidentalis*) APIACEAE

**western sweetroot, licorice-flavored
sweetcicely**
RM, subalpine, montane,
foothills, common, Spring–
Summer, perennial, 2–4 ft.

Robust herb from taproot with dense cluster of erect stout stems. Long-stemmed
basal leaves, alternate on stem; divided
ternate-pinnately 1–3 times; leaflets lanceolate to ovate with toothed margins. Inflorescence a compound umbel of tiny yellow to greenish yellow
flowers. Fruit a linear, glabrous schizocarp with a short
beak-like tip. Grows in mountain meadows, open forests,
oak or aspen woods, on avalanche tracks and moist slopes.
Herbage smells strongly of anise. Native.

Podistera eastwoodiae APIACEAE

Eastwood's springparsley

SR, alpine, subalpine, locally abundant,
Summer, perennial, 2–4 in.

Deciduous herb with many leaf and flower
stems originating at the base. Leaves all basal,
green, pinnate with 3–7 pairs of leaflets; surfaces hairless. Inflorescence an umbel of
yellow flowers. Grows in sunny and shady
locations in the tundra, meadows, and coniferous forests. Similar to *Cymopterus alpinus*,
C. bakeri, and *C. humilis* but has more pinnate leaves; also
tends to be found in slightly more moist areas. Native.

Sanicula graveolens

(*S. nevadensis*) APIACEAE

northern sanicle, Sierra sanicle

NR, MR, subalpine, montane, foothills,
sagebrush steppe, intermountain
parks, grasslands, infrequent,
Spring, perennial, 6–18 in.

Upright flowering stems from taproot. Basal
leaves bright green, pinnate or ternate, deeply
dentate; lowest ones emerging from below
ground, and smaller, alternate up the stem.
Light yellow flowers in compact umbels. Primarily west coast distribution; also in Argentina, Chile. Dry slopes, coniferous forests, ledges in sun,
part shade. Native.

Shoshonea pulvinata APIACEAE

Shoshone carrot

MR, subalpine, montane, endemic,
locally abundant, L Spring–Summer,
perennial, 0.75–3.5 in.

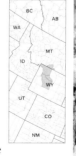

Deciduous, mat-forming herb with short,
dense branches. Leaves all basal, green, 0.5–
1.5 in. long, pinnately divided with 3–7 pairs
of segments (smaller segments linear); surfaces hairless to rough-hairy. Inflorescence
an umbel of yellow flowers. Grows in sunny
and shady locations in the tundra, meadows,
and mixed-coniferous forests. Similar to some
Aletes and *Cymopterus* spp. but tends to form much more
dense mats and is restricted to calcareous soils. Native.

Zizia aptera APIACEAE

meadow zizia, heartleaf golden alexanders
RM, montane, foothills, intermountain
parks, grasslands, wetlands,
common, locally abundant,
Summer, perennial, 11–28 in.
Single- to multistemmed herb with stout
hollow stems. Leaves deciduous. Basal
leaves simple, serrate, with long stems,
sometimes trifoliate. Stem leaves sessile
and trifoliate, more coarsely serrate. Inflorescence an umbel with uneven rays. Flowers yellow.
Grows in riparian areas, moist meadows, seeps. This plant
becomes more widespread and common farther north.
Native.

Oreocarya flava
(*Cryptantha flava*) BORAGINACEAE

yellow cryptantha
MR, SR, pinyon-juniper, sagebrush
steppe, intermountain parks, common,
Spring–E Summer, perennial, 6–14 in.
Flowering stems rise from tufts of silky
gray-green linear foliage. Persistent gray
dead leaves and stems at base. Terminal
clusters of yellow flowers. Widespread in
sandy soil throughout much of the Colorado
Plateau, extending to WY. The commonest yellow oreo-
carya. Native.

Sedum lanceolatum CRASSULACEAE

lanceleaf stonecrop
RM, throughout, common, L Spring–
Summer, perennial, 1.5–10 in.
Brittle decumbent to ascending stems with
small fleshy succulent leaves. Leaves alternate, linear to lanceolate, upper leaves fall
at flowering; lower leaves densely set, incurved to form basal rosettes, blue-green
to yellow-green in shade, reddish green in
exposed sunny sites. Star-shaped flowers in
terminal cymes, 5 petals, typically yellow;
carpels shorter than petals. Sun; open rocky
slopes; rock outcrops, shallow soils. All life zones except
wetlands. Native.

Sedum stenopetalum
(*S. douglasii*) CRASSULACEAE
wormleaf stonecrop
NR, MR, subalpine, montane, foothills,
sagebrush steppe, grasslands,
uncommon, locally abundant, Spring–
Summer, perennial, 2–10 in.
Several branched stems, ascending to erect,
from loose rosettes and horizontal rhizomes.
Fleshy pointed leaves alternate, lanceolate to
linear, flattened, keeled; many leaves fall away
at flowering, leaving behind midribs; upper leaves bear
small plantlets in axils that can take root. Star-shaped flowers in terminal cymes, 5 petals, yellow. Sun, shade; dry
open slopes, rock ledges, scree, forests. Native.

Mentzelia dispersa
(*M. pinetorum*) LOASACEAE
bushy blazingstar
RM, montane, foothills, pinyon-juniper,
sagebrush steppe, grasslands, common,
Spring–Summer, annual, 4–16 in.
Stems ascending to erect, herbaceous, simple
or branched, and barbed; from a taproot. Stem
leaves oblanceolate to linear, alternate, pinnatifid, sessile; basal leaves linear to shallowly
lobed. Yellow, unstalked flowers with 5 petals
in terminal clusters; calyx hairy, bracts egg-shaped. Fruit
a capsule with 15–30 seeds. Found on dry slopes and disturbed sites. Native.

Eriogonum arcuatum
(*E. jamesii* var. *arcuatum*)
POLYGONACEAE
Baker's buckwheat
SR, montane, foothills, pinyon-juniper,
sagebrush steppe, grasslands, common,
Summer–Fall, perennial, 2–32 in.
Many stems form a mat. Leaves grayish,
basal, alternate, oblanceolate-elliptic, 0.2–1.18
in., densely hairy below, woolly tufted above.
5-petaled yellow flowers form a cluster that
branches 1–3 times, and goes from rounded to
flat. Grows in sunny areas, barrens, rock ledges, dry slopes,
and meadows. This has much more yellow and compact
heads than *E. jamesii* and is found at lower elevations than
var. *xanthum*. Very similar to *E. flavum*, with which it may
have integrated near the CO/WY border. Native.

Eriogonum arcuatum var. *xanthum*
(*E. flavum* var. *xanthum*)
POLYGONACEAE
Ivy League wild buckwheat
SR, alpine, subalpine, locally abundant,
Summer, perennial, 1–3 in.
Many stems form a mat, which is rarely
much higher than the foliage, 0.75–3 in.
tall. Leaves all basal, grayish, alternate,
oblanceolate-elliptic, 0.2–1.2 in., densely
hairy below with woolly tufts above. 5-petaled flowers
form a rounded cluster; unbranched. Grows in sunny
areas, barrens, rock ledges, dry slopes, and meadows.
Found in the high elevations of CO, where no other eriogonums are like it. Native.

Eriogonum caespitosum
POLYGONACEAE
matted buckwheat
MR, SR, alpine, subalpine, montane,
foothills, pinyon-juniper, sagebrush
steppe, grasslands, common, Spring–
Summer, perennial, 1.2–4 in.
Herbaceous stems from woody base form
dense, mat-like cushion. Leaves basal, grayish, alternate, oblanceolate, 0.1–0.4 in., dense
white hairs below. 5-petaled flowers form a cluster, orangish yellow, reddish, or rose. Grows in sunny areas, barrens,
rock ledges, coniferous forests, mixed forests, dry slopes,
and meadows. Often found on calcium-rich soils. Native.

Eriogonum flavum POLYGONACEAE
golden buckwheat
RM, subalpine, montane, foothills,
sagebrush steppe, intermountain
parks, grasslands, common,
Summer–Fall, perennial, 2–11 in.
Stems mat-forming and upright. Leaves
basal, green to grayish, alternate,
elliptic-oblanceolate, 0.4–2.4 in.; dense white
hairs below, less above. 5-petaled flowers
form a cluster, yellow fading to gold, orange,
and red. Grows in sunny areas, rock ledges, barrens, dry
slopes, and sage meadows. More plentiful from northern
CO to AB. Native.

Eriogonum umbellatum

POLYGONACEAE
sulphur-flower
RM, throughout, common, L Spring–Fall,
perennial, 2–10 in.

Mat-forming herb or subshrub; leafless flowering stems erect to spreading. Leaves green
to grayish, oblong-ovate to oblanceolate to elliptic, and 0.2–1.6 in. 5-petaled flowers in a
yellow, white, or red umbel. Grows in sunny
areas, rock ledges, scree, barrens, pine parklands, dry slopes, and sage meadows. The most common
eriogonum in the Rockies, with a multitude of varieties
and forms. Found in every habitat, except moist or wet.
Native.

Eriogonum umbellatum var. *porteri* POLYGONACEAE

Porter's sulphur-flower
MR, SR, throughout, common, Summer–Fall,
perennial, 0.5–3 in.
Leafless, erect to spreading stems form a
dense mat. Leaves green, oblong-ovate to
oblanceolate to elliptic, 0.2–0.4 in.; white
below. 5-petaled flowers clustered, yellow,
orange, or reddish. Grows in sunny areas,
rock ledges, scree, barrens, pine parklands,
dry slopes, and sage meadows, in all life zones except
wetlands. This high-elevation variety of *E. umbellatum*
is much more dense, with less woolly leaves and more
pompom-like flowers. Native.

Ivesia gordonii ROSACEAE

alpine ivesia
RM, alpine, subalpine, montane,
foothills, common, locally abundant,
Spring–Summer, perennial, 6–12 in.

Many separate flower and leaf stems originate
from a woody base. Leaves are green, sticky,
hairy, and pinnately compound with 10–25
leaflets; last year's dead leaves persist at base.
Flowers in a rounded cluster; yellow or white
with 5 tiny, insignificant petals. Similar at
first glance to a potentilla or *Geum rossii*, but this species
has narrow leaves, is rarely found with *G. rossii*, and has
smaller, less showy petals than potentillas. Sunny meadows. Native.

Saxifraga chrysantha
(*Hirculus serpyllifolius*)
SAXIFRAGACEAE
golden saxifrage
RM, alpine, locally abundant,
Summer, perennial, 1–6 in.
Herbaceous mat-forming plant with reddish
prostrate to ascending stems; rhizomatous,
not stoloniferous. Leaves in crowded basal
rosettes, with 3–5 alternate, reduced leaves
on stem; narrowly oblanceolate to spatu-
late, fleshy, with smooth to glandular-ciliate margins and
rounded tips. Inflorescence a single flower or a cyme of 2
or 3 flowers with golden yellow petals, sometimes with orange spots at base; sepals bent downward. Meadows, rocky
tundra, on wet talus and scree slopes. Native.

Saxifraga flagellaris
SAXIFRAGACEAE
stoloniferous saxifrage, spider saxifrage
RM, alpine, rare, locally abundant,
Summer, perennial, 1–6 in.
Stoloniferous, weakly rhizomatous herb
with purplish thread-like runners terminating in rosettes. Stems purplish, covered
in glandular hairs. Basal and stem leaves
fleshy and smooth, oblanceolate to spatulate,
with smooth to glandular-ciliate margins. Stem leaves alternate, reduced upward. Inflorescence with 1–3 terminal
flowers. Sepals erect, petals bright yellow (not spotted),
wedge-shaped, with claw-like bases. Scree slopes, fellfields, predominantly on limestone. Native.

Solanum rostratum
(*Androcera rostrata*) SOLANACEAE
buffalobur nightshade
RM, foothills, sagebrush steppe,
grasslands, common, Spring–
Fall, annual, 8–28 in.
Stems erect, herbaceous, usually branched,
hairy, covered with vicious yellow spines.
Leaves alternate, petiolate, pinnate to bipinnate, spiny, with rounded lobes. Yellow
flowers in terminal racemes of 5–15; 5 petals, 5 spiny calyces. Fruit a berry encased in a very spiny calyx. Native to
central U.S.; invasive outside of native range. Sunny, dry
disturbed sites, roadsides, farmland. Showy, painful, and
toxic! Qualifies as native, introduced, and invasive.

Orobanche fasciculata
(*Aphyllon fasciculatum*)

OROBANCHACEAE
clustered broomrape
RM, montane, foothills, sagebrush
steppe, grasslands, common, Spring–
Summer, perennial, 2–10 in.
Stems single or clustered, often branched,
hairy-glandular, yellowish to purple; from a
fleshy root. Stem leaves scaly, alternate, hairy.
4–10 tubular flowers are curved, 5-lobed,
with no bracts; corolla yellow or reddish with purple lines,
yellow patches on lower lip. Fruit an angled capsule,
net-veined. Parasitic plant lacking chlorophyll, parasitizing *Artemisia* spp. When more reddish, easily confused
with *O. uniflora*. Grows on dry, open ground
in steppe ecosystems. Native.

Lithospermum incisum
(*L. angustifolium*) BORAGINACEAE
narrowleaf stoneseed
RM, throughout, common, Spring–
Summer, perennial, 3–15 in.
Stems gray-green, spreading from taprooted
woody crown. Leaves linear to 2–4 in.; all
parts with short hairs. Showy tubular flowers with flared petals produced in upper leaf
axils. Tubes twice as large as corolla. Petals distinctly incised and wavy. Fruit 4 gray shiny nutlets. Grows in sunny
dry meadows, in all life zones except alpine and wetlands.
Native.

Lithospermum multiflorum

BORAGINACEAE
manyflowered stoneseed
MR, SR, subalpine, montane, foothills,
pinyon-juniper, sagebrush steppe,
intermountain parks, locally abundant,
Spring–Summer, perennial, 9–24 in.
Taprooted herb similar to previous, often
taller, with smaller flowers. Corollas twice the
length of the tube. Flowers with round petals.
May form thick colonies on the margins of
pine woods and other shrubby habitats at mid to lower elevations, making an outstanding show most years. Native.

Lonicera involucrata

CAPRIFOLIACEAE
twinberry honeysuckle, black twinberry
RM, subalpine, montane, foothills,
sagebrush steppe, common, Spring–
Summer, perennial, 2–9 ft.
Deciduous, erect shrub with smooth,
greenish, quadrangular twigs, becoming yellowish gray with shredding bark.
Leaves short-stalked, opposite, to 5.5 in.
long; elliptic to ovate, smooth on top, hairy
below. Flowers paired, with hairy yellow to yellowish red
tubular-campanulate, 5-lobed corollas. Corollas cupped by
2 pairs of involucre bracts becoming reddish to purplish
and spreading. Berries shiny, round, and black. Grows
along streams, in meadows, moist forests
and thickets. Birds and mammals eat berries; hummingbirds and butterflies visit
flowers. Native.

Hypericum scouleri HYPERICACEAE
Scouler's St. John's wort
RM, montane, foothills, pinyon-juniper,
sagebrush steppe, intermountain
parks, wetlands, locally abundant,
L Spring–Summer, perennial, 8–28 in.
Erect herbaceous plant from rhizomes and
stolons. Stems simple below, branched above. Leaves opposite, sessile, elliptic, black-dotted along margins. Flowers few to many in loose cyme, yellow, 5 petals, 5 sepals,
black-dotted on margins; shiny, comparatively large central boss of stamens. Widespread in moist
meadows and forests, streambanks. Native.

Linum aristatum
(*Mesynium aristatum*) LINACEAE
bristle flax
MR, SR, grasslands, infrequent, L
Spring–Summer, perennial, 3–7 in.
Ephemeral glabrous herb with few delicate, branching stems from taproot. Leaves
alternate, linear with pointed tips. Flowers solitary, small but showy, yellow or
orange-yellow at branch tips. Sepals bristle-tipped (hence
the epithet). Petals are held for a few hours in the morning
and shed in heat of day. Grows on open, dry, sandy sites
and in prairies and shrublands. Native.

Linum australe
(*Mesynium australe*) LINACEAE
southern flax
RM, intermountain parks,
grasslands, infrequent, L Spring–
E Summer, perennial, 7–14 in.

Herb with erect, wiry stems from taproot. Stems glabrous above and minutely hairy below; sparsely branched above middle, or not at all (*L. aristatum* is glabrous and branched throughout). Alternate linear leaves have pointed tips and small purple glands. Inflorescence a panicle at branch tips with yellow to orange-yellow flowers. Sepals bristle-tipped. Styles shorter than those of *L. aristatum*. Grows in open ponderosa pine forests, dry slopes, and along roads. Native.

Linum rigidum
(*Mesynium rigidum*) LINACEAE
stiffstem flax
RM, grasslands, locally abundant, L
Spring–Summer, annual, 3–8 in.

Glabrous herb with delicate, ascending to spreading stems that branch at base; from taproot. Stems sometimes minutely hairy at base and/or unbranched. Leaves alternate, linear, and glandular-toothed. The 5-petaled flowers, located at branch tips, are open for only a few hours in the morning; they can be a strange shade of caramel-gold unlike any other native plant. Found in dry, open habitats, growing with prairie grasses. Native.

Mentzelia albicaulis
(*Acrolasia albicaulis*) LOASACEAE
whitestem blazingstar
RM, foothills, pinyon-juniper, sagebrush steppe, common, Spring–Summer, annual, 4–16 in.

Several erect white, shiny stems, simple or branched, herbaceous, from a taproot. Leaves sessile, scabrous, oblanceolate to lanceolate or linear, alternate, entire to lobed or deeply pinnatifid. Flowers yellow, 5-petaled, in few-flowered cymes, many stamens, 1 style. Similar to *M. dispersa*, distinguished by observing seeds under magnification. Grows in in variable soil types in sunny, dry disturbed areas. Native.

Eriogonum acaule
(*E. caespitosum* var. *acaule*)
POLYGONACEAE
singlestem buckwheat
MR, SR, montane, pinyon-
juniper, sagebrush steppe, rare,
Summer, perennial, to 2 in.

Low, dense, silver, mat-forming herb. Short
flowering stems are erect and slightly above
the foliage. Leaves tiny, linear, thickened
and silvery-woolly. Flowers yellow, in tiny
closely set clusters, appearing as a mat; stamens protrude
slightly from the petals. Grows in sun, in saltbrush steppe,
clay flats and slopes. Native.

Aquilegia barnebyi
RANUNCULACEAE
oil shale columbine
MR, SR, foothills, pinyon-juniper, endemic,
rare, Spring–Summer, perennial, 1–22 in.
Herb with basal leaves, alternate stem
leaves; 2 or 3 times ternately compound.

Flowers erect or nodding, sepals pinkish and perpendicular to floral axis. Spurs
pink, straight, more or less parallel, evenly
tapered from stout to slender. Petals 5, yellow or cream. Fruit a beaked follicle. Glau-
cous, silvery foliage and yellow flowers not found in other
columbines of region. Confined to steep, shale cliffs in
western CO and eastern UT. Named for English botanist
Rupert Barneby, famed for his work with Fabaceae. Native.

Aquilegia chrysantha
RANUNCULACEAE
golden columbine
SR, montane, foothills, uncommon,
Spring–Fall, perennial, 12–48 in.
Somewhat erect herb with showy yellow
flowers atop 2 or 3 unbranched stems.
Leaves 2 or 3 times ternately divided on long
petioles. Inflorescence of few to several flowers high above semi-evergreen, basal leaves.
Petals 5, long spurs approximately parallel to
spreading; slender, and evenly tapered from base. Sepals
5, perpendicular to floral axis, narrowly ovate, 0.5–1.5 in.
long, somewhat sharp at tip. Fruit a 5-chambered follicle.
Found in moist, shady canyons from foothills to montane
regions. Rare in CO. Native.

Aquilegia flavescens

RANUNCULACEAE
yellow columbine
RM, alpine, subalpine, montane,
common, L Spring–E Summer,
perennial, to 3 ft.

Basal leaves biternately compound, usually glabrous, occasionally glandular to pilose. Leaflets not crowded. Flowers nodding, sepals perpendicular to floral axis, commonly soft buttercream-yellow, sometimes with pink or green tint. Plants most commonly found in the NR at mid to high elevations. Grows in part shade to sun in moist meadows, open forest, streambanks, and cool, rocky slopes. Will hybridize with *A. formosa*, giving the pink or reddish tinge to the flowers. Native.

Ranunculus acris RANUNCULACEAE

tall buttercup, common buttercup
RM, foothills, wetlands, infrequent,
L Spring–Summer, perennial, 12–30 in.

Erect herbaceous plant with 1 to several stems freely branched from stout caudex. Basal leaves 2 or 3 times ternately lobed. Stem leaves similar, alternate. Flowers in loose few-flowered inflorescence, yellow, 5 petals. Fruit an achene, head globose, beak short or long, straight or curved, 0.01–0.04 in. long. Found in moist soils. *Ranunculus* identification requires a key and hand lens or microscope. Introduced.

Ranunculus adoneus

RANUNCULACEAE
alpine buttercup
MR, SR, alpine, subalpine, common,
Spring–Summer, perennial, 3–8 in.

Herb with stems ascending to erect from large caudex. Basal leaves 2 or 3 times dissected. Cauline leaves similar but with shorter petioles. Flowers yellow with 5 petals; early ones low, stems elongating in summer. Fruit an achene, head ovoid, beak awl-shaped, straight. Found in high-elevation meadows, especially at the edge of snowfields. Native.

Ranunculus alismifolius

RANUNCULACEAE

plantainleaf buttercup
RM, alpine, subalpine, montane,
wetlands, common, Spring–
E Summer, perennial, 3–18 in.

Erect herb from caudex. Stems 1 to several, hairy to smooth, almost hollow. Basal leaves narrowly ovate, entire, to 6 in. long. Stem leaves similar but reduced, alternate, sometimes opposite. Upper stem leaves further reduced, without stalks. Inflorescence few to several-flowered cymes. Flowers yellow, petals 5–10 or more, nectary on upper surface, sepals half the length of petals. Fruit a smooth achene with straight or bent beak. Found in wet meadows and streamsides, in which habitats it often forms vast colonies, and in rocky areas. Native.

Ranunculus cardiophyllus

RANUNCULACEAE

heartleaf buttercup
RM, alpine, subalpine, montane,
locally abundant, L Spring–
Summer, perennial, 9–18 in.

Erect herb with branched stems. Basal leaves cordate, 0.5–2.5 in. long, petiole equally long, margins toothed. Stem leaves few, alternate, deeply divided into very slender segments. Inflorescence a cluster of flowers from upper leaf axils. Flowers yellow, 5 or more petals, numerous stamens. The cordate basal leaves, cylindrical fruit heads, and straight-beaked hairy achenes distinguish this species. *R. pedatifidus* has dissected basal leaves and *R. grayi* has smaller petals. Native.

Ranunculus eschscholtzii

RANUNCULACEAE

Eschscholtz's buttercup
RM, alpine, subalpine, locally abundant,
L Spring–Summer, perennial, 3–14 in.

Stems ascending to erect. Foliage smooth. Basal leaves palmately lobed, segments again lobed. Stem leaves few to none, finely lobed. Flowers few, yellow, petals twice the length of the sepals. Fruit a smooth achene, head cylindric or ovoid, straight beak, 0.02–0.08 in. long. Often blooming near snow drifts and along streams. Native.

Ranunculus flammula
(*R. reptans* var. *ovalis*)
RANUNCULACEAE
greater creeping spearwort
RM, subalpine, montane, wetlands, locally
abundant, Summer, perennial, 1–7 in.
Stoloniferous herb, stems sprawling to prostrate. Leaves simple, entire, linear. Basal
leaves on long stalks, stem leaves subsessile.
Flowers usually solitary, long-stalked. Petals yellow, 5; stamens many. Fruit a roundish
achene with slender and straight or curved beak to 0.02 in.
long. Found in lake and pond margins and seeps. Native.

Ranunculus glaberrimus
RANUNCULACEAE
sagebrush buttercup
RM, montane, foothills, pinyon-juniper,
sagebrush steppe, intermountain
parks, grasslands, common, Spring–
E Summer, perennial, 3–12 in.
Ephemeral herb with several simple to
branched ascending stems. Basal leaves narrowly elliptic, margins entire or lobed; stalk
may be much longer than blade. Stem leaves
alternate, sessile, deeply lobed. Inflorescence
a terminal cyme of few flowers. Flowers
shiny yellow, petals 5–10 or more, sepals 5, many stamens.
Fruit an achene, head globose, beak awl-shaped, straight or
curved. Found in meadows and open forests. Native.

Ranunculus gmelinii
(*R. limosus*) RANUNCULACEAE
Gmelin's buttercup
RM, subalpine, montane, foothills, wetlands,
common, Summer, perennial, 12–18 in.
Stoloniferous aquatic or emergent herb with
alternating palmate leaves, often deeply cleft,
floating on water or above. Solitary flowers
from leaf axils. Petals 5 or more, yellow. Several to many stamens. Fruit an achene, head
globose or ovoid, beak narrowly lanceolate,
straight, 0.02–0.04 in. long. Grows in ponds,
shallow streams, and ditches. Native.

Ranunculus hyperboreus
(R. intertextus) RANUNCULACEAE
high northern buttercup
RM, alpine, subalpine, montane,
foothills, wetlands, common, L Spring–
Summer, perennial, 3–18 in.
Stoloniferous aquatic with smooth, prostrate
stems that root at nodes. Basal leaves absent.
Cauline leaves deeply 3-lobed, base blunt or
cordate. Inflorescence solitary terminal or
axillary flowers; yellow sepals and petals,
nectary on petal surface. Fruit an achene, head globose,
beak linear, curved, 0.01–0.02 in. long. Grows in stream
and pond margins, marshes in tundra. Native.

Ranunculus inamoenus
RANUNCULACEAE
graceful buttercup
RM, alpine, subalpine, montane, foothills,
locally abundant, Spring, perennial, 4–16 in.
Stems erect, 3–7 flowers each. Basal leaves
ovate and slightly lobed at tip. Stem leaves
deeply lobed. Flowers yellow, petals 5–10
and just longer than sepals. Fruit a finely
hairy achene, straight or hooked, to 0.02
in. long. Beak 0.02–0.04 in. long. Grows in
meadows and open forests. Native.

Ranunculus jovis RANUNCULACEAE
Utah buttercup
MR, SR, montane, foothills, pinyon-juniper,
sagebrush steppe, infrequent,
Spring–Summer, perennial, 2–7 in.
Ephemeral herb from fleshy roots with 1 to
several stems. Stem leaves on long stalks,
divided into 3–5 lobes, clustered along stem,
longer than basal leaves. Basal leaves similar
but shorter, often lacking. Flowers yellow,
solitary, 5 petals or more. Fruit a globose
cluster of egg-shaped achenes. Blooms in
open areas following snow melt and quickly
goes dormant. Native.

Ranunculus macauleyi

RANUNCULACEAE
Rocky Mountain buttercup
SR, alpine, subalpine, endemic, locally
abundant, L Spring–Summer,
perennial, 3–9 in.

Small, slender herb with 1 or 2 large flowers
per stem. Leaves smooth, green, narrowly
oblanceolate to elliptic, tip rounded or truncate and notched. Flowers yellow, 5 petals or
more, distinctive dark hairs on underside of
sepals. Fruit an achene, head ovoid or cylindric, beak slender
and straight or recurved, 0.02–0.06 in. long. Grows in wet
meadows at high elevations. Native.

Ranunculus macounii

RANUNCULACEAE
Macoun's buttercup
RM, montane, foothills, wetlands, locally
abundant, L Spring–Fall, perennial, 10–36 in.
Coarse herb. Stems erect to somewhat erect,
bristly hairy, may root at nodes. Basal leaves
1 or 2 times ternately divided, toothed. Stem
leaves lanceolate. Inflorescence of numerous
small, yellow flowers on branched stems. Petals longer than sparsely hairy sepals. Fruit an
achene, head globose or ovoid, beak slender

to broadly slender, straight or almost straight, 0.04–0.05 in.
long. Grows in wet and disturbed habitats, moist depressions, ditches, stream and pond margins, and shallow water.
Native.

Ranunculus pedatifidus

RANUNCULACEAE
surefoot buttercup, northern buttercup
RM, alpine, subalpine, locally abundant,
L Spring–E Summer, perennial, 4–12 in.
Compact clumps of 1 to several erect stems,
softly hairy to smooth, not hollow. Basal leaves
deeply divided 7 times on long stalks. Stem
leaves alternate, becoming unstalked and less
divided upward. Inflorescence 1 to several

flowers. Petals 5–10, yellow, ovoid, nectary
on upper surface. Sepals 5. Fruit an achene, head cylindric,
beak lanceolate or awl-shaped, curved, 0.02–0.04 in. long.
Widespread arctic species, extending throughout Rockies at
high elevations. Native.

Ranunculus pygmaeus

RANUNCULACEAE

pygmy buttercup
RM, alpine, rare, Summer–Fall,
perennial, 0.5–2 in.
Tiny arctic herb with short ascending or
erect stems, 1 or 2 flowers each. Basal leaves
kidney-shaped, 3-lobed or more, base blunt,
margins entire. Petals 5 with nectary scale
on upper surface. Fruit an achene, head globose to cylindric, beak awl-shaped, straight
or curved, 0.01–0.03 in. long. Found at high altitudes, often
growing near persisting patches of snow. Native.

Ranunculus ranunculinus
(*Cyrtorhyncha ranunculina*)

RANUNCULACEAE

tadpole buttercup
MR, SR, montane, foothills, sagebrush
steppe, intermountain parks, uncommon,
Spring–Summer, perennial, 4–14 in.
Stems erect and smooth. Basal and stem
leaves ternately or pinnately divided 2 times.
Flowers few, terminal or in leaf axils; yellow, 5 petals narrow, round-tipped, similar in shape to the green sepals. Fruit an
achene, head globose or hemispheric, beak
thread-like, reflexed, brittle, 0.03–0.06 in. long. Grows on
open grassy slopes. Native.

Ranunculus repens RANUNCULACEAE

creeping buttercup
RM, grasslands, infrequent, Spring–
Summer, perennial, 7–20 in.
Stems sprawling to prostrate, may root at
nodes. Leaves ternately divided and lightly
speckled with lighter greenish white. Flowers yellow with 5 egg-shaped petals. Fruit
an achene, head globose or ovoid, beak lanceolate, curved, 0.03–0.05 in. long. Often
produces long runners. Weed of pastures or
gardens. Grows in meadows, lawns, roadsides. Naturalized in many places around
the globe. Introduced.

Ranunculus sceleratus

RANUNCULACEAE
cursed buttercup
RM, montane, foothills, sagebrush
steppe, intermountain parks,
grasslands, wetlands, locally abundant,
L Spring–Summer, annual, 5–24 in.

Coarse buttercup of middle altitudes. Stems
1 to several, erect, smooth, branched, hollow,
rarely root at nodes. Glossy trefoil leaves distinctive. Basal leaves twice deeply 3-lobed,
on long stalks. Stem leaves many, alternate, more deeply
lobed. Small yellow flowers, petals 3–5, nectary on upper
surface; in large cymes. Ovary forms large green cone with
small, deflexed petals. Fruit an achene, head cylindric to
elliptic, beak deltoid, usually straight, 0.01 in.
long. Widespread in moist meadows, shallow
water anywhere. Native.

Geum macrophyllum ROSACEAE

largeleaf avens
RM, subalpine, montane, foothills, common,
L Spring–Summer, perennial, 8–48 in.

Upright herb with hairy stems and leaves.
Basal leaves pinnately compound, 3–10 in.
long, with 4–8 small, paired leaflets and a
large 3- to 5-lobed round to cordate terminal
leaflet. Stem leaves alternate, reduced, often trifoliate. Inflorescence a cyme, bracts subtend flowers. Flowers yellow,
5 roundish petals, numerous stamens and pistils. Fruit an
achene with hooked seeds. Grows in moist meadows, forest openings, and riparian areas. Seeds cling
to socks and clothing. Native.

Geum rossii

(*Acomastylis rossii*) ROSACEAE
Ross' avens
RM, alpine, subalpine, common, L Spring–
Summer, perennial, 0.75–16 in.

Mat-forming herb with hairy stems. Basal
leaves 0.75–4 in. long, pinnately compound
with multiple leaflets, most with 3 or more
narrow segments. Inflorescence a cyme with
1–4 flowers held upright and a few small leaves. Flowers
yellow with 5 petals surrounding numerous stamens and
pistils; sepals green to red in a cup-shape. Height varies with exposure and altitude. Found in high mountain
meadows, tundra, and fellfields. Native.

Potentilla anserina
(*Argentina anserina*) ROSACEAE
silverweed cinquefoil, common silverweed
RM, throughout, common,
Summer, perennial, 2–12 in.

Mat-forming herb. Basal rosettes linked by
long red stolons. Leaves 3–10 in. long, pinnate; 12–25 narrow oval leaflets, rounded
edges, toothed margins; green above,
white-hairy below. Flowers solitary, 0.75 in.
across; 5 broad yellow petals on white-hairy
stalks. Found in all zones except alpine, in seeps, wet
mountain meadows, and along streambanks. The specific epithet is most likely a reference to herbivory by geese
(*Anser* spp.); the plant was also grown for food and medicine. Native.

Potentilla concinna ROSACEAE
elegant cinquefoil, red cinquefoil
RM, alpine, subalpine, montane,
foothills, sagebrush steppe, common,
Spring–Summer, perennial, to 4 in.

Low-growing herb to subshrub; short prostrate to ascending stems from basal rosette.
Leaves cordate to egg-shaped; divided palmately, 5–7 toothed leaflets 0.5–1 in. long.
Surfaces covered in silky hairs that sometimes curl upward; hairs more sparse above. Inflorescence
a cyme of few yellow, 5-petaled flowers. Depending on elevation, flowers appear early in spring, before plant is fully
leafed out. Found on open, dry slopes, meadows, woodlands, and sage meadows. Native.

Potentilla fissa
(*Drymocallis fissa*) ROSACEAE
bigflower cinquefoil
RM, montane, foothills, sagebrush
steppe, common, L Spring–
Summer, perennial, to 1 ft.

Herb. Stems numerous, arranged in a dense
cluster, or slightly spread out from a caudex.
Leaves pinnate, divided into 9–13 rounded
and incised leaflets; surfaces with sparse
hairs above and glandular below. Inflorescence a cyme
of numerous flowers; flowers up to 1 in., with 5 petals.
Lengthy anthers a distinguishing characteristic. Found in
open forests, rocky and dry slopes and meadows. Native.

Potentilla fruticosa
(*Dasiphora fruticosa*) ROSACEAE
shrubby cinquefoil, bush cinquefoil, golden
hardhack, widdy
RM, throughout, common,
Summer, perennial, to 4 ft.

Shrub. Stems upright, spreading to prostrate,
weakly erect or ascending. Alternate leaves
pinnate, with 5 narrowly oval to linear leaflets;
margins entire or sometimes rolled upward.
Yellow flowers single on end of stem, about
1–1.5 in., with 5 petals. Found in many habitats, from
woodlands to rocky slopes, streambeds, and alpine meadows. Native Americans made tea from leaves, and small
animals forage on the fruit. Circumboreal. Native.

Potentilla glandulosa ROSACEAE
sticky cinquefoil
RM, alpine, subalpine, montane, grasslands,
locally abundant, Summer, perennial, to 2 ft.

Erect to ascending, hairy, sticky stems from
loosely branched woody base. Leaves mostly
basal, pinnate, with 5–7 glandular leaflets
to nearly 2.5 in., egg-shaped to round; deep,
nearly rounded double teeth. Inflorescence
widely branched with leafy bracts and short
flower stalks. Yellow to cream-white petals,
slightly shorter to slightly longer than sepals, distinguish
the common RM subspecies: ssp. *glandulosa* (more rare),
ssp. *glabrata*, and ssp. *pseudorupestris*. Mostly found in NR
in meadows, open areas. Native.

Potentilla glaucophylla
(*P. diversifolia*) ROSACEAE
varileaf cinquefoil
RM, alpine, subalpine, common,
Spring–Summer, perennial, to 8 in.

Ascending to erect stems from branching
woody base. Leaves palmate; leaflets 5–7,
lance- to egg-shaped, glaucous, to 1 in., usually nearly hairless. Inflorescence an open
leafy-bracted cyme, stalks straight in fruit. Sepals subtend 5 yellow petals, narrowly triangular, with smaller, skinnier secondary bracts. The type,
common in high-elevation meadows, has lance-shaped
teeth on leaflets' lower half; var. *perdissecta* has narrowly
oval or linear lobes divided three-quarters of the way or
more to midvein. It is difficult to distinguish them where
their ranges overlap. Native.

Potentilla gracilis ROSACEAE

slender cinquefoil
RM, alpine, subalpine, montane,
sagebrush steppe, grasslands, common,
Summer, perennial, to 32 in.

Upright; branched, woody base. Leaves
palmate; leaflets 5–9, inverse lanceolate,
toothed/lobed; gray/green, glandular/hairy.
Flower stems silky-hairy to glandular,
open; many flowers; petals cordate; sepals
lance-shaped, glandular/hairy. Highly vari-
able: glandular green leaves, lobed halfway or more to midvein, var. *brunnescens*; gray-green leaves, toothed less than
halfway, var. *fastigiata*; bicolored leaves, var. *pulcherrima*
(white-hairy below), var. *elmeri* (linear teeth almost to midvein), and var. *flabelliformis* (lance-shaped to
midvein). Dry to moist meadows, open forests, streambanks. Native.

Potentilla hippiana

(*P. effusa*) ROSACEAE

woolly cinquefoil
RM, throughout, common,
Summer, perennial, to 16 in.

Upright stems from thick, branched,
woody base. Leaves pinnate. Leaflets 5–13,
oblong, toothed, gray-green above, thick
white-woolly below, to 1.5 in. Open clusters of numerous flowers on silky, woolly stems; yellow petals notched,
slightly longer than sepals; sepals silky, same color as
bractlets. In var. *effusa*, sepals are woolly and differ in color
from bractlets; leaves gray-green both sides.
Highly variable, crosses with other species.
Found in dry to moist meadows, open mixed
forest, streambanks, disturbed areas to alpine tundra. Native.

Potentilla nivea ROSACEAE

snow cinquefoil
RM, alpine, subalpine, common,
Summer, perennial, to 10 in.

Tufted, mat-forming herb from woody
base, covered with sheaths of leaf remains.
Woolly, hairy stems erect to ascending. Leaflets in 3s,
egg-shaped, toothed to lobed, with long silky hairs and
woolly white hairs beneath; edges rolled backward. Petioles white-woolly. Flowers in clusters of 1–3, with yellow
petals equal to or longer than sepals. Found in high meadows, on rocky ridges and cliffs. Native.

Potentilla norvegica ROSACEAE

Norwegian cinquefoil
RM, subalpine, montane, grasslands,
wetlands, common, L Spring–Summer,
annual, to 2 ft.

Herb with erect, simple or branched stems
from woody base. Base of stems with long
stiff hairs. Leaves with 3 egg-shaped to oval
leaflets; margins with nearly rounded teeth
or lobes pointing upward; surfaces with
some long stiff hairs. Yellow petals smaller
than sepals. Found in moist meadows near streams and
lakeshores, especially in disturbed areas. Circumboreal.
Native.

Potentilla ovina ROSACEAE

sheep cinquefoil
RM, alpine, subalpine, montane, foothills,
common, Summer, perennial, 2–6 in.

Herb with erect to spreading stems, loose
wavy hairs near base; from thick, short,
branching, woody base covered in withered leaf bases. Leaves on short petioles,
mostly basal, pinnate, with 9–21 distinctly
linear-lobed leaflets. The type has variable
grayish hair and more deeply divided lobes;
var. *decurrens* has green hairless leaves, less
division in leaflets. Yellow flowers few on open cyme.
Found on barren and exposed dry slopes. The similar *P.
plattensis* is found in moist meadows or riparian areas and
lacks loose stem hairs. Native.

Potentilla pensylvanica
(*P. bipinnatifida*) ROSACEAE

Pennsylvania cinquefoil
RM, alpine, subalpine, montane,
foothills, sagebrush steppe, grasslands,
common, Summer, perennial, 2–16 in.

Herb with decumbent to erect, hairy to
densely hairy stems from branched woody
base. Leaves mostly basal and stem leaves alternate with shorter petioles; pinnate with
4–11 laciniate-lobed leaflets with sharply
pointed apices. Surfaces nearly hairless or silky-hairy
above and densely white-hairy below. Flowers in compact
cyme; petals and sepals nearly equal. Found in rocky exposed sites, disturbed areas. Varies widely in stature and
hairiness. Native.

Potentilla pulcherrima
(*P. camporum*) ROSACEAE
beautiful cinquefoil
RM, throughout, common,
Summer, perennial, 8–32 in.
Herb with erect to ascending, glandular and
loosely hairy stems from a thick woody base.
Leaves mostly basal, palmate, with 5–9 bicolored leaflets. Surfaces loosely hairy above
to white-woolly below and with red-tipped
glands; margins serrated less than halfway
to midvein, which is a distinguishing feature. Inflorescence an open, spreading cyme with numerous flowers.
Found in dry to moist habitats. Native.

Potentilla recta ROSACEAE
sulphur cinquefoil
RM, montane, foothills, pinyon-
juniper, grasslands, locally abundant,
Spring–Fall, perennial, 1–2 ft.
Herb with erect stems from a woody base;
not rhizomatous. Stem with long hairs perpendicular to it. Leaves mostly along stem,
alternate and palmately divided into 5–7
leaflets; margins serrated about halfway to
midvein. Surfaces sparsely hairy or glandular, green above and below. Inflorescence an
open cyme with stiff hairs and many flowers. Considered
a noxious weed in many states, found in disturbed areas,
along roadsides, and meadows. Can be confused with
many native species, with which it can hybridize. Introduced and invasive.

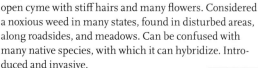

Potentilla subjuga
(*P. osterhoutiana*) ROSACEAE
Colorado cinquefoil
NR, SR, alpine, subalpine, locally
abundant, Summer, perennial, 4–10 in.
Herb to subshrub with tufted stems from a
woody base covered in old leaf scales. Leaves
palmate or almost digitate, usually with 5
leaflets with deep overlapping teeth; usually
1 pair of leaflets connected by a visible rachis
below. Silky hairs above and white-woolly below. Petioles
with varying hairs, spreading at first and becoming flat
later in season. Flowers few to many. Found at higher subalpine and above in meadows, rocky talus slopes, and tundra. Exact range is under debate. Native.

Potentilla uniflora
(*P. ledebouriana*) ROSACEAE
oneflower cinquefoil
RM, alpine, subalpine, common,
Summer, perennial, 2–6 in.

Mat-forming herb. Tufted, erect to ascending stems, short woody base: lower with
stiff straight hairs, upper with long tousled
hairs. Leaves mostly basal, ternate; oval leaflets lobed or toothed nearly halfway to midvein. Upper leaves green with stiff hairs,
lower white with matted woolly hairs. Stem leaves similar,
smaller. Flowers 1 or 2 on stalk. Lance-shaped sepals with
matted hairs, smaller or equal to slightly lobed petals at
tip. Sunny ridgelines, fellfields, talus slopes. Native.

Purshia tridentata ROSACEAE
antelope bitterbrush
RM, montane, foothills, pinyon-juniper,
sagebrush steppe, grasslands, common,
Spring–Summer, perennial, 2–6 ft.

Stems upright to spreading, brown, aging
gray, densely branched. Leaves to 0.75 in.,
semi-evergreen, alternate, clustered at nodes;
wedge-shaped, 3 terminal lobes, no resin dots.
Flowers soft yellow to cream; 5 round to spatulate petals, gold stamens, fragrant; seeds not
plumed. Woodland openings, dry slopes and shrublands.
Native.

Sibbaldia procumbens
(*Potentilla sibbaldii*) ROSACEAE
creeping sibbaldia
RM, alpine, subalpine, montane, common,
Summer–Fall, perennial, 1–3 in.

Herb, mat-forming, from rhizomes. Leaves
trifoliate; wedge-shaped leaflets lobed 3–5
times at apex. Inflorescence 2–15 flowers,
each to 0.25 in., in tight terminal cluster. Petals 5, pale yellow, linear-oblong, alternate with
5 large green sepals twice their size; 5 small
bracts directly beneath sepals. Stamens 5,
small. Red stems and seedheads attract atten-
tion even after flowering. Occurs in dry, rocky flats and
slopes, at edge of receding snowbanks. The only species in
this genus in the Rockies; the rest are native to the Himalayas. Native.

Saxifraga aizoides

(Leptasea aizoides) SAXIFRAGACEAE

yellow mountain saxifrage, evergreen saxifrage

NR, alpine, subalpine, montane, common, Spring–Summer, perennial, 2–6 in.

Herbaceous, rhizomatous (not stoloniferous), mat-forming evergreen; numerous prostrate to erect stems. Leaves smooth, succulent, sessile, linear-oblong; entire margins and spiny tips. Alternate stem leaves resemble basal leaves, but less dense. Inflorescence a several-flowered cyme (occasionally a solitary flower). Spreading sepals alternate with yellow, often orange-dotted petals. 10 greenish, spreading stamens. Ovary 2-carpellate. Occurs in rocky seepage sites, crevices, on streambanks, talus slopes, and the tundra, often on calcareous sites. Circumpolar. Native.

Saxifraga hirculus SAXIFRAGACEAE

yellow marsh saxifrage

MR, SR, alpine, wetlands, uncommon, Summer, perennial, 3–7 in.

Tufted, rhizomatous herb with erect, brownish- or yellowish-hairy stems forming small mats. Leaves in a basal rosette are linear to spatulate and bright green with smooth (or nearly so) surfaces and entire margins; stem leaves similar, alternate, sessile, 3–7 in number, and reducing upward. 1–4 bright yellow, terminal, initially nodding flowers open midsummer. Petals often orange-spotted proximally. Grows along cold boggy streamsides and in wet meadows, often in moss. Circumboreal. Native.

Physalis heterophylla SOLANACEAE

clammy groundcherry

RM, montane, foothills, grasslands, common, L Spring–Summer, perennial, 6–20 in.

Erect, simple or branched, glandular, herbaceous stems. Leaves alternate, simple, entire, petiolate, ovate, glandular. Pale yellow flowers solitary in leaf axils; bell-shaped, nodding; calyx 5-lobed; corolla 5-lobed; 5 stamens. Berries yellowish, spherical, enclosed in papery calyx. Unripe fruits poisonous. Found in sandy soils in disturbed areas, along roadsides, gulches, and in ponderosa woodlands. Native.

Tribulus terrestris ZYGOPHYLLACEAE

puncturevine, goathead
RM, foothills, pinyon-juniper, sagebrush
steppe, grasslands, common, L
Spring–Fall, annual, 1–10 in.

Stems rusty pink, silky to bristly hairs,
spreading close to ground from taproot, or
scrambling over obstacles. Leaves opposite, pinnate, 1–2 in. long; 6–14 oval leaflets,
silky hairs. Flowers single in leaf axils, 0.5 in.
across, 5 egg-shaped petals. Fruit distinct,
hard, 5-part bur; each section with 2 large sharp horns,
posing danger to bike tires, bare feet, pets, etc. An aggressive noxious weed from Europe that resembles some related natives. Sunny roadsides, disturbed sites, trails, farm
fields. Introduced and invasive.

Agoseris glauca ASTERACEAE

pale mountain dandelion, pale agoseris
RM, alpine, subalpine, montane,
pinyon-juniper, sagebrush steppe,
intermountain parks, common,
L Spring–Summer, perennial, 2–24 in.

Herb. Leaves basal, to 18 in. long, lanceolate to
oblanceolate, entire, toothed or lobed, petioles
rarely purplish. Torn leaves excrete a milky
sap. Flower stems leafless; one head per stem.
Involucre cone-shaped; phyllaries in 2 or 3 series, green or
purple, often with purple-black markings; leaves, flower
stems, and phyllaries often hairy. Ray flowers bright yellow, numerous, to 1 in. long. Found in rocky places, along
streams and open meadows. Native.

Agoseris heterophylla
(*Macrorhynchus heterophyllus*)
ASTERACEAE

annual agoseris
RM, foothills, pinyon-juniper, sagebrush
steppe, common, Spring–Fall, annual, to 8 in.

Scapose, slender, lactiferous herb. Leaves in
a basal rosette and mostly erect, to 6 in. long,
oblanceolate and entire, toothed or lobed; surfaces soft to rough hairy. Peduncle ranges
from basally puberulent to apically hairy. Involucres are
hairy and often green to rosy. Ray flowers are many and
are squared at the ends, often serrate, yellow and sometimes drying pink. Plants grow in barrens, disturbed
areas, dry slopes, and other sunny habitats. Native.

Amauriopsis dissecta
(*Bahia dissecta*) ASTERACEAE
ragleaf bahia
MR, SR, montane, foothills, pinyon-juniper,
common, Summer, biennial, 7–36 in.

Herb with 1 erect leafless stem, several
spreading flowerheads; stems reddish, glandular. Leaves in basal rosette, oblanceolate
to linear; 3 finely lobed leaflets, each 1–16 in.
long. Numerous small, yellow, rounded and
somewhat notched rays generally overlap
but may have gaps in between; rays surround a generous
clump of yellow disc flowers; phyllaries hirsute and glandular. Found in disturbed sites, along roadsides, in sandy,
rocky soils, and open forests. Native.

Arnica angustifolia ASTERACEAE
narrowleaf arnica, alpine arnica
RM, alpine, subalpine, montane,
infrequent, locally abundant, L Spring–
Summer, perennial, 2–20 in.

Herb with erect (usually) solitary stems.
Leaves opposite, in 1–5 pairs, lanceolate to
linear, entire. Basal and stem leaves similar, but basal leaves petiolate, and with or
without hairs. 6–16 ray florets, toothed and
yellow, surround yellow discs with yellow anthers. Grows in dry to mesic, sometimes moist,
rocky, calcareous soils. Often strikingly large compared
to surrounding flora. The type is rare in CO, found only
on Taylor Pass, Gunnison County; ssp. *tomentosa* is more
common. Native.

Arnica chamissonis ASTERACEAE
Chamisso arnica
RM, subalpine, montane, foothills,
common, Spring–Summer,
perennial, 8–36 in.

Erect herb, single stems from long slender
rhizomes. Leaves opposite, in 5–10 pairs
along stem, lanceolate; margins slightly
toothed or entire, surfaces hairy, becoming
glandular higher up. Flowerheads to 2 in., in
branched clusters of 1 to several. 10–16 rays surround disc;
blunt bracts with a tuft of white hairs a distinguishing
feature. Grows in moist meadows, conifer forests, and on
streambanks. Similar to *A. montana*, the important medicinal plant from Europe. Native.

Arnica cordifolia ASTERACEAE
heartleaf arnica
RM, subalpine, montane, foothills, common,
L Spring–Summer, perennial, 4–24 in.
Herb with erect, single stems from long slender rhizomes. Leaves opposite, 2–4 pairs on stem, stalked and heart-shaped; margins toothed and surfaces with velvety hairs. Flowerheads generally solitary but up to 3; 6–13 rays surround disc; bracts densely hairy, glandular, pointed and fringed at tips. Grows in moist shady forests and on streambanks. Important summer food source for mule deer and elk. Used by Native Americans medicinally and for rituals. The most common arnica. Native.

Arnica fulgens ASTERACEAE
foothill arnica, hillside arnica
RM, montane, foothills, common,
Spring–Summer, perennial, to 30 in.
Herb with single stem from basal rosette. Leaves at stem base, short petiolate and becoming sessile upward; margins usually entire. Tufts of brown hairs on axils of basal leaves a distinguishing feature. Numerous yellow-orange rays, 0.5–1 in. long, surround yellow disc with glandular and glandless hairs. The similar *A. sororia* lacks glandless hairs. Cypselae brown, hairy, and with white bristly pappi. Found in open meadows, rocky and grassy areas. Native.

Arnica latifolia ASTERACEAE
broadleaf arnica
RM, alpine, subalpine, montane,
common, Summer, perennial, 4–20 in.
Herb with ascending to erect, solitary stems from long slender rhizomes. Leaves opposite, in 2–4 pairs on stem, lanceolate to arrow-shaped, without petioles, and finely toothed; not hairy. Flowerheads generally solitary but up to 3; 8–15 ray flowers surround disc. Found in moist montane conifer forests, subalpine to alpine meadows, and open areas in the mountains. Native.

numerous petals, composite, radial

Arnica lonchophylla ASTERACEAE
longleaf arnica
NR, MR, alpine, subalpine, montane,
intermountain parks, locally abundant,
Summer, perennial, 4–20 in.
Erect herb, typically with solitary stems
(sometimes up to 5) branching only at flowerheads. Leaves toothed and lanceolate,
hairy and glandular; lower leaves petiolate, becoming fewer and reducing upward.
Flowers generally solitary (sometimes up to
5). Found frequently in NR in open montane forests and
rocky meadows. Native.

Arnica longifolia ASTERACEAE
spearleaf arnica
RM, alpine, subalpine, montane, wetlands,
common, Summer–Fall, perennial, 1–2 ft.
Clump-forming herb with many erect
stems. Leaves mostly on stem, lanceolate
and entire, tapering to a point, and not reducing much in size upward; lower leaves
surrounded by a sheath. Phyllaries strongly
pointed. 6–15 yellow ray flowers surround
yellow-orange disc. Found in moist areas,
from riparian to coniferous forests. Native.

Arnica mollis ASTERACEAE
hairy arnica
RM, subalpine, montane, common,
Summer, perennial, 6–24 in.
Clump-forming herb with erect hairy and
sticky stems, usually solitary. Leaves opposite, in 3 or 4 pairs, egg-shaped to lanceolate,
stalked or unstalked; margins irregularly
toothed or entire and surfaces sparsely
hairy. Flowerheads generally solitary but
up to 3; flowers with 6–22 rays surround
the disc. Found on rocky slopes, subalpine
meadows, streambanks and other moist
open areas. Native.

Arnica parryi ASTERACEAE
Parry's arnica, nodding arnica
RM, alpine, subalpine, montane, common,
L Spring–Summer, perennial, 6–20 in.

Herb. Erect stems, single or branched at
flowerheads, from basal rosette that usually
withers when flowering. Basal leaves ovate;
stem leaves lance- to egg-shaped, petiolate, entire, and reducing upward. Yellow discs surrounded by purple-tipped bracts; ray flowers
absent. Found in open forests and meadows,
rarely extending up to alpine zone. Native.

Arnica rydbergii ASTERACEAE
Rydberg's arnica, subalpine arnica
RM, alpine, subalpine, common,
Summer, perennial, 3–14 in.

Herb with erect stems that are solitary or clustered. Basal leaves lanceolate to oval, petiolate,
and in a rosette; stem leaves opposite, in 3 or 4
pairs, lanceolate to spatulate, attached directly
to stem or by short petiole; margins usually
entire and surfaces glandular. Flowerheads
generally solitary but up to 3; 6–10 ray flowers
surround disc. Found on rocky slopes, alpine
meadows, and other exposed dry to moist
areas. Native.

Artemisia frigida ASTERACEAE
prairie sagebrush
RM, throughout, common, Summer–Fall,
perennial, 4–16 in.

Mat-forming, fragrant subshrub with herbaceous stems from a woody crown. Stems
ascending to erect; silvery-woolly. Leaves
silvery-hairy, dense at base; stem leaves alternate, 2 or 3 times ternately divided. Flowers
are small, yellowish, in numerous nodding
heads, in a simple or branched panicle. Fruit
a smooth achene with no pappus. Considered
a host plant for *Castilleja* spp. Found in open
forest, on dry slopes, in dry meadows, and disturbed areas, all life zones except wetlands.
Native.

Artemisia ludoviciana

ASTERACEAE
white sagebrush
RM, subalpine, montane, foothills,
grasslands, common, locally abundant,
Summer–Fall, perennial, 1–3 ft.

Slender erect stems covered in white hairs, from rhizomes. Leaves simple, alternate, sessile, linear to lanceolate, margins entire or with toothed tips, covered in white-woolly hairs, top surface occasionally less hairy to green. Flowers inconspicuous, yellowish, in leafy panicles of numerous heads, dense or loose. Fruit a smooth achene with no pappus. Grows in sunny open prairie and woodlands, disturbed areas, and roadsides. Native.

Artemisia michauxiana
(A. vulgaris ssp. michauxiana)

ASTERACEAE
Michaux's wormwood
RM, alpine, subalpine, montane,
common, Summer, perennial, 5–20 in.

Several stems from woody base; rhizomatous. Leaves alternate, bipinnate into linear segments, green and smooth above, white-woolly below. Yellowish flowers are disciform heads from a spike with bell-shaped involucres; disc and ray flowers present but very small. Fruit a smooth achene. Found on sunny, high rocky slopes and in moist meadows. Native.

Artemisia norvegica
var. saxatilis

(A. arctica) ASTERACEAE
mountain sagewort
RM, alpine, subalpine, montane,
common, Summer, perennial, 7–24 in.

Erect, herbaceous stems, single to several, from a small, branched stem base; smooth to densely hairy; short runners. Basal leaves pinnately divided into linear segments, petiolate, smooth to hairy; few stem leaves, alternate, sessile, smaller toward the terminal end of stem. Flowers yellowish, nodding heads in a narrow spike; ray flowers absent; involucre bracts with dark margins. Fruit a smooth achene. Found in moist or dry meadows, on rocky slopes, and in open forests. Native.

421

Artemisia scopulorum ASTERACEAE
dwarf sagewort
MR, SR, alpine, subalpine, common,
Summer, perennial, 2–14 in.
Herbaceous, gray-green, smooth stems from a
branched, woody base. Basal leaves petiolate,
oblanceolate, bipinnate; stem leaves entire or
pinnate to bipinnate, few, reduced, silky-hairy.
Yellowish nodding flowers, 5–12 in a spike;
involucre bracts with dark margins; ray flowers absent. Fruit a smooth achene. Found
in sunny alpine meadows, rocky places, and in sheltered
areas. Native.

Balsamorhiza hispidula
(*B. hookeri* var. *hispidula*) ASTERACEAE
Hooker's balsamroot, hairy balsamroot
MR, SR, montane, foothills, pinyon-
juniper, sagebrush steppe, locally
abundant, Spring, perennial, 2–16 in.
Solitary flowering stems above bright green
basal leaves. Leaves 6–12 in. long and up to
3 in. wide, hairy and gland-dotted, singly to
doubly pinnate, with pointed tips. Flower
involucre with hairy, lanceolate phyllaries
bell- to dome-shaped, usually 1.2 in. or less in
diameter; ray flowers bright yellow, 0.5–1.75
in. long. Grows in sagebrush meadows, rocky and sandy
sites. Range continues west to NV and southeastern OR.
Native.

Balsamorhiza incana ASTERACEAE
hoary balsamroot
NR, MR, montane, foothills, intermountain
parks, common, Spring–E Summer,
perennial, 8–24 in.
Leaves basal, white to gray, 4–18 in. long by
1–3 in. wide, lanceolate and pinnately divided
to midrib, base triangular, tips rounded, leaf
face usually with soft, tangled hairs. Flowers
solitary; involucre dome-shaped to 1 in. in diameter; outer phyllaries ovate to lanceolate to
0.75 in. long, shorter than the inner phyllaries. Ray flowers bright yellow, 0.75–2 in. long. Found in
grassy meadows and dry, rocky sites. Could be confused
with *B. hookeri*, which also has hairy gray leaves and is
found in parts of ID and UT. Native.

numerous petals, composite, radial

Balsamorhiza macrophylla

ASTERACEAE
cutleaf balsamroot
MR, montane, grasslands, common,
Spring–E Summer, perennial, 12–18 in.
Basal leaves green, 8–20 in. long, sparsely
hairy; lanceolate and pinnately divided,
edges often rolling back so leaf divisions
appear tiered and twisted along central
vein. Flowers usually solitary; involucre
dome-shaped to 1.25 in. in diameter; outer
phyllaries broadly to narrowly lanceolate, to 1.25 in. long.
Ray flowers bright yellow, 1.25–2 in. long. Grows in rocky,
dry sagebrush meadows and conifer forests. May be hybrid
of *B. sagittata* and *B. hispidula*; does not hybridize with
other species. Native.

Balsamorhiza sagittata

ASTERACEAE
arrowleaf balsamroot
RM, montane, foothills, sagebrush
steppe, intermountain parks, common,
Spring–E Summer, perennial, 6–26 in.
Basal leaves on long petioles; leaf triangular to heart-shaped, entire, to 10 in. long,
silvery gray to gray-green, covered in silky
hairs. Flowers solitary, or sometimes up to
3 per stem; involucre dome-shaped or slightly flattened to
1 in. in diameter; outer phyllaries lanceolate or linear, to 1
in. long. Ray flowers bright yellow, to 1.5 in. long. Found in
sagebrush meadows and openings in conifer forests. This
species is known to hybridize with other bal-
samroots where their ranges meet. Native.

Centaurea solstitialis

(*Leucantha solstitialis*) ASTERACEAE
yellow star-thistle
RM, foothills, pinyon-juniper, sagebrush
steppe, grasslands, common, locally
abundant, Spring–Summer, annual, 1–2 ft.
Stems winged, highly branched, shrub-like.
Lower leaves pinnately lobed; upper ones
linear, tomentose, merging with stem
wings. Flowers like small golden thistles, dense disc
flowers, no ray petals; base covered in scale-like phyllaries, each tipped by a vicious spine—use caution! Sunny
disturbed areas, roadsides, gardens, a pernicious pest in
rangelands, agricultural fields. Introduced and invasive.

Coreopsis tinctoria ASTERACEAE
golden tickseed
RM, foothills, pinyon-juniper, sagebrush
steppe, grasslands, common, L
Spring–Summer, annual, 1–2 ft.
Slender erect stems, sometimes with basal
branches. Wispy appearance, leaves pinnate,
lower ones compound, upper less so, linear,
opposite. Terminal flowers in branched clusters of shiny round buds, opening yellow,
or with central red-brown zone; petals have
2 notches, central lobe longest. Reseeds abundantly on
moist streambanks, disturbed sites, and meadows. Attracts pollinators. Native.

Crepis acuminata
(Psilochenia acuminata) ASTERACEAE
tapertip hawksbeard
RM, montane, sagebrush steppe,
grasslands, common, L Spring–
Summer, perennial, 8–28 in.
Swollen woody base with 1–5 stout upright
stems branching near the middle; slightly
hairy near the base. Basal and stem leaves
pinnately lobed about halfway to the midvein, 3–16 in. long and gray-hairy to almost
smooth. Up to 100 flowerheads per stem in
a compound corymb. 5–8 light green phyllaries, lanceolate to 0.5 in. long; 10–18 bright yellow ray flowers to 0.7
in. long. Grows in open places, rocky soil, and sagebrush
meadows. *C. atribarba* and *C. runcinata* have more slender
leaves, the latter lacking deep lobes. Native.

Crepis nana
(Askellia nana) ASTERACEAE
dwarf alpine hawksbeard
RM, alpine, uncommon,
Summer, perennial, 1–8 in.
Low-growing taprooted plant with 1–10 prostrate stems, sometimes branching. Basal
leaves, including long petioles, up to 3.5 in.
long; round or egg-shaped and often purplish;
stem leaves similar, often lacking petioles and
size reduced. Up to 30 flowerheads in rounded compound
corymb, often hidden among leaves; bracts hairless with
5–8 outer ones tapering to a narrow tip; inner bracts twice
as long, purplish and fringed with hairs. Ray flowers yellow, to 0.35 in. long. Found on talus, tundra, moraine and
scree slopes. Native.

numerous petals, composite, radial

Dyssodia papposa
(*Tagetes papposa*) ASTERACEAE
fetid marigold
RM, foothills, pinyon-juniper, sagebrush
steppe, grasslands, common, locally
abundant, Summer, annual, 4–18 in.
Bushy branched plant from single stem,
may be smooth or hairy. Leaves feathery,
pinnately lobed, opposite on lower stems,
may be alternate above; all parts strongly
scented like marigolds when brushed.
Flowers many, at all branch tips; 0.5-in. linear red/orange
bracts surround the compact central disc flowers; 4–8
short yellow ray petals may be present. Fruit an achene.
Found along sunny roadsides, in fields and disturbed sites.
Native.

Encelia nutans
(*Enceliopsis nutans*) ASTERACEAE
nodding sunray
MR, SR, sagebrush steppe, grasslands,
endemic, locally abundant, Spring–
E Summer, perennial, 4–10 in.
Herb. Erect, hairy flower stalks rise singly
from basal leaves; stems and thick rootstock
subterranean. Leaves broad and egg-shaped,
up to 3 in.; surfaces hairless or with stiff,
flattened hairs. Nodding heads of numerous yellow disc
flowers on 4- to 10-in. stalks; rays absent. Phyllaries nearly
equal and lance-shaped. Pappus usually absent. Cypselae notched at tip and hairless, like others in genus.
Found in dry, open areas in heavy soils.
This Colorado Basin endemic is seasonally
drought-deciduous and geophytic. Native.

Enceliopsis nudicaulis ASTERACEAE
nakedstem sunray
MR, SR, sagebrush steppe, intermountain
parks, locally abundant, L Spring–
E Summer, perennial, 6–15 in.
Flowering stems above basal leaves. The
silvery green heart-shaped leaves form a
compact rosette on the ground, very densely
covered with stiff hairs. The flowers are yellow daisies with
gold/orange disc, produced singly on a long pedicel, often
a foot or more in height. The wedge-shaped seeds have distinctive retrorse hairs. Striking herb of sunny areas on dry
shale barrens in lower habitats; enters our range in ID, the
lower Wasatch. Native.

425

Ericameria nana
(Haplopappus nanus) ASTERACEAE
dwarf goldenbush
MR, foothills, pinyon-juniper, sagebrush steppe, common, L Summer–Fall, perennial, 3–18 in.

Low, densely branched resinous shrub. Leaves mainly on upper stems; fleshy, alternate, sticky-resinous, elliptic to spatulate, 0.5 in. long, edges curled in; tiny leaves in axils. Flowerheads clustered at branch tips; 1–7 ray florets with 0.25-in. petals; 4–8 disc florets. Dried involucres often persistent; seeds with 0.25-in. pappus. Found on sunny rocky plains, slopes, and cliffs at mid elevations in the Great Basin, reaching into ID and UT. Native.

Ericameria nauseosa
(Chrysothamnus nauseosus)
ASTERACEAE
rubber rabbitbrush
RM, montane, foothills, pinyon-juniper, sagebrush steppe, intermountain parks, grasslands, common, L Summer–Fall, perennial, 1–6 ft.

Vigorous, variable shrub. Flexible stems blue-green to white, brittle where attached to woody base. Leaves alternate, linear, 1–2.5 in. long, gray-green, stems and leaves with fine white hairs. Small discoid flowers in dense clusters at branch ends; tiny florets tubular, 5 petals fused, star-like at tips, stigma protruding; overall effect is frothy golden mound, tan and persisting in winter. Abundant in most dry lower elevations, roadsides, disturbed sites, washes, forest edges. Native.

Ericameria parryi ASTERACEAE
Parry's rabbitbrush
MR, SR, alpine, subalpine, montane, foothills, pinyon-juniper, sagebrush steppe, common, Summer, perennial, 4–30 in.

Stems greenish when young, turning tan or gray, densely covered in white or grayish fine hairs, spreading to very upright. Leaves alternate, linear, upright, green, may be sticky. Flowers discoid, 5–20 florets larger than other species; in a raceme or spike; phyllaries lanceolate, keeled, sticky. Ray flowers absent. Quite variable. Found in sunny, open slopes, rocky or sandy soils, sagebrush flats, and disturbed sites. Native.

numerous petals, composite, radial

Ericameria suffruticosa
(*Haplopappus suffruticosus*)
ASTERACEAE
singlehead goldenbush
MR, subalpine, montane, common, locally
abundant, Summer, perennial, 6–16 in.
Low shrub with upright stems, fine hairs on
all parts. Alternate leaves to 1.5 in. long, lanceolate, wavy margins, sticky. Flowers 1–3 at
branch tips; compact disc flowers to 0.5 in.
long; leafy bracts below, with leafy-tipped
phyllaries; 1 to several ray flowers likely. Grows on sunny
slopes, rocky ridges, or meadows at high elevations.
Native.

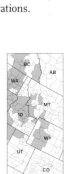

Erigeron linearis
(*E. peucephyllus*) ASTERACEAE
desert yellow fleabane
NR, MR, foothills, sagebrush steppe,
intermountain parks, grasslands, common,
Spring–E Summer, perennial, 3–8 in.
Densely tufted herb, forming low mats 3–8
in. across. One of few yellow erigerons in
the West, the almost silver leaves are 2–4
in. long, narrow, and covered with fine,
stiff hairs, which are distinctive and persist
through flowering. Golden flowerheads 1
in. across. Clasping phyllaries are villous. Widespread at
lower and middle altitudes, primarily in sagebrush steppe,
across the interior Pacific NW. Native.

Eriophyllum lanatum ASTERACEAE
**common woolly sunflower, Oregon
sunshine**
NR, MR, montane, foothills,
grasslands, common, Spring–
Summer, perennial, 4–40 in.
Herb to subshrub with erect or decumbent
white-woolly stems branching from woody
base. Leaves linear to egg-shaped, or pinnately lobed. Single flowers on erect stalks,
with 8–12 rays surrounding numerous yellow disc flowers. Found in rocky, dry areas
from grasslands to forests at moderate elevations. Hybridization among the many varieties occurs. Attracts pollinators. Useful in traditional medicine. Native.

Gaillardia aristata ASTERACEAE
blanketflower
RM, montane, foothills, grasslands,
common, Spring–Summer, perennial, 1–2 ft.
Rough hairy stems, single or branched, from
basal crown. Lower leaves petiolate to 6 in.
long, simple or pinnately cut or notched,
rough with short hairs; upper leaves alternate,
smaller, sessile, entire or with few lobes. Flowers to 3 in. across; mounded dark red-yellow
disc flowers; 12–18 ray flowers, broad at tip,
3-lobed. Variable; many populations are entirely yellow.
Found in open woodlands, sage meadows, and roadsides.
Native.

Grindelia squarrosa ASTERACEAE
curlycup gumweed
RM, montane, foothills, pinyon-
juniper, sagebrush steppe, common,
Summer, perennial, 6–20 in.
Smooth stems, upper half branched. Leaves
smooth, often resinous-sticky, alternate;
upper ones clasping stem, linear to oval, 1–4
in. long; closely set rounded teeth point forward. Sticky flower buds round with recurved
phyllaries evenly spaced, white gummy resin
in center. Dense disc flowers, many outer ray
petals 0.4–0.75 in. long. Rayless forms may be *G. fastigiata*
or other species. Found in sunny forest openings, on disturbed sites, and along roadsides. Native.

Grindelia subalpina ASTERACEAE
subalpine gumweed
MR, SR, subalpine, montane, foothills,
grasslands, common, Summer–Fall,
perennial, 6–15 in.
Smooth stems, upper half branched. Leaves
smooth, often resinous-sticky, alternate,
upper ones clasping stem, linear to oval, 1–4
in. long. Differs from previous by widely
spaced pointed teeth, or may be entire. Sticky
flower buds round with recurved phyllaries
evenly spaced, white gummy resin in center. Dense disc flowers, many outer ray petals 0.4–0.75 in.
long. Found on sunny, open slopes, disturbed sites; sandy
or gravelly soils. Not strictly subalpine, despite common
name. Native.

Gutierrezia sarothrae
(Xanthocephalum sarothrae)
ASTERACEAE

broom snakeweed
RM, montane, foothills, pinyon-juniper,
sagebrush steppe, intermountain
parks, grasslands, common,
Summer–Fall, perennial, 6–20 in.
Subshrub with woody base, slender
branched stems upright, often forming
hemispherical mounds. Leaves alternate,
entire, linear to 2.5 in., smaller on upper stems. Flowers
in small clusters at branch ends; small central disc of 3–9
florets; 2–8 ray flowers 0.25 in. or less. Can be abundant
on roadsides, dry slopes, overgrazed or disturbed sites,
appearing as a collection of golden domes.
Attracts pollinators. Native.

Helenium autumnale ASTERACEAE
common sneezeweed, autumn sneezeweed

RM, montane, foothills, pinyon-
juniper, sagebrush steppe,
grasslands, locally abundant,
Summer–Fall, perennial, 18–48 in.
Plants often densely hairy throughout. Basal
foliage lanceolate, withered at flowering,
distal leaves commonly dentate. Stems conspicuously winged. Ray flowers perpendicular or reflexed
on the ball-shaped inflorescence. Ray flowers yellow, occasionally orange, pistillate and fertile. Disc flowers are
predominantly yellow to brown, moderately hairy. Many
variants. Found along streambeds, in moist
meadows and open forests, along roadsides,
seeps, and wetland areas. Native.

Helianthella parryi ASTERACEAE
Parry's dwarf-sunflower
SR, alpine, subalpine, montane,
common, Summer, perennial, 8–20 in.
Herb with flowering stems above mostly
basal leaves. Leaves lanceolate, under 1
in. wide. Stem leaves reduced. All leaves
roughly hairy. Flowerheads usually solitary
and nodding. Disc and ray flowers yellow; usually 8–10 ray
flowers up to 1.2 in. long. Phyllary bracts behind the flowers are lanceolate, hairy-edged, and imbricate. Found in
aspen and pine forests. Native.

Helianthella quinquenervis
(Helianthus quinquenervis)
ASTERACEAE
fivenerve helianthella
MR, SR, alpine, subalpine,
montane, common, L Spring–
Summer, perennial, 1–5 ft.

Several slender leafy flowering stems above basal leaves. Leaves sparsely hairy (sometimes smooth), up to 4 in. long, lanceolate to egg-shaped; reduced and opposite to subopposite upward. Flowerheads usually solitary and nodding with 13–21 yellow ray flowers. Heads larger than *H. parryi*, with the yellow disc over 1 in. wide. Phyllary bracts are rounded to lanceolate with hairy edges. Found in moist meadows, aspen woodlands. Native.

Helianthella uniflora ASTERACEAE
oneflower helianthella
RM, montane, foothills, sagebrush
steppe, common, Spring–
Summer, perennial, 16–48 in.

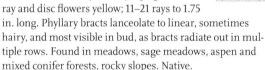

Herb with mostly stem leaves, as basal leaves quickly senesce. Leaves opposite, lanceolate to elliptic, either hairy or smooth, 5–10 in. long. Flowerheads usually solitary, upright. Both ray and disc flowers yellow; 11–21 rays to 1.75 in. long. Phyllary bracts lanceolate to linear, sometimes hairy, and most visible in bud, as bracts radiate out in multiple rows. Found in meadows, sage meadows, aspen and mixed conifer forests, rocky slopes. Native.

Helianthus annuus ASTERACEAE
common sunflower
RM, montane, foothills, sagebrush
steppe, grasslands, common,
Summer–Fall, annual, 2–8 ft.

Thick stems grow quickly, mid-upper portions coarsely branched, all parts rough, hairy. Leaves petiolate; lower opposite to 14 in. long, cordate; upper alternate, size decreasing up stem. Flowers variable; brownish central disc 1–4 in. across with 150 or more florets; showy ray florets 12–30 or more. Edible fruits technically achenes, but shedding their pappus when mature; may be black or striped, glabrous or with small hairs. Hybridizes readily. Found along roadsides, in fields, disturbed sites. Native.

Helianthus nuttallii ASTERACEAE
Nuttall's sunflower
RM, montane, intermountain parks, grasslands, wetlands, common, Summer, perennial, 2–6 ft.
Stems hairy below, more smooth and branched above; rhizomatous roots. Leaves lanceolate, opposite below, may be alternate on upper stems, to 6 in. long. Terminal flowers with yellow central disc less than 1 in. across; 12–21 ray petals to 1 in. long; phyllaries narrow, wavy, pointed, hairy. Most abundant in lowlands, found in moist meadows, along wetland margins, ditches, swales. Native.

Helianthus petiolaris ASTERACEAE
prairie sunflower
RM, sagebrush steppe, grasslands, common, Summer–Fall, annual, 2–4 ft.
Upright stems solitary, or branching from near base, with rough, stiff hairs. Leaves rough, narrow to broadly lanceolate, alternate, 1.5–6 in. long. Terminal flowers; disc brown, 0.5–1 in. across; 15–30 ray petals to 1 in. long. Smaller in all respects than *H. annuus*, but it too hybridizes readily. Can be variable; all forms important for pollinators. Found along sunny roadsides, disturbed sites, dunes; prefers sandy soils. Native.

Helianthus pumilus ASTERACEAE
little sunflower
MR, SR, montane, foothills, grasslands, common, Summer, perennial, 1–2 ft.
Many rough stems from a perennial crown, stiffly hairy, upper ends branching. Leaves oval to lanceolate, opposite, to 1.25 in. long. Flowers 1–6 at branch tips; central disc gold/green to 0.75 in. across; 8–15 ray petals to 1 in. long. Small black seeds within scaly seedhead. Grows in sunny meadows, on dry hillsides, roadcuts, rocky slopes. Native.

Heliomeris multiflora
(*Viguiera multiflora*) ASTERACEAE
showy goldeneye
MR, SR, subalpine, montane,
foothills, common, locally abundant,
L Spring–Fall, perennial, 1–4 ft.

Herbaceous plant from short taproots.
Branching, erect stems finely hairy and
leafy. Leaves mostly opposite, most often
lance-shaped with some variation, often
slightly toothed, coarse, going from
short-stalked to stalkless up the stem. Flowers yellow, 1.2
in. across, with 10–14 ray florets around many disc florets
that form a ball or cone shape. Found in dry, disturbed
areas and openings, meadows, and woodlands. Can be
confused with *Helianthella uniflora*, but is
distinguished by greater numbers of smaller
flowers, rough leaves, and a more branched
structure. Native.

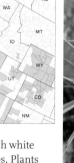

Heterotheca fulcrata
(*H. foliosa*) ASTERACEAE
rockyscree false goldenaster
MR, SR, subalpine, montane, pinyon-
juniper, intermountain parks, uncommon,
Summer–Fall, perennial, 1–2 ft.

Stems are often reddish brown and densely
hairy. Basal leaves are lanceolate and covered with white
hairs. Flowers arranged in open or loose corymbs. Plants
are distinguished by the lanceolate bracts, which are present on most pedicels, subtending the flowers. Found in
sparse gravelly soils, on rocky slopes. Plants
are taller than most members of the genus.
Native.

Heterotheca pumila
(*Chrysopsis alpicola*) ASTERACEAE
alpine false goldenaster
SR, alpine, subalpine, common,
Summer, perennial, to 1 ft.

Multistemmed herb. Leaves to 2.2 in. long,
lanceolate and hairy. Lower leaves senesce
before flowering and will often persist, dry,
until the following growing season. Flowerheads usually
solitary (sometimes up to 9); ray flowers 0.4–0.6 in. long.
Plants grow on scree slopes and tundra. This species,
which can be tall for alpine environments, is restricted to
high elevations in the SR. Native.

Heterotheca villosa
(Chrysopsis villosa) ASTERACEAE
hairy false goldenaster

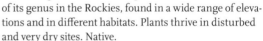

RM, throughout, common, locally abundant, Summer–Fall, perennial, 16 in. Multistemmed herb. Plants form colonies by roots, as well as spread readily by seed. Leaves green to almost silver, to 0.6 in. long, oblanceolate to oblong, hairy. Flowerheads usually solitary. Ray flowers yellow and to 0.8 in. long. Most common representative of its genus in the Rockies, found in a wide range of elevations and in different habitats. Plants thrive in disturbed and very dry sites. Native.

Hieracium scouleri ASTERACEAE
Scouler's woollyweed

NR, MR, subalpine, montane, foothills, sagebrush steppe, grasslands, common, Summer–Fall, perennial, 12–40 in. Rhizomatous herb, stems simple, erect, solitary to few, with milky sap. Herbage sharp hairy below, often glaucous above. Leaves 2–8 in. long, somewhat hairy, linear, mostly entire; reduced, alternate and subsessile upward. Flowers are yellow to orange, dandelion-like, in an open inflorescence. Found in somewhat moist to dry meadows, shrublands, and forest openings. Native.

Hulsea algida
(H. caespitosa) ASTERACEAE
Pacific hulsea, alpinegold

MR, alpine, subalpine, uncommon, L Spring–Summer, perennial, 5–12 in. Coarsely toothed linear leaves, 0.5–1 in. across, in dense, basal tufts. Large golden flowers emerge from woolly buds, often forming an attractive dome of bloom. The entire plant is sticky, with a pervasive, pungent smell. Restricted to steep, often very rough screes in nature. This, the easternmost species in the genus, reaches its southeasternmost limits in our region. Native.

Hymenopappus filifolius

ASTERACEAE
fineleaf hymenopappus
RM, montane, foothills, pinyon-juniper,
sagebrush steppe, intermountain
parks, grasslands, common, L Spring–
Summer, perennial, 4–30 in.

Basal clumps of pinnate, silver filigree leaves,
1–4 in. long, in loose, lacy rosettes. Yellow, rayless flowers in branching panicles on stems
that can be very compact, or tall and rangy.
The 13 distinct varieties that occur in our area are widespread on gravelly, exposed habitats. Native.

Hymenoxys brandegeei

(*Tetraneuris brandegeei*) ASTERACEAE
Brandegee's fournerve daisy
SR, alpine, subalpine, montane,
common, Summer, perennial, 3–10 in.

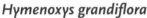

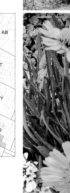

Basal growth from woody branched caudex.
Flowering stems with few alternate linear
leaves decreasing in size, with terminal flowers. Leaves linear, may be forked or lobed,
hairy, 2–4 in. long. Flowers to 1.5 in. across; as
many as 250 disc florets, 14–23 ray florets, petals 0.25–0.35 in. long. Found on sunny, rocky
slopes or in meadows. Similar to *H. grandiflora*, but more southerly. Native.

Hymenoxys grandiflora

(*Tetraneuris grandiflora*) ASTERACEAE
old man of the mountain
MR, SR, alpine, subalpine, common, locally
abundant, Summer, perennial, 3–12 in.

Hairy flowering stems from a branched
woody caudex. Leaves linear with white hairs,
pinnately forked and lobed, alternate on stem.
Flowers solitary, often facing east; showy,
to 3 in. across; up to 400 densely packed
gold-green disc florets, 15–35 ray florets, petals with 1 or 2 notches; phyllaries hairy to
white-woolly. Found on sunny, rocky slopes,
meadows, and ridges. Monocarpic, flowering
after 12–15 years of growth, then dying. Native.

numerous petals, composite, radial

Hymenoxys hoopesii
(Dugaldia hoopesii) ASTERACEAE
orange sneezeweed
MR, SR, subalpine, montane,
intermountain parks, common,
Summer–Fall, perennial, 1–3 ft.
Sturdy vertical stems, glabrous to slightly
hairy, branching at top with 1–12 terminal
flowers. Leaves glabrous, oblong to lanceolate, 3–8 in. long with notable midvein; basal
and alternate up stem. Flowers gold/yellow
to orange, to 3 in. wide; central disc yellow to green/brown;
14–26 ray florets have drooping or twisting 3-lobed petals.
Grows in sunny meadows and forest openings, along roadsides and streambanks. Attracts pollinators. Native.

Hymenoxys richardsonii
ASTERACEAE
Colorado rubberweed
RM, montane, foothills, pinyon-juniper,
sagebrush steppe, grasslands, common,
L Spring–Summer, perennial, 3–18 in.
Many glabrous or lightly hairy upright
stems, branching midway, from branched
woody caudex. Basal leaves, hairy at base,
linear, often forked; alternate on stem,
shorter and forked, 3–5 linear lobes. Flow-
ers 1–7 per stem, 0.75 in. across; 25–75 gold central florets; 7–10 rays, 0.3–0.6 in. long, angled downward, narrow
where attached, with broad 3-lobed tips. The smaller var.
floribunda is less widespread in central and northern areas.
Grows on bare slopes, in gravelly soils, along
roadsides, sage slopes. Native.

Machaeranthera grindelioides
(Xanthisma grindelioides)
ASTERACEAE
rayless tansyaster
RM, montane, pinyon-juniper, sagebrush
steppe, intermountain parks, grasslands,
infrequent, Summer, perennial, 6–18 in.
Compact herb, many stiff stems rising from
a taproot, with many alternate, ovate leaves
1–2 in. long. The spiny, holly-like leaves and twiggy habit
are unusual in low composites where it grows. The involucre has conspicuous, spiny-tipped bracts that curve backward and rayless yellow flowers. Common component of
sunny shale barrens and windswept ridges. Native.

Machaeranthera pinnatifida
(*Haplopappus spinulosum*)
ASTERACEAE
lacy tansyaster, yellow spiny daisy
RM, montane, pinyon-juniper, sagebrush
steppe, intermountain parks, grasslands,
common, Summer, perennial, 6–24 in.

Many wiry stems rising from a stout taproot, clothed with spiny-margined, pinnate
leaves whorled around the stems. These are
branched at the tips with numerous showy
yellow flowers, 1–2 in. across. Widespread in sparse grassland in both the Great Plains and intermountain region.
Native.

Oreochrysum parryi
(*Haplopappus parryi*) ASTERACEAE
Parry's goldenrod
MR, SR, subalpine, montane, common,
Summer–Fall, perennial, to 23 in.
Herb. Erect, usually solitary stems with a purplish base arise from long, thin rhizomes.
Leaves sometimes succulent, alternate, clasping stem, 2.5–6 in. long. Flowers numerous
in corymb-like arrangement, with prominent
yellow rays 0.25–0.4 in., surrounding many
disc flowers. Found in moist to dry forested
areas and meadows. Long rays and leaf-like bracts distinguish it from other "goldenrods." This is the only species
in the genus. Native.

Packera cana
(*Senecio canus*) ASTERACEAE
woolly groundsel
RM, alpine, subalpine, montane,
foothills, grasslands, common, Spring–
Summer, perennial, 4–16 in.
Several herbaceous stems from a taproot; covered in white-woolly hairs. Basal leaves tufted,
ovate to elliptic, petiolate woolly, entire to irregularly lobed; stem leaves sessile, woolly,
alternate, toothed, and strongly reduced toward the top. Flat-topped clusters of 6–15
daisy-shaped flowers; ray and disc flowers present, yellow.
Found on sunny, dry, rocky slopes, forest openings, and
dry meadows. Native.

Packera crocata
(*P. dimorphophylla*) ASTERACEAE
saffron groundsel
MR, SR, alpine, subalpine,
montane, common, L Spring–
Summer, perennial, 4–35 in.

Single (sometimes 2 or 3) herbaceous, glabrous stems from horizontal stem bases. Basal leaves ovate to oblanceolate, petiolate, tapered bases; stem leaves alternate, pinnately lobed or lyrate, sessile, gradually reduced. 7–15 daisy-like flowerheads in rounded clusters; disc and ray flowers present, deep yellow to orange-red. Grows in moist meadows, along trailsides, among rock outcrops and rocky slopes. Native.

Packera fendleri
(*Senecio fendleri*) ASTERACEAE
Fendler's ragwort
SR, subalpine, montane, foothills,
grasslands, common, Spring–
Summer, perennial, 4–16 in.
Loosely tomentose herbaceous stems, 1 to several, from rhizomatous base. Basal leaves petiolate, lanceolate to oblanceolate with tapering bases, margins shallowly pinnatifid or wavy, tomentose; stem leaves alternate, gradually reduced, sessile, lanceolate to oblanceolate, wavy, tomentose. 6–25 daisy-like flowerheads per stem; 6–8 yellow ray flowers, many disc flowers. Grows on dry, rocky slopes, along streamsides, and in disturbed areas. Native.

Packera multilobata
(*Senecio multilobatus*) ASTERACEAE
lobeleaf groundsel
MR, SR, montane, foothills, pinyon-
juniper, sagebrush steppe, common,
Spring–Summer, perennial, 4–20 in.
1–5 loosely clustered, glabrous to sparsely hairy herbaceous stems from woody stem base. Basal leaves petiolate, obovate to oblanceolate, deeply pinnatifid to lyrate; stem leaves alternate, sessile, deeply pinnatifid, reduced. 10–30 yellow, daisy-like flowerheads per stem; 8–13 ray flowers, numerous disc flowers. Found in dry, rocky or sandy soils, in sage meadows and open woodlands. Native.

Packera neomexicana var. mutabilis
(Senecio neomexicanus) ASTERACEAE
New Mexico groundsel
SR, montane, foothills, common,
Spring–Summer, perennial, 8–24 in.

Herbaceous, 1–3 glabrous or tomentose stems from a woody base. Basal leaves lanceolate to oblanceolate, tomentose, margins dentate to crenate; stem leaves alternate, entire to shallowly toothed, abruptly reduced. 3–20 yellow daisy-like flowerheads in rounded clusters; 8 or 13 ray flowers, numerous disc flowers. Grows in sunny meadows and coniferous woodlands. Native.

Packera pseudaurea
(Senecio pseudaureus) ASTERACEAE
falsegold groundsel
RM, montane, foothills, grasslands,
common, Spring–Summer,
perennial, 12–28 in.

Herbaceous, 1–4 glabrous to sparsely hairy stems from simple or branched base. Basal leaves petiolate, ovate to elliptic with bases truncate to cordate, margins pinnately lobed to subentire; stem leaves reduced, alternate, sessile, sometimes clasping, pinnatifid. 5–20 yellow, daisy-like flowerheads in loose or congested arrays. Ray flowers may be absent. In the SR grows var. *flavula*. Grows in moist meadows, forest openings, and along streamsides. Native.

Packera streptanthifolia
(Senecio streptanthifolius)
ASTERACEAE
Rocky Mountain groundsel
RM, subalpine, montane, foothills,
common, Summer, perennial, 4–28 in.

Herbaceous, 1–5 clustered, glabrous stems from woody base. Basal leaves petiolate, thick, rigid, oblong to ovate, margins entire, crenate, or dentate; stem leaves alternate, gradually reduced, becoming sessile, with pinnatifid bases. 6–20 yellow, daisy-like flowerheads in loose clusters; 8–13 ray flowers, numerous disc flowers. Grows in open forests, on rocky, dry hillsides, and moist to dry meadows. Native.

Packera werneriifolia
(*Senecio werneriifolius*) ASTERACEAE
hoary groundsel
MR, SR, alpine, subalpine,
montane, foothills, common,
Summer, perennial, 2–6 in.

Herbaceous, 1–5 clustered, glabrous to
thinly tomentose stems from branched rhizomes. Basal leaves usually sessile, lanceolate to elliptic; margins entire or dentate to
wavy toward tips; stem leaves very reduced,
bract-like, alternate. 1–5 daisy-like, yellow to orange flowerheads in rounded clusters; 8–13 ray flowers (sometimes
absent), numerous disc flowers. Found in sunny, moist
to dry meadows, in forest openings, and on rocky slopes.
Native.

Petradoria pumila ASTERACEAE
rock goldenrod
MR, SR, montane, foothills, pinyon-
juniper, locally abundant, L Spring–
Summer, perennial, to 1 ft.
Stems 1 to many, topping a somewhat woody
base. Basal leaves leathery, linear to lanceolate to 5 in. long with 3–5 veins, withering to gray near base. Stem leaves alternate
and reduced. Flowerheads numerous in a
nearly flat-topped panicle, blooming simultaneously with
2–8 flowers per individual branch. Phyllaries tan with entire margins and tapering to sharply pointed tips; 1–3 ray
flowers yellow to 0.3 in. long. Found on dry slopes. May
be confused with *Gutierrezia sarothrae* or
Chrysothamnus spp. Native.

Picradeniopsis oppositifolia
(*Bahia oppositifolia*) ASTERACEAE
oppositeleaf bahia
RM, pinyon-juniper, sagebrush steppe,
grasslands, common, locally abundant,
Summer, perennial, 2–5 in.
Short tufted plants from rhizomatous roots,
gray-green, branched at base. Leaves pinnate, to 1.5 in., opposite, may have 5 lobes,
but 3 terminal lobes longest and palmate in appearance;
short stiff hairs. Terminal flowers, 30–60 disc florets with
3–8 short ray petals. Sunny plains, clay or gravelly saline
flats, roadsides. Native.

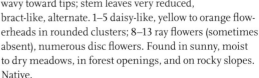

Psilostrophe tagetina ASTERACEAE
woolly paperflower
MR, SR, sagebrush steppe,
grasslands, common, L Spring–
Summer, biennial, 4–18 in.

Basal rosette first year, then mounded,
densely branching. Leaves basal, spatulate,
withered by flowering time; smaller, linear
to spatulate on stems; all parts green-gray
with woolly hairs. Showy flowers 1 in.
across in branched arrays at stem tips; 3–6
lemon-yellow ray flowers are 3-lobed; 6–9 central disc flowers are gold/orange. Flowers dry to a long-lasting papery
tan. Sun; in lower desert and grassland transition zones;
limestone soils, sandy or saline flats, shrublands. Native.

Pyrrocoma crocea
(*Haplopappus croceus*) ASTERACEAE
curlyhead goldenweed
SR, subalpine, montane, intermountain
parks, locally abundant, Spring–E Summer,
perennial, 4–32 in.

Robust herbaceous plants, stems sometimes
hairy. Leaves linear, 3–18 in. long, clasping
stems. Flowerheads single; phyllary bracts in
multiple rows are broad and herbaceous, often
edged in red and sometimes reflexed in bud
and flower. 25–70 bright yellow-orange ray flowers are long
and narrow to 1.4 in. long; disc flowers also yellow to 0.5
in. long. Grows in seasonally moist meadows, forest openings, and along roadsides. The type has the largest flowerheads of the genus. Native.

Pyrrocoma lanceolata
(*Haplopappus lanceolatus*)
ASTERACEAE
lanceleaf goldenweed
RM, montane, sagebrush steppe, locally
abundant, Summer, perennial, 8–20 in.

Single- to multistemmed upright or spreading
herb with basal leaves up to a foot long on petioles; stem leaves much smaller; basal leaves
sharply spiny toothed or entire with pointed
tip, hairy or smooth. Flowers usually 5–20 in panicle-like
array; flowers on short stalks with linear-lanceolate phyllaries in 3 or 4 rows and with a papery base, hairless edges,
tips green. Ray flowers yellow, 18–45, less than 0.5 in. long.
Disc flowers yellow. Grows in moist and alkaline meadows.
Native.

Pyrrocoma uniflora
(*Haplopappus uniflorus*) ASTERACEAE

plantain goldenweed
RM, alpine, subalpine, montane,
sagebrush steppe, locally abundant,
Summer, perennial, 2–16 in.
Herb, sometimes with hairy, reddish stems.
Basal leaves linear to elliptic, 6 in. long by
0.6 in. wide, slightly toothed, narrowly lobed
or entire; often has tufts of hair in leaf axils.
Stem leaves few, reduced, alternate. Flowerheads solitary, rarely up to 4. Phyllary bracts in 2 rows,
green or inner ones with papery bases, narrowly linear,
slightly overlapping. Disc flowers to 0.3 in. long, rays to 0.5
in. long, yellow. Pine forests, alkaline meadows, riparian
areas, near hot springs. Native.

Ratibida columnifera
(*Rudbeckia columnaris*) ASTERACEAE

Mexican hat, prairie coneflower
RM, foothills, grasslands, common,
Summer, perennial, 1–2.5 ft.
Branched stems from basal rosette that
withers by blooming time. Leaves 1–6
in. long, alternate; linear pinnate lobes;
short hairs on leaves and stems. Terminal flowers on slender stems extended
above leaves; 3–7 ray petals 0.75–1.75 in. long, oval with
notched tips, strongly down-curved; yellow, bicolored, or
entirely burgundy-red. Central disc flowers an elongated
gray-green cone, opening brown from the base upward.
Found along roadsides, in forest openings
and meadows. Native.

Rudbeckia hirta ASTERACEAE
black-eyed Susan
RM, montane, foothills, sagebrush
steppe, intermountain parks, common,
locally abundant, L Spring–Summer,
biennial, 1–3 ft.
Herbaceous, erect stems, 1 to several,
branched, hairy. Leaves alternate, lanceolate
to elliptic, hairy, entire margins. Flowerheads with ray and disc flowers. Disc flowers dark purple;
ray flowers 8–20, typically yellow to orange, reflexed; pappus absent. Fruit a small, glabrous, oblong achene. Grows
in open meadows and forests, disturbed sites, and along
roadsides. Several varieties; in the Rockies, it's var. *pulcherrima*. Native.

Rudbeckia laciniata ASTERACEAE
cutleaf coneflower
RM, montane, foothills, grasslands, common,
L Spring–Summer, perennial, 2–10 ft.

Erect, branched herbaceous stems, whitish,
smooth, waxy, from a woody base. Leaves alternate, ovate to lanceolate, mostly trilobed,
deeply pinnatifid with 3–11 lobes, smooth or
hairy below. Flowerheads with 6–13 ray flowers; many disc flowers, yellow; pappus present and short. Fruit a 4-angled achene. Lower
leaves may remain green through winter. Grows in moist
meadows, along streambanks and roadsides, in open
woods and other moist sites. One of the tallest yellow composites in the region. Native.

Scabrethia scabra
(Wyethia scabra) ASTERACEAE
Badlands mule-ears
MR, SR, pinyon-juniper, sagebrush
steppe, common, L Spring–
Summer, perennial, 14–24 in.

Stems and leaves coarse, hairy, sandpapery;
many emerging from woody crown. Leaves
alternate, lanceolate to 6 in. long, prominent
midrib, persisting dried gray-brown on the
stems when dormant in winter. Flowers ter-
minal or on short lateral stems, 4 in. across; ray petals to
1.75 in., central disc gold, aging brown. Showy sun-lover
of the high desert, sandy soils, canyon country between
mountain ranges. Native.

Senecio amplectens
(Ligularia amplectens) ASTERACEAE
showy alpine ragwort
MR, SR, subalpine, montane, common,
L Spring–Summer, perennial, 16–28 in.

Single or loosely clustered stems from rhizomes or branched caudices; herbaceous,
glabrous or sparsely hairy. Leaves alternate, primarily on lower and middle stem,
reduced above, ovate to obovate, petiolate,
purple-tinged, margins dentate. 1–5 nodding,
yellow flowerheads, 13 ray flowers, involucre bracts dark.
Found in sunny to shady forests and meadows. Native.

Senecio amplectens var. holmii
(*Ligularia amplectens* var. *holmii*)
ASTERACEAE
Holm's ragwort
MR, SR, alpine, locally abundant,
Summer, perennial, 5–10 in.

Single or loosely clustered stems from rhizomes or branched caudices; herbaceous, glabrous or sparsely hairy. Leaves primarily basal, ovate to obovate, petiolate, purple-tinged, margins dentate. 1–5 nodding, yellow flowerheads, 13 ray flowers, involucre bracts glabrous, purplish. Shorter and more compact than the type. Found in sunny to shady forests and meadows. Native.

Senecio atratus ASTERACEAE
tall blacktip ragwort
SR, alpine, subalpine, montane, common,
Summer, perennial, 15–30 in.
Herbaceous, 1 to few stems from rhizomes; erect, floccose-tomentose to canescent. Leaves alternate, reduced above, oblong-ovate to oblanceolate, petiolate, margins dentate with dark teeth. Numerous yellow flowerheads in flat-topped cymes, 5 or 8 involucre bracts, 3–5 ray flowers. Found in sunny disturbed areas, along roadsides, and on open slopes in rocky soils. The most common senecio along high roadcuts. Native.

Senecio bigelovii
(*Ligularia bigelovii*) ASTERACEAE
nodding ragwort
SR, subalpine, montane, foothills, common,
L Spring–Summer, perennial, 8–40 in.

Single to few stems from woody base; herbaceous, floccose-tomentose (sometimes glabrous). Leaves alternate, reduced toward top, ovate to lanceolate, bases tapered, margins serrate to dentate or subentire; petiolate below, sessile to clasping above. Numerous yellow, nodding flowerheads with 13–21 involucre bracts, ray flowers absent. Populations have yellow or maroon bracts, the maroon bracts being quite striking. Grows on dry, open hillsides, in meadows and forests. Native.

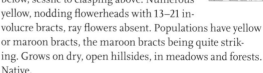

Senecio crassulus ASTERACEAE
thickleaf ragwort
RM, alpine, subalpine, montane, common,
Summer–Fall, perennial, 10–24 in.
Single to few, herbaceous, glabrous stems
from branched rhizomes. Leaves alternate,
thick, elliptic to broadly oblanceolate, entire
to sharply dentate, petiolate below, sessile and
clasping above. 4–12 yellow flowerheads with
8–13 ray flowers in branched, open inflorescence. Grows on sunny, dry to moist slopes, in
meadows and open forests. Native.

Senecio eremophilus ASTERACEAE
desert ragwort
RM, subalpine, montane, foothills, common,
L Spring–Summer, perennial, 1–3 ft.
Single to few, glabrous stems from branched
caudices. Leaves alternate, petiolate or sessile, ovate or lanceolate to narrowly lanceolate,
pinnate to lacerate or dentate. Numerous yellow flowers in corymbs; ray and disc flowers
present, 8–13 ray florets. Highly variable; 2 varieties occur in our region. Found along roadsides and streamsides, in meadows and open
forests. Native.

Senecio fremontii ASTERACEAE
dwarf mountain ragwort
RM, alpine, subalpine, common,
Summer–Fall, perennial, 3–14 in.
Herbaceous stems freely branching from
a spreading, woody base; glabrous, often
purple-tinged. Leaves alternate, petiolate,
ovate or obovate to oblanceolate; margins
laciniate to dentate or subentire; evenly distributed along stems, reduced below. Single
yellow flowerheads at branch tips, 8 ray flowers, disc flowers present. Variable; 2 varieties in our region. Found in open forests and
along roadsides and streamsides. Native.

Senecio integerrimus ASTERACEAE
lambstongue ragwort
RM, alpine, subalpine, montane,
foothills, common, L Spring–
Summer, perennial, 10–14 in.
Herbaceous single erect stems from woody
base; glabrescent, loosely tomentose or villous. Leaves alternate, petiolate below, sessile and reduced above; lanceolate, elliptic, entire or irregularly dentate. Numerous, yellow or cream heads in congested inflorescences, 8–13 ray flowers, 13–21 involucre bracts. Variable; 4 varieties recognized in the Rockies. Grows in sunny open places. Native.

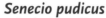

Senecio pudicus
(Ligularia pudica) ASTERACEAE
bashful ragwort
MR, SR, alpine, subalpine, montane,
common, Summer–Fall, perennial, 8–16 in.
Single, sometimes few, glabrous stems
from woody base. Leaves alternate, petiolate
below, reduced and sessile above; narrowly
lanceolate to oblanceolate; margins entire or
dentate. Nodding heads in racemes or panicles; yellow, ray flowers absent. Grows in
sun on rocky slopes and in coniferous and
aspen woodlands. Similar to but smaller than, in all
aspects, *S. bigelovii*. Native.

Senecio serra ASTERACEAE
tall ragwort, sawtooth groundsel
RM, montane, foothills, common,
Summer–Fall, perennial, 16–72 in.
Herbaceous, single or few stems from
branched caudices; glabrous or lightly
floccose-tomentose when young. Leaves
alternate, evenly distributed; petiolate to
subsessile; lanceolate to narrowly lanceolate or elliptic; margins sharply toothed;
lower leaves often withered at flowering.
Numerous yellow flowerheads, 8–13 involucre bracts with black tips; 5–8 ray flowers.
Found in meadows, on moist hillsides and streamsides,
and in aspen forests. Forms large colonies by rhizomes.
Native.

Senecio soldanella
(*Ligularia soldanella*) ASTERACEAE
Colorado ragwort
SR, alpine, locally abundant,
Summer, perennial, 3–8 in.

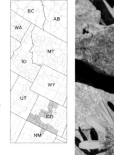

Single herbaceous stems from branched caudices; glabrous, often purple-tinted. Leaves mostly basal, purple-tinged, petiolate, broadly ovate to obovate, weakly dentate to subentire, stem leaves reduced and alternate. Solitary, nodding yellow flowerheads with around 13 ray flowers. Found in coarse scree, on sunny, rocky alpine slopes. Native.

Senecio spartioides
(*S. andersonii*) ASTERACEAE
broom-like ragwort
MR, SR, montane, foothills, pinyon-juniper, grasslands, common,
Summer–Fall, perennial, 10–28 in.

Multiple or single stems from taproots forming woody crowns; herbaceous, erect, glabrous or sparsely hairy. Leaves alternate, narrowly linear to filiform, entire, sessile, evenly distributed. 10–20 yellow flowerheads in corymb-like arrays, 5–13 ray flowers. Grows in sunny, dry disturbed sites, along streambanks, and on hillsides. Native.

Senecio taraxacoides
(*Ligularia taraxacoides*) ASTERACEAE
dandelion ragwort
SR, alpine, subalpine, uncommon,
Summer–Fall, perennial, 2–8 in.

Single or loosely clustered herbaceous stems from branched caudices. Leaves basal, floccose-tomentose, petiolate, oblanceolate to ovate; margins sharply and deeply dentate. 1–3 nodding yellow flowerheads with up to 13 ray flowers, or sometimes none. Uncommon on scree slopes in the alpine. Found only in CO and NM. Native.

Senecio triangularis
(*S. gibbonsii*) ASTERACEAE
arrowleaf ragwort
RM, subalpine, montane, common,
Summer, perennial, 1–5 ft.
Herbaceous, tall upright stems. Leaves alternate, triangular with saw-toothed margins; up to 8 in. long, leaf base 0.75–4 in. wide. Flowerheads 10–30 in a corymb-like array. Ray flowers usually 8, up to 0.5 in. long. Found near streams and in moist meadows. Could be confused with *S. serra*; *S. triangularis* is more common, has broader leaf bases, and is found in wetter sites. Native.

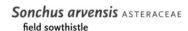

Sonchus arvensis ASTERACEAE
field sowthistle
RM, montane, foothills, wetlands, common, Summer, perennial, 1–6 ft. Erect, solitary, herbaceous, lightly branched stems; smooth below, hairy above; exude milky sap when broken. Leaves alternate, prickly-margined, pinnately lobed to pinnatifid, reduced higher up; clasping bases. Several flowerheads up to 1.5 in. across: all florets including disc have rays, though central ones are smaller, finer, giving fuzzy appearance. Unusual plant with its tall stem with few leaves. Found in disturbed areas, dry to wet meadows, and ditches. Introduced.

Sphaeromeria capitata
(*Tanacetum capitatum*) ASTERACEAE
rock tansy
MR, SR, sagebrush steppe, intermountain parks, infrequent, locally abundant, Spring-E Summer, perennial, 3–7 in.
Compact herb forming prostrate, almost woody mats. Leaves narrowly 3-lobed (or more) in compact rosettes, silvery white with hairs. Spherical clusters of rayless flowers on short upright stems in early summer. Can resemble buckwheats, but entire plant is intensely aromatic. Dry slopes or barrens, sage meadows and gravelly ledges; rare in parts of its range. Native.

Stenotus acaulis
(*Haplopappus acaulis*) ASTERACEAE
stemless mock goldenweed
RM, montane, foothills, pinyon-juniper,
sagebrush steppe, intermountain parks,
common, L Spring–E Summer,
perennial, 2–10 in.

Dense, mat-forming evergreen cushion plant.
Narrow leaves 1–4 in. long in lax rosettes, dark
green and leathery. Flowers are single heads
with 5–7 ray flowers on low stems; deep yellow
verging on orange. Conspicuous in gravelly or shaly areas
in steppe. Quite variable in size, depending on rainfall and
habitat. Native.

Stenotus armerioides
(*Haplopappus armerioides*)
ASTERACEAE
thrift mock goldenweed
RM, foothills, pinyon-juniper, sagebrush
steppe, intermountain parks, common,
L Spring–E Summer, perennial, 6–17 in.

Low clumps, often expanding outward from
bare center of dead leaves and stems. Leaves
basal, stiff, dark green, lanceolate, up to 3 in.
long. Many flowering stems of single heads
with 6–12 lanceolate ray flowers around a
golden disc. Grows on sunny, rocky slopes, ledges,
barrens, and in sage meadows. Native.

Tanacetum vulgare
(*Chrysanthemum vulgare*)
ASTERACEAE
common tansy
RM, foothills, grasslands, locally abundant,
L Summer–Fall, perennial, 1–4 ft.

Spreading rhizomes form dense colonies
with smooth, branched stems. Leaves 4–8
in. long, 1–2 in. wide, fern-like, hairless, dotted with glands, cut pinnately into linear
sharp-toothed lobes. Inflorescence with 20–
200 yellow flowers in flat, dense, button-like
clusters; no ray flowers. Grows in sunny,
disturbed areas, meadows, and urban areas. Brought to
America as a cultivated herb to repel insects and induce
menstruation and abortion; now often considered a noxious weed. Skin irritation possible. Introduced.

numerous petals, composite, radial

Taraxacum lyratum ASTERACEAE
harp dandelion, alpine dandelion
RM, alpine, subalpine, montane,
common, Summer, perennial, 0.4–2 in.
Herbaceous plant from branched taproot.
Stems ascending to erect, glabrous, and
slightly reddish purple. Long leaves form
a basal rosette, linear- to narrowly oblanceolate, pinnately cut into triangular lobes.
Flowers a yellow, solitary head with 35–50
ray florets. Involucre bracts campanulate to
cylindric, very dark green with hints of purple. Found in
dry to well-drained areas on ridges, barrens, and tundra.
Native.

Taraxacum officinale ASTERACEAE
common dandelion
RM, throughout, common,
Spring–Fall, perennial, 2–8 in.
Herbaceous plant from thick taproot. Erect
stems are leafless and tubular, with a hollow interior; they exude a milky sap when
damaged. Long leaves form a basal rosette; pinnately cut into triangular, reflexed
lobes. Flowers a yellow, solitary head with
more than 70 ray florets, 1–2 in. across.
Bracts bend backward around the base,
forming a cup. Fruit a brown to olive achene with long,
parachute-like bristles, easily carried by the wind. Found
in disturbed areas, meadows. One of the most common
and aggressive European species. Introduced and invasive.

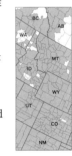

Taraxacum ovinum
(T. ceratophorum) ASTERACEAE
alpine dandelion
RM, alpine, subalpine, montane, common,
Spring–Summer, perennial, 4–7 in.
Herbaceous plant from branched taproot. Stems purple-tinged, ascending to
erect, cobwebby when young, becoming
glabrous in age. Leaves form a basal rosette, with blades narrowly oblanceolate to
linear-oblanceolate or linear-oblong, with
deep margins. Phyllary tips are often swollen and reddish
in color, commonly with horns. Flowers a yellow, solitary head with 40–80 or more ray florets. Found in openings, on tundra, moist meadows, streambanks, and rocky
slopes. Native.

Tetradymia canescens ASTERACEAE

spineless horsebrush
RM, foothills, pinyon-juniper,
sagebrush steppe, common,
Summer–Fall, perennial, 7–28 in.
Compact shrub with sparsely branched,
upright white tomentose stems. Leaves
densely white-haired, linear, 1–2 in. long.
Clusters of orange-yellow disc flowers, each
with 5 reflexed petal-like segments, held in
few-flowered heads with conspicuously exserted stigma. Widespread in sagebrush and juniper
steppe. Native.

Tetraneuris acaulis

(*Hymenoxys acaulis*) ASTERACEAE

**stemless fournerve daisy, stemless
hymenoxys**
RM, throughout, common, L Spring–
Summer, perennial, 1–17 in.
Stemless unless flowering, with rosettes,
often densely tomentose and compact. Leaves
basal, linear to spatulate, 1–2 in. long. Smooth
or lightly hairy flower stems with solitary yellow daisies; ray petals notched at tips, disc
golden. Highly variable and widespread, with
many subspecies. Found on gravelly slopes
and in sage meadows, from Great Plains to alpine tundra,
all life zones except wetlands. Native.

Tetraneuris torreyana

(*Hymenoxys depressa*) ASTERACEAE

Torrey's fournerve daisy
MR, SR, foothills, pinyon-juniper, sagebrush
steppe, intermountain parks,
grasslands, locally abundant, L Spring–
E Summer, perennial, 3–12 in.
Similar to *T. acaulis* in general appearance;
usually shorter, and distinguished by the
margin of the outer involucre bract always
being scarious, as well as its leaves being consistently dotted with glands. Grows on dry
slopes, in meadows and pine parklands. More
limited range and elevation than *T. acaulis*. Native.

Thelesperma filifolium

ASTERACEAE
stiff greenthread
MR, SR, foothills, grasslands, common,
L Spring–Fall, annual/perennial, 10–20 in.
Herbaceous, short-lived, often found growing in colonies. Slender stems wiry, brittle
at base, rising from a central crown. Fine
leaves are opposite, filiform, much-divided,
dark green or slightly glaucous. Showy
Coreopsis-like daisy flowers after rains. Disc
flowers reddish brown to yellow with reddish brown veins;
ray flowers 8, yellow. Found in rocky or sandy soils in open
places, often in disturbed areas. Conspicuous during years
of heavy summer monsoons on Great Plains grasslands
and sparse rangelands. Native.

Thelesperma subnudum

ASTERACEAE
Navajo tea
RM, foothills, pinyon-juniper, sagebrush
steppe, intermountain parks, grasslands,
common, Spring–Summer,
perennial, 4–12 in.
Stemless unless flowering; basal rosettes
from rhizomes forming small colonies.
Leaves opposite, lowest ones petiolate, 3 or
more deep linear lobes; cauline leaves smaller and few,
near base of flower stem. Flowers single, terminal; ray petals variable: 0 or 8, around a gold center of disc flowers.
Found in sunny forest openings, talus slopes, sage meadows. Native.

Tonestus lyallii

(*Haplopappus lyallii*) ASTERACEAE
Lyall's goldenweed
RM, alpine, subalpine, locally abundant,
Summer–Fall, perennial, 3–8 in.
Herbaceous, from branched roots and often
creeping rhizomes. Upright stems tufted,
leafy, and densely glandular. Leaves entire,
alternate, oblanceolate to spoon-shaped,
0.5–2 in. long, becoming reduced up the
stem. Flowers 1–2 in. across, a yellow, solitary head with
15–35 ray florets around a cluster of disc florets. Involucre
bracts a dark greenish purple, forming a hairy cup. Found
on rock ledges, in open forests, sandy slopes, and meadows. Native.

Tonestus pygmaeus
(*Haplopappus pygmaeus*) ASTERACEAE
pygmy goldenweed
SR, alpine, subalpine, common,
locally abundant, L Spring–
Summer, perennial, 0.4–3.5 in.

Herbaceous, forming mounds 3–12 in. wide.
Stems hairy, lacking glands. Leaves alternate,
entire, broadly lanceolate to oblong, 0.4–2 in.
long, curl inward or are flat, densely ciliate,
distinctly veined. Flower a yellow, solitary
head with 10–16 ray florets around a cluster of 43–66 disc
florets; the curves of the ray petals make them appear
crumpled or aged. Phyllaries directly under the flower are
wide and blunt. Found on tundra, alpine meadows, dwarf
coniferous forests, and often in the stony soil
around larger rocks. Native.

Tragopogon dubius
(*T. major*) ASTERACEAE
western salsify
RM, montane, foothills, pinyon-juniper,
sagebrush steppe, intermountain
parks, grasslands, common, Spring–
Summer, annual/biennial, 1–3 ft.

Erect, herbaceous stems woolly when young,
smooth when mature with milky sap. Leaves
alternate, clasping, linear, entire, simple. Flowers solitary
heads, terminal; disc flowers absent, ray flowers yellow,
nodding at maturity. Fruit an achene, slender, brown,
tipped with feathery white hairs, the whole appearing like
a large dandelion seedhead. Found in dis-
turbed areas, meadows, gardens, and along
roadsides. Introduced.

Verbesina encelioides ASTERACEAE
golden crownbeard, cowpen daisy
MR, SR, foothills, pinyon-juniper,
sagebrush steppe, grasslands, common,
Summer–Fall, annual, 9–40 in.

Tall, rank plant. Leaves dusty gray, deltoid or
ovate, deeply dentate on margins. Flowers resemble sunflowers or tall yellow daisies; ray
flowers often have notched or lobed ends. Usually found
on heavily disturbed sites of Great Plains and lower elevations. The strong scent discourages herbivores. Native.

Wyethia amplexicaulis

ASTERACEAE

mule-ears

RM, subalpine, montane, foothills, pinyon-juniper, sagebrush steppe, grasslands, common, locally abundant, Spring–Summer, perennial, 1–2 ft.

Taprooted perennial; all parts glabrous. Basal leaves elliptic-lanceolate; shiny crisp green, leathery, upright to 14 in. long, slightly wavy edge; a few alternate and reduced on flowering stems. Flowers outfacing golden daisies at stem tips, 1 or 2 more in leaf axils below terminal flower; 3–5 in. across; disc flowers age brown. Found in sunny forest openings, grass and sage meadows; often in large colonies. Hybrids with *W. arizonica* can be hard to distinguish. Native.

Wyethia arizonica ASTERACEAE

Arizona mule-ears

SR, montane, sagebrush steppe, common, locally abundant, L Spring– Summer, perennial, 8–30 in.

Flowering stems coarse, hairy. Basal leaves elliptic with wavy edges, distinct petioles; 5–14 in. long by 2–4 in. wide, usually with rough hairs on all parts; flowering stems with smaller narrow alternate leaves. Flowers 1–4 in terminal arrays; 3–5 in. across, hairy sepals; 11–14 ray petals, central disc florets gold, aging brown. Primarily a Four Corners distribution. Found among sagebrush, in meadows and forest openings. Native.

Wyethia ×*magna* ASTERACEAE

mule-ears

SR, montane, sagebrush steppe, grasslands, endemic, infrequent, locally abundant, L Spring– Summer, perennial, 20–30 in.

Basal leaves 8–14 in. long, lanceolate to ovate, usually shiny, glabrous, prominent midvein. Stems slightly hairy with smaller alternate leaves that clasp stem. Flowers terminal, though stems often branch at upper leaf nodes with additional flowers. Flowers to 4 in. across; 10–13 ray petals. Sunny montane forest openings, sage meadows; mainly western CO, possible in adjacent UT, NM. A stable hybrid of *W. amplexicaulis* and *W. arizonica*. Native.

Dryas drummondii ROSACEAE
Drummond's mountain-avens
NR, MR, alpine, subalpine, montane,
foothills, common, locally abundant,
L Spring–Fall, perennial, 1–9 in.

Mat-forming herb. Leaves oblong to elliptic,
0.5–1.5 in. long, round-toothed margins often
roll under; leathery; top dark green, bottom
white and woolly. Leaves stay green long into
winter; die back with new leaves in spring.
Scapes 2–8 in. long, leafless, hairy. Flowers
solitary, nodding to ascending, 8–10 elliptic petals, never
seem to fully open. Calyx covered in dark hairs. Stamens
numerous. Fruit numerous achenes. Occurs from high
to low elevations along streambanks in calcareous soils.
Native.

Solidago canadensis
(*S. altissima*) ASTERACEAE
Canada goldenrod
RM, montane, foothills, grasslands,
common, L Summer–Fall, perennial, 1–6 ft.

Erect and robust unbranched stems from
creeping rhizomes, herbaceous; solitary
or clustered, hairy. Leaves alternate, simple, linear-lanceolate to lanceolate, strongly
3-nerved, densely hairy below, smooth above;
margins serrate for half of length or more. Open or dense
panicle-like inflorescence of flowerheads with yellow ray
and disc flowers; 10–18 ray florets, 2–8 disc florets. Found
along roadsides, in disturbed areas and open woods, on
hillsides. Native.

Solidago missouriensis ASTERACEAE
Missouri goldenrod
RM, montane, foothills, grasslands,
common, Summer–Fall, perennial, 1–3 ft.

Erect, smooth herbaceous stems from a creeping rhizome or woody base; solitary or few,
typically unbranched. Leaves alternate, simple, linear lanceolate to oblanceolate, 3-nerved,
sessile, smooth, reduced upward; margins entire. Terminal panicle-like inflorescence wider
than tall; flowers with 7–13 yellow ray florets, 9–13 yellow
disc florets. Grows in dry, open sites, meadows, disturbed
areas, and roadsides. Native.

numerous petals, radial

numerous petals, elongated clusters, radial

Solidago simplex
(S. spathulata ssp. glutinosa)
ASTERACEAE

Mt. Albert goldenrod, sticky goldenrod
RM, alpine, subalpine, montane, foothills,
common, Summer–Fall, perennial, 2–24 in.
Erect to ascending herbaceous stems from
stout rhizome or woody stem base; solitary
to few, simple, smooth. Basal leaves oblanceolate to spoon-shaped, toothed or entire,
rounded, petiolate; stem leaves alternate,
few. Inflorescence of yellow heads with long peduncles in
paniculate arrays; 8–12 ray florets, 6–31 disc florets. Moist
meadows and forests, rocky slopes, disturbed areas. Native.

Solidago velutina ssp. sparsiflora
(S. sparsiflora) ASTERACEAE
threenerve goldenrod
MR, SR, montane, foothills, sagebrush
steppe, grasslands, common, locally
abundant, Summer–Fall, perennial, 6–32 in.
Erect to ascending single stems from the
tips of rhizomes forming groups; herbaceous, sparsely to densely hairy. Leaves alternate, elliptic to spoon-shaped; short-hairy,
3-nerved, margins entire; basal leaves present at flowering. Dense to open inflorescence of numerous
yellow heads in paniculate arrays; 6–12 ray florets, 5–17
disc florets. Open slopes, mountain meadows, forest clearings and edges, disturbed areas. Native.

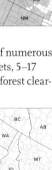

Cirsium parryi ASTERACEAE
Parry's thistle
SR, alpine, subalpine, montane,
endemic, common, L Spring–Summer,
biennial/perennial, 1–6 ft.
Herb with single erect stem, finely hairy to
cobwebby, from taproot. Basal (mostly absent by flowering) and alternate stem leaves,
4–12 in., not decurrent; oblong to lanceolate;
entire, wavy-margined, or pinnatifid; small
spines present. Surfaces smooth and green
above and cobwebby below. Greenish yellow discoid flowers,
1 to many, terminal and in leaf axils, subtended by spiny
bracts. Involucres cobwebby; phyllaries without glutinous
dorsal ridge and spines appressed. Moist meadows, streambanks, open forests. Endemic to CO, NM, AZ. Native.

Cirsium scopulorum
(C. eatonii var. eriocephalum)
ASTERACEAE
mountain thistle
SR, alpine, subalpine, common,
Summer, biennial, 0.5–6 ft.

Herb with erect to ascending stems from
taproot. Basal and alternate stem leaves 1–14
in. long, decurrent, narrowly lanceolate, pinnatifid; marginal spines; mostly smooth
above, white-woolly or cobwebby below. Inflorescence a large, heavy, dense, often nodding cluster
of discoid flowers with yellow, white, or pale pink rays.
Involucres densely white-woolly with 0.4–0.7 in. phyllary
spines. Grows in meadows, forest openings, and on tundra
and scree at high elevations, especially along
the Continental Divide. Native.

Solidago multiradiata ASTERACEAE
Rocky Mountain goldenrod
RM, alpine, subalpine, montane, foothills,
common, Summer–Fall, perennial, 2–20 in.

Erect herbaceous stems from a short rhizome
or branched woody base; slender, smooth to
sparsely hairy. Leaves alternate, oblanceolate
to spoon-shaped, petiolate toward basal end,
clasping higher up; margins ciliate and entire.
Inflorescence a dense cluster of yellow flowers from hairy
branches; 12–18 ray florets, 10–35 disc florets. Hybridizes
with S. simplex at higher elevations. Found in rocky soils
on tundra, slopes, and in meadows. Native.

Solidago nana
(S. nivea) ASTERACEAE
baby goldenrod
RM, montane, foothills, pinyon-juniper,
sagebrush steppe, grasslands, common,
L Summer–Fall, perennial, 4–20 in.

Single to few herbaceous stems from stout
rhizomes or woody, branched stem bases;
decumbent to ascending, hairy. Leaves alternate, oblanceolate to spoon-shaped, petiolate
toward base, sessile higher up, short-hairy,
margins entire to toothed toward tips. Densely packed inflorescences of 30–100 yellow flowers in corymbiform arrays; fewer ray florets (6–10) than disc florets (8–20). Found
in dry to wet alkaline meadows and flats, open woodlands,
and on slopes. Native.

Escobaria missouriensis

CACTACEAE

Missouri foxtail cactus
MR, SR, montane, foothills, pinyon-juniper,
sagebrush steppe, grasslands, infrequent,
L Spring–E Summer, perennial, 1–3 in.
Plants may be solitary or heavily branched
forming large clumps up to a foot across.
Branching and clumping tends to be more
common east of the Continental Divide.
Central spines are absent with 10–20 radial
spines per areole. Spines are straight, yellowish to brown.
Flowers are yellow to cream, sometimes red at base of petals. Bright red fruit. Occurs in sun, dry slopes, and diverse
substrates. Native.

Opuntia fragilis CACTACEAE

brittle pricklypear
RM, montane, foothills, pinyon-juniper,
sagebrush steppe, intermountain parks,
grasslands, common, L Spring–Summer,
perennial, 1–4 in.
Succulent stem segments dark green,
spheric to cylindric; form low mats and de-
tach from each other easily. Each segment
1–2 in. long. Spines are gray with brown
tips; straight. Typically 3–8 spines per areole. Glochids present at each areole tan to brown, inconspicuous. Flowers usually yellow, sometimes red at base
of petals; 1–2 in. across. Fruit is tan, smooth, 1–1.5 in.,
with some areoles bearing 1–6 short spines. Meadows and
woodlands, in sandy or gravelly soils, and
on granite and limestone outcrops. Native.

Opuntia macrorhiza CACTACEAE

twistspine prickly pear
MR, SR, foothills, sagebrush steppe,
grasslands, common, L Spring–
E Summer, perennial, 3–6.5 in.
Succulent lax stem segments dark green,
flattened, obovate to circular, 2–4.5 in. long.
Plants form clumps from tuber-like roots.
Typically 1–4 white to reddish brown spines
per areole toward the edges of the pads, to 2.5 in. Fewer
spines than other padded species. Dense tufts of glochids
present at each areole; pale yellow to red-brown. Yellow
flowers with red basal coloring. Fleshy fruits dull red,
edible. Dry rocky, sandy soils. Native.

Opuntia polyacantha CACTACEAE
plains pricklypear
RM, montane, foothills, pinyon-juniper,
sagebrush steppe, intermountain
parks, grasslands, common, L Spring–
E Summer, perennial, 3.5–5 in.

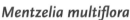

Succulent, flattened, green stem segments
not easily detached; elliptic to broadly ovate.
Stems grow upright, branching outward to
form colonies. Spination variable, often dense;
white to gray spines, many glochids. Simple,
showy flowers; variable: yellow, pink, or orange. Stamens
on most opuntias are thigmonastic: they bend toward the
center when touched by insects (or a finger)—a mecha-
nism that aids pollination. Fruits dry at maturity. Grows in
dry, sandy, gravelly soils in sun. In the western U.S. and northern Mexico, 5 varieties are
recognized. Native.

Mentzelia multiflora
(Nuttallia multiflora) LOASACEAE
Adonis blazingstar
SR, montane, foothills, pinyon-juniper,
sagebrush steppe, grasslands, common,
Spring–Summer, perennial, 16–31 in.

Erect, hairy, herbaceous, whitish stems; usually branched. Leaves alternate, sessile, elliptic
to lanceolate, shallowly to deeply pinnatifid. Yellow (occasionally white) star-like flowers in cymes; 10 petals, open in
late afternoon. Grows in dry, sandy soils, along roadsides,
and in disturbed areas. Native.

Mentzelia speciosa
(Nuttallia speciosa) LOASACEAE
jeweled blazingstar
SR, montane, foothills, pinyon-
juniper, sagebrush steppe, common,
L Spring–Summer, biennial, 1–2 ft.

Stems herbaceous, slender, white, branched,
sometimes perennial. Leaves alternate,
stiff-hairy, lack broad clasping base; linear to
oblanceolate, shallowly pinnatifid. Bright yellow flowers with 10 petals, 5 sepals. Flowers
are brighter yellow than previous species. Grows in sandy
soils in open forest to dry, rocky slopes. Native.

Nuphar polysepala
(N. lutea ssp. polysepala)

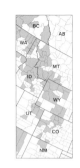

NYMPHAEACEAE

Rocky Mountain pond-lily
RM, subalpine, montane, foothills,
wetlands, infrequent, locally abundant,
Summer, perennial, floating to 12 in.
Aquatic; thick underwater rhizomes in
muddy pond or lake bottoms, 1–8 ft. deep.
Leaves rich green, heart-shaped, 4–16 in.
long; floating or emerging above surface.
Flowers 2–4 in. across; 6–9 showy round sepals, globe-like
on sturdy stem at or above surface. Central stigma
disc-shaped, yellow with radial lines; reddish stamens. In
northern areas, may occur in lakes, ditches, ponds of lower
or mid elevations; in the SR, restricted to
subalpine or montane lakes, less common,
but abundant in some sites. Native.

Trollius albiflorus
(T. laxus) RANUNCULACEAE

American globeflower
RM, alpine, subalpine, montane, common,
L Spring–Fall, perennial, 3–22 in.
Herbaceous perennial with erect stems.
Basal leaves usually stalked, some ses-
sile. Stem leaves alternate, 0.4–0.8 in. long,
deeply palmately divided into 5 toothed or lobed segments.
Flowers solitary, 1–2 in. wide, radially symmetrical. Sepals
5–10, petal-like, yellow or green before bloom, then white.
Petals inconspicuous, stamen-like and concealed under
true stamens. Stamens many. Fruit a follicle. Occurs in
open wet areas, near receding snowbanks. Native.

WHAT DO SCIENTIFIC NAMES MEAN?

Most scientific names, whether Latin or Greek, carry meaning, some simple and some quite complex. They typically reflect either the name of a person who worked with or discovered the plant, or a location, or a particular characteristic of the plant. Learning some of the more common meanings can help you remember a plant's identity and features. Note: for many versions given here, there is also either a male or female equivalent (e.g., *acuminata* but also *acuminatum*).

acer / sharp
acuminata / tapering to a long, pointed tip
adeno / gland
aduncus / hooked
aggregata / clustered
agrestis / growing wild
alatus / winged
albidus, alba / white
algida / cold
alpinus / alpine
alta / tall
amplexicaulis / stem-clasping
angusti / narrow
anserina / goose
anthus / flower
aprica / exposed to the sun
aquifolium / needle-leaved
arenaria / sand-loving
argentea / silvery
arguta / sharp (toothed)
aristatum / with a long, bristle-like tip
arvense / field
asper / rough
atro / dark
atrosanguineus / dark blood-red
aurantiacus / orange-colored

aureum / golden
bi / two
bilobus / two-lobed
blanda / white
boreale / northern
brachy / short
brevi / short
caerulea / sky blue
caespitosus / tufted, sod-forming
canescens / white-hairy
capitatum / headed
carpum / fruit (ed)
caudata / tailed
caulis / stem
cephalus / head
cereum / waxy
cernua / nodding
chamae / on the ground
chima / winter
chiono / snow
chrys / golden
cinereus / ash-colored
cinque / five
coccinea / scarlet
cordi / heart-shaped
cornuta / horned
corona / crown
crassi / fleshy
croceus / saffron-yellow
cunei / wedge-shaped
cuspidata / tipped with a sharp and stiff point
dasy / rough thick
decumbens / lying down
dendron / tree-like
denta / tooth
didymo / twin-like
discolor / of different colors
divari / diverse
divergens / wide-spreading
dumosus / bushy

edulis / edible
elatior / tall and slender
eremo / solitary, lonely
erigeron / early old
erio / woolly
erythro / red
exigua / small
exscapa / stemless
fili / thread-like
flagellaris / whip-like
flavo / yellow
flora / flower (ed)
floribundus / free flowering
foetidissima / very ill-smelling
folium / leaved
formosa / handsome
fruticosa / shrubby, bushy
galericulata / covered with a helmet
glaber / smooth
glauca / bluish green
glottis / tongue
gonum / corner, knee
graveolens / rank-smelling
guttatus / spotted, drop-like
gynus / seed
hetero / mixed, varied
hirsut / rough-hairy
hirta / short-hairy
hydro / water
hyper / above
hypo / under
humifusa / spread over the ground
humilis / dwarf
ifera / bearing
inerme / unarmed
integra / whole
issima / very (superlative)
lacti / milk-like
laevigatus / smooth
lanatus / woolly
lanceolatus / lance-leaf
lasio / hairy
lati / broad
lepto / slender, small
leuco / whitish
luteus / yellow
macro / large

maculata / spotted
mega / large
melano / black
micro / small
mille / thousands, many
mono / one
mucronatus / sharp-pointed
multi / many
nana / dwarf
niger / black
nitidus / shining
nivale / snow
nuda / naked
occidentalis / western
octo / eight
officinalis / healing
oides / like
oligo / few
opsis / head
oreo / mountain
oreophilus / mountain-loving
osmo / odorous
pallida / pale
palustris / marsh-loving
parri / leek-like
parva / small
patens / spreading
pauci / few
pectinata / with narrow, comb-like divisions
philus / loving
phylla / leaf
platy / broad
plena / plentiful, many
pleura / rib
poli / polished
poly / many
pratensis / meadow
procerus / tall
procumbens / lying on its face
prunifolia / plum-leaved
pseudo / false, similar to
pteri / winged
pulcherrima / very beautiful
punctata / dotted
pumila / dwarf
purpureus / purple
pusillus / dwarf

pygmaea / dwarf
racemosus / branched
reni / kidney
repens / creeping
reptans / creeping
rhiza / root
rivularis / of brooks or rivulets
rostrata / beaked
rotundi / round, plump
rupestris / of the rocks
rupicola / living among rocks
rubra / red
rugosa / wrinkled
saligna / willow-leaved
salsuginosus / growing in brackish places
sanguineus / bloody, blood-red
sativa / cultivated
saxatile / found among stones
saxi / stone
saxifraga / rock-breaker
scoparius / broom-like
scopulorum / of the mountains
secunda / facing one side
senecio / old; old man
sepium / growing in hedges
septentrionale / northern
sericea / silky soft-hairy
serotina / late
serra / saw-toothed
speciosa / beautiful

spectabilis / showy
sperma / seed
squarrosus / parts spreading or recurving at ends
stella / star-shaped
stenopetala / with small petals
stolonifera / bearing runners
strepto / twisted, curved
stricta / stiff
sub / just below
sylvestris / of the woods
tenellum / small, frail
tenue / thin, frail
terebinthinus / turpentine
thamnos / bush
thele / nipple
tinctoria / paint, used for dye
toxi / poisonous
trachy / rough
tri / three
uliginosus / marsh
umbellata / umbrella-shaped
uncinatus / hooked
uva-ursi / bear-berry
varians / variable
villosa / downy
virens, viridis / green
viscosa / sticky
vulgatum / common
xanthum / yellow

GLOSSARY

acaulescent: lacking a stem, or so short as to make leaves appear as if they are arising from the ground

achene: small, dry one-seeded fruit that does not split open when ripe

achlorophyllous: having no chlorophyll

acute: ending in a sharp point, with straight sides; less than 90 degree angle

adaxially: on the side of or facing the axis, like the upper surface of a leaf

alpine: found above timberline at high altitude

alternate: arranged singly at different heights along the stem

annual: plant that germinates, flowers, seeds, and dies in one year

anther: pollen-producing part of a stamen

apetalous: no petals

apex: the tip, or uppermost point away from attached end

apomictic: asexual reproduction, like seed formation without fertilization

appressed: pressed flat against another organ, as hairs pressed against the surface of a leaf or stem

aquatic: growing in or on water, floating or rooted to soil at the bottom with submerged stems or shoots

areole: a modified node, visible as small depressions on the surface of cacti from which spines grow

armed: bearing prickles, thorns, or spines

ascending: curving or angling upward from the base

axil: the upper angle between the leaf and the stem

axillary: pertaining to the axil, or in the axil

banner: upper and usually largest petal of a pea-like flower

basal: found at or near the base of a plant or plant part

beak: a narrow, pointed and elongated structure

berry: fleshy fruit with more than one seed within the soft tissue

biennial: plant that completes its life cycle in two years

bilabiate: two lips

biternate: doubly ternate, as where three leaflets are again divided into three

blade: the expanded portion of a leaf

boss: a projection from a surface

bract: small leaf-like structure associated with an inflorescence, usually circling the base of a flower cluster or a composite flowerhead

bractlet: small secondary bract

branch: secondary stem, growing from the main stem

branched: a stem or branch that divides into smaller branches many times

branchlet: a small branch from a large branch; usually terminal

bristles: 1. large, stiff, straight hairs; 2. in the aster family, fine hairs at the top of the flower arising from an inferior ovary

calyx (pl., calyces): whorl of sepals, the lowest or outermost part enclosing the rest of the flower; often green or tan

campanulate: shaped like a bell

capsule: a dry fruit that splits open when ripe, with one or more seed-containing compartments

carmine: vivid red

carpel: one of the ovule-bearing structures that comprises the innermost whorl of a flower

carpellate: with carpels

cartilaginous: resembling cartilage, being flexible but tough

catkin: a spike of tiny pollen-bearing or seed-producing flowers, commonly found on willow, aspen, or birch

caudex: woody base

circumboreal: around the world at northern latitudes

clasp (clasping): surrounding the stem, in part or fully

clavate: club shaped

cleft: split about halfway to the base

cleistogamous: small, closed inconspicuous flowers that self-pollinate

composite: very small flowers crowded into tightly compact heads that superficially resemble a single flower, as in the aster family

compound: a leaf in which the blade is subdivided into separate portions or leaflets

cordate: heart-shaped

corolla: collective term for all the petals in an individual flower, which may be separate or united

corymb: flat-topped inflorescence in which flower stalks arise at different levels on main axis, reaching nearly same height, and outer ones open first

corymbiform: looks like a corymb, but not same structure

crenate: having the margin or surface cut into rounded teeth

cup: cup-like structure on which the parts of the flower are born

cyme: branched inflorescence in which the central flower on the main stem opens before the side flowers

cypselae: a dry, single-seeded fruit that does not open when ripe, formed by a fusion of an inferior ovary with two carpels and a calyx tube; seen in some Asteraceae

deciduous: refers to a plant that loses its leaves at the end of a growing season; also said of plants that are leafless part of the year

decumbent: lying on the ground with the tips pointing upward

dentate: having outward-facing teeth along the margin

disc: in Asteraceae, the part of the head made up of disc flowers

disc flower: the tubular flowers often in the center of composite flowerheads, such as sunflowers and asters; some heads (e.g., thistle, rabbitbrush) have only disc flowers

dissected: cut deeply into fine lobes

distal: side away from the attached end

drupe: fleshy fruit that does not open when ripe and has a stony layer surrounding a single seed, like a peach

duff: organic matter that is decaying on the forest floor

egg-shaped: wider at the base and narrower at the tip

ellipsoid: a body elliptic in long section and circular in cross section

emersed: rising above or standing out of water

entire: descriptive term for a leaf that has smooth margins without teeth, notches, or other divisions

erect: upright from the ground

evergreen: a plant bearing leaves throughout the year

exserted: projecting beyond another structure

filament: stalk of the stamen that holds the anther

fleshy: thick and juicy, often said of plants in the stonecrop family

floccose: having tufts of soft hairs that are often deciduous

florets: small individual flowers in the larger flowerhead, as occur in sunflowers

fluff: light, feather-like particles

follicle: a dry fruit that opens on one side when ripe and that contains many seeds but a single carpel, as in milkweed

fruit: botanically, any ripened ovary where seed is held; can be fleshy, like apples and berries, or dry, like capsules or sunflower seeds

fused: united, as petals to a calyx or to each other; not free

fusiform: shaped like a spindle, tapering toward each end

galea: looks like a helmet or hood

glabrous: hairless

gland: small, round structure that emits a sticky substance on the outer plant surface; sessile or on the end of the hair

glaucous: a covering of the outer surface of leaves or fruits of a bluish white, waxy powder or film, which can be rubbed off

globose: spherical

glochid: fine, stiff hairs, often barbed, arising from the areoles at the base of spines in *Opuntia*, *Cylindropuntia*, and related cacti genera

glutinous: gummy; like glue

gypseous: composed, in some part, of gypsum

hair: thin to thick thread-like growth on the outer surface

head: a dense cluster of small flowers making up the inflorescence and surrounded at the base by bracts; used most often to describe flowers of the aster family

heliotropic: organism that follows the movement of the sun, turning toward it, maximizing its exposure to sunlight

hemiparasitic: attached to, and relying on, the roots of another plant for some nutrients

herb: plants are herbs (or herbaceous) if they have no woody stems

hirsute: bearing coarse, stiff hairs

hispid: rough with bristles or stiff hairs

hybrid: plant created when two different species interbreed

hypanthium (pl., hypanthia): a cup or tube-shaped enlargement at the base of a flower bearing on its rim the stamens, petals, and sepals

inferior ovary: ovary attached below the sepals, petals, and stamens

inflorescence: arrangement of the flowers, or cluster of flowers of a plant

intercostal: positioned in between ribs or nerves

involucre: a circle of bracts at the base of a flowerhead or flower cluster

involute: edges rolled inward to the upper side toward the midrib

irregular: said of flowers that are bilaterally symmetrical, like lobelias

keel: in pea flowers, the lower boat-shaped pair of united petals that enclose the stamens and pistil; found in all pea-like flowers of the legume family

labellum: lip; the median and most distinct petal of an orchid

lacerate: roughly torn; irregularly cut

lactiferous: containing a milky juice

lanceolate: lance-shaped, long and narrow, broadest toward the base

lateral: coming from or on the side

leaf axil: the upper angle between the leaf stalk and the stem

lenticel: a small spot or line of loose corky cells allowing an exchange of gases between living tissue of the stem and the atmosphere

linear: narrow, with parallel sides; as in a long, narrow leaf with nearly parallel margins

lip: upper or lower section of an unequal corolla or calyx

lobe: divisions of a leaf, especially if rounded; or the corolla of a flower with united petals

lyrate: shaped like a lyre, with terminal lobe of pinnate leaf rounded and larger than lower ones

marcescent: withering but not falling off

margin: edge

mat: a form of plant growth in which stems and leaves are very low and interwoven into a dense mass, like moss campion, or a spreading thick tangle, like alpine clover

midrib: central vein of leaf

monocarpic: dies after flowering and bearing fruit one time

mottle: colored spot or blotch on a surface

mycorrhizae: symbiotic relationships between plants and mycorrhizal fungi, starting with fungi colonizing the root system of the plant, providing both improved nutrient and water absorption systems in exchange for carbohydrates that the plant produces

mycotrophic: getting food from a fungal source, namely mycorrhizae

native: growing in a place without the aid of people or because of human activities

nectariferous: with, or producing, nectar

nectary: nectar-producing part of a flower

nodding: bent or drooping downward or forward

node: on stems, the point at which a leaf or flower cluster is, or has been, attached; sometimes the word "joint" is appropriate when there is a swelling at the node

nut: dry fruit containing a single seed

nutlet: small fruit, usually one of several

oblanceolate: lance-shaped but broadest above the middle and tapering toward the base

oblong: longer than wide, rounded

obovate: oval (leaf) shape, more slender near the base

obovoid: inversely egg-shaped, with narrow end toward attachment

opposite: refers to leaf or stem arrangement where two like units are attached to opposite sides of the same node

oval: nearly round

ovary: the part of the pistil that contains ovules and, after fertilization, ripens into a fruit containing the seed

ovate: having an egg or oval shape, with broad end at attachment

ovoid: having a three-dimensional egg shape

palmate: said of a leaf when leaflets, lobes, or veins all spread from the top of the leaf petiole like fingers of a hand

panicle: an inflorescence in which individual flowers are attached to a much-branched flower stalk

papilionaceous: group of flowers (e.g., those from the pea family) that resemble a butterfly

papillate: having small, rounded, fleshy projections

pappus: the modified and mature calyx of florets (tiny flowers making up the flower-head) in the aster family (Asteraceae), usually comprising hairs, bristles, or scales (e.g., dandelion, salsify, sunflower)

parted: deep division, like in a leaf; often

more than halfway to midvein or base

pedicel: the flower stalk of an individual flower in a cluster

peduncle: a stalk bearing a flower or inflorescence

pendent: leaning over or drooping downward; pendulous

perennial: plants that live for several years, even though they may die back to underground living parts in winter

persistent: remaining attached, not falling off the plant for some time

petal: one of the colored or white segments making up the corolla of a flower

petiole: stalk part of the leaf attached to the blade

phyllary: bract on the cup of many members of the aster family

pinnate: a compound leaf with leaflets attached on a long axis; feather-like

pinnatifid: cleft half the distance or more to the midrib, but not meeting it

pistil: the seed-producing organ of a flower, made up of ovary, ovules, stigma, and style

pith (pithy): often continuous central spongy tissue in stems and roots of some vascular plants that may function as storage

plait: pleat or fold, as in some floral parts

pod: a dry fruit that splits open along two sides, releasing seed (legume)

pollen: tiny yellow grains produced in the anther and transferred to the stigma in pollination

pouch: anatomical structure that resembles a pouch

prickle: sharp growth, thorn, or spine, usually restricted to smaller growths

prostrate: trailing or lying flat on the ground

puberulent: covered with fine short hairs

pubescent: covered with fine soft short hairs; also bearing any kind of hairs

raceme: unbranched, elongated cluster of flowers with the oldest flowers at the base

radially symmetrical: said of a flower when the parts of the calyx are alike in size and form, and the parts of the corolla are also alike in size and form

ray flowers: refers to the strap-shaped marginal flowers around a center disc as in the aster family; often thought of as "petals"

recurve: curved toward the back

red-listed: on the IUCN Red List of Threatened Species, which is the world's most comprehensive inventory of the global conservation status of biological species

reduced: diminished in size

reflexed: bent or curved downward or backward

regular flower: flower with parts similar in size and shape and arranged symmetrically; can be divided in many ways to mirror-image halves

reniform: kidney-shaped

resupinate: inverted; upside-down due to twisting of pedicel, as flowers in some orchids

rhizome: creeping underground stem

rhombic: having the shape of a rhombus (a parallelogram with four equal sides and sometimes with no right angles); diamond-shaped

root: underground structure from the base of the stem, anchors the plant and allows for absorption of nutrients and water

rosette: cluster of leaves at ground level, usually in a circle

scalloped: curved projections with sharp depressions between

scapose: with flowers arising from a leafless peduncle from the ground (often a basal rosette)

schizocarp: dry compound fruit that splits into separate one-seeded carpels that remain closed at maturity

scree: steep mass of rock debris with scant soil

scurfy: covered in a scaly deposit or bran-like scales

seed: product of fertilization

sepal: fused or free member of the calyx, usually green and leaf-like

serrate: having saw-like teeth on the margin that point forward or toward apex

sessile: without a stalk or petiole

sheath: vertical coating surrounding the stem at the leaf base

shredding: pulling apart in strings; often said of bark

shrub: a perennial woody plant smaller than a tree, with several to many stems branched from the base

simple: composed of one part, unbranched, undivided; said of a leaf that is not compound

sp. (pl., spp.): abbreviation for "species," used when the exact species is not known or named (e.g., *Rosa* sp., for one species, *Rosa* spp., referring to several species)

spathe: large bract just below and enclosing a spadix

spatulate: said of a leaf broader at the tip and tapering to the base; spatula-shaped

species: a group containing individual plants of the same kind; the word is both singular and plural

spike: unbranched inflorescence with sessile flowers; used here to include a raceme with stalked flowers

spine: sharp, stiff, pointed structure, a modified leaf or stipule, that comes from below the epidermis

spreading: held outward from the point of attachment

spur: a hollow, nectar-containing projection sometimes found as a part of a sepal or petal, as in larkspur or violet

ssp.: abbreviation for "subspecies"

stalk: a specialized flower stem, often referring to the structure supporting the flower

stamen: pollen-producing male organ composed of a stalk (filament) and pollen sacs (anther)

staminode: modified stamen that does not produce pollen

stem: central support of a plant, bearing leaves, flowers, and other organs

stigma: the pollen-receiving part of the pistil

stipules: small appendages at the base of a leaf or leaf stalk in many plants; may be leaf-like or thorn-like, generally in pairs

stolon: stems that spread from the original

plant (runners), producing new above-ground plants as they go

stoloniferous: able to spread via stolons to form expanding colonies

style: the stalk-like part of the pistil connecting the ovary and stigma

subalpine: just below timberline

subentire: almost entire

subshrub: perennial plant with woody stems except terminal part of new growth that dies back annually; a small, low shrub

subtended: occurring immediately below, as bracts just under a flower

suckering: sending out a shoot from roots or lower part of stem

superior ovary: ovary attached above the sepals, petals, and stamens

talus: mass of rock fragments at the base of a cliff

taproot: root system with main primary root that grows vertically downward with smaller lateral roots

teeth: alternating projections and indentations on the margin

tendril: slender, twining or coiling structure from the tip of a leaf or stem, by which a climbing plant grasps for support

tepal: any of the modified leaves making up a perianth which are not differentiated into calyx and corolla

terminal: growing at the tip or end of a branch or stem

ternate: arranged in threes

throat: expanded opening of flowers with fused sepals or petals

tomentose: covered in soft, densely matted woolly hairs

toothed: refers to leaf margins that have points or serrations of various shapes, like the teeth of a saw

trichomes: epidermal hair or hair-like structure

triternate: ternate three times

tube: cylindrical structure formed by fused sepals or petals

tubercle: a small knobby tuber-like prominence

tuft: cluster of short-stemmed leaves and flowers growing from a common point

tufted: stems or leaves in a very tight cluster

twig: in woody plants, the smallest segment, produced during the latest growing season

two-lipped: describes a type of flower found in the figwort, plantain, and mint families; the petals are united or joined into a tube that is expanded at the open end into two lobes, usually of unequal size and rounded or notched, as in penstemons

umbel: a type of flat-topped or rounded inflorescence in which the flower stalks all arise from the same point, like umbrella spokes

variety (var.): a term denoting a minor variation of a species

vascular: pertaining to plants with veins or to the veins in a plant structure

vein: vessels by which water and nutrients are transported; often easily seen in leaves

vernal: pertaining to spring

vine: trailing or climbing plant with long, flexible stem, often supported by tendrils

whorled: three or more leaves or branches arising from a single node, as in bedstraw

wings: in pea-like flowers, the two similar petals at the sides of the flower, between the banner and keel

woody: said of plants with firm stems and branches, remaining alive from season to season

xeric: of, relating to, or requiring only a small amount of moisture

zygomorphic: bilaterally symmetrical

SOURCES AND RESOURCES

This book is intended to be a blend between a portable field guide, a complete list of flowers, and a technical book. As such, with certain genera (e.g., *Penstemon, Antennaria*), more technical guides will be necessary to key out to species, subspecies, and variety. The digital world has also recently provided us with mobile apps and websites that allow the casual botanist to always carry a basic flower identification guide in their pocket, for those times where flower guides are forgotten. In addition, for background information, knowing plant identification terminology is crucial for both seasoned and beginner botanists.

Compiling accurate and complete information on thousands of wildflowers to write complete descriptions with habit, perennation, bloom time, size, color, and habitat information takes hundreds of sources to succeed. These descriptions would never have been possible without obscure research articles, websites, and personal experiences. We would like to give a special shout-out to the following sources for being staples in our research and useful tools for all.

Websites

The Biota of North America Program: North American Vascular Flora (bonap.org). Provides an extensive collection of distribution maps, as well as more specific maps on families, soil types, and climates; served as the basis for all the U.S. maps in this book.

CalPhotos (calphotos.berkeley.edu). A resource for hundreds of high-quality photos of wildflowers.

Celebrating Wildflowers (www.fs.fed.us/ wildflowers). Provides information on native plants, their uses in the ecosystems they inhabit, and general information on wildflower viewing.

E-Flora BC: Electronic Atlas of the Flora of British Columbia (ibis.geog.ubc.ca/biodiversity/eflora). GIS-based maps of the vascular plants, bryophytes, fungi, and lichens of British Columbia.

Flora of North America (efloras.org). Provides detailed descriptions of vascular plants and bryophytes across North America, including scientific and common names, distribution maps, keys, illustrations, habitat and range information, synonymy, chromosomal data, and ethnobotanical uses and toxicity.

Jepson Flora Project (ucjeps.berkeley.edu/ eflora). A guide to the native and naturalized vascular plants of California, including taxonomic information, keys, distribution maps, and illustrations and photos.

Montana Field Guide (fieldguide.mt.gov). Provides information on the ecology, identification, and distribution of Montana's plants, lichens, and general biological communities, with downloadable field guides.

The Plant List (theplantlist.org). An attempt by herbaria, universities, conservatories, gardens, and other organizations around the world to curate a list of all current scientific names of plants and their known synonyms.

Saskatchewan Wildflowers (saskwildflower. ca/native-plant-photos.html). A resource for high-quality photographs that depict micro-details, such as hairs and glands on the stems and leaves of plants.

SEINet (swbiodiversity.org/seinet). A collaboration of many research institutions providing information on the region's flora, including taxonomic information, maps, and photos.

USDA: The PLANTS Database (plants.usda.gov). An easy search tool for basic information on the vascular plants, mosses, liverworts, hornworts, and lichens of the United States.

Wildflowers, Ferns, and Trees of Colorado, New Mexico, Arizona, and Utah (swcoloradowildflowers.com). Compares similar taxa found in the region and provides beautiful pictures, general information, interesting historical facts, and Greek and Latin name meanings.

Wildflower Identification (wildflowersearch.com). Unique search feature where you can select a location and find plants within a certain radius and time frame, filtering by flower type, flower color, family, genus, etc. The site provides many reference links to information and photos from different herbaria, field guides, and government agencies.

WTU Image Collection: Plants of Washington (biology.burke.washington.edu/herbarium/imagecollection.php). Provides photos, distribution maps, descriptions, synonymy, and informational links for the plants and lichens of Washington.

Books

Colorado Flora: Eastern Slope; Colorado Flora: Western Slope by W. A. Weber and R. C. Wittmann. More technical guides to the flora of Colorado, with information on microhabitats, altitudinal ranges, and rare and ancient plants.

Flora of Colorado by Jennifer Ackerfield. With a well-written taxonomic key, this up-to-date flora provides descriptions of each taxon as well as range maps.

Flora of the Pacific Northwest by C. L. Hitchcock and A. Cronquist. A very technical, authoritative key to all the flora of the Pacific Northwest, for the more advanced botanists with knowledge of botanical terms.

Flora of the Yellowstone by Whitney Tilt.

Includes photos, descriptions, and habitat data, with a handy photo key of all the plants in the book at the beginning.

Manual of Montana Vascular Plants by Peter Lesica. A comprehensive field guide to the more than 2,500 species of Montana's vascular plants.

National Audubon Society Field Guide to North American Wildflowers: Western Region. An easy-to-use identification guide to nearly 1,000 wildflowers found in all elevation ranges and habitats in the western United States.

Plant Identification Terminology by J. G. Harris and M. W. Harris. An illustrated glossary that has stood the test of time. Useful for amateurs and experts alike, this guide defines almost any botanical term you will need to know to excel in using technical keys.

Plants of the Rocky Mountains by L. Kershaw, A. MacKinnon, and J. Pojar. A comprehensive guide to plants of our region, including trees, shrubs, wildflowers, grasses, ferns, mosses, and lichens. Historical and general facts keep this guide interesting.

Wildflowers of the Pacific Northwest by M. Turner and P. Gustafson. A Timber Press field guide to the many plants of that region, ranging from the coastal dunes to the high alpine meadows.

Mobile Apps

Colorado Rocky Mountain Wildflowers by Al Schneider. This paid app, an extension of his website (swcoloradowildflowers.com), has pictures of and information on over 500 wildflowers, ferns, shrubs, and trees from Colorado, and often Montana, Wyoming, and New Mexico.

Colorado Wildflowers by Ernie Marx. This free app, an extension of his website (easterncoloradowildflowers.com), has pictures of and information on over 525 plant species growing east of the Continental Divide in Colorado.

PHOTO CREDITS

William Adams, page 111 (middle)

Janét Bare, page 168 (bottom)

Curtis Björk, pages 64 (top), 88 (bottom), 90 (top), 92 (bottom), 93 (middle), 110 (middle), 138 (top), 139 (top), 145 (top, middle), 152 (bottom), 236 (bottom), 237 (top), 240 (bottom), 243 (bottom), 251 (middle), 288 (top), 306 (middle), 310 (middle), 319 (middle), 387 (middle), 415 (bottom), 422 (top), 425 (top)

Todd Boland, pages 53, 54 (top), 56 (bottom), 58 (middle), 60 (top), 65 (top), 68 (bottom), 69 (middle), 71 (bottom), 72 (bottom), 73 (bottom), 78 (middle), 85 (bottom), 90 (middle), 91 (bottom), 121 (top), 122 (bottom), 126 (top), 127 (bottom), 128 (top), 132 (middle), 135 (bottom), 136 (bottom), 137 (middle), 148 (bottom), 152 (middle), 153 (middle), 155 (bottom), 163 (middle), 165 (top), 166 (top), 167 (top), 175 (top), 185 (top), 190 (bottom), 194 (top), 196 (bottom), 210 (top), 211 (bottom), 216 (top), 220 (top), 224 (top), 231 (top), 233 (bottom), 235 (bottom), 241 (middle, bottom), 244 (bottom), 248 (middle), 253 (top), 264 (top), 268 (bottom), 269 (top, middle), 270 (bottom), 272 (top), 273 (bottom), 286 (middle), 291 (bottom), 293 (middle), 298 (bottom), 301 (middle, bottom), 302 (top), 303 (middle), 309 (middle), 315 (top), 316 (bottom), 320 (bottom), 322 (middle), 325 (bottom), 330 (top, middle), 331 (middle), 332 (bottom), 335 (middle), 339 (bottom), 348 (middle), 351 (middle), 352 (middle), 357 (top), 358 (top), 361 (middle), 364 (middle), 365 (top), 366 (top), 372 (top), 377 (top), 379 (bottom), 380 (bottom), 383 (middle), 392 (top), 398 (top), 401 (middle), 408 (middle), 409 (bottom), 410 (bottom), 413 (top, bottom), 414 (top), 416 (middle, bottom), 417 (middle, bottom), 418 (top, bottom), 420 (bottom), 421 (bottom), 423 (bottom), 433 (bottom), 443 (bottom), 446 (middle), 447 (bottom), 453 (bottom), 455 (middle)

Neide Bollinger, page 439 (top)

Barry Breckling, pages 150 (top), 156 (bottom), 183 (bottom), 314 (middle), 402 (middle)

Sharon Chester, page 317 (bottom)

Christopher Christie, pages 160 (middle), 176 (middle), 197 (middle)

Gerald and Buff Corsi, © California Academy of Sciences, page 124 (bottom)

Ann DeBolt, page 21

Pam Eveleigh, page 301 (top)

RT Hawke, page 174 (middle)

Bryan Hobby, pages 341 (middle), 384 (top)

Mike Ireland, page 134 (middle)

Emily Kachergis, page 236 (middle)

Ben Legler, pages 57 (middle), 61 (bottom), 72 (top), 74 (middle, bottom), 79 (top), 88 (top), 90 (bottom), 99 (middle), 104 (middle), 112 (bottom), 117 (bottom), 118 (bottom), 124 (middle), 131 (middle), 137 (top), 147 (middle), 151 (bottom), 159 (top), 163 (bottom), 187 (bottom), 189 (top), 204 (top), 205 (top), 230 (top), 239 (middle), 253 (bottom), 266 (middle), 267 (middle), 271 (top), 278 (top), 280 (top), 283 (middle), 286 (bottom), 287 (middle), 291 (middle), 299 (middle, bottom), 300 (bottom), 304 (middle), 305 (middle), 310 (bottom), 313 (middle), 318 (top), 319 (top), 328 (bottom), 333 (middle), 342 (top), 343 (middle), 348 (bottom), 354 (bottom), 358 (middle), 359 (top, middle, bottom), 360 (bottom), 383 (bottom),

391 (middle), 393 (top, middle), 403 (top, bottom), 405 (middle), 407 (top), 422 (bottom), 424 (top), 432 (middle), 433 (top), 434 (middle), 437 (middle)

Max Licher, page 288 (middle)

Jay Lunn, pages 213 (middle), 309 (bottom)

Ginny Maffitt, pages 167 (middle)

Ernie Marx, pages 64 (middle), 140 (middle), 171 (bottom), 199 (bottom), 223 (middle), 237 (bottom), 411 (top), 435 (top)

Gary A. Monroe, pages 172 (top), 344 (bottom)

Frank Morrey, pages 59 (middle), 62 (middle), 63 (middle), 65 (bottom), 66 (bottom), 68 (middle), 75, 86 (top), 98 (top), 111 (bottom), 113 (bottom), 120 (top), 123 (bottom), 125 (bottom), 127 (top), 136 (top), 141 (top, bottom), 148 (middle), 155 (top, middle), 171 (middle), 172 (middle), 183 (top), 195 (top inset), 195 (middle, bottom), 199 (middle), 200 (middle), 207 (bottom), 210 (bottom), 211 (middle), 214 (top), 221 (middle, bottom), 224 (middle), 226 (bottom), 251 (bottom), 263 (bottom), 268 (top), 273 (middle), 280 (middle), 281 (top), 296 (bottom), 298 (top), 309 (top), 317 (top), 322 (top), 337 (bottom), 355 (middle), 362 (top, bottom), 363 (middle), 364 (top), 372 (bottom), 374 (middle, bottom), 375 (middle), 395 (bottom), 398 (middle), 402 (top), 406 (top), 415 (middle), 431 (bottom), 435 (bottom), 438 (top), 440 (top), 451 (top), 455 (top)

Keir Morse, pages 56 (top), 61 (middle), 65 (middle), 230 (middle), 399 (middle)

Johan Nilsson, pages 85 (top), 98 (middle), 99 (bottom), 100 (middle), 104 (bottom), 119 (top), 131 (bottom), 133 (top), 142 (middle), 160 (top), 191 (top), 201 (top), 204 (middle), 209 (bottom), 215 (middle), 226 (top), 240 (middle), 310 (top), 334 (top), 345 (middle), 376 (top), 401 (bottom)

Jo Panosky, pages 2-3, 7, 38, 59 (top)

Jean Pawek, pages 128 (bottom), 154 (top)

Jim Pisarowicz, page 428 (middle)

Suzanne Putnam, page 22 (top)

©Al Schneider (swcoloradowildflowers. com), pages 60 (bottom), 70 (middle), 77 (bottom), 82 (bottom), 83 (top), 84 (bottom), 92 (top), 96 (top), 105 (top, middle), 108 (middle), 115 (middle), 124 (top), 125 (middle), 129 (bottom), 140 (bottom), 150 (middle), 158 (middle), 160 (bottom), 162 (top), 164 (top), 192 (top), 193 (top), 206 (top), 207 (top), 217 (top), 222 (top), 224 (bottom), 248 (bottom), 252 (top), 262 (top), 303 (bottom), 305 (top), 306 (top), 308 (top), 321 (middle), 329 (middle), 334 (middle), 343 (bottom), 346 (bottom), 355 (top, top inset), 360 (middle), 370 (bottom), 382 (bottom), 385 (middle), 387 (bottom), 396 (top), 410 (top), 415 (top), 416 (top), 419 (bottom), 420 (top), 423 (middle), 425 (middle, bottom), 436 (top), 437 (top), 454 (middle), 455 (bottom)

Alan Schroder, pages 281 (middle)

Lori Skulski, pages 59 (bottom), 107 (middle), 126 (middle), 211 (top), 217 (middle), 263 (top), 277 (bottom), 278 (middle, bottom), 297 (middle), 308 (middle), 320 (top), 328 (middle), 339 (middle), 453 (top)

Mikel R. Stevens, pages 169 (top, middle, bottom), 170 (top), 173 (middle), 175 (middle), 176 (top), 177 (middle), 180 (top, middle), 181 (middle, bottom)

Amy Taylor, page 165 (bottom)

Jeff Thompson, page 192 (bottom)

Karen Vail, pages 54 (middle), 72 (middle), 73 (top), 85 (middle), 86 (middle), 127 (middle), 149 (top), 152 (top), 156 (top, middle), 168 (middle), 212 (middle), 245 (middle), 251 (top), 270 (top), 276 (middle), 279 (top, middle), 283 (top), 289 (top), 291 (top), 292 (middle), 293 (top), 297 (top), 302 (middle), 311 (bottom), 314 (bottom), 316 (middle), 321 (bottom), 335 (top), 338 (middle), 340 (top), 341 (bottom), 366 (middle), 368 (bottom), 377 (bottom), 379 (top), 381 (bottom), 382 (top), 389 (top, middle), 396 (middle)

Linda Vaxvick, pages 213 (bottom), 225 (middle), 284 (bottom), 350 (bottom), 410 (middle)

Gary Waggoner, pages 441 (top), 450 (top)

Phyllis Weyand, Lady Bird Johnson Wildflower Center, page 64 (bottom)

Mary Winter, pages 191 (middle), 203 (bottom)

Loraine Yeatts, pages 55 (top, middle), 71 (middle), 87 (top), 88 (middle), 93 (top), 95 (middle), 112 (top, middle), 117 (middle), 126 (bottom), 136 (middle), 138 (middle), 149 (bottom), 164 (middle), 165 (middle), 171 (top), 173 (top), 175 (bottom), 177 (top), 184 (bottom), 198 (top), 206 (bottom), 208 (bottom), 210 (middle), 222 (bottom), 223 (bottom), 231 (middle), 232 (top), 233 (top), 234 (middle), 238 (top), 247 (top, middle), 260 (bottom), 261 (middle), 272 (middle), 275 (bottom), 276 (bottom), 294 (top), 295 (top), 302 (bottom), 306 (bottom), 308 (bottom), 314 (top, top inset), 331 (bottom), 334 (bottom), 354 (top), 356 (middle), 361 (bottom), 363 (top), 380 (top, middle), 388 (top), 390 (top), 396 (bottom), 399 (bottom), 404 (top), 405 (top, bottom), 412 (top, bottom), 414 (bottom), 420 (middle), 424 (bottom), 426 (top), 429 (bottom), 434 (top), 441 (middle, bottom), 442 (bottom), 443 (top), 445 (top, middle, bottom), 447 (middle), 450 (middle), 456 (top, middle, bottom), 458 (top)

Tom Zeiner, page 222 (middle)

All other photos are by the authors.

INDEX

ABOUT THE AUTHORS

Scott Dressel-Martin

Sonya Anderson has worked since 2006 as a horticulturist at Denver Botanic Gardens, where she maintains the Birds and Bees Walk, the Darlene Radichel Plant Select Garden, and the Steppe Garden. The Birds and Bees Walk is a pollinator education garden displaying a variety of flowers that attract and support pollinators, including native wildflower genera such as *Penstemon*, *Gaillardia*, and *Asclepias*. In 2010 she also began working with Plant Select, a leading non-profit focused on identifying, evaluating, and promoting plants proven to thrive in gardens in the high plains and intermountain region. Native species of *Scutellaria*, *Aquilegia*, and *Eriogonum* are just a few of the stalwarts chosen for this program.

Mike Bone has been a professional horticulturist since the late 1990s and has focused most of his career on propagation and production of plants from steppe climates. Mike began working for the Denver Botanic Gardens in 2002 and currently

serves as the Curator of Steppe Collections, contributing to the Plant Select program and working to collect seeds from plants all around the world as well as extensively throughout the American West. Mike writes for a variety of periodicals and has coauthored or contributed to several books on plants for dryland gardens.

Nick Daniel's lifelong passion for our native flora was instilled in him by his parents as he grew up in Denver. He studied horticulture at Colorado State University and then was hired by the Denver Botanic Gardens. The native flora of the Southern Rocky Mountains and the Four Corners region is his area of focus and passion. Whenever out hiking or camping with his wife, daughter, and dogs, he has a constant focus on the plants surrounding him, and brings this in-situ knowledge and experience to his work at DBG, where he manages several native plant gardens and the cactus and succulent collection.

Dan Johnson has worked in horticulture for over 30 years, including the nursery industry and public gardens. This includes 20 years with Denver Botanic Gardens, currently as Curator of Native Plants and Associate Director of Horticulture. His work has included creation and maintenance of more than a dozen of DBG's gardens, with a focus on xeric and native plants and naturalistic design. Travels have included horticultural exploration with a focus on steppe climates in South Africa, Argentina, Spain, and Pakistan. Publications include the recently revised and expanded *Meet the Natives* wildflower guide and *Steppes*. Forays throughout the West continue to expand his plant palette and knowledge.

Born near the headwaters of the Yampa River, **Panayoti Kelaidis** has observed Rocky Mountain wildflowers from his early childhood. His undergraduate degree was in Chinese, which has been useful on botanical trips to China. He designed the initial plantings of the Rock Alpine Garden, which has featured many native plants first grown regionally and many new to cultivation. A lifelong rock gardener, he helped found the Rocky Mountain chapter of the North American Rock Garden Society, is a near charter member of Colorado Native Plant Society, and was involved with the beginnings of Xeriscape and Plant Select. His hobbies include cooking, reading, and exploring faraway mountains across Eurasia and in South Africa, New Zealand, and the Andes!

Mike Kintgen grew up in Colorado, splitting time between the Front Range and Steamboat Springs, where he first discovered native plants at age five. Since that time he has been able to continue to experience them in both his home gardens and in the wild throughout the American West. Plant-themed travels have taken him from the alpine areas of Montana and Wyoming south to the deserts and steppe of New Mexico, and west to the summits and valleys of Nevada and Utah. He has worked full-time at Denver Botanic Gardens since 2004 in the Rock Alpine Garden. He is currently working on a masters in alpine ecology at Regis University.

Sarada Krishnan is Director of Horticulture and Center for Global Initiatives at Denver Botanic Gardens, where she is responsible for directing the design and maintenance of the horticulture displays and collections and for developing and leading global projects. She earned a BS in horticulture in India, an MS in horticulture from Colorado State University, and a doctorate from the University of Colorado, Boulder. Her doctoral research was on conservation genetics of the wild coffee (*Coffea* spp.) in Madagascar. She is a coffee genetic resource expert, continuing to serve on many global projects and on USDA's National Genetic Resource Advisory Council. During her 11 years at DBG, she has overseen numerous construction projects and establishment of a horticultural trial program and tissue culture lab.

Cindy Newlander studied horticulture at the University of Nebraska and received an MS in public horticulture through the Longwood Graduate Program at the University of Delaware. A Nebraska native, Cindy grew up vegetable gardening alongside her mother, which jumpstarted her interest in plants. At Denver Botanic Gardens, she's led the plant records department since 2002, documenting the extremely diverse living plant collections, including labeling, photographing, and mapping, and was instrumental in developing Gardens Navigator, a web portal into the Gardens' living collections. In her spare time, Cindy enjoys gardening, sand volleyball, and exploring nature with her family.

Savannah Putnam was homeschooled growing up in Rochester, New York, where she was able to spend most of her days catching insects in her backyard and exploring the nearby ponds, meadows, and woods. She took that love of the outdoors and earned a BS in biology at Iowa State University, focusing on plant and insect ecology. Research projects have taken her to agricultural plots in New York and Iowa, prairies in Kansas, and the tundra in Greenland. Chief among other projects for the Denver Botanic Gardens, she worked as the coordinator for this book. In her spare time she enjoys camping, rock climbing, and everything Jane Austen.

Jen Toews joined the Denver Botanic Gardens in 2015 as the Plant Recorder, responsible for researching nomenclature and the accessioning of all plants entering the Gardens. She has an MA in English from University of Colorado, Denver, and a BA in biology from Metropolitan State University

of Denver with an emphasis in botany and ecology. She is a certified Native Plant Master in Jefferson County and is passionate about the flora of the Rocky Mountains, the West Coast, and everything in between. In her free time, Jen enjoys photographing Colorado's diverse plants and their habitats and exploring the region through hiking, backpacking, and road trips.

Katy Wieczorek is a greenhouse horticulturist at Denver Botanic Gardens, where she has the pleasure of propagating plants and collecting seed of species from around the world. She manages a seed herbarium of wild collections and the seed collections of native and non-native plants. She came to DBG with a BA in environmental biology/ecology from Western State Colorado University. She was interested in studying plants from a young age, but the outdoor classroom of the Gunnison Valley solidified that dream. In her spare time, she loves to explore the West, including hiking and running rivers, with her husband, Taylor, and son, Huck.

LEAF FORM

simple

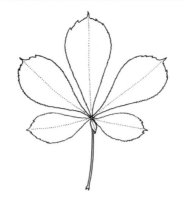

palmately compound

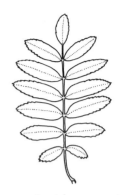

pinnately compound

LEAF SHAPE

linear

lance

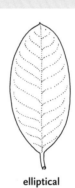

ovate

elliptical

spoon

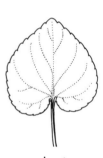

heart

LEAF MARGINS

entire

toothed

lobed

LEAF ARRANGEMENT

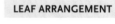

alternate